The Rough Guide to

Zimbabwe

There are more than one hundred and fifty Rough Guide titles
covering destinations from Amsterdam to Zimbabwe

Forthcoming titles include
Argentina • Croatia • Ecuador • Southeast Asia

Rough Guide Reference Series
Classical Music • Country Music • Drum 'n' Bass • English Football
European Football • House • The Internet • Jazz • Music USA • Opera
Reggae • Rock Music • Techno • Unexplained Phenomena • World Music

Rough Guide Phrasebooks
Czech • Dutch • Egyptian Arabic • European Languages • French • German
Greek • Hindi & Urdu • Hungarian • Indonesian • Italian • Japanese
Mandarin Chinese • Mexican Spanish • Polish • Portuguese • Russian
Spanish • Swahili • Thai • Turkish • Vietnamese

Rough Guides on the Internet
www.roughguides.com

ROUGH GUIDE CREDITS

Text editor: Helena Smith
Series editor: Mark Ellingham
Editorial: Martin Dunford, Jonathan Buckley, Jo Mead, Kate Berens, Amanda Tomlin, Ann-Marie Shaw, Paul Gray, Judith Bamber, Orla Duane, Olivia Eccleshall, Ruth Blackmore, Sophie Martin, Geoff Howard, Claire Saunders, Gavin Thomas, Alexander Mark Rogers, Polly Thomas, Joe Staines, Lisa Nellis, Andrew Tomičić, Claire Fogg, Richard Lim, Duncan Clark, Peter Buckley (UK); Andrew Rosenberg, Mary Beth Maioli, Don Bapst, Stephen Timblin (US)
Production: Susanne Hillen, Andy Hilliard, Link Hall, Helen Ostick, Julia Bovis, Michelle Draycott,

Katie Pringle, Robert Evers, Niamh Hatton, Mike Hancock
Cartography: Melissa Baker, Maxine Repath, Nichola Goodliffe, Ed Wright
Picture research: Louise Boulton, Sharon Martins
Online editors: Kelly Cross (US)
Finance: John Fisher, Gary Singh, Edward Downey, Mark Hall, Tim Bill
Marketing & Publicity: Richard Trillo, Niki Smith, David Wearn, Jemima Broadbridge (UK); Jean-Marie Kelly, Myra Campolo, Simon Carloss (US)
Administration: Tania Hummel, Charlotte Marriott, Demelza Dallow

ACKNOWLEDGEMENTS

A big thank you to the many readers of previous editions of this guide who took the trouble to write in with their comments and suggestions:

Sue Adams, Mike Appleton, William Bealey, Joan Belshaw, Tim Brett, Nicholas Burt, Gordon Campbell, Penelope Campbell, Louise Covacic, Angela Cross, Martin Dallimer, Janet Dawson, Jon Edgell, Olivia Finucane, Christopher Fitzgerald, Jake Gordon, Chris and Lisa Green, Jane Hansen, Ruth Harvey, Pirkko Heikkila, Sue Hexler, Yael Hoogland, Garth Jenman, M. Grebby, Julian Heathcote, Jenny Lunnon, Julie McMillan, Iain Mackay, Stewart Meikle, Ruth Mainwairing, Paula

Morris, Charlotte Nutt, Kathryn Prosser, Pat Rapley, P.A. Reavley, Carole Reed, Margaret Riordan, C. Stubley, R. Syme, H. and J. Symons, D.M. Teasdale, Peter Thompson, Miriam Tobolowsky, Tim Waller, A. White, Hugh Wilkins and Leanne Kaufman, Adrian Williams, Mary Willis.

The editor would like to thank the Map Studio, Romsey, Hants; Robert Evers for typesetting; Louise Boulton for the cover; and Nikky Twyman for proofreading.

For individual author acknowledgements, see p.v.

PUBLISHING INFORMATION

This fourth edition published May 2000 by
Rough Guides Ltd, 62–70 Shorts Gardens,
London WC2H 9AB
Distributed by the Penguin Group:
Penguin Books Ltd, 27 Wrights Lane, London W8 5TZ
Penguin Putnam Inc, 375 Hudson Street, New York, NY 10014, USA
Penguin Books Australia Ltd, 487 Maroondah Highway, PO Box 257, Ringwood, Victoria 3134, Australia
Penguin Books Canada Ltd, 10 Alcorn Avenue, Toronto, Ontario, Canada M4V 1E4
Penguin Books (NZ) Ltd, 182–190 Wairau Road, Auckland 10, New Zealand
Typeset in Linotron Univers and Century Old Style to an original design by Andrew Oliver
Printed in England by Clays Ltd, St Ives plc
Illustrations in Part One and Part Three by Edward Briant.

Illustrations on p.1 and p.341 by Tony Pinchuck
© Barbara McCrea and Tony Pinchuck, 2000
No part of this book may be reproduced in any form without permission from the publisher except for the quotation of brief passages in reviews.
432pp – Includes index
A catalogue record for this book is available from the British Library
ISBN 1-85828-532-1

The Rough Guide to
Zimbabwe

written and researched by

Barbara McCrea and Tony Pinchuck

with additional contributions by

Kathy Holden, Andrew Meldrum and
Katharina von Rohr-Games

**ROUGH
GUIDES**

We set out to do something different when the first Rough Guide was published in 1982. Mark Ellingham, just out of university, was travelling in Greece. He brought along the popular guides of the day, but found they were all lacking in some way. They were either strong on ruins and museums but went on for pages without mentioning a beach or taverna. Or they were so conscious of the need to save money that they lost sight of Greece's cultural and historical significance. Also, none of the books told him anything about Greece's contemporary life – its politics, its culture, its people and how they lived.

So, with no job in prospect, Mark decided to write his own guidebook, one which aimed to provide practical information that was second to none, detailing the best beaches and the hottest clubs and restaurants, while also giving hard-hitting accounts of every sight, both famous and obscure, and providing up-to-the-minute information on contemporary culture. It was a guide that encouraged independent travellers to find the best of Greece, and was a great success, getting shortlisted for the Thomas Cook travel guide award, and encouraging Mark, along with three friends, to expand the series.

The Rough Guide list grew rapidly and the letters flooded in, indicating a much broader readership than had been anticipated, but one which uniformly appreciated the Rough Guide mix of practical detail and humour, irreverence and enthusiasm. Things haven't changed. The same four friends who began the series are still the caretakers of the Rough Guide mission today: to provide the most reliable, up-to-date and entertaining information to independent-minded travellers of all ages, on all budgets.

We now publish more than 150 titles and have offices in London and New York. The travel guides are written and researched by a dedicated team of more than 100 authors, based in Britain, Europe, the USA and Australia. We have also created a unique series of phrasebooks to accompany the travel series, along with an acclaimed series of music guides, and a best-selling pocket guide to the Internet and World Wide Web. We also publish comprehensive travel information on our Web site:

www.roughguides.com

HELP US UPDATE

We've gone to a lot of effort to ensure that the fourth edition of *The Rough Guide to Zimbabwe* is accurate and up-to-date. However, things change – places get "discovered", opening hours are notoriously fickle, restaurants and rooms raise prices or lower standards. If you feel we've got it wrong or left something out, we'd like to know, and if you can remember the address, the price, the time, the phone number, so much the better.

We'll credit all contributions, and send a copy of the next edition (or any other Rough Guide if you prefer) for the best letters. Please mark letters: "Rough Guide Zimbabwe Update" and send to:
Rough Guides, 62–70 Shorts Gardens, London WC2H 9AB, or Rough Guides, 4th Floor, 345 Hudson Street, New York, NY 10014. Or send email to: mail@roughguides.co.uk
Online updates about this book can be found on Rough Guides' Web site at www.roughguides.com

THE AUTHORS

Tony Pinchuck launched his travels hitching around South Africa when he was 15. At university he studied African politics, and also drew political cartoon strips, several being banned by the apartheid government, after which he left for the UK. He has since lived in London and Sydney, earning a living as a designer, cartoonist, editor and writer, and has published articles on Southern Africa, as well as ten books, including *Mandela for Beginners*, *The Rough Guide to South Africa* and the forthcoming *Rough Guide to Cape Town*. His latest project has been an experiment in travelling with a child, using his young son, Gabriel, as a guinea pig.

Barbara McCrea was born in Zimbabwe and went to university in South Africa, going on to teach African literature at the University of Durban-Westville for two years, before coming to London in 1983. Driven by homesickness, she wrote *The Rough Guide to Zimbabwe & Botswana* with Tony Pinchuck, before tackling even lengthier travels for the South Africa and Cape Town guides. Besides writing and travelling between South Africa, London and Sydney, she works as a movement education teacher, and looks after her child Gabriel.

ACKNOWLEDGEMENTS

Tony and **Barbara** would like to thank contributors Katharina von Rohr-Games for her meticulous and lively work on Kariba and Harare; Kathy Holden for exceptionally thorough updates of Northern Botswana and Victoria Falls; and Andy Meldrum for his finger-on-the-pulse material on Zimbabwe politics. Thanks also to the following, without whose help there would have been no book: Pat McCrea and Lily Pinchuck for providing us with beds, meals and babysitting while we were writing the book; and our toddler Gabriel for cheerfully regarding his parents' nomadic lifestyle as a rather marvellous game; Mike and Anna Scott in Bulawayo and their delightful kids Monica, Ben and Fenn for putting up with the three of us for weeks on end; Margaret at 18 Lochview Rd, Bulawayo; Peta Jones for her invaluable intelligence on Binga; Dr Andrew Jamieson of the British Airways Travel Clinic in Knysna for his invaluable advice about malaria; Christine Khondji for her good company and ceaseless cheerfulness in exploring rock art; ish Mafundikwa for updating the music section; Manuel Bagorro for information on Harare cultural life; Sharon Bristow and staff at Ecological Safaris for travel information and for facilitating email communication under trying conditions. Thank you also to: Richard Peek at Malalangwe; Sandy and Dennis Paul at Shumba Shaba; Vivi Jedeikin in Harare; staff and management at Touch the Wild; Val Bell at Bulawayo Publicity Association; Styx Mhlanga in Bulawayo; Dee and Jane at Frog & Fern, Chimanimani; Pete & Anna-Simone Hutton in Bulawayo; Thea and Rob Haden-Tebb in the Bvumba; Shirley Lander at Mutare Publicity Association; Loanda and Theo Nel at Hot Springs; Wilderness Safaris; staff at Imire; Mrs De Vries at Kumuna; Martyn Dogerell of *Malindi Station Lodge*; staff and management at Tiger Bay; the English family at Sinamatella for administering first aid to Gabriel when he burnt his foot; Ian Games and Katharina von Rohr-Games for accommodating us in Harare; and the many other unmentioned people in Zimbabwe who gave us their time and assistance. A special thanks to our editor, Helena Smith, for her deft editing, sure-footed guidance of the book on its path to publication and for being an absolute pleasure to work with.

Kathy Holden would like to thank John McKinnel for his companionship and for his help in collecting information; Mack Air and Delta Air for flights; the *Marang Hotel*; Helen at Hartley Safaris; Lindy and Carol-Ann at Okavango Tours and Safaris; Moremi Safaris; Ann, Paul and Laura at Audi Camp; Phil and Kay Potter at *Island Safari Lodge*; *Chobe Safari Lodge*; Kerry and Clive Bradford at Kandahar; Victor Mhondera at Shearwater; Steve Bolnick and Tom of Baobab Safaris; Richard Sheppard at Fawlty Towers and Tony at Serious Fun in Livingstone; Heather Carr-Hartley; Stephen Griesel; Thebe River Safaris; Mags Varley and Di at Backpackers Bazaar; and Elizabeth and Hans at 357 Gibson Rd, Victoria Falls.

CONTENTS

Introduction x

PART THREE CONTEXTS   341

LIST OF MAPS

MAP SYMBOLS

----·-	National boundary	∴	Ruins	★	Bus stop
■-■-■·	Chapter division boundary	◓	Cave	🅿	Petrol station
═══	Main road	🌊	Waterfall	Ⓗ	Hospital
────	Minor road	⚲	Church (regional maps)	ⓘ	Tourist office
────	Unpaved road	⊼	Picnic site	⊠	Post office
─ ─ ─	Footpath	⚑	Golf course		Building
■─■─■	Railway	◓	Swimming pool	✛	Church (town maps)
··········	Waterway	△	Campsite		Park
◆	Point of interest	◉	Accommodation		National park
♦	Border post	■	Restaurant	[ ]	Forest reserve
▲	Peak	✈	Airport		Salt pan
⋏⋏	Hills	✈	Airstrip		Swamp/delta
⋛	Viewpoint				

INTRODUCTION

E asy-going, safe and infinitely hospitable, Zimbabwe is a perfect introduction to Africa – it's hard to imagine not having a good time here. With an extensive tourist infrastructure and good transport links, it remains a straightforward place for visitors to negotiate, despite economic troubles – the country suffered a currency crash in 1998 and inflation levels are high. Many people combine a trip to Zimbabwe with a visit to Botswana's Chobe National Park and the Okavango Delta which are, for that reason, covered in this guide.

Zimbabwe is best known for its excellent and accessible **game reserves** and the **Victoria Falls** – the adventure-sport capital of Africa, which draws backpackers and adrenaline junkies from across the globe. For unadulterated excitement, **whitewater rafting** below the Falls is a must, but there are numerous other ways to scare yourself witless, including bungee jumping off the Victoria Falls bridge, skydiving or riverboarding. Elsewhere in the country, you can track big game on foot with an armed guide, and there's some superb mountain hiking in the **Eastern Highlands**. In terms of game viewing, Zimbabwe, along with Chobe National Park and the Okavango Delta, can hold their own alongside South Africa and Kenya and, if it's **elephants** you're after, the region can't be beaten. While elsewhere in Africa elephants are seriously threatened, in **Chobe** and **Hwange** parks they are present in a superabundance of tens of thousands. You'll also find the rest of the **Big Five** – lions, leopards, buffalo and rhinos – in respectable numbers (though black rhinos hang on only in intensively protected areas). Between them, Zimbabwe and Botswana possess virtually all of Southern Africa's 291 recorded mammal species, and birdwatchers will find six hundred species to get to grips with. The **Okavango Delta** in Botswana is unquestionably one of the world's greatest eco-tourism destinations, combining the unique setting of an inland delta with terrific game viewing.

Human culture in the region goes back tens of thousands of years. Zimbabwe has the greatest concentration of prehistoric **rock art** in the world; finely realized paintings of animals and people in everyday life, ritual and myth, are scattered about the granite rock formations that pepper the country, seen most easily at the **Matopos Hills** near Bulawayo. The fact that you can see in the wild the very animals that feature in murals from 10,000 years ago greatly enriches the experience. Also worthy of exploration are the **stone ruins** from the ancient states that once held domain on this great plateau – **Great Zimbabwe** is just the best known of several hundred complexes.

Physically, Zimbabwe is divided by the central **highveld** plateau, which is covered by massive granite outcrops called **kopjes** (pronounced like "copies"). Because of its malaria-free moderate climate and prime lands, the highveld became the white-dominated political and economic hub of what used to be Rhodesia. Rising from the plateau for 350km along the Mozambique border are the Eastern Highlands, peaking at 2400m in the narrow belt of the **Nyanga** and **Chimanimani mountains**. To the north and south, the plateau falls away through the intermediate **middleveld plateaus**, lying between 900m and 1200m, to the **lowveld** regions, which descend in the north to the Zambezi River Valley on the Zambian border and in the south to the Limpopo and Save River valleys on the South African border. These two lowveld regions share a similar climate and vegetation, quite distinct from that of the high-veld; they have lower rainfall and are hotter. On Zimbabwe's dry western flank, the tree **savannah** of the Hwange area runs across the border to merge with the Kalahari sands of Botswana. It's in these low-lying areas that the major game parks are located, and where malaria is a problem. Across the border from Hwange is Botswana's Chobe Park, and west of here the country is watered by the vast

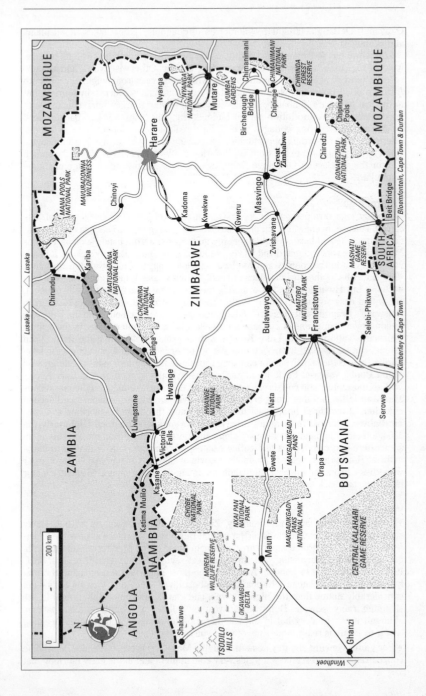

Okavango Delta: 15,000 square kilometres of channels, oxbow lakes, flood plains and islands.

Zimbabwe has well-maintained, lightly used roads which, combined with its relatively small size, make it a perfect country to tour **by car**. Otherwise, you'll find an inexpensive network of buses, trains and planes, with easy access from neighbouring South Africa or on to Botswana. Neither Zimbabwe nor Botswana is overrun by tourists, but in the last ten years Zimbabwe has developed a growing tourism infrastructure with good-quality **accommodation** for all budgets, ranging from well-run backpackers' lodges and self-catering cottages to bed and breakfasts and topnotch safari camps. There are also rewarding opportunities for staying with African families in villages. Good budget transport exists from South Africa and Victoria Falls to Maun, the launch pad for the spectacular Okavango Delta, as well as to Kasane, on the edge of Chobe Game Park.

Where to go

Obviously, your own personal interests – and time – will dictate where you travel. The capital, **Harare**, is enjoyable simply to stroll about, taking in markets, parks, beer gardens, street life and local style; high-energy guitar sounds from bands such as Thomas Mapfumo's Blacks Unlimited and Oliver Mtukudzi burst out of the city's clubs. If this is your first visit to the country and you have only a few days, Zimbabwe's top attraction, **Victoria Falls**, is the obvious place to head. Not only does it have good regional connections, but **Hwange** and **Chobe**, among the best game reserves in the subcontinent, are within easy striking distance. With a week or more you could fly on to safari in Botswana's beautiful and game-rich **Okavango Delta**, or launch out from the Falls on a walking safari led by one of Zimbabwe's excellent licensed hunter-guides in the remote **Chizarira National Park**. **Lake Kariba**, with its prolific waterside game viewing and fishing, can be reached from Victoria Falls by air, or by car and ferry across the lake. Kariba Town is the launch pad for canoeing trips down the Zambezi to the thrillingly wild **Mana Pools National Park**. From Kariba, it's five hours by road back to Harare.

With more time, you could rent a car to circuit the country, taking in the marvellous **Matopos Hills** and their rock art near **Bulawayo**, the country's sepia-toned second city, then strike three hours east to Masvingo and the magnificent ruins at **Great Zimbabwe**. A further three hours' drive east takes you to the **Eastern Highlands**, the 350-kilometre mountainous rampart along the border with Mozambique. This is an area where you can see tea and coffee estates, take in waterfalls, wallow in mineral baths at Hot Springs, relax at mountain resorts or hike in Chimanimani's spectacular wilderness. From the Eastern Highlands' mountain-encircled capital, **Mutare**, it's four hours by road back to Harare.

When to go

Though technically a tropical country, **Zimbabwe** doesn't conform to hot, sticky stereotypes. The highveld climate (Harare and Bulawayo) is as close as possible to perfection, with dry-season temperatures similar to those of the Mediterranean, but without the humidity. Surprisingly, Harare's highest recorded temperature peak of 35°C (95°F) is below that of London. Altitude is the most important determinant: the low-lying areas off the plateau – Kariba, the Zambezi River Valley and Victoria Falls – get considerably hotter than the higher towns, and can be uncomfortably humid in the steaming rainy season. **Botswana**'s weather follows a roughly similar pattern, although it can be very hot in the summer months in Maun and Kasane. Deciding **when to come** is really a question of what you're after.

• For **game viewing**, the **dry season** (roughly May–Oct) is recommended, as wildlife concentrates around scarce water; it's very cold at night and in the early morning, but warm enough for T-shirts in the middle of the day. Temperatures climb towards September – an optimum "spring" month, which combines good wildlife with vegetation coming into flower amidst the dust. October, the hottest month, is the prime time for wildlife, when animals are restricted to a few waterholes.

• The arrival of the **rainy season** in November does much to dampen temperatures. The rains, which last till March, are a time of new growth – a lush and beautiful period. Rain usually comes in the form of afternoon thunderstorms, leaving most of the day clear. There can be several days, or even weeks, between falls. The Eastern Highlands receive the highest rainfall, where you may experience a series of cool wet days.

• **April** and **May**, the "autumn" months, are perhaps ideal for general travels – warm and dry, with the land still fresh from the rains, though long grass may make game viewing more difficult.

SEASONS

• **November to mid-March**. Rainy "summer" season: thunderstorms; hot
• **Mid-March to mid-May**. Post-rainy "autumn" season: limited rainfall; cooling off
• **Mid-May to mid-August**. Cool, dry "winter" season: virtually no rainfall; cool to moderate, but very sunny and clear
• **Mid-August to November**. Warm dry "spring" season: virtually no rainfall; temperatures rise to peak

MEAN TEMPERATURES (°C) AND RAINFALL (MM)

The first figure is the mean **maximum** temperature; the second, the mean **minimum**; and the third, the average rainfall per month.

	Jan	Feb	Mar	April	May	June	July	Aug	Sept	Oct	Nov	Dec
Harare	26	26	26	26	24	22	22	24	27	29	27	26
(Highveld:	16	16	16	13	9	7	7	9	12	15	14	16
1478m)	188	169	80	43	11	5	0	3	8	32	93	189
Beit Bridge	33	33	32	30	28	25	25	28	30	32	32	33
(Lowveld:	22	21	20	17	12	8	8	11	15	19	20	21
457m)	70	50	36	24	5	4	1	1	8	21	39	66
Nyanga	21	21	21	20	18	16	16	18	21	23	22	21
(Eastern	13	13	12	10	8	6	6	7	9	11	12	13
Highlands:	257	219	135	51	17	16	14	15	13	43	125	215
1878m)												
Francistown	30	30	29	27	25	24	24	26	30	33	32	31
(Eastern	17	17	16	13	9	5	5	7	12	16	18	18
Botswana:	106	79	72	19	6	4	0	0	0	23	55	85
1100m)												
Okavango	30	30	30	30	27	25	27	29	32	34	32	31
Delta	20	20	19	16	15	6	5	8	12	16	17	18
(1000m)	150	160	80	30	2	0	0	0	2	6	50	100

BASICS

GETTING THERE FROM BRITAIN AND IRELAND

Most people travel to Zimbabwe by air. There are direct flights to Harare from Britain and Europe, but the opening up of South Africa has turned Johannesburg into the major gateway to the region, with excellent onward air and surface connections, making it a viable alternative springboard into Zimbabwe.

Fares from London to Harare and Johannesburg depend on the season in which you're flying. Roughly speaking, for **Harare**, April and May (except Easter) are **low season**, while July to September and a couple of weeks on either side of Christmas are the **high season**. The rest of the year is the medium-priced **shoulder season**. It's always worth enquiring when the seasons begin and end, as changing your departure date by a few days can potentially make a big difference in price. For Johannesburg, the high and low (known as "basic" on South African Airways) seasons are roughly the same as for Harare, but there are two intermediate seasons: the one confusingly called "low" and the other "shoulder". In any case, you should expect some variation on these dates from one airline to the next. **Overland options** include journeys via North or East Africa, either driving or travelling by rail or on local buses. Organized trips that show you the sights run on a number of routes, some starting in Britain.

FLIGHTS FROM THE UK AND EUROPE

Air Zimbabwe (3 weekly) and British Airways (4 weekly) are the only airlines that fly nonstop from London to **Harare** (both out of Gatwick), a journey taking ten hours – the fastest currently available. Air Zimbabwe has several other direct flights that stop either in Europe or Africa en route to Harare, adding two hours to the journey.

From mainland Europe, a number of the continent's major airlines now sell tickets that involve changing planes in Africa, usually Johannesburg, and continuing your journey to Harare with a local carrier. The one notable exception is Austrian Airlines, which still flies nonstop from Vienna to Harare.

Few people purchase tickets directly from the airlines at the officially quoted prices (around £1000 in high and £700 in low season). You can usually pick up fares for a lot less by booking through travel **agents** (see box on p.5), who will often be able to sell you the same scheduled seat cheaper, although you'll have to start planning this well in advance during peak season. For the latest cheap deals, look through the travel sections of the weekend newspapers – the *Sunday Times* and *Observer* especially – and, if you live in London, *Time Out* magazine and the *Evening Standard* newspaper; you may be able to pick up a return flight to Harare for around £500 in low season. Keep an eye out also for "seat sales" from the airlines throughout the year, which sometimes bring fares in basic season down to around £400, as well as "seat auctions" run by some airlines on their Web sites.

FLIGHTS FROM IRELAND

There are no direct flights **from Ireland** to Zimbabwe or South Africa, and prices tend to be higher than routings from Britain. With the frequency of connections from Belfast and, to an even greater extent, from Dublin to London and several cities on mainland Europe, you shouldn't have a problem arranging a convenient **connection** if you book well in advance.

From Belfast to Johannesburg, KLM fly via Amsterdam and Olympic Airways via Athens, but these can involve a longish delay between flights (anywhere between 2hr and 8hr). **From Dublin**, the choice of flights to Johannesburg is a lot wider and the interval between connections much shorter. Among the airlines flying this route are: Aer Lingus, connecting the main European carriers in Amsterdam, Frankfurt and Zurich;

Air France, 10 Warwick St, 1st Floor, London W1R 5RA (☎020/8742 6600, *www.airfrance.fr*).

Air Namibia, 3 Premier House, Betts Way, Crawley, West Sussex RH10 2GB (☎01293/596654).

Air Zimbabwe, Colette House, 52–55 Piccadilly, London W1V 9AA (☎020/7491 0009).

Alitalia, 4 Portman Square, London W1H 9PS (☎020/7602 7111, *www.alitalia.it*).

Balkan Bulgarian Airlines, 322 Regent St, London W1R 5AB (☎020/7637 7637).

Britannia Airways, London Luton Airport, Luton, Beds LU2 9ND (☎01582/424155, bookings through Bluebird ☎0990/320000, *www.britanniaairways.com*).

British Airways, 156 Regent St, London W1R 5TA, and branches throughout the UK (all enquiries ☎0345/222111, *www.british-airways.com*).

Egyptair, 29–31 Piccadilly, London W1V 0PT (☎020/7734 2395).

Emirates Airlines, 95 Cromwell Rd, London SW7 4DL (☎020/7808 0808, *www.emirates.com*).

Ethiopian Airlines, 4th Floor, 166 Piccadilly, London W1V 9DE (☎020/7491 9119).

Iberia Airlines of Spain, Venture House, 3rd Floor, 27–29 Glasshouse St, London W1R 6SU (☎020/7830 0011, *www.iberia.com*).

KLM Royal Dutch Airlines, ticket office at Terminal 4, Heathrow (reservations ☎0990/750900, *www.klm.nl*).

Kenya Airways, Cirrus House, CFC Building, Bedfont Road, London Heathrow Airport, Staines, Middlesex TW19 7NL (☎01784/888222, *www.kenyaairways.co.uk*).

Lufthansa German Airlines, 7–8 Conduit St, London W1R 9TG (☎0345/737747, *www.lufthansa.co.uk*).

Olympic Airways, 11 Conduit St, London W1R 0LP (☎020/7409 3400).

Sabena, 10 Putney Hill, London SW15 6AA (☎0345/581291, *www.sabena.com*).

South African Airways, St Georges House, 61 Conduit St, London W1R 0NE (☎020/7312 5000, *www.saa.co.za*).

Swissair, Swiss Centre, 10 Wardour St, London W1V 4BJ (☎020/7434 7300, *www.swissair.com*).

Virgin Atlantic Airways, Virgin Megastore, 14–16 Oxford St, London W1N 9FL (☎01293/747747, *www.flyvirgin.com/atlantic/*).

British Midland, connecting with SAA at Heathrow; and Sabena, changing planes at Brussels. Apart from these, your travel agent should be able to arrange a routing to suit you.

When it comes to **packages**, you're best off contacting one of the British-based companies listed in the box above, or booking through one of the agents in the box opposite.

FLIGHTS VIA JOHANNESBURG

Johannesburg International, the busiest airport in Africa, is, unsurprisingly, the most popular gateway into Southern Africa, and flying here may not turn out to be the inconvenience it at first seems. There are regular and easy connections from Johannesburg to Harare, and its air links with Victoria Falls and Bulawayo make it a pretty handy springboard if you're concentrating your travels on western Zimbabwe – a highly plausible possibility. Johannesburg is also the obvious hub if you're combining your visit to Zimbabwe with one to South Africa or any of its neighbouring countries.

South African Airways (SAA), British Airways and Virgin Atlantic fly daily from Heathrow direct to Johannesburg, a journey taking just under twelve hours.

ROUND-THE-WORLD TICKETS

Round-the-world tickets provide an extremely economical way of travelling if you want to include Zimbabwe in an extended tour taking in several countries or continents. Routings almost always include Australia, plus a wide choice of other destinations. A popular combination is London–Harare–Perth (own arrangements to Sydney)–Sydney–Los Angeles–London, which costs under £650 in May and June, or around £950 in September and October. For the same price you can include a flight to Johannesburg (or another African destination) as one leg and make your way overland to Harare, from where you can fly out to Perth or Sydney.

PACKAGE HOLIDAYS

There are quite a number of tour operators and travel agents that specialize in travel to Southern Africa. You can buy **off-the-peg packages** or ask them to organize a **tailor-made** one for you. It's not always cheaper to make arrangements on arrival, especially if you're planning to stay in safari lodges or hotels – which have to charge sales tax inside Zimbabwe, but not if you pay outside the country. Packages start

at around £2000 for Zimbabwe only, £2600 for Zimbabwe and Botswana, for two weeks all in (flights, accommodation, tours). Alternatively, you might consider making reservations for only some parts of your holiday, particularly the more popular

TRAVEL AGENTS IN THE UK

Bridge the World, 47 Chalk Farm Rd, London NW1 8AN (☎020/7209 9494, *www.b-t-w.co.uk*). Specializes in round-the-world tickets, with good deals aimed at the backpacker market.

Council Travel, 28a Poland St, London W1V 3DB (☎020/7437 7767, *www.ciee.org*). Flights, with student discounts.

Flightbookers, 177–178 Tottenham Court Rd, London W1P 0LX (☎020/7757 2444); Gatwick Airport, South Terminal inside the British Rail Station (☎01293/568300); on the Web at *www.flightbookers.net*. Low fares on an extensive offering of scheduled flights.

The London Flight Centre, 131 Earls Court Rd, London SW5 9RH (☎020/7244 6411); 47 Notting Hill Gate, London W11 3JS (☎020/7727 4290); Shop 33, The Broadway Centre, Hammersmith, London W6 9YE (☎020/8748 6777). Long-established agent dealing in discount flights.

North South Travel, Moulsham Mill Centre, Parkway, Chelmsford, Essex CM2 7PX (☎01245/492882). Friendly, competitive agency offering discounted fares worldwide. Profits are used to support projects in the developing world, especially the promotion of sustainable tourism.

STA Travel, 86 Old Brompton Rd, London SW7 3LH; 117 Euston Rd, London NW1 2SX; 38 Store St, London WC1E 7BZ; 11 Goodge St, London W1P 1FE; 85 Shaftesbury Ave, London W1; 40 Bernard St, London WC1N (all London enquiries ☎020/7361 6262); 38 North St, Brighton (☎01273/728282); 25 Queen's Rd, Bristol BS8 1QE (☎0117/929 4399); 38 Sidney St, Cambridge CB2 3HX (☎01223/366966); 27 Forrest Rd, Edinburgh EH1 (☎0131/226 7747); 184 Byres Rd, Glasgow G1 1JH (☎0141/338 6000); 88 Vicar Lane, Leeds LS1 7JH (☎0113/244 9212); 75 Deansgate, Manchester M3 2BW (☎0161/834 0668); 36 George St, Oxford OX1 2OJ (☎01865/792800); 9 St Mary's Place, Newcastle upon Tyne NE1 7PG (☎0191/233 2111); on the Web at *www.statravel.co.uk*; plus branches on university campuses throughout Britain. Worldwide specialists in low-cost flights and tours for students and under-26s, though other customers are welcome.

Trailfinders, 42–50 Earl's Court Rd, London W8 6FT (☎020/7938 3366); 194 Kensington High St, London W8 7RG (☎020/7938 3939); 22–24 The Priory, Queensway, Birmingham B4 6BS (☎0121/236 1234); 48 Corn St, Bristol BS1 1HQ (☎0117/929 9000); 254–284 Sauchiehall St, Glasgow G2 3EH (☎0141/353 2224); 58 Deansgate, Manchester M3 2FF (☎0161/839 6969); on the Web at *www.trailfinders.com*. One of the best-informed and most efficient agents for independent travellers. They produce a very useful quarterly magazine worth scrutinizing for round-the-world routes (for a free copy, call ☎020/7938 3366).

Travel Bag, 52 Regent St, London W1R 6DX; 373–375 The Strand, opposite the *Savoy Hotel*, London WC2R 0JF; 12 High St, Alton, Hants GU34 1BN (Southern Africa enquiries, ☎020/7287 5535). Discount flights worldwide.

The Travel Bug, 125 Gloucester Rd, London SW7 4SF (☎020/7835 2000); 597 Cheetham Hill Rd, Manchester M8 5EJ (☎0161/721 4000). Their Web address is *www.travel-bug.co.uk*. Large range of discounted tickets. Official South African Airways agent.

Travel Cuts, 295 Regent St, London W1 (☎020/7255 2082, *www.travelcuts.co.uk*). Specialists in student/youth travel and round-the-world tickets.

Travel Horizon, 107 Great Portland St, London W1N 5FA (☎020/7580 5000). Agents for Air Namibia and SAA.

Usit Campus, 52 Grosvenor Gardens, London SW1W 0AG (☎020/7730 8111); 541 Bristol Rd, Selly Oak, Birmingham B29 6AU (☎0121/414 1848); 61 Ditchling Rd, Brighton BN1 4SD (☎01273/570226); 37–39 Queen's Rd, Bristol BS8 1QE (☎0117/929 2494); 5 Emmanuel St, Cambridge CB1 1NE (☎01223/324283); 53 Forest Rd, Edinburgh EH1 2QP (☎0131/225 6111, telesales ☎668 3303); 166 Deansgate, Manchester M3 3FE (☎0161/833 2046, telesales ☎273 1721); 105–106 St Aldates, Oxford OX1 1DD (☎01865/242067); on the Web at *www.usitcampusco.uk*. Student/youth travel specialists, with branches also in YHA shops and on university campuses all over Britain.

TOUR OPERATORS IN THE UK

Abercrombie and Kent, Sloane Square House, Holbein Place, London SW1W 8NS (☎020/7730 9600, *www.abercrombiekent.com*). Large upmarket operator with comprehensive and professional programmes in Southern Africa.

Acacia Expeditions 23a Craven Terrace, Lancaster Gate, London W2 3QH (☎020/7706 4700, *www.acacia-africa.com*). Camping-based trips along classic Southern African routes, with an eighteen-day trip that squeezes in all the main sights of Zimbabwe and Botswana.

Africa Travel Centre, 21 Leigh St, London WC1H 9QX (☎020/7387 1211, *www.africatravel.co.uk*). Experienced and knowledgeable Africa specialists with a variety of tailor-made itineraries. Agents for many Southern Africa-based overland operators, including Drifters.

Art of Travel, 21 The Bakehouse, Bakery Place, 119 Altenberg Gardens, London SW11 1JQ (☎020/7738 2038, *www.artoftravel.co.uk*). Highly flexible specialist agent offering fully inclusive holidays to Zimbabwe and South Africa, to suit a range of budgets, using tried-and-tested local operators.

Grenadier Safaris, 11–12 West Stockwell St, Colchester CO1 1HN (☎01206/549585, *james@grenadier.demon.co.uk*). Small but expert agent with genuine knowledge of Southern Africa and an affection for the region based on several years' residence. Highly personalized upmarket trips with great attention to detail.

Hayes & Jarvis, Hayes House, 152 King St, London W6 0QU (☎020/8748 5050). Long-established operator, whose wide-ranging options stretch from budget self-catering and no-frills safaris to luxury tours. Exotic weddings organized.

Kuoni Worldwide, Kuoni House, Dorking, Surrey RH5 4AZ (Africa ☎01306/743000); 33 Maddox St, London W1R (☎020/7499 8636); 2a Barton St, Manchester M2 (☎0161/832 0667). Flexible packages from this reputable long-haul operator, with good deals for families.

Okavango Tours and Safaris, Gadd House, Arcadia Avenue, London N3 2TJ (☎020/8343 3283, *www.okavango.com*). Botswana-based company that are old hands with on-the-ground knowledge of the subcontinent, offering fully flexible and individual tours across South Africa, Zimbabwe and Botswana.

Rainbow Tours, 64 Essex Rd, London N1 8LR (☎020/7226 1004, *rainbow@gn.apc.org*). Southern Africa specialists with trips emphasizing eco-friendly and community-based tourism.

Safari Consultants, Orchard House, Upper Road, Little Cornard, Sudbury, Suffolk CO10 0NZ (☎01787/228494, *bill.safcon@pop3.hiway.co.uk*). Individually tailored holidays across Southern Africa, with particular expertise in activity-based holidays, including walking safaris.

South African Airways Holidays, 12 Coningsby Rd, Peterborough PE3 8XP (☎0870/607 1364). Fly-drive and tailor-made tours using SAA and other main carriers.

Sunvil Discovery, Sunvil House, Upper Square, Old Isleworth, Middlesex TW7 7BJ (☎020/8232 9797, *www.itsnet.co.uk/si/sunvil.htm*). Tailored holidays throughout Southern Africa with programmes dedicated to Zimbabwe and Botswana.

Virgin Holidays, The Galleria, Ground Floor, Station Road, Crawley, West Sussex RH10 1WW (☎01293/617181, *www.virginholidays.co.uk*). Flexible packages in conjunction with Virgin Atlantic Airlines combining South Africa with Zimbabwean destinations.

Worldwide Journeys and Expeditions, 8 Comeragh Rd, London W14 9HP (☎020/7381 8638). Outstanding tailor-made travel programmes by a company that will steer you to the smaller, better-value options in South Africa, Zimbabwe and Botswana.

---

activities and places that may get overbooked. Canoeing trips, whitewater rafting and such frequently visited destinations as the Mana Pools and the Okavango Delta fall into this category. Most of the agents below can offer partial prebooking.

ORGANIZED OVERLAND TRIPS

Several overland operators run **trans-Africa routes** starting in Britain, Europe or Nairobi and working their way down routes through Zimbabwe to Cape Town. Shorter legs are also offered, with the possibility of starting or terminating in Zimbabwe.

A 28-week trip from **London to Cape Town** via West Africa, Kenya and Zimbabwe will cost £4500–5000 (land arrangements only); other routes go via Egypt and Nairobi. For a more modest eleven-week trip from **Nairobi to Cape Town** via Harare, expect to pay in the region of £2000, or around £800 for a three-week trip from **Harare to Cape Town** via Victoria Falls and Namibia. An increasing number of operators are also offering overland trips within Southern Africa, taking in **Zimbabwe and its neighbours**.

OVERLAND OPERATORS IN THE UK

Dragoman, 97 Camp Green, Debenham, Stowmarket, Suffolk IP14 6LA (☎01728/861133, www.dragoman.co.uk). Extended journeys in purpose-built expedition vehicles through Africa. Shorter camping and hotel-based safaris also offered.

Encounter Overland, 267 Old Brompton Rd, London SW5 9JA (☎020/7370 6845, www.encounter-overland.com). Wide range of routes in Southern Africa including six-month treks from London to Cape Town via Nairobi and Harare.

Exodus, 9 Weir Rd, London SW12 0LT (reservations ☎020/8675 5550, brochures ☎020/8673 0859, www.exodustravels.co.uk). Experienced adventure-tour operators running nine-week trips from Kenya to Cape Town and short tours in Southern Africa.

Explore Worldwide, 1 Frederick St, Aldershot, Hants GU11 1LQ (reservations ☎01252/760000, brochures ☎01252/760100, www.explore.co.uk). Journeys inside Southern Africa that take in Namibia, Botswana and Zimbabwe.

Guerba Expeditions, Wessex House, Station Road, Westbury, Wiltshire BA13 3JN (☎01373/826611, www.guerba.co.uk). Range of trans-African overland routes including Nairobi to Cape Town and shorter pick-and-mix trips in Southern Africa that spend time on Lake Kariba, in the Okavango Delta and canoeing on the Zambezi.

Kumuka Expeditions, 40 Earl's Court Rd, London W8 6EJ (☎020/7937 8855, www.kumuka.co.uk). Seven-week journeys from Nairobi to Cape Town, and three-week trips from Victoria Falls to Cape Town.

Oasis Overland, 33 Travellers Way, Hounslow, London TW4 7QB (☎020/8759 5597, oasisoverland@travellersway.demon.co.uk). One of the smaller overland companies, with low prices, such as a three-week "Deserts and Game Parks" tour through Botswana and Namibia to Cape Town.

Truck Africa, 37 Ranelagh Gardens Mansions, Ranelagh Gardens, Fulham, London SW6 3UQ (☎020/7731 6142, www.truckafrica.com). Young and fun, with trips that include one against the grain from Cape Town to Harare.

AIRLINES, AGENTS AND TOUR OPERATORS IN IRELAND

AIRLINES

Aer Lingus, Northern Ireland reservations (☎0645/737747); Dublin reservations (☎01/705 3333). Branches at: 41 Upper O'Connell St, Dublin; 13 St Stephen's Green, Dublin 2; 12 Upper St George's St, Dun Laoghaire; 2 Academy St, Cork (☎021/327155); and 136 O'Connell St, Limerick (☎061/474239).

British Midland, Northern Ireland reservations (☎0345/554554); Dublin reservations (☎01/283 8833).

KLM UK, reservations in Northern Ireland (☎0990/074074); in the Republic (☎0345/445588).

Lufthansa, Dublin airport (☎01/814 4755).

Olympic Airways, Franklin House, 140–142 Pembroke Rd, Ballsbridge, Dublin 4 (☎01/608 0090).

Sabena Airlines, Dublin airport (☎01/844 5454).

Virgin Atlantic, Club Travel Offices, 30 Lower Abbey St, Dublin 1 (☎01/873 3388).

AGENTS AND TOUR OPERATORS

Liffey Travel, 12 Upper O'Connell St, Dublin 1 (☎01/878 8322). Package tour specialists.

Thomas Cook, 11 Donegall Place, Belfast (☎01232/550232 or 554455); 118 Grafton St, Dublin 2 (☎01/677 1721). Package holiday and flight agent with occasional discount offers.

Trailfinders, 4–5 Dawson St, Dublin 2 (☎01/677 7888, www.trailfinders.com). Competitive fares out of all Irish airports, as well as deals on hotels, insurance, tours and car rental worldwide.

USIT, Fountain Centre, College Street, Belfast BT1 6ET (☎01232/324073); 10 Market Parade, Patrick Street, Cork (☎021/270900); 33 Ferryquay St, Derry (☎01504/371888); Aston Quay, Dublin 2 (☎01/602 1777 or 677 8117); Victoria Place, Eyre Square, Galway (☎091/565177); Central Buildings, O'Connell St, Limerick (☎061/415064); 36 Georges St, Waterford (☎051/872601); on the Web at www.campustravel.co.uk. Student and youth specialists.

GETTING THERE FROM NORTH AMERICA

There are no direct flights into Zimbabwe from North America, but direct services do run to Johannesburg from New York, Miami and Atlanta. From there, it's easy to catch a connecting flight into Zimbabwe or to travel overland (for details, see Getting there from South Africa).

Fares from North America to Southern Africa depend on which **season** you're flying in. Low season is mid-January to May, and September to November; high season is June to August, and December to mid-January. Expect small variations on these dates from one airline to the next.

From the US, South African Airways flies nonstop three to four times a week out of **Atlanta**, **Miami** and **New York** to Johannesburg. The round-trip Apex fare out of all three cities to Johannesburg is US$1350 low season and US$1570 high season. **From Johannesburg,**

SAA offers discounted fares to Zimbabwe and Botswana – rates range from US$46 to US$87 one way. It might be cheaper to go from the US into **London**, **Frankfurt** or one of the other European hubs, with onward connections to Johannesburg or Harare. Round-trip fares as low as US$1000 (East Coast) and US$1500 (West Coast) are often available from discounters on these routings. Check the ads in the Sunday travel sections of major newspapers.

From Canada, there are nonstop and direct flights on Canadian Airlines **from Toronto** into New York, London and Frankfurt, connecting with South African Airways flights to Johannesburg. Round-trip fares range from C$1850 (low season) to C$2050 (high season).

Air Canada offers a daily nonstop service **from Vancouver** to Frankfurt or London with onward connections into Africa on South African Airways. Round-trip fares range from C$1860 (low season) to C$2090 (high season). Prices for flights from Vancouver via New York tend to be slightly higher. KLM flies nonstop four times a week from Vancouver to Amsterdam, with onward connections on South African Airways. Round-trip fares range from C$2660 (low season) to C$2900 (high season). It's also possible to reach Johannesburg from Vancouver via nonstop flights to Hong Kong and Singapore, with onward connections to Johannesburg and thence to Zimbabwean destinations.

PACKAGE HOLIDAYS

Most North Americans coming to Zimbabwe and Botswana do so on **packages** which emphasize safaris. Many take in these countries as part of a

---

AIRLINES IN THE US AND CANADA

Air France in US ☎1-800/237-2747, in Canada ☎1-800/667-2747, *www.airfrance.com*.
American Airlines ☎1-800/433-7300, *www.americanair.com*.
British Airways in US ☎1-800/247-9297, in Canada ☎1-800/668-1059, *www.british-airways.com*.
Delta ☎1-800/241-4141, *www.delta-air.com*.
Northwest/KLM in US ☎1-800/374-7747, in

Canada ☎1-800/361-5073, *www.klm.com*.
Sabena ☎1-800/955-2000, *www.sabena-usa.com*.
South African Airways ☎1-800/722-9675, *www.saa-usa.com*.
Swissair in US ☎1-800/221-4750, in Canada ☎1-800/267-9477, *www.swissair.com*.
Virgin Atlantic Airways ☎1-800/862-8621, *www.fly.virgin.com*.

larger African trip, often including both East and Southern Africa, although the notable game areas of Botswana and Zimbabwe are enough to warrant a trip on their own. The most desirable wildlife regions of both countries are concentrated around their northern borders, making them a coherent and manageable region for travel. Obvious highlights include the Okavango Delta and Chobe National Park in Botswana, and Victoria Falls and Hwange National Park – all within a couple of hours of each other by air.

For more generalized packages, the demise of apartheid has opened the whole of Southern Africa into an integrated region. For first-time visitors, highlights are likely to include Cape Town, the Winelands and the Garden Route in South Africa, the Okavango Delta in Botswana, Victoria Falls in Zimbabwe and a major game reserve in one of the three countries.

The more adventurous and those with a bit of time to kill can opt for several weeks travelling **overland** from North Africa to Harare or beyond. A number of operators have well-organized group trips of varying length on the continent. One of the most common routes takes you from Nairobi to Harare over five or six weeks.

FARES

Barring special offers, the cheapest of the airlines' published fares is usually an **Apex** ticket, although this carries certain restrictions. You have to book – and pay – at least 21 days before departure and spend a minimum of seven days abroad (maximum stay three months). Some airlines issue **Special Apex** tickets to **under-24s**, often extending the maximum stay to a year. Many also offer youth or student fares to **under-26s**; a passport or driving licence are sufficient proof of age, though these tickets are subject to availability and can have eccentric booking conditions. It's worth remembering that most cheap return fares involve spending at least one Saturday night away and that many will only give a percentage refund if you need to cancel or alter your journey, so check the restrictions carefully before buying.

You can normally cut costs further by going through a **specialist flight agent**. This can be either a **consolidator**, who buys up blocks of tickets from the airlines and sells them at a discount, or a **discount agent**, who in addition to dealing with discounted flights may also offer special student and youth fares and other travel-related services, such as insurance, car rental and tours. If you travel a lot, **discount travel clubs** are another option – the annual membership fee may be worth it for benefits such as cut-price air tickets and car rental.

Don't automatically assume that tickets purchased through a travel specialist will be cheapest – once you get a quote, check with the airlines for special offers and you may turn up an even better deal. Be advised also that the pool of travel companies is swimming with sharks – never deal with a company that demands cash up front or refuses to accept payment by credit card.

A further possibility is to see if you can arrange a **courier flight**, often from New York to Johannesburg or Harare. The hit-or-miss nature of these makes them most suitable for the single traveller who travels light and has a very flexible schedule. In return for shepherding a parcel through customs and possibly giving up your baggage allowance, you can expect to get a drastically discounted ticket. You'll probably also be restricted in the duration of your stay. Also worth considering is an "**open-jaw**" ticket, which allows you to arrive in one city, travel overland, then depart from another.

If South Africa is only one stop on a longer journey, you might want to consider buying a **round-the-world (RTW) ticket**. Some travel agents can sell you an "off-the-shelf" RTW ticket that will have you touching down in a handful of cities; a typical itinerary would be Boston–London–Johannesburg–Buenos Aires–Lima–New York (US$1950). Others will tailor one to your needs but this is apt to be more expensive.

ROUND-TRIP FARES

Prices quoted below are for round trips and exclude taxes (roughly US$50–65/C$30). They also assume midweek travel; for **weekend travel**, check if the airline hikes its fares on its South Africa routes. SAA, for example, charge the same rates seven days a week, whereas British Airways fares are around US$25 more expensive (each direction) at weekends. Typical lowest standard Apex **fares** to Johannesburg for low/high seasons are: Chicago (US$1650/2050); Los Angeles (US$1750/2150); New York (US$1300/1700); Toronto (C$2650/2950); and Vancouver (C$3100/3350). Low- and high-season **discount/student rates** can be found for New York to Johannesburg for about US$950/1350.

AGENTS AND OPERATORS IN THE US AND CANADA

DISCOUNT AGENTS AND COURIER BROKERS

Air Brokers International, 150 Post St, Suite 620, San Francisco, CA 94108 (☎1-800/883-3273 or 415/397-1383, *www.airbrokers.com*). Consolidator.

Air Courier Association, 15000 W 6th Ave, Suite 203, Golden, CO 80206 (☎1-800/282-1202 or 303/215-0900, *www.aircourier.org*). Courier flight broker.

Council Travel, 205 E 42nd St, New York, NY 10017 (☎1-800/226-8624 or 888/COUNCIL or 212/822-2700, *www.ciee.com*); plus branches in cities across the US. Specialists in student travel.

Educational Travel Center, 438 N Frances St, Madison, WI 53703 (☎1-800/747-5551 or 608/256-5551, *www.edtrav.com*). Student/youth and consolidator fares.

High Adventure Travel, 442 Post St, 4th Floor, San Francisco, CA 94102 (☎1-800/350-0612 or 415/912-5600, *www.highadv.com*). Round-the-world tickets. Their Web site lets you build and price your own RTW itinerary.

Now Voyager, 74 Varick St, Suite 307, New York, NY 10013 (☎212/431-1616, *www.nowvoyagertravel.com*). Courier flight broker and consolidator.

STA Travel, 10 Downing St, New York, NY 10014 (☎1-800/777-0112 or 212/627-3111; *www.sta-travel.com*), plus branches in cities across the US. Worldwide discount travel firm specializing in student/youth fares; also student IDs, travel insurance and car rental.

Travel Cuts, 187 College St, Toronto, ON M5T 1P7 (☎1-800/667-2887 or 416/979-2406, *www.travelcuts.com*); plus branches in cities across Canada. Discount travel organization.

Traveler's Advantage, 3033 S Parker Rd, Suite 900, Aurora, CO 80014 (☎1-800/548-1116, *www.travelersadvantage.com*). Discount travel club.

TOUR OPERATORS

Although phone numbers are given here, you're better off making tour reservations through your **local travel agent**. An agent will make all the phone calls, sort out any hitches and arrange flights, insurance and the like – all at no extra cost to you.

Abercrombie and Kent (☎1-800/323-7308, *www.abercrombiekent.com*). Leading upscale operator with over thirty years of experience organizing African safaris. Package options include a twelve-day "Family Safari" from US$3215 for adults and US$1460 for kids (both packages are land-only).

Adventure Center (☎1-800/227-8747, *www.adventure-center.com*). Wide variety of affordable packages, ranging from a six-day "Zambezi Canoe Safari" to a fifteen-day "Great Zimbabwe Discovery".

Adventures Abroad (☎1-800/665-3998, *www.adventures-abroad.com*). Canada-based company offering small-group and activity tours to Zimbabwe, South Africa and the neighbouring regions.

AfricaTours (☎1-800/235-3692, *www.africasafaris.com*). Moderate to high-end customized tours.

Backroads (☎1-800/462-2848, *www.backroads.com*). Eleven-day hiking/inn trip.

Big Five Tours and Expeditions (☎1-888/244-3483, *www.bigfive.com*). Range of photographic safaris, including an eleven-day "Long Walk to Freedom" from US$2995 (including flights).

Bushtracks (☎1-800/995-8689 or 650/326-8689, *www.bushtracks.com*). Upmarket, customized tours for travellers interested in wildlife photography, at around US$400–450 per day.

International Gay and Lesbian Travel Association (☎1-800/448-8550, *www.iglta.org*). Trade group with lists of gay-owned or gay-friendly travel agents, accommodation and other travel businesses.

Saga Holidays (☎1-800/343-0273). Specialists in group travel for seniors. Saga, and their more education-oriented subsidiary, Road Scholar, offer a choice of packages including "South Africa: A Nation Reborn" (fifteen nights from US$3599, including flights).

Wilderness Travel (☎1-800/368-2794, *www.wildernesstravel.com*). Small-group tours, including a fifteen-day luxury hiking tour for US$4895 (land only).

Worldwide Adventures/Quest Nature Tours (☎1-800/387-1483, *www.worldwidequest.com*). Packages include a nineteen-day mixed-accommodation hiking/game-viewing/cultural tour for US$1495, and a more upscale fourteen-day hotel/lodge-accommodated, game-viewing and birdwatching tour for US$3495 (both land-only).

GETTING THERE FROM AUSTRALIA AND NEW ZEALAND

Southern Africa is an expensive destination for travellers from Australia and New Zealand. Fares are steep, and a ticket to Europe with a stopover in Zimbabwe, or even a round-the-world (RTW) ticket, generally represents better value than a straightforward return.

The only **direct flights** from Australasia to Zimbabwe are the twice-weekly services on Qantas from Sydney via Perth to Harare, one of which touches down in Johannesburg before the last leg to Harare. Flying to Johannesburg offers far more choice, with South African Airways (SAA), Qantas and Air New Zealand all covering the route; some of the Asian (Air Lanka, Malaysia Airlines, Singapore Airlines and Thai Airways) and Middle Eastern (Gulf Air) airlines tend to be less expensive, but their routings often entail more stopovers en route. Air and surface connections are good from Johannesburg to several centres in Zimbabwe (for details, see Getting there from South Africa on p.13).

FARES

Whatever kind of ticket you're after, your first call should be to a specialist travel agent (see p.12), who can fill you in on all the latest **fares** and any **special offers**. If you're a student or under 26, you may be able to undercut some of the prices given here; STA is a good place to start. All the fares quoted are for travel during low or shoulder seasons; flying at peak times (primarily mid-May to Aug and Dec to mid-Jan) can add substantially to these prices. When the airlines have surplus

capacity, special fares to Harare can be as low as A$1700. Otherwise, the best return fares you're likely to find are around A$1900 from the eastern states and A$1650 from Western Australia. From New Zealand, fares start at NZ$2250.

"Open-jaw" tickets enable you to fly into Harare and out of Johannesburg (or vice versa), which can save valuable time spent backtracking; a special SAA fare costs in the region of A$1950 from the east coast (around A$200 less from Perth). If you plan to visit Zimbabwe/South Africa en route to Europe, you can expect to pay around A$2300/NZ$2650.

ROUND-THE-WORLD TICKETS

Round-the-world tickets that take in Zimbabwe/South Africa are worth considering, especially if you have the time to make the most of a few stopovers. Ultimately, your choice of route will depend on where else you want to visit besides Zimbabwe, but possible itineraries include: starting from either Melbourne, Sydney or Brisbane, flying to Harare, then travelling overland to Cape Town, before flying to London, and taking in Amsterdam, New York and San Francisco on the way back home (from A$2250); or, starting from Perth, flying to Denpasar, Casablanca, Istanbul, Nairobi, then down to Harare and Johannesburg on the return leg to Perth (from A$2200).

From New Zealand, you could fly from Auckland to Sydney, Bangkok and London, returning via Harare and Perth to Auckland. Fares for this route start at NZ$2800.

PACKAGE HOLIDAYS AND ORGANIZED TOURS

Package holidays from Australia and New Zealand to Southern Africa (taking in Zimbabwe) tend to be either expensive or of the extended overland variety, although airlines are beginning to put together bargain fly-drive options as demand increases. At the luxury end of the market, tailor-made safaris will set you back around A$6500/NZ$7200 for a two-week trip. **Adventure tours** are worth considering if you want to cover a lot of ground or get to places that could be difficult to reach independently. Contiki offer fully inclusive fourteen-day bus tours, with prices starting from A$4450, including return flights. Companies such as Encounter Overland, Explore Worldwide and Peregrine Adventures run extended camping trips taking in the Zimbabwe and Botswana highlights (20–28 days; A$200–2250, excluding air fares).

AIRLINES, AGENTS AND OPERATORS IN AUSTRALIA AND NEW ZEALAND

AIRLINES

Air Lanka, 64 York St, Sydney (☎02/9321 9234); 6/44 Emily Place, Auckland (☎09/309 2425).

Air New Zealand, 5 Elizabeth St, Sydney (☎13 2476); 139 Queen St, Auckland (☎09/357 3000).

British Airways, Level 19, 259 George St, Sydney (☎02/8904 8800); 154 Queen St, Auckland (☎09/356 8690).

Gulf Air, 64 York St, Sydney (☎02/9244 2199).

Malaysia Airlines, 16 Spring St, Sydney (☎13 2627); 12/12 Swanson St, Auckland (☎09/373 2741 or toll-free ☎0800/657 472).

Qantas, 70 Hunter St, Sydney (☎13 1211); 154 Queen St, Auckland (☎09/357 8900 or ☎0800/808 767).

Singapore Airlines, 17 Bridge St, Sydney (☎13 1011); corner of Albert and Fanshawe streets, Auckland (☎09/303 2129).

South African Airways, 5 Elizabeth St, Sydney (☎02/9223 4402).

Thai Airways, 75 Pitt St, Sydney (☎1300/651 960); 22 Fanshawe St, Auckland (☎09/377 3886).

TRAVEL AGENTS

Anywhere Travel, 345 Anzac Parade, Kingsford, Sydney (☎02/9663 0411).

Budget Travel, 16 Fort St, Auckland, plus branches around the city (☎09/366 0061 or ☎0800/808 040).

Destinations Unlimited, Level 7, 220 Queen St, Auckland (☎09/373 4033).

Flight Centres Australia: 82 Elizabeth St, Sydney, plus offices nationwide (for nearest branch ☎13 1600); New Zealand: 205 Queen St, Auckland (☎09/309 6171), plus offices nationwide (for nearest branch ☎0800/FLIGHTS).

Northern Gateway, 22 Cavenagh St, Darwin (☎08/8941 1394).

STA Travel Australia: 855 George St, Sydney; 256 Flinders St, Melbourne; other offices in state capitals and major universities (for nearest branch ☎13 1776, for sales ☎1300/360 960); New Zealand: 10 High St, Auckland (☎09/309 0458, for sales ☎09/366 6673); plus branches in Wellington, Christchurch, Dunedin, Palmerston North, Hamilton and at major universities; Web site at www.statravelaus.com.au.

Thomas Cook Australia: 175 Pitt St, Sydney; 257 Collins St, Melbourne, plus branches in other state capitals (local branch ☎13 1771, Thomas Cook Direct telesales ☎1800/063 913); New Zealand: 159 Queen St, Auckland (☎09/379 3924).

SPECIALIST OPERATORS

These agents specialize in African travel arrangements, and can help with flights, accommodation and car rental, as well as fully inclusive tours.

Africa Travel Centre, 456 Kent St, Sydney (☎02/9267 3048 or 1800/622 984); 21 Remuera Rd, Auckland (☎09/520 2000).

The Classic Safari Company, 11/465 Kent St, Sydney (☎02/9264 5710); in Western Australia or

the Northern Territory ☎08/9472 7414, or toll-free ☎1800/351 088. Luxury, individually tailored safaris.

Lion Travel, 6/10 Lorne St, Auckland (☎09/373 5942).

TOUR OPERATORS

Abercrombie and Kent, 90 Bridport St, Albert Park, Melbourne (☎03/9699 9766); 14/17 Victoria St, Auckland (☎09/358 4200). Luxury tours of Southern Africa.

African Wildlife Safaris, 1/259 Coventry St, Melbourne (☎03/9696 2899). Upmarket camping and lodge-based safaris to Southern Africa.

Bench International, 36 Clarence St, Sydney (☎02/9290 2877 or 1800/221451). African tours, focusing on wildlife and safaris.

Contiki Holidays for 18–35s, 35 Spring St, Bondi Junction, Sydney (☎02/9511 2200). Frenetic tours for the young and adventurous.

Encounter Overland, Suite 15, 600 Lonsdale St, Melbourne (☎03/9670 1123 or 1800/654 152). Overland tours – from seven days to 34 weeks.

Explore Worldwide, book through Adventure World, 73 Walker St, North Sydney (☎02/9956 7766 or 1800/221 931), plus branches in Melbourne, Brisbane, Adelaide and Perth; 101 Great South Rd, Remuera, Auckland (☎09/524 5118). Small-group tours and treks.

Peregrine Adventures, 258 Lonsdale St, Melbourne (☎03/9663 8611), plus offices in Brisbane, Sydney, Adelaide and Perth. Adventure tours and all-inclusive game safaris throughout Africa.

GETTING THERE FROM SOUTH AFRICA

In Southern Africa, all roads, rail links and air routes lead to Johannesburg, the economic powerhouse and undisputed transport hub of the region. Zimbabwe's two principal cities, Harare and Bulawayo, and its main tourist centre, Victoria Falls, are also well connected to Johannesburg by air, road and rail links.

FLIGHTS

Apart from the frequent connection from Johannesburg, there is a weekly nonstop flight to Harare from Durban and a few flights a week from Cape Town to Harare, stopping en route in Johannesburg. **Flights** from South Africa to Zimbabwe are quick and convenient, with fares dependant on your destination, which season you fly and how long you're staying. South African Airways (SAA) has two seasons, with April, July and December falling into the **high season** and the rest of the year into **low season**. The cheapest fares typically involve minimum stays of around a week and a maximum of a month. On SAA the cheapest return fares you can expect **from Johannesburg** to Bulawayo are US$160/285 (low/high season) and, from Johannesburg to Harare or Victoria Falls, US$295/320. Expect slight variations on other airlines. In addition to SAA, Air Zimbabwe, Zimbabwe Express Airlines and British Airways/Comair offer several flights per day from Johannesburg to Victoria Falls and Harare, and Air Zimbabwe flies nonstop from Johannesburg to Bulawayo twice a week.

If you are travelling around the region taking in a number of destinations in South Africa, Zimbabwe or Namibia, you should definitely consider the SAA **Africa Explorer** scheme, which can save you up to sixty percent on SAA regional and domestic fares. The Africa Explorer must be booked outside South Africa in conjunction with an international ticket to South Africa (you don't have to be flying SAA on the international leg), must include between four and eight sectors, and is valid for a month, with a minimum stay of three days in any one place.

LUXURY COACHES

Luxury coaches are much cheaper and far slower than air travel, but, if you have the time, they offer the added attraction of taking in some of the countryside en route. Of the three main operators plying regional routes, Greyhound, Translux and Trans Zambezi, between them, run a daily service to Harare (18hr; US$50), whereas Greyhound and Translux run one to two buses daily to Bulawayo (13hr; US$40); return fares are precisely double the singles quoted here. All three companies operate out of Park Station in central Johannesburg.

BACKPACKERS' BUSES

One of the big advantages of **backpackers' buses** is that they're the only form of transport that will take you door to door from South Africa to Zimbabwe. Of the two companies that connect the two countries, **Route 49** is the only bus outfit (including the luxury coaches) to run a direct express service from Cape Town to Bulawayo, a twice-weekly journey that takes 24 hours and costs about US$110, including meals and refreshments. A shuttle bus takes passengers to Victoria Falls the following day to arrive mid-morning, but you can spend a few days in Bulawayo if you wish and they'll also drop off passengers on request at Hwange National Park. The fare from Cape Town to Victoria Falls is roughly US$115. They also go from Johannesburg to Victoria Falls via eastern Botswana twice a week (16hr; US$50). A shuttle bus links up with this bus at Nata to take passengers to Maun, one of the few forms of public transport, apart from flying, that will get you to the Okavango Delta. The fare from Johannesburg to Maun is US$75.

JOHANNESBURG DEPARTURE POINTS

All Johannesburg **flights** leave from Johannesburg International Airport (information ☎011/975 9963), still frequently referred to by its former name, Jan Smuts. There's a range of options for getting to the airport from the city or suburbs. Of the scheduled bus services, Impala (every 45min 6.15am–10pm; 30min) goes from Park Station in the city centre and charges around US$7. If you're leaving from the northern suburbs, you'll find it easier to take the Magic Bus (☎011/608 1662; every 30min 5.30am–9.30pm; 30min), which picks up at the *Sandton Sun Hotel* and costs about US$10. The more expensive hotels often offer courtesy buses, while most backpackers' hostels and some smaller guest houses and B&Bs will arrange drop-offs. Taking a **taxi** to the airport is convenient and safe, but be sure to take a metered taxi. Be prepared to pay around US$15 from most areas. Reputable companies include Maxi Taxis (☎011/648 1212), Rose Radio (☎011/725 1111 or 725 3333), Good Hope (☎011/725 6431) and Metro (☎011/484 7975). If you're catching a **luxury coach** or train from **Park Station**, it's highly advisable to get there by taxi, as the station lies in a fairly rough part of the city centre, where you wouldn't want to get lost.

The **Baz Bus** operates a hop-on-hop-off service four times a week from Johannesburg to Victoria Falls, a journey via the Beit Bridge border that takes about eighteen hours; a single fare is in the region of US$60. Baz has a virtual monopoly on providing bus transport to backpackers touring South Africa, with a route from Cape Town to Johannesburg that goes via the Garden Route and Durban. The main reason to use them rather than Route 49 to get to Zimbabwe is if you're putting together an itinerary that includes destinations along their South African network – in which case you should expect to pay US$185 from Cape Town to Victoria Falls, with any number of stops along the way.

TRAINS

Spoornet, South Africa's rail operator, runs one **train** a week from Johannesburg to Bulawayo (27hr; US$55 first class, US$35 second class, US$20 third class). First- and second-class compartments have sleeper accommodation and if you're travelling as a couple you may be able to get a *coupé*, a small private compartment that sleeps two in first class and three in second. Bulawayo is useful if you want to continue by rail all the way to Victoria Falls, as you can catch the evening Zimbabwe National Railways train to the Falls. Tickets are obtainable from the Spoornet reservations offices at the stations in Cape Town (☎021/449 3871) or Johannesburg (☎011/773 2944).

DRIVING AND BORDER REQUIREMENTS

Apart from the border crossing, **driving** from South Africa to Zimbabwe is pretty straightforward. Beit Bridge is the only border post connecting the two countries and can get pretty congested. This provides good reason, if you're heading for western Zimbabwe (Bulawayo, Hwange National Park or Victoria Falls), to approach via Botswana, a route which doesn't

LUXURY COACH AND BACKPACKER BUS COMPANIES

Baz Bus National (☎021/439 2323, fax 439 2343, *info@bazbus.com*). Bookings can also be made through hostels or the Baz offices at the central tourist information centres in Cape Town or Durban. Their Web site (*www.bazbus.com*) has route and pricing information.
Greyhound Cape Town (☎021/418 4310); Bloemfontein (☎051/430 2361); Durban (☎03/309 7830); Johannesburg (☎011/830 1301); Port Elizabeth (☎041/586 4879).
Route 49 Cape Town (☎021/426 5593, *zimcaper@dockside.co.za*).

Trans Zambezi (operating in South Africa as Intercape) Cape Town (☎021/386 4400); Port Elizabeth (☎041/586 0055); Pretoria (☎012/654 4114). Their Web site (*www.intercape.co.za*) has contact numbers.
Translux Cape Town (☎021/405 3333); Durban (☎031/361 8333); East London (☎043/442333); Johannesburg (☎011/774 3333); Port Elizabeth (☎041/507 1333); Pretoria (☎012/315 2333). A useful Web site (*www.translux.co.za*) covers pricing, passes and routes.

add significantly to your journey and will almost certainly save time at the border. As no-one tells you what to do at the Beit Bridge border post and there are no signs giving instructions on the Zimbabwean side, it's worth coming prepared. If you're an AA member, you can save yourself a lot of time by arranging with them the documents you'll need in advance.

For the **South African side** you'll need an **export/import permit** for customs. If you don't have one, you'll need your original car registration documents so they can issue the permit. They will then issue you with a gate pass, after which you go through to Immigration in the same building. The **Zimbabwean side** is more tricky and can seem rather arbitrary and complicated. Often forms have run out and you'll have to queue up twice at each window: once to get the forms, and the second time to get them processed after you've filled them in. You are likely to be accosted by "freelancers", who will offer to provide forms and help you through the process in return for an extortionate fee. They are best ignored. First you must queue up to pay the toll (US$5) to cross the bridge and you'll be given a **toll card**. Next, go to **Immigration** with your filled-in green immigration form; make sure you get your toll card stamped. Next, go to **Customs** with your black-on-white customs declaration form and your temporary import permit (which can be arranged in advance through the AA). Finally, if you haven't already arranged Zimbabwean **third party insurance** through the AA, you must go to a separate building next door to buy this.

GETTING THERE FROM OTHER AFRICAN COUNTRIES

For overland travellers coming down Africa, there are several trodden paths to the south.

From **Malawi**, the quickest route through Mozambique brings you into Zimbabwe's north-eastern corner, a few hours from Harare. The other option from Malawi is much longer, going through Zambia to Livingstone and into Zimbabwe at Victoria Falls, or into Botswana at Kazungula. From **Mozambique**, you can fly from Maputo (2 weekly) or Beira (3 weekly) to Harare. The road between Mutare and Beira is now safe, and minibuses go between the border post on the Mozambique side and the coast.

From **Zambia**, it's straightforward enough to hitch to the Victoria Falls or take a daily coach from Lusaka to Harare. A train connects Dar-es-Salaam in **Tanzania** to Kapiri Mposhi in central Zambia, where it's necessary to change. Another service from a nearby, but separate station goes via Lusaka to Livingstone, from where buses and taxis ply the route to the Zimbabwe border; Victoria Falls town is a short walk across the bridge. There's also a regular coach service between Lusaka and Francistown in Botswana.

Zimbabwe and Botswana are both also directly connected by air to the independent enclave kingdoms of **Lesotho** and **Swaziland** – both within South Africa.

AFRICAN AIR CONNECTIONS

Harare is well connected to a number of destinations in Africa, making multi-stop travel easy. Air Zimbabwe flies between Harare and

---

SOUTH AFRICAN MOBILE SAFARIS COVERING ZIMBABWE AND BOTSWANA

Afroventures Safaris, PO Box 2339, Randburg (☎011/807 3720). Overland safaris in Botswana, Zimbabwe and South Africa, graded according to difficulty. Can be joined in Victoria Falls, Maun or Johannesburg.

Karibu Safari, PO Box 35196, Northway 4065, Durban; 50 Acutt Ave, Rosehill, Durban (☎031/839774). Overland camping trips by truck through Zimbabwe, Botswana, Malawi, Namibia and South Africa, with an upmarket alternative of lodge-based safaris.

---

the following cities: Gaborone, Lilongwe, Lusaka, Nairobi, Dar-es-Salaam, Maputo, Mauritius and Windhoek.

If you plan to head on to further African travels, **Nairobi** is probably the most useful hub to

head for. You can also fly Harare to Addis Ababa nonstop for Ethiopian Airlines' excellent connections across the continent. Alternatively, for West Africa, you can fly direct to Lagos (Balkan Bulgarian Airlines) and Accra (Ghana Airways).

RED TAPE AND VISAS

Citizens of Botswana, Canada, Ireland, Namibia and the UK need only a valid passport, and evidence that they have sufficient funds to support themselves, to enter Zimbabwe for up to ninety days. South Africans are issued with a free visa at their point of entry.

In December 1998, Zimbabwe's Ministry of Home Affairs introduced a system of reciprocal visas and charges, which means that if you're not a citizen of one of the countries mentioned above,

and your country requires Zimbabwean citizens to have visas, you will need one to enter Zimbabwe; but visas are issued at the point of entry and don't have to be arranged in advance, although they do incur a cost. The new regulations and the precipitate way in which they were imposed has been challenged by the Ministry of Tourism, so there's a chance they may be suspended. Check for the latest details when you're due to travel.

Nationals of **EU countries** (apart from the UK and Ireland), **Australia** and the **US** can obtain a single-entry visa, costing US$30, at their port of entry. **Multiple-entry visas** costing US$55 must be obtained in advance from the Department of Immigration in Harare or any Zimbabwean consular or trade mission office outside the country. South Africans requiring multiple-entry visas must also apply in advance, but there's no charge.

If you're a **journalist** coming to Zimbabwe – particularly if you're just going on holiday – consider stating an alternative occupation on your entry form. Anyone even vaguely connected with the media is generally given a 24-hour visa, and must then get accreditation at the Ministry of Home Affairs. However, if you are on a press assignment, it's probably best to say so, otherwise you could get into a tight corner if found out later.

ARRIVING OVERLAND

If travelling overland, make sure things are timed so you don't end up stranded at a closed border post. Most of **Zimbabwe**'s border posts with Zambia, Botswana and South Africa open from 6am to 6pm, seven days a week, apart from Beit Bridge, which opens until 8pm.

DIPLOMATIC MISSIONS ABROAD

Australia, 11 Culgoa Circuit, O'Malley, ACT 2606 (☎06/6286 2700).
Botswana, 1st Floor, IGI Building, PO Box 1232, Gaborone (☎314495).
Canada, 332 Somerset St West, Ottawa, ON, K2P 0J9 (☎613/237 4388).
Germany, Villichgasse 7, 5300 Bonn 2 (☎0228/356071).
Mozambique, Avenue Kenneth Kaunda 816/820, Caixa Postal 743, Maputo (☎1/499404).
South Africa, Bank of Lisbon Building, 37 Sauer St, Johannesburg 2000 (☎011/838 2156); 798 Mertons, Arcadia, Pretoria (☎021/342 5135); 53/55 Fawley Towers, 55c Kuyper St, Zonnebloem, Cape Town (☎021/461 4710).
UK, 429 The Strand, London WC2 0SA (☎020/7836 7755).
USA, 1608 New Hampshire Ave NW, Washington, DC 20009 (☎202/332 7100).
Zambia, 4th Floor, Ulenda House, Cairo Road, Lusaka (☎01/229382).

HEALTH

Zimbabwe is a pretty healthy country for travellers and you can put aside most of the health fears about horrible "tropical" diseases that may be justified in some parts of Africa. Two exceptions to this are HIV, which is rampant (but there's little chance of contracting it other than through unprotected sex), and malaria, which is a potential hazard in certain areas.

The sunny, dry climate and unpolluted air suits most people, and Zimbabwe's temperate central plateau – where Harare and most other major towns are situated – is exceptionally healthy, with a complete absence of malaria. There are generally high standards of hygiene and safe **drinking water** in all tourist areas.

INOCULATIONS

Although no **inoculations** are compulsory if you arrive from the West, it's wise to make sure that your **polio** and **tetanus** jabs are up to date. **Yellow fever** vaccination certificates are necessary if you've come from a country where the disease is endemic, such as Kenya or Tanzania.

Cholera vaccination is unpleasant, pretty ineffective and not recommended unless you are going to be working for a period in terribly deprived areas. Some authorities recommend a course of **typhoid** shots, which for similar reasons is something to think twice about. Despite their terrible reputation, typhoid fever and cholera are both eminently curable, and few (if any) visitors to Southern Africa ever catch them.

A Havrix shot protects against **hepatitis A**, which is caught from contaminated water or food, for a year in the first instance; a booster injection a year later gives protection for a further ten years. Hepatitis B vaccine is only essential for anyone involved in health work. It's spread by the transfer of blood products, usually dirty needles, so most travellers need not worry about it.

If you decide to have an armful of jabs, start organizing them six weeks before departure. If you're going to another African country first and need the yellow fever jab, remember that a yellow fever certificate only becomes valid ten days after you've had the shot.

HOSPITALS

Private clinics are the best bet for visitors to Zimbabwe as **hospitals** tend to be oversubscribed, understaffed and ill-equipped. Clinics will offer more personal treatment, costs are

MEDICAL RESOURCES FOR TRAVELLERS

For a comprehensive and sobering account of the health problems which travellers encounter worldwide, consult the regularly updated **Traveller's Health**, edited by Dr Richard Dawood (OUP; Viking Penguin).

AUSTRALIA AND NEW ZEALAND

Auckland Hospital, Park Road, Grafton, Auckland (☎09/379 7440). Similar services as below.
Travellers' Medical and Vaccination Centre, 7/428 George St, Sydney (☎02/9221 7133); 2/393 Little Bourke St, Melbourne (☎03/9602 5788); 6/29 Gilbert Place, Adelaide (☎08/8212 7522); 6/247 Adelaide St, Brisbane (☎07/3221 9066); 5 Mill St, Perth (☎08/9321 1977); *www.tmvc.com.au*. Up-to-date information on health-risk areas, recommended inoculations and preventative measures for travellers and so on.

BRITAIN AND IRELAND

British Airways Travel Clinic, 156 Regent St, London W1 7RA (Mon–Fri 9.30am–5.15pm, Sat 10am–4pm; ☎020/7439 9584); plus the clinic within Flightbookers, 177 Tottenham Court Rd, London W1P 0LX (Mon–Fri 9.30am–6.30pm, Sat 10am–2pm; ☎020/7757 2504); both are walk-in services, but appointments are available. There are appointment-only branches at 101 Cheapside, London EC2 (Mon–Fri 9am–4.30pm; ☎020/7606 2977), and at the BA terminal in London's Victoria Station (Mon–Fri 8.15–11.30am & 12.30–3.30pm; ☎020/7233 6661). BA also operate around forty regional clinics throughout the country (for the one nearest to you, call ☎01276/685040, or consult *www.britishairways.com*), plus at Gatwick and Heathrow airports.
Healthline (☎0839/337733; code for Zimbabwe ☎61; 49p per minute) and **Health-Fax** (☎0991/991992; code for Zimbabwe ☎269; £1.50 per minute). Up-to-the-minute recorded advice provided by the Hospital for Tropical Diseases on how to stay healthy abroad. Computer-operated system dishes out detailed health information about Zimbabwe and all its neighbouring countries. Health-Fax sends the same information to a fax number you specify, which actually works out cheaper.
Hospital for Tropical Diseases, St Pancras Hospital, 4 St Pancras Way, London NW1 0PE (☎020/7388 9600). Travel clinic offering consultations, jabs and any other medical gear you might need, such as mosquito nets or anti-malaria pills. Consultations cost £15, a fee that is waived if you have jabs as well. Most jabs cost around £10.

---

nowhere as prohibitive as in the US and if you're insured they should certainly pose no problem.

In **remoter parts**, where there are no private clinics, the local health centre or hospital will usually be able to carry out adequate first aid, but be prepared for makeshift solutions rather than the latest treatments.

In emergencies, or for extremely serious conditions, patients are sometimes flown to **Johannesburg**, where the full range of up-to-date treatment is available.

WATER – AND STOMACH UPSETS

Only in extremely remote places do you need to **boil** your water or use **water purification** tablets. **Stomach upsets** from food are equally rare. You'll only find salad and ice – the danger items in some other countries – in hotels and smarter restaurants. Both are perfectly safe and not to be missed. As anywhere, though, **wash** fruit and vegetables as thoroughly as possible, and don't overindulge on fruit – no matter how tempting – when you first arrive.

If you do get a stomach bug, the best cure is lots of water and rest. Papayas, the flesh as well as the pips, are a good tonic to offset the runs.

Avoid jumping for **antibiotics** at the first sign of illness; keep them as a last resort – they don't work on viruses and annihilate your "gut flora" (most of which you want to keep), making you more susceptible next time round. Most upsets will resolve themselves if you adopt a sensible fat-free diet for a couple of days, but if they do persist unabated, or are accompanied by other unusual symptoms, then see a doctor as soon as possible.

MASTA (Medical Advisory Services for Travellers Abroad), School of Hygiene and Tropical Diseases, Keppel Street, London WC1E 7HT (☎020/7631 4408). Commercial service providing detailed "health briefs" for all countries, and a Travellers' Healthline (☎0891/224100; 49p per minute) providing written information tailored to your journey by return of post.

Trailfinders Immunization Centre, 194 Kensington High St, London W8 7RG (Mon–Wed & Fri 9am–5pm, Thurs 9am–6pm, Sat 9.30am–4pm; ☎020/7938 3999). Walk-in advice and inoculation service operated by the respected and knowledgeable travel agency.

SOUTH AFRICA

BA Travel Clinics, Sunninghill Family Medcare Centre, opposite Megawatt Park, Edison Crescent/Maxwell Drive, Sunninghill, Sandton, Johannesburg (☎011/807 3132); Room 1027, Fountain Medical Centre, Heerengracht, Cape Town (☎021/419 3172); Queen Street/Melville Street (☎044/382 6366). The only BA Travel Clinics outside the UK offer good advice on health matters for travellers to Zimbabwe; excellent on the question of the latest precautions for malaria, which they are constantly monitoring. They also administer immunizations, dispense necessary medicines and sell items such as mosquito spray and medical kits. Their Web site (*www.travelclinic.co.za*) has reliable up-to-date information on travellers' health.

USA AND CANADA

Canadian Society for International Health, 1 Nicholas St, Suite 1105, Ottawa, ON K1N 7B7 (☎613/241-5785). Distributes a free pamphlet, *Health Information for Canadian Travellers*, containing an extensive list of travel health centres in Canada.

Center for Disease Control, 1600 Clifton Rd NE, Atlanta, GA 30333 (☎404/639-3311, International Travelers Hotline ☎1-888/232-3228, *www.cdc.gov/travel/travel.html*). Publishes outbreak warnings, suggested inoculations, precautions and other background information for travellers.

International Association for Medical Assistance to Travellers (IAMAT), 417 Center St, Lewiston, NY 14092 (☎716/754-4883), and 40 Regal Rd, Guelph, ON N1K 1B5 (☎519/836-0102). Non-profit organization supported by donations, and providing a list of English-speaking doctors in South Africa, climate charts and leaflets on various diseases and inoculations.

Travel Medicine, 351 Pleasant St, Suite 312, Northampton, MA 01060 (☎1-800/872-8633). Sells first-aid kits, mosquito netting, water filters and other health-related travel products.

Travelers Medical Center, 31 Washington Square, New York, NY 10011 (☎212/982-1600). Consultation service on immunizations and treatment of diseases for people travelling to developing countries.

HEAT AND DUST

The **sun** could be the most dangerous thing you encounter. Sunglasses and a broad-brimmed hat are recommended, especially for children. Ordinary sunscreens and lotions can be bought in pharmacies in Zimbabwe and Botswana, though you should buy the **total block** or **high-protection** variety before you leave. Tanning should be a very gradual process.

If you're not used to dealing with continuous heat over long periods of time, take care to avoid heat exhaustion. Be aware that you may be overheating, and if you start feeling ill – headaches or nausea – get to a cool shady place. Make sure you're getting enough water and that your salt levels aren't depleting.

Botswana is particularly **dusty** – take this on board if you're asthmatic or allergic to dust. If you're just flying in to the Delta and staying near the water, you shouldn't have any problems.

SNAKES, INSECTS AND OTHER UNDESIRABLES

Zimbabwe and Botswana both threaten all sorts of bites, stings and rashes – which rarely, if ever, materialize.

Snakes are common, but hardly ever seen as they get out of the way quickly. Puff adders are the most dangerous because they lie in paths and don't move, but they're not commonly seen by travellers. The best advice if you get bitten is to remember what the snake looked like (kill it if you can, for identification) and get to a clinic or hospital. Most bites are not fatal and the worst thing is to panic: desperate measures with razor blades and tourniquets risk doing more harm than good.

Tick-bite fever is occasionally contracted from walking in the bush, particularly in March and April, when the grass is long and wet. The offending ticks are minute and you're unlikely to spot them. Symptoms appear a week later – swollen glands and severe aching of the bones, backache and fever. Since it is a self-limiting disease, it will run its course in three or four days. Ticks you may find on yourself are not dangerous, just repulsive at first. Make sure you pull out the head as well as the body (it's not painful). A good way of removing small ones is to smear Vaseline or grease over them, making them release their hold.

Scorpions and **spiders** abound but are hardly ever seen unless you turn over logs and stones. If you're collecting wood for a campfire, knock or shake it before picking it up. Contrary to popular myth, scorpion stings and spider bites are painful but almost never fatal. Most are harmless and should be left alone. A simple precaution when camping is to shake out your shoes and clothes in the morning before you get dressed.

Rabies exists in both countries. Be wary of strange animals and go to a clinic if bitten. It can be treated effectively with a course of injections.

MALARIA

Malaria, caused by a parasite carried in the saliva of Anopheles mosquitoes, is endemic in tropical Africa: many Africans have it in their bloodstream and get occasional bouts of fever. It has a variable incubation period of a few days to several weeks, so you can become ill long after being bitten. If you go down with it, you'll know: the fever, shivering and headaches are like severe flu and come in waves, usually beginning in the early evening. Malaria is not infectious but it can be dangerous, and even fatal if not treated quickly.

Protection against malaria is absolutely essential. Although much of Zimbabwe and Botswana, including most of the main towns, is free of malarial mosquitoes, you have to keep taking the tablets to maintain your resistance for when you're bitten by a carrier mosquito – in a low-lying game park, for example. However, remember that no anti-malarial drug is totally effective, and the only reliable protection is to avoid getting bitten.

TABLETS

Doctors can advise on which kind of **preventive tablets** to take – generally the latest anti-resistant creation – and you can buy most without a prescription at a pharmacy before you leave. It's important to keep to a routine and cover the period before and after your trip with doses. Take enough pills with you to cover your entire stay, as the types of tablet sold in Botswana and Zimbabwe are different.

MEDICAL AIR RESCUE SERVICE

Even if your worst nightmare comes true and you catch malaria in Zimbabwe's bush, or fall victim to some other medical misfortune, don't panic. Zimbabwe's **Medical Air Rescue Service**, PO Box HG 969, Highlands, Harare, 2 Fairbridge Ave, Belgravia, Harare (☎04/791074, 790530 or 790391–2, fax 790594, *marketing@mars.co.zw*), can rapidly transfer you from anywhere in the country to a reliable hospital.

Given how inexpensive the service is, a subscription is highly recommended, especially if you're going anywhere remote or are taking part in adventure sports. For **US$1.20 per day**, a MARS subscription will cover evacuation to the most suitable hospital anywhere in Zimbabwe – usually a private one in Harare. During transit they will negotiate with your insurer on your behalf to get you a hospital bed and ensure that all your costs are covered. They can also arrange, should it be necessary, for you to be moved to Johannesburg, and they have facilities in Botswana, Zambia, Mozambique and Malawi and can bring you back from any of these countries to Zimbabwe.

Although most safari operators subscribe to the service, which is available to all their clients, you won't be covered when you're not under their supervision, when travelling to or from their camp. Even if you're covered by travel insurance, there's still good reason to take out MARS cover on top, as insurers tend to insist on bureaucratic procedures before authorizing rescue, such as "vital signs" (for example, blood pressure and oxygen saturation readings), whereas if you have a MARS subscription immediate evacuation is guaranteed. Most insurers also have a "pre-existing conditions" exclusion clause, whereas MARS collects you regardless.

Subscriptions can be taken out in advance and there are plans for Internet credit card transactions (*www.mars.co.zw*) or you can arrange it at their office.

MEDICAL KIT

Most basic medicines and medical gear can be bought in pharmacies in Zimbabwe, so there's no need to lumber yourself with too heavy a **medical kit**. Only in deeply rural areas where few visitors ever go are you likely to be caught short. If you need specialized drugs, bring your own supply, but any first-aid items can be easily replaced. A very **basic kit** should include:

Antibiotics Potentially useful if you're heading off the beaten track. A broad-spectrum variety is best.
Antiseptic cream Bacitracin is a reliable brand. Nelson's natural calendular ointment is invaluable for stings, rashes, cuts, sores or cracked skin.
Bandages One wide and one narrow.
Eyedrops Wonderfully soothing if you're travelling on dusty roads.

Fine tweezers Useful for removing thorns or glass.
Insect repellent Essential in malarial areas (see opposite).
Paracetamol Safer than aspirin for pain and fever relief.
Lip salve/chapstick
Sticking plasters/Band-Aids

NETS, OILS AND COILS

Female Anopheles mosquitoes – the aggressors – are active between dusk and dawn. Sleep under a **mosquito net** when possible, making sure to tuck it under the mattress, and burn mosquito **coils** (which you can buy everywhere) for a peaceful, if noxious, night. Whenever the mosquitoes are particularly bad – and that's not often – cover your exposed parts with something strong. **Insect repellents** containing diethyltoluamide work well, and other locally produced repellents such as *Peaceful Sleep* are widely available. Citronella oil is a help, too, but hardly smells better than the repellents.

Electric mosquito-destroyers that you fit with a pad every night are less pungent than mosquito coils, but you need electricity. Mosquito "buzzers" are useless.

IF YOU FALL ILL

If you contract malaria, you'll need to take a **cure**. Don't compare yourself with local people, who may have considerable immunity. The priority, if you think you might be getting a fever, is treatment. Delay is potentially risky.

Warning signs include flu-like symptoms, fever, diarrhoea and joint pains. If you come down with any of these, from one week after arriving in a malaria zone to three months after leaving, you should immediately see a doctor and have a **blood test**.

BILHARZIA

One ailment which you need to take seriously in both countries is **bilharzia**, carried in all Zimbabwe's waterways outside the Eastern Highlands. Bilharzia (schistosomiasis) is spread

by a tiny, waterborne parasite. These worm-like flukes leave their water-snail hosts and burrow into human skin to multiply in the bloodstream. They work their way to the walls of the intestine or bladder, where they begin to lay eggs.

Avoid swimming in dams and rivers where possible. If you're canoeing or can't avoid the water, have a test when you return home. White water is no guarantee of safety; although the snails favour sheltered areas, the flukes can be swept downstream. The chances are you'll have avoided bilharzia even if you swam in the Zambezi, but it's best to be sure.

Symptoms may be no more than a feeling of lassitude and ill health. Once infection is established, abdominal pain and blood in the urine and stools are common. Fortunately it's easily and effectively treated these days with praziquantel, although the drug can make you feel ill for a few days. No vaccine is available and none foreseen.

AIDS AND SEXUALLY TRANSMITTED DISEASES

Horror stories of rusty syringes and HIV-infected blood transfusions are not relevant to Zimbabwe. Disposable needles are routinely used and the Zimbabwean health authorities have screened all donated blood for **AIDS** for a decade. Zimbabwe was the third country in the world to do so – after the United States and Germany, and some months ahead of Britain. If you're travelling overland, though, and want to play safe, take your own needle and transfusion kit.

Your biggest chance of getting AIDS is through unprotected sex. AIDS, as well as various **venereal diseases**, is widespread in Southern

Africa. Some estimates put HIV incidence at a staggering twenty percent of Zimbabwe's population, and the chance of catching the virus through sexual contact is very real. Follow the usual precautions regarding safer sex: either abstain, or use a condom.

TEETH

Have a thorough **dental checkup** before leaving home. You'll find dentists in the main towns in Zimbabwe; they are listed after doctors at the beginning of each town in the telephone directory.

TRAVEL INSURANCE

Most people will find it essential to take out a good travel insurance policy. This can be quite comprehensive, anticipating anything from lost or stolen baggage and missed connections, to charter companies going bankrupt; however, certain policies (notably in North America) only cover medical costs.

If you plan to participate in adventure activities, watersports, or do some hiking, you'll probably have to pay an extra premium; check carefully that any insurance policy you are considering will cover you in case of an accident. Note also that very few insurers will arrange on-the-spot payments in the event of a major expense or loss; you will usually be reimbursed only after going home. In all cases of loss or theft of goods, you will have to contact the **local police** to have a report made out so that your insurer can process the claim.

BRITAIN AND IRELAND

Most British and Irish travel agents and tour operators will offer you insurance when you book your flight or holiday, and some will insist you take it. These policies are usually reasonable value, though, as ever, you should check the small print. If you feel the cover is inadequate, or you want to compare prices, travel agents, insurance brokers and banks should be able to help. Basic cover for Zimbabwe starts at £30 for seventeen days, £40 for a month, and £120 for three months. If you have a good "all-risks" **home insurance policy**, it may well cover your possessions against loss or theft even when overseas, and many **private medical schemes** also cover you when abroad – make sure you know the procedure and the helpline number.

THE US AND CANADA

US travellers should check their current insurance policies: you may find you are already covered for medical expenses or other losses while abroad. In Canada, provincial health plans typically provide some overseas medical coverage, although they are unlikely to pick up the full tab in the event of a mishap.

Holders of official **student/teacher/youth cards** are entitled to accident coverage and hospital inpatient benefits – the annual membership is far less than the cost of comparable insurance. **Students** may also find that their student health coverage extends during the vacations and for one term beyond the date of last enrolment. **Homeowners' or renters'** insurance often covers theft or loss of documents, money and valuables while overseas.

After exhausting the possibilities above, you might want to contact a specialist travel insurance company; your travel agent can usually recommend one, or see the box below. Travel insurance **policies** vary. Some are comprehensive, while others cover only certain risks (accidents, illnesses, delayed or lost luggage, cancelled flights and so on). In particular, ask whether the policy pays **medical costs** up front or reimburses you later, and whether it provides for medical evacuation to your home country. For policies that include lost or stolen luggage, check exactly what is and isn't covered, and make sure the per-article limit will cover your most valuable possession. Most policies cover only items lost, stolen or damaged while in the custody of an identifiable, responsible third party – hotel porters, airlines, luggage consignment and so on.

The best **premiums** are usually to be had through student/youth travel agencies – rates for STA policies, for example (see box on p.10), are US$35 for up to seven days, US$55 for eight to fifteen days, US$115 for one month, and US$180 for two months.

AUSTRALIA AND NEW ZEALAND

Travel insurance is available from most **travel agents** (see p.12) or direct from **insurance companies** (see box) for periods ranging from a few days to a year or even longer. Most policies are similar in premium and coverage. Two weeks' cover for a trip to Southern Africa should cost roughly A$130/NZ$145, while you can expect to pay around A$190/NZ$210 for a stay of one month, A$270/NZ$310 for two months and A$300/NZ$340 for three months.

TRAVEL INSURANCE COMPANIES

AUSTRALIA AND NEW ZEALAND

Cover More, 9/32 Walker St, North Sydney (☎02/9202 8000 or 1800/251 881).
Ready Plan, 141 Walker St, Dandenong,
Melbourne (☎1300/555 017); 10/63 Albert St, Auckland (☎09/379 3208).

BRITAIN

Columbus Travel Insurance, 17 Devonshire Square, London EC2M 4SQ (☎020/7375 0011, *www.columbusdirect.co.uk*).
Endsleigh Insurance, 97–107 Southampton Row, London WC1B 4AG (☎020/7436 4451, *www.endsleigh.co.uk*).

Frizzell Insurance, Frizzell House, County Gates, Bournemouth, Dorset BH1 2NF (☎01202/292333).
Worldwide, The Business Centre, 1–7 Commercial Rd, Tonbridge, Kent TN12 6YT (☎01892/833338, *www.wwtis.co.uk*).

USA AND CANADA

Access America, PO Box 90310, Richmond, VA 23230 (☎1-800/284-8300).
Carefree Travel Insurance, 100 Garden City Plaza, PO Box 9366, Garden City, NY 11530 (☎1-800/323-3149).
Desjardins Travel Insurance Canada ☎1-
800/463-7830.
Travel Guard, 1145 Clark St, Stevens Point, WI 54481 (☎1-800/826-1300, *www.noelgroup.com*).
Travel Insurance Services, 2930 Camino Diablo, Suite 200, Walnut Creek, CA 94596 (☎1-800/937-1387, *www.travelinsure.com*).

COSTS, MONEY AND BANKS

For visitors there are two economies in Zimbabwe: a tourist one linked to US dollars, which can be moderately to very expensive; and the local Zimbabwe dollar economy, which is relatively cheap for anyone with foreign currency (although not for Zimbabweans). What you spend will depend largely on how you navigate between the two.

Staying in backpackers' lodges, self-catering or eating cheap snacks you could scrape by at under a basic **US$15** a day – less if you're camping. If you plan on staying in more comfortable accommodation with en-suite rooms – B&Bs, guest houses or mid-priced hotels – and you're eating out regularly, you should allow anything between **US$30** and **US$50** a day.

At the top end, staying in exclusive game lodges where everything is included – from drinks and meals down to having your socks washed – will set you back anything between **US$150** and **US$325**.

Transport is inexpensive, especially compared to Europe, Australia or North America. If you use economy buses rather than tourist-oriented alternatives, you can cover large distances for a few

dollars. Luxury coaches and train travel are more expensive but still quite reasonable. Car rental is a relatively expensive option but the only way of reaching some places. Travelling the 440km from Bulawayo to Harare, for example, expect to pay around US$5 by economy bus, US$15 for a sleeper on the train, a similar amount by luxury coach, and US$45 by air. By car it would total roughly US$75 (including fuel) for two-week rental, and about double that for a one-day rental, to cover the distance.

Accommodation is generally cheaper for two or more sharing, except in backpacker lodge dorms, where you can expect to pay US$3.50–5 per person in a dorm (a couple of dollars more if you share a double room). In larger towns, you'll find decent en-suite rooms in apartments, hotels or B&Bs from US$15 per person, rising to a mid-range average of US$35, with luxury accommodation spanning a range from about US$60 to US$100 or more.

On safari, there's a huge gulf in cost between doing it yourself in National Parks accommodation or going for an all-in safari deal. Parks accommodation is excellent value but consequently often oversubscribed, starting at around US$5 per person sharing a self-catering chalet. Private hotels at national parks, such as *Hwange Safari Lodge*, charge around US$95 per person (B&B) – a premium for their proximity to the action, not for their facilities. A typical bush camp or safari lodge in the thick of wildlife country will charge from US$150 per person, rising to just short of US$350 for the most expensive, fully inclusive of meals, game activities (drives, walks or boat trips) and the on-hand expertise of one or more licensed game guides.

Food is cheap if you eat where the locals do and combine it with self-catering. You can easily eat a filling meal of *sadza* and chicken or meat for a couple of US dollars. Moving up a notch

---

PARK ENTRY FEES

On a number of occasions in the late 1990s, the government raised National Parks **entry fees** without notice (at one point in 1999, the weekly entry fee to Hwange and other parks was a whopping US$40), only to reduce them in response to howls of protest from the tourism industry. You should check on the current situation by contacting either the National Parks booking offices or one of the travel agents listed in the book.

need not break the bank either. Breakfast at a Harare café can come out as low as US$2, light lunches like sandwiches and pizzas typically go for under US$3.50, while you should have no difficulty finding a very good main course such as fillet steak or fish at a decent city restaurant for under US$5.

Entrance fees to museums are typically not more than US$2, while galleries tend to be considerably cheaper, but it's at national parks where you'll really feel the pinch, with day entry at the major parks costing US$10 and week entry US$20 per person.

MONEY, THE EXCHANGE RATE AND BANKS

Zimbabwe's currency is the **Zimbabwe dollar** (Z$ or ZWD), often referred to as the "buck". Notes come in 10-, 20- 50 and 100-dollar denominations and there are coins of 1, 5, 10, 20 and 50 cents and Z$1, Z$2 and Z$5. At the time of writing, the exchange rate was roughly Z$40 to the US dollar; Z$60 to the pound sterling; Z$25 to the Australian dollar; and Z$6 to the South African rand.

Usual **bank opening hours** are Monday, Tuesday, Thursday and Friday 8am to 3pm, Wednesday 8am to 1pm, and Saturday 8am to 11am. The ongoing liberalization of the economy has led to a proliferation of private **foreign exchange bureaux** at airports and in all the larger towns and resorts. These are usually fairly quick and efficient and offer competitive rates. Out of hours, you can sometimes change money at hotel cashiers' desks, particularly in larger establishments – but don't count on it if you're not staying there.

The days of strictly scrutinized currency declaration forms in Zimbabwe are thankfully long gone. You will, however, be asked on your arrival form to declare how much money you are bringing into the country to ascertain whether you can sustain yourself throughout your stay. Be sure to use up all your Z$ while in the country, as it's virtually impossible to change them outside the country.

Judging by the number of hustlers around, the currency **black market** in Zimbabwe is flourishing, although it's difficult to see why. Black market trading is a serious offence, and the rates offered on the streets rarely make the risk worth it. In any case, the odds are that the dealer is running a scam, and you may find that the wad of notes offered in exchange for your hard currency is padded out with strips of newspaper.

TRAVELLERS' CHEQUES, CASH AND CREDIT CARDS

Travellers' cheques are the safest way to carry your funds into Zimbabwe, as they can be replaced if lost or stolen. American Express, Visa and Thomas Cook are all widely recognized.

However, they'll be useless if you're heading into remote areas, where you'll need to carry **cash**.

Zimbabwe's fifteen percent sales tax (see box on p.25) is not levied on transactions settled outside the country (prebooking car rental, for example) or inside the country using a **credit card**. The most useful credit cards are Visa and Mastercard, which can also be used to draw cash at **automatic teller machines** (ATMs), found in the cities. American Express, however, is not all that widely accepted in Zimbabwe.

MAPS, BOOKS AND INFORMATION

The Zimbabwe Tourist Organization (ZTO) is underfunded and not a brilliant source of information, but you can sometimes pick up basic maps and information on hotels and organized tours. If there's an office in your country, it may be worth paying a visit just to browse around and whet your appetite. Elsewhere, contact the nearest Zimbabwe diplomatic mission (see Red Tape and Visas, p.16) or an office of Air Zimbabwe.

The best **map** of Zimbabwe is produced by the Automobile Association of Zimbabwe and is available at its branches in Harare, Bulawayo and Mutare, as well as (more expensively) through many newsagents and bookshops in Zimbabwe. The Globetrotter map of the country, although the prettiest available, has some unfortunate inaccuracies.

Zimbabwe is well covered by detailed Ordnance Survey (OS) maps, which are indispensable for walking in any of the national parks. They're available from the Surveyor General's Office, Electra House, Samora Machel Avenue, Harare. The office also has a wealth of maps covering everything that can be mapped, from rainfall patterns to geology and land use; it's fascinating just to browse around.

The **Parks Department** produces useful fact sheets, which are frequently out of stock, but your best chance of finding them is through their office in Harare. They have information on facilities and attractions in most of the national parks. And, finally, local information is available from town publicity associations. These are often very helpful, with up-to-date hotel and camping information, brochures and some useful regional maps.

ZIMBABWE TOURIST OFFICES

Head Office, Ground Floor, Kopje Plaza, 1 Jason Moyo Ave/Rotten Row (☎04/752570, *nkanyepi@africaonline.co.zw*).
Germany, An der Hauptwache, 60313 Frankfurt (☎069/920 7730).
South Africa, Tower Mall, Upper Shopping Level, Carlton Centre, Commissioner Street,

PO Box 9398, Johannesburg 2000 (☎011/331 3137).
UK, 429 Strand, London WC2R 0SA (☎020/7836 7755).
US, Rockefeller Centre, Suite 1905, 1270 Avenue of the Americas, New York, NY 10020 (☎212/332 1090).

SPECIALIST BOOK AND MAP SUPPLIERS

AUSTRALIA AND NEW ZEALAND

The Map Shop, 16a Peel St, Adelaide (☎08/8231 2033).
Mapland, 372 Little Bourke St, Melbourne (☎03/9670 4383).
Perth Map Centre, 884 Hay St, Perth (☎08/9322 5733).

Specialty Maps, 58 Albert St, Auckland (☎09/307 2217).
Travel Bookshop, Shop 3, 175 Liverpool St, Sydney (☎02/9261 8200).
Worldwide Maps and Guides, 187 George St, Brisbane (☎07/3221 4330).

BRITAIN

Blackwell's Map and Travel Shop, 53 Broad St, Oxford OX1 3BQ (☎01865/792792, *bookshop.blackwell.co.uk*).
Daunt Books, 83 Marylebone High St, London W1M 3DE (☎020/7224 2295), and 193 Haverstock Hill, London NW3 4QL (☎020/7794 4006); National Map Centre, 22–24 Caxton St, London SW1H 0QU (☎020/7222 2466, *www.mapsworld.com*); Stanfords, 12–14 Long Acre, London WC2E 9LP (☎020/7836 1321, *sales@stanfords.co.uk*); The Travel Bookshop, 13–15 Blenheim Crescent, London W11 2EE (☎020/7229 5260, *www.thetravelbookshop.co.uk*).
Heffers Map Shop, 3rd Floor, 19 Sidney St, Cambridge CB2 3HL (☎01223/568467, *www.heffers.co.uk*).

James Thin Melven's Bookshop, 29 Union St, Inverness IV1 1QA (☎01463/233500, *www.jthin.co.uk*).
John Smith and Sons, 57–61 St Vincent St, Glasgow G2 5TB (☎0141/221 7472, *www.johnsmith.co.uk*).
The Map Shop, 30a Belvoir St, Leicester LE1 6QH (☎0116/247 1400).
Newcastle Map Centre, 55 Grey St, Newcastle upon Tyne NE1 6EF (☎0191/261 5622).
Stanfords, 29 Corn St, Bristol BS1 1HT (☎0117/929 9966).
Waterstone's, 91 Deansgate, Manchester M3 2BW (☎0161/832 1992, *www.waterstones.co.uk*).

CANADA

Toronto Open Air Books and Maps, 25 Toronto St, Toronto, ON M5C 2R1 (☎416/363-0719).
Ulysses Travel Bookshop, 4176 St-Denis, Montréal H2W 2M5 (☎514/843-9447, *www.ulysses.ca*).

Vancouver International Travel Maps & Books, 552 Seymour St, Vancouver, V6B 3J5 (☎604/687-3320).

IRELAND

Easons Bookshop, 40 O'Connell St, Dublin 1 (☎01/873 3811).
Fred Hanna's Bookshop, 27–29 Nassau St, Dublin 2 (☎01/677 1255).

Waterstone's, Queens Building, 8 Royal Ave, Belfast BT1 1DA (☎01232/247 355); 7 Dawson St, Dublin 2 (☎01/679 1415); 69 Patrick St, Cork (☎021/276 522).

Continues overleaf

SPECIALIST BOOK AND MAP SUPPLIERS continued

SOUTH AFRICA

Travellers Bookshop, King's Warehouse, Victoria Wharf, Waterfront, Cape Town (☎021/425 6880).

USA

California Book Passage, 51 Tamal Vista Blvd, Corte Madera, CA 94925 (☎1-800/999-7909 or 415/927-0960); The Complete Traveler Bookstore, 3207 Fillmore St, San Francisco, CA 94123 (☎415/923-1511, *www.completetraveler.com*); Map Link Inc, 30 S La Patera Lane, Unit 5, Santa Barbara, CA 93117 (☎805/692-6777, *www.maplink.com*); Phileas Fogg's Books & Maps, #87 Stanford Shopping Center, Palo Alto, CA 94304 (☎1-800/533-FOGG, *www.foggs.com*); Sierra Club Bookstore, 6014 College Ave, Oakland, CA 94618 (☎510/658-7470, *www.sierraclubbookstore.com*); Rand McNally, 595 Market St, San Francisco, CA 94105 (☎415/777-3131).

Chicago Rand McNally, 444 N Michigan Ave (☎312/321-1751, *www.randmcnallystore.com*). Rand McNally now have more than twenty stores across the US; call (☎1-800/234-0679) for the address of your nearest store, or for direct-mail maps.

The Complete Traveller Bookstore, 199 Madison Ave, New York (☎212/685-9007); Rand McNally, 150 E 52nd St, New York (☎212/758-7488).

The Map Store Inc, 1636 I St NW, Washington, DC 20006 (☎1-800/544-2659 or 202/628-2608); Travel Books & Language Center, 4437 Wisconsin Ave, Washington, DC (☎1-800/220-2665).

Seattle Elliot Bay Book Company, 101 S Main St (☎1-800/962-5311 or 206/624-6600, *www.elliotbaybook.com\ebbco*).

ZIMBABWE ON THE INTERNET

Don't expect anything too elaborate from Zimbabwe's **Web sites**, but you'll find a fair number of browsable pages providing good news coverage and background, as well as hundreds of sites that are little more than vehicles advertising the tourism industry.

British Airways Travel Clinic
www.travelclinic.co.za. Authoritative health advice and tips from the South African branch of BATC. It draws a distinction between the health risks in South Africa and the rest of the continent – a less paranoid spin on the bugs, bites and bacteria than you'll get in Britain or the US.

CIA World Factbook: Zimbabwe
www.odci.gov/cia/publications/factbook/zi.html. A good basic rundown on Zimbabwe, knocked together by US spooks.

Daily Mail & Guardian *www.mg.co.za*. The South African weekly *Mail & Guardian's* site includes daily news and a homepage dedicated to surveying Southern Africa's online travel resources, as well as Jump*Start (*www.mg.co.za/mg/za1/jump.html*), its excellent launch pad for exploring other links.

Ecoafrica.com *www.ecoafrica.com*. Good site for nature and adventure travel, with information on Zimbabwe and Botswana.

Encyclopedia Zimbabwe Online
www.mediazw.com/index.shtml. Searchable electronic version of the most comprehensive one-volume information resource on Zimbabwe, but now a little out of date.

Financial Gazette *www.fingaz.co.zw*. Online version of Zimbabwe's longest-established independent newspaper, offering good financial and general news about the country.

Stanford University Library Zimbabwe Page
www-sul.stanford.edu/depts/ssrg/africa/zim.html. Outstanding jump site with a selection of very good links on a wide range of topics relating to Zimbabwe, from travel and the environment to more academic topics.

The Universal Currency Converter
www.xe.net/currency. Up-to-date rates from any currency you can think of.

Zimbabwe Independent Online
www.samara.co.zw/zimin. As its name implies, the Web version of the *Independent* provides an unbiased angle on events in Zimbabwe.

GETTING AROUND

As elsewhere in Africa, patience is critical for getting around on public transport. Leave yourself plenty of time for journeys and be prepared for long waits if you take local buses or hitch. Trains are a bit erratic, sometimes arriving spot on time, sometimes hours late. Luxury coaches and air travel, on the other hand, are usually pretty reliable.

BUSES AND COACHES

In the absence of a national bus system, the country is covered by a complex network of private bus companies, which are cheap and often crowded. These **economy buses** run short routes as well as long hauls and offer a more representative experience of how most Zimbabweans travel than the **luxury coaches**, which are undoubtedly more comfortable, with their reclining seats, on-board facilities and air-conditioning.

VOLVOS AND CHICKEN BUSES

Zimbabwe's economy bus network has improved immeasurably since the days of poorly maintained rattling rigs spewing black smoke and providing unreliable services. Known as **chicken buses**, these vehicles are still on the roads, but have been largely replaced since the mid-1990s, when Zimbabwe's fleet was modernized with hundreds of sleek new machines generically known as **Volvos** (a term that's not strictly accurate, as they sport a variety of marques). Volvos are more spacious, have comfortable seats and are faster than chicken buses and now tend to predominate. It hardly needs saying that they're the preferable choice, unless cramped conditions

and frequent breakdowns are part of the experience you're looking for.

Catching economy buses can be confusing. They're not geared to tourism, so clear information is thin on the ground. Several companies often ply the same route with no central coordination, and often you'll receive conflicting information about bus times. Ask around to build up a plausible picture of departure times.

The safest rule, however – certainly in smaller towns – is to **arrive early** at the bus station. Buses often leave at 6am and, although the 6am bus may be delayed for want of passengers until after 7am, it will most likely leave before schedule if it's full. Between the main cities an early start is less crucial, as buses depart throughout the day.

Most centres have a **main bus station** – invariably adjoining the market. Cities have several: one for town services, one for the surrounding area, and another for long-distance routes. In most areas, the long-distance bus station is referred to as the **renkini**. The one for town or the immediate region is usually called the **terminus**. In rural areas the **bus stop** may be under a prominent tree with a hand-painted sign tacked onto the trunk.

With the influx of new buses, services in Zimbabwe have never been more frequent and competition has never been hotter. This is likely to affect you at bus stations, where **touting** for your custom can be annoyingly fierce, especially in the bigger cities, which provides a good reason for waiting at one of the smaller stops on the way out of town, although this carries the risk that the bus may already be full by the time it gets to you. Stiff competition is also the reason why so many of Zimbabwe's economy buses dice with each other, often dangerously, (sometimes hitting 140kph) in an effort to beat their competitors to the next stop and pick up the waiting punters.

A lot of travelling goes on at the **weekend**, especially towards the end of a month and around public holidays, most notably Christmas. Buses get jam-packed, so try to plan your journeys to avoid these times.

On all buses, most people are scrupulously honest, but it pays to watch your **baggage**. Especially during busy periods, **tsotsis** (crooks) prey on travellers, either picking pockets or stealing baggage from the roof rack. Wherever possible, travel light and take your luggage onto the bus, where you can keep an eye on it. Hefty packs are a distinct disadvantage in any case. If there are no luggage racks inside, you may end up with your baggage on your lap if the bus is full, besides having to struggle past dozens of people.

LUXURY COACHES

Luxury coaches run between main centres, stopping at important towns along the way. Apart from flying, they are the most comfortable and reliable form of public transport. Blue Arrow has an effective monopoly on the major **domestic routes**, although the erratic (and consequently not recommended) Express Motorways does sometimes make an appearance. Luxury coaches are efficiently run, keep to an accurate timetable, have on-board refreshments, videos and toilets, are air-conditioned and make scheduled stops for hotel teas. Blue Arrow run services from Harare to Mutare, Harare to Bulawayo and from Bulawayo to Victoria Falls.

TOWN BUSES AND COMMUTER OMNIBUSES

The most frequent, reliable and cheapest public transport in the towns are the privately run **commuter omnibuses** – aka "commuters" or "taxis". Minibuses that run up and down fixed routes at breakneck speed, they tend to operate along the main arteries through the urban centres, but can generally get you to most places you're likely to want to go to. You can hail them anywhere along their route or wait where you see groups of people hanging about the roadside, usually an indication of an official stop. An assistant who travels on the minibus will collect your fare during the journey.

TRAINS

Rail travel is a comfortable and laid-back way of getting around and there are nightly services between **Harare** and **Bulawayo/Mutare**, and between **Bulawayo** and **Victoria Falls**. There are also **international connections** from Bulawayo daily to Gaborone (via Francistown) run by Botswana Railways and weekly from Bulawayo to Johannesburg (via Gaborone) operated by South Africa's Spoornet.

In Zimbabwe National Railways' **sleeper class** (first class), couples can get a *coupé* (small private compartment), but you'll need to go under the same name to fulfil notions of married respectability. If you're travelling alone, you'll share a four-person sleeper compartment. **Standard-** (second) and **economy-class** coaches aren't divided into compartments and have bus-style seating, the main difference between the two being that economy has plastic seats, and standard has velour-upholstered ones, and the fact that economy gets pretty crowded.

Travelling in a sleeper, your seat becomes a bunk, hence throwing in a night's accommodation for the fare. If you're keeping costs down, the berths are comfortable enough in a sleeping bag, but the inexpensive **bedding** offered on the train is well worth it for a night of freshly ironed sheets with plump feather pillows and thick woollen blankets. Someone comes round once the train is moving to make up your bed. **Dinner** – meat and three-veg style – and **drinks** are served on most trains. Don't expect linen tablecloths and silver service. It's all a bit cursory, but can be fun if you're not expecting too much. Take some snacks in case you're delayed in arriving, as they don't do breakfast. Note that due to a programme of upgrading, some dining cars will be temporarily out of commission during 2000 and possibly into 2001, which means that cooked meals may not be available on your train; to avoid a famished night, it's advisable to check on this before you travel.

Initial **reservations** for Zimbabwean trains can be made over the phone, in which case you should ask for a computer reference number, and

LUXURY COACHES AND BACKPACKER BUSES FROM SOUTH AFRICA

A couple of **luxury coachlines** run regular services from Johannesburg to Zimbabwe, as do a couple of **backpacker bus companies**. None of these can be used solely for travel within Zimbabwe, but you may break your journey inside Zimbabwe and resume it a few days later provided you start or terminate your trip outside the country with the same company. For example, if you're travelling from Johannesburg to Victoria Falls, you can break your journey in Bulawayo for a few days. For details of these services, see Getting there from South Africa on p.13.

you must pay for the ticket in person within 48 hours. For South African trains, booking must be done in person at the station and you will be asked to show your passport.

INTERNAL FLIGHTS

Flying between destinations in Zimbabwe is an attractive option if time is short, and **Air Zimbabwe** has regular flights between major towns and tourist destinations. From Harare it has direct services to Bulawayo, Hwange National Park, Kariba and Victoria Falls, as well as connections between Kariba and both Victoria Falls and Hwange National Park. The smaller **Zimbabwe Express Airlines** flies from Harare to both Bulawayo and Victoria Falls. There are no scheduled flights to Great Zimbabwe or the Eastern Highlands and none between Victoria Falls and Hwange National Park, although Zimbabwe Express sneaks what appears to be one onto their timetable but under closer examination turns out to be a rather expensive bus service. The regular single **fare** from **Harare to Bulawayo** is roughly US$55. For around US$115 you can get a single ticket from **Harare to Victoria Falls**, which comes with a free optional stop in Kariba if you're flying on Air Zimbabwe. Standby discounts are available when flights are empty, at the discretion of the duty manager. Both airlines have good connections with South Africa and several South African airlines fly into Zimbabwe (see Getting there from South Africa p.13).

TAXIS

Taxis run in most towns and will pick up any number of people for a single metered fare. They're moderately priced and are certainly worth using to get to nightspots outside city centres.

All official taxis are metered and there's little point in asking for an estimate before you leave – the drivers tend to make up a random underestimate. Few rides, however, should cost more than US$8 and most short trips in town will be closer to US$3.

DRIVING AND CAR RENTAL

Zimbabwe has comparatively little traffic and a relatively well-maintained **tarred road network** covering most of the country. This combination makes for very pleasant driving. In a week – albeit a rather full one – you could hit most of the highlights, and in a fortnight you could do a full circuit of the country. Distances between towns aren't great: the 440km from Harare to Bulawayo takes four to five hours, for example, and it's three or four hours from the capital to the Eastern Highlands.

Car rental is expensive, with Hertz, Avis and Europcar the operators having the most extensive national networks. Among the mid-sized companies that have presences in Harare, Bulawayo and Victoria Falls, you'll find Budget, Elite, Transit and Thrifty.

In these centres you'll also find localized companies offering more competitive prices, but be

---

INTERNATIONAL CAR RENTAL AGENCIES

UK

Avis ☎0990/900500
Budget ☎0800/418 1181

Europcar ☎0345/222525
Hertz ☎0990/996699

AUSTRALIA

Avis ☎1800/225 533
Budget ☎132 727

Hertz ☎133 039

NEW ZEALAND

Avis ☎09/526 2847
Budget ☎09/375 2222

Hertz ☎09/309 0989

NORTH AMERICA

Avis ☎1-800/331-1084
Budget ☎1-800/527-0700

Hertz in the US ☎1-800/654-3001,
in Canada ☎1-800/263-0600

SOUTH AFRICA

Avis ☎0800/021111
Budget ☎0800/117722

Europcar ☎0800/011344
Hertz ☎0800/600136

warned: because their base is narrower, you can't expect the same level of backup as is offered by the larger companies.

If you know exactly when you'll want a car, it's also worth thinking about organizing rental in your home country before you leave – it can work out cheaper. Booking ahead, either from abroad or in Zimbabwe, is wise too at times of heavy demand.

Wherever you book, look through the **small print** before taking a vehicle. The collision damage waiver is usually invalid if you drive on unsurfaced roads. People do take the cars off track, but if anything goes wrong the responsibility and expense are usually yours – check before you drive off.

DRIVING

Driving in this British ex-colony is on the left. Foreign driving **licences** are valid for up to ninety days, indefinitely if they're from the following countries: Botswana, Malawi, Namibia, South Africa, Swaziland or Zambia.

Petrol is easily available in all the towns but, because of the long distances between them, be sure to fill up whenever you can. **Strip roads** – narrow tarred tracks wide enough for only one vehicle – can take some getting used to. They tend to be found only in more remote areas, although you occasionally encounter them near towns. Approaching oncoming traffic, you're supposed to pull off the road with only your right-hand tyres on the tar and your left on the dirt hard shoulder, which feels decidedly hair-raising at first.

A few **words of warning**: because cars are often in poor condition, lights and brakes don't always work well. People tend also to drink and drive as a matter of course. So, always drive defensively and never rely on the good sense of other motorists.

HITCHING

Hitching is easy and generally safe. People aren't afraid to pick up hitchers and they will often go out of their way to be helpful.

There are two types of hitching: either with middle-class people, where payment is not in question, or with people who pick up hitchers to help pay for the journey. "**Paying rides**" may well be obvious, because you'll be with fellow passengers in the back of a pick-up for instance, or not so obvious if it's just you in an ordinary car. In the latter case, enquire if you can make a contribution. Payments never exceed the equivalent of local bus fares, so it's always affordable.

Leaving Bulawayo and Harare, it's easiest to catch a bus or taxi to the outskirts and wait on the main road.

CYCLING

Zimbabwe is great for **cycling** if you have the stamina. Roads are generally in good shape and tarred, and in cities bikes are ideal as there are cycle tracks everywhere alongside the streets. The distances between towns are long, but there are small settlements en route where you can stop at rural stores for a rest and a drink. Zimbabwe's stable inland climate means strong wind isn't a problem, but cycling is nicest during the dry, cool months. Standard **spares** are available in the larger towns and you'll find parts for **mountain bikes** in Harare and Bulawayo, but it's not a bad idea to pack any spares you think you might need. **Bike rental** is possible at Victoria Falls and less readily in Bulawayo and Harare.

ACCOMMODATION

Finding places to stay in Zimbabwe should rarely pose problems. On the lowest of budgets you can rely on campsites throughout the country and there's a wide variety of good accommodation across a broad price range – from under US$5 for a bed in a backpackers' lodge to US$325 per person at its top safari lodges.

HOTELS

The cheapest **hotels** that can be recommended in Zimbabwe are found in the large towns; in Harare, Bulawayo and Mutare, you'll find basic doubles from US$10–15 per person. All but the cheapest are invariably clean and respectable places, with freshly ironed linen and en-suite rooms, while the worst are noisy watering holes doubling up as brothels and are not generally listed in the Guide. Smaller centres usually have a pretty good hotel or two with twin or double rooms from US$25 per person; in tourist areas like Victoria Falls, Kariba and Nyanga, expect to pay US$35 upwards. All the main tourist centres also have several hotels of international standard, with prices between US$55 and US$100.

NATIONAL PARKS ACCOMMODATION

The **National Parks accommodation** lodges, cottages and chalets are some of Zimbabwe's real bargains. Set in the loveliest spots in the parks, they offer outstanding self-catering deals, in one- or two-bedroomed units, at very low rates. All come with basic furniture, fridges, pots and pans, blankets, linen and towels, and are serviced daily.

Most basic are the **chalets**, starting at around US$8 for one double bedroom and providing outside cooking and communal washing facilities. Self-contained **cottages** with kitchen and bathroom start from under US$12. The **lodges**, from US$16, have everything, including crockery and cutlery. Bear in mind, though, that you'll be paying US$20 entrance fee per person on top of this to stay overnight in most national parks, a charge that covers stays of up to a week.

Across the country during school holidays (see p.57) and at weekends near the cities, National Parks places get pretty full and advance **booking** is essential. It's not a bad idea to reserve at other times, too, especially for more popular places like Hwange and Mana Pools. You can book up to six months ahead – not as excessive as it sounds, as some places are in such demand that accommodation is allocated by ballot. Don't be put off, however, if you haven't reserved. You may be lucky if you just turn up, and you can always phone to check on the position if you're in the vicinity.

YOUTH HOSTELS AND BACKPACKERS' LODGES

Harare and Bulawayo each have a **youth hostel** geared to budget travellers. **Backpackers' lodges**, of varying standards, but run along

---

BOOKING FOR NATIONAL PARKS ACCOMMODATION

Harare Central Reservations Office, Borrowdale Road/Sandringham Drive, adjacent to the Botanic Gardens: PO Box CY 826, Causeway, Harare (Mon–Fri 8am–4pm; ☎04/706077–8, fax 726089 or 724914, *NationalParks@gta.gov.zw*).

Bulawayo National Parks, Herbert Chitepo St/Tenth Avenue (Mon–Fri 8am–4pm; ☎09/63646, fax 65592).

ACCOMMODATION PRICE CODES FOR ZIMBABWE

Most accommodation options in our account of Zimbabwe have been given **price codes** to indicate the cost of a single night's lodging. The price on which each code is based is the non-resident rate, **per person sharing**; there is usually a supplement for a single person in a room. Prices for establishments that only offer all-inclusive rates (comprising meals, and perhaps guided tours and other services) have not been coded and are given in US$ (per person per night). Although some establishments still quote prices in Z$, for consistency all Zimbabwe prices in this book are given in US$ (see box on p.25).

① **up to US$7.50** Camping, dorms and doubles at backpacker lodges, with shared washing and cooking facilities as well as National Parks chalets and cottages.

② **US$7.50–15** Budget alternatives a rung up from backpacker lodges, including decent hotels, apartels and rooming houses in Harare, Bulawayo and Mutare. You'll also find one or two self-catering garden cottages in this price range.

③ **US$15–25** You should expect a fair bit more than the basics from the hotels, self-catering cottages, B&Bs and guest houses in this category, and you'll sometimes find places with real flair.

④ **US$25–35** Decent hotels in smaller centres fall into this range, otherwise dominated by B&Bs and guest houses, from which you should expect some style and pretty good service.

⑤ **US$35–45** Some very good hotels in Harare and Bulawayo, with a bit of character. Some of the best B&Bs and guest houses in touristy areas such as Victoria Falls are up here too.

⑥ **US$45–55** Few places fall into this range but it does mark the starting point for luxury hotels, of which there are a couple in Harare and Bulawayo, where you'll get excellent value for money if you want the multi-star works.

⑦ **US$55–75** Mostly upmarket hotels with an international brand.

⑧ **US$75–100** The top hotels in the cities and a handful of luxurious lodge-style guest houses across the country.

⑨ **over US$100** The sky's the limit here. Virtually every private game lodge around the National Parks or wilderness areas.

roughly similar lines, are a more viable option, as the youth hostels fill up fast. There are lodges all over the country, with a particularly high concentration in Harare and Bulawayo. Prices in dorms start at US$3.50 per person. The worst ones are fleapits, but many of the better ones offer an outstanding service to budget travellers, laying on meals and transport. Double rooms go for around US$10.

SELF-CATERING

If backpackers' lodges aren't your bag, self-catering is one of the best budget options in Zimbabwe, with a fair variety of accommodation, from apartels and rooming houses in the cities to stand-alone self-contained cottages. **Apartels**, apartment blocks that have been converted into hotel-style suites, offer some of the best value around: you'll get all the comfort of an en-suite hotel room (phones, TVs, carpets) although not the communal facilities such as bars and restaurants. An advantage, though, is that most have equipped kitchenettes. You'll find such rooms for as little as US$10 per person and you shouldn't pay much more than US$15. Usually cheaper still are **rooming houses**, mostly found in Mutare – developed to cater to Mozambican families on shopping sprees – in converted apartment blocks or houses. You'll have your own room and, while some are en suite, you may have to share washing, toilet and kitchen facilities with other guests. Prices are comparable to double rooms in backpackers' lodges.

Cottages, along similar lines to National Parks lodges, are rented out privately in several areas from around US$20 per night, depending on the number of beds. You'll find a few in suburban gardens in the cities, but they're more common at resorts, particularly Kariba, where they offer a good budget option in the face of a dearth of backpackers' hostels, especially if there are several of you sharing.

BUSH CAMPS AND SAFARI LODGES

The ultimate place to stay in Zimbabwe is in a **bush camp**, set in a remote part of the country, with wildlife roaming through. You pay (from US$150 to several times that) not for conventional luxury but for the privilege of being in one of the world's great wilderness areas – and for the personal expertise of a professional guide constantly on hand. Accommodation is very variable, as is location. You'll find stilted "tree-houses", walk-in tents, thatched chalets, old farmhouses, stone lodges and houseboats.

SAFARI FARMS AND COUNTRY LODGES

Since the beginning of the 1990s, a large number of farms have restyled themselves as **country lodges**. The emphasis is on intimacy and personalized service. You're made to feel a guest in someone's home (which indeed most of them are). They're all over the country, some near towns and others near game-viewing areas.

Those near towns provide a rural alternative to staying in the impersonal upmarket city hotels. The remoter ones are run as **safari farms**, set in their own game estates. The animals you'll see may include predators and antelope, but will usually represent only a small selection of Zimbabwean game. Most safari farms are no replacement for the real thing, but do provide a less demanding way of retreating to the country; Prices range from US$30 to US$200. See Safaris on p.42 for booking details.

BED AND BREAKFASTS, GUEST HOUSES AND LODGES

The distinction between **bed and breakfasts** and guest houses is fairly blurred in Zimbabwe. As a general rule of thumb, B&Bs in Zimbabwe are closer to the British model than the American, with accommodation normally consisting of a (commonly en-suite) room in someone's home. Breakfast is included in the price, which is usually US$15–25 per person for a double. **Guest houses** usually consist of en-suite custom-built accommodation that is a touch more stylish and more expensive than B&Bs.

CAMPING

If you don't want to rely on hotels as a fall-back, then **camping** is a recommended option, with prices generally under US$3 per person per night. The white Rhodesian passion for outdoor life has left campsites in all but the remotest parts. In towns, too, a tent will prove a big money-saver.

On the whole, **campsites** are generally well maintained. They provide good cooking and washing facilities, and there's usually an attendant, which greatly reduces the chances of theft. On the minus side, summer heat can make sleeping under nylon a bit of a sweat and in the national parks it's hardly any dearer to stay in a chalet. Taking a tent means you'll never be stuck for somewhere to stay, but it's worth trying to anticipate how much you'll actually use it. As for camping supplies, a **portable stove** is useful, though there are usually plentiful stocks of firewood and fireplaces.

WHAT TO TAKE

You can get most necessary items in Zimbabwe, although in the remote rural areas you shouldn't expect more than the barest of essentials. Locally manufactured products, however, such as shoes and clothes, are easy to come by and usually quite cheap. As far as food is concerned, unless you're on a macrobiotic diet, you'll have no problem finding a good selection, particularly in the major towns.

CLOTHES

You can generally get away with a few light clothes in Zimbabwe. But don't be fooled by average temperature figures. The weather is capricious and even in midsummer night temperatures can plummet in some places.

From the end of August to October, take light cotton clothes, a long-sleeved T-shirt and a sweater or jacket. The same goes for the period from November to March, though in this **rainy season** it's just as well to include a light plastic mac or hooded jacket. A light woollen jumper is a good idea, even in summer, if you're visiting the cooler Eastern Highlands, or planning on early-morning game drives. Tracksuits are good game-viewing gear too, allowing you to peel off as the day warms, and are practical for camping all year round.

From August to May, shorts or a light skirt are well worth having, and **sunglasses** are recommended all year round. **Hats** or caps are indispensable if you're spending a lot of time outdoors, for example canoeing or walking. A length of light cotton cloth, available from fabric shops in Zimbabwe, is extremely useful as a wrap to ward off the fierce summer sun, and can double as a makeshift towel.

Lightweight, quick-drying **walking boots** or shoes are a must if you're planning any energetic activities. Leave behind waterproof, heavy-duty leather hiking boots: while they may be excellent for European hikes, they weigh far too much and you'll just sweat in them. For less ambitious walks and scrambles, tennis or running shoes are ideal.

For **game viewing** you'll need dark or neutral-coloured clothes. Plain green or khaki gear available from army surplus shops is perfect. White might look stylish but it's not a good idea; in white clothes you stand out like a beacon to the animals you're discreetly trying to watch. And don't take camouflage clothes of any kind: they're illegal for civilians.

Finally, it's worth being forewarned about the Southern African idiosyncrasy of "**smart-casual wear**", demanded by many Western-style hotels after 6pm – cocktail time, in other words. Exactly what they mean by it is somewhat ad hoc and most of it applies to men. Shorts are out, as are jeans. Trainers are usually acceptable but sandals aren't. If you take a pair of slacks, closed shoes and a smartish shirt with a collar (short sleeves are OK), you should pass. Smart-casual doesn't appear to apply to women, unless you're looking really scruffy.

FOOD AND DRINK

Local food in Zimbabwe is a mishmash of traditional staples and English colonial diet – a very bland combination indeed. Standard dishes are either downmarket maize porridge and stew, or more upmarket meat and two veg. Fortunately the meat is very good and cheap – steaks are not to be missed – and you'll find a range of international food in all the larger towns, which breaks the monotony of ubiquitous burgers, chips, pizzas and fried chicken takeaways, or more expensive sit-down cuisine. And there are those mainstays of white Southern Africa: braaivleis (barbecue) and biltong (dried meat).

You'll find all the usual drinks, but beer in various guises is the commonest. Zimbabwe produces its own drinkable wines and also spirits, and, like Botswana, imports a wide range of foreign liquor.

EATING IN ZIMBABWE

The traditional diet in Zimbabwe tends to be a variation on local produce: maize and beef. The local staple is **sadza** and relish, *sadza* being a stiff maize porridge cooked quickly and energetically – a process which entails some skill. Relish can be any kind of stew, sometimes based on vegetables but most commonly **nyama** (meat). The meat is unspecified – it can be goat, mutton, beef or chicken – but is usually unpalatably plain.

If you stay at hotels and stick to the city centre, you'll come across traditional fare as a curiosity on most menus. For a more authentic experience,

you'll need to go to one of the many cheap eating houses around the bus or train stations which, besides *sadza*, serve deep-fried doughy concoctions, chips, filling buns and an unending supply of Coca-Cola. *Sadza* is usually steaming and freshly cooked. One **vegetarian** option at these places, which often sell a few groceries as well, is to buy a tin of baked beans and have that with *sadza*, instead of meat, or, even better, a tin of "Sumu and beans" which consists of spicy, chunky tomato, onion and baked beans. Plain Sumu, without the beans, has a fair amount of chilli.

Bread, both brown and white, has become so expensive that it's now a luxury for many black families. Brown bread is available only in the big centres and not always in hotels. The national preference is definitely for white loaves, which are also somewhat cheaper.

STREET FOOD AND BREAKFAST

Street food, sold around bus stations, varies according to season, but you'll find boiled or roasted corn on the cob (*chibage*), peanuts, some varieties of beans, hard-boiled eggs and lots of fruit. Out of working-class areas and into the middle-class-dominated city centres, there's a noticeable absence of street food. Instead, you find Western-style cafés, restaurants and burger joints.

Food in hotels, restaurants and snack bars is solidly British-based – old familiars such as tomato sauce, pickles, baked beans, peanut butter, marmalade and cornflakes. English **breakfasts** are always on offer at the large hotels, suitable for vegetarians too. You can stuff yourself with fruit and fruit juice, cereal, eggs, bacon, sausages (and even steak sometimes), cheese, toast, scones and jam.

BUFFETS AND BARBECUES

If you skip breakfast and want a big lunch, the larger hotels do **buffets** of equally good value, with huge spreads of salad, cold cuts and puddings. Although they may appear at first sight to be expensive, you'll probably eat enough to last you the rest of the day. Among all this, you'll still find enough to eat if you're a vegetarian, and some places will give you a discount if you're not eating meat.

Barbecues – *braaivleis* – are an integral part of the social scene in Southern Africa. The centre of attraction is a slab of steak to gorge on and *boerewors*, a delicious spicy sausage of Afrikaans origin. A pot of *sadza* may well be on offer as an accompaniment at these occasions. Every campsite in the country will have a place to cook outdoors and "**braai**" your meat.

The other meat speciality to try is **biltong** – sun-dried, salted meat cut into strips. It can be made from beef or, much tastier, from game, and is available from most butchers, or from supermarkets. Biltong is an invaluable camping food, but you can't always get it during the summer months, when the sun is too hot for proper curing of the meat. **Game** meat – including crocodile tail, shoulder of impala, and warthog – is on offer at some of the expensive hotels.

FRUIT AND VEGETABLES

Although Zimbabwe has no distinctive cuisine, the range of **fruit** and **vegetables** is special. Interesting vegetables to try include members of the marrow variety – gem squash, butternut and pumpkin. Avocados are plentiful, cheap and delicious. Recommended fruits include guavas, pawpaws (papaya), lady-finger bananas and mangos. At markets you'll also see unfamiliar wild fruit, often delicious – but ask to sample before buying.

CAMPING FOODS

Zimbabwe has a limited range of **lightweight food**. If you're doing some serious hiking you'll probably manage on local goods, but it's worth considering bringing the odd packet with you. Locally, maize meal is extremely cheap and you can make either a thin porridge in the morning, or clods of *sadza* as part of a main meal. Other lightweight food includes dried milk, Pronutro breakfast food (a nutritionally balanced, and not unpalatable concoction developed in South Africa), crispbread, biltong, packeted soup, groundnuts and dried slices of mango. Cheese is always available, as are tinned meat and beans, suitable fruit and vegetables, brown rice and pretty awful pasta.

For four-wheel-driving and camping, fresh produce which keeps includes potatoes, cabbages, onions, carrots, oranges and lemons. Buy oil and vinegar in screw-top containers, rather than tops which can pop off from the pressure. Dust gets in everywhere, so packet food such as dried milk or sugar should be decanted into screw-top containers. Keep a day or two's worth of food at hand in a separate, easy-to-reach box, and leave the rest in a food trunk.

DRINKING

Alcohol – mainly **beer** – is cheap, and is consumed in large quantities in both Zimbabwe and Botswana. Beer comes as lager, pilsener or *chibuku*. In Zimbabwe, all that distinguishes the locally brewed lagers is brand name, among them Castle, Lion, Black Label, or the more expensive Centenary, Zambezi and Bohlinger. Beer is always ordered by name brand, as loyalty is strong. Lager is served ice-cold; you won't find warm British bitter.

It takes a bit of courage to drink **chibuku** – a thick mixture more like porridge than lager, served in large containers. It's not available in hotels or bars, only in working-class beer halls and beer gardens. Finely atmospheric focal points of social life as they are, the beer halls are not recommended for women on their own.

The ceremonial brewing and drinking of beer is an integral part of African life, for occasions ranging from marking a rite of passage to getting a new job. Even beer drunk at urban gardens is drunk ritualistically: the bucket-sized mugs are passed from one person to the next, or momentarily set down while people talk or exchange greetings. Night-time drinking happens in small shebeens in the high-density areas. You'd need to be invited to one of these, firstly to find it, and secondly to feel at all comfortable once you're in.

WINE

Zimbabwe produces its own **wine**, a product that is improving all the time. Even up to the early 1990s, Zimbabweans were quick to joke about the local product, describing it variously as paint stripper or rat poison. Those days are gone and Zimbabweans will now proudly tell you that the country's wines consistently win bronze and silver medals – although no gold to date – at international competitions. The most serious competition, however, comes from South Africa. The easing of import restrictions has brought often excellent Cape wines onto Zimbabwe's supermarket and bottle-store shelves – at several times the price of the local product. You may even find there's nothing else available in some restaurants, which is a great pity.

SOFT DRINKS

Extremely cheap non-alcoholic drinks include Coca-Cola and also one of Zimbabwe's best products, Mazoe orange and lime squashes, which retain the gorgeous flavour of the fruit – not sickly-sweet or chemical-ridden. Zimbabwe has several varieties of bottled water – both still and sparkling – mostly from springs in the Eastern Highlands.

One soft-drink speciality in both countries is the **rock shandy**, a mix of lemonade, soda water and Angostura bitters with ice and a slice of lemon. In Zimbabwe, Malawi shandies are a slightly sweeter alternative, which replaces the lemonade with ginger beer. If you're offered a "Zambezi cocktail", refuse politely unless you want water – a little local joke.

PHOTOGRAPHY

Zimbabwe is immensely photogenic and, with any kind of camera, you can get beautiful pictures. What kind of camera you take depends on how much weight you're prepared to carry, how much like a tourist you want to look, and whether you want to photograph animals.

Small, compact cameras are great because you can keep them unobtrusively in your pocket and whip them out for a quick shot. But they're hopeless for wildlife – a nearby lion will end up a furry speck in savannah. Compacts can also be potentially dangerous – tales abound of tourists with little cameras sneaking up too close for comfort to big game and ending up in very sticky predicaments.

If you take your photography seriously, you'll probably want a single-lens reflex camera (SLR) and two or three lenses – a heavy and cumbersome option. For decent wildlife photography you definitely need a **telephoto lens**. A 300mm lens is a good all-rounder; any bigger and you'll need a tripod. The smallest you could get away with for animals is 200mm, while 400mm is the best for birds. All long lenses need fast film, or you'll find you're restricted to the largest apertures, and hence the narrowest depth of focus. If you simply want good snaps from your SLR, think about one well-chosen zoom lens.

One problem is the **heat**. Never leave your camera or films lying in the sun. The film in a camera left exposed on a car seat, for instance, will be completely ruined. Keep rolls of film cool in the middle of your clothes or sleeping bag.

LIGHT READINGS

You really have to rely on a judicious combination of the camera's **light readings** and your own common sense. The contrast between light and shade can be huge, so expose for the subject and not the general scene. This can mean setting your camera to manual, approaching the subject to get a reading and then using that. With a zoom you can zoom in for a reading and then return. Some of the new multi-mode cameras will do much of this for you.

If you're photographing black people, especially in strong light, use more exposure than usual, otherwise they'll be underexposed; the light and your eyes (which are more sophisticated than any camera) can deceive you.

Early morning and late afternoon are the best times for photography. At midday, with the sun overhead, the light is flat and everything is lost in glare.

FILM

Film is readily available in Zimbabwe. Don't let anyone tell you it's unnecessary to have fast film because the sun is so bright in Africa. Even if you opt for a compact with a fast lens (ie one that's very light-sensitive) you'll need at least some 400 ASA film if you want to take pictures at dawn and dusk and in heavy cloud or forest. With long lenses on an SLR, fast film is essential.

SUBJECTS AND PEOPLE

As for subjects, **animal photography** is a question of patience and resisting taking endless pictures of nothing happening. If you can't get close enough, don't waste your film. While taking photos, try keeping both eyes open and, in a vehicle, always turn off your engine.

You should always ask before taking **photographs of people** or, for example, of a dwelling decorated with colourful paintings. Some kind of interaction and exchange is customarily implied; people often ask for a copy of the photograph and you'll end up with several names and addresses and a list of promises.

TRAVELLING IN RURAL AREAS

Out in the wilds, you will need to tune into local sensitivities – and avoid some obvious pitfalls. You'll undoubtedly commit some unwitting faux pas, but people are tolerant if they can see you're making an effort and are commonly too polite anyway to point out the error of your ways. Always remember that you are the stranger.

BEHAVIOUR

You should always **ask** before helping yourself to borehole or tap-water in rural areas – travellers are never refused. And if you come across a **breakdown** on a remote road, the form is to stop and offer assistance – yours may be the first vehicle in a week.

Women are expected to be modest, so wearing shorts, or short skirts, away from tourist areas is not a good idea. Nor is the display of affection in public. Sharing food on a bus will create goodwill, but it's not usual to do so, except with a friend.

If you're travelling alone, people may find it very odd that you do so by choice, as being alone is regarded as a great affliction by many rural people. There's also common surprise and deep regret and condolences if you're the right age but haven't had any children.

GETTING INFORMATION

If you want reliable information, the way you frame **questions** is vitally important. People generally dislike disappointing a visitor, so when you ask "Is it far?", you will invariably hear "Oh no, not far at all." So, if you don't want to go astray, don't ask leading questions. It's better to ask "How long does it take you on foot/by bicycle?" By the same token, don't ask distances. The need to know specific numbers of kilometres or miles is rarely uppermost in people's minds in Africa.

Lastly, when asking about **road conditions** in remote parts of Zimbabwe ask "How long ago has a car/bicycle passed here?", and not "Is this road passable?" It may be passable for cattle and people but not for cars.

CAMPING IN THE BUSH

Camping in the bush throughout **Botswana**, you'll find that people won't be suspicious and will be easy about you setting up camp in the middle of nowhere, although it is always polite to ask permission from the local chief if you're near a settlement.

In **Zimbabwe**, the situation is somewhat different. Land distribution patterns haven't yet changed significantly from colonial days. Generally the best land is fenced off in the hands of private farmers and the rest is called "communal land" (formerly "tribal trust lands"), with large numbers of peasant farmers.

Little more than a decade ago, rural people in the communal lands were in the midst of bitter and bloody conflict. The only whites in these areas at the time were those connected with the army, the government or missions. Today, while there are aid workers about, you still don't find people holidaying in the communal lands, and there's certainly nothing in the way of campsites or tourist facilities.

This is not to say that Zimbabwe's communal lands are off limits: you could have a fascinating and rewarding time in rural areas, where you'll find people terrifically friendly. You could ask for lodgings in a village hut, or stay in former district commissioners' or government officials' accommodation in some of the bigger settlements. But do make yourself known to the district administrator so as to avoid arousing any concern or suspicion at your behaviour.

NATIONAL PARKS

Zimbabwe's national parks, administered by the Department of National Parks and Wildlife Management, are sanctuaries free of human settlement, except of course for tourist lodges and campsites. Of the eleven national parks, seven are primarily game reserves, the remainder being areas of outstanding natural beauty.

The game parks are: **Gonarezhou**, **Chizarira**, **Kazuma Pan**, **Mana Pools**, **Matusadona**, **Hwange** and **Zambezi**. Other areas have been designated as of unique cultural or scenic importance: **Chimanimani** (montane vegetation), **Matobo** (granite rock formations and rock art), **Nyanga** (scenery and grasslands) and **Victoria Falls** (the Falls themselves).

Game reserves are unfenced and animals are free to come and go, but they rarely venture into areas of human habitation. Reserves frequently abut on hunting areas, which tend to prevent animals wandering into rural farmland. In any case, animals tend to shy away from land occupied by people and domestic stock.

If you're **camping out** in a national park, there's little to fear from animals so long as you take a common-sense attitude. Safety hints are given on p.144. Rogue elephants and man-eating lions aren't serious dangers you need to worry about. Wildlife shies away from people, and accidents invariably result from reckless human behaviour that threatens animals – rather than vice versa.

Entrance fees for most national parks, paid at the reception office when you arrive, are US$10 for day entry and half that for under-16s; one-week unlimited entrance is US$20 for adults. Unless you've prebooked **accommodation**, that too can be arranged, if available, at reception on arrival, as can camping.

The parks and reserves are all open to private visits. With one or two notable and very exclusive exceptions, there is virtually no private accommodation within the national parks, but accommodation and facilities provided by the Department of National Parks are decent and clean, if sometimes in need of redecoration.

Apart from Hwange – the most accessible of the game parks and serviced by reasonably priced game drives – the reserves are negotiable only in private cars or by going on organized safaris or game drives. Transport options for each park are outlined in the relevant chapters.

SAFARIS

Everyone wants to see big game on their African trip. Prepare to put away your watch and your preconceptions and relax. Even if you don't encounter the lioness with cubs that someone else saw half an hour ago, you're bound to be repeatedly rewarded with the unexpected: a bat-eared fox resting in the grass, a dung beetle determinedly rolling a ball of elephant droppings, or a large grey mongoose stalking through the grass.

Spotting game takes skill and experience. It's easier than you'd think to mistake a rhino for a large boulder, or to miss Leo in the tall lion-coloured grass – African game is after all designed with camouflage in mind. Having someone knowledgeable to point things out makes it that much easier to have a good time.

Zimbabwe scores high as a wildlife destination precisely because it is eminently well endowed with first-class **game guides**. Although it's a pity not to take advantage of this resource, it's still possible to do it yourself more cheaply.

Safari operators are listed under their area in the guide. The main safari regions in Zimbabwe are **Kariba**, the **Middle** and **Lower Zambezi** and **Mana Pools** (Chapter 2), **Hwange** and **Victoria Falls** (Chapter 4), and **Gonarezhou** (Chapter 5). In Botswana the chief areas are **Chobe** (Chapter 8) and the **Okavango Delta** (Chapter 9).

DO IT YOURSELF

The most basic way to see game is to catch a bus close to the parks and stay in National Parks accommodation – or to camp. For anyone on a tight budget it may be the only chance of getting into a national park and you won't be tied down by a fixed itinerary. In Zimbabwe, National Parks accommodation – geared mainly to locals – is cheap. And, if you're carrying a tent, you can take advantage of the excellent campsites for next to nothing.

Busing cuts down your options of viable destinations and, unless you're steel-nerved, intrepid and have endless time, it really isn't worth attempting anywhere more ambitious than **Hwange National Park**'s Main Camp. You could do a lot worse. Main Camp is one of the best places to catch sight of a wide spectrum of game

in a small area. From here you can catch minibuses or more personalized game drives into the park.

MOBILE SAFARIS

The least expensive of the package deals, **mobile safaris** offer the chance to get off the beaten track with a professional. You'll camp rather than stay in luxury lodges or fixed bush camps, but that doesn't mean you'll be excessively uncomfortable. While some mobile safaris do expect clients to share chores, many others are fully serviced. In the top-of-the-range versions, you'll sleep under canvas on camp beds, be woken in the morning with tea and arrive back at camp to cooked meals.

Most mobile safaris set out from one of the main centres and set up tents in the National Parks campsites. **Prices** start at US$120 per person per day.

BUSH CAMPS AND SAFARI LODGES

Traditional safaris based in **bush camps or safari lodges** are still immensely popular. Zimbabwe's best camps and lodges are located either in national parks or in adjacent game-rich concessions.

Guests at the more exclusive places usually number between twelve and sixteen, giving an intimate atmosphere with the chance to talk to guides during meals. Some of the larger lodges resemble hotels and lack this personal feel.

Animals are often free to wander through the grounds, and you'll get a very direct experience of the wild. It's not uncommon for guests to peer through a window at a bush camp to see antelope grazing a few metres away or even a languid lion padding by. Many safari lodges have their own waterholes, where you can watch animals drinking from the safety of your room or the bar.

Accommodation is under canvas or in more permanent thatched structures. Chalets frequently have en-suite toilets and bush showers (a hoisted bucket of hot water with a shower nozzle attached) behind reed screens but open to the elements – one of the great thrills of the bush is taking a shower under the southern sky as an elephant strolls by.

Food is usually good and plentiful. On a typical day at a camp or lodge you're woken at dawn for tea or coffee followed by guided game viewing: a drive, walk or trip on the water depending on where you are. Outings are restricted to no more than seven people, which means personalized attention. Mid-morning you return for breakfast. After that, there's the chance to spend until lunch on a viewing platform or in a hide (blind) just quietly watching the passing scene. Late-afternoon game viewing is a repeat of early morning, but culminating with sundowners as the light fades.

Prices, from US$150 per person per day, are fully inclusive of accommodation, food and game activities.

ACTIVITY AND SPECIALIST SAFARIS

Safaris – in Zimbabwe at least – aren't just about sitting in Land Rovers and looking at animals. If you're moderately fit and active and game drives sound too sedentary, there are walking, canoeing, horse-riding and even elephant-back safaris. **Walking safaris** take groups of up to six people headed by a tracker and a licensed guide. Trips are supported by a back-up vehicle, which carries all supplies as well as your personal effects. All you carry is your own camera, binoculars and anything else you may feel you need for half a day's walking.

Supported trips are based at a tented camp where you eat and from which you take morning and afternoon walks. You will see fewer animals than you would from a vehicle but what you do see is more intensely experienced.

Part of the excitement of this kind of trip is in the actual tracking of the animal you're trying to see. There's a real sense of achievement when you finally catch sight of that rhino after a three-hour trek. But no less important is the insight you gain into the bush from your guide, who will point out the minutiae of insect, bird and plant life, which seems part of the backdrop until you realize how integral it is to the whole system.

Canoeing safaris vary from those where participants muck in and help cater, to those where it's all laid on. All go down either the **Upper Zambezi** above Victoria Falls or the **Lower Zambezi** beyond Lake Kariba, and some include sections of walking. **Whitewater kayaking** on the Upper Zambezi above the Victoria Falls has the added frisson of negotiating rapids at intervals between paddling down the river through the Zambezi National Park.

Horse safaris from Victoria Falls are open to experienced riders, who can go on excursions of several days, or novices, who are restricted to shorter stints. There's nothing like riding close to a herd of buffalo, who allow horses far closer than they ever would lone humans. More exciting still are outward-bound horse safaris in the Mavuradonna Mountains, heading out into the wilderness and spending nights in bush camps.

With 640 recorded **bird** species, Zimbabwe has a lot to offer birdwatchers. All licensed guides know a lot about the subject, but a particularly good bet would be a specialist **bird safari**, as run by Peter Ginn Birding Safaris (PO Box 44, Marondera; ☎ & fax 079/23411, *pgbs@mango.zw*).

And for something completely different you can even go riding **elephants**, at *Elephant Camp* near Victoria Falls. Since starting in the early 1990s, it has become an incredibly popular pursuit and gets booked out. The elephants aren't wild, having all been born in captivity, and are used to human company.

COMMUNICATIONS, POST AND PHONE SERVICES

Communication in Zimbabwe can be an intensely frustrating experience and you'll need to learn patience to avoid going mad. It can take a while just to get a line, and when you do there's no guarantee you'll get a connection or that the number you're phoning is even working, a situation that has been partly alleviated by the introduction of mobile phone networks. The postal service, while reliable and safe, is painfully slow. The best hope of making contact is via email, which is becoming fairly widely adopted, but it, of course, ultimately relies on the phone network.

POST

The **postal service** retains a colonial flavour, with British-style signs in post offices instructing you how to use services and pack parcels. On the whole, mail services are reliable, if slow – though letters do occasionally fail to arrive. If you are sending anything of value, it's wise to register it.

Post offices generally open at 8.30am, and close at 4pm Monday to Friday and at 11.30am on Saturdays. **Airmail** letters to Europe don't cost much and take about a week to arrive on average. Aerogrammes are available and are even cheaper, and save the hassle of carrying a pad. All post offices (their addresses are given in the listings for the main towns and cities) offer **poste restante** facilities.

PHONE

If you were relying on the land-line phone network (referred to locally as "PTC" after the government-owned Post & Telecommunication Corporation) to make your arrangements in Zimbabwe, forget it. The phone system is so congested and antediluvian that you can spend hours trying one number and still not get through. After several years, the network was still in the process of being modernized at the beginning of the new millennium – don't hold your breath. Having said that, international connections are much quicker and easier than local calls, with clearer lines to overseas numbers than to places close by. In fact, it's usually much easier to make calls to Zimbabwe from outside the country than within it. There are plenty of **public call boxes** and a growing number of **card phones** in the cities, though you can expect to queue for public phones, especially in Harare and Bulawayo. A more convenient option is to use one of the **communications bureaux** in the towns, where there are several phones connected to a computer and you pay once you've successfully made your call.

MOBILE PHONES

The dire state of telecommunications in Zimbabwe has been partly improved by the introduction of three **mobile phone networks**, but their coverage is still limited to the major urban areas. However, as with international calls, it is usually easier to get

---

PHONE NUMBER CHANGES AND DIRECTORY ENQUIRIES

Zimbabwe is currently in the process of upgrading to a digital telephone network – though when the project will be completed is anyone's guess. At the time of writing, work had been finished in Harare, but as areas outside the capital become affected, you'll find that some of the phone numbers quoted in this book have changed. Telephone **directory enquiries** if you experience problems: local ☎962, trunk ☎968 and international ☎965.

INTERNATIONAL PHONE CODES

Phoning Zimbabwe from outside the country

Country code: **263**

Zimbabwe's internal trunk codes begin with 0. Drop this digit (just after the country code) when phoning from abroad.

International calls from Zimbabwe

International access code: **00**

Country codes
Australia 61 (+6 to +8hr)
Britain 44 (-1 to -2hr)
Canada 1 (-6 to -10hr)
Ireland 353 (-1 to -2hr)
New Zealand 64 (+10hr)
US 1 (-6 to -10hr)

The following Southern African countries share the **same time zone** as Zimbabwe:

Country codes
Botswana 267
Malawi 265
Mozambique 258
Namibia 264
South Africa 27
Zambia 260

connections from a mobile (known in Zimbabwe as a "cell phone") even if you're phoning a number on the PTC network. Largest of the two mobile networks are the PTC-owned **NetOne** and the more dynamic privately owned **Econet**. If you have a GSM (digital) mobile handset, you can easily use it on either network by buying a pay-as-you-go starter pack that includes a SIMM card, which you insert in the phone to provide your personal line and phone number. In addition to this you'll need to buy airtime cards. The good news is that Zimbabwe has among the cheapest mobile **call rates** in the world: a one-minute peak rate call costs US$0.15 to PTC numbers anywhere in Zimbabwe.

THE MEDIA

Despite the government's heavy-handed control of large sections of the news media, Zimbabwe boasts a healthy range of papers, magazines and books. And with the country boasting one of Africa's best music scenes, local radio can be a major attraction.

THE PRESS

You'll see a fair quantity of **magazines and newspapers** on sale at bookshops and on city-centre street corners. Most are in English, although you'll also encounter Shona and Ndebele publications.

There are two main national dailies: the *Herald* based in Harare and the *Chronicle* in Bulawayo. Along with several other publications, they fall under the Zimbabwe Mass Media Trust, a State-owned organization formed in 1981 to foster a press more sympathetic to the government, which has achieved the desired result. The *Chronicle* had its hour of glory during the "Willowgate" car corruption scandal of 1988, when the editor, Geoff Nyarota, pursued some valiant investigative reporting, stood up to the Minister of Defence and eventually caused the minister's resignation. By the late 1990s the government had consolidated its control over the two newspapers and they became little more than propaganda sheets. In 1999, a third daily, the *Daily News*, was launched headed by Nyarota; it provides more independent and critical coverage of events, but it has failed to attract advertisers and may not survive.

On **Sundays** in Harare you can pick up the *Sunday Mail*, the government's most fervent supporter, and the *Sunday News* in Bulawayo. The independent Sunday paper, the *Standard*, is a more interesting read. In 1999, the *Standard*'s editor and chief reporter were arrested and allegedly tortured by government officials infuriated by a story about resistance in the army to the Congo war. The two privately owned, weekly newspapers whose importance cannot be over-emphasized are the *Financial Gazette*, published on Thursdays, and the *Zimbabwe Independent*, published on Fridays. Both papers are business-oriented financial news and hard-hitting political commentaries. Although they are keen competitors, together the two papers have helped to set the agenda for change, exposing the corruption of the Mugabe government and articulating the need for a new constitution, better management of the economy and better governance.

For the best news coverage of Southern Africa, pick up the South African *Mail & Guardian*, which comes out on Fridays. In addition to good regional coverage you get the bonus of stories from Britain's *Guardian*, which owns a share in the paper.

Outside Harare and Bulawayo you might also check out the **local weeklies**. These tend to be quaintly parochial: reading the letters pages feels almost voyeuristic. In the Eastern Highlands, look for the *Manica Post* and in Gweru the *Midlands Observer*.

Of the **monthly magazines**, the popular *Parade* achieves a lively mix of feature articles, sport, politics and gossip, while the resilient *Moto* is definitely worth a read. A critical and readable journal of analysis and opinion, *Moto* was founded in 1959 by Mambo Press (a Catholic publishing house), and reflected African views through the 1960s until its 1974 banning. It resumed publication in 1980, failed due to lack of money in 1981 and bounced back in 1982, fighting on contemporary issues like land reform. Women's issues are highlighted in *Speak Out*, a magazine published by the Women's Action Group.

BOOK PUBLISHING AND BOOKSHOPS

Zimbabwe's flourishing **publishing industry** produces fiction, poetry, drama, folk tales and children's literature. **Zimbabwe Publishing House** and **Baobab** concentrate on high-quality literature, while **Pacesetters** and **Drumbeat** produce fast-paced light reading. (For more on the literary scene, see Writing from Zimbabwe on p.381, and Books on p.388.)

There's also a wealth of well-produced and very readable school texts for all levels that provide excellent introductory material on history, geography and other aspects of Zimbabwe, and a comprehensive array of reference material on flora, fauna, culture and geography.

Bookshops can be found all over the country, the largest chain being Kingstons. A modest selection of the latest British novels is available, but at higher prices than in the UK. Bring novels with you to swap or give away, and take the opportunity to sample the excellent and reasonably priced locally published books. The *Book Café* at the Fife Avenue shops, and Mambo Press in Harare, are worth visiting for their wide selections of African literature, while the Book Centre near the *Meikles Hotel* usually has a good selection of travel books. *Ndoro Coffee Bar* on First Street has a limited, but quality, selection of African books.

BROADCASTING

Zimbabwe has four radio stations and a TV channel, plus TV2 in Harare. **Radio 1** is the station for the "mature listener", with a mixture of easy listening, light classical, jazz and pop as well as talk shows; **Radio 2** – "the music lovers' station" – broadcasts in Shona and Ndebele and plays local and South African jive; **Radio 3** is the chart-oriented station, serving a mixed menu of local jive, Europop, funk, rap, reggae, rock and so on; and **Radio 4** is largely educational (Radios 1 and 3 are in stereo). The radio news broadcasts are unmitigated government propaganda, but the lively talk shows often highlight criticism of the government.

Although there are some locally produced **television** programmes, it's cheaper for ZBC (Zimbabwe Broadcasting Corporation) to import programmes, hence the large quantity of American, British and Australian padding. The ZBC evening news, at 8pm, is geared primarily towards its most prominent viewer, Robert Mugabe. Its blatantly partisan coverage would be infuriating – if it weren't so boring. Broadcasts are in colour, though many TVs are still black and white. A second channel, **Joy TV**, began broadcasting in 1998. It has limited evening hours and notably carries the BBC International News at 9pm.

BBC WORLD SERVICES AND VOA

If you want to keep up with world news, tune into the **BBC World Service**, which gives wider coverage than local stations, and broadcasts some excellent programmes in its **Africa Service**. There can be considerable variation in reception, so it's worth surfing the airwaves to find the sharpest frequency. As a rule of thumb, the lower **short-wave** ones (below 7000kHz) tend to provide better reception from late afternoon and throughout the evening, while the higher ones are usually better during the early morning till about midday. **Frequencies** tend to change seasonally, so it's best to find out current wavelengths from the World Service Web site (*www.bbc.co.uk/worldservice/schedules/safrica.htm*), or by simply experimenting. Having said that, the **medium wave** transmissions on 1197kHz (daily local time 1pm–7.15am) have remained consistently in service and also tend to offer the best reception.

The **Voice of America**'s English-language service to Africa broadcasts throughout the day on 909kHz (medium wave) as well as on a number of short-wave frequencies. A complete list of current schedules is available on their Web site (*www.voa.gov/allsked.html#E*).

MUSIC AND DRAMA

For live music listings, scan the entertainment pages of the press (see **The Media, p.46**) and look for roughly printed posters wrapped around lampposts and on walls – every weekend brings a choice of bands competing for punters. Details on specific venues are included through the Guide, and a personal selection of names to look out for is given in the Contexts piece on Zimbabwean music (see p.373).

There's no awe of megastars in Zimbabwe; musicians work hard for a living, and have to play often. **Harare** is the best place to see and hear them; the biggest events come at month-ends, when the names, like Thomas Mapfumo, hold *pungwes* – derived from the term used at all-night rallies held by guerrillas during the war – till the early hours. As economic times have become tougher, several popular music venues have become rougher, with foreign visitors being pick-pocketed inside and mugged outside. Check with locals about the safety of nightclubs.

Music and performance from Zimbabwe's **oral tradition** is less well-known outside the country. A few collections of **folk tales** and **praise poetry** have been published in translation, but the tradition lives on and develops most effectively through **drama**. Find out about productions by affiliates of the Association of Community Theatres as well as those by the University of Zimbabwe theatre group in Harare and independent groups such as **Amakhosi** in Bulawayo. Watch the press for current events. Most publishers have a drama list, which includes play scripts from Zimbabwe. In Harare, venues for theatre include the **Alliance Française**, on Herbert Chitepo Avenue and Ninth Street, and **Theatre in the Park** by the National Gallery. The **Book Café** also features some theatre offerings in the evenings, including the sensational stand-up comedian Edgar Langeveldt. Bursting on the scene in 1999, he won a devoted following for his vicious send-ups of Robert Mugabe, Michael Jackson and Zimbabwe's white, black and coloured (mixed-race) communities.

TAPES AND CDS

The widest selection of Zimbabwean music is available on cassette tapes, while only a few local musicians are on CD.

There are two record companies: **Gramma Records** and the **Zimbabwe Music Corporation** (**ZMC**). The fact that they pay no advances and low royalties to their groups enables them to take chances with recordings, which ensures that a large number of groups get onto tape, only to disappear if they show no instant profit. Much of the music recommended in the Contexts section on music (see p.373) may well prove to be unavailable – the negative flip side of small runs – and reissues are sporadic. But combing the smaller **record shops** often produces a rare gem – try downtown.

The best places for recordings, not surprisingly, are Harare and Bulawayo – the top shops are listed under these cities in the Shopping sections.

SPORTS AND OUTDOOR ACTIVITES

White Rhodesians had a formidable taste for sports and the great outdoors. Although many left after Independence, the tradition has continued and even expanded. Outstanding public sports facilities exist all over the country and other more exciting activities, taking in the wild, are now becoming more common. On the spectator front, soccer is a national obsession, as are cricket and horse-racing.

PARTICIPATORY SPORTS

Every town of any size has at least one public **swimming pool** – wonderful outdoor Olympic-sized places. Bathing is also an option in **mountain pools**, particularly in the Eastern Highlands, which are bilharzia-free.

Tennis is becoming a popular game, with a growing number of blacks taking up the sport. Zimbabwe's amazing Black brothers (who are white), Byron and Wayne, have done very well in the Davis Cup, beating highly rated contenders from Australia and Chile. Tennis courts are plentiful; if you're a keen player planning on a long stay, be sure to bring a racket. Harare and Bulawayo are dotted with sports clubs and they will accept non-members for a reasonable fee. For the odd casual game, you'll find little-used courts at many of the national parks – and rackets to rent.

Many of the national parks also have small artificial lakes, where **fishing** is permitted with a licence obtainable from the park's reception – they'll also rent rowing boats where available. There's more exciting fishing at parks and resorts along the Zambezi and at Lake Kariba. The most sought-after catches include trout and bream, but the ultimate fishy adversary has to be the fighting tiger fish: tiger-fishing fanatics have a Tiger Tournament on Lake Kariba every October. You can buy tackle in the big cities or rent at resorts, but if you need anything fancy bring it along.

Finally, if **golf** is your game, bring your clubs – every town in Zimbabwe has at least one golf course.

SPECTATOR SPORTS

Like most African countries, Zimbabwe's national sport is **soccer**, which draws crowds of between 30,000 and 45,000 for big matches. The game is played in both rural and urban areas, but the competitive league structure is confined to the towns and cities. The **season** runs from February to November.

From provincial level, amateur teams seek promotion to the first-division **Super League**, involving fourteen or so teams. Apart from the league there are four major club **competitions**: the Chibuku Trophy, the BAT Rosebowl, the Natbrew Cup and the Rothmans Shield. For most of the past decade, Dynamos have dominated Zimbabwe's club soccer; among other **teams** worth looking out for are Highlanders, Zimbabwe Saints, CAPS United and Black Rhinos (the army team).

Horse-racing ranks as one of Zimbabwe's most popular spectator sports. Cutting across all race and class divisions, the annual tote turnover tops US$4.5 million – a huge figure for a small developing country. A number of events take place at the country's two main venues: Ascot in Bulawayo and Borrowdale Park in Harare. The principal racing **season** is May to July.

As far as international competition goes, **cricket** is Zimbabwe's most successful sport. Every year, two international sides come for month-long tours. Most have been beaten by the home team in limited-overs matches, although Zimbabwe has only won about half of its first-class competitions. In the 1999 World Cup, Zimbabwe's national team did very well, reaching the semi-finals. At **national level** the premier events are the Rothmans National League and the Logan Cup. Matches are played on a limited-overs basis on Sundays. Because of the longer daylight hours, cricket in Zimbabwe is a summer game.

OUTDOOR ACTIVITIES

The post-Independence revival of Zimbabwean tourism brought some exciting outdoor options that combine **adventure activities** with Zimbabwe's natural attractions: full details are given in the relevant chapters throughout this book.

Three Zambezi adventures must share the top spot as the most thrilling experiences available. For the ultimate one-day adrenaline surge, **whitewater rafting** on the rapids below the Victoria Falls can't be beaten (see p.203), and it's become a big attraction of the Falls in its own right; the rafting is undeniably thrilling, but there have been some fatal accidents. Some of the rafting companies also offer body surfing through the rapids with a small "boogey board". **Bungee jumping** off the historic Victoria Falls Bridge to the Zambezi 111m below is an undeniable adrenaline thrill, billed as the highest commercial bungee jump in the world. Another adventure involves three or more days **canoeing** down the Zambezi through some of Zimbabwe's wildest and best game country (see pp.136–140).

Another exciting way to see wildlife is from horseback, and a couple of operators offer the option of **riding** into big game country, in the Mavuradona Mountains and from Victoria Falls. For some less demanding riding, you can rent horses very cheaply in some of the national parks, although – obviously enough – only at ones with no big cats.

Hiking safaris, too, are an exciting way to experience the wild in a way that just isn't possible from the confines of a vehicle. There's a choice of going out with a licensed guide with everything laid on, which doesn't come cheap but is always good value, or self-catering outings with National Park game scouts, which is far cheaper. And, for less organized hiking and climbing, you'll find miles and miles of eminently walkable wilderness all over Zimbabwe.

CRAFTS

In spite of the shortages of certain high-tech goods, there's a lot worth buying in Zimbabwe – and not just tourist souvenirs.

The country produces its own fine **cotton** and you can get a good range of commercially made clothes and fabrics. Local prints, with vibrant designs and bold colours, are well worth looking at; they make useful multi-purpose wraps and easily transported souvenirs. A number of local artists also work with cottons to produce a distinctive and refined Zimbabwean school of **batik**, that appears on sale both as lengths of fabric or made up into garments – surprisingly cheap for handmade goods. Look for this type of stuff at the craft shops in Harare or visit the artists at home.

Much of the **carving** you'll come across, both in wood and stone, is of the repetitive "laughing hippo" school – not really worth buying when there's so much more creative work about. There are some real artists working in softwoods, and **Zimbabwe's stone carvers** represent a significant international art movement. In 1983 the London *Sunday Telegraph*'s art critic wrote that "it is extraordinary to think that of the ten leading sculptor-carvers in the world, perhaps five come from one single African tribe [ie the Shona]". His **top three** were Sylvester Mubayi, Joseph Ndandarika and Nicholas Mukomberanwa. You

can see and possibly buy their work, as well as stunning sculpture by other big names, from Harare's commercial **galleries**. If you have an eye for it, you can also pick up cheap (but potentially valuable) work by unknowns at the **National Gallery shops** in Harare and Bulawayo, or from the sculptors' community at **Tengenenge** (see p.107).

In addition, good-quality **crafts** are available all over the country, at curio shops, at some of the markets in larger centres or from roadside stalls. Items to look for include distinctive **baskets**, which vary from region to region.

In Bulawayo and around Victoria Falls, look out for **Batonga crafts**, often antique family heirlooms that won't be around for much longer, and pipes and hardwood stools. Many of the common items – walking sticks, grass hats, and full-colour wooden chickens and guinea fowls from Zambia – retain considerable vibrancy.

Easy-to-carry souvenirs include a range of Zimbabwe **T-shirts** decorated with above-average designs, and beautifully polished egg-shaped **stones**. And of course there's a host of rigorously commercial and tacky tourist bits and pieces, from ghastly stuffed animals to that copper clock in the shape of Zimbabwe that you always wanted for your front room.

TROUBLE

Violent crime is thankfully rare in Zimbabwe. However, in a country of great extremes of wealth and poverty, it would be a miracle if there wasn't some theft. Visitors are therefore advised to take all the usual precautions.

CRIME

If you're robbed in Zimbabwe, you're unlikely to be aware of it while it's happening. **Pickpockets** are quite common, though by taking a few simple precautions and being aware you can minimize the risk.

Be particularly mindful when in and around bus stations and markets – places where there are large numbers of people milling around. And carry your valuables where you can keep an eye on them; in crowded places, keep your bag or rucksack in front of you, rather than on your back, where nimble fingers can't dip into your goods without you noticing. You also should avoid leaving valuables in **vehicles** – another major target for thieves.

DRUGS

All you're likely to come across in Zimbabwe is *dagga* or *mbanje* (cannabis in dried leaf form), which grows quite happily in Zimbabwe and can occasionally be seen alongside footpaths or at bus stops. Growing it is a criminal offence (as is using it); seldom a week passes without press coverage of yet another *mbanje* queen going to jail.

SEXUAL ATTITUDES AND HARASSMENT

Despite a liberation struggle that saw **women** fighting and dying alongside men, gender distinctions still run deep in Zimbabwe. Even in urban areas, African women are still expected to show due respect to men, though more extreme practices seem likely to dwindle as increasing numbers of women take up paid employment. Attitudes to black women are quite restrictive and there have been clampdowns on single women out at night in Harare, including mass arrests and trumped-up accusations of prostitution. Tourists are unlikely to experience any of this, although women on their own are considered fair game by men.

Context is important, however, and if you want to avoid **harassment** you'll have to steer clear of certain places: cheaper hotels, bars and jive joints. Even if you're obviously with a male companion, many **drunks** at nightspots will not be put off. The alternative is to go out anyway but to let the suggestions pass – if you're a white woman the danger of sexual assault is minimal. There have been reports of single women being hassled on trains by drunks, but there are separate compartments for males and females and they can be locked from the inside. Away from drunks, women can walk quite freely without fear of catcalls or being pestered.

THE POLICE

Most Zimbabwean **police** are friendly and polite and you're unlikely to have much contact with them unless you're robbed. If you do have any dealings, then a respectful response is likely to pay off. Police resources are limited – they don't even have vehicles in some places – so don't place too much hope on seeing your goods again. It's worth weighing up the value and likelihood of getting your stuff back against the hassle of filling in forms and answering questions, which is often done with great thoroughness by policemen genuinely keen to help. For **insurance** purposes or replacement of **travellers' cheques** and **passports**, you'll have no choice. Be sure to get a copy of the police report stating what you've lost or had stolen, to give to embassies, insurers or travellers' cheque companies.

TRAVELLERS WITH DISABILITIES

Perhaps because Zimbabweans fought a war within living memory, they show little more curiosity about disability than you would normally encounter in the UK or US. On the whole, you can expect the usual Zimbabwean friendliness and consideration.

Getting to Zimbabwe need pose no problem, as both Air Zimbabwe and British Airways are sympathetic to disabled travellers, although you should give them advance warning that you may need assistance.

In general, **buildings** outside Harare are low-rise, with one or two storeys, and are often quite spacious, so access is easy as a rule. Hotels and hostels are also usually low-rise, with ground-floor accommodation. However, because of the tendency for rain to fall in heavy bursts, most buildings have an entrance step, and take care of the **floors**, which are often highly polished.

Kerbs in main town centres tend to be 50cm or so from street level (also because of the heavy rain showers). They are therefore difficult to climb and quite impossible to negotiate in a self-propelled wheelchair. In **Harare**, dropped kerbs are reasonably common and you should have little problem getting around the centre in a wheelchair. However, they're quite steep: once you've committed yourself, there's no going back. Dropped kerbs are rarer in **Bulawayo** (despite the fact the city has an internationally famous disabled mayor) and never appear on opposite sides of the road, but at least the roads are wide so it's not too severe a hardship to remain in the gutter for a while.

In **suburban areas** of Zimbabwean towns and cities, kerbs are often lower, but the surfaces of both the roads and pavements are correspondingly poor, which can make it just as difficult to get around. **Outside the main cities**, pavements are more of a rarity, and indeed almost all roads and paths bar the main highways are rough tracks. Sandy and stony, they are difficult surfaces for a wheelchair to negotiate and walking can be a problem if you have trouble with uneven surfaces. Any tarmac is regarded as being for vehicles, and pedestrians, cyclists and wheelchair users are expected to move to the verge. Failure to comply with this convention can have drastic consequences.

It's worth bearing in mind that even the most basic Western wheelchair is likely to be considerably more sophisticated than anything available in Zimbabwe, so if you are able, and decide, to walk around, find someone to look after it and be prepared to tip them for their efforts.

PLANNING A HOLIDAY

There are **organized tours** and holidays specifically for people with disabilities – the contacts in the box on p.54 will be able to put you in touch with specialists for trips to Zimbabwe. If you want to be more independent, it's important to become an authority on where you must be self-reliant and where you can expect help, especially regarding transport and accommodation. If you do not use a wheelchair all the time but your walking capabilities are limited, remember that you are likely to need to cover greater distances while travelling (often over rougher terrain and in hotter temperatures) than you are used to. If you do use a wheelchair, have it serviced before you go and take a repair kit with you.

Read your **travel insurance** small print carefully to make sure that people with a pre-existing medical condition are not excluded. Tripscope (see box on p.54) can provide a current list of appropriate insurers. Use your travel agent to make your journey as straightforward as possible; airline or bus companies can cope better if they are expecting you, with a wheelchair provided at airports and staff primed to help. A **medical certificate** of your fitness to travel, provided by your doctor, is also extremely useful, and some airlines or insurance companies may insist on it. Make sure you have extra supplies of drugs – carried with you if you fly – and a prescription including the generic name, in case of emergency. Carry spares of any clothing or equipment that might be hard to find; if there's an association representing people with your disability, contact them early in the planning process.

SPECIFIC SITES

What follows is a disabled traveller's rundown of some of Zimbabwe's main tourist spots, highlighting the kind of problems and pitfalls you're likely to encounter at specific sites. The list is by no means exhaustive, but, used in conjunction with the accounts featured in the Guide, it should help you to plan your trip.

MBARE MARKET

With its narrow walkways, Harare's bustling **Mbare Market** is far from ideal wheelchair territory. Nevertheless, if you can cope with the restricted views – mainly of bottoms – the whole place is quite an experience. The main hall for crafts and gifts stands at the top of two very high steps. If you decide to leave your chair, make sure someone keeps an eye on it. Some of the outer areas of the market don't have established stalls and the paths through them are effectively off limits to wheelchair users.

DOMBASHAWA AND NGOMAKURIRA ROCK PAINTINGS

Dombashawa cave, famous for its San rock art, lies about a kilometre from the car park and, although the early stages might be travelled in a wheelchair, there is a steep scramble at the end – only worth the effort if you are really into cave painting. Unless you have unlimited energy, forget the cave at **Ngomakurira**, which requires the climbing technique of a mountain goat to reach.

TENGENENGE

The sculpture park at **Tengenenge** is not well set out for disabled visitors. Its loose sand and gravel paths are difficult to negotiate in a wheelchair (at least without the help of a strong pusher), and the way the pieces of sculptures are packed together can make the site tricky to walk round if you are unsteady on your feet in confined spaces. However, the site is well worth the effort, and Shona sculpture enthusiasts with mobility problems should not be deterred.

HIPPO POOLS

Hippo Pools is flat and grassy, and easy to get around. The paths in the immediate vicinity are generally firm and can be negotiated in a wheelchair with the assistance of a strong pusher, although they tend to peter out the farther from camp you venture.

MATOBO NATIONAL PARK

Much of the **Matobo National Park's** stunning scenery is visible from a car, but the bare rocks can make walking quite difficult. The cave paint-ings that are such a feature of the area are usually quite a scramble from the roadside, and tend to be only worth the effort if you are a real rock art fan.

A steady climb over bare rock for about a kilometre from the car park, **Rhodes's Grave** is not reachable by wheelchair, but the view from the top makes it worth the effort. The chalets at Maleme Dam are single-storey. However, not all are situated near the toilet block, so when you check in ask for one that is.

VICTORIA FALLS

As with many of Zimbabwe's main tourist sites, **Victoria Falls** is relatively uncongested, so movement around the site is fairly easy. Moreover, the main viewing points can be reached without difficulty, thanks to generally level and well-surfaced access paths.

HWANGE NATIONAL PARK

Access to the **Hwange National Park** is only possible by car. The chalets and lodges at Main Camp are single-storey, but most of the site as a whole is covered by a fine layer of sand that has drifted in places, making life difficult for wheelchair users. The main viewing platforms have good strong handrails. At Nyamandlovu platform, however, it is possible (although strictly speaking against the rules) to sit at the base if the climb presents a problem.

GREAT ZIMBABWE

The sprawling archeological site of **Great Zimbabwe** encompasses a large area crossed by sand and gravel paths. It is too spread out to explore on foot, and the nature of the paths means that a good strong pusher is recommended.

The site's principal highlight, the Great Enclosure, can be reached by wheelchair, but you'll need to be prepared to get out if you want to explore a bit. The older structures are up a steep hill and accessible only to the very fit and determined.

NYANGA NATIONAL PARK

Ideal walking country, **Nyanga National Park** is not well geared to disabled people. However, some magnificent scenery can be seen from, or within easy distance of, the roadsides.

World's View is easily accessible by car, and can be comfortably explored on foot. For

accommodation, the single-storey *Troutbeck Inn* is recommended rather than the *Rainbow Nyanga Hotel*, which occupies a hilly site with a number of steps. The National Park lodges are fully accessible.

by Will Bee

BEFORE YOU LEAVE: USEFUL ORGANIZATIONS

AUSTRALIA AND NEW ZEALAND

ACROD (Australian Council for Rehabilitation of the Disabled), PO Box 60, Curtin, ACT 2605 (☎02/6282 4333). General travel information.

Disabled Persons Assembly, 173–175 Victoria St, Wellington (☎04/811 9100). Advice and travel information.

CANADA

Jewish Rehabilitation Hospital, 3205 Place Alton Goldbloom, Chomedy Laval, PQ H7V 1R2 (☎514/688 9550 ext 226). Guidebooks and travel information.

Kéroul, 4545 Av Pierre de Coubertin, CP 10, Station M, Montréal, PQ H1V 3R2 (☎514/252-3104). Organization promoting and facilitating travel for mobility-impaired people, primarily in Québec.

Twin Peaks Press, Box 129, Vancouver, WA 98666 (☎206/694-2462 or 1-800/637-2256). Publisher of the *Directory of Travel Agencies for the Disabled* (C$19.95), listing more than 370 agencies worldwide; *Travel for the Disabled* (C$19.95); the *Directory of Accessible Van Rentals* (C$12.95); and *Wheelchair Vagabond* (C$18.95), loaded with personal tips. Postage and packing C$5 for first title, C$3 each extra one.

UK

Access Travel, 16 Haweswater Ave, Astley, Lancs M29 7BL (☎01942/888844). Tour operator that can arrange flights, transfer and accommodation. This is a small business: staff personally check out places before recommendation and can provide firsthand impressions on conditions in South Africa, guarantee accommodation standards and recommend suitable places to stay on game farms as well as other places of interest. ATOL bonded and established for five years.

Holiday Care Service, 2nd Floor, Imperial Building, Victoria Road, Horley, Surrey RH6 7PZ (☎01293/774535). Provides free lists of accessible accommodation abroad – European, American and long-haul destinations, including South Africa – plus a list of accessible attrac-

tions in the UK. Information on financial help for holidays available.

RADAR (Royal Association for Disability and Rehabilitation), 12 City Forum, 250 City Rd, London EC1V 8AF (☎020/7250 3222, Minicom ☎020/7250 4119). Produce an annual holiday guide for long-haul destinations including South Africa, but information tends to be rather basic (£7.50 inc p&p).

Tripscope, The Courtyard, Evelyn Road, London W4 5JL (☎020/8994 9294). Registered charity providing a national telephone information service offering useful advice for first-time disabled air travellers, and they can provide an up-to-date list of insurers offering appropriate policies for your needs.

USA

Mobility International USA, PO Box 10767, Eugene, OR 97440 (voice & TDD ☎541/343-1284). Information and referral services, access guides, tours and exchange programmes. Annual membership US$35 (includes quarterly newsletter).

SATH (Society for the Advancement of

Travel for the Handicapped), 347 Fifth Ave, New York, NY 10016 (☎212/447-7284). Non-profit-making travel industry referral service that passes queries on to its members.

Travel Information Service (☎215/456-9600). Telephone-only information and referral service for disabled travellers.

TRAVELLING WITH CHILDREN

Holidaying with children is straightforward in Zimbabwe and you'll find people friendly, attentive and accepting of babies and young children. The following is aimed principally at families with under-5s.

Flying to Zimbabwe with toddlers is the only considerable challenge, especially as the long-haul flight is bound to disrupt sleeping and eating routines. Although children up to 24 months only pay ten percent of the adult fare, the illusion that this is a bargain rapidly evaporates when you realize that they get no seat or baggage allowance. Given this, you'd be well advised to secure bulkhead seats and reserve a **bassinet** or sky cot, which can be attached to the bulkhead. Bassinets are usually allocated to babies under six months, though some airlines use weight (under 10kg) as the criterion. When you reconfirm your flights, check that your seat and bassinet are still available. A child who has a seat will usually be charged fifty percent of the adult fare and is entitled to a full baggage allowance. For getting to and from the aircraft, and for use during your stay, take a lightweight collapsible **buggy** – not counted as part of your luggage allowance. A child-carrier backpack is another useful accessory.

Given the size of the country, you're likely to be **driving** long distances, something you should think about carefully to avoid grizzly children. Aim to go slowly and plan a route that allows frequent stops – or perhaps take trains or flights between centres.

Game viewing can also be boring for young children, since it too involves a lot of driving – and disappointment, should the promised beasts fail to put in an appearance. Plus, of course, toddlers won't particularly enjoy watching animals from afar and through a window. If they are old enough to enjoy the experience, make sure they have their own binoculars. To get in closer, some animal parks, such as Imire, about an hour from Harare, have semi-tame animals that should do the trick, while snake and reptile parks are an old favourite that you'll encounter at tourist centres such as Victoria Falls.

Family accommodation is plentiful and hotels often have rooms with extra beds or inter-connecting rooms. Kids usually stay for half-price. Self-catering options are worth considering, as most such establishments often have a good deal of space to play in, and there'll often be a pool. Note that many safari camps don't allow children under 12, so you'll have to self-cater or camp at the national parks.

Eating out with a baby or toddler is easy, particularly if you go to an outdoor venue where they can get on unhindered with their exploration of the world. Some **restaurants** have highchairs and do small portions. If in doubt there's always the ubiquitous family-oriented chains such as Spur or Wimpy. Breast-feeding is practised by the majority of mothers wherever they are, though you won't see many white women doing it in public. There are very few **baby rooms** in public places for changing or feeding.

You can buy disposable **nappies** in the major centres (British or US brands are better than South African ones), as well as wipes, bottles, formula and dummies. High-street pharmacies and the Clicks chain are the best places to buy baby goods.

Health and hygiene standards are high and there are plenty of good doctors and hospitals should you need them. **Malaria** affects some of the major tourist areas (see p.20), so you might want to think carefully about visiting such areas, as the preventatives aren't recommended for under-2s. For toddlers, chloroquine is available as a syrup, while proguanil is only available in tablet form – not the easiest thing to get down little throats. Avoid Victoria Falls, Hwange and the Zambezi Valley in summer. Malarial zones carry a considerably reduced risk in winter, when it's unusual to find mosquitoes, so if you're set on going this is the best time. Take mosquito nets, cover children from head to toe between dusk and dawn, and use a good repellent. For protection against the **sun**, see p.19.

DIRECTORY

AIRPORT TAX of US$20 is payable on leaving Zimbabwe. It can be paid in Zimbabwe dollars to the equivalent value – a good way to use up notes you can't export. You can buy the necessary stamp, which you should stick to your plane ticket, at banks or at the airport bureau de change just before checking in.

CONTRACEPTIVES Condoms are available from pharmacies, as are contraceptive pills – on prescription – but to ensure the continued use of your particular type bring your own supplies.

ELECTRICITY is 220 volts; both round- and square-pin sockets are used.

EMERGENCIES General ☎999; police ☎995; fire ☎993; ambulance ☎994. Doctors are listed in the two telephone directories at the front of each town or city section.

GAY AND LESBIAN LIFE Homosexuality is illegal in Zimbabwe, and official statements deny that it exists among blacks, while white society remains largely macho and homophobic. In 1995 the whole issue made international headlines when the government put pressure on the organizers of the prestigious Zimbabwe International Book Fair to prevent gays being represented at the event. Despite pressure from the US and neighbouring South Africa, President Mugabe made a personal intervention, likening gays to "pigs and dogs" and asserting that in his opinion "gays have no rights"– sadly, a sentiment with

considerable popular support in Zimbabwe. In the end, gays were barred from the fair, in spite of the ironic fact that its theme for the year was "Human Rights and Justice". Things have not improved since then. Gay men and women nevertheless continue to campaign through GALZ (Gays and Lesbians of Zimbabwe), contacted by post at Private Bag A1631, Avondale, Harare.

OPENING HOURS Most things start early in Zimbabwe, and shops are no exception, opening at 8am, and closing at 5pm on weekdays and at noon or 1pm on Saturdays. You can usually expect shops to close between 1pm and 2pm for lunch during the week in small places, although this isn't cast in stone. A few large city-centre super-markets have late opening hours, while small suburban grocers and cafés selling basics also stay open after 5pm.

TAMPONS are available from supermarkets and general stores. If you do get caught out in a small village that's run out, you'll always be able to get panty pads.

TIME is GMT +2hr, US Eastern Standard Time +7hr, Australian Eastern Standard Time -8hr. Daylight is roughly 6am to 6pm, slightly extended in midsummer.

TIPS are rarely added to bills and are obviously appreciated. About ten percent or loose change, depending on the bill, should do.

TOILETS Public ones aren't that common, although you will find some in the big cities, rarely with any paper. Those around the tearooms and restaurants of department stores are always quite salubrious and do have toilet rolls. In rural areas you'll come across long-drop toilets – holes you squat over – and the ingenious Blair toilets, invented in Zimbabwe.

TOPLESS BATHING is completely unacceptable in Zimbabwe – in fact it's an arrestable offence.

WORK Unless you line up a job or voluntary work before leaving for Zimbabwe, you have very little chance of getting employment. Particular skills are sometimes in demand, but you're unlikely to be granted a work permit while hundreds of thousands of Zimbabweans remain unemployed.

HOLIDAYS

Public holidays

January 1 New Year's Day
Easter Good Friday to Easter Monday
April 18 Independence Day
May 1 Workers' Day

May 25 Africa Day
August 11 Heroes' Day
August 12 Armed Forces Day
December 25 & 26 Christmas & Boxing Day

School holidays (approximate)

Early December to mid-January
Mid-April to mid-May

Early August to mid-September

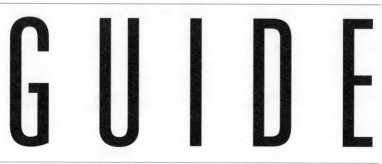

PART TWO

THE

GUIDE

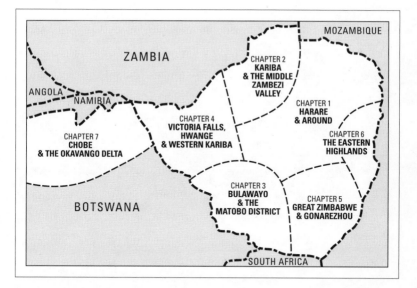

CHAPTER ONE

HARARE AND AROUND

A fter two decades of independence, Harare has avoided the fate of numerous large African cities and remains a slow-paced, unthreatening centre to spend time in. The unrivalled metropolitan centre of Zimbabwe, it still exudes the parochial respectability of an English provincial capital. But familiarly First World as it may all initially seem, Harare's spacious cityscape of flowering trees and tracts of red earth running between broad streets and exuberant gardens quickly remind you that you're in Africa.

In the absence of compelling sights, there are a number of ways to pass a few easy hours – or even days. Harare has several **museums**, including a first-class collection of local **sculpture**, good **craft shops** and some pleasant outdoor cafés.

Sights in the **suburbs** include the **Botanic Gardens** and **Mukuvisi Woodlands**, as well as the excellent **Beit Gallery** at the National Archives. A little beyond the city limits you'll find **rock paintings** at Dombashawa and Ngomakurira, set in typical Zimbabwean granite country, as well as **Lake Chivero** with its caged snakes and two dozen rhinos. Further afield, a couple of **private game ranches** provide a refuge if you want to get out of the city. Given half a day's travelling, you can plunge into the wild country of the **Mavuradonna range** in the north, which offers horse safaris and Africa's largest sculptors' colony, while to its southeast, the thrilling **Umfurudzi Safari Area**, a couple of hours from Harare, sees the Big Five from time to time.

South of Harare, the **Midlands** occupy the centre of the country and are usually seen through a window en route between the capital and Bulawayo or Masvingo – as much of them as anyone needs to see. Primarily farming and mining country with moderately attractive scenery, the only real reasons to break a journey here are to stop for the night (and there are several good places) or to visit Gweru's **Antelope Park**, with its eighty lions – and the chance to walk with a lion cub.

Harare is also an easy place to make **travel arrangements** for more exciting parts. As a base or springboard for countrywide travels, the capital is, as you'd expect, very well connected, with excellent tarred roads radiating out to most places you're likely to want to go. Kariba and Bulawayo are five hours away in opposite directions **by road**, while Nyanga in the Eastern Highlands and Great Zimbabwe to the south are a mere three hours distant. Although there is no direct link by road to Victoria Falls and Hwange (you have to go via Bulawayo), you can reach them from Kariba, taking the ferry westwards along the lake. **By train**, head east to Mutare, or south to Bulawayo, and thence to Victoria Falls. Inevitably, too, Harare is also the centre of all domestic and international **flights**.

ACCOMMODATION PRICE CODES

Hotels and other accommodation options in Zimbabwe have been categorized according to the **price codes** given below, which indicate the cost, per person sharing, of a night's lodging. For a full explanation, see p.33.

① under US$7.50   ④ US$25–35   ⑦ US$55–75
② US$7.50–15   ⑤ US$35–45   ⑧ US$75–100
③ US$15–25   ⑥ US$45–55   ⑨ over US$100

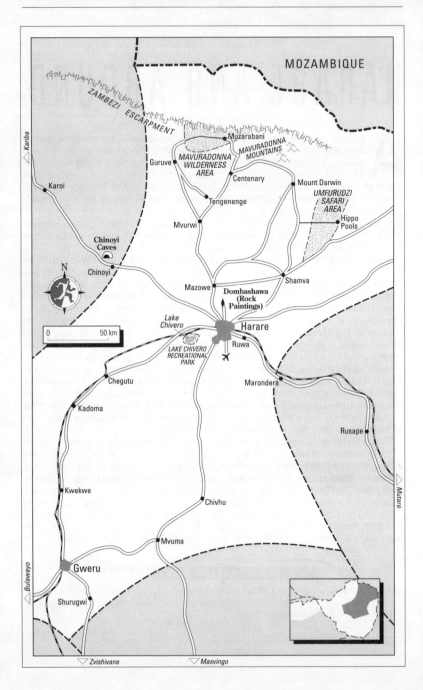

HARARE

HARARE is predominantly sedate and clean, most of what you see on the streets owing its origins to Western influences, from a slightly old-fashioned penchant for suits, collars and ties to fast-food restaurants and flash cars. You won't find anything like the vibrant chaos, traditional garb or colourful markets familiar in West Africa. But, as the nation's showpiece, it has attracted resources denied elsewhere, and in many ways stands apart from the rest of the country. Gleaming glass towers erected over the last two decades proclaim post-Independence prosperity in striking contrast with the lacklustre, 1960s slabs that give the place its provincial feel.

Colonial planning still divides rich and poor. The influx of white immigrants over the last ninety years and the presence of a ready black workforce provided a development blueprint for Harare as an affluent town with elegant suburbs and hidden **working-class districts**. Walk through the downmarket, downtown **Kopje** and **Robert Mugabe Road** quarters and you'll discover a bustling area of ageing buildings and shops selling bric-a-brac and essentials. Mingling with the street clamour, the beat of local music thumps out from a hundred shop-counter record players. A couple of kilometres further on you hit **Mbare** – a "high-density suburb" with its huge sprawling market, and also the country's biggest bus station, hub of the public transport network.

Some history

In the late nineteenth century, the swampy area that is now Harare was the domain of **Chief Neharawa** of Seki – until the arrival of white settlers from South Africa, bankrolled by Cecil John Rhodes's British South Africa Company (BSAC). On **September 13, 1890**, the Union Jack was hoisted in the heart of the modern city centre on the site of present African Unity Square and a fortress, called **Fort Salisbury** (after Robert Arthur Talbot Gascoyne-Cecil, third marquess of Salisbury, who was then the British prime minister), was quickly erected.

The settlement was intended as a base for working the **goldfields** of the Zambezi Valley, which speculators believed matched the ore-rich veins of South Africa. This was wishful thinking, yet the unlikely marshland became the country's main urban centre as settlers were enticed by the promise of large farms and substantial mining claims. The town took its earliest shape from the traders who haphazardly set up shop at the foot of the Kopje; in 1891, Captain Thomas Ross was brought in by the BSAC to impose some town planning on the dangerously organic growth that was taking place. The result was the collision of two street grids: Ross incorporated the existing plots below the Kopje and created a rectangular grid parallel to Pioneer Street, ensuring that future development would be constrained by a second grid of martial regularity, aligned due north.

During the 1890s, Salisbury's commercial centre shifted east from the Kopje to the district around present-day **Africa Unity Square**. At the same time, **racial segregation** crept in. The first "location" for black workers was a dismal affair a kilometre south of Kopje, with a white superintendent and a nine o'clock curfew. Not surprisingly, few blacks were enticed to settle. It was only after the suppression of the First Chimurenga

Important note: the stretch of **Chancellor Avenue**, leading north off North Avenue past the **President's Residence**, is off limits from 6pm to 6am. A barrier operated by armed troops is usually lowered between these hours. The restriction is to be taken very seriously – several motorists have been shot dead for venturing down this no-go street during prohibited hours, even on occasion with the boom raised. If the **president's cavalcade** is passing anywhere in town, you're required by law to stop and pull over.

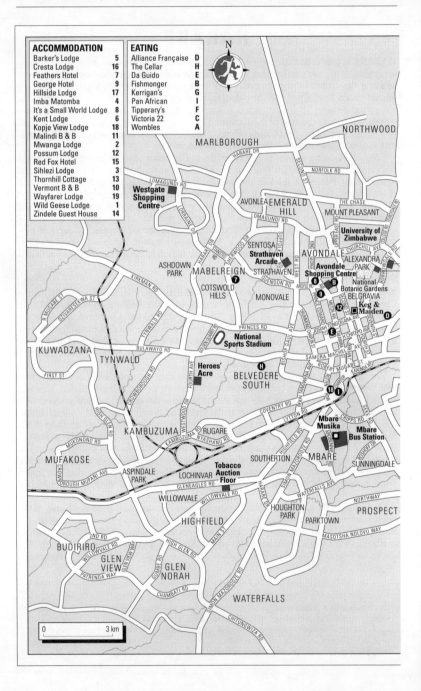

ACCOMMODATION

Barker's Lodge	5
Cresta Lodge	16
Feathers Hotel	7
George Hotel	9
Hillside Lodge	17
Imba Matomba	4
It's a Small World Lodge	8
Kent Lodge	6
Kopje View Lodge	18
Malindi B & B	11
Mwanga Lodge	2
Possum Lodge	12
Red Fox Hotel	15
Sihlezi Lodge	3
Thornhill Cottage	13
Vermont B & B	10
Wayfarer Lodge	19
Wild Geese Lodge	1
Zindele Guest House	14

EATING

Alliance Française	D
The Cellar	H
Da Guido	E
Fishmonger	B
Kerrigan's	G
Pan African	I
Tipperary's	F
Victoria 22	C
Wombles	A

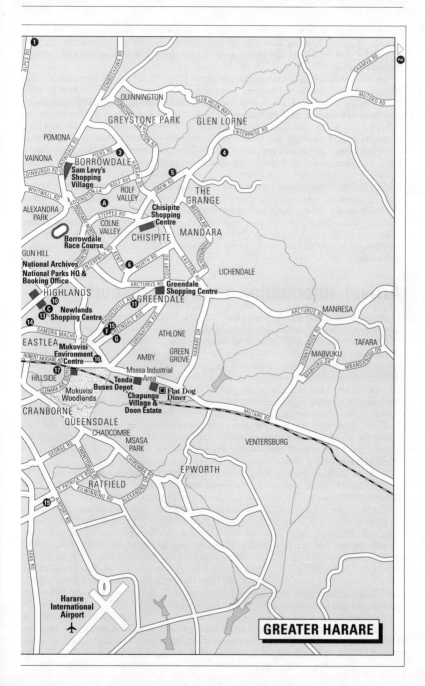

GREATER HARARE

(liberation war) in 1896, and the imposition of **taxes** to force blacks to work in town, that the workers' housing shortage became serious. In 1907 a new location was built across the Mukuvisi River in a choice spot near the town cemetery, abattoir and sewage disposal works.

Salisbury was officially recognized as a city in 1923, when it became the capital of the British colony of Southern Rhodesia. But the real boost came after World War II, when it was made **capital** of the newly formed **Federation of Southern Rhodesia, Northern Rhodesia and Nyasaland**. The city expanded with new enterprises and industry, and by the time the Federation broke up in 1963, the industrial base was firmly established. Following the Unilateral Declaration of Independence in 1965, construction slowed down, and reached a standstill by the time the Smith regime capitulated. The pace picked up dramatically after **Independence**, with an energy that made up for the stagnant years of sanctions and continued apace to the end of the century. At the beginning of the millennium, Harare is a conundrum – a city that has never looked more prosperous, even as the country faces unprecedented **economic crisis**. There are more smart shops, shiny cars, interesting buildings and chic cafés on its streets than ever before, but there are also more street kids, pickpockets and hustlers. Harare is again as divided as it was under the segregationist policies of the white minority government, only now the ever-widening gulf is between rich and poor rather than black and white.

Arrival, information and city transport

Unprepossessing **Harare Airport** (☎04/575111), 15km southeast of the city centre, is split into adjacent domestic and international terminals. A new international terminal, under construction in 2000, should alleviate the dismal atmosphere and ease congestion, but no fixed completion date is on the cards. Air Zimbabwe (daily 5.30am–8pm), on the bottom floor of the international terminal, is the handling agent for most airlines flying in and out of Harare and also deals with lost luggage and property. Most facilities are open from the first flight of the day till the last one at night and include several **bureaux de change** in the main airport building, as well as a kiosk selling curios, magazines, books and snacks, and a communications bureau with phone, fax and email facilities. A viewing terrace, bar and restaurant (nominal entrance fee) is the only option for tea, drinks and sit-down meals. Just outside the main building, and difficult to miss, you'll find a **post office** (Mon–Fri 8.30am–1pm & 2–4pm, Sat 8–11.30am) and a **left luggage office** (6am–10pm; US$1.20 per item per 24hr period).

Metered **taxis** are thick on the ground and, especially if there are two or more of you, provide the cheapest and most convenient way of getting into town. Airport Taxis (☎04/572463) charge US$5–6 to go into the city centre and US$7–8 to the more distant northern suburbs. Licensed taxi drivers in Zimbabwe are generally straight, but there's an outside chance of being stung for more than you expect because the driver takes a long and circuitous route. To avoid this there's always the option of taking one of the **shuttle buses** that charge a fixed fare, but are usually pricier. Hotellink (☎04/736787 or 702199) operates a door-to-door service that costs a flat US$5 per person to the city centre, but you could be left hanging about if the bus has just left. More convenient, but twice as expensive, is to book ahead and have them meet you. Bushbeat (☎04/572949, fax 572956, *vfrtours@internet.co.zw*; booking essential), is another company that meets passengers and takes them anywhere in Harare for around US$12.

Many hotels, guest houses and lodges will also provide free **transfers** for guests from the airport, provided arrangements are made prior to arrival. Most upmarket city-centre hotels charge around US$10 for a minibus transfer, while many out of town lodges include airport pick-up in their tariff. Of Zimbabwe's **car rental** companies, Avis, Budget, Elite, Europcar, Hertz and Thrifty (see p.95) have booths outside the international terminal.

LUXURY COACH AND SEMI-LUXURY COACH ARRIVAL AND DEPARTURE POINTS

BUSLINE	TELEPHONE	TERMINAL	DESTINATION
Blue Arrow	☎04/621055–7 ☎04/729517	Blue Arrow	Bulawayo, Mutare
Exodus	☎04/703979	Roadport	Johannesburg
Express Motorways	☎04/796934 ☎04/791227	Roadport	Bulawayo, Johannesburg, Mutare
Greyhound	☎04/621055–7 ☎04/729517	Blue Arrow	Johannesburg
Powercoach	☎04/668716–7	Roadport	Kariba, Lusaka
Translux	☎04/725132 ☎04/705295	Roadport	Johannesburg
Trans Zambezi	☎04/722163 ☎04/722172	Roadport	Johannesburg
UTC	☎04/770623–34	UTC	Kariba

TERMINALS

Blue Arrow, Chester House, Speke Avenue, between Third and Fourth streets
Roadport, Robert Mugabe Road/Fifth Street
UTC, Park Street/Jason Moyo Avenue

Arrival

The Roadport was constructed during the second half of the 1990s in an attempt to provide Harare with a centralized terminal for its luxury and semi-luxury **coaches**, and, although some of these services do now use it, others have retained their own arrival and departure points (see box). Having said that, without exception all the luxury coaches start or end their journeys in the city centre, close to taxis or within walking distance of the hotels in the Avenues. With few exceptions, long-distance **Volvo** and **chicken buses** terminate at Mbare bus station, although many pass through the centre on the way; from Mbare, catch a city bus or taxi.

Designed along the lines of an airport, the **Roadport**, on the corner of Robert Mugabe Road and Fifth Street, is a rather glitzy building housing desks of several bus and coach companies (see box), with an arrival point at the rear where buses pull in and out. Each bus company has its own check-in desk, where you can also book and collect tickets. The desks are mainly open from 8am till 5pm, but occasionally they will stay open longer, depending on the departure and arrival times of their buses. Facilities include an **information desk** (8am–5pm; ☎04/702828 or 728315), a **bureau de change** (8am–9pm), a small **curio shop** that also sells crisps and sweets, a **restaurant** with a comprehensive and reasonably priced menu, and a waiting lounge with several toilets and TV screens. Should you need a **taxi**, the Taxi Co-operative Society has an office here and there is a **communications bureau** offering phone, Internet and email facilities.

Although one or two long-distance Volvo buses use the Roadport, most, along with the chicken buses, leave from **Mbare bus station**, off Ardbennie Road near the market, from where you can get buses to most places in Zimbabwe; over a hundred companies ply their trade from here. Although the bus terminus appears chaotic, there are in fact separate bays allocated for each final destination. Generally you can't book a seat, but should simply turn up at the bus station on the day you intend to travel.

Trains pull into the station at the southern end of the city centre. Most central places are within walking distance, but if you need a taxi head for the rank outside the station in Kenneth Kaunda Avenue. Failing that, try the one at *Meikles Hotel*, four blocks up on Third Street.

Information

Paradoxically, the capital is about the worst centre in the country for gathering **information**, which is thin on the ground and pretty poorly coordinated. A starting point is the **Publicity Association** (Mon–Fri 8am–noon & 1–4pm) on the Second Street side of African Unity Square, where staff usually appear reluctant to part with information, although you can sometimes get answers to specific questions. They do, however, have a chaotic noticeboard, where you can find information about tours, car rental, places to stay and so on; they also sell a colour city map and publish the moderately useful monthly *What's on in Harare*, which lists coming events and is sometimes available from their office. For specific information about **concerts** and **movies**, your best bet is the otherwise dull *Herald*, which is sold on street corners in the centre as well as at all the bookshops and newsagents.

Probably the best source of information for backpackers is through the informal channel of lodges. Many of the better ones have good **noticeboards** and some even keep files of useful literature about other lodges around the country, plus tours, adventure activities and transport.

The **Automobile Association of Zimbabwe** (AA), 57 Samora Machel Ave, opposite the Crowne Plaza Monomotapa (Mon–Fri 8.30am–4.30pm, Sat 8–11am; ☎04/752779), is an invaluable source of maps of destinations in Zimbabwe and South Africa, particularly their excellent *AA Road Map of Zimbabwe*, which is the most up to date there is and is cheaper here than at the bookshops and newsagents. Additional useful services available to members of other motoring organizations worldwide include their touring leaflets with general information about major tourist areas, weekly road reports describing the latest detours and surface conditions, and the hotel booking service, which reserves accommodation in Zimbabwe or neighbouring countries for the price of the phone call or fax.

If you're staying more than a night or two and spending time in the suburbs, a **street atlas** is indispensable; the best is the beautifully clear and regularly updated *Mobil Harare Street Atlas*, available from bookshops such as Kingstons or CNA (see p.93).

City transport

Harare's city centre is small enough to be easily and comfortably negotiated on **foot**. Otherwise, by far the easiest option in a city with crowded public transport is a **taxi**. They're usually easy to find, with ranks all over the city centre, and you'll always find some outside *Meikles Hotel* and around Africa Unity Square. Fares work out at around US$0.40 per kilometre, so you can expect to pay under US$1 for most short hops within the centre and US$5–6 from town to the airport (see Listings, p.97, for details of ranks and phone numbers).

SECURITY IN CENTRAL HARARE

Although muggings are on the increase, central Harare is no more dangerous than most cities, even at night. Theft is a major problem, however, and vigilance pays.

• **Pickpockets** are the major threat, so watch out in crowded places: the bus stations and the market are favourite hunting grounds for nimble-fingered criminals. There have also been a number of incidents in the National Gallery and the adjacent Harare Gardens.

• **Don't engage with strangers** who approach you; a favourite scam is for a well-dressed and well-spoken person to show a sponsorship form ostensibly for a good cause such as the disabled; while you're distracted dealing with it, you'll be approached from behind, jostled and relieved of your valuables.

• **Travelling by car** you should always make sure to lock it, and don't leave valuables inside – car break-ins are common. Equally, don't leave *anything* on display as some thieves will smash a window to steal something as seemingly trivial as a tape or an article of clothing. In the city centre use car parks that are guarded by an attendant, or park in one of the multi-storey parkades.

• **At night** be on guard coming out of restaurants, pubs and clubs in the vicinity of the city centre or the Avenues.

• **Don't carry valuables** if you don't have to – use safes or lock-up facilities at your accommodation.

The city's rather erratic style of driving makes **cycling** in the centre dangerous, but in the suburbs it's an option worth considering. Cycle rental has taken a dive as too many bicycles were being stolen or mistreated, but a couple of backpackers' lodges (see p.71) still offer bikes to their guests and one dealer sells bikes with a guarantee to buy them back minus a reasonable monthly depreciation (see p.94).

Buses are the least viable way of getting around, as they are infrequent and usually full. Like buses, **commuters** follow fixed routes and take a number of passengers. They charge a cheap flat rate for any distance (around US$0.40), but it takes a while to work out routes – it's worthwhile only if you're planning a long stay. Plentiful and convenient, they stop when passengers want to get on or off, rather than having fixed stops like buses. To catch one, flag it down as it passes, or look out for unofficial stops, easy to spot by the congregations of people at the roadside, especially during the rush hour. Be warned, though, that they are routinely crammed beyond their legal capacity and tend to tear around.

Tours

Tours of sights in the city, suburbs and out of town, such as Mbare market, Mukuvisi Woodlands and Chapungu Village, cost from $US20 per person for half a day and are well worth considering if you can't be bothered struggling with commuter buses. One of the best operators is Bushbeat Trails, who are booked through VFR Tours, Kilwinning Road, Hatfield (☎04/572949, fax 572956, *vfrtours@internet.co.zw*), and offer a wide choice of excursions in and around Harare with itineraries that include historical and craft tours, commercial farm visits, visits to the Tobacco Auction Floors and full-day trips to Lake Chivero. Very professional, well informed and flexible, they are responsive to special requests. Other reputable companies that run city tours include UTC, Park Street/Jason Moyo Avenue (☎04/770623 to 770634), a long-established operator; the recommended Mhuka Wild Tours, 170 Union Ave (☎04/729576 or 735358, *mtours@icon.co.zw*), who also make trips outside Harare; and Southern African Touring Services (SATS), Sabi House, 18 Park St (☎04/753535, *sats@samara.co.zw*), which isn't too reliable about returning calls, but has a delightful and well-informed tour guide.

Accommodation

There has never been more choice of **accommodation** in Harare, particularly with the opening up of establishments in the suburbs and the proliferation of B&Bs and guest houses. Despite this growth in supply there hasn't been any noticeable drop in bed rates and, backpackers' lodges aside, you may have to put in a little work to find somewhere inexpensive to stay.

The four- and five-star **international hotels** are expensive, while **mid-range** places tend to fill up fast; most are clean, well serviced, with swimming pools, and within easy walking distance of the centre. Options at the bottom of the range can be slightly seedy, as some **inexpensive hotels** double up as brothels: the listings below stick to the more respectable places. Your best option, if you're on a tight budget, is the **backpackers' lodges** that have mushroomed during the 1990s to cater for the influx of shoestring travellers. Most are old houses, often near the centre, with bedrooms converted into small dorms or double rooms. Cooking facilities are provided, and some lodges even have gardens and pools.

A good area to start looking for somewhere central that's also inexpensive or mid-priced is the **Avenues** – the chunk northeast of the Harare Gardens (usually referred to simply as "the gardens") between Second Street and Enterprise Road. Lined with jacaranda and flamboyant trees, these quiet streets are where you'll find the oldest colonial-style town houses, with their colonnaded verandahs and shady gardens.

If being in the thick of the city doesn't top your agenda, you'll have a lot more choice and you'll find a plentiful choice of inexpensive and moderately priced B&Bs and guest houses in the **suburbs**. Most prestigious of these areas are the elite suburbs, to the north and east of the city, where the streets are leafy, the gardens extensive and the houses large, but the atmosphere owes more to Middle America or Australia than to Central Africa. It's worth bearing in mind that unless you have your own transport you'll need to rely on taxis or minibuses to travel the five or more kilometres into town.

For a more extravagant option you can stay even further from the centre at one of the **game farms** or **country lodges**, just outside the capital. Firmly at top end of the scale, these establishments offer a tranquil alternative to the big hotels and often have wildlife (usually antelope) on the property. Many visitors choose to spend their first or last night in Zimbabwe at one of these places.

Backpackers' lodges

Backpackers and Overlanders Lodge, Twentydales Road Extension, corner of Delport Road (☎04/575715, fax 575719, *conxshon@samara.co.zw*). First-class backpackers' lodge a couple of kilometres from the airport, with double rooms, dorms (including an exclusive one for women), a thatched A-frame building with four double rooms, individual double-room cottages and camping, plus a swimming pool and garden. Regular transfers are provided to and from the city centre, airport and train station, and you can self-cater or eat their reasonably priced evening meal. ①.

BED AND BREAKFAST BOOKINGS

Affordable Accommodation (☎04/302190, fax 744594, mobile 091/308656, *bednbrea @cornish.icon.co.zw*) is a **B&B booking agency** based in Harare that deals in reasonably priced, good-quality accommodation in private homes or self-contained flats in suburbs near the city centre. All accommodation is pleasantly furnished, with good security, usually a pool, TV and phone and fax facilities, and they all offer meals and a laundry service as optional extras. Daily rates range from US$25 to US$40 per person.

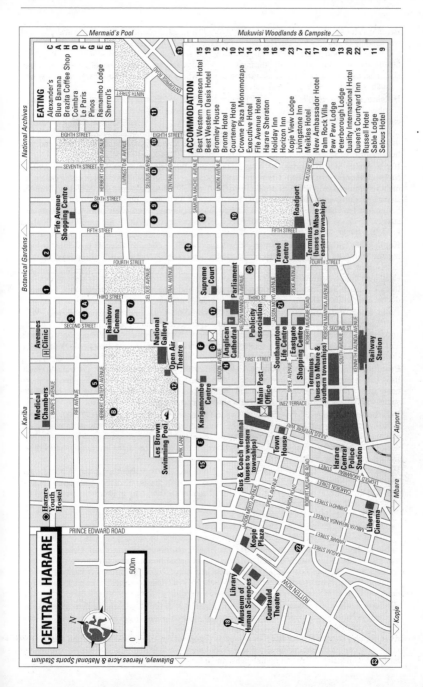

CENTRAL HARARE

EATING

Alexander's	C
Blue Banana	A
Brazita Coffee Shop	H
Coimbra	D
Le Paris	F
Pinos	G
Ramambo Lodge	E
Sherrol's	B

ACCOMMODATION

Best Western Jameson Hotel	15
Best Western Oasis Hotel	19
Bromley House	5
Bronte Hotel	2
Courteney Hotel	10
Crowne Plaza Monomotapa	12
Executive Hotel	14
Fife Avenue Hotel	3
Harare Sheraton	18
Holiday Inn	16
Horizon Inn	4
Kopje View Lodge	23
Livingstone Inn	7
Meikles Hotel	21
New Ambassador Hotel	17
Palm Rock Villa	8
Paw Paw Lodge	6
Peterborough Lodge	13
Quality International Hotel	20
Queen's Courtyard Inn	22
Russell Hotel	1
Sable Lodge	11
Selous Hotel	9

Bromley House, 182 Herbert Chitepo Ave (☎04/724072, *gensec@cra.icon.co.zw*). Centrally located women-only hostel opposite the Harare Gardens that's been in business for fifty years, offering safe and friendly accommodation. Dead cheap with spotlessly clean dorms, the downer is that it quickly fills up with students, particularly during term time. Packed lunches and evening meals are available, plus use of the garden and a convivial lounge, where you'll meet fellow travellers and young Zimbabweans. Rate includes breakfast. ①.

Hillside Lodge, 71 Hillside Rd, Hillside (☎04/747961, *hillside@samara.co.zw*). Relaxed former farmhouse set in beautiful shady gardens east of the centre, which is 10min away by car. The apparent chaos is more than mitigated by the easygoing approach of Rod and Nathalie, who leave guests to get on with it and will pay your taxi fare from the airport. Home-cooked meals are available and there's a bar, free tea and coffee, as well as email access. Camping, dorms, double rooms and tree houses for two. ①.

It's a Small World Lodge, 72 King George Rd, Avondale (☎ & fax 04/335341 or 335176, *backpack@harare.iafrica.com*). Unexceptional backpackers' lodge about 4km north of the centre, its main recommendation being its proximity to the Avondale shopping centre. Initial pick-up from the airport, bus or train stations is free, and there's a pool, TV lounge, phone, fax and email facilities, bottomless tea and coffee as well as a kitchen for self-catering, reasonably priced breakfasts and snacks, braais on Fridays and a laundry service. Dorms and doubles in the garden. ①. Doubles inside the house. ②.

Kopje View Lodge, 33 Fort Rd (☎04/705680, fax 724996). A cheap and decent hostel that is looking the worse for wear, just south of the central shopping district opposite the power plant on Rotten Row, a busy double carriageway. Separate male and female dorms and private rooms are clean but could do with better furniture and less worn-out mattresses, while their rock garden isn't the ideal place for camping. Pick-ups from airport and meals by arrangement only. Camping, dorms and doubles. ①.

Palm Rock Villa, 39 Selous Ave (☎04/724550 or 700691, *palmrockvilla@hotmail.com*). Well-maintained lodge in the Avenues in a small turn-of-the-century house with nine three-bed dorms and five double rooms. Only self-catering is on offer, with a well-equipped kitchen, plenty of men's and women's showers and toilets, secure off-street parking, email access, luggage lock-ups and a thatched outdoor area in a neat little garden with braai facilities. Dorms and doubles. ①.

Paw Paw Lodge, 262 Herbert Chitepo Ave (☎04/720102, *paw-paw@icon.co.zw*). Central and essentially tatty hostel that has covered its cracks with a fresh coat of paint that can't disguise the shortcomings of a rather unsavoury kitchen and outdoor showers. A dirt-cheap and friendly place all the same, with email facilities and a small curio shop. Dorms, singles and doubles. ①.

Peterborough Lodge, 11 Peterborough Ave, off Samora Machel Avenue (☎04/776990). Spotless, exclusively self-catering lodge just east of the city centre geared more to volunteers on postings or students than to backpackers, and frequently full. Facilities include a pleasant garden with plenty of deck chairs and a TV lounge, and although there's little privacy the rates are highly competitive. Dorms and doubles. ①.

Possum Lodge, 7 Deary Ave, Belgravia (☎04/726851, fax 722803, *possum@zol.co.zw*). A friendly and well-run owner-managed establishment off busy Second Street that is one of the most popular budget places in town, 20min walk from the centre. Email and fax facilities and an excellent travel agent are on site, as well as bike rental, bar, home-cooked food and a snack menu or self-catering. Lots of free extras include pick-ups from the airport and train station, luggage storage and safe, mail holding, braai nights, volleyball, games room, swimming pool and a book exchange. The six dorms in the house sleep four to fourteen people, and there are doubles in sheds in the garden as well as camping. ①.

Sable Lodge, 95 Selous Ave (☎04/726017, fax 706670, *rmardon@samara.co.zw*). Deservedly popular city-centre lodge run by helpful staff in a colonial-style house that was renovated in 1999. It features stripped pine floors, a swimming pool, kitchen, TV lounge, off-street parking and fax facilities as well as an on-site travel agency. Meals are available on request. Camping, dorms and doubles. ①.

Wayfarer Lodge, 47 Jesmond Rd, Logan Park, Hatfield (☎ & fax 04/572125, *wayfarer@icon.co.zw*). Pleasant, enthusiastically run hostel set in a quiet shady garden 4km from the airport. All-day breakfast, vegetarian and meat dishes are available at reasonable prices, or you can self-cater and there's a bar, laundry service and fax facilities as well as organized day-trips, night outings and safaris. The range of accommodation includes camping, traditional-style thatched huts with single beds, wooden sheds with stable doors and double beds, and a two-person tree house. ①.

Guest houses and B&Bs

Horizon Inn, 107 Fife Ave/Second Street (☎04/724917–8, fax 724900). Good-value establishment in the Avenues that offers clean, budget en-suite doubles. Limited self-catering is possible and all rooms come with TV; some have extra bunk beds for groups or families. The only drawbacks are the lack of a garden or lounge, and the environs, which can be slightly dodgy after dark. ②.

Kent Lodge, 43 Kent Rd, off Enterprise Road, Chisipite (☎ & fax 04/495029, *bookings@kentlodge.icon.co.zw*). Guest house in quiet suburbs about 8km northeast of the centre, in a converted family home set in a shady garden with a pool and patio. Nine en-suite rooms all have TVs and safes. Dinner is available on request, and a photocopier, fax, computer, as well as Internet and email facilities, are available to guests, as is a large, cosy lounge with a fireplace. ③.

Livingstone Inn, Livingstone Avenue/Third Street (☎04/738593). Centrally situated low-cost accommodation in an apartment block that underwent a face-lift in 1999 and is working hard to offer value for money. Clean en-suite rooms and discounted long-stay rates that make it popular with students, volunteer workers and businesspeople. A food hall in an adjacent shopping centre offers cheap takeaways and is an added attraction. ②.

Malindi Bed and Breakfast, 19 Alfred Rd, Greendale (☎04/495701, fax 495889, *malindi@ africaonline.co.zw*). Warmly hosted and immaculately clean accommodation in a family home with large gracious gardens in a quiet suburb 10min drive from the city centre. The main house has three large en-suite double rooms and there's a self-contained cottage in the garden with two double rooms, a fully fitted kitchen, bathroom and lounge. A pool and braai area are available to guests, and you can rent mountain bikes. ③.

Sihlezi Lodge, 12 Circle Close, off Harare Drive, Borrowdale (☎ & fax 04/884028, *sihlezi@ samara.co.zw*). Large house with seven comfortable, spacious double rooms and two thatched stone cottages all with TVs and phones, 5min drive from Sam Levy's Shopping Village in the upmarket northern suburbs. Ethnic decor and a large indigenous garden give the feel of a safari lodge rather than a guest house. Dinner available. ⑤.

Thornhill Cottage, 10 York Ave, Highlands (☎ & fax 04/776406, mobile 091/316621, *thornhill@primenet.co.zw*). Self-contained thatched cottage that sleeps two, set in a large garden lined with palms, in a quiet avenue 5km east of the city. Smart and excellent value for money. Booking essential. ④.

Vermont B&B, 5 Leeds Close, off Oxford Avenue, Highlands (☎04/776579, fax 746695). Two double rooms in a secure and private self-contained cottage with small rooms in the grounds of a family home, 5km east of the Avenues. Rooms share a small kitchen/diner, where breakfast is served. Clean, comfortable and a little claustrophobic, but would suit a family. ④.

Zindele Guest House, 6 Caithness Rd, Highlands (☎04/776136, fax 776137, *zindele@pci.co.zw*). Suburban bungalow with seven functional doubles, five of them en suite (the other two with detached bathrooms) in a quiet street with secure parking 3km east of the centre. Andrew, the friendly cook, is on hand to knock up your ingredients into a delicious dinner at no extra charge. ②.

Inexpensive hotels

Executive Hotel, Fourth Street/Samora Machel Avenue (☎ & fax 04/701807–9). Don't be put off by the mouldy exterior of this centrally situated, converted apartment block: inside you'll find large, clean en-suite rooms. The hotel's *Gecko's Restaurant* isn't worth traipsing out for, but is fine if you feel like staying in, with reasonably priced steaks and pasta dishes. Bargain accommodation considering its standard and location. ②.

Feathers Hotel, Sherwood Drive, Mabelreign (☎04/228472 or 228473, fax 339501, *feathers@zol.co.zw*). Light, clean rooms in a large farm-style hotel with a pool and garden, about 10km from the centre in the western suburbs close to Westgate Shopping Centre. Excellent value but likely to be inconvenient unless you have your own transport. ②.

Fife Avenue Hotel, 102 Fife Ave/Second Street (☎04/707031–3, fax 707034). One of the least expensive hotels in the Avenues, but a clean and respectable one, making it highly popular with tourists and business travellers. Its multi-storey accommodation was completely refurbished in 1999, and it has comfortable en-suite rooms, a pool, a quiet bar, a breakfast terrace and a motel atmosphere. Good value. ③

George Hotel, King George Road, Avondale (☎04/336677–9, fax 339501, *rundog@harare.iafrica.co*). Pleasant, friendly, if rather ordinary hotel a couple of kilometres north of the centre, opposite Avondale Shopping Centre. Shabby furniture, but otherwise perfectly adequate and respectable. ③.

Red Fox Hotel, Greendale Avenue/Stewart Road (☎04/495466). Decent country-style hotel in an incongruous mock-Tudor style opposite Honeydew Farm in the eastern suburbs. A fair way out of town, but excellent value at only a touch more than backpackers' lodge prices. An option worth considering if you have your own transport. ②.

Russell Hotel, 116 Baines Ave (☎04/791895–7). Functional multi-storey stubby block next door to Italian and Portuguese restaurants and 10 min walk from city centre. Plenty of acceptable rooms in the main hotel and cheaper ones in its annexe on Second Street. Nothing fancy, though there is a pool. ②.

Selous Hotel, Selous Avenue/Sixth Street (☎04/727940 or 727948–9 or 702116, fax 727885, *selhotel@ samara.co.zw*). One of the best-value hotels in the Avenues, with friendly service, clean, comfortable surroundings and 52 en-suite rooms. Secure parking, a garden terrace and lounge are reserved for guests, while the *Penthouse Restaurant* on the top floor offers a superb view of Harare. ②.

Moderate hotels

Best Western Oasis Hotel, 124 Nelson Mandela Ave (☎04/704217–9, fax 790865, *oasgc@ samara.co.zw*). Fully serviced hotel 5min walk from the centre, with bright and friendly atmosphere, early-morning tea and newspapers, pool and patio bar. ⑥.

Bronte Hotel, 132 Baines Ave (☎04/707522–7, fax 721429). Comfortable en-suite rooms in a gracious colonial building in the Avenues, with enchanting gardens and courteous service. Highly recommended and excellent value for money. Cheaper, but far less appealing rooms are available opposite the main hotel in the Baines Wing Annexe. ④–⑤.

Courteney Hotel, Selous Avenue/Eighth Street (☎04/706411–4, fax 708709). Unattractive 1970s decor is the hallmark of this otherwise decent hotel in the Avenues, which is only recommended if the *Bronte* is full. A small enclosed garden, pool and free morning papers are added touches, and its *L'Escargot* restaurant is highly rated. ⑤.

New Ambassador Hotel, 88 Union Ave (☎04/708121–4, fax 708126). Friendly and convenient hotel with marbled and pastel interiors, bang in the centre opposite Parliament. All rooms en suite with TV and phone. ⑤.

Quality International Hotel, Nelson Mandela Avenue/Fourth Street (☎04/794461–9, fax 722894 or 708997, *quality@id.co.zw*). Reasonable but somewhat anonymous central hotel with air-conditioning, safes and TV in every room. Inexpensive airport transfers by arrangement. ⑤.

Queen's Courtyard Inn, Robert Mugabe Road/Kaguvi Street (☎04/755899 or 759508, fax 759382, *qcourt@africaonline.co.zw*). Located on a busy road in the Kopje area just southwest of the city centre, Zimbabwe's oldest registered hotel, built in 1899, was renovated in 1998 to recreate the original ambience, featuring a reading room, lounge, bar and a courtyard restaurant. ⑤.

Expensive hotels and lodges

Barker's Lodge, 1 Masasa Lane, Kambanji, Glen Lorne (☎04/499081 or 499076, fax 499065, *barhol@harare.iafrica.com*). Eight luxury en-suite chalets with their own verandah, TV, phone and Internet facilities, in landscaped gardens in the salubrious northern suburbs, 15km northeast of the centre. Poolside bar, lounge and tennis court. The owners, Duncan and Yvette Barker, are nationally renowned cooks and serve expensive but memorable five-course gourmet dinners. ⑨.

Best Western Jameson Hotel, Samora Machel Avenue/Park Street (☎04/774106–774112, fax 774119, *jamgm@samara.co.zw*). Best value of the expensive hotels, located in the heart of town, 5min walk from the Gardens and able to offer all the facilities you'd expect in the top rung. ⑦.

Cresta Lodge, Samora Machel Avenue/Robert Mugabe Road, Coronation Park (☎04/487154, 487157, 487006 or 487008, fax 487009, *lodgeres@samara.co.zw*). Upmarket facilities at competitive rates, 6km east of the city. All rooms come with satellite TV and air-conditioning, and the hairdressing and beauty salons, gift shop, bureau de change, pool, lounge, bar, restaurant and coffee shop mean you need never leave the hotel. Free airport transfer on request. ⑦.

Crowne Plaza Monomotapa, 54 Park Lane (☎04/704501–30, fax 791920, *crowneplaza@crownep. zimsun.co.zw*). The third tallest building in the city centre, with tremendous views, all its rooms overlooking the Harare Gardens – ask for the upper floors. Conveniently adjacent to the National Gallery and the Olympic-sized Les Brown swimming pool. ⑧.

Harare Sheraton, Pennefather Avenue (☎04/772633 or 772612, fax 774648 or 774668, *sheraton@ harare.iafrica.com*). Part of the international chain, this Yugoslav-designed, post-Independence building's exterior has become a landmark of Harare, but once inside you could be anywhere. Features several restaurants and bars, pool, gym, tennis court and sauna. ⑨.

Holiday Inn, Samora Machel Avenue/Fifth Street (☎04/795611 to 795629, fax 727267 or 738956, *hih@hih.zimsun.co.zw*). Most casual of the hotels in this bracket, with a nice pool, free accommodation for children under 19 sharing their parents' room, and babysitters on request. ⑦.

Imba Matombo, 3 Albert Glen Close, Glen Lorne (☎04/499013–4, fax 499071 or 494508, *imba@harare.iafrica.com*). Thatched, colonial-style home in one of Harare's opulent suburbs with views over the surrounding countryside. Cottages and rooms are tastefully and individually furnished, some with their own verandah and lounge. Railway sleeper furniture and African artefacts, tennis court, 25m pool and connoisseur meals around the grand dinner table all add to the posh ambience. Full board ⑨.

Meikles Hotel, Third Street/Jason Moyo Avenue (☎04/707721 or 795655, fax 707753 or 707754, *meikles@harare.iafrica.com*). Overbloated hotel that trades on an inflated reputation as the capital's best. With views across Africa Unity Square, you don't get more central, or expensive, than this. ⑨.

Country lodges and guest houses

None of the places listed below is more than an hour's drive from town, many on large properties that offer activities such as birdwatching, horse-riding, canoeing or walking. Several have some plains game on their estate, but don't expect too much in terms of game viewing. (If you're looking for an animal experience rather than a night in the country, you'd be better off heading for Imire or Bally Vaughan private game reserves, both easy drives from town; see p.102). At the upper end of the range the establishments listed here offer solid country-style luxury for weekends away or first and last nights in Zimbabwe, while a couple of the cheaper options are conveniently situated near the airport in a pleasant farming district. Few accept walk-ins, but all offer free or inexpensive transfers to and from town and the airport. The luxury places do an all-inclusive rate, which covers meals, drinks, walks and drives.

Changamire Lodge, Box WGT 480, Harare (☎ & fax 04/305878, *armadilo@mail.pci.co.zw*). Comfortable accommodation with an ethnic feel in four brick-and-thatch A-frame chalets on a private game reserve (plains game only) along the Gwebi River, 55km from Harare. Pool, fishing, sundowner cruises, game drives, walks and tobacco-farm tour available to guests. To get there, take the Kariba road; turn left down a dirt road just after the 52km peg and follow the signs for the remaining 3km. The rate inclusive of all meals and activities is US$180 per person.

Landela Lodge, Box 66293, Kopje, Harare (☎04/734044–6, fax 708119, *res@landela.co.zw*). Wonderful farmhouse near Ruwa, 35min east of the airport, off the Mutare road, with lush gardens and superb food. Highly recommended and a great option if international hotels pall. Sightseeing trips into town can be arranged, as well as visits to a nearby game farm where you can ride. US$140 per person all in.

Mbizi Game Park and Lodges, Twentydales Road extension off Delport Road, Box UA 358, Harare (☎04/700676–8 or 575720, fax 700812, *accommo@mbizipark.icon.co.zw*). Renovated colonial farmhouse with en-suite double rooms with ethnic interiors, and self-catering bush cottages that sleep up to six, on the banks of the Ruwa and Munyami rivers. Abundant birdlife and plains game, including giraffes. Some 22km from Harare, it's also a very convenient 10km from the airport. Activities include canoeing, fishing, birdwatching and horse-riding on the four-square-kilometre property. Free transfers to town or airport. Self-catering US$80 per cottage, plus US$5 per person per activity; half-board including all activities US$90 per person.

Setanga Lodge, Box 175, Ruwa (☎ & fax 073/2381, *setalodge@yahoo.com*). Exceptionally friendly guest house on a smallholding, not far from the airport. Some 25km from Harare off the Mutare road, next to the well-signposted Ruwa Country Club, it's a good place to spend your first or last few days in Zimbabwe; there are thatched chalets in the gardens and a twin room with its own entrance in the main house, all en suite. Orphaned antelopes roam free and the birdlife is good. Guests have access to facilities at the country club, which has an eighteen-hole golf course, and moderately priced dinners are available. B&B rate US$30 per person sharing.

Shields Safaris, Cockington Estates, Darwendale (☎04/704781 or 704786, fax 738754, *premier@samara.co.zw*). Lodges at three sites within the Squatodzi Valley Game Park, just under 100km west of Harare: two simple thatched houses overlooking a lake, a three-bedroom self-catering cottage and a fully serviced stone-and-thatch lodge. Activities include game drives, fishing, bird-watching, canoeing and nature walks. Self-catering US$40 per person; fully inclusive US$100.

Thetford House, PO Box 6485, Harare (☎04/795841 or 795844, mobile 011/607906, fax 795845–6, *angie@runwild.co.zw*). Large, English-style country mansion in the hilly Christon Bank area approximately 60km north of the centre, with views over the Mazowe Valley and Dam: cream teas and Sunday lunches. Half-board US$75 per person; full board including game drives in a small game park, horse-rides, drinks, return transfers, shopping trips and laundry US$150.

Wild Geese Lodge, PO Box BW 198, Harare (☎04/860466 or 860275, fax 860276, *geese@africaonline.co.zw*). Cottages with private verandahs, and a main lodge with a pool, dining room and bar with shiny parquet floors, fresh flowers and starched linen. Set at the head of the Mazowe Valley just outside the northern suburbs, about 12km from town, next to Wingate Golf Club; you can enjoy panoramic views over savannah grasslands towards the mountains. Airport transfers and trips into town can be arranged, as well as horse-riding through the valley, where plains game and a variety of birds can be spotted. US$126 per person B&B; activities and other meals extra. A couple of slightly less expensive chalets are also available.

The City

In common with every town in Zimbabwe that came into existence during the colonial period, Harare's town planning still bears the marks of an earlier obsession with racial segregation. Today the **city centre** is the most integrated of Harare's districts, both racially and in terms of class: you'll see white farmers, black tycoons and the poor from the townships all rubbing shoulders here. Harare's oldest African quarter, **Mbare**, lies just 3km south of the centre and, unlike the former whites-only suburbs, retains its racially exclusive character. A world apart are the **northern suburbs** such as Avondale and Borrowdale, established by Rhodesia's white elite, who did their best to emulate English gentility with vast tended gardens, golf courses, the Botanic Gardens and the Borrowdale racetrack. These areas have undoubtedly changed their complexion, if not status, although they still remain disproportionately white. On the other side of the train tracks lie the less affluent **southern suburbs**, separated from the north by grey belt of industrial areas. During the heyday of white Rhodesia these faded off into the **African townships** that included Epworth, Mufakose and Kuwadzana and were kept out of sight, and mind, at a comfortable distance from the living quarters of the city's white population.

The City centre

Harare's **city centre** splits up quite neatly into functional districts. The **main commercial area**, with smart shops, banks and restaurants, is largely confined to the section west of Fourth Street, around **Africa Unity Square** and up to the **Harare Gardens**. **First Street** is an attractive pedestrian mall where you can sit at outdoor cafés and survey the passing scene. The distinctively curving *Monomatapa Hotel*, scraping more sky than most, makes an effective landmark. **Jason Moyo Avenue**, between Second and Fourth streets, is a tourist strip, lined by the Publicity Association information offices, *Meikles Hotel* and the adjacent Southampton Life Centre with its travel agents and curio shops and the Air Zimbabwe terminal around the corner in Third Street. On the southwest side of the centre, in the **Kopje area**, the roads suddenly skew off centre and you're in a different city. From here zip over the Kopje itself, and you'll find yourself in Harare's townships, hidden from view – and conscience – by the hill.

Africa Unity Square, Parliament and the Cathedral

Africa Unity Square, a fountain-decked piazza jazzed up by an exuberant fringe of flower sellers, marks the heart of the capital and vibrates with both colonial and post-Independence resonances. Formerly called Cecil Square, to honour Cecil John Rhodes, it's the spot where colonial Harare was founded on September 13, 1890, with the ceremonial hoisting of the British flag, a fact still recalled in the layout of the square's paths, which follow the pattern of the Union Jack. Obviously in no doubt that the locals didn't go along with this annexation of African real estate to the Empire, the British pioneers immediately set about erecting a fort on the site. In 1988 the square shed its colonial name in favour of the present one to celebrate the unification of ZANU-PF and ZAPU, Zimbabwe's two main parties.

North of the square, across Nelson Mandela Avenue, the **Parliament Buildings** were going to be a hotel when construction began in 1895. However, the outbreak of the First Chimurenga (anti-colonial uprising) brought building to a standstill as troops putting down the rebellion were billeted in the unfinished shell. When the developers went bust in 1898, the British South Africa Company (BSAC) took it over to use as a post office, but soon after the newly formed Legislative Assembly was installed. As the first session sat in 1899, the builders were still at work. For **guided tours** or seats in the **visitors gallery** during debates, apply to the Chief Information Officer, Parliament of Zimbabwe, PO Box 8055, Causeway, Harare.

On the western edge of the same square, Harare's sandstone **Anglican Cathedral**, at the corner of Nelson Mandela Avenue and Second Street, took fifty years to complete after inception in 1913. The designer, British-born Sir Herbert Baker, was then South Africa's leading architect and was responsible for the Union Buildings in Pretoria, and South Africa House overlooking London's Trafalgar Square; he also worked on the design of New Delhi with Lutyens, the master of imperial architecture. Baker wanted the Harare cathedral to have a cylindrical bell tower as a reference to the conical tower at Great Zimbabwe – a rare acknowledgement of indigenous forms – but this eccentric idea was, sadly, overruled. The sombreness of the interior, with its starkly impressive solid granite columns, is relieved by the cartoon-like murals of the stations of the cross. If you're lucky you may hear Shona women at choir practice, using traditional percussion, and for some beautiful vernacular hymns look in on a Shona Eucharist (times are posted outside the Cathedral).

Harare Gardens and around

Largest and loveliest of the city centre's public spaces, the **Harare Gardens** are well manicured and well used. On afternoons schoolkids loll about doing homework, and on weekends wedding parties parade around, the women in white chiffon and shiny red fancy dress, the men charcoal-suited. People stroll the thoroughfare that cuts through from Park Lane to Herbert Chitepo Avenue, and it's a good place to take a break and contemplate the city. On Sundays, around late morning and lunchtime, a big market brings a bit of bustle to the gardens, and makes a pleasant place to go craft hunting. This isn't a place to come after dark, though, as there have been some muggings in the gardens.

At their southern end, on Park Lane, the **Crowne Plaza Monomatapa Hotel** (frequently referred to as "Monos"), is one of the few buildings in Harare that dates from the 1970s, the height of the war years, when guns came before bricks, and is one of the few modern buildings to make reference to the meandering walls of Great Zimbabwe – and thus the country's ancient architectural tradition. Its height and distinctive form make it an ideal beacon for orientation around the centre.

The National Gallery of Zimbabwe

Within spitting distance of the Monomatapa and just to its east, the **National Gallery of Zimbabwe** (daily except Mon 9am–5pm; US$0.50, Sun free), Julius Nyerere Way and Park Lane, was opened in 1957 and from the outset promoted local talent irrespective of race. An initial interest in painting was soon overtaken when the curators became aware of **stone sculptures** by Joram Mariga. In the 1960s a workshop was founded, with stone being brought in from Nyanga and given to the employees, and Zimbabwe's formidable movement in sculpture was established. Initially, under the directorship of Frank McEwan, it produced works geared towards European expectations, but since the 1980s the emphasis has become truly national and the movement has gained world recognition. Modern stone sculpture gets a good showing in the permanent collection in the well-populated **sculpture garden**, inhabited by mythological creatures and beast-humans frozen in mid-transformation. **Bernard Matemera**, master of this species conversion, has a number of distinctively distorted works scattered about. Amongst other big names, the **Takawira brothers** drag exquisitely refined busts from unfinished rough-hewn stone.

Temporary exhibitions inside the cash-strapped gallery tend to be varied and of uneven quality. So far Zimbabwe has spawned no movement in painting or allied visual arts that can match its stone sculpture in confidence or originality, which isn't to say you won't find something sparkling by an individual artist. Past exhibitions have included the Longman Biennale of works by women artists, visiting shows sponsored by the embassies, West African textiles, an exhibition by final-year art students and the annual display of award-winning architectural designs. It's also worth keeping an eye open for the new wave of **landscape painting**, which has emerged as artists have lost their enthusiasm for politically motivated themes. The gallery owns a significant collection of traditional works, drawn from throughout the continent, mostly **West African sculpture** and crafts, which sadly aren't always on display. A bimonthly **newsletter**, available from the gallery, lists current and forthcoming events.

Eastgate Centre

Two blocks due south of Africa Unity Square, the **Eastgate Centre**, between Speke Avenue and Robert Mugabe Road, is arguably the most interesting post-Independence building in the city centre. With its curious Tudoresque chimneys and *Blade Runner* interior, it's unquestionably the most startling.

Eastgate, completed in 1996, is the result of a brief to minimize mechanical air-conditioning by making use of natural ventilation. According to the architects, Pearce Partnership, Eastgate is a reaction against the modernist notion that buildings are "machines for living in". Instead, they started from the principle that their building was an **ecosystem**, and found inspiration by studying termitaries in the Zimbabwean savannah – the tall earthy mounds occupied by termite colonies. To regulate the temperature in termitaries, the insects build them with chambers inside, which employ convection to draw cooling air through the mound. Eastgate adopts the same principle, using its chimneys to discharge coolant air drawn in through low-level inlets and up through the building. The building's distinctive **structure** is also part of the solution. Two slender nine-storey slabs connected by bridges form a shopping arcade that seamlessly links Second and Third streets. They also expose the maximum possible surface given the site, so optimizing radiation to regulate the internal temperature.

The architects claim that Eastgate uses 35 percent less **energy** than comparable buildings in central Harare and it has the added edge that, during the capital's frequent power cuts, its ventilation system still works.

Robert Mugabe Road

The greatest concentration of Harare's historic buildings – many of them low-key but highly rewarding – lie along **Robert Mugabe Road**. Walk down the section between Second Street and Julius Nyerere Way and you'll see over half a dozen notable facades, several with cast-iron balconies and columns with beautiful filigree capitals, dating from 1910 to 1923. **Fereday & Sons** at no. 72 started off as a gun, ammunition and cycle dealer in the 1920s, and is now one of the best camping shops in Harare. It's worth entering the building for the intact period interior, even if the original exterior cast-iron columns have been displaced by undistinguished concrete ones.

Some other fine buildings lie further west, close to the Kopje area, on the way to the Museum of Human Sciences. Among these are **Vasan's Footwear**, between Chinoyi and Cameron streets, a 1902 building that originally served as an outfitters, with a typical turn-of-the-century pavement canopy supported on slender columns. Way more monumental is **India House**, between Harare and Mbuya Nehanda streets, constructed in 1901 as the headquarters of the *Rhodesia Herald* newspaper. Its imposing Edwardian facade has Italianate features such as pedimented upper-floor windows and fluted pilasters typical of the style. On the other side of Harare Street, the **Queen's Courtyard Inn**, known as the *Queen's Hotel* when it was built 1900, was renovated in 1998 to restore its historic appearance. Characteristic of its colonial style is a tin roof and wraparound verandah under the protection of a deep overhang.

The Museum of Human Sciences

Five minutes' walk from the west end of Robert Mugabe Avenue, the capital's relatively modest **Museum of Human Sciences**, on Rotten Row (daily 9am–5pm; US$2), is knocked into a cocked hat by the excellent Museum of Natural History in Bulawayo (see p.157). Previously known as the Queen Victoria Museum, the building has a giant concrete snail, pangolin, praying mantis and chameleon standing guard outside, and amidst the motley collection of didactic bric-a-brac inside – freshwater aquaria, a history of life, the world and everything – two exceptionally well-displayed galleries stand out. One is the **habitat exhibition** in the **natural sciences gallery**, a sure draw for any wildlife enthusiast en route to the game parks. The displays recreate Zimbabwe's variety of landscapes so realistically that you're left wondering how they got the granite kopje, adorned with appropriate flora and fauna, inside. The other habitat displays are equally good – and more informative than a dozen books. Another excellent diorama is a reconstructed **Shona village**, which has life-size mud huts, people and vegetation.

From far earlier times, there's a reconstruction of a fast-moving **dinosaur** – half bird, half lizard and warm-blooded; in one place in the Zambezi Valley, over twenty of these small predators were found in a group.

The Sheraton Hotel and Harare International Conference Centre

About 300m west of the museum is the **Sheraton Hotel and Harare International Conference Centre**, which was the most controversial post-Independence building when construction was completed in the early 1990s. A shimmering gilt glass slab of monumental proportions, it provides a curious transition from the streets of Third World Harare to a brassy Midas-world where everything that can be is gold, from the gold-tinted windows, gold light fittings and gold-finished furniture down to the guests' gold watches and medallions. The building was the work of the former-Yugoslavian Energoprojekt company, who brought in their own building teams and materials to produce this piece of theatre. Rumour has it that the government wanted Zimbabweans to work on the project and, when they persisted in this demand in mid-construction, Energoprojekt deserted, taking their drawings with them and leaving local architects to work it all out.

Mbare

If Harare has a heart, **Mbare** must be it – it's a quarter that should on no account be missed. Once away from the orderly centre, you plunge into a distinctly African city of which vibrant Mbare is the liveliest part – still close to the centre (3km), and with streams of people walking down the road and hanging about the run-down blocks of flats. Poverty is all around, though you're unlikely to see anything desperate. Begging is, however, on the increase (as are muggings) and only a foolhardy visitor would wander around here alone after dark; women on their own are especially vulnerable. In general, unless you're feeling pretty confident about where you're going, it's advisable to take a tour or go with someone who knows their way around as there have been incidents of visitors asking directions and being literally led down a blind alley to be robbed.

Called Harare Township during the colonial days, Mbare's new name comes from a chief who once held court on the Kopje. The quarter is the decades-old trading area for Africans bringing their produce in from the country, and it remains so today, hosting the country's biggest **market** – known as the *musika* – at the nexus of all road transport. Leave by bus from here for the rural areas or the provincial towns and you'll be part of a vast throng of travellers, especially at weekends and holidays.

Getting to Mbare from central Harare is easy. Regular buses leave from the city terminus on Angwa Street/South Avenue. You can also pick up commuter omnibuses in Market Square, opposite the Roadport on the corner of Fourth Street and Robert Mugabe Road, although regular taxis are a lot less hassle.

The market

In 1981, following Independence, the City Council developed Mbare's trading area by adopting the idea of "communal markets" being successfully propagated at the time in China, and laid on washing facilities and covered stalls for traders. The enormous complex of the **musika**, which lines Chaminuka Street, nowadays has endless different sections, selling produce, clothes, crafts, live poultry, traditional medicines and the unrecognizable. This is also your chance to try *chibuku* at one of the **beer halls**, or some **street food**. The **fresh produce** area is a banquet of bright-coloured fruits and vegetables – mounds of the stuff for bulk buyers or smaller carefully arranged piles if you just want a salad's worth; either way, this is the cheapest place in town for fruit and veg. Expect to be approached by a market porter who will trail after you, usually with a wheelbarrow, carrying your purchases for a tip.

In another part of the *musika*, **secondhand gear** ranges from piles of clothes on the pavement to old plastic bottles and bags. In this relatively litter-free country, little is thrown away, everything is recyclable and almost anything broken can be cobbled together again. Invention is boundless – one stall sells buckled spectacle frames and broken sunshades. Look out, too, for the sandals made from worn-down tyres with crossover straps. It's a standing joke in Harare that if you get something ripped off, the secondhand market at Mbare is the first place to look. **Herbal medicines** are sold at several stalls and you can track down traditional healers (*n'angas*) who work in the area. The stalls are a mishmash of skins and seed pods, things in bottles, bunches of dried plants, and prized items like cowrie shells and gemsbok (oryx antelope) tails. The government has passed a bill strengthening the position of *n'angas*; an association was formed in 1981 and there's now some cooperation between modern and traditional practices. Some spirit medium *n'angas* are concerned only with the cause of the illness, while others just treat the physical symptoms.

Mbare is also one of the best places around for **souvenirs**, with **baskets** and **carved work** being common. Look out for hand-lathed objects such as snuffboxes wrought from exotic woods, which are very popular with African women, for whom smoking is traditionally prohibited. Hand-beaten copper and brass **bracelets** are good buys. Traders are open to bargaining, and although they're tough dealers you should be able to pick up goods more cheaply here than at the town craft shops.

The Canon Paterson Art Centre

Just north of the market is the **Canon Paterson Art Centre**, on the corner of Chaminuka Street and Mbare Road (daily 8am–5pm; free), where you can watch **stone sculptors** working. By contrast with places such as Chapungu (see p.83), you won't find big names here; the centre is dedicated to providing an outlet for any craftworker/ artist and for this reason they will accept into their ranks anyone with the requisite skills. This means there's no quality control, so you stand a fair chance of confronting a sea of indifferent work, but by the same token there's the chance of spotting some real talent and paying a fraction of the prices you'll pay at the commercial city galleries and shops.

The centre's small **shop** is crammed full of carved elephants, Zimbabwe birds and the like. Often the stone itself (serpentine, rather than much softer and less attractive soapstone) is more beautiful than the pieces themselves, but small sculptures are inexpensive and easy enough to transport; should you fall in love with something larger, they will happily pack, crate and ship it anywhere in the world for you.

The suburbs

The once exclusively white areas of the capital are a monument to the suburban dream. But half a dozen worthwhile attractions are tucked away here, often conveniently close together, making it possible to combine two in a single excursion. None is more than twenty minutes' drive from the centre and even if you don't have your own car you'll be able to get there by commuter omnibus or taxi, which shouldn't cost an arm and a leg. In the north, just beyond the Avenues, the tremendously enjoyable **National Botanic Gardens** and nearby **National Archives of Zimbabwe** are rewarding showcases for the country's human and natural history. South of these, and less than 3km east of the city, **Mukuvisi Woodland Nature Reserve and Environment Centre** is a great place for kids, with a playground and the chance to see cute baby elephants being fed, while 500m further east **Chapungu Village and Sculpture Park** is one of the pleasantest places in town to look at stone carvings and watch craftspeople at work. In the west, towards the high-density suburbs, **Heroes' Acre**, a monument to the luminaries of the liberation struggle, is a curiosity of African socialist realism rather than a substantial sight, but one worth visiting if you are interested in Zimbabwe's history and politics. Finally, appropriately housed in the spluttering industrial areas south of Heroes' Acre, the **Tobacco Auction Floors** offer the chance to see the world's biggest such institution and to marvel at the rapid-fire speech of the auctioneers.

The National Botanic Gardens

Fronting up to the northern suburbs, the **National Botanic Gardens**, Sandringham Drive, Alexandra Park (daily 8am–6pm; free), are Zimbabwe's answer to London's Kew, a peaceful place where you can immerse yourself in African vegetation, neatly divided into ecological zones. There's a fine collection of the continent's **trees**, including most of Zimbabwe's 750 species, while large areas are closely cropped **parkland** with ponds ideal for picnicking or lazy afternoons. A **restaurant** (see p.84), signposted from the car park, does teas and snacks on the lawn.

The gardens are about ten minutes by car and thirty on foot from the centre: go north up Fifth Street, which becomes Sandringham Drive, and the main entrance is on the right. Otherwise, catch any bus down Second Street and get off at Downie Avenue, where there's another entrance.

The National Archives of Zimbabwe

About 1km east of the Gardens, the **National Archives of Zimbabwe**, signposted off Ruth Taylor Road, Gun Hill (Mon–Fri 8.30am–4pm; US$0.50), house the most rewarding museum in Harare, the **Beit Trust Gallery**, on the first floor. A rich reserve of historic books, documents, newspapers, stamps, objects and paintings relating to Zimbabwe's history, the museum's outstanding feature is its collection on the lower level of original Victorian oil paintings of Southern African subjects. Most notable of these is a clutch of documentary landscapes by the well-known nineteenth-century adventurer, artist and diarist **Thomas Baines**, who became a fellow of the Royal Geographical Society in 1887 in recognition of his achievements. Baines accompanied a number of expeditions as a chronicler, including David Livingstone's exploration of the Zambezi in 1858 and one undertaken by James Chapman to the Victoria Falls in 1861. Describing a painting from the latter excursion, art critic Celia Winter Irving writes that "his works convey with realism the flow of the water, the wetness of the spray, the transparency of the spume and the crashing and rising of the torrent. Today, the artistic merit of Baines' work is measured equal to its documentary worth."

On the same level, **historic books** and **antique maps** of Africa dating back to the mid-sixteenth century include original African travelogues by Portuguese adventurers, with scientific and ethnographic coverage that reads like science fiction; one antique colour plate shows a fantastic hippo baring jagged carnivorous fangs. The **newspaper display** on the same floor, traces Zimbabwe's history in press reports, through federation, UDI and post-Independence – interesting not just for the history, but the way events were reported at different times. Climb the spiral stairs from here and you'll reach the **Chimurenga exhibition**, with informative displays on both liberation struggles and some pretty gruesome photographs relating to the hanging by the British of the organizers of the anti-colonial uprising of the 1890s.

You can buy excellent, and reasonably priced reproductions of some of the paintings and antique maps on display in the Beit Trust Gallery; ask at the reception desk.

Mukuvisi Woodland Nature Reserve and Environment Centre

Tucked away in Harare's southeastern suburbs, just 2.5km from the centre, is the msasa-vegetated **Mukuvisi Woodland Nature Reserve and Environment Centre**, Hillside Road Extension, corner of Glenara Avenue South (daily 8am–5pm; US$0.50). Now stocked with antelope including eland, waterbuck, impala and waterbuck, as well as elephants and rhino, it already had resident populations of steenbok, duiker, hares and guinea fowl when the enclosure was erected in 1980. Luckily for the wildlife, City Council attempts to put up a housing estate here were quashed when concerned residents appealed to the High Court. Orphaned elephant calves, hand-reared at the woodlands, are a popular attraction, and easily seen at feeding times from the **viewing platform**, which is signposted from the entrance. As feeding takes place throughout the day, your best bet is to ask at the entrance booth when the next session is due.

Not far from the entrance, a **walk-in aviary** gives a great chance to get close to some of Zimbabwe's indigenous species, especially waterfowl, while other enclosures house crocs, tortoises and terrapins. For intrepid urban adventuring, join one of the two-hour **walking safaris** (daily 2.30pm; US$1 per adult), or the **horse-rides** (daily 8.30am & 3pm; US$2; booking essential) that allow you to get up really close to wildlife. Most of the 1.7-square-kilometre woodland is open to all for walking and is thoroughly pleasant. There have been odd reports of muggings, but you should be perfectly safe if you stick to the western section around the entrance gate and kiosk. Over 230 **bird species** have been recorded: lucky ornithologists may spot the ground-nesting nightjars or some of the wildfowl. Most of the region's trees grow here in the last patch of indigenous woodland inside the city limits.

You can get teas and canned drinks from the **refreshment kiosk** near the entrance (daily 8am–5pm), which has outdoor seating and a children's playground. Also around the reserve entrance, the Wildlife Society of Zimbabwe's **Woodland Shop** (Mon–Fri 8am–5pm, Sat & Sun 9am–5pm) sells an excellent range of souvenirs and outdoor goods that includes T-shirts, camping equipment, maps and field guides.

Chapungu Sculpture Park and around

Chapungu Sculpture Park, attached to the Chapungu Village, Doon Estate, 1 Harrow Rd (Mon–Fri 8am–6pm, Sat & Sun 9am–6pm; US$0.25), about 1km east of Mukuvisi off the Mutare road, near the *Cresta Lodge*, is one of the nicest places in Harare to view sculpture. You'll find plenty of quality affordable pieces by unknown artists and the opportunity to see sculptors at work; various tour operators run trips out here (see p.69). Another outstanding reason to come is the **Doon Estate craft complex** that houses fifteen outlets selling diverse goods, many of them of a very high quality (see Shopping, p.92).

Chapungu Village (same details as for the Sculpture Park), promises an "insight into the cultural and traditional life of Zimbabwe"; there's limited interest in the small reconstructed traditional Shona village and, if you come over the weekend, you'll be able to catch some tourist-orientated traditional dancing (Sat & Sun 3–5pm).

Nearby, more crafts are on display at the **Danhiko Project**, an outlet for disabled craftworkers, about 500m west of Doon Estate on the Mutare road (see Shopping, p.92).

Heroes' Acre

The undeniably imposing shrine to the liberation struggle at **Heroes' Acre**, a combination of abstract monumental architecture, sculptures and friezes in an Afro-Asian version of socialist realism, lies about 5km west of the city centre along Bulawayo Road (daily 8am–4.30pm; donation). One of the soldiers guarding the place will guide you up the monumental black staircase, give you a rundown on the entombed heroes and provide a commentary on the two friezes. The hefty granite slabs scale to a crescendo at the **eternal flame** – actually an electric light switched on nightly – echoed in the flag raised by the triumphant figures of the foreground **monument to the unknown soldier**. On the lower first tier, burnished slabs bear down on the **graves of heroes** of the revolution, while another series of unmarked stones waits eerily for tomorrow's luminaries. In 1999, following the death of Joshua Nkomo, founder of ZAPU and the putative father of Zimbabwe's liberation struggle, his remains were brought from Bulawayo to be interred here, despite his own wish to be buried in his home turf of Matabeleland.

Two rather didactic **friezes** in bronze relief flank the monument. The first traces **oppression**: vicious BSAP cops (the Rhodesian police force continued to bear the name of the British South Africa Police right up until Independence) and toothy dogs savage youngsters and a mother and child, while the outraged parents organize opposition, eventually sending their children across the border for military training. The second frieze depicts the **armed struggle**, with large dashes of heroism culminating in a triumphalist, Leninesque Robert Mugabe declaiming to the masses. A small site **museum** by the entrance houses a collection of photographs, mostly black-and-white, of the political figures buried here. There's also brief coverage of colonialism and the liberation struggle.

To **get there** from the city centre by **car**, head west along Samora Machel Avenue, which becomes Bulawayo Road. The entrance to Heroes' Acre is on the left, about 500m after the National Sports Stadium, which you'll see looming on your right. It's about another kilometre to the monument itself. You can also catch any Bulawayo **bus**, or the Warren Park bus (15min) from a block past the *Jameson Hotel* on Samora Machel Avenue. The prospect of the steep one-kilometre walk from the entrance to the memorial may encourage you to go the whole way by **taxi**.

Tobacco Auction Floors

Also west of the city, but some 4.5km due south of Heroes' Acre, the **Tobacco Auction Floors**, Gleneagles Road, between Ranham and Eltham roads, Willowvale (Mon–Fri 8am–noon; free), are the world's largest. You're welcome to wander around and ask the staff any questions, but there isn't an official tour organized by the floors themselves, although they are included in most city tours. Up-to-date information on sales and prices of tobacco are on display, and watching the traders, especially the motormouth auctioneers, can be quite entertaining.

Eating

There's no shortage of places to eat in central Harare, most of them not too imaginative or stylish, but there are some notable exceptions. If you're looking for something African, there's a small choice of reasonable restaurants or you can have **sadza ne nyama** (maize porridge and meat stew), the staple diet in Zimbabwe, for next to nothing. While not specifically Zimbabwean, spicy piri-piri chicken is a familiar regional speciality imported from neighbouring Mozambique. If you prefer a juicy **steak**, you won't do better anywhere in the world. **Vegetarian restaurants** are a concept yet to hit Harare, but a growing number of establishments offer meat-free dishes. Try the Italian or Indian restaurants listed below, or starters at the Greek restaurants, which can make filling vegetarian meals in themselves. Failing that, most chefs will find an impromptu solution.

Most mid-range and upmarket **hotels** offer buffet breakfasts, lunches and dinners for a fixed fee and also have coffee shops or snack bars, which non-residents are welcome to use. The **coffee bars** listed below tend to open early and are good places to have breakfast; they offer vegetarian options and European menus. **Fast-food** and **takeaway** joints are enormously popular with black and white Zimbabweans and are consequently spreading like wildfire across Harare. You'll find these at most shopping centres and street malls, and although they may be handy they're not necessarily a cheaper option than sitting down at a restaurant or snack bar. Many **pubs and clubs** also serve food (see below).

Coffee, snacks and light meals

Book Café, above OK Bazaars, Fife Avenue Shopping Centre, Avenues (☎04/792551). Attached to Grassroots, one of Harare's best bookshops, this is a great place to have good coffee and reasonable snacks, with vegetarian and meat options. Wednesday is African night, when dishes from around the continent are served, and Tuesday is vegetarian night. The café is also a well-known venue for jazz bands, stand-up comedians and literature evenings. Internet and email facilities, which you must book, are also available. Mon 10am–6pm, Tues–Sat 10am–10.30pm; closed Sun.

Botanic Gardens Restaurant, Botanic Gardens, Sandringham Drive, Alexandra Park. Close to the main entrance on the extension to Fifth Street, this is the only place in Harare where you can have a peaceful cup of tea away from traffic and noise. Seating is under a large thatched terrace or outside in the gardens. The obvious place to stop after a walk in the park: decent breakfasts, snacks and afternoon teas in the best surroundings in Harare. Daily 8am–6pm.

Brazita Coffee Shop, 17 Southampton Arcade, Union Avenue. Indoor and outdoor seating, homemade cakes and snacks at a reliable city-centre café. Daily 7am–5pm.

Fournos Bakery, 144 Samora Machel Ave. French-style patisserie in the city, selling expensive but excellent cakes, breads and pastries with outdoor seating and hot meals, including bagels, pasta and meat dishes. Daily 7am–11pm.

Italian Bakery, Avondale Shopping Centre, next to the cinema (☎04/339732). Incredibly popular Italian- and Ethiopian-run eatery, where its worth queuing for the best cappuccinos, pastries, filled pittas and pizzas in town. Also a licensed bar, occasional live music in the evenings and outdoor seating. Daily 6.45am–midnight.

Kerrygan's Coffee Shop, 16 Greendale Ave, next to Honeydew Farm, Greendale. Smart, brisk café in a thatched rondavel with a verandah in the grounds of a garden nursery. English breakfast and home-cooked snacks include salads, crepes, soups and sandwiches or full meals such as roast beef or butter fish, all beautifully presented and reasonably priced. Mon–Fri 8am–4.30pm, Sat 8am–noon.

Le Café, Alliance Française (☎04/720777). Hugely popular café with outdoor terrace and patio garden. Baked potatoes and delicious sandwiches, enormous omelettes and great cappuccinos. Sloth-like service is part of the relaxed charm. Mon–Sat 8am–10pm, Sun 8am–6pm.

Le Paris, Samora Machel Avenue, between First and Second streets. French-style pavement coffee bar in the city centre, serving good breakfasts and a variety of cheap kebabs and other meat dishes with some vegetarian options. Daily for breakfast till 4.45pm.

News Café, Newlands Shopping Centre. Enterprise Road, Highlands. Trendy café/bar on a busy road, serving all sorts of fancy goodies at moderate prices including *zivas*, a Yemeni layered dough, folded and toasted with a choice of fillings. Mon–Fri 7.30am till late, Sat & Sun 9am till late.

Scoop, Avondale Shopping Centre. Excellent Italian *gelati* in over thirty flavours draws in the eager punters; you can also sit outdoors and have a cup of coffee.

African restaurants

Café Afrique, *Cresta Oasis Hotel*, 124 Nelson Mandela Ave. A good but pricey bet in the city centre, if you want to sample a variety of indigenous dishes from around the continent as part of a bigger lunch or dinner buffet. Daily 6.30am–10pm.

Pan African at the National Handicraft Centre, Chinhoyi Street/Grant Street, Kopje (☎04/737660). More a café than a restaurant, this is a good place to try inexpensive Zimbabwean staple food. Dinner must be booked. Mon–Sat 9am–5pm and open erratically in the evenings.

Ramambo Lodge, 1st Floor, BB House, Samora Machel Avenue/Leopold Takawira Street (☎04/775345). Safari-lodge-themed restaurant in the city that's a bit of a tourist trap but is still a good place to try expensive game dishes. The menu includes Zimbabwean fish (freshwater, of course) as well as vegetarian specialities. At lunchtimes you eat to the strains of marimbas and to the rhythms of traditional dancing in the evening. Mon–Sat 12.30–2.20pm & 5.30–11.30pm.

European restaurants

Alexander's, 7 Livingstone Ave, Avenues (☎04/700340). Converted home with some outdoor seating and moderately priced meals with a French flavour. Mon–Sat 12.30–2.30pm & 7–11pm.

Aphrodite Taverna, Strathaven Shopping Centre, near Avondale (☎04/339135). Casual and quiet venue with good Greek food at moderate prices. Daily noon–2.30pm & 6.30–10pm.

The Cellar, Marimba Shopping Centre, Samora Machel Avenue, Belvedere (☎04/740371). Fairly expensive but good restaurant that claims to have the most diverse menu in the country. As the name suggests, the restaurant is underground with an upstairs bar for waiting diners. Daily for lunch and dinner.

Coimbra, 61 Selous Ave, Avenues (☎04/700237). Their speciality, spicy piri-piri chicken, is better and cheaper than *Nandos* and a good reason to eat at this mid-priced Portuguese restaurant. Daily except Mon noon–2pm & 6–10pm.

Da Guido, Montagu Shopping Centre, Josiah Chinamano Avenue, Avenues (☎04/723349). Arguably the best value in town at this popular and moderately priced Italian restaurant, which has excellent daily specials. Daily noon–2pm & 6–10pm.

Fishmonger, 50 East Rd, Avondale (☎04/308164). A wide selection of expensive but excellent seafood, including calamari, prawns and a terrific variety of line fish. Served in a converted turn-of-the-century house with an informal atmosphere in the salubrious northern suburbs. It's also one of the very few places in town where you can eat in a pretty garden. Daily 12.30–3pm & Tues–Sat 6.30–10.30pm.

La Dolce Vita, upper floor next to the cinema, Avondale Shopping Centre (☎04/334824). Highly rated Italian restaurant and music bar with a sophisticated air: excellent food prepared from fresh ingredients bought daily by the chef. Expensive, but a real treat. Mon–Fri 12.30–2pm & 6.30–10.30pm, Sat 6.30–10.30pm.

L'Escargot, *Courteney Hotel*, Selous Avenue/Eighth Street, Avenues (☎04/704409). Excellent à la carte menu with lots of moderate-to-expensive seafood in a formal atmosphere. A separate wine bar provides somewhere to hang out while the food is being prepared. Mon–Fri lunch and dinner, Sat dinner only.

Pinos, 73 Union Ave (☎04/792303). Smack in the middle of town, so a good place to stop after shopping: expensive seafood specialities, salads and meat dishes. Daily noon–2.30pm & 6.30–10.30pm.

St Elmo's, Avondale Shopping Centre, Avondale. Part of a South African chain that dishes up fabulous cheap pizzas with generous toppings and salads at reasonable prices; has a fully licensed bar. As popular as the Italian bakery next door, it tends to fill up after movies. Mon–Thurs 11am–11pm, Fri & Sat 11am–midnight, Sun 11am–10pm.

Sherrol's in the Park, Harare Gardens (☎04/705323). An Italian menu boasting the best minestrone in town, available indoorsin the rather good and moderately priced restaurant, while outside you can enjoy unexceptional cheap snacks in an exceptional setting in the middle of the gardens. Restaurant open Tues–Fri for lunch and Tues–Sat for dinner; patio open daily during the day.

Tipperary's, 54 Fife Ave/Leopold Takawira Street, Avenues (☎04/722210); 19 Greendale Ave, opposite Honeydew Farm (☎04/481097). Imitation Irish taverns with an à la carte menu, a standard selection of pub grub, but particularly known for its moderately priced steaks. Daily noon–3pm & 6–10pm.

Victoria 22, 22 Victoria Drive, Highlands (☎04/776429). Harare's most expensive and exclusive restaurant has indoor or garden seating and food and service that are both uniformly outstanding. The five-course Italian set menu changes fortnightly, but always includes various antipastos, homemade pasta with a selection of sauces, meat, poultry and fish and Italian desserts. They will cater for vegetarians by prior arrangement. Booking essential. Dinner only Mon–Sat from 7pm; closed Aug & Christmas.

Wombles, Ballantyne Park Shopping Arcade, Borrowdale (☎04/882747). Cosy English-style restaurant/pub, with a fireplace, wooden beams, excellent bar food and Mexican specialities at moderate prices. Alternatively, you can eat at the much more expensive and stylish à la carte restaurant next door, famous for its steaks and weekly specials, which are often seafood. Mon–Sat noon–2.30pm & 7–9.30pm.

Asian restaurants

Blue Banana, 109 Fife Ave, Avenues (☎04/746152). Authentic Thai cuisine prepared in a smart exotic environment with lots of cushions, and indoor and outdoor seating on the floor or at tables. Extensive and reasonably priced menu. Mon–Fri lunch and dinner, Sat dinner only, closed Sun.

Manchurian, Second Street Extension, Avondale (☎04/336166). Moderately priced eat-as-much-as-you-want Mongolian-barbecue stir-fry, where the chef cooks your choice of meats, fish and vegetables, spiced by you, on a central hotplate. Very tasty, sociable and good value for money.

Sitar Restaurant, Newlands Shopping Centre, Highlands (☎04/746215). Authentic Indian atmosphere and excellent, moderately priced Tandoori food with varied vegetarian possibilities. Slow service, but the food is hot and freshly prepared. Mon–Fri & Sun lunch and dinner, Sat dinner only.

Teppanyake, *The Sheraton*, Pennefather Avenue, just outside the city centre (☎04/774674). As the name suggests, Japanese *teppanyake* cuisine is on the expensive three-course set menu, which offers both seafood and meat options cooked at your table. A curiosity, or perhaps advantage, is that the restaurant also doubles up as the *Komba Hari* steakhouse, which means that if your eating companions don't fancy raw fish, they can tuck into a slab of beef while you savour your sushi. Mon–Fri lunch and dinner, Sat dinner only.

Takeaway and fast food

The Big Mac has yet to hit Zimbabwe's streets, but burgers, pies, pizzas, chicken and chips are consumed in vast quantities by a population ravenous for fast food. Catering to this mounting appetite, a number of **food malls**, where several outlets share a central seating area, have sprung up across town, mostly in or near shopping centres and business or industrial areas. Many **restaurants**, notably the Asian ones listed on p.86, offer a takeaway service, as do some **cafés**, which sell snacks and pastries over the counter.

Chicken Inn. City-centre branches: Speke Avenue and First Street. Suburban branches: Kelvin Corner, Graniteside; 43 Mutare Rd, Msasa; and Second Street Extension, Alexandra Park. A highly popular local chain that does dead-cheap bread-crumbed chicken, in the style of *KFC*.

Chinese Take Away. Avenues branch: Fife Avenue Shopping Centre; suburban branches: King George Avenue, Avondale; and Newlands Shopping Centre, Enterprise Road. The usual selection of Chinese foods, mostly good and cheap.

Eastgate Shopping Centre, Second Street/Robert Mugabe Road, city centre. Devotes its second floor to a food mall with a variety of unusual as well as standard fast-food joints: a health bar, where you can eat delicious fresh salads and low-fat snacks; a booth selling curries and samosas; and a rib joint.

Golden Reef, 43 Mutare Rd, Msasa. The only fast-food place in town where you can get half-decent fish and chips at a reasonable price.

Nandos. City-centre branches: Nelson Mandela Avenue, next to OK Bazaars; Speke Avenue; Leopold Takawira Street; Samora Machel Avenue/Fourth Street. Suburban branches: Pomona Shopping Centre, Borrowdale; Avondale Shopping Centre; Westgate Shopping Centre; Chisipite Shopping Centre. Portuguese-style grilled piri-piri chicken, delicious and reliable but relatively expensive.

Pizza Inn. City-centre branches: Nelson Mandela Avenue and Speke Avenue. Suburban branches: Sam Levy's Village, Borrowdale; Second Street Extension next to Reps Theatre; Chisipite Shopping Centre; Westgate Shopping Centre. Good pizzas with a variety of toppings at cheap to medium prices, depending on size and topping.

Steers. City-centre branches: Nelson Mandela Avenue/First Street; Samora Machel Avenue opposite *Holiday Inn*; Speke Avenue. Suburban branches: Chisipite Shopping Centre; Newlands Shopping Centre, Enterprise Road. Burgers and steak rolls from a long-established South African chain.

Wimpy. City-centre branches: First Street; Eastgate Shopping Centre. Suburban branches: Sam Levy's Village; Borrowdale; Avondale Shopping Centre; Westgate Shopping Centre. Globally uniform burgers, breakfasts and ice creams. Decent value for money. The Eastgate Shopping Centre branch has outdoor seating.

Drinking, music and nightlife

Convivial places where you can simply sit down and have a quiet drink are not as common in Harare as you might expect, and those **bars** that exist are frequently attached to hotels. For more sedate – and often a little sedative – imbibing, the upmarket hotels with their "smart-casual" after-dark dress code are an obvious choice. There are plenty of cheap street bars in and around town, but they tend to get very raucous, particularly as the evening wears on. English- or Irish-themed pubs, where you can enjoy a beer and grab some grub, began to make an appearance in the late 1990s. You'll also find a few **sports bars** dotted about with satellite TVs, predominantly frequented by the city's white residents and foreign visitors eager to see the national cricket side or their football team on a large screen. Some of the **cafés** (listed on p.84) have a licensed bar and stay open late enough for you to enjoy a few drinks after movies and frequently put on live entertainment in the evenings.

Given that most activities in Zimbabwe are accompanied by drinking, it should come as no surprise that **dancing and music** are no exception; apart from the occasional big concert held at one of the stadiums or other large venues, much of the city's nightlife tends to take place at the bars and clubs listed on p.88. Harare audiences are still very divided, with the city's black elite turning to US sounds, whereas traditional music has become the preserve of locals with strong rural roots – and visitors in search of the exotic. Listening to **Zimbabwean pop** is largely an urban, working-class pastime. The biggest events are at the end of each month – right after payday. This is the time when you'll catch the big names, such as **Thomas Mapfumo** or **Oliver Mtukudzi**. Till the early hours they hold **pungwes** – a term derived from the word for all-night rallies organized by guerrillas during the liberation war. The best known *pungwe* is held every October at the Gwanzura Stadium in Highfield: it runs over a 24-hour period, starting around 2pm with nonstop performances in both Shona and English by actors and singers. **Albert Nyathi**, an Ndebele actor who recites his own poetry, made his name here and has been a regular ever since.

To find a gig, look at the posters wrapped around poles or tree trunks, or pasted up around town. The *Herald* also advertises major gigs and has a listing of nightclubs. **Daytime concerts**, staged occasionally in one of the stadiums or gardens, tend to be fun, family-oriented affairs. On Sundays and national holidays (such as Independence Day), concerts with imported stars or local big names take place in the National or Rufaro stadiums. Look out, too, for daytime events at all the out-of-town venues.

Harare bars and clubs

Archipelago, Linquenda House, Nelson Mandela Avenue. Tacky, but reasonable cocktail bar and dance spot popular with hookers, aid workers and volunteers.

Bizarre Bar, George Square, Kamfinsa Shopping Centre, Greendale. Small, smoky bar with psychedelic paintings and dizzy decor. Grills and excellent pizzas served all night. Regular venue for amateur and professional bands, some better than others; lots of blues and rock (usually Wed, Fri & Sat evenings). Seating is limited and on a busy night you might be asked to leave your table the second you've finished. Daily Mon–Sat 5pm till late.

Flat Dog Diner, 5 Harrow Rd, next to Chapungu Village, Msasa (☎04/498409). Casual bar, serving mid-priced seafood including Mozambique prawns. Outdoor seating and occasional live music; phone for details. Daily noon–3pm & 6–9.30pm.

The Freckle and Phart, *George Hotel* (☎04/336677). Very laid-back and slightly run-down but friendly and respectable pub-style venue: indoor and outdoor seating and several snooker tables. Live music Fri and Sat eves.

Harare Beer Engine, Park Street/Samora Machel Avenue next to the *Jameson*. Casual but smart English-style pub with wood and copper decor, selling one draught lager and one bitter brewed to an English recipe. Sport is screened on their TV and an eclectic range of live bands perform, usually on Wednesday and Thursday nights. Mon–Sat 11.30am–midnight.

Keg and Maiden, Harare Sports Club, Josiah Tongogara Avenue, Avenues (☎04/702669). Overlooking the cricket grounds, the clubhouse, which was built in 1936 with big gables, high ceilings and wooden floors, makes an outstanding venue for a pub. It gets absolutely packed when major sports events are screened, but it's a great place to socialize and meet a local (mainly white) sporting crowd. Daily noon–midnight.

Keg and Sable, Sam Levy's Village, Borrowdale. Imitation English pub that has some outdoor seating and serves local and South African draught beers as well as bar snacks and basket foods. Guinness was taken off the slate due to the high import duties. Another place to catch sporting events via their satellite TV service. Daily noon–11pm.

The Londoner, Strathaven Shopping Centre. Friendly sports diner with a choice of a big screen and a general scrum, or the more intimate option of taking your own table with a personal TV.

Old Crow Bar, next to the *Courteney Hotel*, Selous Avenue, Avenues. Turn-of-the-century colonial tin-roofed railway cottage with small outdoor section houses a popular drinking spot for locals and visitors. Daily 11.30am–3pm & 5–9.30pm.

Sandro's, 50 Union Ave, corner of Julius Nyerere Way. One of Harare's more respectable nightspots, it's the fashionable haunt of government officials and journalists, with cabaret shows and restaurants.

Sports Diner, 134 Samora Machel Ave above the Food Court at the Mobil service station opposite *Holiday Inn* (☎04/720986, *sportsdiner@internet.co.zw*). Popular and excellent central venue with a constantly changing live programme that includes jazz, blues and Latin sounds. Regular events include traditional dancing and African theatre; there's a big screen for watching sport and snacks, and larger meals are available. Phone to find out what's currently on.

Stars Bar, *Sheraton*, off city centre (☎04/772633, US$2.50). Glitzy hotel bar with fierce air-conditioning and expensive drinks, but regular live music featuring some of Zimbabwe's top musicians. Regular programme includes jazz, rising Shona/reggae star Andy Brown, Luck Street Blues and disco. Phone for details. Daily except Mon 8pm–2am.

Out of town

While going drinking and jiving in the African townships holds out the promise of an interesting cultural experience, it's one you'd be advised to forego unless you go with someone who knows the scene. Out of town a couple of places are visited safely by tourists, but you'll need a car to get to them. Going alone is a poor idea, especially if you're a woman. Of these, the *Seven Miles Motel*, along the Masvingo Road, looks more run-down from the outside than it is, and has bands every Saturday from 4pm till late, while *The Skyline Motel*, at the nineteen-kilometre peg on the Masvingo Road is reckoned by some to be the best music venue in Zimbabwe and you'll find consistently excellent bands playing in the garden at weekends. Go in the evening and bop to the setting sun, while your steak sizzles. No need to take your own meat: buy it there and braai it yourself.

Entertainment

The arts are flourishing in Harare, despite an undertow of economic crisis, whose turbulence has in fact thrown up opportunities for experimentation and satire. While novelists and musicians such Thomas Mapfumo have been commenting on the shortcomings of the white-minority and post-Independence governments since the 1960s, the emergence of a critical **theatre** in the late 1990s was something quite new. For the first time, actors began openly satirizing political leaders and audiences were comfortable to applaud openly, making the local theatre a space definitely worth watching.

Members of the 200-strong **Zimbabwe Association of Community Theatre** (ZACT) can regularly be seen performing at the **Theatre in the Park**, just outside the Crowne Plaza Monomotapa in the Harare Gardens. Plays explore pressing issues such as HIV/AIDS, foreign aid and sexual abuse, and, although the quality of performances is uneven and sometimes didactic, you may strike on something really exciting; tickets are cheap enough to make the risk worth taking. In the dry season the programme covers several different plays a month, less during the rainy months, with approximately two-week runs. Harare's leading theatre company, **Over the Edge**, pushes the boundaries of political comedy and social satire with its romping farces. Rooted in repertory theatre, it has matured into a group that holds its own internationally. The most regular **formal theatre** consists of eminently missable musicals and drawing-room dramas at the large Reps Theatre auditorium down Second Street Extension; the theatre's small auditorium has more interesting productions from time to time.

Traditional dancing, or touristy versions of it, aren't hard to find, but the capital also has its own **contemporary dance** troupe, **Tambuka**, which has its made a name locally and internationally and is well worth catching.

Film

Action-packed Hollywood **movies** are favoured by Zimbabwean cinema audiences and most major big-screen films make it to Harare, but don't expect anything too arty or esoteric. Check the *Herald* for what's on. The **central cinemas** are the five-screen Rainbow on Park Lane, the six-screen Ster-Kinekor complex in the Eastgate Centre on the corner of Second Street and Robert Mugabe Road and the Liberty Theatre at 50 Cameron St, which specializes in kung fu, violence and mayhem. In the **suburbs** your choice is the three-cinema complex at Avondale Shopping Centre, just north of the Avenues, comprising the Seven Arts, the Elite 100 and the Vistarama, while, further out in the northwest, Westgate Shopping Centre has a four-screen Ster-Kinekor complex.

Festivals

Despite Zimbabwe's economic woes, the **arts** seem to be flourishing here as never before. The towering event on the cultural calendar is the Zimbabwe International Book Fair, while the still-young Festival of the Arts is definitely worth keeping an eye on.

The Harare International Festival of the Arts

In 1998 the capital hosted the first **Harare International Festival of the Arts** (HIFA): if its initial output is anything to go by, and you're thinking about coming out in April or May, it's definitely worth taking in the festival. HIFA aims to showcase local culture in its broadest sense (taking in crafts, popular music, visual arts and theatre), but within an international context. According to festival director Manuel Bagorro, "This is principally a celebration of Zimbabwean arts, but it's also an arena for exchanging ideas and skills across continents." The 1999 festival took over venues in central Harare for five days and staged seventy performances as diverse as Latin American dance, flamenco from Spain, Zimbabwean music played by big names such as Oliver Mtukudzi and Stella Chiweshe as well as up-and-coming bands, political satire from the Bulawayo-based Amakhosi Theatre Company and Edgar Langeveld's local brand of stand-up comedy. In addition, there was a large market, where you could pick up local craftwork or talk to gallery owners about stone sculpture. In future the festival is expected to extend over six or more days.

For **further information**, check out the HIFA Web site which is located at: *www. zimbabwe-interactive.com/hifa*.

Film festivals

Normally scheduled for September with a two-week run, the extremely popular fledgling **Harare Film Festival** was initiated in 1998 and features four films each day (12.30pm, 3pm, 5.30pm & 8.30pm), at one of the Avondale cinemas. An international event, the 1999 festival featured work from 23 countries, including South Africa, Denmark, Iran and a joint Belgian/Democratic Republic of Congo production. Although there was nothing from Zimbabwe, in years the country has something to show, this is the best place to catch it. Programmes are available at the box office for US$0.25 and you should book in advance as tickets move fast.

A number of smaller film festivals make their appearance throughout the year – usually embassies bringing a few films from their country to Zimbabwe. Most notable of these is the annual **French Film Festival**, usually held in October, consisting mostly of contemporary French films but also the odd classic, all with English subtitles. Organized by the Alliance Française (☎04/720777 or 738497), the festival uses one of Harare's cinema's to show all the films, but this changes every year, so you'll need to check details nearer the time.

The Zimbabwe International Book Fair

Sub-Saharan Africa's most important and prestigious publishing event, the **Zimbabwe International Book Fair**, is held in the Harare Sculpture Garden, behind the National Gallery, each year during the first week in August. The largest gathering on the continent of African and international publishers, booksellers and writers, it includes two closed professional days and two public days, where you can browse stands and see some of the latest African books and periodicals. Each year's fair has a theme with linked events, such as workshops and lectures.

The Heritage Exhibition

Scheduled for the last three months of the year, the **Heritage Exhibition** displays contemporary Zimbabwean painting, sculpture, ceramics and textiles. It starts at the National Gallery in Harare, before going to Bulawayo and then Mutare. As the exhibition relies on funding, it sometimes fails to get off the ground and in 1999 had to be cancelled for lack of support. An international section provides a space for foreigners resident in Zimbabwe to exhibit their work. Buyers can only collect their purchase when the exhibition is finished.

Shopping

There's little exotic about the actual experience of shopping in central Harare: malls, department stores and supermarkets give the place a humdrum feel. Nevertheless, it's an excellent place to buy crafts and a few distinctly Zimbabwean items. **Crafts** worth buying include wall hangings and fabrics, inventive handmade wire toys and African printed fabrics. A growing network of informal African commercial links has meant the influx of traders from around the continent bringing West African **carvings** and Ethiopian silver **jewellery**. You can pick up wonderful items of **clothing** such as locally printed T-shirts with designs by leading Zimbabwean artists, extremely cheap and lively canvas shoes for adults and kids, and desert boots. **Stone sculptures** by internationally acclaimed Shona carvers make more expensive and more substantial souvenirs – or investments. Locally produced **CDs** and **cassette tapes** are extremely reasonable.

For curios, crafts and CDs, head for the city centre, and the more colourful Kopje area for African fabrics. The most interesting place to buy souvenirs and food, however, is Mbare Market (see p.80), while if you're keen on sculpture crafs see p.78.

Food

Grocers are liberally distributed throughout Harare and **food shopping** is easy. Try the big **supermarkets** – OK, Bon Marché or TM – or one of the **delicatessens** in the Avenues selling slightly more exciting foods. Of these, the Fife Avenue shopping centre is recommended and is open seven days a week till 8pm, while the **greengrocer** in the central Parkade Shopping Centre is comparatively expensive but dependable for good fruit and vegetables. All over the city, you'll find modest **roadside markets** where traders sell fruit and veg by the handful-sized pile, wrapped in newspaper. If you're mobile, try Honeydew Farm shop, on Greendale Avenue, opposite the *Red Fox Hotel* just off the Mutare Road: the shop has a wide selection of produce, including excellent fresh vegetables, honey, jams, home-made goodies and fish. At the opposite end of town, Farmer's Market in the Westgate Centre is the next best place for fresh produce and also sells great home-made sausages and pickles.

Crafts, clothing and fabrics

Harare has a surfeit of **souvenir shops**, but as the quality of **curios** varies greatly it's worth looking around. There are several curio shops around First Street if you aren't too particular, and you're also likely to be pestered by people in the street selling small stone carvings – a laughing hippo or grinning elephant – which are cheaper than those sold at official curio outlets. A growing phenomenon is **informal markets**, congregations of stalls selling a range of carvings, crafts, furniture and textiles, which you'll find along roadsides all over Harare. They can be good places for a bit of low-key haggling and you should be able to pick up souvenirs more cheaply here than in the shops, even if the goods on sale tend to be a little repetitive. The biggest (and growing all the time) are just outside Westgate Shopping Centre on Lomagundi Road; across the road from Sam Levy's Village on Borrowdale Road; just outside Newlands Shopping Centre in Highlands; on the corner of Sherwood Drive and Princess Road; the Craft Co-operative on the Bulawayo Road just west of Heroes' Acre; opposite *Meikles Hotel* on Jason Moyo Avenue; and in the Harare Gardens next to the National Gallery. Shops selling better-quality **arts and crafts** are thinner on the ground, and are listed below.

Colourful **printed cottons** are available all over, but the cavernous Adam Brothers on South Avenue, which is packed with prints from Zimbabwe, Zambia and Malawi, is especially recommended. They also have a more spacious shop on Kenneth Kaunda Avenue. Plaza Oriental, 27 Robert Mugabe Rd (toward *Queens Courtyard Inn*), is the best shop for Java prints with a terrific selection, well displayed on the walls. If you're in Zimbabwe for a while, consider using one of the African **tailors**, who can make up whatever you want from local fabrics for a modest fee – find one through the fabric shops or enquire from one of the men you'll see sewing at old treadle machines on the street. Bright *tackies* (pumps), sneakers and desert boots are available very cheaply throughout Zimbabwe at any of the Bata chain of **shoe stores**.

Danhiko Project, 123 Mutare Rd, opposite Jaggers Superstore. Part of a programme for people with disabilities, it sells colourful and distinctive Danhiko products (prints, dyed cloths, bags, clothes and wooden carvings), available with a hefty mark-up at the better craft shops in town.

Dendera Gallery, 65 Speke Ave, between First and Second streets. The most upmarket of the craft shops with a superb collection of domestic and ritual artefacts from Southern and West Africa, musical instruments, masks, textiles and baskets. It's not cheap, but is the place to go if you are looking for something old. It also sells exceptional amber and Ethiopian silver jewellery, and beautiful necklaces and bracelets fashioned from clear-glass trading beads.

Doon Estate, 1 Harrow Rd, off Mutare Road next to Chapungu. Complex of fifteen shops selling an enormous variety of high-quality Zimbabwe-made items. Kudhinda Fabrics transform colourful potato and screen prints into stunning designs for cushion covers, wall hangings, table mats, clothes and bags; The Works, Fair Trade Shop (which also has a branch in the centre on Julius Nyerere Way/Samora Machel Avenue) incorporates a huge selection of products designed by over thirty Southern African artists, including wacky screen printed T-shirts, natural oils and soaps, gift wrap and recycled paper products; and other shops specialize in wrought-iron sculptures and artefacts, greetings cards, mahogany or teak furniture, toys, candlesticks – one even sells hand-made Belgium chocolates. A terrific place to browse and shop, with a tea garden selling cakes and drinks. Mon–Fri 8am–5pm, Sat 8am–1pm.

Jairos Jiri, Park Lane Building, Julius Nyerere Way. One of the countrywide chain selling crafts by disabled craft workers, close to the Monomatapa Crowne Plaza and the National Gallery. Worth browsing, though the Bulawayo shop is better stocked.

Limited Edition, Eastgate Centre, Second Street/Robert Mugabe Road. Small selection of good-quality clothing, jewellery, prints and traditional arts and crafts.

National Gallery Shop, National Gallery, Julius Nyerere Way/Park Lane. Range of books, publications, local arts and crafts, and sculpture. Much of the latter is mediocre, but there are always one or two pieces that stand out. The selection of local crafts isn't bad and the prices competitive with the shops in town.

National Handicraft Centre, Grant/Chinoyi Street. Spacious and modern craft outlet in the Kopje district where you're left to browse. A little out of the centre, but worth it for the great collection of reasonably priced basketware, drawn from various regions and the best of its kind in Harare.

Ndoro Trading, First Street, between Samora Machel and Union avenues. Zimbabwe's most stylish contemporary craft outlet, with a carefully selected and unusual range.

Rado Arts, Union Avenue/First Street; Karigamombe Centre, 53 Samora Machel Ave. Good selection of masks and West African artefacts.

Trading Company, First Street between Samora Machel and Union avenues; Southampton Life Centre, Jason Moyo Avenue/Second Street; Avondale Shopping Centre. Top of the list if you're after ethnic cushion covers and interior fabrics; their high-quality batik clothes, bolsters and tableware are particularly good value.

Books and music

Zimbabwe has a small but flourishing book industry that is constantly turning out first-rate non-fiction and highly readable novels; Harare has made a major impact in the book world with the annual Zimbabwe International Book Fair (see p.90), Africa's premier publishing event. Despite this, few of the city's **bookshops** are likely to blow you away with their size or range and, apart from Grassroots, they're not really places to browse, though you'll always find some interesting local books on their shelves. Most places stock a fair range of British or American pulp fiction.

For **music** Harare has a small choice of promising places, where you'll usually be able to get some informed advice about what's hot and what's not on the local scene. Also worth a look are the many small record shops and pavement vendors in the Charter Road area; some sell **traditional instruments**, as do most of the craft shops listed.

Book Centre, Eastgate Centre, Second Street/Robert Mugabe Road; 40 Angwa St; Sam Levy's Village, Borrowdale; and Westgate Shopping Centre. A fair selection of novels and natural history titles from the national bookshop chain.

Booklovers' Paradise and Exchange, 5 Sudbury Ave, Monavale. Good bet for secondhand paperback fiction.

CNA, 80 Robert Mugabe Rd; Sam Levy's Village, Borrowdale; Westgate Shopping Centre. South African chain tackling Kingston's on their home turf, but barely distinguishable, apart from the fact that they sell CDs.

Grassroots, attached to the *Book Café*, above OK Bazaars, Fife Avenue Mall. Fine selection of books covering social issues, politics and history as well as the best selection of novels in the country and of books about Zimbabwe.

House of Books, Sam Levy's Village, Borrowdale. Large secondhand bookshop with a wide and slightly chaotic collection that demands time to browse.

Kingstons, Jason Moyo Avenue/Second Street; George Silundika Avenue; 55 Samora Machel Ave; Westgate Shopping Centre; and Sam Levy's Village, Borrowdale. Stationery, newspapers, periodicals and a wide selection of coffee-table tomes and general-interest paperbacks.

EMBASSIES AND HIGH COMMISSIONS

Angola Doncaster House, 26 Speke Ave/Angwa Street (☎04/770075 or 770076).

Australia 4th Floor, Karigamombe Centre, 53 Samora Machel Ave (☎04/757774 or 781557).

Botswana 22 Phillips Ave, Belgravia (☎04/729552, 793492 or 793493).

Canada 45 Baines Ave (☎04/733881 or 733885).

Germany 14 Samora Machel Ave (☎04/707075).

Malawi 42 Harare St (☎04/752137–9).

Mozambique 152 Herbert Chitepo Ave (☎04/793654).

Namibia 31a Lincoln Rd, Avondale (☎04/304855 or 304856).

Netherlands 2 Arden Rd, Highlands (☎04/776701 to 776706).

New Zealand 8th Floor, Green Bridge, Eastgate Centre, Second Street/Robert Mugabe Road (☎04/759221–24).

South Africa 7 Elcombe Ave/Second Street, Belgravia (☎04/753147–9).

United Kingdom 7th Floor, Corner House, Samora Machel Avenue/Leopold Takawira Avenue (☎04/772990).

USA 172 Herbert Chitepo Ave (☎04/794521).

Zambia Zambia House, 48 Union Ave (☎04/773777 or 773781).

Mambo Bookshop, Mutual House, Speke Avenue. Outlet of Zimbabwe's Catholic (and socially concerned) publishing house that has decent history and politics shelves, but unsurprisingly the religious department is where it really shines.

Music, 86 Rezende St. Mostly secondhand LPs.

Ndoro Trading, First Street, between Samora Machel and Union avenues. Small, expertly selected choice of Zimbabwean and Southern African CDs, but not cheap.

Pop Shop, First Street/Nelson Mandela Avenue. The selection of records here is tops, making this a good last stop to stock up on music before leaving.

Spinalong, Hungwe House, George Silundika Avenue; Eastgate Centre, Second Street/Robert Mugabe Road; 69 Jason Moyo Ave; Barbour's Department Store, First Street; and Sam Levy's Village, Borrowdale. National music chain that stocks a broad selection of West African, Zimbabwean and transatlantic sounds.

Treasure Trove, Second Street/George Silundika Avenue. Secondhand bookshop that will sometimes make exchanges as well.

Listings

Airlines Air Malawi, Throgmorton House, Samora Machel Avenue/Julius Nyerere Way (☎04/752563); Air Namibia, Travel Plaza, 29 Mazowe St (☎04/732094); Air Tanzania, Ujamaa House, 23 Baines Ave (☎04/752537/8); Air Zimbabwe, 3rd Floor, Eastgate Centre, Third Street (☎04/705175 or 707926), and airport (☎04/575111, reservations ☎04/575021); Air Zambezi, Travel Plaza, 29 Mazowe St (☎04/706532); American Airlines, 8th Floor, Southampton Life Centre, Jason Moyo Avenue/Second Street (☎04/733071 or 733072); Balkan Airlines, Trustee House, 55 Samora Machel Ave (☎04/759271); British Airways, 5th Floor, Southampton Life Centre, Jason Moyo Avenue/Second Street, or Travel Plaza, 29 Mazowe St, or desks at *Meikles* and *Sheraton* hotels (central information line ☎04/747400 or 737200); Ethiopian Airlines, CABS Centre, Jason Moyo Avenue (☎04/790705 or 790706); Kenya Airways, 4th Floor, Three Anchor House, Jason Moyo Avenue (☎04/774083 or 774084); KLM Royal Dutch Airlines, 1st Floor, Finsure House, Union Avenue/Second Street (☎04/706559); Lufthansa German Airlines, 2nd Floor, East Wing, 99 Jason Moyo Ave (☎04/793861); Qantas, 5th Floor, Karigamombe Centre, 53 Samora Machel Ave (☎04/751228); South African Airways, 2nd Floor, Takura House, 69–71 Union Ave (☎04/738922 or 738928); TAP Air Portugal, Travel Plaza, 29 Mazowe St (☎04/706231 or 706232); Zimbabwe Express Airlines, Kurima House, 89 Nelson Mandela Ave (☎04/729681 or 708867).

American Express is represented by Rennies Travel, 2nd Floor, Eastgate Centre (☎04/705591).

Automobile Association, Fanum House, 57 Samora Machel Ave, between First and Angwa streets (Mon–Fri 8.30am–4pm, Sat 8–11am; ☎04/752779, fax 752522, *aazhohre@zol.co.zw*).

Banks Branches are scattered all over town, with head offices as follows: Barclays, First Street/Jason Moyo Avenue; Commercial Bank of Zimbabwe (CBZ), 60 Union Ave; First Bank, Old Reserve Bank Building, 76 Samora Machel Ave; Metropolitan Bank, 7th Floor, Metropolitan House, 3 Central Ave; Standard Chartered, John Boyne House, Speke Avenue; Zimbank, First Street/Speke Avenue.

Bike rental, some of the backpackers' lodges including *Possum Lodge* and *It's a Small World* rent out bicycles, but only to guests. Manica Cycles, 103 Manica Rd, next to Eastgate Centre (☎04/722236), will sell you a bike and guarantee to buy it back from you at the same price minus a pretty reasonable depreciation of US$10 per month.

Bureaux de change Most banks have a foreign exchange counter and there are numerous bureaux de change across town, all of them licensed and reputable. Several at the airport open with first arrivals and close with the last plane coming in. Bureaux de change in town include CFX (Mon–Sat 9am–4pm), Newlands Shopping Centre; Angwa Street/Jason Moyo Avenue; Sam Levy's Village, Borrowdale; and Enterprise Road/Londonderry Avenue (closed Sat). FX Moneycorp is at 100 Jason Moyo Ave (Mon–Fri 8am–5pm, Sat 8am–noon); 169 Fife Ave; Orbit Travel, Kensington Shopping Centre; and Newlands Shopping Centre. Also: Thomas Cook (Mon–Fri 8am–4.30pm); Rennies Travel, Vanguard Centre, 104 Jason Moyo Ave; Manica Travel, Eastgate Centre; and Westgate Shopping Centre (Mon–Fri 8am–4.30pm, Sat 8–11am; Avos (Mon–Fri 9am–5pm, Sat 9am–noon), 160 Samora Machel Ave/Seventh Street.

Camping equipment Bushtec, 10 Borrowdale Lane, behind Sam Levy's Village; Travel Plaza, 29 Mazowe St; Feredays, 72 Robert Mugabe Rd; Westgate Shopping Centre, next to Farmer's Market;

and Sam Levy's Village, Borrowdale. All the shops specialize in camping gear with both locally made and imported equipment. Rooneys Hire Service, 142 Seke Rd, Graniteside (☎04/771557, *zimhire@cst.co.zw*), rents out camping equipment.

Car rental The big international companies have the broadest network throughout Zimbabwe, with offices in major towns and resorts – especially useful if you want to drive only one way and drop off in another centre. These are: Avis, airport (daily 7am–9pm; ☎04/575144); next to *Meikles Hotel* (Mon–Sat 7am–5pm; ☎04/575431–3 or 575558–9, fax 575481); Budget, airport (daily 7am–9pm; ☎04/575421, fax 575422); 145 Samora Machel Ave, city centre (Mon–Fri 8am–5pm, Sat & Sun 8am–noon; ☎04/701858 or 701859, fax 701860); Europcar, airport (open daily 7am–9pm ☎04/575592, fax 575593); 19 Samora Machel Ave (daily 6.30am–6pm; ☎04/752559–752561, fax 752083, *europcar@primenet.co.zw*); and Hertz, airport (daily 7am–9pm; ☎ & fax 04/575206); Beverley Court, Nelson Mandela Avenue (Mon–Fri 8am–5pm, Sat & Sun 8–11.30am; ☎04/706254, 706038 or 706039, fax 792793, *hertzzim@harare.iafrica.com*); *Meikles Hotel* (Mon–Fri 8am–5pm, Sat & Sun 8–11.30am; ☎04/795655). The growing number of smaller local companies are invariably cheaper, but make sure they offer some backup in the event of a breakdown. Of these the longest-established are: Elite, airport (daily 6.30am–8pm; ☎ & fax 04/575411); 95 Belvedere Rd, Belvedere, near the *Sheraton* (Mon–Sat 8am–5pm); Thrifty, airport (8am–8pm), 10 Samora Machel Ave, under Bell's Car Hire (daily 8am–5pm; ☎04/736787, *bell@africaonline.co.zw*); Truck and Car Hire, Nelson Mandela Avenue/Fifth Street, opposite the *Cresta Oasis* (☎ & fax 04/721259, 721388, 721895 or 732370, *carhire@africaonline.co.zw*); and MCM Car Rental, 158 Samora Machel Ave (☎702180–2, fax 702209, mobile 011/401861–2, *mcm@primenetzw.com*).

Doctors are listed in the front of the Harare telephone directory, but many are private practitioners with full patient lists. The Avenues Clinic (☎04/251140/80/90), Mazowe Street/Baines Avenue and Medical Chambers, 60 Baines Ave, are both recommended, accept private patients and are central, with several resident doctors and a dentist. If for any reason they can't treat you, they will refer you to a suitable doctor or hospital. Dentists and pharmacies are also listed in the phone book, after medical practitioners.

Emergencies police ☎04/995; ambulance ☎04/994; fire ☎04/993; general ☎04/999; MARS private ambulance ☎04/734513–5 or 727540.

Galleries Harare has a crop of good commercial galleries dealing mainly in sculpture, where the enthusiast can browse works by Zimbabwe's established names. Gallery Delta, "Robert Paul's Old House", 110 Livingstone Ave/Ninth Street (daily 8.30am–5pm), has worthwhile exhibitions of graphics, textiles and ceramics. Matombo Gallery, 114 Leopold Takawira St (Mon–Fri 8am–6pm, Sat 8am–1pm), displays works by big and lesser-known names. Founded by the renowned sculptor David Mutasa, Nyati Gallery, Spitzkop Road (17.5km out of town on the Bulawayo road), is a sculpture garden where you can watch artists at work; it's worth visiting particularly if you're out Lake Chivero (Lake McIlwaine) way. Stone Dynamics Sculpture Gallery, 56 Samora Machel Ave (Mon–Fri 8am–5.30pm, Sat 8.30am–1pm), emphasizes work by the so-called "second-generation artists" – newcomers developing on the work of 1960s veterans. Vukutiwa Gallery, a 20min walk from the centre at Blakiston Street/Harvey Brown Avenue (daily 9am–6pm), has a crowded sculpture garden, arranged around the swimming pool of a once-grand house; Pierre Gallery, 14 Maasdorp Ave, Alexandra Park (daily 9am–5.30pm), exhibits stone, metal and wood sculpture as well as paintings of Zimbabwe. National Handicraft Centre, Chinhoyi Street/Grant Street (Mon–Fri 8am–5pm, Sat & Sun 9am–5pm), has batiks, stone and wood carvings made by several art and craft cooperatives; Fine Wood Art Museum, 30 Arundel School Rd, Mount Pleasant (daily 10am–4pm), stock a large selection of baskets, wood carvings and pottery; and the Innerspace Gallery at Westgate Shopping Centre (Tues–Fri 10am–5pm, Sun 10am–1pm; closed Mon & Sat), is an upmarket place with exhibits changing regularly but mostly comprised of paintings and prints depicting landscapes and life in Zimbabwe.

Hospitals Neither the Parirenyatwa Hospital, Mazowe Street/Josiah Tongogara Avenue (☎04/794411), which is the state-run general hospital, nor the Wilkens, Princes Road (☎04/741864–72), which specializes in infectious diseases, is recommended as a first port of call, given the long queues and indifferent treatment you can expect. Far better to contact one of the clinics listed above under Doctors.

Immigration Linquenda House, Nelson Mandela Avenue (between First and Second streets), for visa extensions.

Internet and email Many of the backpackers' lodges and larger hotels listed under Accommodation offer Internet, email and fax facilities to their guests. These aside, Internet cafés are springing up all over Harare and include *Internet Village*, Kenneth Kaunda Avenue, opposite the train station (daily 7am–10pm); *Clicnet*, Batanai Gardens, First Street/Jason Moyo Avenue (Mon–Sat 8am–6pm); Chainbridge Business Centre at the *Sheraton Hotel* (open daily 24hr; ☎04/758637, *huishcor@africaonline.co.zw*); *Internet Café*, 4th Floor, Eastgate Centre, Second Street/Robert Mugabe Avenue (Mon–Fri 8am–5pm; ☎04/758194–6, *info@icafe.co.zw*); *The B.O.S.S.* above TM Supermarket, Borrowdale, next to Sam Levy's Village (Mon–Fri 8am–5pm; ☎04/885765); and the *Book Café*.

Laundry Most hotels, guest houses and backpackers' lodges offer laundry service, but should you be stuck, head for the place on Fife Avenue/Sixth Street (Mon, Tues, Thurs & Fri 7.30am–6pm, Wed 7.30am–2pm, Sun 9am–noon; ☎04/72017 or 724459).

Left luggage at the station "cloakroom" costs a few cents per day per item. The one at the airport (daily 6am–10pm) charges US$3 per 24hr. All backpackers' lodges have lock-up safes and left-luggage storage free of charge for guests, as do most hotels and guest houses.

Libraries Harare City Library, Jason Moyo Avenue/Rotten Row (Mon–Fri 9am–5.30pm, Sat 9am–1pm; ☎04/751834/5) has the best collection of books, but there are local branches in Mount Pleasant, Greendale, Highlands, Hatfield and Mabelreign; National Parks Library at Parks headquarters next to the Botanic Gardens (Mon–Fri 8am–4.30pm; ☎04/703376 or 707624); charge a small daily user fee but have a good selection of natural history books; British Council, 23 Jason Moyo Ave (Tues–Fri 10am–6pm, Sat 9am–1pm; ☎04/790627–9). The British Council is members-only, but you can join immediately if you bring suitable identification and Z$300 to cover the annual charge. They have a reading room and a wide choice of British publications, newspapers (often out of date) and periodicals.

Maps The Surveyor General's Office, Electra House, Samora Machel Avenue (near the *Jameson Hotel*), PO Box 8099, Causeway, has the best maps available of Zimbabwe, covering more or less anything you're likely to need, including hiking maps. Most bookshops, including CNA, Kingstons and Book Centre, sell road maps of Harare, other major towns and Zimbabwe, and the AA is also a good source of maps.

Mobile phones The three network providers are: Net-One, Rotten Row, 16th Floor, Kopje Plaza Building (☎04/707295); Econet, 2 Old Mutare Rd, Coronation Park (☎04/486121); and Telecel 202 Seke Road, Graniteside (☎04/748321–9). In addition to these, scores of outlets, all over the city centre and at all the shopping malls, such as mobile phone shops, newsagents, furniture dealers and supermarkets, sell pay-as-you-go starter packs and airtime cards. The only snag has been the shortage of the starter packs (though not airtime cards), with Econet the most consistently reliable.

National Parks bookings Accommodation for most national parks throughout the country is best arranged in advance through the Central Reservations Office, Borrowdale Road/Sandringham Drive, adjacent to the Botanic Gardens: PO Box CY 826, Causeway, Harare (Mon–Fri 8am–4pm; ☎04/706077–8, fax 726089 or 724914, *NationalParks@gta.gov.zw*).

Parking on the main streets is generally safe in the centre during the day, if often congested. There are often metered spaces or you have to buy a prepaid ticket from a parking official supposedly wearing a white coat; the ticket ought to be displayed in the car window, but many people don't bother paying as meters are often jammed and the officials are either well camouflaged or not present. Multi-storey parking garages or "parkades" charge on average less than US$0.50 per car per day, making them an attractive option. There are parkades (daily 6am–11pm) opposite the main post office, Julius Nyerere Way/Nelson Mandela Avenue; and First Street (entrance on Union Avenue or Samora Machel Avenue). Supervised car parks are dotted around town, most notably on Fourth Street/George Silundika Avenue; Leopold Takawira Street/Park Lane; and by the central police station.

Pharmacies are open during normal shopping hours and listed in the front of the telephone directory. The QV Pharmacy on Angwa Street/Union Avenue is open longest (8am–midnight).

Post office Most suburbs have a post office and the centrally located ones (Mon–Fri 8.30am–4pm, Sat 8am–noon) are on Union Avenue opposite the Parkade Shopping Centre; Inez Terrace, between Nelson Mandela and Jason Moyo avenues; and Central Avenue/Third Street.

Shippers and packers Air-Link, Boshoff Drive/Conald Road, Graniteside (☎04/755020 or 755025), can collect, pack, airfreight and ship even awkward-shaped goods.

Swimming pool The Les Brown Pool is an Olympic-sized affair off Park Lane, opposite *Monomatapa Hotel* (mid-May to mid-Aug daily 11am–4pm; rest of the year daily 10am–6.25pm). Other pools include the Mount Pleasant, behind the shops on The Chase; Greendale, Elizabeth Road/Grove Road; Highlands, Dromore Road, off Kew Drive.

Taxis can be called by phone and are metered (check that the meter is working; if not, agree on the price before you start your journey). Recommended firms are Rixi (☎04/753080–2); A1 (☎04/703334, 725371 or 725283) and Creamline (☎04/703333). Avondale Taxis (☎04/335883 or 332463–4) are reliable but more expensive. There are also a number of ranks outside the station in Kenneth Kaunda Avenue; the east side of Africa Unity Square; near the Civic Centre on Kaguvi Street; and others peppered around the centre, especially at the big hotels and shopping centres. (Beware pirate companies, of which there are plenty, particularly in the Mbare and Kopje areas. It can be hard to recognize them but often they will have poorly painted logos on the side of the cab, won't have meters and the drivers are usually excessively pushy.)

Telephone booths and bureaux Booths are scattered around the centre and in shopping arcades and food malls, usually functional and well used. In the centre, use the ones on First Street mall or outside the *Monomatapa Hotel*. You can buy phone cards from the post office, which is your other option when making expensive calls, as you will otherwise never have enough change to cover the cost. There are several telephone bureaux in Harare, where you pay a receptionist when you finish rather than using coins – easier and cheaper for long-distance calls. Among them you'll find one at Fife Avenue Shopping Centre (open during shopping hours); and one in Barts House, 2nd Floor, Room 10, Jason Moyo Avenue/Leopold Takawira Street (Mon–Sat 7am–6pm, Sun noon–6pm).

Thomas Cook Jason Moyo Avenue/Fourth Street (☎04/728961).

Travel agents are all over the place. Highly recommended for flights and other travel arrangements are The Travel Company, 2nd Floor, Travel Centre, Third Street/Jason Moyo Avenue (☎04/700541 or 731774–6, fax 700542, *travel@harare.iafrica.com*), and ITC Destinations, First Floor, *New Queen's Hotel*, Robert Mugabe Road (☎04/757564–6, fax 757255). Run Wild, 3rd Floor, Southampton Life Centre, Jason Moyo Avenue (☎04/795841, *runwild@africaonline.co.zw*), is good for tours within Zimbabwe and Southern Africa; Safari Par Excellence, 26a Blakiston St/Josiah Chinamano Avenue (☎04/700911–2), for tours and adventure activities in Zimbabwe and Zambia; The Wacko Travel Company, 4th Floor, Eastgate Centre (☎04/773965 or 758194–6, *wacko@harare.iafrica.com*), for Southern Africa and adventure activities; and VFR Tours, 34 Kilwinning Rd, Hatfield (☎04/572949, after hours 570459, fax 572956, *vfrtours@internet.co.zw*), for tours in Zimbabwe. For budget travel arrangements, Wildlife Expeditions at Possum Lodge, 7 Deary Ave, Belgravia (☎ & fax 04/722804, *wildlife@icon.co.zw*), offers possibly the most personal service and the best selection, is great for advice, very helpful and will arrange all your bookings in and out of the country.

AROUND HARARE

If you're spending some time in Harare, a number of nearby destinations make pleasant breaks, although they aren't really worth a special excursion if you only plan a brief stay in the capital. **Lake Chivero** is a popular weekend outing for Hararians and there's a string of low-key wildlife distractions along the way. **Ewanrigg Botanical Gardens**, too, are a pleasant place to spend a few hours. If the Matopos Hills (see p.166), with their typically Zimbabwean rock kopjes, aren't on your itinerary, then it's worth making a trip to **Dombashawa** north of Harare to see the inspiring granite formations and rock paintings. Accommodation at Lake Chivero is detailed below; other places to stay within easy reach of Harare are listed on p.75.

Lake Chivero

The damming of the Hunyani River in 1952 to provide year-round water for Harare's growing population opened up an accessible "Recreation Park" around the artificial lake. Though very much a resort for Harare weekend trippers, **LAKE CHIVERO**, 32km southwest of Harare (and known until the early 1990s as Lake McIlwaine), is pretty enough – msasa-clad hills encircling wide stretches of water – and has the lure of game viewing in the national park on the southern side. The northern side, which is generally a place for just a day out, is more developed and commercialized, but to the south there are National Parks **chalets** for a more restful weekend; southern shore wilderness purists curl up their lips at the thought of the developed north side, while north coast enthusiasts descend en masse for braais and boating.

Practicalities

Four roads branch off the Harare–Bulawayo Road and lead to the lake. Each provides access to a separate set of attractions along the lake: the first turn-off, 16km from the city, leads to the peaceful **northern reaches** of the lake, which are good for picnics; at the 23-kilometre peg a road slithers off to **Snake World** and the **Lion and Cheetah Park**; the third branch, 5km beyond, takes you to the hotel, bird gardens and cabins at **Kuimba Shiri**; while the final branch, 4km further south along the highway, after you cross the Hunyani River, goes to the **Lake Chivero National Park** on the southern shore. All the roads and tracks are well maintained and regularly graded, making them easy to negotiate in an ordinary car. There's no public transport to Chivero; regular **buses** from Mbare pass this way and you can get off at any of the turn-offs, but you'll need your own transport to get around the Lion and Cheetah Park or the national park.

Organized **tours** are available through Harare-based companies, including Bushbeat Trails (bookings: VFR Tours, Kilwinning Road, Hatfield; ☎04/572949, fax 572956, *vfrtours@internet.co.zw*); UTC, Park Street/Jason Moyo Avenue (☎04/770623–34), a long-established operator; Mhuka Wild Tours, 170 Union Ave (☎04/729576 or 735358, *mtours@icon.co.zw*), which also takes trips outside Harare; and Southern African Touring Services (SATS), Sabi House, 18 Park St (☎04/753535, *sats@samara.co.zw*). All do day-trips to the national park, and the Lion and Cheetah Park, and on request they'll also take you to any of the other attractions in the area. **Prices** (US$26–45) depend on the itinerary and length of the trip. If you want to stay overnight at lake accommodation, they are flexible and will collect you the next day at a small extra charge.

Accommodation

Visitors can stay overnight in one of the basic but comfortable and clean lakefront *Admiral's Cabins* (bookings through Kuimba Shiri ☎062/2309, fax 2308; ②), or you can camp (①) at the adjacent campsite or the one operated by National Parks, just to its west. The *Hunyani Hills Hotel* (☎062/2236 or 2633; ②), about 2km west of the cabins along the lake, is the nicest place to stay on the north shore; you can have tea in the garden, survey the lake and stroll along the shore to get a view of the dam wall. On the southern shore, National Parks rents out chalets and lodges that sleep up to five people and cost US$12–20 (depending on the number of beds) for the whole unit per night; of these, *Kingfisher Lodge* has the best view of the lake. Bear in mind, though, that in addition to the cost of the chalet you'll have to pay US$20 Park entrance fee per person to stay for up to a week. Book through National Parks Central Reservations Office, Borrowdale Road/Sandringham Drive, adjacent to the Botanic Gardens (Mon–Fri 8am–4pm; PO Box CY 826, Causeway, Harare; ☎04/706077–8, fax 726089 or 724914, *NationalParks@gta.gov.zw*), or direct through Lake Chivero National Park (☎062/27342). The most luxurious place to stay on the lake and the closest to town is *Harare Safari Lodge*, Box ST 172, Harare (☎04/690202, fax 690288, *joyboat@telco.co.zw*; B&B ⑧, full board ⑨), which has rock-and-thatch lodges, a self-catering cottage with fully equipped kitchen, and twin tents on decks under thatch on the northern bank. It lies 29km from the city centre; follow signs from the turn-off 16km from the city.

Snake World and the Lion and Cheetah Park

Closest to Harare of the institutionalized Chivero attractions, **Snake World**, at the 23-kilometre peg (daily 8am–5.30pm; US$1), harbours a representative sample of Zimbabwe's snakes coiled behind glass-fronted cages; you're allowed to handle some of the safer ones. A couple of kilometres further along the same branch road, the **Lion and Cheetah Park** (daily 8am–5.30pm; US$7) is run by the same outfit. A drive-through section (you need your own vehicle) takes you through several acres of indigenous bush stocked with lions, normally elusive cheetahs, a couple of elephants, giraffes and some plains game. The park may have served as a fantasy African wilderness for the 1989 remake of *King Solomon's Mines*, but the reality is less romantic: the cats are fenced off from the herbivores, head off to small shelters for the night, and eat beef fed to them, rather than hunting for a living. This is not say they're tame: in 1989, one unfortunate – a fundamentalist Christian trying to emulate the Roman martyrs – crept into their enclosure at night, and all that was found the next day was a driving licence and some car keys.

Also on site is a series of desperately small enclosures that offer scant stimulation for the inmates, amongst them a chimpanzee from Tanzania and a giant tortoise from the Galapagos, allegedly aged 255.

Kuimba Shiri

Some 5km southwest of Snake World along the Bulawayo highway, a road branches off at the Turnpike garage and leads to the bird gardens and accommodation at **Kuimba Shiri** (daily 8am–5pm; US$1.20). The name means "singing bird" in Shona – an apt sobriquet, as the site along the lakeshore attracts wild waterfowl and lakeshore species that come to mingle with the indigenous birds kept in the open-plan bird park. Previously known as Larvon Bird Gardens, this is the best of the Chivero attractions and has decent-sized aviaries, some of which you can walk through, with enough other attractions to justify making a day of it. Displays provide interesting information about the birds, or for more depth ask at reception for a guided tour. A new large enclosure houses raptors including African fish eagles, which fly around, nest and generally behave as they would in the wild.

A **tea garden**, **restaurant** and **bar** on large lawns under msasa trees completes the picture for a pleasant day out, with the additional draws of **falconry demonstrations** (daily 4pm), a swimming pool and, at weekends, live **jazz**. **Speedboat rental** can be arranged, and Mvuu Wilderness (☎04/335362) launch their double-decker pontoon onto the lake for daily breakfast (US$12), lunch (US$25) and dinner (US$30) **cruises**. Trips last two hours and meals are included in the price; a sunset cruise (US$20) has a cash bar on board and serves snacks. Booking is advisable, especially at weekends. Accommodation is available in cabins or at the *Hunyani Hills Hotel* (see p.98).

Lake Chivero National Park

With the wonderful exception of over two dozen white rhino, there's no big game in the **Lake Chivero National Park**, lining the southern shore of the lake (daily dawn–dusk; day entry US$20, overnight up to seven days US$40). There are, however, plenty of antelope, giraffe, zebra and smaller mammals to compensate, and a wide variety of waterbirds – as well as bird species favouring the msasa woodland. The lake provides a good opportunity to spot smaller denizens, too, like reptiles, amphibians, butterflies and other insects; look out for the tiny white-and-pink tree frogs clinging onto branches. The prettiest time for a visit is September, when the msasas confoundingly unfurl their autumn-coloured spring leaves in preparation for the rains.

The park is fairly small and well covered by a network of game drives. A **map**, usually available at the National Parks booking office in Harare or at the park entry gate, helps with orientation, but if they're out of stock you should be fine, as the well-marked loops and tracks make it hard to get lost. You'll invariably see zebra and antelope in open grassy areas, and giraffe browsing in more wooded spaces. Accompanied **horse-riding** is an excellent way to see the park, and it can get you really close to the rhinos. Book at the Parks headquarters for a ride, which costs US$5 per person for ninety minutes, plus a flat rate of US$4 for the guard who goes out with you. You can also go on **game walks** around Bushman's Point (see below), but again you need to be accompanied by a game guard.

Camping isn't allowed in the park but **accommodation** is available close to the water in fully equipped National Parks lodges (see Accommodation, p.98).

Bushman's Point and Crocodile Rock paintings

A number of **rock paintings** are scattered within a two-kilometre radius of the National Park entrance gate and the warden's office at Crocodile Rock smack in the middle of the park on the lakeshore, just under 10km from the main gate. **Bushman's Point**, at the southeastern tip of the park, is the only area where **walking** is permitted, but you need a car to get there. This thickly wooded waterside area is alive with foraging *dassies* (rock rabbits) and, on a rock face overlooking the shoreline path, are some faded rock paintings. Look for the line of thirteen identical kneeling figures at the bottom of the face – thought to be a dance chorus. Also low down are three figures with sticks, standing, sitting and recumbent, which overlie some striped forms.

Another rock painting site is at **Crocodile Rock**, for which you'll need transport and a Parks guide. They are well worth seeing, though – two large crocs, one painted belly up, make a unique panel with nine hunters to the left of them executed in great detail – and the rock is the most attractive of the park's several designated **picnic sites**. It is the haunt of herons and pied kingfishers rather than crocodiles, and has a marvellous view over the lake.

Ewanrigg Botanical Gardens

Set in commercial farmlands, **Ewanrigg Botanical Gardens** (daily 6am–6pm; US$5), about 40km northeast town, is a lovely place to spend the day – although the steep entrance fee slapped on in 1999 is a definite disincentive. They are most famous for **cycads** and **aloes** – red-hot-poker-like succulents whose flowers span the spectrum from yellow to a brilliant red – but there's also a herbarium and a water garden. During the week you can have a walk in solitude, but at weekends the place fills up with trippers out for a lunchtime braai using the fireplaces and picnic spots provided. The most impressive time to visit is midwinter, when the aloes are in flower; it's rather dusty and dried out in August and September before the pre-rains flowering. For the traditional **herb garden**, head through the aloes and up steep steps colonnaded by thickly planted young trees. Down on the other side you'll find the **water garden**. Bear left through an open grassy area, planted with trees and massive bamboos, to get back to the entrance gate.

To get there by public transport, take the Shamva **bus** from Mbare and ask to be put down at the Ewanrigg turn-off; the gate is about 1km down the dirt road. **By car**, drive out on the Enterprise Road, taking the Shamva fork about 15km from the city centre – Ewanrigg is signposted.

Chinamora rock paintings

There's a multitude of painted caves in the communal lands around Harare. The two best-known sites are at **Dombashawa** and **Ngomakurira**, in the Chinamora

Communal Lands north of the city limits. Dombashawa, 30km north of the city centre, is well visited and you're unlikely to be alone, while Ngomakurira, 10km further on, is a lonelier and altogether more arresting spot.

Transport to either site is straightforward. For both you should take one of the frequent Bindura **buses** that go via Dombashawa from Mbare bus station. Buses leave central Harare from the OK Supermarket on Cameron Street and either pass along Second Street or Chancellor Avenue and past Borrowdale racetrack. You could try catching one en route; the route out of town is interesting in itself, passing by the mansions, pools and flourishing gardens of Harare's plushest area, which is immediately followed by Hatcliffe, one of the most extensive townships, which drifts off into the communal lands. For Dombashawa, get off at its turn-off, and for Ngomakurira continue on to the Sasa Road stop; both are signposted from the main road.

By **car** or **hitching**, take the Borrowdale/Dombashawa road. For Dombashawa, turn right at the sign 30km from Harare. The car park for the main cave is just under a kilometre further on, and the cave is a twenty-minute walk along a clear path up the hillside. Dombashawa is included in **tours** from Harare taken by Mhuka Wild Tours, 170 Union Ave (☎ & fax 04/729576, *mtours@icon.co.zw*); Southern African Touring Services (SATS), Sabi House, 18 Park St (☎04/753535, *sats@samara.co.zw*); and Top Class Tours, PO Box CY 2919, Harare (☎ & fax 04/734312, *topclasstours@hotmail.com*). **Prices** are in the region of US$40.

Dombashawa

The attraction of **Dombashawa** (daily 9am–6pm; US$2) lies in the enormous whale-back rocks of the site, which you can clamber over to gain vantage points. The paintings themselves are, by comparison, disappointing, having fallen victim to fire, smoke, vandalism, graffiti and cleaning. The largest collection of paintings spreads out on the inner walls of the **main cave**, where buffalo, zebra, elephant, kudu and rhino keep human figures company. One of the most interesting groups, in a cleft 20m left of the main cave, has an indistinct elephant harassed by hunters. Slightly further on, but off to the right, are some human and semi-human figures, believed to be associated with rain-making ceremonies. Around the area, several other clefts and small areas of rock are also daubed with pictures (now pale and delicate) of animals and people.

Just outside the main entrance you'll see a dense forest of **uapaca trees**, known locally as *mahobohobo*, which, according to local legend, have magical properties. The story goes that a local farmer tried to fell some of these trees to clear land, but on successive occasions he would return the following day only to find them standing up again. It was realized that the trees had unusual powers, and the forest was declared sacred and preserved.

A small **interpretation centre**, next to the parking lot at the foot of the hill, gives an interesting overview of the local geology, history, vegetation and rock art, with astonishing facts about the age of some of these works, which archeologists believe date back 4000 to 13,000 years. A small shop sells snacks and drinks, and there's an adjoining picnic site, which gets overrun at weekends and on public holidays.

Ngomakurira

To reach **Ngomakurira** (daily 8am–5pm; US$2), carry on along the main road for 10km past the Dombashawa turn-off. Turn right at the signposted Sasa Road, and there's parking 1.5km from the main road. For the half-hour walk up to the site, it's worth considering taking a guide, whose fee is included in the entrance fee, although a tip is normally given at the conclusion of the walk. There have been several muggings in these hills – another good reason to go accompanied. From the large isolated tree on the left at the foot of Ngomakurira's massive dome, walk along a path between maize fields to the base of the hill, then take one of the paths which lead up to a wooded valley watered by a clear stream and rock pools. The stream leads to the bottom of a sheer cliff on which you'll find the numerous faint but beautiful paintings: the route is marked by arrows painted onto the trees and rocks. A small shop at the site sells pricey curios such as ceramic pots and carvings as well as cold drinks, home-made peanut butter and tomato sauce.

The site

Some say that Ngomakurira, literally "the place where the spirits beat the drums", takes its name from the echoes one hears in this perfect amphitheatre. It's a powerful and otherworldly place, abundant with elegant paintings decorating the bottom of the Day-Glo-orange-stained cliff. In such an enclosed space its sweep and height are enormously magnified and, when you sit on the back of the granite hump opposite, you can hear your own words perfectly, mockingly reproduced by the ancestors.

The **paintings** here include four huge **elephants**, rated amongst the best of their type by Peter Garlake, Zimbabwe's leading rock art expert. There is no shortage of other fine renderings, either, with some fascinating scenes of **human groups**. One shows a man, arms raised in terror, being clubbed by another. It was scenes like these that led some anthropologists to impose an interpretation of ritual regicide (king-killing) on Southern African Stone age Art. One conclusion was that such motifs could not have been produced by hunter-gatherers like the **San** (see p.343), although more recent theory points out that the lifestyles depicted in the paintings are very similar to those of San groups like the !Kung. And the regicide theory sounds, in any case, somewhat sensational, there being no evidence of such acts having been carried out anywhere in the country.

Bally Vaughan and Imire private game parks

The countryside surrounding the capital consists predominantly of private farms and communal lands – indigenous game was shoved off to the fringes of the country ages ago. What reserves you find around Harare are miles tamer than anything in the big-game country around Hwange, the Zambezi or Limpopo valleys. Having said that, a couple of small private **game parks** do give you the chance to get close to large African animals – elephants, rhinos, cheetahs and lions – in a controlled environment, making them ideal places for families with under- 12s, who are likely to be bored on safari.

Bally Vaughan Game Park

Closer to Harare of the two is **Bally Vaughan Game Park**, set in granite country among lush, wooded highveld plains, 44km north of Harare on the Shamva road (Box HG886; ☎04/776341 or 746521–9 or 074/2775, fax 04/746546 or 074/2430, *gamepark@mango.zw*). Conducted game drives and walks take in the park's plains game and you can also go canoeing or ride an elephant. An on-site animal orphanage has enclosed lions, leopards and small cats, and there's a bird sanctuary, too. **Accommodation** is available at the park's luxury *Mwanga Lodge* for US$120, inclusive of all meals, drinks and activities. No drop-ins are allowed, but **day-trips** can be arranged from Harare for US$26 per person.

Imire Safari Ranch

Imire Safari Ranch at Wedza, 110km east of Harare (Box BW 1711, Harare; ☎04/733391, 733396 or 728493–4, fax 731856 or 728492, *imire@id.co.zw*), was one of the first places in Zimbabwe to experiment with schooling African elephants, using bonding and reward, something that had once been considered impossible. Although elephant riding is what attracts many visitors to Imire, director Barbara Travers is quick to emphasize that this isn't a circus and the ranch aims to provide a total wildlife experience, which includes game drives on the 45-square-kilometre estate in search of the ranch's plains game, visits to the lion and rhino enclosures (Imire is well-known for its successful rhino-breeding programme), and elephant and rhino feeding, in which guests are encouraged to take part. During your stay you can also visit some fine San rock paintings at Markwe Cave, on an adjoining farm, and Mukuyu, the better of Zimbabwe's two wineries, thirty minutes away by car on the Hwedza road.

Day-trips to Imire can be arranged from Harare for US$70 including lunch, drinks and a game drive, but staying one or two nights is recommended. **Accommodation** is available at the ranch's *Sable Lodge* in seven comfortable chalets and a family room inside the old farmstead, where breakfast and a generous dinner is served in winter in front of a blazing fire. The rate, inclusive of transfers to and from Harare, all meals and activities, is US$160, but significant discounts are available throughout the year.

THE MIDLANDS

For visitors, the **Midlands** hold few attractions. The region declares itself the heart of Zimbabwe, a claim that does bear a grain of truth as it's rich in gold, asbestos, nickel and chrome, and forms the base for the country's important textile and steel industries. More importantly, though, the Midlands occupies the physical heart of Zimbabwe, which means that if you're travelling between Harare and the south, you can't avoid it unless you fly. This isn't a hardship as its landscapes are reasonably attractive even if there's nothing dramatically interesting. (The most significant tourist highlights of the Midlands – the wonderful stone ruins at Danangombe and Naletale – are covered in Chapter Four with Kame, as they are sited midway between Gweru and Bulawayo.)

Two main arteries cut through this heartland, each splaying out from Harare. The **Masvingo route**, the shortest one if you're travelling between Johannesburg and Harare, whips through the insignificant centres of Chivu and Mvuma. Far more promising is the **Bulawayo route**, which takes in the larger towns of Gweru, Kwekwe and Kadoma, between them providing ample opportunity for pleasant refreshment or overnight stops, should you want to break your journey.

The towns on the Harare–Bulawayo road see few tourists, but were well visited by **elephant hunters** in the past. The Portuguese set up an ivory-trading post in the eighteenth century near Chegutu, and after they departed the hunters stayed; in fact, so many people came up to Chegutu from Bulawayo in the second half of the last century that the route became known as Hunters' Road.

Chegutu and Kadoma

First stop down the line towards Bulawayo is the cotton and cattle-farming settlement of **CHEGUTU**, 105km southwest of Harare, a village that's quiet even by Midlands standards. These days, its only noteworthy features are the two Viscount aircraft shells parked on the southern outskirts of town next to the main road, which serve as a restaurant.

KADOMA, 35km southwest of Chegutu, the centre of a major cotton-growing and mining district, is larger and a far better place to break a journey. The nicest stop for the night or refreshment is the reasonably priced *Cotton Country Inn*, 32 Herbert Chitepo St, well signposted just off the commercial centre of town (mobile ☎011/211641; ③), which has ten bright and simply furnished en-suite double rooms and also serves a well-priced breakfast, lunch and dinner on an airy terrace with a fountain. The very smart *Kadoma Ranch Motel*, 1.5km north of town on the Bulawayo Road (☎068/2106, 3944 or 3946, fax 2325; ⑥), targets business travellers and is where inter-city coaches break for tea or a meal. Beyond that, Kadoma is a typical colonial railway town, bypassed by the main road, with well-preserved buildings a short hop from the station. What bustle there is happens around the nearby **Cameron Square**, planted with palms, gumtrees and jacarandas. Fronting the square is the *Grand Hotel*, its elegant facade recalling the gold-rush days when it hosted dancing girls, hunters and prospectors, but these days it's best admired from the outside.

Kwekwe

The Harare–Bulawayo road passes the scarred, mine-dumped outskirts of **KWEKWE**, the least attractive of the Midlands towns, characterized by hunched office blocks, its downtown district aspiring to city-centre status. Walk 100m and you're in the suburbs among downmarket shops. Older, more photogenic buildings are concentrated a block up, in Second Street.

Kwekwe was built on **gold**, growing up as a mining settlement for the rich surrounding reefs, and its one tourist attraction is the **National Museum of Goldmining** (daily 9am–5pm; US$2). A treat if you enjoy antique machinery – suction pumps, engines and rock crushers – it's otherwise not inspiring, apart from the amazing **Paper House**. This, century-old structure, made from wire-reinforced papier-mâché, was Zimbabwe's first prefabricated building. It has stood since 1894, when it was shipped out from England as a residence for the general manager of Kwekwe's Globe and Phoenix Mine. In fact you can get an excellent view of the house without paying, by looking through the fence just to the right of the entrance.

Like most of Zimbabwe's mines, the Globe and Phoenix operated on **ancient diggings**, which had been run using manual implements, or fires lit against rocks to make them crack. Gold-mining already had a thousand-year history here, and trade in the precious metal was one of the ways the ruling classes consolidated their power. In the sixteenth century, gold brought the first **European interference** in the region with the arrival of Portuguese; their attempts at conquest and control flopped, but not before they'd brought in Spanish experts to develop the ancient workings.

In the late nineteenth century, after the defeat of Lobengula, the **British** flooded into the district. The gold rush never came to much, but by the 1930s one in every thirty whites was a small-scale prospector. Today a few big mines pull in the bucks, but there are still some determined prospectors. In the northeast, Shona women continue to pan the Mazowe and Luenha rivers with wooden trays, and transport their finds in porcupine quills.

Practicalities

Kwekwe is not a place to linger, but your best bet for meals or a bed is the *Golden Mile Motel* (☎055/23711; ③), 2km out on the Bulawayo road, where Blue Arrow **coaches** set down and pick up; it has the added advantage of a swimming pool. If you're driving, you'd be miles better off continuing for another forty minutes to Kadoma in the north or Gweru to the south. Outside Kwekwe, 55km east on the Mvuma road, is the competitively priced accommodation at *Mopani Park Farm* (mobile ☎011/716837, *jahadwin@hotmail.com*; ②). Set in a black rhino conservancy, it isn't really a viable overnight stop between Harare and Bulawayo as it's some distance off the main road. What you come for is excellent and affordable **horse-riding** – the chance of polo-crosse lessons or a hack through the bush with the added attraction of game viewing. The varied accommodation consists of a two-bedded thatch-and-brick house on a dam, some rondavels, two tree houses and a dorm that sleeps fifteen. Full bar facilities and meals are on offer, or you can self-cater. Transfers are available from Kwekwe by prior arrangement.

Gweru and the Antelope Park

GWERU, 62km south of Kwekwe, was established in the 1890s as a staging post between Bulawayo and Harare. Today it is mainly a goods marshalling centre, linked by rail to South Africa, Mozambique and Zimbabwe's major towns. As a stop-off between Bulawayo and Harare it's no tourist magnet, but an agreeable place nonetheless; with wide streets and some lovely colonial architecture blooming among the ubiquitous 1960s blocks, the town seems to bask in a permanent Sunday-afternoon glow. Less than ten minutes' drive from town brings you to the **Antelope Park**, where you can see **lions** en masse – one of the best reasons to stop off in the Midlands.

Arrival and accommodation

Blue Arrow and Express Motorways **coaches** stop at the *Fairmile Motel*, and economy **buses** at the Kudzenai terminus by the town market (behind the *Midlands Hotel*). **Commuter omnibuses** use the terminal on the corner of Leopold Takawira Avenue and Sixth Street, while the **train station**, with connections to Harare and Bulawayo, is located at the end of Tenth Street. **Taxis** line up both at the *Midlands Hotel* and the bus terminus.

Gweru has a reasonable quantity of **accommodation**, much of it indifferent, but two more-than-decent places are the reasonably priced *Fairmile Motel*, 1.6km south of the city on the Bulawayo Road (☎054/24144, fax 23189; ③), an airy motel set in large gardens with a children's playground and a swimming pool and a car rental company in the lobby; and the less expensive and good-value *Twin Peaks*, 5km south of town on the Shurugwi road (☎054/23762 or 26885, fax 23762; ③), which has four-teen thatched chalets with showers arranged around a garden with a pond. Further

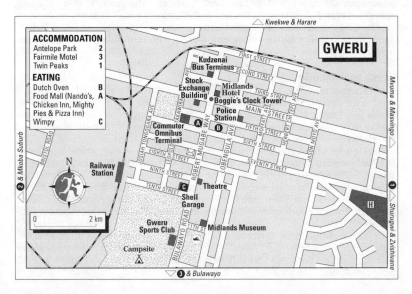

out of town, the *Antelope Park* (☎0541/52172, mobile 091/205956), offers camping (①) and self-catering chalets (②) in a quiet rural setting and the choice of buffet meals or food packs, which you can cook yourself.

The Town

Of the town's limited "tourist attractions", the unfortunately named **Boggie's Clock Tower** deserves some kind of booby prize. "Erected by Mrs Jeannie Boggie in memory of her husband Major Boggie", it stands at the junction of Main Street and Robert Mugabe Way, the two major axes. The peeling **Stock Exchange Building**, built in 1898 a little further along Main Street, warrants at least a quick look, despite its state of neglect. Now owned by the Ministry of Mines, it's a splendid example of colonial architecture and the oldest building of consequence in the city, constructed after the defeat of the First Chimurenga – a reflection of business confidence.

The **Midlands Museum** on Lobengula Avenue (daily 9am–5pm; US$2) is another possible place to while away some time, with its impressive display of firepower from both world wars: guns, aircraft and grenades. The attached aircraft museum appropriately houses a collection of planes – Gweru's Thornhill military air base is the country's largest. The town is also the home of the Zimbabwe Military Academy, which trains officer cadets and junior officers.

The Antelope Park

Gweru's, indeed the Midlands', highlight is its **Antelope Park** (mobile ☎011/205956, *conolly3@icon.co.zw*), some 8km southwest of town on the road through the industrial estate, noted for its cohort of around **eighty lions**, who lay on incredible symphonies of roaring at night. The cats are penned to keep them off the backs of the park's herbivores – giraffe, zebra, kudu and tsessebe – but their enclosures are sizable and they're in excellent condition. Under the management of Andrew Connolly, who has an excellent rapport with the animals, the park has a friendly and relaxed air, making it one of the nicest and least expensive places to overnight (see above) between Bulawayo and Harare. On the banks of a river, it offers **cruises**, an excellent way to see some wonderful birds in the area, and other activities include **game drives**, guided **horse-riding** and walking with **lion cubs**, all for US$10 per person.

Eating and nightlife

For restaurant **food**, you've a choice, a little out of town, of a standard slap-up hotel meal at the *Fairmile*, 1.6km south of town, or *Twin Peaks*, 5km from the centre, the town's best eatery, which does reasonably priced rolls and salad bowls or more substantial steak, chicken, fish or vegetarian dishes. In the centre of town, the closest thing Gweru has to a European-style café is the *Dutch Oven* (7.45am–8pm; closed Sun), on Fifth Street between Lobengula Avenue and Robert Mugabe Way, which does breakfasts and standard sit-down chicken, pies and chips. Predictable fast food is available at *Wimpy*, in the forecourt of the Shell filling station, on the corner of Tenth Street and Bulawayo Road, or for a wider choice make for the food mall on the corner of Robert Mugabe Way and Sixth Street, which brings together branches of *Nandos* and *Chicken Inn*, both of which knock up decent poultry, along with *Mighty Pies* and *Pizza Inn* franchises.

Regular **nightlife** in the centre of this provincial town amounts to drinking at the *Carrousel Bar* upstairs at the *Midland Hotel* in Main Street, which is a lot less sleazy than the *Dandaro* downstairs, or Hollywood movies at the Embassy Cinema in Fifth Street, off Robert Mugabe Way.

NORTH OF HARARE

Four roads radiate **north from Harare**, terminating at small towns on the edge of the Zambezi escarpment where it drops away to the remote, arid areas on the Mozambique border. The towns here have always been outposts, vulnerable to guerrilla attack and suffering severely during the bush war which had its origins in the region. Long before the Independence struggle, the spiritual inspiration for the **First Chimurenga** was conjured here and two famous early liberation heroes, Mbuya Nehanda and Mapondera (see box on p.110), operated locally.

The most travelled road in this region leads northwest to Kariba – apart from farmers and peasants, few people travel the others. One you might want to follow heads off through the citrus farms of Mazowe to Mvurwi and Guruve, the nearest town to the marvellous sculpture community at **Tengenenge**. Further attractions lie north beyond Mvurwi, on the edge of the Zambezi lowlands, where the middleveld plateau rises in the upward swoop of the **Mavuradonna Mountains**. This is one of the wildest regions of Zimbabwe, and is home to the country's most adventurous – and best – horse-riding safari centres. The broken hilly country on the eastern side of this district was recently designated as a hiking area, and is most easily approached from the village of Centenary. For this and **Hippo Pools Camp**, off the road to Mount Darwin in the **Umfurudzi Safari Area** further east, you'll need your own transport.

Tengenenge

If Harare has awakened your interest in Zimbabwean sculpture, don't miss **TENGENENGE**, two hours north of Harare by car. This artists' community just south of the Zambezi escarpment in the rolling grassy hills of the Great Dyke requires some motivation to reach, but it's an extraordinary place and well worth the effort. Part of the final section of road is on gravel; you'll know you're nearly there when you come across sentinel sculptures lining the way.

The sculpture community

So prolific is the output of Africa's largest artists' community that acres of land around Tengenenge seem to have been planted with sculptural works – primitive, crude, representational and grotesque. Sculptures perch on walls, windowsills and above the doors of derelict buildings; others stand on wooden plinths driven into the ground or lie tossed aside in the grass. You can walk around the village looking at the carvings and chat to sculptors chipping away at new works. Almost everything is for sale and, if you're looking for a quality bargain by an unknown, this is definitely the place.

Tengenenge was one of the great formative influences in Zimbabwe's sculpture revolution. When **Tom Blomefield** took over the farm here after World War II, he began by ploughing with oxen until he discovered **chrome** on his lands, which earned him enough money in two years to make bricks to build drying sheds and to employ someone to manage his tobacco production. Then came UDI, sanctions and the collapse of the tobacco industry. Blomefield decided to chuck it all in and become an artist. But with an entire black workforce to consider, he thought of absorbing their labour in arts and crafts groups. Miraculously, around this time, huge deposits of **serpentine** (the beautifully mottled stone in yellowish to almost black shades of green) were discovered on the farm. Blomefield was joined by **Lemani Moses**, a Malawian sculptor, and gradually the place began to attract people from all over. This was one of the hottest areas during the bush war, but Tengenenge was left alone. Blomefield believes this was because he always showed due respect to the local chief and respected the ancestral spirits, frequently arousing the ire of the local church, which was doing its best to suppress them.

Workers at Tengenenge come from Angola, Malawi, Zambia and as far away as Tanzania, and each brings a distinctive tradition which has breathed diversity into the Zimbabwe sculpture movement. Each culture has its own cosmology of **gods, ancestors and spirits** that influence humans in different ways and make all sorts of demands. The Shona supergod **Mwari** is a disinterested figure approached through the ancestors, while **Kalunga**, god of the Angolan Mbunda people, is very personal. The Malawian **Chewa** and **Yao** cultures express religion through very formal ritual dances using masks, highly stylized mask-like sculptures being one hallmark of their work. Local **Shona** sculptors, too, frequently draw on folklore; cautionary tales and transformations of people into beasts are common subjects.

There are now over a hundred artists associated with the farm, some of them affiliates producing at home and using Tengenenge's distribution channels, but many resident and stipended if their talent is insufficiently recognized by the commercial art world to make ends meet. Several of Zimbabwe's big names are products of this community, and artists like **Bernard Matemera** still live here. Matemera was the winner of the 1986 Delhi sculpture triennial, produced a ten-tonne stone sculpture for the non-aligned conference in Titograd and has several pieces in the National Gallery in Harare. Others, like **Henry Munyaradzi**, have exhibited in Europe, America and Australia.

If you come on Tengenenge's birthday (February 22) or Independence Day (April 18), you can expect to be treated to wild, inebriated celebrations in which secret dance societies compete publicly, in ghoulish, satirical and bawdy displays.

Practicalities

Travelling to Tengenenge **by car**, turn on to Gurungwe Road 12km before Guruve at the 35.5-kilometre peg, and follow the signs for Tengenenge. The first 10km or so of this road are tarred, followed by about 5km of poor gravel track. Getting there by **public transport** is a far more difficult proposition, only for the very determined: take a bus from Mbare to Mvurwi and change there for **Guruve**, getting off at the Gurungwe Road turn-off mentioned above; from here, walking is the only way to tackle the remaining 18km to Tengenenge. If you get stuck overnight, Guruve's one **hotel** has cheap doubles. Otherwise the best **accommodation** is at Tengenenge itself, where there are simple huts for rent and plenty of space for camping. Food is also available, and visitors are welcome to try their hand at some sculpture, but be prepared to fit into African village life if you choose to stay. The nearest upmarket alternative is *Kopje Tops Camp* in the Mavuradonna (see p.110).

Companies running organized **tours** out to Tengenenge from Harare include Stonegate Safaris, St Brelades Close, Borrowdale (☎04/870698), who charge around US$85, and Bushbeat Trails, who are booked through VFR Tours, Kilwinnig Road, Hatfield (☎04/5729 4934, fax 572956, *vfrtours@internet.co.zw*), and do a similar trip for US$55. Both take a full day, include lunch and are popular, so booking well ahead is recommended.

The Mavuradonna Wilderness

Relatively unknown, even to many Zimbabweans, the **Mavuradonna Wilderness Area**, around 190km from Harare, is one of the country's wildest conservation regions, an uncultivated and mountainous tract that was a no-go area for many years during the bush war. Largely hunted out before 1988, this beautiful and unpopulated part of the country was restocked in 1992 and poaching has been virtually eliminated. Game typi-

MUTOTA: THE MAVURADONNA SPIRIT MEDIUM

The spirit medium **Mutota**, a renowned local religious figure, wields enormous influence in the Mavuradonna area. From time to time even white farmers send him the customary offering of bolts of black-and-white cloth to ensure good rains, or to bring harm to poachers; this usually has to be done through a Shona intermediary, as he finds the odour of whites offensive. Whether the farmers offer their tribute through genuine belief or for political reasons is a moot point.

The story goes that the current Mutota – a young Mozambican in his early thirties who doesn't speak the local language – was called in a dream after the old incumbent died. Guided only by this visitation, he walked hundreds of kilometres through difficult terrain to take over the mediumship here in neighbouring Zimbabwe. During trances, he takes on the persona of the **mhondoro** – the lion spirit of an ancestor – conveying his message in leonine growls and roars, which are then translated by an interpreter.

cal of such mountainous country is present, including leopard, sable, zebra, kudu, reedbuck, warthog, bushpig, bushbuck, duiker, klipspringer and grysbok. There are also growing but small herds of eland and buffalo and small resident breeding herds of elephants whose numbers swell during the dry season as bulls migrate up from the Zambezi Valley.

Surprisingly, the hidden wilderness lies just two hours' easy drive (mostly on metalled roads) from Harare. Elephants have, over many years, worn paths into deep valleys tangled with bamboo thickets and streams that support palms and waterberries. Their routes, negotiable only on horseback or on foot, provide the only tracks here, threading through open countryside and rocky outcrops. The views across the Great Dyke, a massive fault looming out of the landscape, are always beautiful.

San hunter-gatherers (see p.343) have left their mark on scattered rock faces – often quite literally, in the form of small terracotta-coloured hand prints. Depicting animals, humans and geometric forms, many of the paintings have yet to be scientifically investigated, leaving much to interpretation.

Accommodation and getting there

There are only two **places to stay** – one budget, the other upmarket and geared mainly to riding safaris (see p.110) – in the Mavuradonna Wilderness, which is a controlled area managed on behalf of the local council under the Campfire scheme (see p.233 for details). For budget travellers, the **Community Headquarters Camp**, east of the Muzarabani road offers simple accommodation in 22 thatched A-frame shelters, with basic washing and toilet facilities and sites for four tents. You have to bring everything you need, including food and drinking water, although built-in braai places mean you won't need a cooker. A network of waymarked trails of various lengths leads from the camp, but approach the nearby waterfall with care, as it can be treacherous. **Booking** for the camp, which costs under US$5 per two-person shelter, must be made in Harare through the Wildlife Society Shop, PO Box GD 800, Greendale (☎04/731596 or ☎ & fax 04/700451) at Mukuvisi Woodlands (see p.82).

To get to Mavuradonna **by car**, take Second Street Extension out of Harare to Mazowe. Turn left here and continue past Centenary, keeping to the tar on the Muzarabani road. At the fifty-kilometre peg, turn right at the Mavuradonna Wilderness Community Headquarters Camp – it is a short walk off the main road some distance before the village. Two to three **buses** leave Mbare terminus for Mazurabani each day; ask to be dropped at the turning for the Community Headquarters Camp, from where it's a two-hundred metre walk to the camp.

Riding safaris

The ultimate way to penetrate the valleys, peaks and hidden corners of the Mavuradonna is on horseback. For experienced equestrians, Carew Safaris operates adventurous **riding safaris** deep into the wilderness area. Other less ambitious trips, offering some of the best-run and most exciting riding in Zimbabwe, start from *Kopje Tops Camp*, where non-riders can also stay in stone and adobe en-suite lodges, each carefully positioned for maximum privacy. Led by one of Zimbabwe's handful of woman professional hunter-guides – formidably competent and thoroughly knowledgeable about the local flora and fauna – rides head for the Bat Caves pole and thatch bush camp, which can be used as a base for exploring the Tingwa Valley and surrounding area. All supplies are portered in, so you carry very little. On more intrepid excursions you can leave behind the security of the fixed camp to reach the remotest tracts, exploring precipitous paths or following elephant herds – you sleep in caves or under the stars and carry whatever you need.

Trips as short as two days can be arranged, but safaris are normally for a minimum of four and a maximum of ten days, and **cost** US$220 per person per night; transfers from Harare by road cost US$65 per person each way. Air charters can be arranged to or from Mana Pools, Kariba, Chikwenya or Harare on request. Bookings are made through Geoffrey Carew, Private Bag 295A, Harare (☎058/404 or 551, *carew@ vcarewsafaris.com*). Alternatively, in the UK, you can book through any of the major African safari specialists.

The Palm Reserve

Guests at *Kopje Tops Camp* can visit the **Palm Reserve**, a small concentration of **raffia palms**. These incredible trees, which sport the longest leaves in the world, live only

---

MAPONDERA – ZIMBABWE'S ROBIN HOOD

An inspirational outlaw-hero, **Mapondera** was an early **freedom fighter**, whose stamping ground was the Zambezi Valley, near the Mavuradonnas. In the late nineteenth century, he would slip eel-like across the river, between British and Portuguese territory, avoiding the armies of both. An independent warrior-ruler, descended from a Rozvi royal family, he put up a firm resistance to **colonial rule** and rejected the hut tax. In 1894 Mapondera and a band of followers fled from a settler force sent to arrest them. They emerged from their refuge to raid administrative offices, ambush tax collectors and burn shops they felt were exploiting the peasants.

To the government he was nothing more than a bloody murderer, but the Zimbabwean and Mozambican peasants who fed and sheltered Mapondera passed a different judgement. For several years he and his army held out against the white invaders. In 1901, with an army numbering nearly a thousand, he attacked their settlement at **Mount Darwin**, notorious as a place of fighting during the Second Chimurenga, and nearly wiped it out. But, in the end, it was a stalemate. Mapondera continued his campaign for several more years under increasing pressure from the multiplying forces of colonial control. As white influence on both sides of the Zambezi closed in, his operational zone became restricted. Hunted by the Portuguese and British, unable to get food or grow crops, and exhausted by nearly a decade on the run, he returned to his home at Mount Nyota, resigned to defeat. He sent a final message to his people saying that the old order was now finished and offering words for the new: "I leave my children here. They must look after themselves."

Soon afterwards he was arrested, tried and sentenced to a hefty seven years. He found confinement unbearable, went on hunger strike, and starved himself to death. Mapondera was honoured by the Mugabe government as a folk hero: a building in Harare is named after him.

twenty or thirty years, producing exquisite waxy amber cones. Growing on the confluence of crystal-clear streams, no one is quite sure how the isolated pockets of palms came to be where they are. One theory is that they were brought with trading Portuguese, and have clearly found an environment very much to their liking.

Umfurudzi Safari Area

Of the few established attractions in the north, the **Hippo Pools** and **Sunungukai camps** in the 740-square-kilometre **UMFURUDZI SAFARI AREA** are the two most worthy of mention, offering hutted accommodation, river walks, game viewing and plenty of peace and quiet. Situated on the banks of the Mazowe River in beautiful broken granite country, they are both highly recommended as weekend retreats from Harare, or as stop-offs if you're touring the northern circuit around Mount Darwin and Centenary.

Umfurudzi's **vegetation** consists predominantly of miombo woodland and granite kopjes with patches of marshy vlei and grassland, large mopani trees and some huge baobabs. This habitat is ideal country for sable antelope, which thrive here in several herds, one of them fifty strong. Other common **wildlife** species include kudu, duiker, impala, warthog, wildebeest, zebra, hippo, vervet monkey, baboon, dassie and klipspringer. Leopards, bushbabies and hyenas are frequently heard at night but rarely seen, while less common occasional visitors include lions and eland. The area is also excellent for **birds**: almost three hundred species have been spotted here.

The Hippo Pools Camp

The **Hippo Pools Camp**, 160km from Harare, consisting of **chalets** and a **campsite**, is a commercial operation administered by National Parks (day entry US$10, week entry US$20). Hunting is forbidden, but you can fish, canoe and walk along the Mazowe River, and there's a fair amount of game in the area, with the big five making rare appearances. Several outdoor **activities** can be undertaken from the camp, including **walking** along a fifty-kilometre network of trails that have been cut in a perimeter around the camp, with a seven-kilometre conducted hike every Saturday morning. Roads in the safari area are only suitable for 4WD or high-clearance vehicles, but guided **game drives** go out every Saturday afternoon and are also available at other times on request. When the Mazowe River is in full spate, it's navigable for 3–4km and **canoes** can be rented for this purpose. Guided walks, game drives and canoeing all **cost** US$10.

Transfers costing US$10 each way are available from Harare (Mon & Fri 3pm) and from Hippo Pools (Mon 5am & Fri 8am). If you're **driving**, head north out of Harare along Enterprise Road, following signs to Shamva (the road is poor in parts and ideally you'll need a high-clearance vehicle, though saloon cars can make it). Continue past Shamva Mine, 90km from the capital, and Madziwa Mine entrance, at the 99-kilometre peg. A little beyond this the road forks and you should take the right branch onto a gravel road. After 700m you'll reach the gates of Madziwa Mine Secondary School on the left. Make a sharp right past a reservoir, through the market and bus terminus, and turn right at the Hippo Pools sign attached to a tree. Take the road round the perimeter of the mine till it hits a tarred road, onto which you should take a left and continue for 8km to Amms Mine. The road again becomes gravel and traces the perimeter of the mine till it reaches a National Parks sign at a fork. Bear right and continue for 6km till you reach a sign indicating that Hippo Pools is 12.5km further. Follow the sign left and continue to the camp, ignoring all branches off the road.

Accommodation consists of three thatched chalets (③), each with its own fully equipped kitchen, lounge, dining room, toilets and showers. Linen is provided but not towels, and it's recommended that you bring additional bedding in winter. There are also some smaller basic cabins (②) that come unequipped and share washing facilities, and a shady campsite (①). Given the limited amount of accommodation, **booking** is essential and can be done in Harare through Goliath Safaris, *Bronte Hotel*, Baines Avenue/Fourth Street, the Avenues (☎04/739836–8, fax 708843). Rather pricey breakfasts and evening **meals** are available at Hippo Pools Camp.

Sunungukai Camp

Sunungukai Camp (book through Campfire, 15 Phillips Ave, Belgravia, Harare; ☎04/790570; ③) has the double advantage of being both cheaper than Hippo Pools and offering the chance of experiencing African village life at first hand. The camp was developed as part of the Campfire Programme, which enables local villagers to channel revenue from tourism into projects that benefit the whole community, such as building schools and clinics. It's a pretty basic setup, with a campsite, four bucket showers, water from a borehole and a communal kitchen. Local guides can take you to San rock paintings and a sacred mountain – the "Breathing Mountain" of Mushambanhaka – or show you around villagers' homes.

Sunungukai is two hours by (mostly tarred) road north of Harare; full directions are given when you book. Two economy **buses** leave daily from Mbare bus terminus (1pm & 4pm); the bus is routed "Nyava via Shamva, Mazoe Bridge" or "Nhakiwa via Bindura, Glendale" and the stop to ask for is Nyagande, a small village 1500m from the camp. The journey takes around three hours, with frequent stops; departure times, as everywhere else in Zimbabwe, are approximate.

travel details

Harare is, unsurprisingly, the nexus of travel, with excellent and lightly used tarred **roads** to Mutare, Masvingo, Bulawayo and Kariba. Hwange and Victoria Falls, though, are reached by road from Bulawayo, not Harare. There are overnight **rail** services to Bulawayo and Mutare with comfortable sleepers, while Bulawayo and the Midlands are well served by **luxury coaches** at least once a day, with one of the Sunday services continuing through to Victoria Falls. Coaches run to Mutare five times each week, and to Masvingo at the weekend only. Slow and crowded **local buses** from Mbare will take you almost anywhere, starting at undefined times early each day. **Domestic flights** are excellent value, with countrywide connections daily, though none to Mutare, which only has a military airport. They are sometimes prone to delays, but international flights leave punctually.

Trains

Harare to: Bulawayo via Kwekwe, Gweru and Shangani, for Danangombe and Naletale ruins (daily at 8pm; 9hr); Mutare (daily 9.30pm; 8hr 30min).

Luxury coaches

Details of departure points and operators for coach services from Harare are listed on p.67.
Harare to: Bulawayo via Chivhu (1 daily, Fri 2 daily; 6hr); via Kwekwe and Gweru (Thurs 1 daily, Fri & Sun 2 daily; 6hr); Johannesburg (1–2 daily; 16–18hr); Kariba (7 daily; 5hr); Lusaka (Tues & Fri 1 daily; 9hr); Mutare (Wed, Fri & Sun 1 daily; 4hr 15min).

Volvos, chicken buses and commuters

Every day more that a hundred bus companies send out **Volvo** and **chicken buses** from Mbare *musika* to every corner of Zimbabwe. Amid the scrum at the Mbare bus station, accurate timetables are quite impossible to determine, if they exist at all. As a rule of thumb, most buses head out in the morning, often as early as 5am or 6am, with the greatest proportion leaving before lunch, so your best bet, if you're using this form of transport, is to turn up at the bus station as early as possible, find the stand for your destination and be prepared to ask around – and to wait. In addition to long-distance routes, scores of **commuter omnibuses** run services along the main roads.

Flights

Air Zimbabwe (UM), the national carrier, has the most extensive **domestic network** connecting Harare with Bulawayo and several tourist centres. Zimbabwe Express (Z) has a considerably smaller network and it's worth noting that there are no scheduled flights to either Mutare (for the Eastern Highlands) or Masvingo (for Great Zimbabwe). As for **regional connections**, Johannesburg, less than two hours away by air, is served by Air Zimbabwe, Zimbabwe Express, British Airways/Comair (BA) and South African Airways (SA); it's the transport hub of Southern Africa, and is the obvious place to make for should you wish to travel elsewhere in the region. Air Zimbabwe also has direct connections, at least once a week to several other African destinations: Dar-es-Salaam, Lilongwe, Lusaka, Mauritius, Nairobi and Windhoek.

Harare to: Bulawayo (4 daily; 50min; UM & Z); Cape Town (Mon & Fri 1 daily; 4hr 30min; UM); Durban (Sun direct 1 daily; 2hr 10min; UM); Hwange National Park (Tues, Thur & Sat 1 daily; 2hr; UM); Johannesburg (5–6 daily; 1hr 40min; UM, BA, Z & SA); Kariba (1 daily; 45min; UM); Victoria Falls (3–4 daily; 1hr; UM & Z).

CHAPTER TWO

KARIBA AND THE MIDDLE ZAMBEZI VALLEY

Zimbabwe's northern border is formed by the Zambezi River, which is dammed at Kariba to form the vast artificial Lake Kariba. The river traverses some of the wildest and hottest parts of the country, with Mana Pools National Park, below the dam, the wildlife centrepiece: a place where you'll see animals without the slightest effort, and where walking in a group – the big attraction – is permitted, provided you are used to the bush and observe safety procedures.

The **lake** itself has a strange quality – hardly surprising given that a whole valley was drowned to create it, and a people, the Batonga, moved out. From the shallows, dead treetops poke out, while camel-hump formations dominate the lakeshore, sprouting grotesque baobabs and desiccated mopane woodland. Amid the creeks and islands, however, lies the rewarding **Matusadona National Park**.

Independent access to these wildlife areas is, unfortunately, neither easy nor cheap, and this is a part of the country where it is generally worth joining an organized expedition. Many of these tours (see p.142 for details of operators) are adventurous and fairly intrepid options. If you want a taste of African expedition life, with the reassurance of an experienced guide or leader, it's hard to beat the excitement of a **canoeing trip** down the Zambezi, taking in Mana Pools en route, or a **backpacking safari** in one of the three national parks, ensuring equally close encounters with big game.

Kariba Town, five hours by road from Harare and well connected by air, is the hub of Zambezi tourism, promoted as a fabulous riviera but perhaps a little defeated by its own hype. While the blues of mountain and lake are very beautiful, there's nothing much to do here without a boat and fishing gear. Kariba is often the first stop for visitors doing the

---

ACCOMMODATION PRICE CODES

Hotels and other accommodation options in Zimbabwe have been categorized according to the **price codes** given below, which indicate the cost, per person sharing, of a night's lodging. For a full explanation, see p.33.

① under US$7.50   ④ US$25–35   ⑦ US$55–75
② US$7.50–15   ⑤ US$35–45   ⑧ US$75–100
③ US$15–25   ⑥ US$45–55   ⑨ over US$100

"milk run" – Kariba, Hwange National Park and Victoria Falls. If you're **circuiting the country**, the **Kariba ferry** conveniently connects the northeast of Zimbabwe to its west.

Travelling overland, one of Zimbabwe's longest hauls by road runs through the dusty and remote **back routes** south of the lake. Starting at Harare, the road veers west at **Karoi** into some of the country's least developed communal lands, scattered with stilt-perched lookout huts, maize fields and sandy villages. A full day's drive, or two days on a chicken bus, brings you to **Binga**, the thoroughly untouristy centre of Lake Kariba's west (for coverage of western Lake Kariba, see Chapter Four).

THE ROAD FROM HARARE

The towns diminish steadily in size as you head northwest from Harare towards Kariba. None particularly merits a night's stop, though all have at least one hotel should the

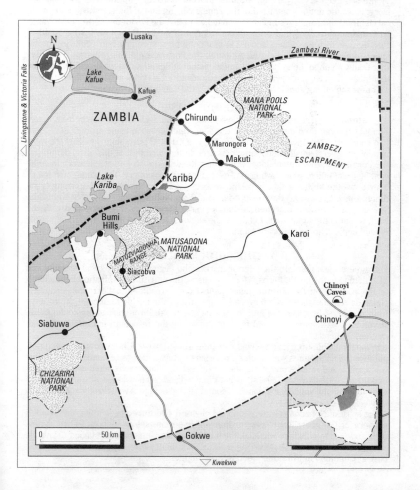

need arise. Tobacco and maize farms line the route to the escarpment, with a scenic highlight as you cross the **Great Dyke**, a massive topographic spine which bisects the highveld plateau and is the source of many springs and streams.

Among the **buses** heading to Kariba out of Harare are several daily chicken and Volvo buses that leave from Mbare bus station, the Powercoach semi-luxury bus (to Kariba and Lusaka), which uses the Roadport, and the UTC minibus that departs from

---

ZAMBEZI VALLEY HISTORY

The Zambezi Valley has been inhabited since the first **hunter-gatherers** lived there, and Bantu-speaking **Iron Age farmers** have navigated the river for centuries. Numerous Iron Age sites are scattered along the Zambezi, including the **Ingombe Ilede** burial site near Chirundu, which showed that external trade had reached this far up the Zambezi by the sixth century AD. Later, **Muslim merchants** traded up the river for gold and ivory: romantic notions persisted of the Zambezi being one of the gateways to the biblical Ophir. At the Zambezi's Indian Ocean delta in 1497, the Portuguese adventurer Vasco da Gama supposedly found Arab dhows laden with gold dust. Hot on his heels, other **Portuguese** fortune-seekers arrived in large numbers, spending four centuries on the lower Zambezi in search of riches. Although the Portuguese didn't penetrate much further than Chirundu, below the lake, in the sixteenth century, this was considerably further inland than any European had previously advanced in Africa and, from their reports, we know something about the Mutapa State of the Zambezi Escarpment.

THE MUTAPAS

The **Mutapas** were originally Shona-speakers, who had drifted north from Great Zimbabwe some time during its disintegration (final collapse came around 1450), and had conquered the Tavara – another Shona group. The Mutapa state was only the most famous of several small Shona kingdoms around the northeast at this time, though for the Portuguese, the Mutapa king, whom they knew as the Monomatapa, was a magnificent figure of untold wealth who ruled over an enormous empire. The empire was in fact a myth, but the Mutapas did control the important Zambezi trade route. According to tradition, the Mutapas had their own Adam and Eve: **Nebedza** and his sister **Nehanda**. Nehanda is Zimbabwe's archetypal mother-earth heroine, closely associated with the land, which is the fundamental element of religious, social and material life, the source of food and the home of the ancestors.

THE CHIMURENGAS

Portuguese incursion into the interior marked the beginnings of colonial brutality and bloodletting in the north. Perhaps for this reason, the **spiritual inspiration** behind both of the past century's **Chimurengas** came from here. In both liberation struggles, Nehanda rematerialized as a powerful figure, urging the people to liberate the country from the white invaders. On both occasions she spoke through mediums, who themselves took on her persona and became known by the respectful title *Mbuya* (grandmother) Nehanda.

In the First Chimurenga, a Nehanda medium from Mazowe, **Charwe**, encouraged people to avoid all dealings with whites. As far as the authorities were concerned, Charwe was a witch and rabble-rouser and she was arrested. Photographs taken just before her execution in Salisbury, in 1898, show her dignified and self-possessed; she's said to have gone to her death singing and dancing, confident that her spirit would return for final victory.

The spirit of Nehanda re-emerged in the **Second Chimurenga**, winning the people's support for the guerrillas. When mediums of important spirits such as Nehanda gave their approval to efforts to win back the land, many peasants were persuaded to join the struggle. In 1972, ZANLA guerrillas secretly took the medium over the border to their base at Chifombo in Mozambique to rally the fighters.

its terminus on the corner of Park Street and Jason Moyo Avenue. If you're bent on **hitching**, Saturday is best, when people drive from the capital to Kariba for the weekend; if you're wondering what's in the small sacks people wave at you from the roadside, they contain worms for bream fishing at Kariba.

Chinoyi

CHINOYI, 115km northwest of Harare, is a farming and mining centre, which remained a white stronghold well into the 1990s but has now become far more mixed as a result of the government's land redistribution policies. The petrol stations are all most people see of the town, though it has a claim to fame in its much vaunted **caves**, and a place in history as the spot where the Second Chimurenga began, on April 28, 1966, with the killing of seven ZANLA guerrillas in a confrontation with Rhodesian forces. The date is celebrated as the annual Chimurenga Day, and a memorial to the "Gallant Chinoyi Seven" has been erected in the town.

The **Chinoyi Caves** (daily 6am–6pm; US$10), enclosed by a recreational park 8km north of the town, make an interesting break on an otherwise dull journey to Kariba. The labyrinth of the caves centres on the legendary **Sleeping Pool**, whose waters appear strikingly deep and vivid blue as you approach via the passage, though the none-too-fragrant odour does its best to deflate the dreamy atmosphere promised by the name. The best time to see the pool is at noon, when light pours from a natural skylight onto the still surface. If you don't find caves claustrophobic, descend into **Dark Cave**, nearby, which has steps and electric lighting until you get to the viewing platform at the end of the tunnel. There's a good view from here of the Sleeping Pool, overhung by stalactites in shades of blue that vary with the time of day. Numerous passages and galleries lead off from the Dark Cave for more serious exploration. As all tracks are well signposted, you can easily explore without the help of a guide.

Archeologists have found ancient traces of troglodyte occupation in these subterranean dolomite chambers; in the 1830s the Nguni are supposed to have used them as a place of execution, and later in the century Chief Chinoyi used them as a refuge from Ndebele raiders.

Practicalities

If you want to stay at Chinoyi Caves, there's an unappealing National Parks **campsite** within the recreational park, adjacent to the local prison, and a far nicer one closer to town in the grounds of the *Orange Grove Motel* (☎067/22785–6, fax 23095) 1.5km north of the town centre on the Karoi Road (the continuation of Independence Way), which offers adequate, functional en-suite **rooms** (②) facing the car park. The more comfortable and marginally more expensive *Chinoyi Caves Motel* (☎ & fax 067/22340; ③), 8km north of the town next to the caves, lies on the Karoi Road, the major truck route to Zambia and Malawi, making it a noisy option, but an agreeable one apart from that. The motel has twenty en-suite chalets and a large terrace under mature fig trees where reasonably priced food is served; there's also a small and dark but elegant bar and restaurant. A pool is available to guests, but casual visitors pay US$2.50 for a swim.

Karoi, Makuti and Chirundu

Under a Rhodesian government land settlement scheme, many white farmers moved into the area around **KAROI** between 1945 and 1950, the farms identifiable by their tobacco-curing sheds and tall brick chimneys. *Karoi* is a Shona term meaning "place of the sorceresses", which accounts for the town logo of a witch on a broomstick, and it marks the start of the bizarrely named **Nicolle Hostes Highway** – 400km of gruelling dirt to Matusadona, Chizarira and Binga.

If you're looking for **accommodation**, the run-down **campsite** overlooking the dam (take the first road to your right just before you get to the town junction) should be avoided, as security could be a problem and there's no water in the dilapidated ablution block. Head instead for the more salubrious one at *Spring Fever Homecraft*, 5km north of town (see below) or one of the two Karoi **hotels**, the smarter of which is the *Twin River Inn*, 1km north of the town on the Chirundu Road (☎064/6845, fax 6846; ③), rebuilt in 1995 in a mock-colonial style with Dutch gables and sixteen semi-detached en-suite rondavels arranged in a semicircle. The less stylish *Karoi Hotel* (☎064/6317 or 6283, fax 6856; ②), in the centre of town, glories in 1970s decor, with plastic chairs and turquoise walls; its 35 rooms are clean but dark and airless.

Both hotels have a **restaurant** and **bar** but, again, the *Twin River* scores with the *Caroline's Restaurant* and the *Dubble Puddle Bar*, a very sociable drinking place. The *Twin River* also has a good **tea garden** with a takeaway counter and an excellent shop selling curios, bait for fishing and all sorts of camping gadgets. Another recommended refreshment stop is *Spring Fever Homecraft and Teagarden* (daily 7.30am–5pm) next to the Mobil garage, 5km north of Karoi en route to Kariba. Home-made cakes and scones, breakfast and hot lunches are available both in the garden, which is attached to a garden nursery, and under a large thatched restaurant. The adjacent craft shop sells all sorts of locally made goodies, from jams and cookies to greeting cards, tea cosies and children's clothes. A **campsite** lies behind the nursery on two acres of lawn, but there's little shade and the proximity to the road makes it rather noisy.

Makuti

En route to Kariba or Mana, everyone stops for drinks at *Cloud's End Hotel* (☎063/526 or 451; ②) in **MAKUTI**, the highest point in the vicinity, on the Chirundu and Harare Road just past the turn-off to Kariba before the road begins to tumble down into the Zambezi Valley. Extremely popular and often fully booked, this is one of the classic stopovers and seems frozen in time, with stupendous views over the valley, a terrace restaurant and the famous *Cloud's End* bar, a real hunter's grotto with buffalo heads leering from the walls. All of the en-suite rooms have valley views, though otherwise they're pretty average. The village consists of little more than the hotel, plus an adjacent filling station that's always open and a basic grocery store (daily 6am–6pm), which are the last places for petrol and supplies before Mana Pools.

Chirundu

CHIRUNDU, 63km further north, is equally small, despite its border status as the point where you cross the Zambezi River into Zambia. There are daily chicken and Volvo **buses** from Mbare bus station, and the daily Powercoach bus from the Roadport in Harare runs right through to Lusaka. You can get small **rooms** with slightly tatty bathrooms at the inexpensive, colonial-style *Chirundu Valley Hotel* (☎0637/618, fax 664; ③), which attracts tourists, business travellers and truckers. They also have family rooms, which are even cheaper, and the steaks here are excellent. Don't be put off by the hotel's array of parked trucks and trailers lining up for the border crossing – through reception are lawns backing onto woodland, and a swimming pool which draws thirsty elephants and buffalo from time to time. A one-kilometre walk from the hotel to the top of the hill gives magnificent views of the Zambezi with game on the banks, but keep a wary lookout for elephants, especially in the late afternoon. Since the hotel frequently hosts recreational fishermen, it's possible to rent boats and get onto the water, though you should look out for hippos and elephants.

Also a haunt of anglers, *Tiger Safaris* (☎ & fax 063/7633) offers self-catering "fishermen's cottages" along the Zambezi in sight of the Chirundu Bridge, but these are equally suitable as a pleasant overnight stop if you fancy spending time in archetypal jungly riverine forest, dripping with Tarzan-esque lianas. The snag is you need a 4WD vehicle to get there. Take the turn-off from the main road opposite the Total garage and continue down the sandy track for 1.2km, following the almost-illegible blue-and-yellow "Tiger Safaris" signs. The fully serviced cottages (US$70 per cottage), each with its own terrace and four beds, are weather-beaten, rustic and romantic: bring your own food, drinks, towels and fishing tackle. Boats can be rented by the day.

KARIBA AND THE MATUSADONA NATIONAL PARK

Kariba offers a remarkable choice of activities. For those who want a few days lazing by the pool, the **town resort** has all the facilities: a boon, since the lake (except for its deepest central reaches) is frustratingly out of bounds for swimming, due to crocodiles and bilharzia. With more adventurous pursuits in mind, there are a host of **wildlife safari** options, including the **Matusadona National Park**, with its massive dry-season herds of buffalo and elephant and dazzling array of lakeshore animals and birds. And there's the chance of gliding down the Zambezi by **canoe**, on one- to ten-day safaris headed for Mana or beyond.

The Zambezi, downstream from Kariba, creates a hunting enclave which spreads across 10,000 square kilometres to the Mozambique border, consisting of the Charara, Sapi, Chewore, Dande and Doma Safari areas. In the centre of all this is **Mana Pools**, a unique wildlife sanctuary, where, because of the open terrain, the National Park authorities allow walking without guides, and weapons are prohibited.

Kariba Town

Engineers faced with the problem of building a road from the escarpment down the hills to **KARIBA** turned to the ancient paths worn by **elephants**, who knew the easiest descent. The road twists around massive bush-clad hills to the lakeside; as you near the water, look out for elephants crossing the road or tugging at trees.

Orientation, arrival, information and city transport

The precise location of Kariba Town is perplexing, as there's nothing much on the main road besides a Total filling station as you enter the town from the east, and a Shell garage near the border post. Every few kilometres, however, a small turn-off disappears through the trees to one of the lakeside resorts. Stretched over 12km, each of the **hotels** and **campsites** has its own hill-cupped bay, cut off from the next by the undulating landscape.

There are two commercial and residential centres – **Kariba Heights**, perched 600m above the lake, and **Mahombekombe** township on the shore. Before Independence, the Heights was the white residential area, with its palpably cooler temperatures and lofty views – it features a good coffee shop, a bank, Internet café, pharmacy, grocery and curio shops (see Listings, p.130). Set slightly back from the commercial fishing harbour and creeping up Sugar Loaf Hill, Mahombekombe was

KARIBA TO VICTORIA FALLS AND HWANGE NATIONAL PARK

AIR AND ROAD ROUTES

Four **direct flights** a week connect Kariba with Victoria Falls and three a week with Hwange National Park, making this the quickest way of covering these distances. By **car**, the most comfortable and shortest option is to take the ferry between Kariba and Mlibizi (see below), from where it's 134km to Hwange's Main Camp and 152km to the Falls, both along tar. If you're bent on driving the whole way, the quickest overland route between Kariba and Victoria Falls is to cross into Zambia, rather than travel around the south side of the lake via Siabuwa, as the road on the Zambian side of the lake is in much better condition. This is also the preferable route if you want to go by public transport, and the daily Powercoach **bus** from Harare to Lusaka passes through Kariba and Kafue. From here you can catch one of the daily buses that go between Lusaka and Victoria Falls via Kafue.

SPEED PASSENGER FERRIES

The **Kariba ferry** between Kariba town and Mlibizi is by far the easiest way to journey the length of the lake, saving the circuitous 1250-kilometre route you have to follow to drive to Victoria Falls via Bulawayo on tarred roads – the route you'd have to take if you're not in a high-clearance vehicle. (With such a vehicle and an intrepid spirit you can trace the southern shore of the lake along 322km of rough dirt road that goes through dry, wild country between Karoi and meets the tar 18km south of Binga.) But, while the ferry voyage has an *African Queen* romance to it, through wild country all the way, the experience rather depends on who you're sitting next to and how active the boozers are: people often rave it up for the entire 24-hour journey.

The adult passenger **fare** is US$80 (children US$40) for a reclining seat, including meals, tea and coffee; 4WD vehicles are carried for US$80 and sedans for US$57. If you only go as far as Tashinga or Bumi, you pay one third of the full fare and with each successive stop the fare goes up; as far as Binga, you'll pay US$64. Fares are cheaper for South Africans and Zimbabweans. The ferry is often booked up months in advance and you need to pay half the cost to secure your reservation two weeks before sailing. After this, seats are sold off, so keep on enquiring if you're told it's full. Without a car, your

built to house construction workers and continues to be the main residential area for fishermen and people working in the tourist industry. It has the nearest shops and post office to the resorts and it's where the **buses** arrive, although most also pull in en route at **Nyamhunga** (built in the 1970s near the airport to increase housing for Africans), and a few stop at the lakeside resorts.

By air, you arrive at Kariba airport, about 10km east of town just off the main road from Makuti. The inexpensive UTC minibus meets all flights and will drop you off anywhere within the town, or at the harbour if you're connecting to Fothergill Island or one of the resorts further afield. For two people, taking a taxi may work out cheaper than the bus, depending on the distance. There are no facilities at the airport apart from a small kiosk selling drinks and curios.

Chicken and Volvo buses from Harare stop at Mahombekombe bus terminus, from where it's a three-kilometre walk to the *MOTH* campsite and chalets or *Tamarind Lodges* (see p.124). However, some buses go on as far as the Swift Depot, which is much closer. The Kariba Ferries **passenger speed ferry** service uses Andorra Harbour, south of Mahombekombe; for details of **DDF ferries**, see the box above.

Information

Kariba's excellent **publicity bureau** (☎061/3213–4 or 2328, *karibapa@samara.co.zw*) is sited at the Observation Point, which overlooks the dam wall. This is the obvious chances of getting on are better. On board, there's an outside sun deck, a cash bar, food (even for vegetarians) and a shaded lounge, but you're unlikely to spot many animals en route as the ferry sails in the centre of the lake. Nevertheless, it's still worth bringing your binoculars.

Daily (except Wed) **departures** leave Kariba at 9am, and from Mlibizi daily (except Thurs) at 7am. For **bookings**, timetables and further details, contact Kariba Ferries Ltd at Andorra Harbour, PO Box 70, Kariba (☎061/2460); at their Harare head office (☎04/614162–7); or in South Africa through Reservations Frontline in Johannesburg (☎011/789 2440, fax 886 4837, *rfline@iafrica.com*). **Boarding** is a bit of a scramble, so go as early as possible and try to check the day before to confirm that you're booked.

DDF ECONOMY FERRIES

DDF (District Development Fund) Shipping Services, next to Peter's Point by the dam wall (☎061/2694 or 3207, fax 2349), runs pretty basic boats, more like old fishing rigs than fast high-tech vessels: you have to bring all your own food and drinks. A sleeping bag and mattress roll will give you some comfort and reading matter is essential, especially if you're heading for Binga. The **Kariba–Tashinga–Bumi Hills–Chalala** ferry leaves Kariba on Tuesday at 10.30am and returns on Wednesday at the same time. It costs US$12 to Tashinga (4hr) and US$13 to Bumi Hills (5hr).

The **Kariba–Chalala–Binga** boat leaves fortnightly on Thursday and returns to Kariba the following Monday. The journey to Binga takes three days and costs US$30. Passengers can just turn up on the morning of travel but if you intend to bring a **vehicle** across you must book. The rule of thumb is that if your journey is less than 100km, you pay US$30 for your car; over 100km, between US$40 and US$50.

GETTING FROM MLIBIZI TO VICTORIA FALLS OR HWANGE

A daily Country Boy economy **bus** leaves Binga at around 5am and passes through Mlibizi on its way to Victoria Falls. A considerably more expensive but faster and more comfortable alternative is to arrange a **transfer** through the *Mlibizi Zambezi Resort* (☎015/272) at the ferry terminal, who will put you in contact with a local man who plies the route.

starting point for a general town orientation and to get information and advice about activities around Kariba. You can browse through well-organized binders covering everything from flights, ferries, boat rental and cruises to accommodation, canoeing trips and safaris in the National Parks. One folder is dedicated to descriptions and pictures of all the rentable houseboats on Kariba, plus there's detailed background on the dam, the lake's ecology and the history of the Batonga people, numerous displays, photographs, maps and small exhibits of traditional musical instruments, as well as umpteen folders with interesting press cuttings and pictures illustrating the local history. A small shop sells the only available **map** of Kariba, books on the region, postcards, a few curios and ice cream.

City transport

Without a car, you can reckon on doing a lot of walking around Kariba. An irregular **bus** service connects the Swift Depot with Mahombekombe, Heights and Nyamhunga about every half-hour, and ZUPCO buses travel between Heights, Mahombekombe and Nyamhunga every two hours, stopping at the turn-offs to all of the lakeside resorts. **Hitching** along the main road isn't all that easy because the sharp curves and steep gradients make stopping both difficult and hazardous and the myriad branches usually mean a walk at least part of the way. **On foot**, rather than climbing up to the main road, you can cut distances drastically by following any of the well-worn paths directly along the shorefront. During the dry season, keep an eye open for elephants, which sometimes wander about Kariba's hills and shoreline.

More convenient options are taxis or car rental (see Listings), both of which are available in town. For information about **tours**, **safaris** and **cruises** from Kariba, see Kariba activities on p.127.

Accommodation

Kariba **hotels** used to be popular weekend destinations for people from Harare, especially during the winter when the town is much warmer than the capital. Since 1997, when the Zimbabwe dollar took a nosedive, this has all changed, as many Zimbabweans can no longer afford to stay at the big hotels and instead opt for **camping** or staying at the **self-catering** chalets which tend to fill up fast. Nowadays the larger hotels and **resorts** with their pools and air-conditioned rooms get booked up during the Christmas and July school holidays, when they are inundated by well-to-do South Africans and Zambians.

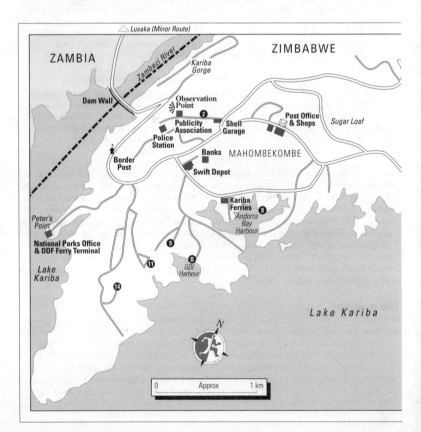

Self-catering and camping

Caribbea Bay Self-catering, *Caribbea Bay* (see p.125). Self-catering chalets at *Caribbea Bay* that are a little more basic than the hotel rooms. Hotel facilities open to self-caterers. Minimum of four and maximum of eight people per chalet. ②.

Cerruti Self-catering Lodges, 40km east of Kariba (☎ & fax 061/2815; Harare office ☎ & fax 04/750665). Five-star self-catering on the lakeshore in five luxury lodges built in 1999. Each sleeps up to nine and has a spacious kitchen and lounge, comes fully equipped and is set in large landscaped gardens with a swimming pool and children's playground. Ideal for families, but bring all your own supplies, as there is no restaurant or shop. To get there, take the Makuti Road past the airport turn-off; turn right at the Charara sign and proceed for 7km past the NAU (National Angler's Union). Two sharing ④, three or more sharing ③.

Friends in the Harbour, Kariba Boating Safaris, Andorra Harbour (☎061/2227, fax 2553). Basic but clean rooms in the very relaxed and friendly atmosphere of a two-storey brick home on the edge of Andorra Harbour. Two doubles and two singles share washing and toilet facilities and you're free to use the large open-plan lounge, small garden with shaded terrace and pool. Beakfast available on request. ②.

Kariba Breezes Backpacker Dorms, *Kariba Breezes Hotel* (see p.125). Camping on a separate site next to the hotel complex; individual sites each have their own tap, braai area and electricity, and there are two six-bed dorms with their own bathrooms. Guests may use the hotel facilities. ①.

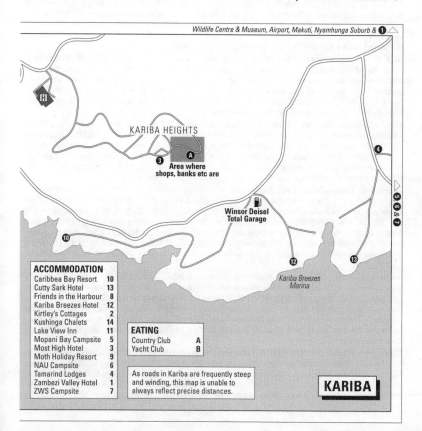

Wildlife Centre & Museum, Airport, Makuti, Nyamhunga Suburb & ❶

KARIBA HEIGHTS

Area where
shops, banks etc are

Winsor Deisel
Total Garage

Kariba Breezes
Marina

ACCOMMODATION

Caribbea Bay Resort	10
Cutty Sark Hotel	13
Friends in the Harbour	8
Kariba Breezes Hotel	12
Kirtley's Cottages	2
Kushinga Chalets	14
Lake View Inn	11
Mopani Bay Campsite	5
Most High Hotel	3
Moth Holiday Resort	9
NAU Campsite	6
Tamarind Lodges	4
Zambezi Valley Hotel	1
ZWS Campsite	7

EATING

Country Club	A
Yacht Club	B

As roads in Kariba are frequently steep and winding, this map is unable to always reflect precise distances.

KARIBA

Kirtley's Cottages, near Observation Point (PO Box 297, Kariba; ☎061/2846). Two separate cottages built into the rock with private wooden deck set amongst the steep rocky slopes within the grounds of a private home. Very secluded with pool and terrace overlooking the Zambezi Gorge, a fun rock garden and a cosy quiet atmosphere. Mrs Kirtley, who is besotted with her cats, is exceptionally friendly, will collect you from town and cooks up fabulous breakfasts and dinners, included in her rate. ③.

Kushinga Chalets, southwest of Mahombekombe, adjacent to *Lake View Inn* (PO Box 113, Kariba; ☎061/2645 or 3041–3, fax 2827, *buffalo@harare.iafrica.com*). Self-catering holiday complex built in 1997, with seven self-contained chalets under thatch on steep slopes overlooking the lake. Each of the two-, four-, six- or twelve-bedded units is built in raked terraces to give the feeling you've got it all to yourself. The separate small campsite, crowded in high season, has miniature thatched A-frames for two. Immaculately maintained, the complex has a pool and low-key outdoor restaurant serving reasonably priced meals and snacks. To get there, go past the Ministry of Fisheries, bear left and follow the signs. Camping and A-frames ①, chalets ②.

Lion's Club Campsite, next to the *MOTH* campsite. The cheapest camping in town right on the lakeshore under indigenous trees. Run by a friendly Kariba old-timer who lives in a caravan with his terrier, the site is run-down (especially the washing area), but as a result it's also fairly quiet, providing a refreshing break if you want escape the lager-swilling fraternity. Cold room and deep-freeze space available at minimal cost. ①.

Mopani Bay Campsite, 1.5km southeast of *Tamarind Lodges* (PO Box 182, Nzhou Drive; ☎061/2555, fax 2593). Friendly and secure campsite managed by the Kariba People's Project with proceeds going to rent reduction for poor families. Well located in mature mopane forest with individual camping spots, plenty of washing facilities, a pool, laundry service and a shop selling cold beers, drinks and snacks. Tents, mattresses and chairs for rent. To get there, turn left 500m past *Tamarind Lodges* and proceed just over 1km to the campsite. ①.

MOTH Holiday Resort, 3km south of Mahombekombe (c/o The Warden, PO Box 67, Kariba; ☎ & fax 061/2809). Cheap, popular and shady campsite that gets crowded at peak times, with tents with beds and linen, self-catering rooms and basic chalets. Laundry service, firewood, braai meat and refreshments are on sale and free transfers are available to *Lake View Inn* every evening. On foot it's 15 min via a short cut up the hill to the inn, where *MOTH* residents can use the pool at any time. Booking recommended. All accommodation ①.

NAU (National Anglers Union) Campsite, (PO Box 17, Kariba, 40km east of Kariba on the Charara Estuary ☎061/2667, fax 2659). This old-fashioned fishing camp offers the largest campsite on the lake and the promise of a quiet spot among the old trees, even in season. Basic self-catering chalets with private verandahs that sleep up to eight are also on offer; watch out for elephants, which regularly walk through the camp. A small shop sells basic groceries, and there's a filling station and a pool. Camping ①, chalets ②.

Nyanyana Camp, 28km from Kariba (book through National Parks central reservations in Harare; at Peter's Point in Kariba ☎061/2257; or direct ☎061/2898). National Parks camp on the lakeshore in the Charara Safari Area, 5km off the Makuti road, which gives a perfect chance to get into the wild with game, including elephants. Apart from camping, you can rent two en-suite lodges that resemble suburban bungalows, each with five beds and a fully fitted kitchen, where the pink ceilings and red lounge suites are rather at odds with the surrounding bush. The weekly entrance permit to the safari area is US$20 per person. Lodges US$20 for up to five people. Camping ①.

Tamarind Lodges, Nzhou Drive on the way to the *Cutty Sark Hotel* and *Kariba Breezes Marina*, PO Box 1, Kariba (☎061/2948, *tamarind@zambezi.net*). To the dismay and disbelief of many conservationists, this place was built smack in the middle of a designated wildlife corridor, severing an important migratory path for game. If this doesn't bother you, it's one of the nicest self-catering options available in Kariba, with 22 individual four- and six-bedded open-plan stone cottages. Braai areas and garden but no pool or shop. You can use the facilities at the *Cutty Sark Hotel* 500m further south. Four sharing ①; two sharing ②.

Zimbabwe Wildlife Society (ZWS) Campsite, on the border of the Charara Safari Area. Similar to Nyanyana, this site is on a peninsula with ample opportunity to spot game including elephant and buffalo. You have to self-cater, but there are four canvas tents to rent with two beds in each: handy if you don't have your own. An education centre and museum began construction in 1999 and will be managed by the ZWS. In summer, pitch your tent under one of the few large trees, to beat the blazing sun. To get there from Kariba, take the Mukuti Road past the airport and turn right at the

Nyanyana and Crocodile Farm turn-off; follow the road and bear right past the bream farm and follow the signs to the campsite. Camping or on-site tents with beds ①.

Hotels

Caribbea Bay Resort, (Zimbabwe Sun Hotels, Travel Centre, 93 Jason Moyo Ave, Harare ☎04/736644–5, fax 736646, *zimsuncro@zimsun.gaia.co.zw*; or direct ☎061/2452–7, fax 2765 or 2789). The architects must have been inspired by the Flintstones when they dreamed up this pink Swiss cheese of a building that's actually supposed to resemble a Spanish villa. Despite the fact that it's ostentatious, tacky and expensive, punters just love it – especially kids. All rooms have air-conditioning, TV and telephones, and it's all topped off with a lakeside pool, bar, two restaurants, a good curio shop and the only casino in town. ⑦.

Cutty Sark Hotel, (PO Box 80, Kariba; ☎061/2321 or 3314–6, fax 2575, *indmar@harare.iafrica.com*). Excellent value for money in quaintly furnished bungalows facing the lake; the hotel is friendly, with a large pool in lush gardens set in 72 acres of indigenous bush. There's a choice of bars and restaurants, but everyone, including the staff, are well into the holiday spirit, so don't expect snappy service. A good base to arrange activities, as a couple of car rental companies and several safari operators have desks here. ③.

Kariba Breezes, (PO Box 3, Kariba; ☎061/2433 or 2434, fax 2767). Slightly characterless resort, where you should ask for a lake view. The 43 modern, light and spacious double chalets have private verandahs and bathrooms. Most relaxed of the large lakeside establishments, its snack-bar terrace serves excellent burgers. Pool, and on-site marina where you can rent a boat with a driver. ④.

Lake View Inn, (Travel Centre, 93 Jason Moyo Ave, Harare ☎04/736644–5, fax 736646, *zimsuncro @zimsun.gaia.co.zw*; or direct ☎061/2411–2, fax 2329). Quieter and classier than the rest of the pack, although the rooms aren't exceptional, the inn sits above the lake some distance from the main cluster of big hotels and offers peaceful surroundings with superb views over the water from the large overhanging terrace – the perfect spot for breakfast or romantic sundowners. It's a steep climb down from the main hotel. ⑤.

Most High Hotel, Kariba Heights (PO Box 88, Kariba; ☎ & fax 061/2964–5, *mosthigh@samara.co.zw*). A squeaky-clean Christian-run hotel 2min walk from the shops and the Country Club. It might not have immediate access to the water but offers spectacular and panoramic lake views. Not a good choice for sundowners (the hotel is dry) or dirty weekends (couples must bring proof of being married to share a room). A large restaurant offers home-cooked meals and the garden has a pool, basketball court and braai area. If the strong Christian context doesn't bother you, you'll find it comfortable, homely and friendly. ⑤.

Zambezi Valley Hotel, Nyamhunga opposite Barclays Bank (PO Box 105, Kariba; ☎2994, fax 2926). Close to the airport and a totally different scene to the lakeside hotels, this offers a good venue to meet black Zimbabweans and listen to live music in the beer garden most weekends. Rooms are clean, en-suite, comfortable and most are air-conditioned, if a little dark and cluttered with furniture. A cultural centre next to the hotel puts on entertainment such as traditional music, marimba playing, dancing and braais, as well as displays on the history of the Zambezi Valley and local crafts. ③.

The Town

Nobody comes to Kariba for the town. It's often too hot to do anything other than lie around, have an iced something or other, and maybe rouse yourself to go on a cruise. If you can beat the torpor, then take in the **Santa Barbara Chapel**, built in memory of the workers who died during the construction of the dam, and have a look at the **dam wall** itself.

The **Njaya Cultural Village**, a few hundred metres southwest of the Mohombekombe shops behind the Shell garage, sells a selection of curios, but the main attraction is the performances (Wed & Sat 8–9.30pm) by local Batonga and Mozambican Chamunga dancers as well as marimba concerts. The westerly turn-off at the garage leads up to the **Observation Point**, from where you can see the wall in its entirety – 128m high and 579m wide at its base, with the pent-up Zambezi, when in flood, leaping through the gates to the gorge below. A small gathering of **curio sellers**

THE FALL AND RISE OF LAKE KARIBA

Many animals, and not a few people, died in the creation of **Lake Kariba**, so that **hydro-electric power** could be harnessed to feed industry in Zambia and Zimbabwe. The dam was, at the time, the largest in the world, and its size and strength remain awesome. Its arching form is like a vast, Roman load-bearing arch turned on its side; the convex shape absorbs the pressure, and the base, straining to spring apart, is solidly checked by the ancient gorge walls.

The Batonga, who suffered most of all by being shoved off their ancestral riverside lands into the harsh interior, were convinced that the wrathful river god **Nyaminyami** would destroy the dam project. In July 1957, the first confirmation of their belief was delivered, as a once-in-10,000-years storm saw the Zambezi burst through the coffer dam to destroy months of work. Later, the angry god whipped up a tempest, which swept away the Zimbabwe–Zambia roadbridge, and soon afterwards turned his attention to the suspension footbridge, which went the same way. When the rains stopped, Nyaminyami sent unusually murderous temperatures: workers died from heatstroke and the tools had to be carried in buckets of water. Eighteen men also perished when they fell into wet concrete during construction. The wall was, of course, eventually completed, but to some Batonga the battle isn't over – and there are nervous reports of cracks.

Since being built, the lake's biggest crisis has been the **drought** of the 1980s and early 1990s, which saw water levels sink below the level necessary to supply the country's hydroelectricity needs. Zimbabwe experienced frequent power cuts and in the end was obliged to buy in electricity from South Africa. By the mid-1990s, the reservoir was still only a quarter full, but all this changed after unusually **heavy rains** at the end of 1998 and beginning of 1999 in Angola and Zambia, the main catchment areas for the Zambezi, as well as high rainfall in minor catchments in Zimbabwe. By June 1999 the water level of Lake Kariba had risen just short of its maximum level of 489m. Much of the previously exposed shoreline became submerged and peninsulas such as Spurwing and Fothergill, which had both ceased to be islands in 1989, were once again cut off from the mainland.

The sudden rise of the water level could have a series of effects on the **lake ecology**. Fringe grassland, an important food source for game in winter when most of the mainland vegetation has desiccated, is now submerged, with the potential for widespread starvation among herbivores. The lakeshore was also the place where game used to congregate to feed or drink, leaving a large build-up of nutrients along the shore in the form of dung. Where previously this would have been recycled as nutrients for grass, a huge wealth of organic matter has now been released into the water, where it could fuel the growth of weeds and tip the chemical and ecological balance of the lake. Referred to as **eutrophication**, this process has the potential, if not controlled, to alter fish stocks seriously and capsize the fishing industry.

As for **tourism**, the lake now looks more spectacular than ever, but there's a distinct downside, because the grassy shore where game was most easily spotted has flooded. The current water's edge now consists of dense bush, scrub and woodland, which means that watching game from a boat isn't as the breeze it was for most of the 1990s. But as the level drops, which it's bound to do, this will improve. Despite the problems of a rising water level, the sluice gates were still closed in July 1999, as the lake authorities were reluctant to gamble on when the next good rains would come, particularly since much of the country relies on Lake Kariba for its water and electricity.

in the observation point car park sells mainly crochet tablecloths and bedspreads, but if you need a little extra help conquering the slopes of Kariba this is the best place to buy an intricately carved Nyaminyami (the fish-headed river god with snake's tail) walking stick. Other than that there is a good choice of carvings, straw hats and baskets. On the way to the vantage point you'll come across a display with a giant mural of Kariba dam with some interesting facts, and the Kariba **information bureau** (see

Information, p.120) has an office here where you can gen up on the local ecology and the people of the lake.

To **walk on the wall**, you have to cross the border into Zambia. The main road that goes past the Shell garage continues southwest and does a U-turn a couple of kilometres on, before reaching the border post. For a quick visit, just leave your passport with the border officials and collect it on your way back – no fees, long forms or currency declarations are involved.

The Santa Barbara Chapel

The dam's main construction contracts went to an Italian company, and thus the **Santa Barbara Chapel** (daily 7am–5pm; free) in Kariba Heights that commemorates those who died is dedicated to an Italian saint. The chapel is a poignant place, built in a circular form to represent the coffer dam, with a trellised front open to the elements. The church's adaptation to the climate is perhaps the most interesting thing about the building, but it's not honestly worth much effort to get to, except on Sunday mornings (7.45–9am), when the traditional singing of the mainly black congregation floats out.

The Wildlife Information Centre and Museum

The **Wildlife Information Centre and Museum** (daily 8.30am–4.30pm), run by the Zimbabwe Wildlife Society (ZWS), is definitely worth a visit. You can't miss the large thatched building on the Makuti road, just by the airport turn-off. Several **shops** sell crafts and curios including batiks, carvings, wind chimes, pottery and books. ZWS have their own **information centre** here, mostly displaying books, pamphlets and information on PEAK (Programme for Environmental Awareness in Kariba), a project to educate schools and the community about the sustainable use of local natural resources. A small display on anti-poaching has a large collection of snares and traps collected by rangers over the years, while upstairs the little **museum** (small entrance fee) has a couple of interesting cabinets with examples of local fauna and flora, a few stuffed birds and some small mammals. A separate section devoted to the lake provides an impressive and interesting summary of its ecology, particularly the impact of weeds on the fishing industry and a small display of stuffed and mounted fish. Refreshments and snacks are available in the teahouse and garden at the back, where you can also picnic.

Kariba activities

It's no surprise that most of the activities around Kariba centre around getting onto the lake; in addition, you have a choice of short cruises or longer trips that involve overnighting on the lake and seeing game. If you're short of time there's the option of one-day safaris that leave from Kariba. For fully fledged canoeing and walking safaris that start out from Kariba, see p.137 and pp.138-139.

Tours and one-day safaris

Chipembere Safaris (PO Box 9, Kariba; ☎ & fax 061/2946, *chipsaf@zambezi.net*). One-day foot safaris in the Matusadona National Park with licensed professional guide Steve Pope. Transfers from Kariba by speedboat make this ideal if you're short of time but want to take a walk on the wild side. Costs around US$45 per person (minimum four), including lunch and drinks.

Graeme Lemon Walking Safaris PO Box 281, Kariba (☎ & fax 061/2538, *lemon@samara.co.zw*). One-day excursions, featuring boating, walking and driving for US$90 including breakfast and lunch.

River Horse Safaris, *Kariba Breezes Hotel*, Kariba (☎ & fax 061/2422 or 2447, *riverhse@icon.co.zw*). Day-trips from Kariba to the Charara Safari Area with optional canoeing, a game walk and boat cruise from US$30 to US$85.

Safari Par Excellence, 26a Blakiston St/Josiah Chinamano Avenue, Harare (☎04/700911–2); or at the *Cutty Sark Hotel*, Kariba (☎061/3332). Four-in-one game drive, walk, canoe trip and return boat cruise from Kariba packed into one day for US$95.

Sobek, c/o Run Wild, 3rd Floor, Southampton Life Centre, Jason Moyo Avenue, Harare (☎04/795841, *runwild@africaonline.co.zw*); or PO Box 281, Kariba (☎ & fax 061/2538, *lemon@zambezi.net*). One-day 22km canoe trail through the Kariba Gorge, including transfers and lunch for US$75.

UTC, desks at *Cutty Sark, Caribbea Bay*, and *Lake View Inn* (☎061/3312, 2376 or 2662). One of the oldest operators in the business offering daily visits to the Heights, the Dam Wall and Observation Point (US$12), and game drives to the Kaburi Wilderness (from US$20) with pick-ups from all lake-front hotels.

Cruises

Sundowner cruises are a Kariba institution: you can enjoy gorgeous sunsets, beer in hand, after the day's heat has subsided. Having booked, you'll be driven to the harbour from the *Cutty Sark, Lake View Inn* or *Caribbea Bay* hotels. **Full-day cruises** to Fothergill and Spurwing islands are the only ones that offer any serious prospect of seeing very much in the way of wildlife. These trips also include a stop for lunch and the chance to swim in safe, deep waters well away from the shore – and from bilharzia parasites or the snapping jaws of crocs and hippos.

River Bank Cruises, *Cutty Sark Hotel* (PO Box 337, Kariba; ☎ & fax 061/3141). Pretty similar programme to UTC, but a touch more expensive, with better food, usually braais.

UTC *Lake View Inn, Caribbea Bay* and *Cutty Sark Hotel* (☎061/3312, 2376 or 2662). Daily cruises from US$8 for 90min to US$30 for a day on the lake, as well as a full-day trip (5hr) that takes in Fothergill and Spurwing islands.

Houseboats

Houseboating is a great way to see the lake at your leisure; you can sleep on the roof under the stars or in a comfortable cabin, and meander down creeks for fishing, game viewing, birdwatching or just idling with a drink on the water. Boats go with drivers and, generally, six to twelve passengers on board (some take up to fifty), provide all cutlery, crockery and linen and usually have a splash pool, sun deck, plenty of board games and a well-stocked bar on board.

Over a hundred houseboats are available for rental in Kariba and the number is growing. Many conservationists want this controlled, because the boats contribute substantially to **pollution** in the lake and can be an eyesore in the picturesque spots of the shoreline, which is where they invariably moor. You may even find you can't get a decent snap of the shoreline and wildlife because, wherever you point your camera, your viewfinder is cluttered with houseboats.

Departures are from one of the three main harbours – Marineland next to *Caribbea Bay*, the Kariba Breezes Marina and Andorra – all good places to gather information about the boats, sailing times and prices, as is the publicity bureau at the Observation Point (see Information, p.120). **Costs** vary from US$30 to US$300 per person per day, depending on what's included in the package and the level of luxury you want. One of the best budget deals is offered by Wildlife Expeditions at Possum Lodge, 7 Deary Ave, Belgravia, Harare (☎ & fax 04/722804, *wildlife@icon.co.zw*), who arrange **backpacker specials** on a private houseboat at US$130 per person for three days, with all meals and some drinks included. A walking safari from the boat into Matusadona is available at an extra cost. Two other reputable agents in **Harare** who can organize houseboat rental are Run Wild, 3rd Floor, Southampton Life Centre, Jason Moyo Avenue (☎04/795841, *runwild@africaonline.co.zw*), and Rhino Rendezvous, 169 Second Street Extension, Belgravia (☎04/745642–8), which has the most comprehensive selection of houseboats in town.

At **Kariba** two friendly and helpful agents based at Andorra Harbour are Kariba Boating and Safaris, PO Box 266, Kariba (☎ & fax 061/2227 or 2922–3), and Anchorage Marina, PO Box 61, Kariba (☎061/2245 or 2280), which can also be booked through their Harare representative at 1 Eton Close, Northwood (☎04/301860). Once on a houseboat, you usually stay on board till you return to Kariba, as the law restricts cruisers to the Kariba basin and for safety reasons you're only allowed to wander within 50m of your boat. If you're keen on a combined houseboat and walking safari, you'll need to hire an armed professional guide, who is licensed to take you outside the fifty-metre cordon.

Sailing and paddle-steamer safaris

Sailing on the lake and off its shoreline is a marvellous way to see game, as the silence of the yacht lets you get extremely close to wild animals. Sail Safaris, 4 Cheshire Rd, Mount Pleasant, Harare (☎04/339123, fax 339045, *sailsaf@harare.iafrica.com*), which also has a desk at the *Cutty Sark Hotel*, offers four- and seven-day **safaris** during April and October on a catamaran that accommodates up to six passengers. You can learn to sail with a professional skipper on board or, if you're over 23 and an experienced sailor (you'll need proof), you captain your own boat. Nights are spent beached on the shore, you sleep in the cabin and meals are prepared by the crew. A central deck and a large forward trampoline offer good helming positions for birdwatching, sunbathing or fishing. The **cost** for a four-day excursion, including airport transfers, park entrance fees, meals and soft drinks, starts at around US$400 per person for six passengers (rising to US$650 if there are only two of you) and around US$570 for seven days (rising to US$955 for two people). No children under the age of 8 are allowed.

If you can't see lions on the Mississippi you can always catch a **paddle steamer** on Kariba. *The Southern Belle Zambezi Paddle Steamer*, 3 Bath Rd, Belgravia, Harare (☎04/791131 or 739908, fax 720188, *sbelle@id.co.zw*), is an opulent vessel with 22 en-suite and air-conditioned double cabins. The interior is grand, dinners come with silver service and a sun deck with a pool provides the chance to idle or swim off the extravagance. Scheduled three-day cruises leave every month (enquire for details) and you moor each night at Spurwing, Tashinga and Nyodza, where you can disembark for activities such as fishing or walks, drives and speedboat cruises to view game. A fully inclusive three-night package costs US$325 per person.

Eating, drinking and nightlife

Considering that Lake Kariba is Zimbabwe's major fishing ground, it's ironical that there is very little **fresh fish** about. If you eat fish here, chances are it was caught in the lake, frozen in town and sent straight to Harare, from where it would have to be reimported. One of the few places you can buy fresh fish is Irving and Johnson (I&J), a large fishing company on the lake near Mahombekombe Spar. If you fancy a quick snack, try a plate of the local speciality, crunchy fried *kapenta* (tiny fish). The other, more expensive, regional dish is **crocodile tail**, a surprisingly light and delicate meat.

The best places for snacks, refreshments and à la carte meals are the **hotels**. Boasting the best views across the lake to the Matusadona Range, the *Lakeview Inn* terrace is worth visiting for a drink or for their gargantuan breakfasts. Kariba's only decent **takeaway** joint is the massively popular *Polly's* (Mon & Tues 8am–5pm, Thurs–Sun 8am–7pm) at Windsor Diesel, where you'll find reasonably priced burgers, pies, sandwiches, chicken and chips and their excellent, if disappointingly small, pizzas. A few tables and chairs outside provide seating for customers, but watch out for the notorious thieves – baboons and monkeys – who will do their best to snatch your dinner. For **sadza and relish**, you'll find a number of places around the Mahombekombe and Nyamhunga market areas, of which *The Stew Pot*, behind the Barclays Bank in Mahombekombe, does dead-cheap takeaway *sadza* with meat stew or fish.

In **Kariba Heights**, the *Fox on Toast*, principally an excellent curio shop with unusual crafts, also serves great home-made cheesecake with a free cup of filter coffee on their verandah, while the great drawcard at the *Country Club* (Tues–Sun for lunch and dinner; non-members' entrance fee US$0.25), in the same vicinity, is its fabulous views over the lake, making it ideal for a sundowner. Despite the exclusive-sounding name, the ageing vinyl tables give the appearance of a students' union bar, but the beers are the cheapest in town, the food terrific, and the service polite and friendly.

In a similar vein, but right **on the lake** at the GDI Harbour, is the *Yacht Club* (daily 7am–11pm), a favourite hangout for white locals. Totally unpretentious, you can get cheap meals at this relaxed place that's more about beer and good cheer than slick boats; it features a large pool, trampoline and deck above the garden.

For campers, self-catering is the cheap option and the most central supermarket (daily 6am–7.30pm) is next to Windsor Diesel Total garage, which has **basic supplies** and is handy if you're driving through town. For a bigger choice of fruit, vegetables and groceries, try the markets in the high-density suburbs, or the moderately stocked Spar supermarket in Mahombekombe and the much bigger one in Nyamhunga (both daily 8am–7pm). The Heights also has a small supermarket (Mon, Tues, Thurs & Fri 8.30am–1pm & 2–4.30pm, Wed & Sat 8.30am–1pm) and a swimwear boutique that curiously also sells fruit, vegetables, snacks and basic groceries (Mon–Fri 7.30am–5pm, Sat & Sun 8am–1pm).

Listings

Airlines Air Zimbabwe should be contacted through their Harare office (☎04/705175 or 707926), as should Air Zambezi (☎04/729831 or 734824, fax 706291 or 708119, *airzamb@harare.iafrica.com*).

Automobile Association, represented by Kariba Service Station (☎061/2918).

Banks Barclays Bank has branches in Kariba Heights; in Mahombekombe, opposite the Swift Depot; and in Nyamhunga.

Bureau de change Heights (daily 7.30am–4.30pm). All the hotels offer bureau de change facilities, but rates are often not as good as at the bank or the office at the Heights.

Car rental Hertz has desks at the *Cutty Sark Hotel* (☎061/2321), *Caribbea Bay* (☎061/2452–7 ext 1517) and *Lake View Inn* (☎061/2411 or 2662), while Europcar has an office at Windsor Diesel Total garage (☎061/3318) and *Caribbea Bay* (☎061/2573).

Doctors, of whom there are only two, are listed under Medical practitioners at the beginning of the Kariba section of the telephone directory. They are Dr Knight, 11 Libuyu Ave (☎061/2819), and Dr Masvosva in Nyamhunga (☎061/2989).

Emergencies general ☎999; ambulance ☎994; police 995.

Ferries Kariba Ferries, Andorra Harbour (PO Box 70, Kariba; ☎061/2460; or at their Harare head office ☎04/614162–7; or in South Africa through Reservations Frontline in Johannesburg (☎011/789 2440, fax 886 4837, *rfline@iafrica.com*), which runs comfortable express ferries across the lake. DDF (District Development Fund) Shipping Services, next to Peter's Point by the dam wall (☎061/2694 or 3207, fax 2349), operates cheap, basic services across the lake.

Laundry next to Kariba House Boats near the *MOTH* campsite.

Pharmacy in the Heights (Mon, Tues, Thurs & Fri 8.30am–1pm & 2–4.30pm, Wed & Sat 8.30am–1pm).

Post office in Heights and Mahombekombe (Mon–Fri 8am–3.30pm, Sat 8–11.30am).

Taxis Pass Taxis (☎061/2866) is the only radio taxi company in town, and you'll find cabs waiting at all the resorts. UTC has offices at *Caribbea Bay*, *Cutty Sark* and *Lake View Inn*, and runs between all the resorts.

Matusadona National Park

It is the **Matusadona Mountains** that form a backdrop to all those picturesque shots of Kariba sunsets, with drowned treetops in the foreground. The

MATUSADONNA NATIONAL PARK (6am–6pm; day entry US$10, week entry US$20; prior accommodation bookings obligatory for overnight trips), which harbours all the big game, borders the southern lakeshore and rolls over the Zambezi Escarpment into wild, largely inaccessible hills and valleys. The lakeshore with its inlets, gorges, bays and islands is the most easily reached area of the park, but there are also rewarding walks (with guides) up the river valleys, where you'll find ebonies, acacias, thick jesse bush, mopane trees and plenty of game, including the park's 250 lions.

Most people experience Matusadona by splurging on one of the excellent **safari camps** bordering the National Park, from where you can see the massive dry season herds of buffalo and elephant and a dazzling array of other lakeshore animals and birds. Alternatively, a handful of safari companies, some based at Kariba, organize **camping, walking** or **canoeing safaris** (see p.137 & pp.138–139) in Matusadona and around the Eastern Basin. The attraction of walking through the park lies in following the rivers, which run into Lake Kariba and attract a great diversity of game.

It's not really worth coming to Matusadona for just one night, so take adequate supplies and book as far in advance as possible through National Parks (see Accommodation on p.133). Without transport or a fishing rod, your activities will be restricted to lazing around the camp, watching birds and beasts wandering through. A National Parks scout may be available to take you walking, but they are often out dealing with poachers or shooting crop-destroying "problem animals" in adjacent communal lands.

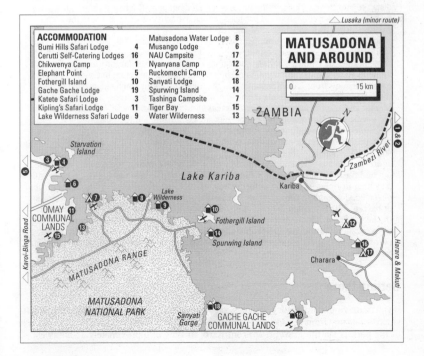

ACCOMMODATION

Bumi Hills Safari Lodge	4	Matusadona Water Lodge	8
Cerutti Self-Catering Lodges	16	Musango Lodge	6
Chikwenya Camp	1	NAU Campsite	17
Elephant Point	5	Nyanyana Camp	12
Fothergill Island	10	Ruckomechi Camp	2
Gache Gache Lodge	19	Sanyati Lodge	18
Katete Safari Lodge	3	Spurwing Island	14
Kipling's Safari Lodge	11	Tashinga Campsite	7
Lake Wilderness Safari Lodge	9	Tiger Bay	15
		Water Wilderness	13

MATUSADONA AND AROUND

0   15 km

THE LAKE ECOLOGY

Matusadona and Chete Safari Area received some of the five thousand animals saved, in 1959, from the flooding Zambezi Valley. There were pitiful stories of animals moving to higher and higher ground as the waters rose, and being besieged on shrinking islands with diminishing food supplies: Starvation Island had one of the biggest concentrations of stranded animals. Many thousands died and much of the money for the project (one of the earliest wildlife mass appeals) arrived too late. But **Operation Noah**, mounted by conservationist Rupert Fothergill, fought hard against the inevitable. Not only big game, but also the less obvious snakes and tortoises, were bundled off to the mainland. Charles Nicholls' book *Operation Noah* recounts the story.

Nearly 5200 square kilometres of wilderness died with the valley. Desolate trees, still with branches poking from the water thirty years on, bear vivid testimony to the destruction. But all is not gloom and doom: a new ecology has replaced the old in a turn of events that shows the resilience of the natural world. Fish eagles and darter colonies nest in the branches and the decaying wood feeds underwater life. Buffalo and elephants graze on green swards of lakeside torpedo grass (*Panicum repens*), which miraculously saved the day for the young lake slowly being choked by notorious Kariba weed. In this crisis, weed-eating grasshoppers were introduced and arsenic-based poisons considered to clear the floating strangler which blocked all navigation in the west. Mysteriously, it began to die off on its own, piling up on newly barren shores and creating a mulch in which torpedo grass rapidly seeded. Torpedo grass is able to survive long periods underwater, yet it also thrives when water levels sink during the dry season or droughts. The grass is gradually exposed to provide lush grazing for wildlife forced down to the lake when inland grazing and water becomes exhausted. Once the rains begin, the animals disperse into the interior and the grass is covered again by the rising water. This movement to the water echoes an old pre-lake pattern, when game came down to the Zambezi riverine forest, as it still does at Mana.

Aquatic life is rich. Apart from tigerfish, people catch bream, pink lady, chessa, barbel, mudsucker, eel, bottlenose and huge vundu. Freshwater sponges and tiny jellyfish are some of the less familiar species. The Zambezi provided a habitat for the same fish now found in Kariba, with the exception of the tiny sardine-like kapenta, introduced for commercial fishing from Lake Tanganyika in the 1960s. At night you'll see myriad lights on the lake from kapenta rigs attracting the fish into deep water nets, and you can walk around and see the kapenta drying on racks in Mahombekombe; it's cheap and sold in big plastic bags throughout the country as an accompaniment to *sadza*.

Trawling is a tough job – contract-based, wet, uncomfortable and dangerous. Fishermen working for commercial companies have a more reliable income, though it's still low. The gill-net fishermen, however – freelancers after the big fish – live along the shoreline and are plagued by completely unpredictable catches. Some waters are fished out and the strict allocation of fishing territory prevents them moving elsewhere, with poaching in richer waters an unfortunate consequence. The fishing villages are rather deserted, despondent places; wives and families generally live inland, coaxing crops out of barren soil. The catch is dried and salted, and sold in communal areas surrounding the lake, or else sold fresh to commercial boats that do the rounds of the camps, usually for a pittance. To address the problems of distribution, low prices and fishing rights, a number of fishing cooperatives have been formed, some successfully increasing profits for their members.

Getting there

If you're **driving**, only the dry season is recommended to attempt the 468-kilometre gut-shaking journey from Harare, and you'll need 4WD or a high-clearance vehicle. Access to the park is via the gravel road from Karoi to Binga. Approximately 150km west of

Karoi, a signposted turn-off leads into the park through the Vulunduli gate. With your own vehicle, you could easily and rewardingly combine a trip to Matusadona with Chizarira. One way of getting to Matusadona, but a long shot if you don't have a car, is to catch one of the **ferries** that runs across the lake. The DDF ferry runs from Kariba's Andorra Harbour, and a more comfortable and more expensive service (daily except Wed) is operated by Kariba Ferries between Kariba and Mlibizi (see box on p.120).

Accommodation

The only cheap way of spending a night in Matusadona is by camping at the **National Parks campsites**. Apart from the three exclusive parks lodges, you won't find the afford-able chalets you get at many of Zimbabwe's other national parks. The most comfortable way to see Lake Kariba and the Matusadona wildlife is in one of the **bush camps** on the fringes of the park. These are stylish, thatched places with swimming pools that, unlike the Kariba resorts, are able to offer superb game watching, walking and cruising or canoeing. There is daily transport to all camps, by air or boat. Other options for getting into Matusadona are mooring offshore in a **houseboat** (see p.128) or joining one of the **organized safaris** that explore the park on foot or by canoe (see p.137).

National Parks campsites and lodges

Only a few visitors make it to the National Parks **campsites** (①) at **Sanyati** or the very appealing main one at **Tashinga** (6am–6pm; ☎061/2577), the park headquarters, which is bigger than Sanyati and has an airstrip. Both camps have tents for rent, but Tashinga is better stocked and also rents canoes. In either case you'd be advised to make sure they've got what you need and also to book before arriving. Neither has shops or fuel supplies, so bring all you need. Tashinga can be a thrilling place, where you can see game without having to go anywhere: rhinos and elephants sometimes cruise through camp, bushbuck raid the rubbish bins, Egyptian slit-faced bats roost in the toilets, and the birdlife is quite outstanding.

In addition, three fabulous National Parks camps line the shore at **Ume**, **Muuyu** and **Mbalabala**, designed for the exclusive use of one party each (lodges up to twelve people US$40, campsites US$12), for a minimum of a week's stay. For **reservations**, write

---

SANYATI BRIDGE CAMPSITE

Some 124km west of Karoi, en route to Matusadona or Binga, the **Sanyati Bridge campsite** is more than a convenient overnight stop. A Campfire community project, it occupies a tranquil spot overlooking the Sanyati River and has panoramic views of the surrounding mountains and the Sanyati Valley. Game is plentiful in the area, as are love-ly walks of 3–15km to Mawindo and Gandavaroyi falls, the Den of Baboons and Manyenyedzi Dam, which provides excellent barbel and bream fishing. A guide can accompany you, or take a ten-minute stroll to the river (look out for crocs). The **campsite** (①) is a cleared site amongst the endless mopane, but there are also three basic but immaculate thatched mud **rondavels** with two beds and bedding (①). Facilities include a basic kitchen area with a primus stove, some utensils and braai area, a bucket shower with hot water and a long-drop toilet, but most impressive is the fridge-freezer in the office, where you can buy wonderfully cold beers. They also sell soft drinks, crisps and toothpaste. Staff are friendly and the place well cared for; if you enjoy roughing it you could easily hang around this congenial place for a couple of days. To get here from Karoi, head north just before the Sanyati bridge, following the clearly signposted road that reaches the campsite after 1km.

to the Central Booking Office, Department of National Parks, Box CY140, Causeway, Harare, or, better still, go to their headquarters at the Botanic Gardens in the capital (Mon–Fri 7.45am–4.45pm; ☎04/706077–8, fax 726089, *NationalParks@gta.gov.zw*) or their office at Peter's Point in Kariba (☎061/2257, fax 2938).

Luxury lodges and camps

The most luxurious access to Lake Kariba and the Matusadona wildlife is via the **bush camps** or **luxury lodges** situated along the southern shores or on islands in one of the two bays that flank the national park. *Fothergill, Spurwing, Gache-Gache* and *Sanyati* lodges, to the east of the park, are referred to as the **Sanyati Bay lodges**, while the others are known as the **Ume Bay lodges**, after the inlet that defines the western side of Matusadona.

Transfers, either by air or boat, are arranged at an additional charge when you book. Depending on the distance from Kariba town, air transfer prices hover around US$60 one way, and boat transfers are only marginally cheaper. All the lodges below operate full-board **tariffs** (unless otherwise stated), and the rate (per person per night) normally includes activities such as game drives, cruises, walks and canoeing. The tariff can vary considerably between high season (May–Nov) and low season (Dec–April).

Bumi Hills Safari Lodge, Zimbabwe Sun Hotels; direct PO Box 41, Kariba (☎061/2352–3, fax 2354). The oldest and best-known lodge in the area, more like a chic hotel (forty beds) than a bush camp, situated way above the lake overlooking the water, with game coming regularly to drink. Its open layout with long corridors, arches, tiled floors and abundant cast-iron chandeliers evokes a Roman villa and serves as a cool refuge from the often scorching summer days. Has a small natural history museum, a shady garden with a pool and a large terrace bar and dining area, plus walking trails and game viewing by boat or 4WD. US$280.

Chura Bay Bush Camp, adjacent to and administered by *Tiger Bay* (see p.135). The least expensive private camp around the Matusadona, with accommodation in six two-bedded tents under thatch sharing ablutions as well as a dining and lounge area. *Chura* is in a secluded bay about 1km from *Tiger Bay*'s main lodge in very tranquil surroundings that see loads of passing game. You can self-cater here or pay a little extra for three-course meals and a full breakfast. Self-catering US$20, full board US$30; game activities extra.

Elephant Point, Run Wild (☎04/795841–4, fax 795845–6, *runwild@africaonline.co.zw*); or Zambezi Expeditions, Box 281, Kariba (☎ & fax 061/2538, *lemon@zambezi.net*). Small camp with fourteen beds in luxury tents on raised platforms overlooking Sibilobilo Lagoon. Real bush adventure with some of the best professional guides in the business to enhance your experience of the prolific birdlife and game. Boating, canoeing, walking and fishing as well as visits to a local Batonga village are included in the rate. Low season US$190, high season US$230.

Fothergill Island, Zimbabwe Sun Hotels; direct Private Bag 2081, Kariba; (☎061/2253, fax 2240). One of the largest lodges in the area, 35km from Kariba, caters for forty guests. Fothergill, like its neighbour, Spurwing, became a peninsula joined to the mainland in 1989 after the level of the lake dropped due to successive seasons of poor rains, but since the good rains of the late 1990s is once again an island. Surrounded by indigenous woodland, it has all the trimmings of an upmarket camp, including a large pool, an excellent reference library and a selection of wildlife videos, but lacks the personal touch of the smaller establishments. US$265.

Gache Gache Lodge, Landela Safaris, Travel Plaza, 29 Mazowe St, Harare (☎04/734044–6, fax 708119, *res@landela.co.zw*); direct through PO Box 370, Kariba (☎061/2902 or 2905). The most laidback and best camouflaged of the Sanyati Bay lodges overlooks the Gache Gache Estuary in a Campfire concession that adjoins the Charara Safari area, providing immediate access to the surrounding mopane woodlands and Zambezi Escarpment. Accommodation is in twenty well-spaced, open-fronted cottages under thatch. Night game drives, canoeing and fishing are some of the activities available and the birdwatching is outstanding. Since this is the only unfenced camp in the area, game wanders through and grazes close to the lodge, particularly at night, making it thrilling, but unsuitable for small children. Low season US$220, high season US$275.

Katete Safari Lodge, Zimbabwe Sun Hotels; direct through PO Box 41, Kariba (☎061/2807–8, fax 2892). Sixteen twin-bedded luxury chalets and a two-storey main lodge set above the lake with expansive views. Situated close to Bumi Hills and 60km southwest of Kariba town in protected state land, its surrounding environment is mopane scrub and shade has been created by placing all facilities under thatch and by planting fast-growing fig trees. The interiors have the whiff of an English manor, using Victorian-style furnishings and fabrics, cast-iron bathtubs and framed etchings decorating whitewashed stone walls. Despite the formal interiors, you're never allowed to forget where you are, as wild vegetation encroaches and there are no manicured lawns. Game walks and drives, boat cruises, fishing and cultural tours to traditional villages form part of the package. US$285.

Kipling's Safari Lodge, Zimbabwe Sun Hotels (Travel Centre, Jason Moyo Avenue, Harare; ☎04/736644–5, fax 736646). Pompous twenty-bed lodge opened in 1996 close to the mouth of the Ume River with views of the lake and the Matusadona Mountains. Despite the use of natural materials and standard ethnic motifs, the place seems detached from its natural surroundings, while individual rondavels, named after Rudyard Kipling's poems, sport four-poster beds with carved headboards, adding to the grandiosity. The viewing deck has a broad wooden rail etched with animal spoor for identification and there are all the usual activities including a trip to a crocodile farm and a local village. Low season US$226, high season US$290; air transfer US$129 return.

Lake Wilderness Safari Lodge, Buffalo Safaris, PO Box 113, Kariba (☎061/2645, 3041–3, fax 2827, *buffalo@harare.iafrica.com*). Pontoon safari lodges, floating in a game-rich bay within Matusadona National Park occasionally moved along the shoreline to follow wildlife, accommodate eight to twelve people below, and the upper deck serves for game viewing, dining and sunbathing. Depending on the season you may be able to assist in wildlife research, a unique opportunity to learn about the local ecology and game. Walks, game drives, fishing, boating and canoeing are included in the rate and a minimum of three nights must be booked to take part in all activities. Fully inclusive high-season rate US$168, low season US$137; boat transfer US$75 return.

Musango Lodge, Private Bag 2019, Kariba (☎061/2899 or 2391, fax 3242, *musango@mail.pci.co.zw*). Comfortable walk-in tents under thatch on a small island close to the Ume River between Bumi Hills and Tashinga, with views of the lake and outside showers built into rocks. Operated in partnership with the local community through the Campfire project, it offers highly personalized service under the direction of professional guide and ex-warden of Matusadona, Steve Edwards, whose priority is to retain the natural integrity of the island, so that buildings blend into their environment. Guests dine at a communal circular table, although private candlelit dinners on a pontoon can be arranged. Trips to Matusadona are part of the package, and specialized bird walks and game drives are on hand. The place is full of fossils and dinosaur finds from the Kariba area – a product of Steve's obsession with paleontology. Low season US$220, high season US$260.

Sanyati Lodge (☎04/722233 or 720291, fax 720360, *sanyati@icon.co.zw*). One of Zimbabwe's top lodges, with stone-and-thatch buildings, on the steep slopes of the Zambezi Escarpment at the mouth of the Sanyati Gorge. The entire lodge was rebuilt in 1997 with meticulous attention to detail. Features of the air-conditioned chalets are solid mahogany doors and cane furniture, brass fittings and plush white cushions, cast-iron bathtubs, separate showers built into the rock walls and private verandahs with canvas hammocks stretched between trees. Excellent seven-course dinners are served on the wooden deck and you can pass spare moments in the small library or watching satellite TV. A posh place, it dines out on the fact that it has hosted the likes of Prince Philip, but the atmosphere may prove a little frosty for some. No children under 12. Low season US$195, high season US$290.

Spurwing Island, PO Box 101, Kariba (☎061/2466 or 2269, fax 2301, *spurwing@zambezi.net*). Started as a fishing retreat by white tobacco farmers, *Spurwing* is now unquestionably one of the best lodges, a casual friendly place with views from all accommodation. The eleven twin-bedded tents under thatch, six stone-and-thatch twin cabins and three chalets are quite close together, which may impinge on your privacy but is ideal if you enjoy a social scene. Like Fothergill, Spurwing became an island again in February 1999, after a decade of being joined to the mainland. The camp is surrounded by an electric fence and it's one of the few Matusadona lodges that welcomes children. Meals and the usual activities, including good fishing, are included in the rate, but drinks and laundry are not. US$230, under-12s half price, under-3s free.

Tiger Bay, Conquest Tours, 2 King George Court, King George Road, Avondale, Harare (☎ & fax 04/308960, *conquest@samara.co.zw*); or direct (☎061/2569 or 2709, *Tigerbay@pci.co.zw*). Least expensive and most relaxed of all the Kariba lakeshore lodges, situated in the Ume Estuary with terrifically beautiful shoreline gardens of dense subtropical vegetation and lots of mature indigenous trees and a large pool. Accommodation is in A-frames, and the main lodge has a cosy upstairs bar and lounge, all under thatch with a dining terrace. Despite suffering from neglect, it's a comfortable and convivial place and offers all the usual game activities, with particular attention to fishing. Less expensive still is *Chura Bay*, its sister camp (see p.134). Full board US$80 (including activities US$150), children half-price.

Water Wilderness, Wilderness Safaris, PO Box 288, Victoria Falls, Elephant's Walk (☎013/3371–3, fax 4224 or 5942, *wildlodges@telconet.co.zw*). Interesting and unusual lodge consisting of five floating wooden chalets (four twin-bedded and one double), rebuilt in 1999, each with its own bathroom and verandah, just off the shoreline of Matusadona National Park. Guests either canoe or commute by means of the camp's motorized pontoon between their accommodation and the "mother ship", which houses the dining area, bar and viewing-deck-cum-lounge. A professional guide is available to conduct game-viewing activities, as well as a cordon bleu chef, who can cater for vegetarians. Surrounded by water but close to the mainland, this is a great place to see game and birds, but the confinement could lead to cabin fever. No children under 14. Jan–June US$250, July–Dec US$325.

Many of the places listed here fall under the central management of **Zimbabwe Sun Hotels**, who are based at the Travel Centre, 93 Jason Moyo Ave, Harare (☎04/736644–5, fax 736646, *zimsuncro@zimsun.gaia.co.zw*); where local addresses are given, they can also be contacted directly.

The Park

You'll certainly see **elephants** drinking and frolicking in the water, and, if you're lucky, swimming. Most animals, including – surprisingly enough – **lions**, can swim well; one lioness was seen swimming 30m into the lake in hot pursuit of a fleeing impala. Elephants swim using their trunks as snorkels. One remarkable (and photographed) story records an epic thirty-hour swim by two young bull elephants who crossed the lake from Matusadona, and passed Spurwing to land on a beach between two hotels at Kariba. Altruistic, even when exhausted, the one in front inflated his lungs for buoyancy, while the other placed his front feet on the leader's back and did the paddling. Every hour or so they swapped over and finally made it, trunks and legs white from long immersion. The conclusion was that they were following ancient migration routes long since cut off, but still patterned into their memories.

In 1984 Matusadona was declared an **Intensive Protection Zone** (IPZ) for black rhinos that were facing extinction due to poaching. There are now believed to be fifty of the animals, making this the most likely place you'll see them in the wild in Zimbabwe. Tashinga is the base for the **baby rhino project**, where injured or orphaned animals are given refuge until they're old enough or well enough to fend for themselves, when they're released back into the park. All the private lodges in the area include a trip to the sanctuary among their excursions and you may even get the chance to feed a rhino toddler. In 1994, several **cheetahs** were relocated from the lowveld, as it was thought they'd thrive in the open grassland along the lake's foreshore. Sadly, three were killed when the plane bringing them in crashed, but the others are doing well.

Many people come to Matusadona to **fish**, particularly for the fierce **tigerfish** you'll undoubtedly see mounted in hotel bars – glassy-eyed and open-mouthed to display their razor teeth. Prime fishing months are September and October, when Kariba hosts an international tiger contest. The big thing about tigerfish is their fighting ability: they make determined rushes, followed by an impressive leap from the water to shake the hook. **Sanyati Gorge**, a narrow tear in the map on the eastern boundary of the park, is a creek navigable for about 12km and has a reputation for having plenty of tigerfish just waiting for combat.

Kariba to Kanyemba: canoeing the Zambezi

Gliding for a few days down the Zambezi through stunning wilderness areas is one of Zimbabwe's great travel experiences: spend the money and steel your nerves.

CANOEING AND WALKING SAFARIS

There are few roads in the Matusadona, making it a superb place for **hiking** and **canoeing**, with an excellent chance of encountering wildlife.

Buffalo Safaris, PO Box 113, Kariba (☎061/2645 or 3041–3, fax 2827, *buffalo@harare.iafrica.com*). Hans van der Heiden, an ex-game ranger and hunter who is a professional guide, has houseboats along the Matusadona National Park's shore, which he uses as bases for safaris that include walking, fishing and lakeside game viewing by canoe.

Graeme Lemon Walking Safaris, PO Box 281, Kariba (☎ & fax 061/2538, *lemon@samara.co.zw*). One of Zimbabwe's top professional hunter-guides runs four-day/three-night walking safaris in the Matusadona and canoe trips to order. Shorter trips, including one-day excursions, are also available by arrangement. US$200 per day.

Khangela Safaris, PO Box FM 296, Famona, Bulawayo (mobile ☎091/234676 or 346630, *scott@gatorzw.com*). Walking adventures in Matusadona alone, or combined with other national parks, led by energetic professional guide, Mike Scott. Rate fully inclusive of meals and road transfers: US$130 per person per day. Group discounts.

Safari Par Excellence, 26a Blakiston St/Josiah Chinamano Avenue, Harare (☎04/700911–2); or at the *Cutty Sark Hotel*, Kariba (☎061/3332). Large long-established company that runs Matusadona Wilderness Trails accompanied by professional guides from April to November, either as self-contained backpacking and camping trips (US$160) or walks to and from semi-permanent tented camps with vehicle support (US$230). Return boat transfer US$80.

Sengwa Sanyati Camp, Craig McCrae, Sengwa Safaris, c/o Zambezi Safari & Travel, Kariba Heights behind the supermarket opposite the Town Council (☎061/2532 or 3351, fax 2291, *sengwa@pci.co.zw* or *info@zambezi.com*). The most luxurious of the Matusadona walking safaris, this is based at a temporary tented camp under bamboo shelters. Basic, but comfortable, the tents have private verandahs with views over the lake, and great meals are cooked over an open fire. The friendly team is led by Craig McCrae and professional guide Gary Winggate, who takes you on game walks and drives, or game viewing along the shore by speedboat. Fully inclusive rate US$200 per person per day. Return boat transfer.

Depending on the depth of your pocket and your adrenaline reserves, you can take on the whole course, from **Kariba to Kanyemba**, in nine days, or do a portion of the river in three or four. Once on a trip, in theory you won't come across other canoes as each party is allocated a slot, but it's not unknown for trips to leave too early or too late. In two-person canoes, moving with the current, paddling isn't too strenuous, although it can be very hot from November to February, and in August and September strong winds can make it tough going.

Being in a silent vessel is a great way to approach game. You can get right up to watering elephants and skim past grazing buffalo, heads rising quizzically as you pass by. Herds of antelope splash through the shallows from one sandbank to the next and, if you're lucky, you'll see lions on the bank shading under an acacia or mahogany. The water itself is exquisite, changing colour and texture during the day. And of course there are fabulous sunsets.

You don't need to have had previous canoeing experience, but obviously it helps; you may feel rather vulnerable setting off on this massive river having just signed an indemnity form. Take a hat, sunglasses, loads of sunscreen and a *kikoi* for your legs – the sun reflected off the water is fierce. However, the **pace** is leisurely, with frequent stops for campfire meals and walks on the banks; some guides allow swimming in shallow places they regard as safe from crocodiles. **Camping** is usually on sandy islands where there is less game, although you're still sure to be regaled with the sounds of the African night as you lie under your mosquito net close to the fire: lions and hyenas calling, something being chased in the grass, baboons shrieking in alarm and hippos stomping around. In a very rare incident in 1992, a tourist was attacked by a lion which had crossed from the mainland, with Zambezi water levels exceptionally low from the drought.

You'll certainly see all the hippos and crocodiles you ever wanted to. **Crocodiles** are generally very shy creatures, slithering off the bank as you approach, but when they fancy a snack they can also be ruthless and effective hunters. Make sure you listen when your guide tells you to avoid a particular stretch of water. To avoid **hippos** you should steer very close to the bank and shallows when passing – they always make for the deep water. One or two territorial old bulls can make fearsome displays on occasion, but the canoe leaders know the channels where they lurk and warn you beforehand that Mad

ZAMBEZI CANOEING AND WALKING SAFARIS

The operators listed below use experienced and licensed (but unarmed) **canoe guides**; they are allowed to take you on the water, as well as on walks on the riverbanks, but are not allowed to wander more than 50m from the water or from where your canoe is moored. This can be a bit frustrating on days when you don't have to paddle more than 25km, which can be quite quickly covered, and have long rest periods on the riverbank, but can't fill your time with a wilderness hike. However, most have a good knowledge of birdlife and flora and fauna and carry reference books. The Chirundu–Mana trip takes place year-round, but longer safaris, such as Chirundu–Kanyemba, only from March to December. The variation in prices between different companies is usually to do with the level of participation in setting up camp, the quality of food and service, and amount of alcohol provided. It's also worth noting that many companies drop their prices in low season (Nov–June), and that residents of Zimbabwe and the rest of Southern Africa pay less than the non-resident prices quoted below. Whoever you go with, though, **book in advance**, as the trips fill up. Prices below are all-inclusive (except alcohol) rates per person for the entire trip in the high season unless otherwise specified. Low-season rates are approximately twenty percent less.

CANOEING

Buffalo Safaris, Hans van der Heiden, PO Box 113, Kariba (☎061/2645 or 3041–3, fax 2827, *buffalo@harare.iafrica.com*). Hugely reputable and long-established operator offering year-round, two- to nine-night trips with weekly departures from Kariba, Chirundu or Mana Pools. Prices range from US$315 per person for the two-night Kariba–Chirundu section, to US$977 for seven nights on the Kariba–Kanyemba stretch; three nights for Chirundu–Mana costs US$525. Substantial discounts in low season.

Chipembere Safaris, PO Box 9, Kariba (☎ & fax 061/2946, *chipsaf@zambezi.net*). Steve Pope has been in the business since 1982 and has always kept his safaris small and personal. He only covers the Chirundu–Mana Pools route, departing every Sunday of the year. Pick-ups available from all the main hotels in Kariba and at the *Cloud's End Hotel* in Makuti, returning to Kariba on Wednesday afternoon. The inexpensive rates reflect the fact that this is a client-participation safari, meaning you are expected to help with camp chores as well as loading and unloading canoes. High season US$375, low season US$325.

Goliath Safaris, PO Box CH 294, Harare; *Bronte Hotel*, 132 Baines Ave, the Avenues, Harare (☎ & fax 04/708843 or 739836, *goliath@id.co.zw*). Canoeing throughout the year from Chirundu to Mana Pools (three nights US$478) and Mana Pools to Kanyemba (four nights US$575), with weekly departures and free transfers from Harare.

River Horse Safaris, *Kariba Breezes Hotel*, Kariba (☎ & fax 061/2422 or 2447, *riverhse@icon.co.zw*). Two-night Kariba–Chirundu canoeing safaris for US$300; three nights Chirundu–Mana at US$395, five nights Kariba–Mana for US$460.

Max or Harry has to be negotiated. The dangers from wildlife are very real, and there are occasionally fatalities (usually due to clients doing something they shouldn't) and numerous incidents involving hippos – especially cows protecting their calves – capsizing canoes. But, bearing in mind that hundreds of canoes go down the Zambezi every year, incidents are few and the canoeing outfits have a good safety record.

Itineraries

Safaris begin at Kariba, Chirundu or Mana. **From Kariba**, you paddle through the steep gorge below the dam wall into the wide country of the Middle Valley flood plains. It takes three days **to Chirundu** (about US$315), and five or six **to Mana** (US$460–620), an obvious goal. The Kariba–Chirundu section is perhaps the least interesting part of the river – you can expect little game and it's a pity to get so close to the real wilderness of

---

Safari Par Excellence, 26a Blakiston St/Josiah Chinamano Avenue, Harare (☎04/700911–2); or at the *Cutty Sark Hotel*, Kariba (☎061/3332). Two- or three-night participatory or luxury canoe safaris overnighting at lodges and camps on the Zambian side of the river. Luxury trips run between April and December, the others throughout the year. Three-night luxury trips (US$795), and three-night (US$395) or two-night (US$295) participatory camping safaris.

Shearwater, *Kariba Breezes Hotel*, Kariba (PO Box 229, Kariba; ☎061/2265, fax 2459, *swakari@id.co.zw*). Friendly and efficient crew who take sufficient time to brief you before embarking on the safari. Almost identical trails to Buffalo (see opposite) but slightly cheaper.

Sobek, c/o Run Wild, 3rd Floor, Southampton Life Centre, Jason Moyo Avenue, Harare (☎04/795841, *runwild@africaonline.co.zw*); or PO Box 281, Kariba (☎ & fax 061/2538, *lemon@zambezi.net*). Canoe safaris with several departures a week along the Zambian bank of the river. Collections and transfers to Zambia available from all Kariba hotels. Three nights Chirundu–Lower Zambezi National Park staying in luxury tented camps (US$575); Zambezi Weekender (Fri–Sun; US$175) with early-morning hikes, a sunset cruise and a 22-kilometre canoe trail through Kariba Gorge.

WALKING SAFARIS

Chipembere Safaris (contact details opposite). Exclusive walking safaris in the Chitake Wilderness south of Mana Pools from May to October, when the only source of water is the perennial spring, which attracts large game concentrations. Guide Steve Pope has spent so much time here that the resident lions have become semi-habituated to his presence, making this a good bet if you want to watch big cats at close quarters. Accommodation at the base camp is in basic but perfectly adequate tents. Discounts available for standby bookings (a week or less before the date of the trip). Four-day, three-night safaris cost US$460 in high season and US$395 in low.

Goliath Safaris (contact details opposite). A hiking trail from May to October following the Chitake River down the Zambezi Escarpment into Mana Pools. A maximum of 15km is covered per day and porters carry equipment, although you'll have to carry your own personal effects in a backpack. This safari can be combined with either the Mana–Kanyemba canoe trail or the tented safari staying at Chimombe camp (see Luxury camps, p.143).

Graeme Lemon Walking Safaris PO Box 281, Kariba (☎ & fax 061/2538, *lemon@samara.co.zw*). One of the best teams in the business which takes you through the rough terrain of Matusadona on a no-frills wilderness experience. On the Elephant Trail you carry your own backpack and sleep in a basic tented camp, which is packed up each morning. Porters can take your stuff if you don't want to carry a pack. The Lion Trail guides clients along the lakeshore in search of big cats. Luggage goes by boat with porters, who set up camp in a fresh bay each evening, leaving enough time for a sunset cruise before dinner. Elephant Trail US$160 per night, Lion Trail US$210 per night.

Mana without touching it. Nevertheless, this stretch can be convenient if you're already at Kariba, and the Kariba gorge is spectacular. The longest trip, nine days from Kariba **to Kanyemba** (US$980), passes mostly through completely wild country.

The **Chirundu–Mana** trip (four days and three nights) is the most popular, costing US$375–500. A great deal of the trips on this section run through channels, past sandbanks and islands, with the Zambian Escarpment mountains flanking the river all the way.

Mana–Kanyemba (US$575–630) or **Chirundu–Kanyemba** (US$800) are even more exciting, with the added thrill of coping with whirlpools in the precipitous **Mpata Gorge**. Ironstone cliffs with baobabs growing from them replace savannah, creating a magnificent entrance to the chasm. You exit by way of "the gate", a triangular-shaped granite outcrop where the river widens again. Towards Kanyemba, as the hills disappear, huts and farmlands claim the riverbanks in a transition from a magical, elemental realm to the more worldly. Many of the people here are **VaDema**, who until they were removed from their land in the Chewore Safari Area were the only hunter-gatherers left in Zimbabwe and now till instead of hunt. A genetic defect giving a small percentage of the VaDema the appearance of having a couple of toes missing gave rise to the nickname the "Three-toed People".

Transfers are arranged from **Kariba or Harare** to starting points at **Chirundu** and **Mana** and back out again at the end of the trip, but only some companies include this in the cost of the safari. The best option of all is to arrange your own party of at least six friends to do the trip.

Mana Pools National Park

At **MANA POOLS NATIONAL PARK** (open throughout the year; campsites closed Oct–May if rains prevent access; day entry U$10, week entry US$20), the Zambezi meanders through a wide valley, repeatedly splaying out into islands, channels and sandbanks, and with escarpments rising dramatically on either side. Looking across to Zambia, the land appears as an alluring quilt of blue mountains descending into another tract of wilderness – the Luangwa Valley. On the Zimbabwe side, alluvial river terraces, reaching inland for several kilometres, flank the fifty-kilometre river frontage of the national park.

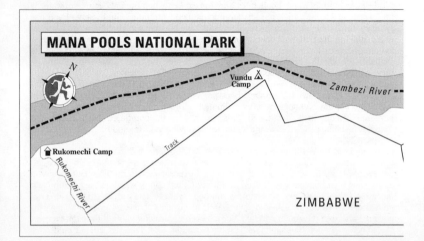

Along these banks are the pools which give Mana its name – depressions filled with water in abandoned river channels. **Chine** and **Long Pool** hold water throughout the year, and attract large animal concentrations in the dry season. Magnificent trees grow on the fertile terraces; the enduring image of Mana is of thorn trees, *Acacia albida*, which create park-like expanses on the riverbank, before giving way to dense stands of dark-green mahogany, figs, sausage trees, rain trees, tamarinds and tawny *vetivaria* grass. Away from the water, the valley floor is a harsh environment, especially in the dry season. Spiky *jesse* bush deters any thoughts of walking, mopanes are stark and life-less, while baobabs punctuate the greys and browns. Several baobabs, in fact, remain tenaciously in the middle of the park's main road, which splits to accommodate them.

The great attraction of Mana, though, is the **wildlife** – and, specifically, the possibil-ities of close contact, because due to its open terrain you're allowed to **explore on foot** without a licensed guide, as long as you are not alone. This doesn't, however, mean there's nothing to worry about. Lions roar nightly around the riverbank campsite and elephants, stepping carefully over guy ropes, think nothing of investigating tents and cars if they smell fresh fruit, or fancy the seed pods beneath the tree you've chosen. After dark, hyenas and honey badgers prowl about, and anything edible, even shoes, will be chewed up. There have been some fatalities and heart-stopping incidents over the years because of tourists' lack of bush experience – mainly through people wanting to get too close to animals for the sake of a good photograph. You must follow certain fundamental bush rules (see p.144) and, if you do so, the whole place is enormously thrilling and rewarding. Unless you've walked in the bush before, it's much safer to explore the Mana area on an organized walk (see p.144).

Getting there

By car, the 400km from Harare to Mana takes six hours on the Chirundu–Lusaka road. This is tarred to the park turn-off at the foot of the escarpment. You need to get an **entry permit** by 3.30pm from **Marongora** (10.30am for day entries), a National Parks outpost on top of the escarpment halfway between Makuti and the Mana turn-off, before winding 80km into the valley and across the dry-river-bed country to

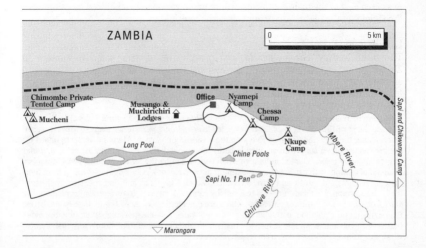

Nyamepi Camp. Should you miss the entrance deadline, you can use the basic camp-site at Marongora and check in at 7.30am the following morning, when the office opens. The road takes around three hours to drive and is exceedingly rough, but you don't need a 4WD.

Without your own vehicle, the only other ways to see the park are on a **canoe** or **walking safari** that takes in Mana, or to **fly** into the private *Chikwenya* or *Ruckomechi* **luxury bush camps**. There is no cheap way to do it: intrepid **hitchers** have succeeded, but local supplies are nonexistent, it is illegal to hitch and you've no guarantee of getting a lift out again. Nor do many **car rental** companies allow their vehicles to go to Mana because of the rough roads, although a few Harare-based firms offer 4WD vehicles – ring around to find the best deals, as fleets and companies change all the time. There are **no buses** to Mana.

Accommodation and walking safaris

National Parks have several campsites, but the two National Parks **lodges**, Musangu and Muchirichiri, are so popular that they're allocated on a lottery system. The campsites and lodges are all on the river, where you'll be serenaded by hippos and other sounds of the night. Booking for the lodges at the main parks office in Harare opens six months before the time you want to go. Lodges sleep eight and go for the usual modest National Parks cost.

If you have your own car, you'll probably be **camping** – campsites also need prior booking. If you haven't already booked in Harare through Central Reservations Office, Borrowdale Road/Sandringham Drive, adjacent to the Botanic Gardens; PO Box CY 826, Causeway, Harare (Mon–Fri 8am–4pm; ☎04/706077–8, fax 726089 or 724914, *NationalParks@gta.gov.zw*), you can try doing so through Marongora (☎063/533 or 512–3). **Nyamepi**, by the park headquarters, is a large site and gets a bit crowded at peak times; buffalo graze around the office, and elephant amble through. Secluded and 8km west of Nyamepi, **Mucheni** has four campsites, and **Nkupe**, a few kilometres east of Nyamepi, accommodates a single group of up to twelve people. There are no facilities at Mana and your last chance to buy food supplies and to fill up your car is at Makuti. One reasonably priced option, and certainly an adventurous one, is to explore Mana as part of a guided **backpacking trail** on the Zambezi flood plain in the wilderness area east of the main campsites, where game viewing is maximized by camping in the vicinity of the places where animals come to drink.

Luxury camps

The three **luxury camps** in the area provide the ultimate safari experience in Zimbabwe: set on the river and with professional guides and an abundance of birds and animals, they have prices to match. Most clients fly into *Chikwenya* and *Ruckomechi* from Kariba in very small planes, though some reach *Ruckomechi* by road and boat. *Chimombe* is reached by road from Harare.

Chikwenya, Wilderness Safaris, Elephant's Walk Shopping Centre, Victoria Falls (PO Box 288, Victoria Falls; ☎013/3371–3, fax 4224 or 5942, *wildzim@telconet.co.zw* or *wildlodges@telconet.co.zw*). Overlooking the Sapi and Zambezi rivers on the eastern boundary of Mana Pools, tents raised off the ground are all en suite with an outside bath, communal dining and lounge/bar area, all under large mahogany trees. Situated in its own small concession on the eastern boundary of Mana is a small luxury camp, with capacity for a maximum of twelve people. Guests are picked up from their thatched chalets after dusk and have an armed escort – elephant and lion regularly walk right through the camp. Meals are under a marvellous canopy of riverine trees and you can look at the stars from the en-suite shower and toilet, which are open to the sky. Activities include game drives, river cruising on a pontoon, early-morning escorted walks and late-morning sitting in game hides perusing the changing wildlife displays. This is undoubtedly one of Zimbabwe's top bush camps, with rates from US$338 per day; transfer US$280 return.

Chimombe, Goliath Safaris, *Bronte Hotel*, 132 Baines Ave, the Avenues, Harare (PO Box CH 294, Harare; ☎ & fax 04/708843 or 739836, *goliath@id.co.zw*). Tented safari camp at Mucheni, in the centre of the park along the riverfront, with en-suite toilets and communal showers. Clients go for three nights, during which you go on early-morning walks in the park, game drives and afternoon canoe trails along the shoreline. Fully inclusive rate for three nights and three full days including free road transfer from Harare (about 7hr each way) is US$575 per person.

Ruckomechi Camp Wilderness Safaris, Elephant's Walk Shopping Centre, Victoria Falls (PO Box 288, Victoria Falls; ☎013/3371–3, fax 4224 or 5942, *wildzim@telconet.co.zw* or *wildlodges@telconet.co.zw*). Fabulous. If you stay at only one safari camp in Zimbabwe, it should be this one. Located in an enormous stand of acacias and mahoganies on the western reaches of the Mana Pools flood plain, *Ruckomechi* is a stylish place that can welcome a maximum of twenty guests. Its advantages include a wide choice of game-viewing activities, canoeing, an extensive area for game spotting and an ample number of guides. Lions are plentiful in the area, and you'd be unlucky not to see one over a three-day stay. Besides en-suite chalets, the camp boasts a marvellous roofless bathroom on the high riverbank, with one side completely open to the water. Daily all-inclusive rates start at US$325 per person in high season (July–Dec), and US$250 at other times; transfer by speedboat from Chirundu costs US$125 per person, US$240 by light aircraft from Kariba.

The park

Mana Pools was declared a **world heritage site** by UNESCO in 1984, and the number of visitors to the park is strictly controlled. There are no striped combis here to wheel the dust, nor other ugly products of tourism. Mana experiences similar **seasonal game movements** to Kariba. Soon after the rains, when food and water in the deep bush begins to dry out, the animals move to the Zambezi to find enough food to carry them through the dry season. By October, Mana's abundant wildlife is concentrated around the pools and river.

Elephant are so common you become quite blasé about seeing them, while **buffalo** congregate in herds up to two thousand strong. **Impala**, **waterbuck** and **zebra** are everywhere and numerous predators stalk in their wake. Nearly everyone sees **lions**; **cheetahs** are rare, but around in small numbers, as are packs of **wild dogs** and secretive **leopards**. **Nyala antelope**, found only at Mana and Gonarezhou, are a special sight not to be confused with **kudu** or hefty **eland** browsing off the mahoganies.

Dawn is the best chance for seeing **hippos** on land, before they move into the water. Creatures of habit, they use well-worn paths up the bank where they graze at night, crunching up long grey sausage-tree pods. They also have similar underwater paths on the river bed. The crescent-shaped seed pods of the *Acacia albida* are gourmet delicacies for elephant and buffalo; each tree bears several hundred pounds of them, which elephants shake to get down or vacuum from the ground underneath. The trees have a reverse foliage cycle, their leaves developing during the dry season to nourish and shade animals on the riverbank, and falling once the rains begin and the animals move to fresher grazing.

The **birdlife** at Mana will leave you gasping, with over 350 species recorded. Brilliant **scarlet carmine bee-eaters** nest in colonies on the riverbank, keen-eyed **fish eagles** watch from treetops, while solitary **goliath herons** wade through the shallows searching for fish and frogs. You'll see the brilliant flashes of **kingfishers** and numerous **geese** and **storks**. Away from the river, look for **hornbills**, **eagles**, **kites** and Zambezi chickens – a long-standing local name for **guinea fowl** – especially the less common crested ones.

What's most appealing of all, perhaps, is not having to go on long game drives to see animals. Besides campsite action you can go to the permanent **Long Pool** near Nyamepi or the rarely dry **Chine Pool** – both good places to spend a couple of hours watching creatures coming to drink. Hippo and croc spotting at Long Pool is always fun, even when nothing much else turns up. Chine Pool, 1km south of Mana River Drive, straddles the river terraces and valley hinterland, attracting animals such as sable and nyala antelope, which don't come to terrace woodlands very often.

SAFETY CONSIDERATIONS

In order to enjoy the **walking** at Mana without feeling paralysed by fear, you need to know some basics. Meeting a lion on foot feels very different from staring at one from a safari vehicle. Most animals, though, aren't out to get you and will only cause problems if surprised, scared or threatened, any of which you *can* do unwittingly. To forestall disaster (accidents are rare), follow this eight-point survivor's guide to tramping the bush.

1. Keep a **safe distance**, especially from large animals like buffalo and elephant, and when taking photographs.
2. **Don't run** if you come across a **lion**: stand still, keep quiet, then back off slowly. Running triggers their impulse to chase. Remember, too, as you fill your viewfinder, both lions and hyenas may defend their kills if you come near them.
3. Stay well clear of **cow elephant herds** with calves. Get downwind and detour or let them pass.
4. Don't cut off an **animal's retreat**. Hippos on land usually make for the river; land mammals, for dense bush or woodland.
5. **Keep a keen lookout** at all times and don't enter thick bush or grass, where your visibility is severely reduced.
6. Leave **white clothes** at home: they're a loud announcement of your presence to the animals you're trying to see.
7. **Bilharzia** isn't common on this stretch of the river, but **crocodiles** are. Watch out when you draw water.
8. **Fresh fruit** (particularly oranges) courts disaster: elephants possess a remarkable sense of smell and have been known to totally trash cars to get at it. And, if any succeed, they may be shot as a consequence.

You're sure to be regaled with some **horror stories** about Mana. Often it's the same bush myth recycled: the man who had his face ripped off by a hyena, or the hunter who retreated from a buffalo up a tree and had the soles of his dangling feet licked away (through shoes and all!) by the vindictive beast's abrasive tongue, or the person who got trapped all night in the campsite loo by a herd of elephants. A few people have been injured or lost their lives at Mana over the years, but when the orchestra of the night begins, remember you're safe in your tent, but not if you sleep out in the open. **Hyenas** come to the campsites nightly, finding even such unlikely items as shoes, tin trunks of food and unwashed pots and pans very attractive.

---

travel details

Economy buses

The length of these routes, and Zambezi Valley road conditions, compound the usual vagueness of local bus times. On the Karoi–Binga road, buses break down more than is usual elsewhere and the drivers often set off when they wake up. Many of the buses start somewhere else and what's happened en route is a mystery. Ask around. The best advice is to be there as early as the locals.

Chirundu to: Harare (several daily; 8hr); Lusaka (several daily; 7hr).

Kariba to: Harare (several daily; 8hr).

Semi-luxury coaches

Various coach companies take on the Harare–Kariba route from time to time, then stop because of unprofitability. Check with local hotels in Kariba or the publicity association in Harare (p.68) for the latest. At the time of writing, Powercoach was running a daily service between the Roadport in Harare and Lusaka via Kariba.

Kariba to: Harare (daily; 5hr); Lusaka (daily; 3hr 30min).

Ferries

Passenger speed ferries run from Kariba to Mlibizi daily except Wednesdays with request-only stops at Binga, Bumi or Tashinga. The **District Development Fund** (DDF) operates a cheaper but slower, less convenient and less comfortable service between Kariba and Binga, Tashinga and Mlibizi (for details, see the box on p.120).

Flights

Kariba is served by flights on Air Zimbabwe and the smaller carrier, Air Zambezi.

Kariba to Harare (1–2 daily; 45min); Hwange (3 weekly; 50min); Victoria Falls (4 weekly; 50min).

CHAPTER THREE

BULAWAYO AND THE MATOBO DISTRICT

Set apart by its Ndebele language and history from the rest of this Shona-speaking country, **Bulawayo** is often bypassed by travellers. This is a pity, for Zimbabwe's second city is as interesting as the capital. Although Bulawayo's citizens have long considered their city to have suffered unjust neglect at the expense of Harare, the upside is that there has been little demolition or hasty redevelopment, and the wide, regularly gridded streets remain studded with gracious colonial-era buildings. Overall, in fact, the city has something of a sepia-toned feel, compounded by rather conservative dress and ageing cars, and a slow, laid-back ambience that makes it a thoroughly pleasant place to stroll about and explore.

Perhaps the best reason to visit the city is for the nearby **Matopos Hills** and **Matobo National Park**. Although such granite outcrops can be found all over the country, the Dali-esque compositions of lichen-streaked balancing rocks and grassy valleys are at their best at Matopos. The world's highest concentration of prehistoric **rock paintings** is found here, too, and you can spend days climbing kopjes and discovering painted caves and rock shelters – human history in the area goes back more than 100,000 years. Much later, the **Torwa** and **Rozwi** states had court centres in the Bulawayo region, the remains of which lie scattered in the countryside. None competes with Great Zimbabwe in size but the local style is exemplified by the beautifully laid walls at **Kame**, 22km west of Bulawayo.

Since colonial times, Bulawayo has served as a **transport hub** between the African hinterland and the continent's southern tip. It's the jumping-off point for Hwange, Victoria Falls, the western shores of Lake Kariba and onward journeys to Zambia, Botswana and South Africa, as well as being well positioned for eastward travel to Great Zimbabwe and the Highlands.

ACCOMMODATION PRICE CODES

Hotels and other accommodation options in Zimbabwe have been categorized according to the **price codes** given below, which indicate the cost, per person sharing, of a night's lodging. For a full explanation, see p.33.

① under US$7.50	④ US$25–35	⑦ US$55–75
② US$7.50–15	⑤ US$35–45	⑧ US$75–100
③ US$15–25	⑥ US$45–55	⑨ over US$100

BULAWAYO

Arriving in **BULAWAYO** is like jumping back fifty years. More like the set of an old movie than a modern African city, the town stood in for late 1950s Johannesburg for the shooting of *A World Apart*, the film about South African anti-apartheid activist Ruth First. The South African connection actually goes deeper than that. In the nineteenth century, Bulawayo was the capital of the **Ndebele state** and the majority language, Sindebele, is very close to the original Zulu. In the wake of the Matabeleland

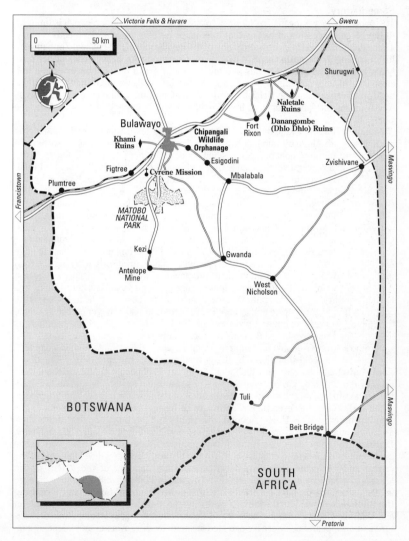

clampdown of the 1980s (see p.358) and a local sense of abject neglect by the capital, a small group of activists dreams of seceding from Zimbabwe and uniting with their notional Zulu kin in South Africa. And on the cultural front, Bulawayo's lively indigenous pop **music** looks as much to Jo'burg jive for inspiration as it does to Harare's Shona sounds. Tourist attractions in town are few, but the city has a couple of Zimbabwe's finest museums: the **National Gallery** here is more dynamic than its counterpart in the capital, and the **Museum of Natural History** was once rated the best in Central Africa, a status that probably still stands.

Some history

The name *Bulawayo* means, in Ndebele, "place of slaughter", a reference, it is thought, to the fierce succession of battles that took place here in the late nineteenth century. These culminated in the accession of one of the key figures of pre-colonial Zimbabwean history, **King Lobengula**, in 1870. His reign, peppered with heavy doses of heroism, lying, betrayal and murder, reads like mythology or grand opera. This era came to a close in 1894, with Lobengula's death, and the Ndebele collapse following the relentless northwards advance of the **British South Africa Company**, which was in the process of colonizing the lands north of the Limpopo. For a summary of these events, see Contexts, p.348.

Although Bulawayo kept its name, the new **colonial town** was re-sited along a classic British grid. Almost immediately it was at the centre of a mining rush: within two months, four hundred gold prospectors had acquired licences, and within ten years the population had reached six thousand. Quick to see an opportunity, the Standard Bank of South Africa set up its first branch in a tent, guarded day and night by the Matabeleland Mounted Police. In 1898, as the proposed Cape to Cairo **railway** reached Bulawayo, the town developed into an important clearing house for goods from the colonies further north, and became the country's main communications centre.

Resistance to the white invasion, however, hadn't ended in 1894. While the First Chimurenga marked the last great survival struggle of the old societies, colonial rule brought new forms of protest. Bulawayo – because of its strong industrial base in engineering, metal founding, manufacturing, garment making, printing, packaging and food production – was at the forefront of the development of worker organizations. The first African **trade union**, the Rhodesian Industrial and Commercial Workers Union, was formed here in 1927; African railway workers staged a successful strike in 1945, and the country's first general strike began here in 1948. **Joshua Nkomo**, general secretary of the railway workers' union and president of the TUC, later emerged in the 1950s as leader of the Bulawayo-based **African National Congress**.

Nkomo's strong regional following in Matabeleland led inevitably to much bad feeling when he was cold-shouldered by the government after **Independence**. The **dissident years** that followed – in which tens of thousands of people in Matabeleland were brutally murdered by government forces – posed a threat to stability, and fuelled fears that tribal warfare might sound the death knell of the new Zimbabwe. The grievances of the early 1980s, however, turned out not to be beyond negotiated settlement.

With the May 1988 **Unity Accord**, dissidents left the bush and laid down their arms. Joshua Nkomo became vice president and the formerly jailed Zipra leader, **Dumisa Dabengwa**, became Home Affairs minister. A second national university has been built in Bulawayo to equalize some of the disparity between developments in the capital and neglected Bulawayo. Horrific evidence, though, of the extent of the killings, particularly by the notorious Fifth Brigade in 1983 and 1984, began to emerge in 1992, when the drought revealed skeletons down dried-out mine shafts. **Breaking the Silence**, a report into the killings by the independent Legal Resources Foundation and Catholic Commission for Justice and Peace, alleged that systematic murder, torture and disappearances were a calculated strategy by the government to destroy support for ZAPU on its home turf. But the findings were suppressed by Catholic bishops, who feared arousing the ire of President Mugabe, until 1997 when a copy came into the hands of the London *Guardian* and it was subsequently published on the Web. As expected, Mugabe, whose government had consistently denied the killings, attacked the "mischief makers who wear religious garb and publish reports that are meant to divide us".

During the end of the 1990s, Joshua Nkomo's fading from the political scene, as he battled prostate cancer, cleared the way for the revival by others of his old political party, now called **Zapu 2000**, which pledged to fight discrimination against Ndebele-speakers. But **Nkomo's death** in 1999 at the age of 83 created renewed tension around Bulawayo and at his burial at Heroes Acre in Harare, Mugabe attempted to reassure Ndebele-speakers that "my government will treat Matabeleland just as it did when Nkomo was alive". As the *Guardian* correspondent Andrew Meldrum wryly commented: "That is exactly what the Ndebele are afraid of."

Arrival, information and city transport

However you **arrive** in Bulawayo, getting into the city centre should present few problems. Many of the backpackers' lodges and other budget places meet every coach and train and tout aggressively; to avoid having to deal with the hard sell, arrange your accommodation in advance.

The airport
Bulawayo's quaintly old-fashioned international **airport** (☎09/226491–3), 22km north of town on Robert Mugabe Way, sees flights from Harare and Johannesburg. A number of companies offer **transfers** to town, among them DFK Tours (☎09/75742) and DNR Shuttle Services and Tour Operators (☎09/45137, mobile ☎091/315200), both of which need to be booked and will charge around US$10 per person to drop you off anywhere in Greater Bulawayo. More convenient and usually cheaper are the **taxis** that wait at the airport, but if they're all taken, you can phone the reliable Rixi Taxis (☎09/60666 or 61933); the fare to the city centre shouldn't work out at much over US$6, irrespective of the number of passengers. For **car rental**, Avis, Elite, Europcar and Hertz have desks downstairs in the airport. An upstairs **restaurant**, which opens onto a balcony overlooking the runway, serves reasonably priced teas, toasted sandwiches, steaks and drinks, and is a very pleasant place to wait.

Intercity coaches and buses
Blue Arrow **luxury coaches** drop passengers from Harare and Victoria Falls at their office opposite City Hall, dead in the centre of town, at Unifreight House, 73a Fife St, which is also used by Greyhound and Translux coaches from Johannesburg. The Trans Zambezi from Johannesburg stops within spitting distance, at the corner of Leopold Takawira Avenue and Robert Mugabe Way, outside the Publicity Association offices.

Of the two **backpacker buses** that connect South Africa with Victoria Falls, both the Baz Bus from Johannesburg and Route 49 from Cape Town pass through Bulawayo, where they'll drop passengers at their accommodation.

There is no central arrival point for **Volvos** and **chicken buses**, but most long-distance buses leave from two main terminals, one serving the western section of the country and the other east. From **eastern Zimbabwe**, including Harare, Beit Bridge, Chiredzi and the Eastern Highlands, economy buses arrive at the **Renkini terminus**, about 2km west of the centre, in Sixth Avenue Extension, opposite the Mzilikazi Police Station in the high-density areas. From there, commuter omnibuses head into town, although you may prefer to avoid the hassle and take a taxi. Buses from **western Zimbabwe**, including

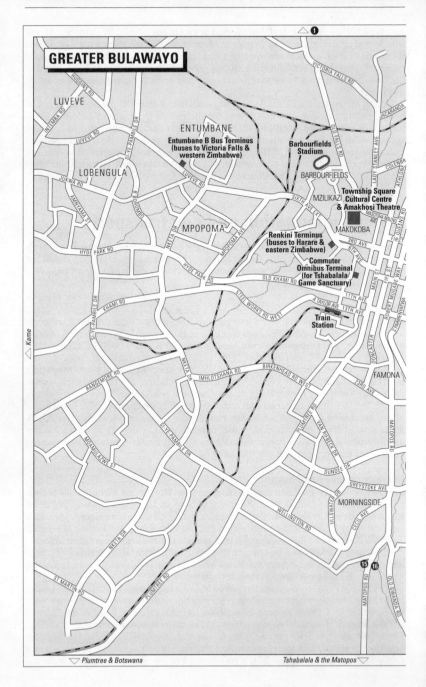

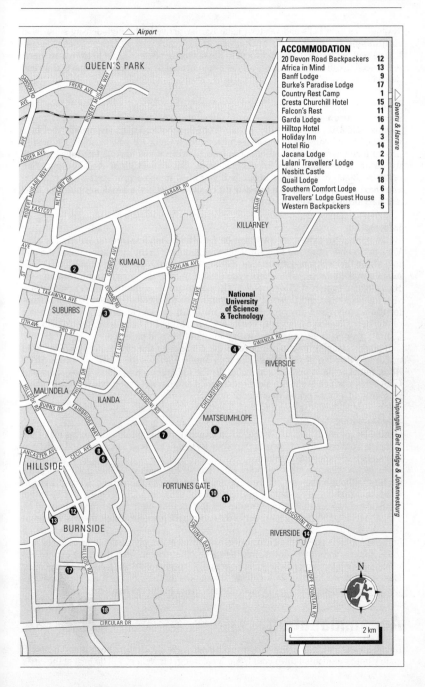

△ Airport

QUEEN'S PARK

ACCOMMODATION

20 Devon Road Backpackers	12
Africa in Mind	13
Banff Lodge	9
Burke's Paradise Lodge	17
Country Rest Camp	1
Cresta Churchill Hotel	15
Falcon's Rest	11
Garda Lodge	16
Hilltop Hotel	4
Holiday Inn	3
Hotel Rio	14
Jacana Lodge	2
Lalani Travellers' Lodge	10
Nesbitt Castle	7
Quail Lodge	18
Southern Comfort Lodge	6
Travellers' Lodge Guest House	8
Western Backpackers	5

△ Gweru & Harare

△ Chipangali, Beit Bridge & Johannesburg

KILLARNEY

KUMALO

SUBURBS

National University of Science & Technology

RIVERSIDE

MALINDELA

ILANDA

MATSEUMHLOPE

HILLSIDE

FORTUNES GATE

BURNSIDE

RIVERSIDE

CIRCULAR DR

N

0   2 km

Hwange, Victoria Falls and western Lake Kariba, arrive in the high-density suburbs at **Entumbane B terminus**, about 6km west of the centre, just off Luveve Road (the continuation of Sixth Extension), adjacent to the shopping centre. To get to town from here, you'll need to call a taxi or hail one of the frequent commuter omnibuses that tear up and down the Luveve Road.

Trains

Bulawayo's **train station**, at the end of Lobengula Street (enquiries ☎09/322411, reservations ☎322310), is a short hop by taxi from the centre. Trains are usually met by a gaggle of lodge and tour-company representatives eager for your custom; it's best to pre-arrange your accommodation, or at least to pretend you have. A **left-luggage** facility (Mon 6am–9pm, Tues–Fri 6.30am–9pm, Sat 6am–3.30pm & 3.30–9pm, Sun 6.30am–2.30pm & 4.30–9pm) is handy if you need to leave your stuff while you plan your next move, and there's a **bureau de change** as well as a **kiosk** serving pies, teas and fizzy drinks on platform one.

Information

Bulawayo has an extremely switched-on **Publicity Association** on Robert Mugabe Way, between Eighth and Leopold Takawira avenues, in the car park outside the city hall (Mon–Fri 8.30am–4.45pm, Sat 8.30am–noon; ☎09/60867 or 72969, fax 60868, *bulawayo@telconet.co.zw*), where you'll find maps and touring information for Bulawayo and the rest of Zimbabwe. They also run an accommodation booking service for Bulawayo and the rest of the country that costs well under US$1. Booking for the Matopos and any of Zimbabwe's **national parks** can be done at the corner of Herbert Chitepo Street and Tenth Avenue (Mon–Fri 8am–4pm; ☎09/63646, fax 65592); it's best to go in person, with plenty of time and patience.

If you're planning to explore beyond the confines of the city centre, you'll need to invest in a detailed **street atlas**. The only one available is the *Mobil Bulawayo Street Atlas*, found at most bookshops, including the ubiquitous Kingstons, Book Mart and CNA chains, which are fortunately rather good and not too expensive; it's worth shopping around a bit as prices vary significantly.

City transport

Central Bulawayo is easy to get around on foot and, although the wide streets make the distance from one side of town to the other feel endless, most places around town can be reached in under thirty minutes.

Bulawayo's flatness, its wide, quiet suburban streets and cycle lanes make it ideal for **cycling**, although the city centre isn't much fun, due to the erratic driving. Bear in mind, too, that if you're staying in the outer suburbs distances to town can be huge. **Taxis** are cheap for short trips (around US$0.40 per kilometre), and can be booked by telephone (see Listings, p.165). Otherwise, the best places to catch them are around the City Hall area, particularly in the public car park. A cheaper option if you're staying in the suburbs is one of the **commuter omnibuses** that ply all the main arteries into town. You can wave them down anywhere along the road or catch them at a central terminal, one of the main ones being in Lobengula Street around Sixth Avenue Extension. **Buses** are more practicable for destinations outside the city, such as the Chpangali Wildlife Orphanage and the Matopos (details given in the guide where relevant).

Accommodation

Bulawayo has a wide range of **accommodation**, from backpacker hostels and B&Bs to luxury hotels and out-of-town country lodges. Budget travellers will do best at the city's

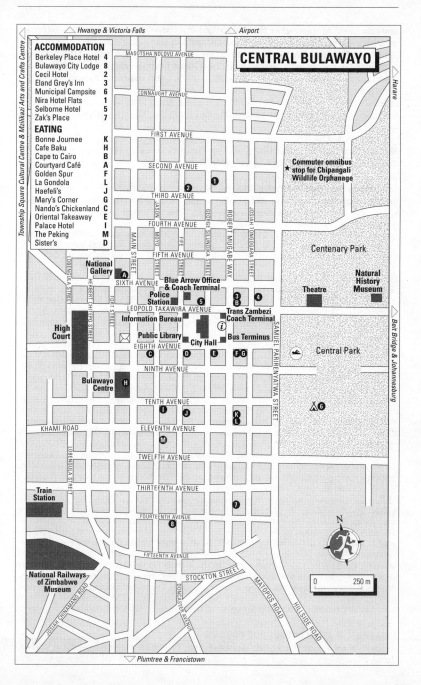

CENTRAL BULAWAYO

ACCOMMODATION
Berkeley Place Hotel	4
Bulawayo City Lodge	8
Cecil Hotel	2
Eland Grey's Inn	3
Municipal Campsite	6
Nira Hotel Flats	1
Selborne Hotel	5
Zak's Place	7

EATING
Bonne Journee	K
Cafe Baku	H
Cape to Cairo	B
Courtyard Café	A
Golden Spur	F
La Gondola	L
Haefeli's	J
Mary's Corner	G
Nando's Chickenland	C
Oriental Takeaway	E
Palace Hotel	I
The Peking	M
Sister's	D

Hwange & Victoria Falls
Airport
Harare
Beit Bridge & Johannesburg
Plumtree & Francistown

Township Square Cultural Centre & Mzilikazi Arts and Crafts Centre

MASOTSHA NDLOVU AVENUE
CONNAUGHT AVENUE
FIRST AVENUE
SECOND AVENUE
THIRD AVENUE
FOURTH AVENUE
FIFTH AVENUE
SIXTH AVENUE
LEOPOLD TAKAWIRA AVENUE
EIGHTH AVENUE
NINTH AVENUE
TENTH AVENUE
ELEVENTH AVENUE
TWELFTH AVENUE
THIRTEENTH AVENUE
FOURTEENTH AVENUE
FIFTEENTH AVENUE
STOCKTON STREET

LOBENGULA STREET
HERBERT CHITEPO STREET
FORT STREET
MAIN STREET
JASON MOYO
FIFE STREET
GEORGE SILUNDIKA STREET
ROBERT MUGABE WAY
JOSIAH TONGOGARA STREET
SAMUEL PARIRENYATWA STREET
KHAMI ROAD
JOSIAH CHINAMANO ROAD
DONCASTER AVENUE
MATOPOS ROAD
HILLSIDE ROAD

Commuter omnibus stop for Chipangali Wildlife Orphanage

Centenary Park
Central Park

National Gallery
Theatre
Natural History Museum

Blue Arrow Office & Coach Terminal
Police Station
Trans Zambezi Coach Terminal
Information Bureau
Public Library
City Hall
Bus Terminus

High Court
Bulawayo Centre
Train Station
National Railways of Zimbabwe Museum

0   250 m

N

backpackers' lodges rather than its cheap hotels which, especially in the centre, are invariably seedy. If you don't fancy the backpacker scene there are also several inexpensive and decent **apartels** in the city centre: hotel-style rooms without the full range of facilities in converted apartment blocks. **Guest houses** and better **hotels**, which tend to draw business travellers, generally offer a good standard of comfort, but are often overpriced. At the top of the scale, small safari operators have blossomed, and it's certainly an option to stay out of town on a **game farm** at an all-inclusive rate, rather than a city hotel; several places have opened up in the **Matopos** if you plan to head straight there (see p.167).

Note that hotels tend to fill up during the Trade Fair at the end of April, so book ahead at that time. The excellent Publicity Association in City Hall has the most up-to-date information on all types of accommodation.

Campsites and backpackers' lodges

20 Devon Road Backpackers, 20 Devon Rd, Hillside (☎ & fax 09/41501). Two four-bed dorms and two doubles (one in a caravan in the garden) in a suburban bungalow 6km from the city, originally an old farmstead but refurbished in 1999. More intimate than most hostels, it targets young professionals and is greatly favoured by foreign volunteers for its congenial bar and pool room. Cooked meals are available, as is self-catering, with Hillside shops just 1km away. The hostel meets guests by prior arrangement, or will refund your taxi fare from town. Camping, dorms and doubles ①.

Berkeley Place Hotel, 71 Josiah Tongogara St, between Sixth and Leopold Takawira avenues (☎ & fax 09/67701). Basic but clean rooms in a popular converted residential hotel, smack in the city centre. Of the 42 rooms, 32 have their own showers, but all share toilets. A recommended budget option if you're not into the backpacker scene. They meet all intercity coaches and trains. ①.

Burke's Paradise Lodge, 11 Inverleith Drive, Burnside (☎ & fax 09/46481). A great place to fill in those white patches with some nude sunbathing, *Burke's*, 6km south of the centre, is unquestionably the coolest hostel in town. Set in twelve rambling acres of peaceful garden, it has a block of five no-frills double rooms next to the pool, and a detached cottage that contains a five-bed dorm, kitchen and a small shop selling bread, cheese, milk, oats, fruit and vegetables. The owners, who live on the same property, are friendly and obliging, and can arrange lifts into town if you want to hit the nightspots. Phone for free collection from coach or train. Camping, dorms and doubles ①.

Country Rest Camp, 19km peg on Falls Road, then 2km down a dirt road (☎09/229551 or 229240, fax 66525, mobile ☎011/212369). Six thatched self-catering cottages with twin beds and a bunk on a working farm. Braai packs for sale and meals on request. Good, cheap accommodation that is handy as an overnight stop enroute to Vic Falls. Cottages sharing ablutions and camping ①, en-suite cottages ②.

Lalani Travellers' Lodge, 5 Derwent Rd, Matseumhlope (☎09/41935). Spick suburban house with six reasonably priced and comfortable, if impersonal, rooms. A couple of the bedrooms inside the main house share a bathroom and are much cheaper. Well signposted off the Esigodini Road, 6km from the centre. Standard rooms ①, en-suite rooms ②.

Municipal Campsite, off Jason Moyo Avenue, opposite the museum. Adjoining the park, this immaculate site is shaded by jacarandas and palms and has the advantage of being a stone's throw from Josiah Tongogara Street swimming pool. A few chalets are available, and although there's no kitchen you can braai and picnic. The site also has 24hr supervision, and you can leave your luggage in the guard's hut during the day. Take a taxi at night, as muggings are on the increase. Camping and chalets ①.

Western Backpackers, 5 Nottingham Rd, Hillcrest (☎ & fax 09/44100, mobile ☎091/224424). Weather-beaten but clean suburban-house-turned-hostel with two dorms sleeping five people, four doubles and a run-down garden. Its greatest asset is Rachel, the good-humoured and friendly house mother, who meets every train and intercity bus. Free morning and afternoon minibus shuttles to town and they run their own budget Matopos and township tours. Camping, dorms and doubles ①.

Inexpensive guest houses and apartels

Africa in Mind, 17 Limerick Rd, Hillside (☎09/43130). Two stylish and excellent-value double rondavels decorated with black-and-white prints and carvings, in a magnificent indigenous succulent garden owned by artist Anna-Simone and knowledgeable former teacher Pete Hutton, who loves talking about Zimbabwe. Each of the comfortable, cool rondavels has its own private terrace, braai area and a well-equipped kitchen, and the pool is available to guests. ③.

Banff Lodge, Banff Road/Leander Avenue, Hillside (☎09/43176–7, fax 44402, *banff@acacia.samara*). Four double and six single rooms looking onto a garden in a characterful single-storey tin-roofed house dating from the early twentieth century. Furnishings from the same period, floral prints, ceiling fans, pool sun deck with loungers and the excellent *New Orleans* restaurant (see p.161) give it the feeling of a small hotel. Booking advised as it's very popular. ③.

Bulawayo City Lodge, Fourteenth Avenue/Fife Street (☎09/67824, 69220 or 69265, *ketan @acacia.samara.co.zw*). Sixteen comfortable en-suite rooms with two double beds in a pleasantly converted apartment block, 5min walk from the City Hall. Good value for the level of comfort, with carpets, ceiling fans and TVs in all rooms, and continental breakfast. Free airport transfers on request. ②.

Falcon's Rest, 17 Greendale Rd, Matseumhlope (☎09/45859). Amazingly, this luxurious, calm home, with beautiful indigenous trees, a pool and granite boulders in the garden, is the cheapest place to stay in one of the more salubrious suburbs, 6km from town, off the Esigodini Road. You won't remain anonymous in the hands of hospitable Mrs Betty Burton, who gives guests the run of her home, including the kitchen. Two bright upstairs bedrooms share a bathroom, while another two are en suite. ②.

Nira Holiday Flats, 41 George Silundika St (☎09/79961–3). Eleven quiet and clean two-bedroom apartments in two stubby blocks that amount to somewhat lifeless crash pads, 800m from the City Hall and coach stops. Rooms are rented individually, so you could find yourself sharing the kitchen and bathroom with someone else. Parties are discouraged and the place is secure, with a 24hr guard at the gate and a reception desk. ②.

Travellers' Lodge Guest House, 2 Banff Rd, Hillside (☎ & fax 09/46059, *travellersguest@telconet. co.zw*). Low-key friendly place in the suburbs that has eleven small functional rooms with showers opening onto a garden and swimming pool. Pine furniture, plain ethnic prints and railway sleeper benches are part of the look. ③.

Zak's Place, 129 Robert Mugabe Way (☎09/540129–30, fax 540190, *zaksplace@telconet.co.zw*). The best value for money in the centre at its more salubrious southern end, 1km from City Hall. Built as an apartment block and refurbished in 1999, the airy en-suite rooms, ranged around a terrace, have carved wooden doors and headboards, parquet flooring, ceiling fans and upholstered wooden easy chairs. Less stuffy than the hotels, but easily as comfortable. ③.

Mid-priced hotels and guest houses

Cecil Hotel, 43 Fife St/Third Avenue (☎ & fax 09/540539). A few minutes from the centre, this is an interesting fusion of an old-fashioned Rhodesian hotel (stuffed animal heads leer down from the walls), with a watering hole popular with black Zimbabweans, where the disco cooks every night and the beer garden in the courtyard hums any time of day. The en-suite rooms are clean but well overdue for refurbishment; ask for an upstairs room if you're not in a party mood. ③.

Eland Grey's Inn, 73a Robert Mugabe Way/Leopold Takawira Avenue (☎09/540318, fax 540319). Thirty-one small but fresh en-suite rooms in a 1960s hotel diagonally opposite the City Hall, refurbished in 1999 and decorated with lime-sponged walls, wood-graining and bright fabrics. A two-bedroom self-catering flat with its own kitchen is rented for US$40 and is suitable for families. ③.

Garda Lodge, 167 Matopos Rd, Hillside (☎ & fax 09/43824, mobile ☎091 330 673, Six en-suite doubles built in an Italian-owned thatched row to the side of a family house, on the Matopos Road opposite the *Cresta Churchill*, almost 6km from the centre. Each unit, with wicker furniture, satellite TV and tea-making facilities, has outside seating, as well as the use of a small pool in the garden and an airy thatched bar where breakfast is served. Dinner on request. ③.

Hilltop Hotel, Gwanda Road (☎09/72493, fax 68657, *hilltop@telconet.co.zw*). Wholesome 1960s American-style motel, 6km south of town on the way to Johannesburg, with a dated ambience. Spacious rooms are furnished with wicker furniture and ceiling fans. ③.

Quail Lodge, 7 Quail Rd, Burnside (☎ & fax 09/45087). Relaxed family home on five acres, 8km south of the centre, run by artist Karen Roselt. Steps from a thatched verandah lead down to the garden and fenced-in pool. The decor is bright and ethnic, and the rooms feel comfortably personal, hung with paintings and photos. There's a thatched cottage set apart from the main house with stone floors and a double bed, and two rooms inside, each with their own bathrooms. Children welcome and self-catering possible. Under-2s free, under-12s half-price. ⑤.

Hotel Rio, 139 Old Esigodini Rd, Riverside (☎09/41384–5, fax 49407, *hotrio@acacia.samara.co.zw*). Friendly owner-managed 1930s motel set in fourteen acres of garden, 11km from town, with seventeen comfortable double and three family rooms. Modernized and well maintained, it's a family friendly place with large well-kept lawns, a children's playground, swimming pool, aviaries with exotic birds and ostriches, and a pony that hangs about the lawns during the week and earns its keep on Sundays giving rides to kids. ③.

Selborne Hotel, George Silundika Street/Leopold Takawira Avenue (☎09/76630, fax 76335, *selborne@africaonline.co.zw*). Well maintained, but a touch old-fashioned, its 1930s facade and fixtures give this popular (and often full) hotel more character than most of the upmarket accommodation in town. Smack in the centre, some rooms have balconies looking onto the City Hall opposite, and the highly regarded *Olav's Bistro* (see p.161) is on site. ⑤.

Southern Comfort Lodge, 22 Jaywick Rd, Matsheumhlope (☎09/41340, fax 76425, mobile ☎011/604337, *southcom@telconet.co.zw*). Six twin-bedded brick-and-thatch chalets with log furniture, set on fifteen acres overlooking a small dam, signposted 6km from the centre, off the Esigodini Road. Family-run, kids are welcome, though there's no self-catering. Dinner can be arranged. ⑤.

Expensive hotels and guest houses

Cresta Churchill, Matopos Road/Moffat Avenue, Hillside (☎09/46956, fax 46551). Excellent-value three-star hotel, 5.5km south of the city centre, that can match the comfort of any of the more expensive hotels without the hefty price tag. ⑥.

Holiday Inn, Ascot Centre/Milnerton Drive (☎09/72464). Part of the chain of predictable but comfortable hotels, with a swimming pool and steakhouse. Its next to Ascot shopping centre and post office, 2km south of town, off the road to Johannesburg. ⑦.

Jacana Lodge, 21a Clark Rd, Suburbs (☎09/79528–9, fax 78275, mobile ☎011/207513, *omvjacana@ telconet.co.zw*). If you've got kids, and money to burn, this is an excellent choice with four two-bed and two three-bed self-catering cottages built on a large property with well-kept gardens and paved areas, 10min walk from the Natural History Museum and Centenary Park. The purpose-built cottages are spacious and come with phone, TV and secure parking. There's a pool, tennis court and an outdoor area for breakfast and drinks. Cots provided; under-twos free, and under-tens half-price. ⑧.

Nesbitt Castle, 6 Percy Ave, Hillside (☎09/427726). Luxurious suites, mainly for businesspeople, in a mock castle, complete with armoury and shadows: built by an eccentric former mayor of Bulawayo. The most expensive place in town, but certainly the most interesting, with excellent food. Half-board ⑨.

The City

As the only city between Johannesburg and Victoria Falls, Bulawayo is often used simply as a stopover – a shame really, since its attractions can easily fill a few days. A trip to the stunning Matobo Hills is the main reason to dally, but the city has several decent attractions, including the National Gallery in a restored colonial building; the country's best museum, the Museum of Natural History; and excellent township cultural tours which take in the Township Square Cultural Centre, where you can sample Zimbabwe's arts and theatre scene.

City Hall and the National Gallery

The centre of Bulawayo is marked by **City Hall**, flanked by **Leopold Takawira Avenue**, which heads out of town to link up with Johannesburg 873km to the south. A few hundred metres west of the hall, the **National Gallery** on the corner of Takawira and Main Street (Tues–Sun 9am–5pm; US$0.30), housed in Douslin House, a splendidly restored Edwardian-colonial mansion, is well worth a visit, if only because – unlike most exhibitions of Zimbabwean art – it isn't dominated by stone sculpture. The permanent collection showcases work in a variety of different mediums, among them cultural artefacts from Matabeleland such as baskets, sitting mats and other woven products as well as work by local painters, and there's usually a visiting exhibition. A number of studios lining the courtyard are open to artists and the public are encouraged to visit them as they work; most offer pieces for sale. The gallery has the excellent Sabona **shop**, which is as worth visiting for its interior decor as for the goods it sells, including high-quality crafts, CDs and books, several of which are by the gallery's director Yvonne Vera, a noted and controversial novelist. There's a delightful **restaurant** in the courtyard (see p.160).

Centenary Park and the Museum of Natural History

Down Leopold Takawira, about 500m east of the City Hall, the boundary of the town centre is abruptly marked by a kilometre-wide swath of parkland that divides it off from Bulawayo's oldest suburbs, imaginatively called "Suburbs". The shade of **Centenary Park**, north of the road, is welcoming after a walk up Bulawayo's wide streets. Although not the most inspiring park, it is especially good for kids. On the east side are a large **aviary** and pens with small **antelope**, a **miniature railway** that chugs around a pond squawking and quacking with splashing waterfowl, the usual swings-and-round-about **playground**, and a place under the trees for tea and ice creams – all very Sunday-afternoonish.

Central Park, almost a continuation of Centenary Park, but on the south side of Leopold Takawira, is a much nicer space, with more trees, flowers and lawns and a large illuminated fountain. Best of all, it includes the **Samuel Parirenyatwa Street Swimming Pool** (Sept–May 10am–2pm & 3–6pm), on the town side of the park, with its pleasingly antiquated 1930s changing booths, and lawns and palm trees for lazing about in the sun.

The Museum of Natural History

On the corner of Takawira and Park roads, on the eastern edge of Centenary Park, the **Museum of Natural History** (daily 9am–5pm; US$2) is the must-see of Bulawayo, the highlight of the city's cultural offerings. Imaginative exhibits not only cover the usual natural history topics of wildlife and botany, but also extend into ethnography, geology and history. The strength of the collection is that it concentrates exclusively on Zimbabwe, without spreading itself too thinly.

The **wildlife gallery** gives excellent background on Zimbabwe's fauna – superb preparation if you're planning to go off to Hwange. The extensive **ornithological collection**, with endless stuffed birds crammed like battery hens into boxes, is a little off-putting, but the dioramas of **indigenous mammals** are excellent and include the second-largest mounted elephant in the world, which very nearly reaches the ceiling of its ground-floor home. Surprisingly interesting displays of gold, emeralds and the other minerals found in Zimbabwe are on show in the **geological section**, which is partly designed to simulate a mine shaft. The adjoining outdoor display of mining antiques demonstrates how the industry operated in the nineteenth and early twentieth centuries.

The **ethnographic collection**, which includes some superb carved wooden stools and headrests, is a kind of yardstick for assessing modern curios. But, for social and historical coverage, the **Hall of Man** is the best thing in the building. It gives amazingly comprehensive insights into all aspects of the region's **history**, from ancient prehistory to the twentieth century. Human activity is handled in terms of social practices – hunting, mining, art, healing, war and trade – before culminating in the **Hall of Chiefs**, devoted to Mzilikazi, Lobengula and stacks of Cecil Rhodes memorabilia.

In a forgotten shady spot behind the western side of the museum, you'll find a **statue of Rhodes** himself dozing off in the company of his colleague and friend Alfred Beit. In earlier times, Rhodes occupied an imposing position in the middle of Eighth Avenue and

Main Street, framed by the powerfully symbolic High Court; at Independence the statue was pulled from its pedestal, to be kicked and beaten by bystanders.

Railway Museum

Behind the station, the **National Railways of Zimbabwe Museum**, Prospect Avenue, Raylton (Tues–Fri 8.30am–4pm, Sat & Sun noon–5pm; US$0.15), is a dusty reverie of nostalgia. Created by and for railway enthusiasts, its collection of steam-age artefacts is pretty interesting just to potter around, although it's rather let down by an absence of interpretative or background information. If you're a steam fan, of course, you'll find the visit rewarding just for the chance to stroll around pristine engines and fiddle with the knobs and levers. But there's enough to interest everyone: place settings, with Minton china, silver cutlery and the menu from one of the royal visits of the 1940s and 1950s; turn-of-the-century letters from Secretary of State for the Colonies Joseph Chamberlain endorsing the extension of the Bechuanaland Railway to Lake Tanganyika; and decommissioned Rhodesian Railway dining cars. **Rhodes's private coach** is a treat – a really lavish construction, used on many trips after 1895, including the one which carried his body 2500km from the Cape to Bulawayo on his death in 1902.

The townships

Bulawayo's town planning is atypical of Southern Africa, because of the proximity of some African townships to the city centre. In fact, the northeastern corner of the city around Lobengula Street and Third Avenue has always been a transitional zone where the African buses terminated and cheap shops predominated. Around the **Lobengula Street** bus terminal, several street vendors sell fruit and vegetables from small stalls. As soon as you cross Lobengula you're in **Makokoba**, Bulawayo's oldest African township ("high-density suburb"). The easiest way to get a flavour of the area is to visit **Township Square**, on the corner of Basch Street and the Old Falls Road, which you can safely do on your own, or – even better – go on one of the township tours and venture into the surrounding areas (see box). If you're feeling confident, you could also venture on to **Makokoba Market**, the city's largest, but you'll need to take either a taxi or commuter omnibus. This is definitely worthwhile, with stalls selling local delicacies like **dried mopane worms** (sold by the cupful), plus **herbal medicines** and a good selection of **baskets** and **beads** not especially intended for tourists. Another place visitors can and do visit easily on their own is the **Mzilikazi Art and Craft Centre**, in the suburb adjacent to Makakoba's northwest boundary – also a port of call on any of the organized tours.

Township Square Cultural Centre and the Amakhosi Theatre

Conceived by local playwright, Cont Mhlanga, **Township Square Cultural Centre** was started in 1994 with NGO donor funding, although its history dates back to the nineteenth century and the era of Ndebele king, Mzilikazi, when national dance festivals were a regular feature of cultural life. In keeping with the traditional ethos, the buildings have been designed in Ndebele style, and the restaurant serves authentic African food. The centre aims to act a physical and spiritual base for performing artists throughout the region and is home to the annual Inxusa Festival (see box on p.162). There's an open-air theatre that seats an audience of over 1200, and the centre is home to the pioneering **Amakhosi Theatre** Company, also founded by Cont Mhlanga, which puts on cutting-edge performances and offers training in performance and music. Among their productions has been *Somkhence*, Zimbabwe's first ethnic opera.

The lawn is apparently shaped in the outline of Africa (although you need to be told to see it) and a walkway is planted with an arcade of indigenous trees, each with a tra-

---

TOWNSHIP TOURS

One of the best things to do in Bulawayo is join one of Umzabalazo's **"People to People Tours"** guided by playwright and theatre director **Styx Mhlanga**, who is himself a resident of Makokoba and takes small groups around his home turf. "Facilitator" is probably a more accurate term for his role than "guide", as he encourages you to chew the fat with drinkers in beer halls, chat to traders at market stalls or to take time with a traditional herbalist, making this a very different experience to the average tour, where you see everything through a bus window and the passing scene is interpreted by your tour guide. The approximately three-hour tour takes in Township Square Cultural Centre, MaKhumalo's beer hall (one of Africa's biggest), Makokoba Market and Mzilikazi Art and Craft Centre. Mhlanga also hosts evening meals with a family in Mzilikazi township, and music tours around four of Bulawayo's top jazz spots. **Bookings** can be made through Studio 6, National Art Gallery, 75 Main St (☎09/72939, fax 78053–4), and tours cost US$10 per person. Another recommended company running township visits is **Face to Face Tours**, PO Box 3677, Bulawayo (☎09/78053–4), which does much the same thing, with a very reliable and affable guide.

---

ditional significance that is used here to symbolize something to do with the arts. The tree closest to the fountain is a Mukiwa planted by Britain's royal thespian, Prince Edward, and represents international cultural exchange.

Tshabalala Game Sanctuary

The main appeal of the small **Tshabalala Game Sanctuary**, 8km south of town on the Matopos Road (daily 6am–6pm; US$10), is that it offers an opportunity to walk or ride a horse to spot giraffe, kudu, zebra, impala, wildebeest, tsessebe and many species of birds, free from the fear of stumbling into dangerous game such as big cats, elephants or rhino. It's a modest place, set in flat thornbush country, where the animals are free to roam in a natural setting. Driving around the sanctuary is possible, but riding is the most rewarding way to see and get close up to the animals. Book for accompanied rides, which are fine for novices, at the park entrance. The best times to go are early morning and late afternoon.

If you don't have the energy to rent a bike (see p.164) and cycle to the sanctuary, take one of the commuter omnibuses that heads down Matopos Road from the terminal on the corner of Eighth Avenue Extension and Basch Street, to **Retreat**, from where you'll have to walk or hitch the last couple of kilometres to the entrance. Another option is to join one of the **tours** to Tshabalala: those offered by Chamboko, 113a Josiah Tongogara St (☎09/76838 or 61857), and African Wanderer, (☎09/72736), are recommended.

Chipangali Wildlife Orphanage

A favourite place for family weekend outings, the **Chipangali Wildlife Orphanage**, 23km southeast of town on Leopold Takawira Avenue, which becomes the Gwanda/Johannesburg road (daily except Mon 10am–5pm; US$2 ☎09/72179 or 70764, fax 46460), is a good place to see the big cats head-on, as well as other African animals you may not have spotted in game parks. The sick, abandoned or orphaned animals are penned up, which gives the place the feeling of a zoo, but they're relocated when possible to the wild after rehabilitation. Feeding time (around 3.30pm) is when you'll see all the lions and other predators snarling and growling over hunks of meat.

To get there by public transport, catch a Gwanda or Esigodini **bus** or **commuter omnibus** on the corner of Samuel Parirenyatwa Street and Second Avenue. The tour operators that go to Tshabalala also offer trips to Chipangali. You can spend the night in quite basic but comfortable enough **chalets** (①), just behind the tearoom, with communal ablutions and cooking

Eating and drinking

Without any regional cuisine to speak of, Bulawayo's food is sometimes pretty good but rarely a revelation. Places serving **snacks** and **light meals** tend to open only during the day, along with the **sadza** spots and greasy takeaways around the train station and bus terminals. Apart from the places listed below, Bulawayo shares the rest of the country's taste for **takeaways**, and you'll find numerous places down Jason Moyo and Fife streets as well as Robert Mugabe Way, selling pies, pizzas, chicken and burgers. Something that has only arrived over the past five years, and still a rarity, are the continental-style pavement **cafés**, where you can relax over a pretty good cup of coffee and a roll. **Hotels** such as the *Selborne* do good buffet lunches with generous salad selections, and **steakhouses** are another safe bet, serving great-value Zimbabwean meat for lunch or dinner. Some of the more old-fashioned restaurants cater for a predominantly white clientele, with formal dress codes and night-time dinner dancing.

As far as **prices** go, you should be able to sit down to an inexpensive main course for under US$2.50; a mid-priced one at a decent eatery will set you back US$2.50–4. Anything above this is pricey for Bulawayo – you'd be most unlikely to find a dish that busts US$7.50.

Cafés, takeaways and snacks

Café Baku, Bulawayo Centre, Main Street. Self-consciously chic European-style café with arty wrought-iron furniture, good coffee and overpriced salami or prosciutto rolls. A young mixed crowd brings it to life after dark. Daily 9am–late.

Bonne Journee, 105 Robert Mugabe Way. A cheap family friendly hangout out that, despite its French-sounding name, is Portuguese-owned and does burgers, mixed grills, fish, kebabs, excellent *piri-piri* chicken and good coffee. Daily except Tues 8am–9pm.

Courtyard Café, at the National Gallery, 75 Main St/Leopold Takawira Avenue. The most congenial spot in town for tea or lunch, with fresh flowers, stripped wooden floors, tables inside or out, and decent salads, pastas and steaks. Daily except Mon 9am–4.30pm.

Eskimo Hut, at the entrance to Showgrounds. Very popular for drive-in ice creams and takeaways.

Haefeli's, 103 Fife St, between Tenth and Eleventh avenues. Far less pretentious than *Baku*, this is the only other European-style café in town, where you can sit down and have a good sandwich and decent coffee indoors or on the pavement. One of the few places still open after 10pm, making it a popular after-movies hangout. Mon–Fri 7am–11pm, Sat & Sun till midnight.

Mary's Corner, 88 Josiah Tongogara St, between Eighth and Ninth avenues. Good, old-fashioned roast-and-three-veg set meals served at lunchtime. Good value and handy for the campsite. Mon–Fri 7.30am–4pm, Sat 8am–noon.

Nando's Chickenland, Jason Moyo Street/Eighth Avenue. More expensive than the average takeaway joint, but serves excellent grilled *piri-piri* chicken, hot and spicy as you like, from the hugely successful South African franchise. Mon–Thurs 9am–11pm, Sat & Sun 9am–1am.

Oriental Takeaway, 85b George Silundika St/Eighth Avenue (☎09/72567). The best pies in town including beef pasties, chicken and mushroom, creamy fish or tangier alternatives such as their spicy chicken roll. Free city-centre deliveries for orders over US$0.50. Mon–Fri 9am–5pm, Sat 8.30am–2pm.

Palace Hotel, Jason Moyo Street/Tenth Avenue. Essentially a beer garden with palm trees that serves meat-and-chips dishes at lunchtime. A good place to meet black Zimbabweans.

Sister's, 2nd Floor, Haddon & Sly, Fife Street/Eighth Avenue. Imaginative, reasonably priced food at one of the most popular lunchtime eateries in the surreal setting of a defunct and empty department store (a move of location for the restaurant is on the cards). Choice includes bagels and flower salads, a selection of scrumptious cakes and desserts (their strawberry and vanilla terrine with butterscotch sauce is something else). Recommended for vegetarians. Daytime only.

Restaurants

Cape to Cairo, Robert Mugabe Way/Leopold Takawira Avenue. Specializes in game dishes and Zimbabwean fish. Mon–Fri noon–3pm & 6–10pm, Sat 6–10pm.

Capri, Eleventh Avenue/George Silundika Street. Good pizza oven, home-made pasta with great sauces (try the smoked salmon carbonara) and tasty seafood at reasonable prices, although their liquor prices are stiff. Tues–Fri 12.30–2pm & 6.30–10pm, Sat & Mon eves only.

Cattleman Steakhouse, Josiah Tongogara Street/Tenth Avenue. Excellent charcoal-grilled steaks and a table of salads.

The Coach House, Nesbitt Castle, 6 Percy Ave, Hillside (✿09/42735–6). A delightful venue for Bulawayo's most stylish tea or coffee, served on the lawn with a choice of muffins, scones or cake for not much over US$1. Their five-course dinners can seem a touch over-formal, though, and are the most expensive in town. No under-12s. Booking essential for tea or dinner. Daily till midnight for dinner.

Golden Spur, 85 Robert Mugabe Way (between Eighth and Ninth avenues). One of the most popular steakhouses in Bulawayo. Vegetarians steer clear. Mon–Fri lunch and dinner, Sat dinner.

La Gondola, 106 Robert Mugabe Way, between Tenth and Eleventh avenues (✿09/61884). Posh seafood restaurant with a bar that opens week nights at 4.30pm for pre-dinner drinks. Mon–Thurs 11am–2.30pm & 6–10pm, Fri 11am–2.30pm & 6pm–midnight, Sat 6pm–midnight.

New Orleans, *Banff Lodge*, Banff Road/Leander Avenue, Hillside (✿09/43176). Favoured by locals for a special night out, the rich, moderately priced dishes come draped in thick cheesy sauces with a liberal use of cream. A formal place, but the atmosphere is warm and the daily specials are always good, with at least one vegetarian option. Booking essential. Daily 12.15–2pm & 7–9pm; closed Tues lunch.

Olav's Bistro, *Selborne Hotel*, George Silundika Street/Leopold Takawira Avenue (✿09/65741). One of Bulawayo's most stylish, some say pretentious, restaurants, decorated with formal green upholstery and matching waiters' uniforms. The expensive French and Norwegian cuisine includes Scandinavian salmon, scampi and their "seafood symphony" platter.

The Peking, Treger House, Jason Moyo Street, between Eleventh and Twelfth avenues. Reasonable and recommended Chinese food. Mon–Fri noon–2pm & 6–10pm, Sat 6–10pm.

Beer gardens

Beer gardens are a must if you want to get to grips with how Zimbabweans live in the townships. And they're fun – people will always chat to you, after they've stared a while. Essentially daytime places, serving *chibuku*, braaied meat and *sadza*, they're open from 10.30am to late. One of the easiest township drinking places to find is at the **Amakhosi Theatre** (see p.163), Township Square, Old Falls Road/Basch Street, at the northwest corner of the city centre as it merges with Makokoba high-density suburb. A safe and relaxed venue, it's a good place to meet people, with a convivial bar in the evenings that serves both traditional and bottled beers. During the day you can queue up to get cheap *sadza* lunches in the canteen.

Entertainment and nightlife

Films and any other **entertainment** on offer in Bulawayo, including occasional classical music concerts in the City Hall, are listed in the *Chronicle*; as elsewhere in Zimbabwe, look out for posters wrapped around trees advertising live local music.

Live music and nightclubs

When it comes to music, Bulawayo is a lot quieter than Harare, but you'd be unlucky not to find some **live music** in Bulawayo on any weekend, and there's invariably something good at the end of the month. Hotels are the most common venues, though big concerts do occasionally take place at the White City Stadium in the western townships. Here in Matabeleland you should look out for the local brand of **pop**, which, with

ANNUAL FESTIVALS

Every year at the end of April and beginning of May, Bulawayo hosts the three-week **Inxusa Festival** at the Amakhosi Theatre, Township Square Cultural Centre, featuring music, theatre, dance and poetry. Billed as a "celebration of African culture and inter-disciplinary arts" it has a sharp edge of political and social comment. Past performers have included musicians Oliver Mutukudzi, Andy Brown, Leonard Zhakarta, Simon Chimbetu, the Lumbumbashi All-Stars, as well as the Tumbuka Dance Troupe. The 1999 festival staged 150 events with over 500 artists from ten countries.

The week-long **Festival e' Nkundleni**, held at the end of November or beginning of December, doesn't confine itself to formal venues, but spills into the town with performances, exhibitions and craft markets. Initiated in 1992, it takes place in Bulawayo's streets, theatres, pubs and department stores and includes dance, music, poetry and theatre from Zimbabwe and international visiting groups.

its strong South African *mbaqanga* influence, caused a revolution in Zimbabwean pop in the late 1960s by displacing the previously dominant rumba rhythms from former Zaire (now the Democratic Republic of Congo). Current proponents of the style include **Chase Skuza** and **Olben Moyo**.

Two excellent local **jazz bands** that perform at the *Alabama* are **Jazz Impacto**, with their distinctive sax sound that fuses South African *kwela* with Afro-jazz and makes sweet listening, and – even better – is **Strive**, with distinct influences traceable to South African diva Miriam Makeba, whose rhythms force you stand up and swing.

If you're lucky enough, your visit to Bulawayo may coincide with a performance by one of the city's accomplished **marimba groups** (see p.374). The marimba, a type of xylophone that nearly died out following the forced migrations of the colonial era, was revived in the 1960s at Bulawayo's renowned **Kwanongoma College**, whose orchestra, the **Kwanongoma Marimba Ensemble**, ranks among the best in the country and is well worth keeping an eye out for.

Two internationally known local groups, **Black Umfolosi** and **Black Spear**, do traditional a cappella singing, after the style of South Africa's Ladysmith Black Mambazo.

Clubs tend to play American **disco** and **funk** and are not the places to find Zimbabwean music. If you do venture out on to the seamier side of the town, watch out at the end of the evening for "the girls", who are great to dance with, but may insist on accompanying you home.

VENUES

The Alabama, *Bulawayo Rainbow Hotel*, Josiah Tongogara Street/Tenth Avenue. The only place in town where you'll catch good live sounds every night of the week (see above).

Cecil Hotel, Fife Street/Third Avenue (☎09/60295). Nightly disco playing mid-Atlantic pop and some local stuff.

New Waverley Hotel, 133–134 Lobengula St/Thirteenth Avenue. Raucous venue opposite the train station, hosting end-of-month gigs in the beer garden and live bands on Friday nights. Entrance is free unless a visiting big name is playing.

Silver Fox, Robert Mugabe Way/Tenth Avenue. Local music and disco.

Talk of the Town, in the Monte Carlo Centre, Fife Street/Twelfth Avenue. One of Zimbabwe's hottest clubs, with a mix of house, jive and reggae.

Township Square Cultural Centre, Old Falls Road/Basch Street (☎09/76673 or 79379). The best place to sample bona fide traditional Zimbabwean music and dance (see p.163).

Cinema and theatre

There are two Rainbow **cinemas** in town: the spanking-new four-screen City 1, 2, 3 and 4 at the Bulawayo Centre, Main Street, shows pretty bland Hollywood fare (the type of thing you may well have seen on the flight over), while the older Elite 400, Robert Mugabe Way, shows action double features. As for drama, the only **theatre** where you're likely to find something local on a regular basis is the Amakhosi at the Township Square Cultural Centre, on the corner of the Old Falls Road and Basch Street. The Bulawayo Theatre in Centenary Park, Leopold Takawira Avenue, occasionally hosts interesting visiting productions, and the large and small city halls are usual venues for concerts and shows. Check the *Chronicle* for entertainment listings.

Football

Zimbabweans are passionate about soccer and a good place to catch some of this enthusiasm is at one of the matches held at **Barbourfields Stadium** in Mzilikazi township, Vera Road, opposite the Mzilikazi Art and Craft Centre. The western stand, nicknamed "Soweto", is best avoided, as this is where local supporters and *tsotsis* (thugs) hang out and where fights are most likely to break out. Rather, sit in the special enclosure, which is generally regarded as safer.

Shopping

Most of the useful **shops** in Bulawayo lie within five minutes' walk of the City Hall. The relatively new Bulawayo Centre, where there's a pharmacy, record shop, newsagent, Internet café, travel agent, shoe and clothes shops, is the poshest mall in town and the place to go if you're looking for better-quality goods. Probably the most colourful area to shop in Bulawayo is the African street market in the vicinity of the corner of Fifth Avenue and Fife Street, which is a lot more atmospheric than the Bulawayo Centre.

Groceries and food

Access Family Supermarket, Fife Street/Leopold Takawira Avenue, opposite the main police station. The only grocery shop in the centre and recommended for general supplies, with a good selection of vegetables.

Farm Fresh Vegetables, 122 Robert Mugabe Way. Excellent for a wide range of vegetables, eggs, dairy products, cakes and outstanding home-made pastas, cold meats and cheeses.

Haefeli's Swiss Bakery, Fife Street/Tenth Avenue. Its long-standing reputation throughout the city's middle-class suburbs ensures that this excellent bakery is always buzzing. Wide choice of loaves, including rye with or without caraway seeds and tasty filled rolls.

Solomon's Supermarket, 56b Fife Ave. The closest thing Bulawayo has to a deli, where you can buy relatively exotic foods such as olive oil, and Jewish specialities including matzos.

TM Supermarket, Ascot Shopping Centre, Leopold Takawira Avenue/Ascot Way. A good place for groceries and booze, especially local and South African wines, at Bulawayo's most upmarket (which isn't saying much) shopping centre.

Walter's Bakery, Robert Mugabe Way/Twelfth Avenue. Fine Italian bakery where you'll get exceptionally good *ciabatta*.

Books and music

Book Mart, 103 George Silundika, between Tenth and Eleventh avenues. Book exchange with a variable stock.

CNA, Bulawayo Centre, Main Street. Good source of newspapers and magazines, including South Africa's *Mail & Guardian*, international weekly editions of the British *Guardian* and *Telegraph* as well *Time*, *Newsweek* and many publications with an African slant. Also has a small but reasonable selection of field guides and pulp fiction.

Kingstons, 91 Jason Moyo St. One of the better-stocked bookshops in town and a good bet for maps and field guides.

Ndoro Trading, Shop 2, Pioneer House, Eighth Avenue. Small but well-chosen selection of Zimbabwean and African CDs.

Sabona Gallery Shop, National Gallery, 75 Main St. Choice selection of Zimbabwean CDs, novels and art books.

Spinalong, Bulawayo Centre, Main Street. The largest record shop in town with a decent number of CDs and tapes by local and African performers.

Vigne Bookshop, 122 Fife St. The only bookshop in town with knowledgeable staff and a reasonable selection.

Crafts and souvenirs

Jairos Jiri, Robert Mugabe Way, behind the City Hall. One of the better branches of this chain, found in the main towns, selling products by disabled craftworkers, cards and a wide selection of local handmade goods. There's a large array of Matabeleland baskets, local pottery, the usual unexceptional soapstone carvings and some good Ndebele beadwork, notably dolls. You're under no pressure to buy, so browse as long as you like.

Ndoro Trading, Shop 2, Pioneer House, Eighth Avenue. Small shop selling a limited choice of the best in Zimbabwean crafts, a good collection of T-shirts, cards and contemporary crafts.

Sabona Gallery Shop, National Gallery, 75 Main St. Specialists in the art and crafts of Matabeleland, with some fine baskets, sculptures, woodcarvings and modern street crafts such as wire cars and motorbikes made out of tin cans.

Listings

Airlines Air Zimbabwe, Trager House, Jason Moyo Street (☎09/72051); South African Airways, Ground Floor, Africa House, Fife Street/Tenth Avenue (☎09/71337); Zimbabwe Express Airlines, Shop 6, Fidelity Life Centre, Fife Street/Eleventh Avenue (☎09/229797 or 229775).

American Express Manica Travel, Fidelity Life Centre, Fife Street/Eleventh Avenue (☎09/540531 or 540535).

Automobile Association Fanum House, Leopold Takawira Avenue/Josiah Tongogara Street (Mon–Fri 8.30am–4.30pm, Sat 8–11am; ☎09/70063, Harare emergency and after-hours ☎04/707959). Very friendly and helpful, and stocks the best (their own) map of Zimbabwe.

Banks Banks are easy to find in the city centre and all have foreign currency counters, where you can change cash or travellers' cheques. Amongst them are Barclays, Main Street/Eighth Avenue; Commercial Bank of Zimbabwe (CBZ), 81a Main St (opposite the central post office); First Bank, Mezzanine Floor, Parkade Centre, 93 Fife St/Ninth Avenue; Standard Chartered, Fife Street/Tenth Avenue. There are also several banks at the Ascot Shops, Leopold Takawira Avenue/Ascot Way, which is handy for the eastern and southern suburbs. Hours are: Mon, Tues, Thurs & Fri 8am–3pm, Wed 8am–1pm, Sat 8–11.30am.

Bike rental Dra-Gama Tourist Services, Office 9, Shamrock House, Eighth Avenue/Josiah Tongogara Street (☎09/72739), and Circle Court Tours and Safaris, 101 York House, Eighth Avenue/Herbert Chitepo Street (☎09/540150, fax 75230), rent mountain bikes for about US$10 per day.

Bureaux de change There are about ten bureaux de change in Bulawayo, all of them authorized and legal, and most of the banks will also change foreign currency. In the city centre you'll find: Barnford's, Shop 52, Bulawayo Centre, Main Street/Ninth Avenue; CFX Foreign Exchange, 97 Robert Mugabe Way; Express, Solomon's, 56b Fife St; FX Moneycorp, Jairos Jiri Craft Shop, Leopold Takawira Avenue/Robert Mugabe Way.

Camping equipment Eezee Kamping, 99 George Silundika St/Tenth Avenue. The best place for camping and fishing gear and safari clothes, but nothing too sophisticated.

Car rental The larger companies with offices in both town and at the airport are: Avis, Robert Mugabe Way/Tenth Avenue (☎09/68571 or 61306); Elite, 17 Woolwich Rd, Thorngrove (☎09/72587); Europcar, 9a Africa House, Fife Street (☎09/67925 or 74157); Hertz, George Silundika Street/Fourteenth Avenue (☎74701 or 61402). Other companies include: Budget, 106 Josiah Tongogara Ave, between Tenth and Eleventh avenues (☎09/72543 or 65566, mobile ☎011/601533); Thrifty, 88a Robert Mugabe Way (☎09/63683); and, cheapest in town, Transit Car Hire, 86 Robert Mugabe Ave/Eighth Avenue (☎09/76495–6, mobile ☎011/201058).

Doctors and dentists are listed in the front of the Bulawayo section of the telephone directory. See also Hospitals and clinics.

Emergencies General emergency ☎999; ambulance ☎994; fire ☎993; and police ☎995. See also: Medical Air Rescue Services.

Hospitals and clinics The government hospitals aren't recommended, but there are several alternatives. In the city centre, Galen House, 93 Josiah Tongogara St/Ninth Avenue (☎09/540051–4), operates a 24hr pop-in emergency service, which tends to be rather full during the day but is a lot better at night; and The Family Centre, 92 Parirenyatwa St (Mon–Fri 8am–1pm & 2–5pm, Sat 8–11am, duty doctor contactable by phone at other times on ☎09/76666, 68702 or 68096), is a friendly group general practice that's a good first port of call for non-emergencies, but you'll need an appointment. In the suburbs, 3km from the centre, the private Mater Dei Hospital, Browning Road, off Hillside Road/Burns Drive, Malindela (☎09/46516), has a spanking-new casualty department, built in 1999.

Immigration department Old Income Tax Building, next to the National Parks booking office, Tenth Avenue/Herbert Chitepo Street (☎09/65621). Best to go in person.

Internet and email The most switched-on Internet café in Bulawayo with the fastest connections is AfriNet Surfing, Shop 59, Bulawayo Centre, Main Street, between Ninth and Tenth avenues (Mon–Fri 9am–6pm, Sat 9am–1pm; ☎09/70324, *secbird@harare.iafrica.com*); and the coolest in the country is Evernet – The Surfer's Paradise, in a laid-back suburban home at 33a Clark Rd, Suburbs (daily 8am–8pm; ☎09/60032 or 78410, fax 79353, *parpatch@telconet.co.zw*), which offers free transport from town and has a pool table, darts, music and a swimming pool, as well as snacks and coffee.

Laundry 109a Josiah Tongogara St, between Eleventh and Twelfth avenues (daily); and Fife Street Launderette, Fidelity Life Centre, Fife Street/Tenth Avenue (Mon, Tues, Thurs & Fri 7.30am–5pm, Wed & Sat 8am–2pm).

Medical Air Rescue Service (MARS), 42 Robert Mugabe Way (☎09/60351 or 78946, ambulance calls ☎64082), offers a superior ambulance and paramedic service to the state-run one, but if you haven't taken out a subscription (see Basics, p.20) you'll be expected to give a guarantee that you'll pay before leaving Zimbabwe.

Mobile phone Econet's Buddie pay-as-you-go starter packs and airtime recharge cards can be bought at numerous outlets in town, including the kiosk in Meikles, Jason Moyo Street/Leopold Takawira Avenue, and the Econet shop upstairs in Bulawayo Centre, Main Street. The CNA newsagent in Bulawayo Centre sells the equivalent for the NetOne network (not always available).

Money transfers Western Union, upstairs, Bulawayo Centre, Main Street/Ninth Avenue, can transfer money from almost anywhere in the world and claims to complete transactions from Europe, the US and Australasia in 15min and from South Africa in around 3hr.

National Parks Bookings Herbert Chitepo Street/Tenth Avenue (Mon–Fri 8am–4pm; ☎09/63646, fax 65592).

Pharmacies Bulawayo's best pharmacy is the busy Plus Two, 94b Robert Mugabe Way, near the City Hall (☎09/68667–8), which has the best stocks and is able to provide reliable advice on minor complaints. After hours, the town's pharmacies jointly operate the Chemists' Emergency Service, 86c Robert Mugabe Way (Mon–Fri 5–9pm, Sat 1–9pm, Sun 9am–9pm; ☎09/69781).

Photos Of the several 1hr processing places around town, Gold Print has the best reputation, with branches at Selous House, Jason Moyo/Tenth Avenue, and Meikles, 64a Herbert Chitepo St.

Police The Central Police Station is on Leopold Takawira Avenue/Fife Street (☎09/72516).

Post office Main branch at Main Street/Eighth Avenue (Mon–Fri 9am–5.30pm, Sat 9am–12.30pm); branch offices in the suburbs.

Swimming pool Samuel Parirenyatwa Street Baths (Sept–May 10am–2pm & 3–6pm).

Taxis Rixi ☎09/60666 or 61933.

Telephone booths and bureaux There are public call boxes all over town with long queues, making it preferable to use one of the phone bureaux such as Tshaka's Communications, Ground Floor, Bulawayo Centre, Main Street, which has plenty of phones and rarely has queues. Local calls cost about US$0.10 for 3min and about US$0.40 per min for calls to Harare or mobile phones.

Travel agents There's no shortage of travel agents, but if in doubt one of the best is Eco Logical Safaris, Shop 58, Bulawayo Centre, Main Street (☎09/61189, fax 540590, *cbristow@ acacia.samara.co.zw*), a friendly, well-informed agency that's particularly good for advice and all travel arrangements in Zimbabwe. Other reputable agencies include: Sunshine Tours, Bulawayo Centre, Main Street, between Ninth and Tenth avenues (☎09/67791, fax 74832, *sunshine@acacia.samara.co.zw*); Gemsbok Safaris, Eighth Avenue/Jason Moyo Street (☎ & fax 09/70009, *gemsbok@acacia.samara. co.zw*); and Manica Travel, Fidelity Life Centre, Fife Street (☎09/540531 or 540535), recommended for booking coach tickets.

AROUND BULAWAYO

A place of incredible power and beauty, the **Matopos Range** is the most compelling reason to explore the **Bulawayo area**. Here, among the smooth granites of whale-backed hills and crenellated castle kopjes, the descendants of Zimbabwe's earliest **hunter-gatherer** inhabitants painted elegant images on the walls of overhangs and in weather-scooped caves. These paintings survive to be seen today in the **Matobo National Park**, which also offers some of the best hiking in the country and reasonable game viewing in its game park. Although now officially known as the Matobo Hills, you'll invariably hear the colonial term "Matopos" used, and see both versions in print.

The hills themselves have the appearance of volcanic eruptions, though they are in fact geologically extremely ancient, having lain covered for thousands of millennia by softer material. This covering has been gradually worn down to the present-day ground level, exposing the previously buried hills – an impressive illustration of just how hard these rocks are.

Besides the Matopos, the area around Bulawayo takes in the beautiful and deserted stone ruins at **Kame**, a convenient half-day's outing from the city. Other stone ruin sites lie, far less accessibly, off the Harare road at **Naletale** and **Danangombe**, best visited on an overnight jaunt, staying at one of the guest farms nearby.

Matobo National Park

Many people visit **Matobo National Park** (day entry US$10, week entry US$20), some 50km south from Bulawayo, for a day, but it's well worth spending longer here, in the park itself or at one of the luxury lodges on the perimeter. The landscape is staggering, and there's miles of walking, as well as the world's highest concentration of ancient rock paintings, leopards and black eagles.

The park is punctuated with very beautiful dams, the easiest to reach from Bulawayo being **Maleme Dam**, which has National Parks lodges, camping, horse-riding, tennis and some short walks to nearby painted caves. Most day-trippers head here for a picnic, stopping off on the way at **World's View**, topped by the grave of Cecil Rhodes. The remote **Toghwe Wilderness Area**, with campsites at **Toghwana** and **Mtsheleli dams**, and two of Zimbabwe's finest **painted caves**, is another day-trip. Also, the **game park** in the **Whovi Wilderness area**, although modest compared to Zimbabwe's great game parks, provides a wonderful granite backdrop to views of its grazing and browsing herds and, most thrilling, regular sightings of white rhino.

Some history

While giving the appearance of being one of Africa's unchanging places, Matobo National Park is really a colonial invention, the story of which is fraught with politics and competing black and white ideologies.

From the early days after the defeat of the First Chimurenga, the white Matopos settlers were worried about a supposed threat to their heritage posed by the presence of blacks on the quasi-sacred site of Rhodes's grave. Later, with the consolidation of racial segregation, concerted attempts were made to shove the black peasant farmers elsewhere. However, even as the whites were developing their theories that Africans were hopeless farmers who were destroying the wild game and upsetting the balance of nature, African ideologies arose in parallel, mirroring white claims to the land. By the 1940s, when attempts to shift Africans hotted up, there was a growing consciousness of the hills as a holy place of Ndebele tradition (see box on p.172), and white accusations of black land mismanagement were countered by the blacks' claims to have been farming the region effectively for centuries before white settlers arrived.

For over a decade, Africans successfully opposed removal, both through the courts and by passive resistance campaigns, but, by 1962, a scheme was approved to clear part of the Matopos to create a national park. Residents were deported south to the Khumalo and east to the Gulati Tribal Trust Lands. African resentment was manifest in the destruction of fences, the lighting of veld fires and petrol-bombing of the park office. The furore was closely linked with burgeoning **nationalist politics**: the young Robert Mugabe even threatened to dig up Rhodes's grave and send the body to England. Through the 1960s, fence cutting and resistance continued. **ZIPRA guerrillas**, who arrived in the 1970s, took refuge in the perfect hideouts offered by the hills, gaining the support of local people, who believed that the park would be returned to them after the war.

It was perhaps the failure of this to materialize that prompted **dissidents** to return to the Matopos Hills in the early 1980s. Although it's still difficult to gauge, they appear to have had the support of frustrated peasants who felt betrayed by the government. The government sent in troops, who brutally murdered and repressed people all over Matabeleland, although much was hushed up at the time.

Following the **Unity Accord** and amnesty in 1988, the Matopos was once again peaceful, although the government declined to give back the national park to its former residents – to deregulate an area nominated for world heritage status would damage its international reputation. The farmlands are now a wilderness and the cultural life that once thrived here is gone – the **rain shrines** inside the park are deserted. Ironically, it's outside the confines of the heritage-preserving national park, in the adjoining communal lands, that spiritual shrines like Njelele are still flourishing.

Accommodation

National Parks accommodation is available at Maleme Dam (see p.171), which gets pretty full in peak season, but during the week and outside school holidays a lodge is easy enough to come by. Although Maleme Dam rest camp is the only place with roofed accommodation, it is possible to camp at several different sites in the park.

In common with all Zimbabwe's National Parks, most of the places to stay are in **private accommodation** just outside the park boundaries, where there are a couple of reasonably priced places, as well as some superb luxury lodges. The nearest **petrol** is back at Bulawayo, and it's best to bring everything you'll need while you're here from the city. Shopping is restricted to basic **groceries** at Maleme Rest Camp (open daily), and much the same at Fryer's or Inungu Store, 10km from Maleme, also open daily (if

---

MASIYE CAMP

Imaginatively designed and built by two local Ndebele women, **Masiye Camp** (book through Enterprise House, Twelfth Avenue/Josiah Tongogara Street, Bulawayo; PO Box AC800, Bulawayo; ☎09/60727, mobile ☎091/224508, *samasiye@telconet.co.zw*) is a beautiful place at the edge of a dam set among rocks and shady vegetation; all profits from Masiye go to a Salvation Army-sponsored project to assist AIDS orphans. It has five **double huts** (①) with communal ablutions and two small en-suite **family units** (③) built into the rocks, as well as two larger two-bedroom units (③). There's also a platform on top of a kopje, should you wish to sleep under the stars. You can self-cater or buy cooked **traditional meals**. Among the **activities** are canoeing on the dam, walks to rock paintings with a local guide, plus visits to a village blacksmith or peasant farmer. There are plans for three-day guided walks with porters, overnighting at camps along the way, and a **tearoom** is open to the public (7.30am–7pm). The camp is well signposted along the Toghwana/Inanke road.

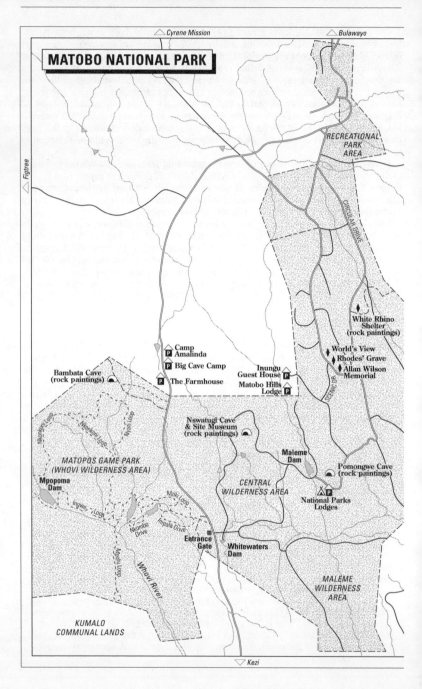

△ Cyrene Mission   △ Bulawayo

MATOBO NATIONAL PARK

△ Figtree

RECREATIONAL
PARK
AREA

CIRCULAR DRIVE

White Rhino
Shelter
(rock paintings)

World's View
Rhodes' Grave
Allan Wilson
Memorial

SCENIC DR.

Camp
Amalinda
Big Cave Camp
The Farmhouse

Inungu
Guest House
Matobo Hills
Lodge

Bambata Cave
(rock paintings)

Nswatugi Cave
& Site Museum
(rock paintings)

Nkonjwe Loop
Nkantoni Loop
Nyan Loop

MATOPOS GAME PARK
(WHOVI WILDERNESS AREA)

Maleme
Dam

Pomongwe Cave
(rock paintings)

CENTRAL
WILDERNESS
AREA

National Parks
Lodges

Mpopoma
Dam

Maziki Loop

Ingwe Loop

Nkombo
Drive

Impala Drive

Mpofu Loop

Whovi River

Entrance
Gate

Whitewaters
Dam

MALEME
WILDERNESS
AREA

KUMALO
COMMUNAL LANDS

▽ Kezi

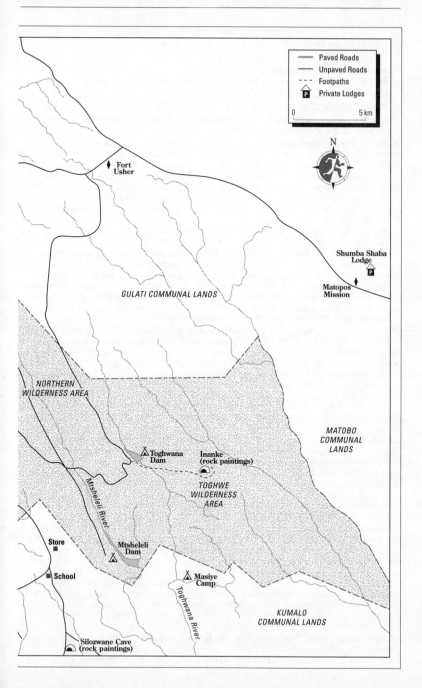

Paved Roads
Unpaved Roads
Footpaths
P Private Lodges
0   5 km

N

Fort
Usher

Shumba Shaba
Lodge
P

Matopos
Mission

GULATI COMMUNAL LANDS

*NORTHERN
WILDERNESS AREA*

*MATOBO
COMMUNAL
LANDS*

Toghwana
Dam

Inanke
(rock paintings)

*TOGHWE
WILDERNESS
AREA*

Mtsheleli River

Store

Mtsheleli
Dam

School

Masiye
Camp

Toghwana River

*KUMALO
COMMUNAL
LANDS*

Silozwane Cave
(rock paintings)

its closed, hoot and the owners who live behind the store will come and open it). For directions to the store, see *Inungu Guest House* (below).

Private lodges and camps

In the last few years, several **exclusive camps** and **lodges** have opened up in dramatic settings on the edge of the national park, all of them in the hills, and some nearer to the National Park than others. Prices listed below are for all-in rates, and are lower for Zimbabweans and South Africans. Transfers from Bulawayo cost extra, but you can drive to all of the lodges in an ordinary car.

Big Cave Camp, signposted off the Matopos Road at the 46km peg, close to the Game Park entrance, PO Box 88, Bulawayo (bookings ☎ & fax 09/77176, mobile ☎011/602848, camp ☎083/8245, *bigcave@harare.iafrica.com*). The most impressive feature of this small camp with seven A-frame chalets is the stunning setting on top of a huge whaleback granite hill, surrounded by 360-degree views of kopjes and valleys. The stone-and-thatch chalets are small, but the French windows opening onto decks compensate. Activities include guided hikes, horse-riding, game drives, rock-art visits and raptor walks. Full board US$95 per person, inclusive of two activities US$195, under-12s half-price.

Camp Amalinda, signposted at the 45km peg on the Matopos Road, close to the Game Park entrance (book through Londa Mela Safaris, 23 Old Gwanda Rd; PO Box 9088, Hillside, Bulawayo ☎09/43954, 46430 or 46443, fax 46436; camp ☎083–8/268, *amalinda@acacia.samara.co.zw*) This camp positively oozes sophisticated luxury and leisured wealth. Ten spacious thatched suites with private terraces nestle amongst boulders and the dining area sits beneath a granite overhang. A stunningly set swimming pool appears suspended on a lip of granite with sunbeds to take in views across a dam. Activities include game drives, tracking rhinos with a professional guide, horse-riding and elephant-back trails (US$50 per person). There's an airstrip if you want to fly in. Fully inclusive US$220, Nov–April discounts and under-12s half-price.

The Farmhouse, Signposted at the 48km peg along the Matopos Road, near the Game Park entrance (☎09/654991 or 70008, fax 654991, mobile ☎091/231318, *farmhouse@gatorzw.com*). One of the few mid-range options, this is a relaxed, attractive and informal B&B with twelve small white-washed self-contained cottages at the foot of a towering granite outcrop. Set on four-square-kilometre property, there are large lawns around the farmhouse itself and tables under umbrellas leading to a swimming pool with waterfall. Self-catering is available or you can order meals at the farmhouse. Among the activities on offer are game drives in the national park, horse-riding, guided walks to look at black eagles or rhinos (the owner is a professional guide) and trips to Bambata Cave. B&B US$55, half board US$65, full board, activities and transfers US$180, under-12s half-price.

Inungu Guest House, next to Fryer's Store, 10km from Maleme Dam, can be booked through Sunshine Tours Bulawayo Centre, Main Street, between Ninth and Tenth avenues (☎09/67791, fax 74832, *sunshine@acacia.samara.co.zw*). One of the cheapest Matopos stays, in a scenic area not far from Rhodes's grave, *Inungu Guest House* sleeps six and is for the use of one self-catering party at a time. Style is not one of its strong points, but it's a popular and pleasant place nevertheless. From Maleme, follow the main road to World's View for 3.5km and take the second turning to the left (after the Pomongwe cave turn-off); after about 6km, bear left and the guest house and shop are on your right 1km further on. B&B US$12.

Malalangwe, Impi Safaris, PO Box 2723, Bulawayo (book through Top of the Range ☎09/41748, or direct ☎09/3183 or 3129, *stonehil@acacia.samara.co.zw*). Luxurious, well-run camp on a magnificent game farm, with a good share of rock paintings and archeological remains, on the western edge of the Matopos range, 1hr from Bulawayo at Marula on the Plumtree Road. Environmental awareness is high on the agenda as the owner, Richard Peek, is a well-known naturalist, and if you're keen on birds, botany, mammals or archeology, this is one of the very best places in the country to come to. The BBC used Malalangwe to film black eagles, and guests can even participate in ongoing data-collecting projects concerning nesting birds or elands. Activities include game drives and walks. Full board and activities Jan 6–June 30 US$140, July 1–Jan 5 US$170. Trips to Matobo National Park extra. Children welcome.

Matobo Hills Lodge, Touch the Wild, 46 George Silundika St, PO Box 3447, Bulawayo (☎09/540922, 540944, 540967–8, fax 229088, *touchwld@harare.iafrica.com*). Closest of the lodges to Maleme and Rhodes's Grave, and set high up in the hills, with great views, lawns, sunbeds and a pool. The decor is ethnic, and the carpeted rooms are hotel-like, rather than safari camp in feel – with up to 34 guests, it lacks the intimacy of the smaller camps. There is a resident professional game guide, and trips to rock paintings, Rhodes's Grave and the game park are offered. Half-board US$127, full-board US$144, fully inclusive US$269.

The Rock Tented Camp, signposted 59km west of Bulawayo on the Plumtree Road, then another 10km (☎09/60575, mobile ☎091/301845). Party time in the western Matopos foothills en route to Botswana, where you can sleep in one of six walk-in tents with twin beds and shared ablutions or pitch your own in a campsite that has seen groups as large as 150. A thatch-roofed lounge has a juke-box and satellite TV, and opens to a lawn and views into shallow valley of grassy woodland. You can self-cater or buy braai packs and have your food cooked by camp staff. To get there, look out for the large sign 59km from Bulawayo and take the dirt road for 10km. Activities include elephant rides and hiking. Full board in walk-in tents US$25, accommodation only US$15, camping in own tent US$5.

Shashani Lodge, signposted 59km from Bulawayo on the Plumtree Road, then another 11km (☎09/60575, mobile ☎091/301845). Six modest but comfortably furnished en-suite brick chalets on top of a granite formation, with balconies overlooking a huge valley in the Matopos foothills, dominated by a massive bald-headed *gomo*. A pool deck overlooks lawns and the valley. There are three elephants, which you can ride, and two lions in an enclosure. Fully inclusive rate (excluding drinks) US$130.

Shumba Shaba Lodge, signposted off the Old Gwanda Road, just beyond the Matopos Mission, 75min from Bulawayo on dirt roads; Zindele Safaris, 140 Fife St, Bulawayo (Bulawayo office ☎09/64128, lodge ☎088/662, *zindele@telconet.co.zw*). Three stylish thatched units perched on a huge granite whaleback known as Red Lion, with truly spectacular views (you can watch the sun rise over the hills from your bed). Each chalet is designed for maximum privacy and one is perfect for a family. Hosted by friendly owners Denis and Sandy Paul, it's an ideal place to chill out, walk, visit rock paintings, mountain-bike, or ride with Sandy, a highly skilled equestrian. Self-drive B&B rate US$50, fully inclusive of transfers from Bulawayo, all meals and two activities US$165.

Seeing the park

The best ways to see the park are **by car** or on one of the recommended **tours** offered by Bulawayo-based companies. There's no public transport to the Matopos, but if you're prepared to walk there are fairly regular local **buses** from Bulawayo to Kezi, stopping at the edge of the park. Ask to be dropped off at the road leading to Maleme Dam; from here it's about a twelve-kilometre walk to Maleme, taking you past the Nswatugi cave rock painting and site museum. **Cycling** the 50km from Bulawayo is fine, but heavy going in summer, and it's certainly not possible to cycle there and back in one day. One less strenuous option is to take your bike on the bus and save it for getting around the park. If you're **hitching**, get the Matopos Road bus from Lobengula Street terminus to Retreat (the last stop) before thumbing. Weekends are not difficult, but during the week the road is extremely quiet.

Tours

One of the best ways of seeing the hills, especially if you only have a day in hand, is to take a **tour from Bulawayo** with African Wanderer (☎09/72736), who are excellent on rock art, history and culture; the recommended Black Rhino (☎09/41662, *blackrhino@hotmail.com*), Chamboko (☎09/76838 or 61857) and Africa Dawn (☎09/74941) do half- or full-day trips. Prices are in the region of US$50 (excluding park entry fees) for a full day. Some of the **backpackers' lodges** in Bulawayo, such as *Western*, do slightly cheaper outings that throw in a night's free accommodation in Bulawayo.

Maleme Dam (the Central Wilderness Area)

Maleme Dam, with its parks accommodation, is the usual first stop on a good tarred road from Bulawayo. The popular route by car to Maleme from Bulawayo takes you past **White Rhino Shelter**, with the best rock art in the rare outline style, and **World's View**, the colonial equivalent of the liberation struggle's Heroes' Acre in Harare. Maleme is good for walking, or just scrambling over boulders. One exciting short walk

THE MWARI CULT IN MATOPOS

As the Great Zimbabwe state in the east of the country disintegrated, its Shona-speaking inhabitants dispersed, looking for new homes. Some, known as the **Torwa**, went west and eventually arrived in the **Matopos** region, establishing themselves around the fifteenth century as the ruling class of the district, with a headquarters at Kame. Imitating their predecessors at Great Zimbabwe, the Torwa built up a large centralized state, over which they ruled until the arrival in the 1680s of the **Rozvi**, another Shona-speaking group from the Mutapa state in the northeast. The Rozvi conquered and took control of the Torwa state, but without destroying it.

It was under the Rozvi that the **cult of Mwari**, the supreme creator, became dominant. Mwari wasn't the exclusive focus of all religious life, and wasn't a personal god: the ancestral spirits still held sway in the lives of ordinary people, while Mwari, as the deity of politics, dealt with matters of state. Most important of these was the bringing of rain – the basis of all economic life.

The Rozvi *mambo*, or king, had the power to intercede with Mwari, and when custom was broken the god would administer punishments in the form of sickness or natural disasters. On these occasions the *mambo* would consult Mwari and become possessed by the *mhondoro*, the original ancestor, a cross between Adam and god, whose spirit had entered a lion. A Mwari priesthood mediated between the possessed king and the people, interpreting the leonine growls of the possessed ruler, passing judgement and punishments, and restoring the natural order.

At the turn of the nineteenth century the religious headquarters of the Rozvi state was in the Matopos and the political capital at Danangombe. The state was in the throes of a political revolution and a **power struggle** that had been developing between the Mwari priesthood and the secular *mambo* came to a head. According to oral tradition, the *mambo* became fed up with the god's interference. When the king heard Mwari's voice coming from the top of his favourite wife's hut, "using a flintlock gun acquired from the Portuguese", he fired at the roof, whereupon the voice moved into the hut and the *mambo* razed the building to the ground. The voice kept on speaking from trees, grass and rocks, and when the *mambo* continued to harass it the voice finally in a "wrathful tone" told the *mambo* that, because he had chased Mwari away, in his place would come "men wearing skins".

The skin-clad men came in the form of **Nguni raiders** – waves of them wearing animal hides. These warriors were by-products of battles taking place in South Africa, where Zulu conquests of the early nineteenth century pushed northwards a series of ruthless refugee armies, which raged through the Rozvi state. When the first bloodthirsty forces under **Zwangendaba** swept through, the *mambo* fled to the Matopos and in despair threw himself off a kopje. Zwangendaba's invasion broke down what remained of the already divided Rozvi state; by the time Mzilikazi's **Ndebele** arrived, the softening-up process was complete and Rozvi country was quickly conquered. The Ndebele forged the tattered fragments into a new, well-controlled and centralized state, occupying present-day southwest Zimbabwe.

The **priesthood** of the Mwari cult retreated to the caves of the Matopos, where Mzilikazi, eager to be on good terms with the local god – a wise move, considering the *mambo*'s fate – sent regular offerings to the shrines. In more recent years, the cult survived even the colonialists. During the 1946 drought many white farmers paid for rain dances to be held in National Park caves; acknowledging the still-potent force of the cult, ZAPU leader **Joshua Nkomo** held regular rallies during the liberation struggle at **Njelele**, one of the biggest rain shrines in the Matopos. It is taboo for outsiders to visit these shrine caves.

goes over vertiginous hills to the barely visible paintings in **Pomongwe cave**, though the outstanding prehistoric images of Nswatugi Cave, 7km in the other direction, are much better. The remote Toghwe Wilderness Area with campsites at Toghwana and Mtsheleli dams is a full day's walk from Maleme.

The dam and around

Right at the centre of the park, **Maleme Dam** provides a good base for day-trips into the other parts. It is also a good place to get your bearings – and an idea of the terrain – before heading off into the wilder east.

You can stay in **National Parks accommodation** or **camp** – barely cheaper than the one-roomed chalets – along the dam but, if possible, it's worth forking out a little extra to stay in one of the two so-called "**luxury lodges**", *Fish Eagle* and *Black Eagle*, if they're available, perched like their namesakes high among the rocks, and treating you to a superb panorama when you wake. Book ahead through the Bulawayo National Parks Booking Agency, Herbert Chitepo Street/Tenth Avenue (Mon–Fri 8am–4pm; ☎09/63646, fax 65592).

There's enough of interest in the Matopos to keep you busy for a week, and one of the best ways to see the area are on foot or **horseback**. Rides leave at 8.30am and 3.30pm and cost US$20 for ninety minutes. You'll see animals on most outings: herds of **sable antelope**, **impala** and **zebra** graze in valleys outside the confines of the park and **kudu** and **bushbuck** are to be seen in the grass. There's no shortage of **baboons and monkeys** – keep the windows and doors of your chalet closed during the day, to stop them from investigating your groceries. Around Maleme you'll also hear the whistling calls of **klipspringer** antelope, which leap up rock faces. Dassies are everywhere, and high on unreachable boulders you'll see the nests of one of the world's largest concentration of **black eagles**. **Leopards** also adore this rocky, cave-riddled terrain but, as usual, you'd be lucky to see one.

The dam area offers **walks** appropriate to all energy levels. A half-hour ramble takes you over the hill to **Pomongwe Cave** and **site museum** (8am–4.30pm) or, to avoid the climb, stroll the 2.5km along the road. The cross-kopje route is the more interesting, but not for vertigo sufferers; its start is signposted and the route waymarked. Steep in parts, it takes you over the hilltop, with a magnificent view and a descent into a thickly wooded granite amphitheatre with a giant cave at one end.

The **cave** is impressive, though its paintings have been annihilated by a well-intentioned smearing of glycerine in the 1920s, supposed to preserve them; it seems unbelievable to have oiled the whole cave before experimenting on a small part. However, this is an important archeological site and digs have uncovered tens of thousands of Stone Age implements and artefacts as well as Iron Age pottery. It's estimated that people lived here for at least 50,000 years. Many of the objects unearthed are displayed in the modest **site museum**.

Nswatugi Cave

Some of the best rock paintings of the area adorn the walls of nearby **Nswatugi Cave**: this is *the* place to visit if you've time for only one site. The animals are beautifully realized, full of life and movement, and will knock on the head any ideas about rock art

---

VISITING THE SITES

A single US$2 ticket is valid for World's View as well as Nswatugi and Pomongwe caves and the game park, but you can't buy tickets at Nswatugi, so make sure you already have one before trawling out. At the time of writing, entry to all the other caves described was free.

being crude or primitive. You only need look at the superb giraffe series or the delicate kudu to realize that these result from an intimate knowledge and years of keen observation of the subject. An informative **site interpretation display**, overseen by an attendant, provides useful background. Nswatugi was one of the shrines in which people used to dance for rain before they were removed from the area in 1962.

To get to the cave, **drive** or **walk** the 7km of road from the Parks lodges past the dam; the road is pretty poor in parts, so you'll need to take it very slowly and it may be advisable for passengers to get out and walk the short sections that are particularly rutted in order to raise your car's clearance. It's easy-going on foot.

World's View (Malindidzimu)

Included on every tour to Matopos, **World's View** (US$2; ticket also valid for Pomongwe and Nswatugi caves and the game park), signposted off the tarred Bulawayo/Maleme Road, 10km north of the dam, is a spectacular place, whatever you think of Cecil John Rhodes. The bald granite mountain he chose for his burial place, a

---

MATOPOS ROCK ART

The best of the **Matopos rock paintings** compare favourably with Stone Age art anywhere in the world. Yet the handful that are reproduced represent only a small fraction of the hundreds that exist in these hills – all of them within a relatively small radius, and some reachable without a car.

Over the last century, anthropologists, archeologists and historians have speculated as to the meanings of the paintings. Many **theories** were simple projections of what they knew about sites elsewhere in the world – or the imposition of their own, private assumptions. One eminent archeologist, basing his conclusions on art deep in caves in Spain, suggested that both arose from the symbolic use of sympathetic magic – the depiction of a dead animal would ensure a successful hunt. Others have concluded that the paintings depict aspects of daily life – menus of animals and plants in the area. Newer ideas reject such interpretations. Zimbabwean rock art is unlikely to be an expression of sympathetic magic, which is unknown in any African hunting society; nor is it simply a menu – the remains of animals found at sites don't correlate with the pictures. Researchers now believe the images were concerned with the way people thought about human existence and actions, depicted through animal icons or metaphors.

The problem with attempting to interpret the paintings by means of an understanding of the people who painted them, though, is that no one knows exactly who they were, beyond the idea that they were **Stone Age hunter-gatherer** predecessors of today's Zimbabweans – possibly San ("Bushmen") hunter-gatherers who roamed all over Southern Africa until quite recently. It seems likely that the images were executed between twenty thousand and two thousand years ago.

Many of the paintings have **religious themes**, which share features with the San focus on the ritual dance. This is used to take people into a **trance state** in which a potency or vital force called *n/um* is released. During trance, the experience of feeling stretched out is often described and some trancers have visions of light or movement. These elongated figures appear in rock art and the visions described correlate with the paintings.

As the picture of **hunter-gatherer cosmology** is built up, it may become possible to develop a more sophisticated interpretation of the paintings. Some tentative connections suggest that kudu are a symbol of potency, elephants are associated with rain, and baboons with legends in which they taught human beings to dance and sing.

For more information on the subject, the best **books** by far are Nick Walker's *The Painted Hills*, a field guide which is normally available at the Maleme Camp shop, while Peter Garlake's *The Hunter's Vision*, which is usually available in town, provides the most authoritative interpretation and background (see Books, p.390).

sacred site known to the Ndebele as *Malindidzimu*, "Place of Benevolent Spirits", has a 360-degree panorama over lonely granite hills and valleys. One of the astonishing things about the site is that it involves only a short climb to give views you'd normally have to climb a high mountain to achieve; in *Voices from the Rocks*, Terence Ranger, the foremost historian of the region, maintains that Rhodes consciously planned the grave as a place of pilgrimage, since it was "easy enough for a grandmother to manage". Certainly, it still stands as a symbolic memorial to settler endeavour.

Rhodes's Grave and the Allan Wilson Memorial

As requested in his will, **Rhodes's Grave** was cut into the rock and a simple brass plaque placed over it. Six years before his death, Rhodes had gone riding in these hills and found this grandiose spot, having long planned to be buried in the country which bore his name. When he died in Cape Town in 1902, his body was taken by train to Bulawayo (presumably on ice). Nearly two weeks later, the cortege of coaches, carriages, carts, horses, bicycles and pedestrians left the city for Rhodes's hut on the Matopos farm, stopping overnight before continuing to the top. The old colonialist was then given a traditional salute by assembled Ndebele chiefs (making Rhodes the only commoner to be granted the honour), who asked for shots not to be let off by the firing party, since it was a sacred site. An **interpretation display** at the foot of the hill has a collection of old photographs covering Rhodes's life.

Contrasting with this quiet resting place and erected at Rhodes's request on the same hilltop, the **Allan Wilson Memorial** commemorates the so-called **Shangani Patrol**, further turning *Malindidzimu* into a monument for white Rhodesia. This odd stone confection is visible for miles, and recalls events after Bulawayo fell to the British South Africa Company in 1893. Wilson was part of a hot-pursuit team running to ground the fleeing Lobengula, and his patrol went ahead of the main column but, just as they were approaching the Ndebele king, the Shangani River flooded, separating them from reinforcements. On December 4, the entire party of 34 was wiped out by the Ndebele, who suffered over a hundred casualties in the day-long battle. The white men were first buried where they fell, then transferred to Great Zimbabwe, and finally brought to the present position in 1904, when the memorial was erected. Romantically heroic reliefs around the plinth depict the members of the party.

White Rhino Shelter

For some extremely fine **outline paintings**, continue 2km north past the World's View turn-off to **White Rhino Shelter**. The paintings are in a small overhang along a clearly marked footpath off the Circular Drive.

The series of wildebeest painted here in different postures has been used to refute the idea that rock art is often used to conjure up a successful hunt. Why would someone interested in the animal purely as meat take the trouble to make subtle distinctions in posture, goes the argument, when one position would be as good as another? Line paintings are quite rare in Zimbabwe and seem to have been executed for only a short experimental period. Some of the most beautiful of all Stone Age paintings were done in this style, in outline only, before being superseded by more elaborate, polychrome works. The outline rhinos of the shelter are to the right, and there's also a black rhino head. The polychrome figures of humans and animals, including a lion, date from a later period (probably executed within the last 1000 years).

Bambata Cave

The oldest art object found in Zimbabwe, a 40,000-year-old stone tool that was engraved 8500 years ago with a grid pattern, was excavated at **Bambata Cave** (free), 10km north of the game park entrance. The **paintings** on the cave walls are estimated at being between 2000 and 8500 years old and include, on the left, depictions of wildebeest, zebra, kudu, tesessebe, impala, rhino, lion, eland, giraffe, roan, reedbuck, sable and a bushpig. On the right you can see people in several trance-related postures, including squatting with hands on hips. The lines seen on many paintings are believed to relate to representations of energy and the transfer of power.

The **car park** for the cave is signposted 8km north of the game park entrance, the last 3km along a very rough road. From here it's another two waymarked kilometres along a clear path through woodland and over a granite whaleback. The walk itself, which takes about thirty minutes, is fabulous, with splendid views across the castellated kopjes and domed hills.

Matopos game park (Whovi Wilderness Area)

The **Matopos game park**, aka the Whovi Wilderness Area (daily dawn–dusk; US$2;,free if you are staying at Maleme Dam), 50km from Bulawayo, approached directly on the Kezi Road, or via Maleme and Nswatugi, is one of the easiest places in Zimbabwe to see **rhino**, and undoubtedly one of the country's most beautiful parks. Many of the animals in the park have been reintroduced, but it's National Parks policy only to replace animals in areas which their species has previously inhabited. White rhinos were brought back after a lengthy absence on the strength of very accurate rock paintings at White Rhino Shelter, which show not some generalized animal, but clearly distinguish it from its hook-lipped ("black") relative (see p.175). Rhinos have done so well here that a number were sent in 1999 to Sinamatella in Hwange in order to build up numbers there.

One of the most thrilling ways to see the rhino is on horseback (though you are not absolutely guaranteed a sighting), from the stables at Whitewaters, just south of the entrance to the game park. Escorted rides, which cost US$20 per person, must be booked in advance, either at the Whitewaters office, or at the Maleme office, and go at 8.30am and 3pm for ninety minutes. The horses are docile and slow, so beginners are welcome.

Besides **rhinos**, you can normally also see giraffe, zebra and a variety of antelope, though no elephants or lions. You'll need your own car to get into the park or you can take one of the many organized **day-tours** which include it (see p.171). Walking is not permitted in the park, apart from near viewing and picnicking points, though the private lodges around the park do offer game walks for their clients. **Mpopoma Dam**, where most people picnic, has the added bonus of several hippos.

Toghwe Wilderness Area

Completely undeveloped bar a couple of campsites, the **Toghwe Wilderness Area** in the east of the Matobo Park offers adventurous hiking and great mountain biking. With a single road brushing along its western flank, connecting **Mtsheleli** and **Toghwana dams** to the main road, walking is the only way to penetrate it. The outstanding focus, **Inanke Cave**, with its excellent paintings, makes a challenging expedition from Toghwana Dam, while **Silozwane Cave**, just outside the park, but more accessible from **Mtsheleli Dam**, is also impressively decorated. Hitching from Maleme to the Toghwe dams is a long shot and you should be prepared to **hike**. It is a long, but pleasant, hike of about 18km to Mtsheleli or Toghwana Dam, along a deserted road that twists around granite outcrops, descending and rising from valleys. There are **campsites** at both dams, where drinking water should be boiled.

Silozwane Cave

Of the two notable **rock art sites** in the area, **Silozwane**, 11km southwest of **Mtsheleli Dam** in the Khumalo Communal Land, is the easier to reach. From the Cave road, take a left fork just before you get to the school and continue for about 2km along a decrepit track, which virtually collapses into the river in places. It is signposted, but only just. Don't be lured to continue along the good gravel road you're on: the road to the cave is a rude track. From the car park, the route heads through forest and up the side of a steep *dwala* (smooth granite hill).

There's a strange atmosphere as you climb the bald rock faces, escaping the worka-day existence below. You hear village sounds, donkeys braying, people talking and cowbells tinkling distantly on the edge of the unearthly silence. **Silozwane Cave** is a surprise on this smooth rock-sea – a sudden scooped-out cavity. A few steps closer, and you make out a series of huge human figures emerging from the grey granulated wall. At first these appear to be just a reddish blur smeared along the lower part of the wall, but closer approach reveals a richly detailed surface of image over image in a multi-tude of sizes and styles. Human figures are bold, clear and plentiful. To the right of centre, some two-metre serpent-like creatures with antelope heads look as if they are being ridden by humans, fish and animals, while to the left an especially comical giraffe with a cartoon head seems crude next to the better-observed one nearby. The closer you get, the easier it is to pick out animals, humans and abstract shapes from the swirling jumble of figures – painted, faded, peeling and overpainted.

Inanke Cave

Surpassing Silozwane, the paintings at **Inanke Cave**, a seven-kilometre trek east of Toghwana Dam, mark the highest expression of local prehistoric art. The cave is teas-ingly tricky to find, but marked at regular intervals by painted arrows and small cairns. Should you lose your way, don't try short cuts. Do your best to retrace your steps – it's easy to become disoriented in the hills and after a while the endless valleys and ranges start to look alike. The walk itself is fabulous, along a wooded stream in a valley with an enormous granite cliff on one side where black eagles nest, over hills and through open grassland dotted with kopjes. En route you'll pass two small overhangs with paint-ings, as well as a well-preserved iron-smelting furnace. The final ascent to the cave, up bare rock, is very steep, but the richness and complexity of the paintings is sufficient reward. Ten minutes' climb further takes you to the bald summit, with its tremendous views in all directions.

Cyrene Mission

CYRENE MISSION, 40km south of Bulawayo on the northern edge of Matobo National Park, is worth a visit for anyone interested in African art. Named after Simon of Cyrene, the African who helped carry Christ's cross, it was founded in 1939 by one **Canon Paterson**, a Scottish reformed atheist who studied art in England – and who later founded the Art Centre in Harare.

From the beginning, the aim of the Mission was to teach self-sufficiency. Pupils were instructed in farming, building and carpentry in order to construct, furnish and deco-rate their own homes. Art was also compulsory and students were given the chance to experiment. Paterson was firmly against imposing the Western artistic tradition on stu-dents and no reproductions were put up on walls. Instead, kids were given a sheet of paper and told to draw, and the buildings are now decorated with their work.

The simple, thatched **Chapel** is decorated with murals and carved furniture, which blend African and Christian mythology in a number of scenes from Ndebele history. The paintings are in a naive style, African-influenced but not wholly African. Some of the more symbolic stutter towards lifelessness, but they are at their best when depict-ing stories using familiar local imagery. The *Good Samaritan* spread, for example, is inspired by local rural life, with its *daga* (dried mud) huts and the earthy colours of the

Matabeleland countryside. Another success is the *Parable of the Talents*, which blends stylized huts, rocks, trees, plants and people into a whirling abstract composition.

To get to the Mission from Bulawayo, hitch or take the Figtree or Plumtree **bus** from Renkini terminus and walk the remaining 2km from the main road. From the Matopos, it's 12km from the northern gate, past the arboretum and one of the campsites in the recreational park; the Mission is on a minor detour back to the main Bulawayo road, so hitching is not recommended from this side.

The Torwa centres: Kame, and Naletale and Danangombe ruins

Some of Zimbabwe's best **stone ruins** stand within striking distance of Bulawayo. All of them are dwarfed in size by Great Zimbabwe (see Chapter Five), but, built later in the Torwa period, they are in many ways more sophisticated and reflect a development of the state's masonry traditions. The largest site – and the closest to Bulawayo – is the Torwa capital, **Kame**, just outside the city limits. Further out, off the Gweru road in Midlands farming country, lie **Danangombe**, a subsequent Torwa headquarters, and tiny **Naletale**, perhaps the finest expression of the style.

The Torwa state and architecture

From the tenth to mid-nineteenth centuries, southwestern Zimbabwe enjoyed a political continuity almost without precedent in Africa. By the twelfth century, offshoot states of **Great Zimbabwe** had walled capitals in the area and were living alongside people of the local "**Leopard's Kopje**" culture, an urban society under a wealthy ruling class. Cattle and gold were the bedrock of Leopard's Kopje wealth, and the elite were often buried with objects covered in the precious metal. They were able to organize teams of labour to produce stone platforms on hillsides, on which their houses were built.

The relationship between the two cultures is unclear, but it is known that by the time Great Zimbabwe collapsed in the fifteenth century the southwest had been pulled together into a single state. This **Torwa state** was a progressive development of its Great Zimbabwe predecessor in the southeast. Although less extensive, it was more efficient, introducing improvements in architecture, pottery and urban layout, and changes in the economy.

Combining Zimbabwe masonry skills with the Leopard's Kopje stone platform tradition, the Torwa produced beautifully decorated **court complexes**. The old hill platforms were enlarged and turned into huge stages by the accomplished use of retaining walls and the decorative possibilities of stone walling.

Kame

The largest concentration of stone wall terracing at **KAME** (sometimes still spelled "Khami"; daily 8am–5pm; US$5) surrounds the ruler's personal hill complex above the Kame River. Like his Great Zimbabwe counterpart, the ruler (or *mambo*) lived in great privacy, with his hill-perched court surrounded by the *zimbabwes* of the ruling class. A secret passage went under the platforms to his palace, its top forming the pavement of the courtyard.

As you ascend the stairs to the **upper platform**, you can see remains of the posts that held up the *daga* roof: elephant tusks once lined the passage. On the lowest step, a secret room was uncovered during excavations in 1947. Royal regalia had been hidden there at some time, perhaps when Kame was set alight during the invasion around 1680, when the *Rozvi* ("destroyers") of the Changamire dynasty swooped down from the Zambezi and conquered the Torwa. The spears and axes of copper and iron, ivory carvings and drinking pots with the *mambo*'s traditional red-and-black pattern are housed in the Natural History Museum in Bulawayo.

Several stone platforms south of the hill complex probably belonged to acolytes – wives or courtiers – of the *mambo*. The walks around this part of the site can be steep, but worthwhile, revealing such details as a **tsoro game** carved in stone. The board, of which there are several examples at Kame, has four rows of holes, with usually about fourteen holes per row. Like a cross between backgammon, chess and Chinese checkers, *tsoro* is still played today throughout Central Africa, under a variety of names. The speed of play achieved by participants, involving remarkable mental arithmetic feats, can be quite bewildering.

On the east side of the hill, to the north and west of the stone structures, are the remains of **huts** belonging to the ordinary people who occupied most of the site. These commoners didn't build their homes on platforms, so the mud walls have by now all but collapsed, and consequently there's a lot less to see.

Among the finds interpreted in the small **museum** – worth a quick look before you explore the site – are some that date back 100,000 years, providing evidence of a human presence at the site long before Kame was built. A useful pamphlet, *A Trail Guide to the Khami National Monument*, is on sale at the museum.

Getting to Kame

Kame stands on a minor road 22km to the west of Bulawayo. If you're **driving** or **cycling**, follow Eleventh Avenue (near Bulawayo train station) out of town through the very unappealing industrial area. Without a car, the best bet is to take one of the reasonably priced (US$25–30) excursions run by African Wanderer (☎09/72736) or Chamboko (☎09/76838 or 61857). Kame doesn't see many visitors, so hitching is a non-starter.

Naletale and Danangombe

Naletale and **Danangombe** (US$5 for both sites), set in isolated ranching country roughly ninety minutes' drive from Bulawayo on dirt roads signposted off the Harare Road, are equally rewarding sites, but harder to reach than Kame. If you're driving, it's possible to stop off en route to Harare, Naletale being the more direct to reach. Take the signposted road which starts 16km north of **Shangani**, a simple farming settlement, for 21km to reach Naletale. Danangombe is signposted immediately south of Shangani, near the station, and is a 23-kilometre drive. It's not practical to drive between the two, as there is no direct road linking them.

If you don't have access to your own transport, and/or if you feel like spending a couple of days in the area, the best option is to contact Jabulani Safaris (☎050/3303 or ☎ & fax 088/603), who arrange transfers from Shangani or Gweru. Their **game farm**, *Bon Accord*, with four double en-suite chalets and one family chalet, abuts the ruins and has bush walks, game drives, canoeing and fishing. There's no big game, but you'll see antelope, giraffe, zebra and wildebeest.

Tariffs, including all meals (no self-catering), drives and tours, are US$120 per person (R400 for South Africans). Driving, the farm is 25km from Shangani, on the dirt Greystone Road. Another game farm, *Embukisweni Safari Lodge* (☎050/2708 or 09/79726, fax 64108, mobile ☎011/601702), 55km south of Shangani, is less convenient for Naletale, but compensates with some ruins on the farm itself and a lovely setting in granite outcrops, with a reasonable all-inclusive rate of US$65 per person.

Naletale

The most interesting of all the *zimbabwes*, **NALETALE** stands at the top of a natural granite dome. As you gaze onto the wooded valley, it's difficult to imagine a better prospect, with trees growing between the long-deserted walls and *daga* hut fragments. The site is small in size – you could do a circuit of the whole place in fifteen minutes – but it's easy to while away half a day wandering about.

From close up, the **walls** don't look terribly special, but step back from the north-west section, the best preserved, and take in the patterning. Better still, lie down, prop your head on one of the pillow-sized rocks scattered about, and just gaze. The tapestried wall is, without doubt, the pinnacle of the Zimbabwe–Kame masonry tradition, the only one standing that includes all five types of patterning: chevron, chequer, herringbone, cord and ironstone. The outer wall, originally topped by small towers with mono-

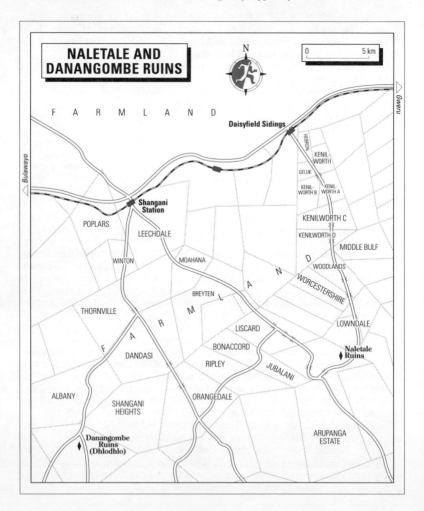

liths, enclosed a large raised platform, which was surrounded by a number of court-yards and other smaller platforms. When Donald Randall McIver, the first professional archeologist to investigate Great Zimbabwe, dug here, he found elephant tusks embedded in the remains of one of the huts.

A path leads up to the site itself from a picnic site and parking place at the bottom of the hill. It's possible to **camp** there, but you should ask for permission from the attendant, who lives in a house on the right of the car park turn-off (and will show you round if you want).

Danangombe (Dhlo Dhlo)

DANANGOMBE, better known by its old name **Dhlo Dhlo**, is equally enjoyable to explore: you can clamber about the ruins and sit high up on rocks in the shade to look out over the rolling countryside. The site became the capital of the Torwa State after Kame was razed to the ground during a combined attack by a dissident Torwa leader and the Portuguese forces of Sismundo Dias Bayao. Later, in their eagerness to pilfer the riches of Danangombe, European treasure hunters managed to destroy many of the buildings by treating them as gold-mining stakes: unworked gold and jewellery were systematically removed. Early digs found a silver chalice, a bell and medallions of six-teenth-century Portuguese origin. The walls that remain reveal beautiful decorative motifs similar to those at Kame.

South to Beit Bridge

Bulawayo to Beit Bridge is one of the major arteries to South Africa – a four-hour journey through remote and dry country. Nevertheless, the area holds several game

---

MISSIONARIES IN ZIMBABWE

Missionary support was a major source of strength to **Rhodes** in his advance into Central Africa. However, many missionaries believed that neither their teaching nor white settlement could be effective until the power of the Matabele was broken. **Lobengula**, in particular, scorned missionary teachings, which he felt consisted mainly of passing the buck for human misdeeds to Christ. He observed that the doctrine was what one might expect from whites because "whenever they did anything wrong they always wanted to throw the blame onto others".

The early missionary lessons literally fell on deaf ears. At the site of the **Jesuit Mission** next to Old Bulawayo you can see the graves of two missionaries murdered in the 1896 Chimurenga, along with their one and only convert, who was deaf and dumb. **African converts** were particularly vulnerable to attack during the uprising, and Bernard Mizeki, one of the first African proselytes, was killed. But, once the uprising was defeated, the way was prepared for the full introduction of Christianity, which is now the predominant religion in Zimbabwe. Inside two years, the American Brethren of Christ had established one of the first fully fledged missions in the Matopos hills, while by 1909 there were more black than white Anglicans in Rhodesia.

Subsequently, the church began to concentrate on developing schools, clinics and hospitals – often attached to the old missions. Mission schools have educated many of Zimbabwe's leading figures, Robert Mugabe among them, and in the latter years of white rule they became increasingly involved in politics. During the 1950s a number of church leaders were outspoken against right-wing trends, and many guerrilla fighters received mission support during the struggle for independence. At this time, gross atrocities were committed against missionaries, blamed by the Smith government on guerrillas, but claimed by nationalists to be the work of government forces committing outrages for propaganda purposes.

farms, most notably the Bubiana Wildlife Conservancy, an hour's drive from the small town of West Nicholson, halfway to Beit Bridge.

Gwanda, West Nicholson and the Bubiana Conservancy

One of the only stopping-off places if you're heading straight for the border is the tiny settlement of **GWANDA**, 126km south of Bulawayo, whose bored traffic cops lie in wait for unsuspecting speedsters along the main road to West Nicholson. Along the main road through town, the *Gwanda Hotel* (☎084/2476, 2751; ②) is an old-fashioned two-storey place badly in need of a lick of paint, with a pleasant courtyard garden by the pool; it's worth paying the extra dollar or two to stay in the newer King Leisure suites, where the beds don't sag and there are TVs and fridges.

One of the few other night stops along the Bulawayo–Beit Bridge road, 95km south of Gwanda, is *Tod's Guest House* (☎016/5403; ③), which trades on the fact that it's "exactly halfway between Victoria Falls and Johannesburg" (530km in each direction). A pretty neglected place, you could see it as a cultural experience – a Rhodesian motel, lost somewhere in the 1960s amid the red-earthed and thorn-treed expanses of the lowveld, with wide verandahs, animal skulls on every wall, very old wildlife photographs and dark, ancient furniture. Petrol and diesel are available and you can camp and braai.

In the vicinity of **West Nicholson**, 44km further south, a number of farmers got together in 1991 and pooled their ranches to create a wildlife zone, primarily in an attempt to save the local rhino population. The 1600-square-kilometre **Bubiana Conservancy** that resulted encompasses grassland, thorn trees and dry, rocky hills, harbouring one of Matabeleland's top game lodges. Beautifully situated high amongst the granite boulders, *Barberton Lodge*, Box FM 444, Famona, Bulawayo (☎09/64638, mobile 011/211854), is a great place to clock up some of the 335 species of birds recorded in the Conservancy, track black rhino and view elephants, big cats and plains game. Most guests fly in from Bulawayo (US$120 return), but self-driving, 50km of it along dirt, is possible. The fully inclusive rate for accommodation, meals, drinks and activities is US$160, but a cheaper option is their bush camp, which works out at US$120 all-in.

Beit Bridge

Though no one would willingly choose to spend the night in **BEIT BRIDGE**, you may need to if the border has closed when you arrive. (For the lowdown on crossing the Beit Bridge border, see Basics, p.4). Fortunately, there are some perfectly reputable **hotels** in the settlement or along the main road leading to the border. The first as you head into town from the north, and the most expensive, is the *Holiday Inn Express* (☎086/3001 or 53371–2, fax 3375, *hiebeit@hiebeit.zimsun.co.zw*; ③), 3.5km north of the border on the Bulawayo road, a slick air-conditioned machine for sleeping in, housed in a surprisingly unobtrusive building opened at the end of 1998, with 104 rooms in three two-storey wings capped by a corrugated-iron roof; all rooms are en suite and have TVs and modem points. There's a breakfast room but no restaurant, so if you want something to eat at other times of day you'll either have to go to the *Nevada Spur* steakhouse over the road or drive the 3km into town for a bite at one of the other hotels. The cheapest place to stay in the sweaty settlement itself is *Peter's Motel* (☎ & fax 086/2309; ①), signposted from the main road, a worn but clean 1960s motel that more than justifies its bargain rate, with air-conditioned en-suite rooms with TVs, arranged around a swimming pool under shady lowveld trees. Spicker is the *Beit Bridge Inn* (☎086/2214 or 3360, fax 2413; ②), opposite *Peter's* across a dusty square, a sparklingly clean, three-storey hotel refurbished in 1999 with cool ceramic-tiled floors and wicker furniture in the air-conditioned en-suite bedrooms; outside there's a shady sitting area by the pool.

ROUTES TO SOUTH AFRICA

The usual way to Johannesburg from Bulawayo is through **Beit Bridge**, Zimbabwe's busiest border post, where you can expect long queues in the trying heat. An alternative route west of Bulawayo goes into Botswana via **Plumtree** border post before heading south, and can be quicker than the Beit Bridge road, with far less traffic; the Plumtree border is also more direct if you're heading for Cape Town. To get to **Johannesburg** via Botswana, strike south through Francistown, where, should you need to break your journey, there are a couple of decent places to stay. At Serule, 84km south of Francistown, take the tarred road to Selebi-Pikwe, then onto Sherwood Ranch and the South African border crossing at Martin's Drift. Once in South Africa, the R35 takes you directly to Potgietersrus, where you join the N1 for Johannesburg. For **Cape Town**, the shortest route is to continue along the main road from Serule through Mahalapye, Gaborone and Lobatse, and on to the Ramatlabama border post. Across the border you join up with South Africa's N18, which connects with the N12, passing through Kimberley and finally the N1, leading directly to Cape Town.

travel details

Trains

These are the details given in timetables, but, in general, don't expect trains to run on time.

Bulawayo to: Gaborone (daily 2.30pm; 16hr), via Francistown (7hr); Harare (daily 8pm; 9hr), via Gweru and Kwekwe; Johannesburg (Thurs 9am; 27hr), via Francistown and Gaborone; Victoria Falls (1 daily 7pm; 12hr).

Luxury coaches

The only luxury coach service that operates from Bulawayo to destinations within Zimbabwe is Blue Arrow, Unifreight House, 73a Fife St, Bulawayo (☎09/65548). From Bulawayo to Johannesburg, there's the choice of Greyhound (contact as for Blue Arrow) or Translux in Johannesburg (☎00 27 11/774 3333).

Bulawayo to: Harare via Kwekwe (4 weekly; 6hr), via Chivu (daily; 6hr); Johannesburg (daily; 14hr); Victoria Falls (3 weekly; 6hr), via Dete for Hwange National Park and Hwange town.

Backpacker buses

Both the Route 49 and Baz Bus between South Africa and Victoria Falls drop off and pick up passengers in Bulawayo. Although you may get off the bus and spend a few days in Bulawayo, your journey with them has to begin or terminate in South Africa. **Route 49** (mobile ☎011/709078) goes between Cape Town and Bulawayo twice a week in each direction, and likewise between Bulawayo and Victoria Falls. **Baz Bus** (mobile ☎011/704242, *info@bazbus.com*) goes between Johannesburg and Victoria Falls four times a week via Bulawayo.

Volvos and chicken buses

You'll find buses to most destinations; this is no more than an attempt to give an idea of main routes you're likely to use. Frequencies and journey times given below are very approximate, so always check information at Bulawayo's Publicity Association or the bus station before setting out. Arrive early to get a place, and pay on the bus.

Bulawayo to: Beit Bridge (1 daily; 6hr); Binga (4 daily; 7hr); Dete Crossroads, for Hwange National Park (4 daily; 3hr); Harare (5 or more daily 5–11am; 7hr or longer); Kezi for the Matopos (1 daily; 2hr); Masvingo (2–3 daily 6–8.30am; 5hr); Plumtree (1 daily; 4hr); Victoria Falls (8 daily; 10hr).

Flights

Bulawayo to: Harare (4 daily; 50min); Johannesburg (5 weekly; 1hr 30min).

CHAPTER FOUR

VICTORIA FALLS,
HWANGE
AND WESTERN KARIBA

Victoria Falls is one of Southern Africa's essential points of pilgrimage. The town, which aptly takes its name from its fabulous attraction, developed initially to serve a relatively modest influx of visitors, but in the 1990s became Zimbabwe's busiest tourism honey pot, drawing over a million visitors a year. Even South Africa, which has good transport connections with the region, now cheekily sells Vic Falls as one of its attractions.

Capitalizing on its potential, entrepreneurs have made the Falls Africa's **adventure and extreme sport** hub, with a host of activities to tempt an extended stay: the world's most adrenaline-charged one-day **whitewater rafting** and **riverboarding** trips surge through the gorge below the Falls, and the **bungee jumping** from the bridge overhead provides one of the highest commercial leaps anywhere. If that's not enough, try **abseiling**, **cable-sliding** or **high-wiring** in one of the Batoka gorges. As Victoria Falls has become bloated with success, a number of operators have shifted shop to **Livingstone**, 10km away in Zambia, which is pulling in a growing number of backpackers who want a more authentically African experience, or simply an affordable bed for the night. There's a constant traffic between the two towns, and you can visit with relative ease.

With all the adrenaline and testosterone pumping around Victoria Falls, its easy to forget that the town is also one of the best bases in the country to start a **safari**. Trips leave from Victoria Falls for remote and adventurous regions such as Chizarira National Park (see p.230) and Mana Pools (see Chapter Two) but, closer

ACCOMMODATION PRICE CODES

Hotels and other accommodation options in Zimbabwe have been categorized according to the **price codes** given below, which indicate the cost, per person sharing, of a night's lodging. For a full explanation, see p.33.

① under US$7.50	④ US$25–35	⑦ US$55–75
② US$7.50–15	⑤ US$35–45	⑧ US$75–100
③ US$15–25	⑥ US$45–55	⑨ over US$100

to home, thousands of square kilometres west and south of the Falls comprise a patchwork of national parks, safari areas and private wildlife concessions where you can go game viewing by canoe on the Upper Zambezi, or stay on dry land and head out by 4WD vehicle, on foot, horse or even elephant back. Here too, **safari lodges and bush camps**, although far from cheap, promise truly exciting experiences of the bush, and the personalized expert attention you'll get makes them worth saving up for.

Among the wildlife reserves, impressive **Zambezi National Park**, which begins on the outskirts of Victoria Falls town, is famed for its herds of beautiful sable antelope. However, Zimbabwe's wildlife showpiece is the extensive **Hwange National Park**, just 100km south of Victoria Falls by road. The most accessible of the country's wildlife parks, Hwange has easy game viewing and low-cost accommodation, as well as luxury game lodges and smaller exclusive bush camps for real safari style.

Although Harare is usually thought of as the springboard for **Lake Kariba**, Victoria Falls is actually substantially closer, at just 260km on good tarred roads to **Mlibizi** on the low-key western edge of the lake. **Binga**, some 80km beyond Mlibizi, is the area's most interesting lakeside settlement, with traditional Batonga villages, several tourist lodges and some budget accommodation.

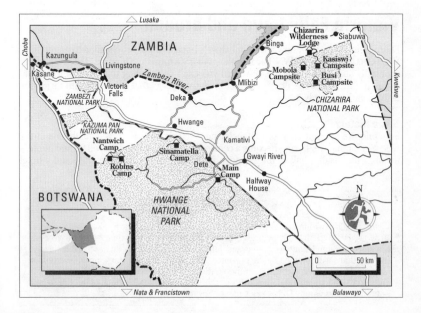

VICTORIA FALLS

The energy and power of the nearly two-kilometre width of the **Zambezi River** thundering 100m down a sheer chasm is a pretty compelling sight and, combined with the clouds of sunlit spray and rainbows, reason enough to spend a day or two gazing at **Victoria Falls**. But the banks of the river, before it takes the plunge, are enticing too – a wonderful place to contemplate the **palm-dotted islands** and the water, which changes from sheeny pink at dawn to metallic blue at dusk. And, for closer views, you can take a river **cruise**.

The **rainforest** fed by the spray of the Falls, with its ilala palms, white river-sand, fiery sunsets and more or less constant humidity makes for a lush landscape like nothing else in Zimbabwe. Immediately surrounding the Falls is the **Victoria Falls National Park**, where you can see antelope, warthog and vervet monkeys in the rainforest amid the spray.

Beginning a few kilometres upstream, the **Zambezi National Park** extends for forty forested kilometres along the river, with dry bush and grassland further inland. Stalked by a wide range of Zimbabwe's wildlife, this is one of the many diversions that make it possible to spend days around the Victoria Falls.

At the centre of all this lies **Victoria Falls town**, unashamedly geared towards tourism, which provides a springboard for the Falls themselves, but has expanded into a host of diversions, especially **adventure activities**. Each of its scattered hotels exists as a self-contained resort, from which guests venture out to stroll down to the water, visit the curio shops, or to take part in the standard excursions – a flight or a cruise. Precisely because of the town's success, visitors weary of its incessant commercialism are making their way across to the older town of **Livingstone** in Zambia, which has a more established identity that isn't tied up with tourism, but where accommodation and travel agents have recently begun to spring up.

Victoria Falls town and around

During the 1990s, a century after Zimbabwe's hoped-for gold rush failed to materialize, **VICTORIA FALLS TOWN** became the country's tourism Klondike. There's nothing especially attractive about the town, and you can't help feeling that everyone's on the make, but this gives the place an undoubted raw energy that goes well with its idenity as the continent's adventure capital.

Some history
Set amid the flat, hot bush of Matabeleland, Victoria Falls town is actually one of the oldest in Zimbabwe, having become a centre for intrepid traders, travellers and hunters through the second half of the nineteenth century. By the 1890s a store and a hotel

---

BORDER CROSSINGS

Victoria Falls is within easy striking distance of three other countries: **Zambia** is a short stroll across the Falls railway bridge (see opposite), while less than hour's drive away you can cross into Namibia or Botswana. Like Zambia, **Botswana** makes a viable day-trip and one that's well justified by the presence of **Chobe National Park**, probably the best place in Africa to see elephants en masse during the dry season. **Day-trips from Vic Falls** to Chobe are covered on p.201. For more extensive explorations of the Chobe and Botswana's **Okavango Delta**, see Chapter Seven.

complete with roulette wheel had been built, though the town was temporarily abandoned following an outbreak of malaria and blackwater fever; the settlement moved to higher ground away from the river, at Livingstone, across the newly completed **railway bridge**. The town on the Zimbabwean side of the river only really came back into its own in the late 1960s, when hotels, banks and, most importantly, an airport were built.

At the end of 1991 the airport was upgraded to international standards – for the benefit of visiting leaders coming "on retreat" at the conclusion of the Commonwealth Heads of Government meeting. With the rapid influx of tourists, the town continues to expand. New facilities and accommodation have sprung up in the fertile entrepreneurial grounds around the Falls, and environmentalists are seriously questioning whether the whole show is sustainable.

Getting there

In keeping with its status as Zimbabwe's tourism hub, Victoria Falls is well served by **transport** from Harare, Bulawayo and South Africa, as well as less frequent services from Botswana and Namibia.

By train
The slowest, but arguably pleasantest way to get to the Falls is on the **Bulawayo–Vic Falls train**. It's a fourteen-hour overnight affair that leaves Bulawayo daily at 7pm and can be hot in summer and freezing in winter. There are sometimes inexplicably long delays and stops at the tiniest of junctions, so it's a good idea not to book any activities for the morning of your arrival. However, the journey is worth the time to view some of Zimbabwe's best wildlife areas from the comfort of a self-contained compartment. At dawn on the second day of the trip, you travel through remote bush, and there are good chances of seeing **game** such as antelope, zebra, or perhaps even one of the Big Five watching the train as it chugs past. On its return leg from the Falls, the train passes through some of this area at dusk, an equally prime time for viewing game. **Victoria Falls station** itself is delightful – an Edwardian concoction shaded by flame-flowered flamboyants, sweet-smelling frangipanis and syringas, and with a platform boasting a pond and palm trees. From the ceremonial exit (High British Empire), you can stroll down a colonnade of trees to the *Victoria Falls Hotel* (see p.194); for the town's main street, walk north along the platform.

By air
By air you at arrive Victoria Falls International airport, 20km south of town on the Bulawayo road, which sees direct flights from Harare, Kariba, Johannesburg, Maun and Windhoek. A UTC **shuttle bus** connects the airport with town for US$8 per person or, less expensively, you can book with Riti Transfers (☎013/4528) who charge US$3.50 for a minimum of two people. If there are three or more of you, a taxi can work out cheaper still, provided you get a straight driver. It should cost about US$10: anything over US$13 is a rip-off. Meters don't always work or aren't always used, so negotiate your fare before you set off. If you've already booked B&B accommodation, check whether they offer airport transfers, as this can work out cheapest of all and is bound to be more reliable. Most of the larger hotels have shuttle buses that charge about US$10 per person.

By car
By car, Vic Falls is 440km from Bulawayo, and 875km from Harare, all on tarred roads. The stretch between Bulawayo and the Falls is very isolated and, once you leave Bulawayo, there are no filling stations, or any signs of human habitation, for 160km till

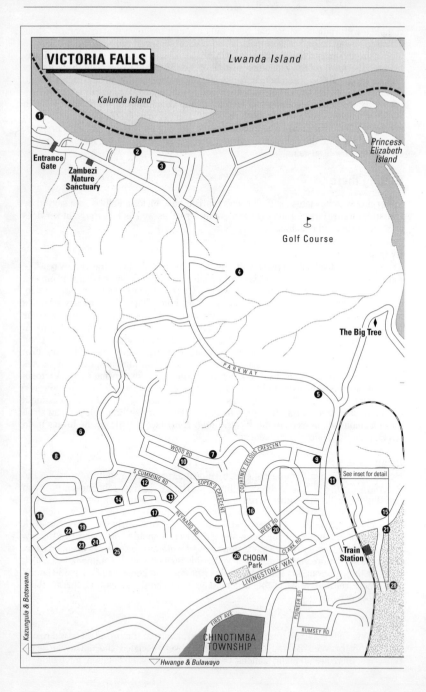

VICTORIA FALLS

Lwanda Island

Kalunda Island

Princess
Elizabeth
Island

Entrance
Gate

Zambezi
Nature
Sanctuary

Golf Course

The Big Tree

PARKWAY

WOOD RD

S CUMMING RD

SOPER'S CRESCENT

COURTNEY SELOUS CRESCENT

REYNARD RD

WEST RD

CLARK RD

See inset for detail

Train
Station

CHOGM
Park

LIVINGSTONE WAY

PIONEER RD

FIRST AVE

RUMSEY RD

CHINOTIMBA
TOWNSHIP

Kazungula & Botswana

Hwange & Bulawayo

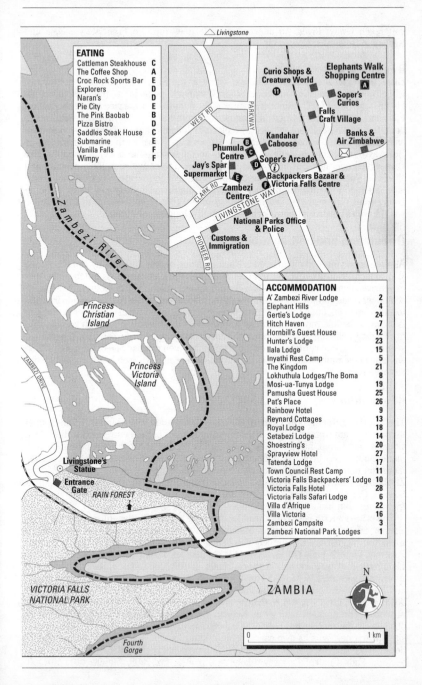

△ Livingstone

EATING

Cattleman Steakhouse	C
The Coffee Shop	A
Croc Rock Sports Bar	E
Explorers	D
Naran's	D
Pie City	E
The Pink Baobab	B
Pizza Bistro	D
Saddles Steak House	C
Submarine	E
Vanilla Falls	F
Wimpy	F

Curio Shops & Creature World ⑪

Elephants Walk Shopping Centre Ⓐ

Soper's Curios

Falls Craft Village

Kandahar Caboose

Phumula Centre Ⓑ Ⓒ

Soper's Arcade Ⓓ ⓘ

Jay's Spar Supermarket Ⓔ

Banks & Air Zimbabwe

Backpackers Bazaar & Victoria Falls Centre Ⓕ

Zambezi Centre

National Parks Office & Police

Customs & Immigration

WEST RD

PARKWAY

CLARK RD

LIVINGSTONE WAY

PIONEER RD

Zambezi River

Princess Christian Island

Princess Victoria Island

ZAMBEZI DRIVE

Livingstone's Statue

Entrance Gate

RAIN FOREST

VICTORIA FALLS NATIONAL PARK

ZAMBIA

Fourth Gorge

ACCOMMODATION

A' Zambezi River Lodge	2
Elephant Hills	4
Gertie's Lodge	24
Hitch Haven	7
Hornbill's Guest House	12
Hunter's Lodge	23
Ilala Lodge	15
Inyathi Rest Camp	5
The Kingdom	21
Lokhuthula Lodges/The Boma	8
Mosi-ua-Tunya Lodge	19
Pamusha Guest House	25
Pat's Place	26
Rainbow Hotel	9
Reynard Cottages	13
Royal Lodge	18
Setabezi Lodge	14
Shoestring's	20
Sprayview Hotel	27
Tatenda Lodge	17
Town Council Rest Camp	11
Victoria Falls Backpackers' Lodge	10
Victoria Falls Hotel	28
Victoria Falls Safari Lodge	6
Villa d'Afrique	22
Villa Victoria	16
Zambezi Campsite	3
Zambezi National Park Lodges	1

N

0 _____ 1 km

you reach Gwayi River. An alternative route goes through Francistown, Nata and Kasane in Botswana, also on tar.

By coach or bus

Blue Arrow coaches from Bulawayo arrive at the Shearwater offices on Parkway, while the twice-weekly Intercape from Windhoek pulls in at the post office in Livingstone Way. UTC minibuses run a daily door-to-door service between Victoria Falls and Hwange and a twice-daily one to and from Kasane. **Backpacker minibuses** operated by Route 49 leave twice a week from Johannesburg (via Francistown, Nata and Kasane in Botswana) and once a week from Cape Town (with an overnight stop in Bulawayo), dropping passengers off at any accommodation in town, as does the **Baz Bus**, which operates four hop-on, hop-off services a week between Johannesburg and Vic Falls. **Volvos** and **chicken buses** from Bulawayo and Western Lake Kariba terminate in Chinotimba township, but you can ask the driver to drop you off en route on Livingstone Way near the *Sprayview Hotel* (see p.193). If you end up in Chinotimba, you'll have to take a taxi or walk the remaining kilometre into town.

Orientation and getting around

All the shops you're likely to need are strung along or just off Parkway or Livingstone Way, which leads straight to the **Falls National Park** entrance. As much of the less expensive accommodation is 2–3km from the town centre, you're bound to find yourself doing some commuting. A number of the places renting out rooms provide free lifts to and from town, but if they don't you'll need to make your own arrangements. **Cycling** is the most flexible way to get around, and several places rent bikes, which you can take overnight (including to the Zambezi National Park lodges or to Zambia). If pedalling seems a sweat, **car rental** can also be arranged, or you can use one of the **taxis**, which shouldn't cost more than US$2 to get you anywhere in town (see Listings on p.207 for all three services).

Information

The **Tourist Information Centre**, Parkway/Livingstone Way (Mon–Fri 8am–1pm & 2–5pm, Sat 8am–1pm; ☎013/4202), conveniently right in the centre next to the Town Council Rest Camp, has a slightly haphazard collection of brochures and other information, but it may be worth popping in to find out the latest information about accommodation options (although they don't arrange bookings). Another possibility is the **Zimbabwe Tourism Authority**, opposite Elephant's Walk shopping centre, near Soper's Curios (Mon–Fri 8am–4pm; ☎013/4376, fax 4387), which scores high for friendliness but lacks hard information and brochures.

   The private sector is streets ahead for anything to do with adventure activities, packages or safaris. Among a number of helpful **travel agencies** and **adventure companies**, the biggest are the fiercely competing Safari Par Excellence Phumula Centre, Parkway, Victoria Falls (☎013/2054, 4424 or 2190, fax 4510, *spevfa@africaonline.co.zw*); Livingstone Way/Parkway, Victoria Falls (☎013/2051, fax 4510); Livingstone Adventure Centre, 216 Mosi-O-Tunya Rd, Livingstone (☎03/321320, *atd@zamnet.zm*); and Shearwater, Soper's Arcade, Parkway Drive, Victoria Falls (☎013/4471-3, 4513, 4648 or 3392, fax 4341, *raft.res@shearwater.co.zw*), each of which will push their own products. The smaller, family-run Kandahar Canoeing Safaris (☎013/3589, 2279 or 4502, fax 2014, mobile ☎011/405930, *adrift@africaonline.co.zw*), in the caboose opposite Shearwater, sells its own canoeing and rafting products, but is well informed, and books most activities around the Falls. Independent Backpackers' Bazaar, Shop 5, Victoria Falls Centre, Parkway (daily; ☎013/5828, fax 2208, mobile ☎011/404960, *backpack@africaonline.co.zw*), is a particularly helpful place to book all adventure activities, transfers or anything to do with the Zambian side, while the **National Parks** office, at the Bulawayo end of Livingstone Way (☎013/4222), is the place to make bookings for the Zambezi National Park.

Accommodation

Up to the mid-1990s, **accommodation** in Victoria Falls was limited to hotels or camping and rock-bottom chalets at the Town Council Rest Camp. This has all changed, and now you'll find the whole gamut of places to stay, including B&Bs, guest houses, self-catering accommodation and backpackers' lodges. Places right in the centre of town tend to be at a premium and tend to be moderately priced or expensive; the less expensive places are generally 2–3km from the centre of town. Most places have mosquito nets, a swimming pool, TV and, if they're self-catering, a braai area; if any of these are vital to you, ask before checking in.

Outside town, a number of **luxury safari lodges** provide a pricey but unquestionably interesting alternative to staying in town. National Parks also offer inexpensive (and thus hugely popular) self-catering accommodation in the bush, 6km outside of town along Parkway. Be warned, however, that the increasing numbers of visitors arriving in the country's premier resort mean a bed for the night is by no means guaranteed. This applies particularly to reasonably priced establishments and from July to mid-January and in April. Advance **booking**, especially for budget places, is essential. It's also worth considering staying in Livingstone, where a lot of new places are springing up (see p.210).

Camping and backpackers' lodges

Hitch Haven, 332 Wood Rd (mobile ☎011/405945, *online@acacia.samara.co.zw*). Dismal and cramped, but cheap dorms with bunk beds, 1.75km from the centre. With only one stove in the kitchen, things could get a bit hectic if everyone gets the munchies at once, but cooked meals are available. Large dusty garden with a pool. Twenty percent discount for Baz Bus passengers and free transfers from the train station. Dorms and camping ①.

Inyathi Rest Camp, 2km from town along Parkway (PO Box 300 Chinotimba Township; ☎ & fax 013/2345, mobile ☎011/607034). Deservedly popular budget place in spotless grounds with small gardens: it fills up fast. Basic thatched rooms, with slightly saggy beds and shared washing facilities. Six-person cottages share kitchens and bathrooms. The grassy campsite is miles better than the one in town, making it well worth the extra distance. Booking advised. Rooms (minimum three) and camping ①, cottages ②.

Pat's Place, 209 West Drive (☎013/4375). Dorms and simple carpeted doubles (among the cheapest en-suite rooms in town) with ceiling fans, 750m from the centre. The separate kitchen area is small and the place is generally a bit sparse, but a Jacuzzi offers some respite. Dorms and doubles ①.

Shoestrings, 12 West Drive (mobile ☎011/800731, *shoestringhre@pc2000.co.zw*). Backpackers' hostel with dorms that sleep four to eight people, and en-suite doubles, set in large grounds with a lovely pool, an easy 500m from town. Bar and handy noticeboard covers various activities. Dorms ①, doubles ②.

Town Council Rest Camp, Livingstone Way/Parkway, PO Box 41, Victoria Falls. Cheap and shabby accommodation bang in the centre, in segregated men's and women's mini-hostels and run-down chalets where all the basics are provided, including pots, pans, a small fridge and firewood for braaing outside. Washing facilities are in dilapidated shared blocks. Two-bedroom en-suite cottages are also on offer, as well as a large sandy campsite. ①.

Victoria Falls Backpackers' Lodge, 357 Gibson Rd. Popular and friendly hostel 1.75km from town, set in a shady, beautifully landscaped garden with a waterfall cascading into the swimming pool. Open-air kitchen and dining area under thatch and reasonably priced basics such as bread, drinks and snacks are on sale. Dorms, slightly stark doubles and two charming A-frame huts all share washing facilities. Bikes can be rented and free transfers are offered when the managers go into town. Recommended. ②.

Zambezi Campsite, next to *A'Zambezi Lodge*, 5km from town along Parkway. Also known as Lathi Caravan Park, it's not as convenient for the town centre as the Town Council campsite is, but is a far pleasanter alternative, with splendid views of the water and easy access to the Zambezi National Park. ①.

Self-catering   ⟨3

Hornbill's Guest House, 376 Squire Cummings Rd (☎031/4495). Four twin air-conditioned rooms (one en suite), 2km from town in shady grounds. Spacious, well-equipped kitchen for self-catering and breakfast available, but not included in rate. ③.

Lokhuthula Lodges, off Parkway, about 2.5km from town (☎013/3211–20, fax 3205, *saflodge@vsl.gaia.co.zw*). Beautifully designed self-catering lodges that are part of the *Victoria Falls Safari Lodge* development, and share many of the same facilities. Two- and three-bedroom lodges sleep six or eight and, while expensive for a couple, are fair value for four or more sharing (mid-Jan to March, June, Oct to mid-Dec), outside the high season, especially with a standby discount of up to forty percent. US$160–205 per lodge per day (depending on time of year).

Pamusha Guest House, 583 Manyika Rd (PO Box 82, Victoria Falls; ☎013/4367, fax 5870, mobile ☎011/800588). Stylishly decorated en-suite rooms with tiled floors, reed ceilings, built-in cupboards and ceiling fans in deeply shaded grounds surrounded by high walls, about 3km from the centre along the *Sprayview* turn-off. A separate building houses a self-catering kitchen. ④.

Reynard Cottages, 403 Reynard Rd (☎013/2103 or 4418, *senanga@telcovic.co.zw* or *reynard@teconet.co.zw*). Small, simply decorated en-suite double rooms, 1.5km from town, in a complex away from the main house with a kitchen and dining area in a separate building. The grounds are grassy with some shade. ④.

Setabezi Lodge, 504 Baobab Rd (☎ & fax 013/2381, mobile ☎011/404 300, *setalodge@yahoo.com*). Spacious, light and tastefully decorated rooms (all, bar one, en suite), 2km from the centre, with tiled flooring and ceiling fans. Well-equipped kitchen and spacious grounds. A separate bungalow has its own lounge, kitchen and en-suite bedrooms. Transfers to and from town or airport compare favourably with taxis. ⑤.

Tatenda Lodge, 541 Reynard Rd (PO Box 105, Victoria Falls; ☎013/3460, ☎ & fax 3349, mobile ☎011/406 510). Small, barely furnished chalets 1.5km from town, cramped around small patches of green. Two small rather sparse kitchen areas are shared by guests. The garden provides space to relax, and there's a sunken bar by the pool. ③.

Villa d'Afrique, 645 Mahogany Rd (Private Bag 5951; ☎ & fax 013/5945, mobile ☎011/400044, *villadafrique@telconet.co.zw*). Tiled fully equipped, self-catering villas arranged around a swimming pool, with two air-conditioned twin rooms, 2.5km from town. Lunch and dinner available, as well as transfers to town. Two sharing ⑥, four sharing ⑤.

Villa Victoria, 165 Courtenay Selous Crescent (PO Box 274, Victoria Falls; ☎ & fax 013/4386, mobile ☎011/212263). Spacious and stark single and double en-suite rooms in small grounds, 2km from the centre. A kitchen and separate dining and sitting rooms are available if you're self-catering. ③.

Zambezi National Park Lodges, 7km from town down Parkway, (book through National Parks Central Reservations Office, Borrowdale Road/Sandringham Drive, adjacent to the Botanic Gardens; PO Box CY 826, Causeway, Harare; ☎04/706077–8, fax 726089 or 724914, *NationalParks@gta.gov.zw*). Wonderfully sited self-catering lodges set back from the river for maximum isolation – with riverine forest separating each – so you really do feel alone. In the swaths cleared between the lodge and the river you'll spot buck, monkeys, warthogs and plenty of birds. Occasionally, elephants stray into the lodge gardens and in the dry season they sometimes swim across from the mainland to the islands of Lwanda and Kalunda opposite the lodges, midway between Zimbabwe and Zambia. The lodges are almost always full, but it might be worth going there in the afternoon to check for vacancies. ①.

B&Bs and guest houses

Gertie's Lodge, 597 Nguhwuma Crescent (book through Zimfari Travel & Tours, Harare, ☎04/870495–7, fax 883539, *zimfari@harare.iafrica.com*; direct ☎ & fax 013/2002, *jtsgerti@telconet.co.zw*). Two-storey, semi-detached rondavels sleeping four to six people, 2.5km from town, with thatched roofs, ceiling fans and an ample lounge. Separate communal dining room, lounge and bar area with a large aquarium. No self-catering, but light snacks, sandwiches, lunches, packed meals, dinners or braais are available on request. ⑤.

Hunter's Lodge, 598 Nguhwuma Crescent (PO Box 132, Victoria Falls; ☎ & fax 013/5977, mobile ☎011/208367, *senanga@telcovic.co.zw*). Six en-suite bedrooms, 2.5km from town, with their own fridges, some complimentary drinks, ceiling fans under thatch and a shared kitchen. A three-bedroom cottage accommodating up to eight people is also available. Twenty percent discount for Baz Bus passengers and free transfers from the train station. No under-12s. B&B or bed-only rate ④.

Mosi-ua-Tunya Lodge, 609 Mahogany Rd (PO Box 165, Victoria Falls; ☎013/4336, fax 4639, *moslodge@telcovic.co.zw*). Two ethnic-styled, double-storey lodges with thatched roofs and air-conditioning, 2.5km from the centre. One has six smallish en-suite bedrooms and a fully equipped kitchen, while the other is better suited to families and large groups, with four large bedrooms on two floors. Rate includes a full English or vegetarian breakfast. ④.

Royal Lodge, 517 Jacaranda Crescent (☎013/2063, ☎ & fax 2099, mobile ☎011/405173, *royaldge@telcovic.co.zw*). Modern air-conditioned and carpeted rooms (some en suite and some with adjacent private bathrooms), with two double beds and wildlife murals, 3km from the centre. The honeymoon suite has a small fridge complete with a bottle of bubbly. Lunch and dinner on request. ⑤.

Hotels and upmarket lodges

A'Zambezi River Lodge, 5km out of town along Parkway (☎013/4561, fax 4536, 5835 or 4511, *reservations@zambezi.com.zw*). A pleasant escape adjacent to the Zambezi National Park, built in a semicircle with rooms facing the river. It claims to have the largest thatched roof in the world, and warthogs, monkeys and occasionally other animals roam about the grounds. A courtesy bus operates for residents without their own transport so it's easy to get to and from the centre. ⑨.

Elephant Hills, 3km out of town just off Parkway (book through PO Box 8221, Harare; or ☎013/4793, fax 4655, *reservations@ehic.zimsun.co.zw*). Hideously obtrusive white elephant, with piped muzak throughout, this is arguably the most controversial development at the Falls. ⑨.

Ilala Lodge, Livingstone Way, PO Box 18 (☎013/4737, fax 4417, mobile ☎011/401814, *ilalazws@coldfire.dnet.co.zw*). Highly recommended lodge where rooms look onto manicured lawns receding into indigenous forest, from which small game emerges in the mornings and late afternoons. Retains a fairly intimate feel by limiting guest numbers. ⑨.

The Kingdom, Parkway/Mallet Drive (PO Box 90; ☎4275, fax 4782, *reservations@kingdom.zimsun.co.zw*). Double rooms with a bunk bed for kids, along the main drag, at an over-the-top hotel labouring under its African-fantasy themes with wrought-iron Matabele warriors, glitzy public spaces and a casino. Family rooms in which the kids pay for breakfast only. ⑨.

Rainbow Hotel, Parkway/Courtney Selous Crescent (PO Box 150; ☎013/4585, fax 4654, mobile ☎011/204567, *frontoffice@rainbowhotel.co.zw*). Comfortable 1960s Spanish-style hotel with the attraction of a bar *in* the swimming pool. ⑧.

Sprayview Hotel, Livingstone Way/Renard Road (PO Box 70; ☎013/4344, fax 4713, *sprayv@africaonline.co.zw*). Cheapest of the Vic Falls hotels, with en-suite bedrooms, about 20min

---

THE VICTORIA FALLS HOTEL

The **Victoria Falls** is Zimbabwe's grandest hotel – and must be seen even if you can't afford to stay. The first visitors to the Falls had to eat and sleep in the train at the station, but in 1905, just after the railway arrived, work began on the construction of a wood and corrugated-iron hotel, close to the terminus. That shack has come a long way, with the avenue of scented trees from the station heralding the hotel's fabulous colonial style and impeccable service. Guests, largely foreign tourists, enjoy rich-*bwana* fantasies here, sipping drinks on the terrace, which opens onto views of the low greeny grey hills of Zambia rising behind the filter of spray. It's all part of the careful setting – the site was chosen for its view of the second gorge and the daring railway bridge.

The short walk from the hotel was too much for Edwardian tourists, so a trolley took them down to the Falls. A number of old snaps in Bulawayo's Railway Museum show well-dressed ladies and gents being pushed by black "trolley boys". The tracks were pulled up some time ago but the remaining path is still a thoroughfare, the trolleymen replaced by hustlers hawking curios.

on foot from the centre. It has a pleasantly nostalgic 1950s colonial atmosphere plus a daytime crèche and large pool. ⑤.

Victoria Falls Hotel, Mallet Drive, opposite the train station (PO Box 10; ☎013/4203, fax 4586, *vicfallshotel@tvfh.zimsun.co.zw*). The place to splurge, it positively oozes bygone elegance, with grand public spaces and white-gloved waiters in starched uniforms (see box on p.193). ⑨.

Victoria Falls Safari Lodge, off Parkway, 2.5km from town (☎013/4714, fax 3205; book from London ☎0171/225 0164, Johannesburg ☎011/331 8911, or Victoria Falls ☎013/4728, *saflodge@saflodge.co.zw*). The most imaginative hotel development at the Falls, thatched with large cool spaces and outdoor eating on a deck that overlooks miles of bush and a waterhole that attracts game. An hourly shuttle bus takes guests to and from town. ⑨.

Out-of-town safari lodges

For visitors wanting to combine game viewing with a visit to the Falls, a number of **lodges** outside town offer luxury in the bush, with game drives, walks or, in some cases, cruises thrown into the all-inclusive price – expect to pay upwards of US$250 (prices given are per person per night). Although some may seem far out of town, by Zimbabwean standards they aren't, and all are packaged as adjuncts to a Falls visit. Transfers to and from Victoria Falls or the airport are provided.

The Elephant Camp, 25km west of Victoria Falls, next to Zambezi National Park. Book through Wild Horizons, Parkway, PO Box 159, Victoria Falls (☎013/2313 or 2001, fax 4349, *wildhori@samara.co.zw*). Accommodating no more than eight guests on a 140-square-kilometre private game reserve, the camp centres around four trained, tame young African elephants. Elephant-back safaris are a focal activity, but these aren't so much children's fun-fair rides as a serious part of fostering an understanding of the animals. You can also pet the elephants, or opt for conventional game-viewing activities, including drives in the neighbouring national park, night excursions and guided walks. High season (July 1–Jan 4) US$450, low season (Jan 5–June 30) US$345.

Imbabala Safari Camp, 72km from town on the Kazungula road. Book through Wild Horizons, Parkway, PO Box 159, Victoria Falls (☎013/2313 or 2001, fax 4349, *wildhori@samara.co.zw*). On the Zambezi flood plain, near the Botswana border; you can see the meeting point of four countries (Zimbabwe, Botswana, Namibia and Zambia) from lawns which slope down to the water. Accommodation is in A-frame, en-suite chalets, catering to a maximum of eighteen guests; lie on your bed and watch the reflected sun set on the river. Excellent guides, good game viewing with elephants galore and outstanding opportunities for birdwatching, with species present that don't occur elsewhere in Zimbabwe. High season (July 1–Jan 4) US$260, low season (Jan 5–June 30) US$225.

Masuwe Lodge, 7km from Victoria Falls to the Masuwe turn-off along the main airport road, and then several kilometres along a private dirt track. Book through Landela Safaris, Travel Plaza, 29 Mazowe St; PO Box 66293, Kopje, Harare (☎04/734043–6, fax 708119, *res@landela.co.zw*). Set in its own concession, with promising prospects for game viewing. A broad range of habitats means birdwatching is also good, with common sightings of birds of prey. Large walk-in tents (consciously recreating an *Out of Africa* ambience) sit on stilted wooden decks providing panoramas of the surrounding bush. The lounge/dining room juts out over a valley, and some dramatic views. Low season US$220, high season US$275.

Sekuti's Drift, 25km out of town, next to the Zambezi National Park. Book through Landela Safaris (see *Masuwe Lodge* above for details). Hilltop re-creation of a nineteenth-century colonial homestead on private safari land, with a green tin roof and polished verandahs, which outdoes even the *Victoria Falls Hotel*. Maximum of twenty guests. Low season US$220, high season US$275,

Tongabezi, Zambia. Book through Private Bag 31, Livingstone, Zambia (☎03/323235 or 323296, fax 323224, *tonga@zamnet.zm*). On the Zambian side and geared more to style than game viewing: it's certainly a beautiful place. Some rooms provide the thrill of sleeping in a four-poster bed on a deck overlooking the Zambezi; other accommodation is in comfortable cottages, and there's also their thoroughly relaxed Sindabezi Island Camp in the middle of the Zambezi, where you can play out Robinson Crusoe fantasies in comfort. This intimate camp sleeps a maximum of eight people (and Horace the resident hippo), has outdoor sofas by the fire, and a dining room under the stars that offers a choice of seven main courses cooked to order. Low-season: cottages US$250, houses US$295; high-season: cottages US$300, houses US$375.

The Falls

When Livingstone arrived at the **Victoria Falls**, and named them after his queen, they already had a pretty catchy name – **Mosi oa Tunya**, "The Smoke That Thunders" – bestowed by the **Makololo**, who, like Livingstone, were newcomers to the region. Following the early eighteenth-century Zulu expansion (in what is today South Africa's KwaZulu Natal province), a refugee fragment had fled north, finally coming to rest around the Falls. They became the Makololo and held domain here briefly during the nineteenth century, ruling over the local tribes.

Stone Age tools uncovered in the area record that humans were living around the Falls for two million years before that. The Zambian side has a dig showing finds at different depths corresponding to different epochs, and the museum in Livingstone has a fine collection of stone tools found at the dig.

Victoria Falls National Park

The moment you arrive in Victoria Falls town, hear the roar and see the mist rising half a kilometre skywards, you'll be itching to get down the main street to the **Victoria Falls National Park** (daily 6am–6pm; US$10). A walk from here through the rainforest will take at least an hour. At full moon you can see the faint lunar rainbow (night entrance at full moon US$20). The Falls are at their most impressive in **April** and **May**, when the river is in full spate, although the dense spray can sometimes obscure the views, which are clearest, if somewhat less spectacular, in **September** and **October** at the end of the dry season. The best **times of day** to visit are around opening and closing, when the light is at its best and fellow tourists relatively sparse. Take waterproof protection (waterproofs can be rented in town – see Listings p.207 – or from the touts at the entrance) for your camera and other vulnerable possessions.

THE CHASM AND DEVIL'S CATARACT

You can walk all along the side of the **chasm** opposite the park entrance, through the woods with their sudden spray showers – be aware that some of the most vertiginous drops are unfenced, with just the occasional thorn bush as a barrier. In the dry season, when the Falls are lowest, you'll probably escape a soaking, but once the rains have swelled the Zambezi you'll get the full force of the spray; wear a swimming costume or raincoat. The wettest viewpoints are those directly opposite the Main Falls, in the areas unprotected by trees.

The first view that you get, at the western end of the chasm, is known as **Devil's Cataract**. Turning left from here takes you to a statue of **David Livingstone**, beyond which the river path leads off upstream. It's hard to avoid Livingstone in this neck of the woods. His commanding effigy overlooking Devil's Cataract portrays the qualities expected from a famous explorer – will and determination. More critical accounts record that he was pig-headed, selfish and sanctimonious but, nevertheless, anti-slavery campaigning was part of his reason for exploring the Zambezi.

THE HIPPO'S TALE

A **San folk tale** relates how the first **hippo** begged the Creator's permission to live in the water, which it loved more than the earth, the sun, the moon or the stars. However, the application was rejected: such a big mouth with such teeth would soon devour all the fish. The hippo begged again, promising to eat nothing in the water, and to emerge at night to graze on the grass and plants of the earth, but once again permission was denied. Finally, the hippo agreed to emerge daily and scatter its dung, so all the creatures could examine them for fishbones.

Livingstone's reverential account that "on sights as beautiful as this Angels in their flight must have gazed" has become one of the clichés of the Victoria Falls: a phrase that's even been reassembled to package the daily air tours – "The Flight of the Angels" – that flit above the chasm. To Livingstone, however, there was a real element of revelation in his vision of Mosi oa Tunya; he wrote of how local chieftains used two of the islands right on the lip of the Falls as "sacred spots for worshipping the deity".

OTHER FALLS AND DANGER POINT
Wander through the rainforest beyond Devil's Cataract and you will see the other falls that roar down the mile-wide fissure: **Main**, **Horseshoe**, **Rainbow** and the **Eastern Cataract**. A highlight is **Danger Point**, at the eastern end, where your walk on the Zimbabwean side finishes with a dizzy promontory near the Victoria Falls Bridge. From the rocks here you can look down into the frightening depths of the abyss, and also get great views of the eastern half of the Falls and the **Boiling Pot**, a seething whirlpool where two branches of the river collide. It can be wet and slippery at the viewpoint, with deluges of spray; during the flood season you won't see much, but when the river is lower it's mesmerizing.

The Town

It doesn't take long to realize that Victoria Falls has become a tourism theme park, so don't be too surprised if you find that much of what there is to do around town centres around shopping or other ways of separating you from your money. Among the less-hyped Falls activities are the **Zambezi river walk** and visits to the **Zambezi National Park**.

Soper's Curios and the Falls Craft Village
The curio shops around the Falls Craft Village, behind the post office and banks, are grouped together in a conglomeration which spills over down Parkway. The first stall was opened in 1903 by the earliest white settler, Percy Clarke, and in 1910 one Jack Soper opened a shop next door with a crocodile pool to attract customers. **Soper's Curios** (Mon–Sat 8.30am–5pm, Sun 9am–1pm) is still there, as is the pool (a new and larger one), with large **crocs** snoozing in the slimy water. For an eclectic mix of antiques and airport art, Studio Africana is worth a look. Some things aren't actually for sale – like the carved wooden **ape god** from Zaire, with a head made from a smoked gorilla skull – but if you want something old this is the place. In a sort of **indoor market** nearby, local women compete with each other to sell **crochet ware**, **baskets**, **carvings** and **bracelets** – it's cheaper and has considerably more buzz than the curio shops, but is not as easy to browse.

RAINFOREST WILDLIFE

The rainforest is eminently explorable and there's plenty of **wildlife** about. Baboons, monkeys, waterbuck, warthog and banded mongooses roam around, while the four hundred or so species of **birds** include Livingstone's lourie with its bright leaf-green breast and crimson flight feathers, the comical trumpeter hornbill, the paradise flycatcher, the nectar-feeding sunbird and more common bulbuls, warblers, barbets and shrikes.

Butterflies are numerous too, blowing through the mist between rainbows and shiny grass. During the rainy season, the undergrowth acquires a special luxuriance, with large blood lilies scarlet among the mosses and ferns. Wild yellow gladioli grow in patches of open grassland, while palms, ebonies, figs, mahoganies and waterberries thrive in the rich, moist soil.

DANGER: HIPPOS, LIONS AND MONEYCHANGERS

Vic Falls is a pretty wild place, despite its urban development. Although most people never encounter them, animals do make occasional appearances. Don't be lulled by the apparent tranquillity of the **Zambezi riverside walk**: watch out for **hippos** leaving the river at dusk for their bankside browse. They return to the water first thing next day, so watch out then too, and avoid blocking their route to the water. During the day they emerge occasionally to scatter their dung on land with a vigorous tail movement, but otherwise all you're likely to see of them are noses and ears above water far upriver from people. Be alert as well to the fact that other species of **wildlife**, including crocodiles, lions, elephants and buffalo, sometimes venture onto the path. A danger you're far more likely come across in town is **currency sharks** offering to change money at advantageous rates. Unless you're after a roll of old newspaper strips, you'll do a lot better at a bank or bureau de change.

The **Falls Craft Village** proper (Mon–Sat 8.30am–4.30pm, Sun 9am–12.30pm; US$5, children US$2) is set to one side of the curio shops, and consists of a mishmash collection of nineteenth-century huts from all over the country with displays of how indigenous Zimbabweans used to live. More interesting, if a little startling, is bumping into one of the two **fortune-telling** *n'angas* huddled in the darkness of one of the exhibit huts and for a few dollars they'll tell your fortune. Though they work out of context here, *n'angas* are widely used in Zimbabwe, by town and country dwellers, as healers and interpreters of the workings of the ever-present ancestors. They have a deep knowledge of illness and both herbal and ritualistic ways of dealing with it. Since Independence, the government has actively encouraged their profession.

Creature World
Creature World (daily 8am–5pm; US$1.60, children US$0.80), clearly signposted among the curio shops and diagonally opposite Soper's Curios, can be diverting for an hour or two. The snake attendant has a great line in ghoulish information (where snakes like to hide, how likely they are to bite you, how long you'll live if they do), and concludes with graphic descriptions of agonizing death. And if you've always wondered how those lifelike animals in museums are created, go to the **taxidermy workshop** in Elephant's Walk Shopping Centre, where they have mounts on display in various stages of completion and people who'll happily tell you some of the secrets of their morbidly fascinating work. The shop explores the depths of bad taste for all pockets: a copper ashtray plinthed on an impala leg goes for a few dollars, while there's a lion-skin rug (with snarling head) for those with more money than taste.

The Zambezi Nature Sanctuary
The **Zambezi Nature Sanctuary** (daily 8am–5pm; US$3), 7km up Parkway just past the *A'Zambezi*, is *the* place to see loads of **crocodiles**. Also known as Spencer's Creek Crocodile Farm, the sanctuary serves the dual purpose of restocking the badly depleted river and rearing the much-maligned reptiles for their skin; every year the Sanctuary collects about 2500 eggs, a proportion of which are hatched, reared and returned (some as healthy three-year-olds). Crocodiles have an important **ecological role** in balancing the fish population, eating predators which prey on the marketable fish such as bream. You can also see lions, leopards, servals and caracals, as well as birds, trees and an aquarium. **Feeding times** for the crocs are 11.15am and 3.45pm, and for the lions it's 4pm.

Without a car, the easiest ways to get here are to **cycle** down Parkway, or to take a **taxi**. There's a pleasant tea kiosk at the sanctuary, and an interesting little museum and curio shop.

RIVER WALKS FOR FREE

If you don't fancy forking out for any of the organized trips, you can walk or cycle up the river towards the Zambezi National Park. Outside the Victoria Falls National Park fence, just beyond Livingstone's statue, a four-kilometre riverside path leads to the *A'Zambezi River Lodge*, then 6km back along the road. You'll probably be alone, as most people don't venture upstream beyond the first rapids. This excursion can be conveniently combined with a visit to the Zambezi Nature Sanctuary and the A'Zambezi, but be wary of **wildlife** (see box on p.197).

Upriver, riverine forest flourishes and the water is smoother and quieter. If it's blistering, just walk 1km or so to the **Big Tree** and come back along Zambezi Drive and Parkway, which brings you to the doorstep of the campsite. The Big Tree, a large baobab, is no crowd-puller, but it has historical interest: early pioneers camped here and it became a traditional gathering place for crossing the river to the Old Drift Settlement and later to Livingstone.

Zambezi National Park

A few hundred metres upstream from the Nature Sanctuary you reach the end of Parkway and the gate to the **Zambezi National Park** (daily 6am–6pm; day entry US$10, week entry US$20), the most accessible area of the Upper Zambezi. You can ride rented bikes to lodges at the park's edge, but not into the park itself. If you can get a booking, stay overnight in the park's **lodges** (see Accommodation, p.193).

The park is best known for its large herds of **sable antelope**. Elephants and rhinos are gratifyingly common, and kudu, impala, waterbuck, zebra, lion, leopard and hyena can be spotted too. With a car, you can reach lovely riverside **picnic sites** to recline in palmy shade and contemplate the flow, although increasing numbers of boats and planes are spoiling the peace. The bizarre fruits under the palm trees that look like cricket balls or exotic animal droppings are the remains of **mulala fruits**, much prized by elephants. They eat them whole, digesting the succulent outer fruit and depositing the inner seed in a ready-made grow bag. Remarkably, the old seasonal elephant migration routes are marked by effectively dispersed cross-country lines of ilala palms. In the riverine woods you'll also find ebony trees, figs and *Acacia albida*.

Two main **roads** run through the park, the most popular being Zambezi Drive, which continues past the lodges along the river. The other option is to take the turn-off 6km south of town on the Bulawayo road to join Chamabonda Drive, which follows the course of the Masuwe River.

Walks lead along the river in front of the lodges. Keep your eyes peeled for smaller animals: **turtles** bask on the banks and splash waterwards for safety and you can even see baby **crocodiles** on tree branches that stroke the water's surface. Beware any bigger specimens, and the occasional elephant that wanders through. **Birds** are also prolific: cormorants, darters and kingfishers perch on half-submerged dead trees waiting for the right fish to swim by. Hadedas wander about on the grassy margins: the name of these large grey birds is inspired by their raucous call, a familiar Zambezi sound.

Boats, planes and village visits

Most visitors to Vic Falls want to get onto the river at least once and there are countless ways of doing this, the least demanding being the traditional booze cruises that have been around as long as anyone can remember; flights over the Falls that are another old favourite. If Vic Falls leaves the impression that Zimbabwean culture is about heavy drinking and adventure sports, going on a guided visit to an African village will give you some idea of the country's real cultural roots.

Cruises and jetboats

The most famous of local leisure activities are the "**booze cruises**", ranging in price between US$12 and US$30, which sometimes include drinks. Dabula Safaris offers a good deal and limits the number of passengers, or enquire at Backpackers' Bazaar, Kandahar or one of the booking agents in town (see box on p.200). The last (early evening) departure is the best time to be on the river, with the darkening forest back-lit by a molten sky. Though the launches don't berth en route, they do pause for photographs, and you're bound to see hippos and perhaps elephants on the banks and islands. Morning and afternoon cruises stop at Kandahar Island for tea: monkeys will try to steal your biscuits.

Jetboats, on the other hand, are able to get the parts booze cruisers cannot reach, as they are shallow, propeller-free craft that can whisk you through rapids in safety and comfort, navigating remote and tranquil sections of the river that were previously only accessible to canoes. You can get close to the Falls during low water or launch out on a five-hour safari 25km upstream into the Zambezi National Park (US$100 per person), or take a two-hour morning, lunch or evening cruise for around US$50. Book through Toad Hall Tours (☎ & fax 013/4641, *thtours@africaonline.co.zw*); Zambezi Jetboat Journeys, The United Adventure Co (☎ & fax 013/4631 or 2233, mobile ☎011/207518); or any agent in town.

Flights

To conservationists on the ground, the proliferation of flying machines buzzing over the Falls is a major irritant that has eroded the calm of this previously tranquil environment. It's undeniable, though, that from the air things look different; soaring above the spray, the sheer immensity of the gorge and Falls is dramatically revealed. Formerly, the only airborne joyrides on offer here were in a five-seater light aeroplane – now you can also choose a seaplane, helicopter, microlight or ultralight aircraft. "**The Flight of the Angels**" (about US$55), the oldest-established of the aerial excursions, lasts fifteen minutes, and the price covers transport to the airport; longer, 75-minute options include a game flight; and expect to pay from US$75 for a fifteen-minute trip in a **helicopter**.

Microlights and **ultralights** (from US$70) bear a strong resemblance to airborne 50cc motorbikes – it's just you and the pilot. Flights lasting around 35 minutes take in views of local villages, the gorge, the rainforest, Zambezi National Park and, of course, the Falls themselves. According to aficionados, the main difference between the two is safety. Ultralights, bookable through most agents or Bush Birds Flying Safaris (☎013/3398, fax 2411, *ulazim@samara.co.zw*), are rated the less risky of the two, partly because of their design, and partly because pilots hold commercial licences.

Village visits

The majority of Zimbabweans still live rural subsistence lives, yet most visitors leave the country without having set foot in a typical village outside some artificial romanticized reconstructions. Baobab Safaris offer the chance to correct the stereotypes, to find out how people really live and to meet them. The tour, established with a village development committee (a proportion of the fee goes to the village), takes you to **Monde**, 14km from Victoria Falls. Here you'll learn about traditional building methods, sample indigenous foods, meet a healer, visit the fields and talk to craftspeople. The tours, which leave at 8.30am and 2pm by arrangement, cost US$45 per person and can be booked directly through Baobab Safaris (☎ & fax 013/4283, mobile ☎011/404981, *baobab@telconet.co.zw*) or any agent at Victoria Falls.

Game drives and safaris

It's easy to be blinded by the hype of the Falls and to forget that it's situated close to several of the most significant **wildlife areas** in Southern Africa. On its doorstep, the

ADVENTURE ACTIVITY AND SAFARI OPERATORS

Unless otherwise specified, the recommended operators listed below are based in Victoria Falls.

Abseil Zambia, near Livingstone Adventure Centre, Livingstone; PO Box 61023 (☎03/323454, *abseil@outpost.co.zm*). Abseiling and high-wiring.

Adrift see Kandahar Canoeing Safaris.

African Extreme Bungi, PO Box 60353, Livingstone (☎03/324231 or 324156, mobile ☎011/405868, fax 324238, *reservations@bungi.co.zw*). Bungee jumping.

Baobab Safaris, PO Box 196, Victoria Falls (☎013/4283 or 2158, mobile ☎011/404981, *safaris@telconet.co.zw*). Walking and mobile safaris.

Bundu Adventures, 208 Parkway, opposite the campsite (☎013/3523, mobile ☎011/210946 or 406209), or PO Box 60773, Livingstone (☎03/324407, fax 324406, *zambezi@zamnet.zm*). Whitewater rafting.

Charles Brightman see Ivan Carter Safaris.

The Elephant Company, PO Box 125, Victoria Falls, Zimbabwe (☎013/4471–2, *reservations@elephants.co.zw*). Elephant-back safaris.

Frontiers Rafting, Phumula Arcade, 3 Parkway, Victoria Falls (☎013/5800–1, fax 5801). Canoeing and whitewater rafting.

Ivan Carter Safaris (Charles Brightman), 487 Marula Crescent (☎ & fax 013/5821, mobile ☎011/209144, *candt@africaonline.co.zw*). Foot safaris.

Kandahar Canoeing Safaris, caboose opposite Shearwater, Soper's Arcade, Parkway (☎013/3589, 2279 or 4502, fax 2014, mobile ☎011/405930, *adrift@africaonline.co.zw*). Canoeing under the Kandahar brand; the same company offers whitewater rafting using the international Adrift name.

Khangela Safaris, PO Box FM 296, Famona, Bulawayo (☎09/49733, fax 78081, mobile ☎091/ 234676 or 023/406981, *scott@gatorzw.com*). Foot safaris.

Leon Varley Walking Safaris, Backpackers' Bazaar, Shop 5, Victoria Falls Centre, Parkway (☎013/5828, fax 2208, mobile ☎011/404960, *backpack@africaonline.co.zw*). Foot safaris.

Safari Par Excellence, Phumula Centre, Parkway, Victoria Falls (☎013/2054, 4424 or 2190, fax 4510, *spevfa@africaonline.co.zw*); Livingstone Way/Parkway, Victoria Falls (☎013/2051; fax 4510); and Livingstone Adventure Centre, 216 Mosi-O-Tunya Rd, Livingstone (☎03/321320, *atd@zamnet.zm*). Whitewater rafting and riverboarding.

Serious Fun, 216 Mosi-O-Tunya Rd, Livingstone (☎03/323912, *seriousfun@zamnet.zm*). River surfing (aka riverboarding).

Shearwater Adventures, Soper's Arcade, Parkway Drive, Victoria Falls (☎013/4471–3, 4513, 4648 or 3392, fax 4341, *raft.res@shearwater.co.zw*). Whitewater rafting and riverboarding.

Tandemania, PO Box CT383, Shop 20b, Soper's Arcade, Parkway (mobile ☎011/211092 or 211093, *tandem@telcovic.co.zw*). Skydiving.

Thebe River Safaris, PO Box 5, Kasane, Botswana (from Zimbabwe ☎00267/650314, *thebe@info.bw*).

Touch the Wild, desks at *Elephant Hills Hotel*, *The Kingdom* and *Victoria Falls Hotel*. Game drives, guided walks and one-day safaris.

Ulinda Safari Trails, PO Box 229, Victoria Falls (☎013/2078). Hwange and Chobe multi-day safaris.

Wild Horizons, PO Box 159, Vic Falls Centre, Parkway (☎013/2313 or 2004, *wildhori @samara.co.zw*). Foot and elephant-back safaris.

Zambezi Horse Trails, book through Backpackers' Bazaar, Shop 5, Victoria Falls Centre, Parkway (☎013/5828, fax 2208, mobile ☎011/404960, *backpack@africaonline.co.zw*), or most other agents in town.

Zambezi National Park is a good place for to see African mammals, but about an hour by car are Chobe and Hwange national parks, the flagship game reserves of Botswana and Zimbabwe. In a similar vicinity you'll find Kazuma Pan National Park and Vic Falls is also the springboard for the marvellous and remote Chizarira National Park. A range of organized activities can be booked at the Falls, from three-hour outings in vehicles, on horse- or elephant back, to multi-day walking safaris. Contact details for the activities listed below are given in the box opposite.

Game drives in the Zambezi and Hwange national parks

Touch the Wild's excellent **game drives** in the nearby game reserve are a down-to-earth way of enjoying the area's natural splendours. The Zambezi National Park (see p.198 for a full treatment) runs along the southern bank of the Zambezi towards Botswana. During the three-hour trips, you may see elephant, buffalo, lion, zebra and many different species of antelope – worth it for whistle-stoppers, but not if Hwange's on your itinerary. Touch the Wild pick up from central hotels at 6am and 3.30pm daily in summer (8am & 3pm in winter); book through them.

Victoria Falls also makes an excellent starting point for one-day – and longer – safaris into northern Hwange and Chobe in neighbouring Botswana. The two-hour drive to **Hwange National Park** (see p.213) takes you through State Forest and the Matetsi safari area, so the game viewing starts almost straight away. Trips leave at around 6am and you get back to town by 7pm. Ulinda Safari Trails, led by one of Zimbabwe's few women professional hunter-guides, and Touch the Wild, among the longest-established operators in the Hwange area, both go to Hwange for the day. Prices are around US$100, including meals; Ulinda also does a two-day/two-night camping excursion to Hwange for around US$350.

Day-trips to Chobe National Park

Botswana's **Chobe National Park** is Africa's top **elephant sanctuary**, with a population estimated at as many as 50,000 (for full coverage of Chobe, see Chapter Seven, p.201). Touching Botswana's river-bounded northern frontier, the parts near Zimbabwe consist of beautiful flood plain with abundant birds and the continent's southernmost population of **red lechwe** antelope. Even if you don't plan to include Botswana in your itinerary, it would be a pity to miss out on Chobe, as it's only an hour by car from Victoria Falls or Livingstone, making it a manageable day-trip.

Just about any operator offering game drives also does Chobe day-trips. Most are pretty similar – only the prices vary. **From Victoria Falls**, the most expensive is UTC, one of the longest-established companies, which charges around US$150 per person for a day-trip. The smaller companies charge around US$120: Ultimate Africa Safaris, PO Box 224, Victoria Falls (☎013/3564, *ultimate@africaonline.co.zw*), and Baobab Safaris, PO Box 196, Victoria Falls (☎013/4283 or 2158, mobile ☎011/404981, *safaris@telconet.co.zw*), are recommended. An equally reputable company is the Botswana-based Thebe River Safaris, PO Box 5, Kasane, Botswana (from Victoria Falls ☎00267/650314, *thebe@info.bw*). Zimbabwean **car rental** companies won't let you cross the border with one of their cars without their written permission.

Canoeing on the Upper Zambezi

One of the most interesting of Vic Falls' aquatic attractions is **canoeing** on the Upper Zambezi, under the supervision of licensed guides. Trips include walking on the islands, and looking at flora and fauna. Craft on one-day trips are stable, highly manoeuvrable two-person inflatables – you're most unlikely to experience the duckings that sometimes happen in faster, less stable eskimo-style kayaks. And, should you end up in the Zambezi, you'll be soaked but safe – guides and assistants are on hand to haul you out if you capsize. Guides are trained professionals and safety is primary; you'll get first-class commentary on local natural history. There are hippos, though, which can be aggressive at times and get that adrenaline pumping as you paddle hard to get past.

Kandahar Canoe Safaris is the longest-established operator on the Upper Zambezi. A family run business, it takes small, personal, quiet and safe **canoe** safaris, including a three-hour Sundowner Wine Route (US$45), a one-day canoeing safari (US$85) and a number of longer overnight canoe safaris (US$150–400). Nights are spent in fully ser-viced riverside campsites and the silence of a canoe provides an unparalleled game-viewing platform, devoid of engine fumes and noise. Similar trips are operated by Frontiers.

Foot safaris in northwestern Zimbabwe

Foot safaris are a lot more interesting than driving around in search of game. Though you'll actually see fewer animals than on a drive, because you cover less ground, what you do see is more intensely witnessed. There's nothing like hearing branches crack-ing next to you and glimpsing the horns of a buffalo as it turns tail and crashes into the thicket.

Guides are reassuringly armed and the stringent standards necessary to obtain a licence in Zimbabwe ensure they're able not only to halt a charging elephant, but also know everything you ever wanted to know about the bush. Before you set out, there's an interesting safety talk about what to do if you meet a lion or encounter enraged buf-falo, elephant or rhino. In reality you probably won't have such encounters, but the thought certainly keeps you on your toes. All walks include meals or refreshments in beautiful spots on the riverbank.

For **short outings**, Charles Brightman of Ivan Carter Safaris offers two-hour morn-ing or afternoon walks in the natural surrounds of the *Victoria Falls Safari Lodge*'s estate, as well as half- and full-day hikes in the Zambezi National Park. Similar packages are offered by Kazuma Trails and Tatenda Safaris.

For **multi-day walking adventures**, it's difficult to beat Khangela and Leon Varley Walking safaris, some of the most exciting foot safaris anywhere in Zimbabwe. They take substantial excursions into the dramatic broken country of rarely visited Chizarira National Park (see p.230) – great fun and highly recommended. Both also do longer and more ambitious safaris that take in any combination of national parks, including Chizarira, Kazuma Pan and Zambezi National Park as well as Matusadona and Hwange. Varley's backpacking safaris (you carry your own gear) cost US$130 per person per day, or US$190 with a support vehicle carrying everything (low-season discounts avail-able Nov–April). On almost all of Khangela's trips, which are outstanding value at US$130 per person per day, your gear is carried for you. On the pricier Pioneer Trails, operated by Wild Horizons, you walk and camp in Hwange and Kazuma Pan national parks and need to be fit enough to take on at least 10km per day. Prices start at US$175 per person per day (participating in camp duties), rising to US$275 if you want to restrict your exertions to walking. Steve Bolnick of Baobab Safaris is another recom-mended hunter-guide, offering great-value budget packages (US$230 for three days, fully inclusive) once a week to Hwange from the Falls. Bolnick is one of the few Zimbabwean professional guides licensed to operate in **Botswana**, giving you the chance of a package that includes walking in Hwange, the Zambezi National Park and Chobe for US$165–250 per person per day (depending on the level of luxury).

Kazuma Pan National Park

Kazuma Pan, in Zimbabwe, south of the Falls on the Botswana border, was first opened to the public in 1987 and you can still only visit with a licensed guide. There's no accommodation here – it remains strictly a wilderness area. The landscape in the 315-square-kilometre park is unique in Zimbabwe, but similar to the great pans in

Botswana: miles of treeless, open grassland rich in game. The depression is surrounded by dense teak forests well watered seasonally with streams and rock pools.

Kazuma Trails (☎ & fax 013/3368, mobile ☎011/404947) or Leon Varley Walking Safaris (book through Backpackers' Bazaar, Shop 5, Victoria Falls Centre, Parkway (☎013/5828, fax 2208, mobile ☎011/404960, *backpack@africaonline.co.zw*), will pick you up at the Falls for **walking expeditions** to the pan. You may see rare species such as roan antelope, gemsbok, tsessebe, cheetah, black rhino, bat-eared fox and wild dogs, as well as lion, elephant and buffalo. In fact, about the only animals you won't see here are hippos. When the pans fill – as they do every few years – an extraordinary variety of **waterbirds** thrives here. Montagu's harriers are frequent visitors and the rare wattled crane actually breeds in the park. One of Kazuma's curiosities is a small variety of **fish** – as yet unidentified – which remains dormant during dry years and becomes active when it's wet; how it survives prolonged drought remains a mystery.

Horse safaris

Another prime way to see game is on **horseback**. The Zambezi Horse Trails outings give a rare chance to see the bush, accompanied by informed commentary. Two-hour rides start at the outskirts of town and follow the river to end up at the national park boundary. Full-day rides last from 9.30am until 4pm and include lunch, and for experienced riders an overnight outing is also available. Prices start at around US$50 for two-and-a-half-hour rides, which are open to novices. For the experienced, the choice ranges from half-day rides to four-night fully backed-up safaris, with prices from US$70. Bookings can be made through most agents in town.

Elephant-back rides

One of the most exciting and interesting ways of game viewing is on **elephant** back – something that saw a phenomenal growth in the second half of the 1990s. Elephant Back Safaris (book through Wild Horizons or any agent) and The Elephant Company offer morning (6–11.30am) and afternoon (3–7pm) safaris, which aim to give you an "experience of an elephant" rather than simply a ride on one. You'll gain some insight into the nature of these magnificent beasts, as well as getting a unique perspective on other wildlife. The price of about US$125 includes a full English brunch, or drinks and snacks, as well as transfers to the camp. A combined morning and afternoon safari with a night spent at *The Elephant Camp* (see Accommodation) can also be arranged, but is pretty expensive.

Adventure activities

Victoria Falls has become a major centre for **adventure activities**. Whitewater rafting was established in the 1980s as an attraction to rival the Falls themselves, and has since been joined by bungee jumping, riverboarding, abseiling cable-sliding and even sky-diving. Contact details for the activities listed below are given in the box on p.200.

Whitewater rafting

Riding the rapids has become one of Zimbabwe's biggest attractions, rivalling even the Falls themselves in popularity. The section starting in the gorge is reckoned to be the most exciting one-day commercial trip in the world and, despite the well-publicized deaths – averaging about two a year since 1992 – punters keep coming in increasing numbers. In fact, the run is reckoned to be relatively safe for its level of difficulty, almost as if it was designed especially for rafting. The eighteen to twenty **rapids**, including several grade fives (the most difficult commercially runnable category) are immediately followed by stretches of calm in which "long swimmers" (people who have fallen overboard and gone adrift) can be quickly retrieved, thus combining the maximum adrenaline surge with a relative degree of safety. If at times you feel like the ball in a massive pinball machine, the names given to the rapids – Devil's Toilet Bowl, Gnashing Jaws of Death, Overland Truck Eater, Terminator and Oblivion – do nothing to dispel the sensation.

Most people go down in an inflatable **oared raft**, steered by a trained oarsman who does all the work while you shift your weight when instructed and occasionally fall out. If this all sounds too passive, you could opt for a **paddle raft**, in which the passengers help to steer using paddles. Given a well-coordinated team, this is a more precise way to navigate the rapids, which means the raft is less likely to flip over. But because you have to perch on the edge of the craft, leaning out to paddle, you're much more likely to get thrown out. Whichever way you do the trip, though, the most strenuous part is the steep 230-metre climb out of the gorge at the end of the day.

The Zimbabwe stretch has the advantage of avoiding the bureaucracy of the border crossing, but if you opt for a trip starting in Zambia most **operators** will arrange to get you there. Shearwater, which operates from the Zimbabwe side, and Safari Par Excellence, which operates on both sides of the river, account for seventy percent of Vic Falls rafting business. Frontiers and an excellent newcomer, Adrift, also operate on the Zimbabwe side, while several other companies, including Bundu, launch from Zambia. One-day trips cost around US$95. Book well in advance to ensure a place; weekends are invariably fully reserved by Zimbabweans. The "high-water" trips go from mid-January to March and during June and July, and the "low-water" runs (when, naturally, the rapids are at their fiercest) from August to some time in December or January, depending on river levels. No rafting takes place in April or May.

Besides scrambling down to it and walking, rafting is the only way you'll get into the hundred-metre-deep **Batoka Gorge**, which had never been navigated until the now-defunct Sobek achieved it in 1981. Apart from day-trips, there are two-day and week-long **marathon excursions** right the way through the gorge to the mouth of the **Matetsi River**, near Deka – special but expensive trips that only operate from August to December and July to January. A third of the way through, you come to the **Moemba Falls**, which are exceptionally beautiful even if they're nothing on the scale of the big ones. They're also very rarely visited; few people even know of their existence and there are no marked roads in the vicinity – just 4WD tracks.

Riverboarding

In **riverboarding**, reminiscent of riding coastal breakers, you surf the river and "boogie" the Zambezi's rapids on a specially designed board. After a lesson on basic skills in calm water, you continue downstream taking progressively bigger rapids, stopping to ride stationary waves at "surf-spots". You can choose between a half-day, a full day, a riverboarding/rafting combination or an overnight trip. Shearwater runs trips on the Zimbabwe side, Safari Par Excellence on both banks, and Serious Fun, which uses the term "river surfing", sets out from Zambia. Half-day trips start at about US$95 and run from approximately July to January, while full days, offered year-round, will set you back about US$125.

Bungee jumping

In keeping with the town's gung-ho image is African Extreme's 111-metre plunge from the Victoria Falls Bridge, no longer the highest commercial **bungee jump** in the world, but quite possibly the most spectacular. If voluntarily hurtling into a gorge tethered to the end of an elastic band (albeit a thick one) sounds dangerous, rest assured that there have been no deaths so far. There have, however, been reports of spinal injuries, and even detached retinas. At US$90, it will probably be the most expensive ten seconds of your life.

Sky diving

More conventional than bungee jumping, and arguably more rewarding, are the two types of **sky dives** offered by Tandemania. If you want the thrill of free-falling from 3000m, but not the hassle of training, try the tandem jump, where you are harnessed to an instructor. After thirty seconds the parachute opens and you canopy ride for about five minutes before coming in for a piggyback landing, in which the instructor takes the full weight. Alternatively, opt for a one-day course that usually allows you to jump by mid-afternoon. You leave the plane at about 1000m, attached by a static line that opens the chute automatically. Tandem jumps cost US$160; the day training and jump is US$110, with the option of additional dives for US$20 plus US$5 for gear rental.

Abseiling and high wiring

If bungee jumping and skydiving don't do the trick, abseiling and high-wiring offer a couple other ways to get down. In **abseiling**, you are gently lowered down a rockface from a platform at the top of Batoka Gorge, attached to main and safety ropes; you can either walk back out of the gorge or get hauled up. The world's first commercial **high wire** consists of a cable 75m above the ground, spanning 135m across the gorge. After being securely attached to the cable via a safety harness, you take a flying leap or running dive over the edge of the gorge. Given that's it's as easy as falling off a log, no experience is required. The price tag of around US$95 includes a light breakfast and lunch (preferably eaten after the leap), a full day of either activity as many times as you like, and sundowners if you survive till the end of the day. Book through Vic Falls agents or Abseil Zambia in Livingstone.

Eating and drinking

The hotel dining rooms and terraces pose stiff competition to the growing number of **restaurants** springing up in town. All of the hotels offer à la carte menus with something affordable for lunch, as well as midday and evening braais; of those in the centre, *Ilala Lodge*, which does a very good mid-priced Mongolian barbecue, has the best reputation for food; it's on Livingstone Way. Most of the restaurants, cafés and takeaways are concentrated around the arcades in Parkway.

The Boma, *Lokhutula Lodge*, 2.5km from the centre. Popular and frequently full: good-value outdoor breakfast, lunch and dinner menus, including excellent eat-all-you-like evening braais that come with a huge choice of meats, salads and first-class desserts, for under US$17. A cheaper vegetarian alternative is also available. Traditional dancing and Zimbabwean traditional food make this an entertaining evening out.

The Cattleman Steakhouse, Pumula Centre, Clark Road. The ultimate place to eat any cut of beef you can think of, served in a variety of sauces; moderately priced.

The Coffee Shop, Elephant's Walk Shopping Centre. Nourishing sandwiches and quiches at very reasonable prices, as well as great filter coffee and delicious home-made muffins and cakes in a tropically landscaped courtyard. Daily 8.30am–6pm.

Eat-Za-Pizza, 307 Parkway (☎013/2049). Cheap burgers and submarine sandwiches, and moderately priced pizzas which you can have delivered. Daily 10am–midnight.

Explorers The cheapest food in town, and lots of it, with daily specials and a really good Sunday roast. Daily 11.30am–11.30pm.

The Meeting Place, opposite Elephant's Walk Shopping Centre. Quick and cheap lunch at a small free-standing snack bar; the simple garden tables have views of the sculptures at the Living Stone Gallery.

Naran's, Soper's Arcade in Parkway. Not a place to linger, but one of the town's cheapest places to eat, serving vegetable curries and good *sadza*.

Pink Baobab, Parkway. Breakfasts, snacks, light meals, teas and great coffee served throughout the day in a lovely garden. Particularly pleasant in the morning, it's a congenial venue for postcard writing. Daily 7am–3.30pm.

Pizza Bistro, Soper's Arcade in Parkway. The best pizzas in town – although there's not exactly stiff competition. Mon–Sat 7am–9.30pm.

Pride Rock, at Zambezi Nature Sanctuary. Similar menu and prices to the *Boma*, but their party trick is bringing the food to your table on sword skewers – you slip off what you want. Tame lions and a leopard (best not fed at table) lurk in enclosures and add to the African experience. Daily 6.30–10pm.

Saddles Steak Ranch, Phumula Centre. Bog-standard South African steakhouse franchise offering moderately priced steaks, burgers, pizzas and grills. Daily noon–2.30pm & 6–10.30pm.

Vanilla Falls, near *Wimpy* in Livingstone Way. The best ice cream and frozen yoghurt in town.

Victoria Falls Safari Lodge (☎013/3201–4). Pricy but rather good set dinners in an exceptional setting overlooking an illuminated waterhole. Also an excellent and affordable spot for sundowners.

Wimpy, Parkway/Livingstone Way. Better beefburgers and coffee than you might expect, but otherwise the usual bland stuff from this worldwide franchise. Mon–Thurs & Sun 7am–9pm, Fri & Sat 7am–10pm.

Nightlife and entertainment

At Victoria Falls, **nightlife** is generally synonymous with drinking, but there are a few alternatives. High-rollers should check out the **casinos** at the *Elephant Hills* and *Kingdom* hotels, where you'll be relieved of your remaining cash faster than it takes to bungee jump. More educational is a potentially fascinating **night game drive** onto a private reserve, though after five hours beetling about in the bush trying to make out animals in the spotlight the trip can become something of an ordeal. Most drives include a stop at a bush enclosure, where you're served a dinner of hot dogs with a choice of umpteen sauces in the dark. Sightings of hyenas and other nocturnals rarely encountered during the day are almost guaranteed.

Tribal dancing, by contrast, is short and sweet, with performances nightly from 6.30pm to 8pm at the Falls Craft Village for about US$15. The masks are impressive and the stilt dancing particularly worth seeing; a brief explanation precedes each performance, putting the dances in some kind of context. The *Victoria Falls Hotel* has dancing every evening (around 7.30–8pm) for those dining at the *Jungle Junction*, as does the *Elephant Hills* (7–8pm; US$10). During the day there's free traditional singing and dancing for about half an hour (daily 11am & 4pm) outside the Elephant's Walk Shopping Centre, where you'll also find buskers during the rest of the day. If you prefer taking part rather than observing, the very un-African Down Time **disco** at *Ilala Lodge* is the place to go.

Bars

Every one of the hotels has at least one drinking hole, while some have several. Surprisingly though, few seem to make anything of the superb views on their doorsteps. If you want to enjoy the river with your drink, your best bet is one of the many booze cruises that float along the Upper Zambezi every evening (see p.199 for details). Beer halls at the Town Council Rest Camp and near the Chinotimba taxi ranks are the places to meet Zimbabweans.

Croc Rock Sports Bar and Nite Club, Zambezi Centre. 24hr sports bar with pool tables and several TVs indoors, plus an outdoor section in a courtyard. Reasonably priced chicken and salads.

Down Time, *Ilala Lodge*. One of the most popular spots in town gets 'em hopping in its bar and disco. Cover charge of US$3 is waived if you're having a meal at the lodge.

Explorers, Soper's Arcade, Parkway. Loud and lively joint, with whitewater videos and pounding music, where rafters hang out after a hard day on the river. Midday and evening meals served.

The Kingdom. Noted for its top-floor bar, with the best views across the gorge and into Zambia.

Victoria Falls Hotel. The antithesis of *Explorers*, offering sedate terrace drinks with views of the bridge and the spray rising into the reddening sky. The quietest place to drink in town.

Victoria Falls Safari Lodge. The bar on the impressive timber deck overlooks the hotel's floodlit private waterhole, where in the dry season you stand a chance of seeing exciting wildlife.

Listings

Airlines Air Zimbabwe (☎013/4316, 4518 or 4665) has offices in the main administrative block, Livingstone Way, opposite the *Kingdom*, and deals with South African Airways; Zimbabwe Express (☎013/5992, fax 2123, mobile ☎011/203902), in Elephant's Walk Shopping Centre or at the airport. **Airport** ☎013/4250.

Banks In the same block as Air Zimbabwe in Livingstone Way (Mon, Tues, Thurs & Fri 8am–3pm, Wed 8am–1pm & Sat 8–11.30am). There are also bureaux de change in Parkway. Standard Chartered has a branch at the *Kingdom*.

Bike rental About fifteen companies, mostly down Parkway, rent bikes. Among these are Baobab, outside the restaurant with the same name, and Campsite Bicycle Hire, next door to Kandahar's caboose, which is cheaper than most. Rates are generally around US$1 per hour or US$8 for a full day. It's worth checking out a few places, as the condition of the bikes varies.

Camping equipment Raincoat & Camping Equipment Hire Services, 307 Parkway Rd, behind *Eat-Za-Pizza* (☎013/4528) rents anything you need for camping, including towels and torches and fishing tackle.

Car rental Budget, Zambezi Centre (☎013/2243), offers the best deal in town. Others are Avis on Livingstone Way at the Shell Station adjacent to the *Kingdom* (☎013/4532–5); Hertz on Parkway at the UTC offices (☎013/4297); Car and Truck Rental, Zambezi Centre; Eurocar at the *Sprayview*; Transit Car and Truck Hire (☎013/ 2109), 18 Soper's Centre.

Doctor Dr Nyoni, Victoria Falls Surgery, West Drive, off Parkway (Mon–Fri 9am–7pm, Sat 9am–1pm, Sun 10–11am; ☎013/3356).

Emergencies Police ☎995; fire ☎993; ambulance ☎994; general ☎999; Medical Air Rescue Service (see below).

Groceries For self-catering, the best place to stock up is Jay's Spar, behind Soper's Arcade. Also handy, especially when Spar is closed, is the 7–11 store, 306 Parkway, next to Frontiers.

Internet and email services *Blue Lizard Internet Café* in the Croc & Paddle, Elephant's Walk Shopping Centre; *Cyber Café* (9am–7pm; ☎013/4684–5), Soper's Arcade, Parkway; and Internet Village, Soper's Arcade. Charges are around US$3 for 15min, to US$9 for 1hr).

Laundry Mosi-oa-Tunya Laundry (Mon–Fri 8am–5pm, Sat 8am–noon) behind the caboose on Parkway is pricey; the Town Council Rest Camp offers cheaper laundry services; and most B&Bs and self-catering places have reasonably priced services.

Medical Air Rescue Service MARS, 162 Courtney Selous Ave (☎013/4764, emergency ☎4646, fax 4764, *marketing@mars.co.zw*) operates a private ambulance and paramedic service.

Pharmacy Victoria Falls Pharmacy, Phumula Centre, Parkway near Safari Par Excellence and also at the *Kingdom*'s Great Enclosure (Mon–Fri 8am–5pm, Sat 8.30am–1pm, Sun 9am–noon; ☎013/4403, mobile ☎011/405270 or 405269, after hours ☎013/4336 or 3339).

Photos Zambezi Memories, Shop 4, Phumula Centre (daily 7.30–6pm) offers a 1hr photo service developing slides or prints, and also sells batteries and disposable cameras.

Police Livingstone Way (open 24hr; ☎013/4206 or 4401).

Post office is on Livingstone Way near the banks (Mon–Fri 8am–4pm, Sat 8–11.30am).

Raincoat rental Raincoat & Camping Equipment Hire Services, 307 Parkway Rd, behind *Eat-Za Pizza*. Advisable if you don't want to get drenched at the Falls.

Safari and adventure bookings Backpackers' Bazaar, Shop 5, Victoria Falls Centre, Parkway (daily; ☎013/5828, fax 2208, mobile ☎011/404960, *backpack@africaonline.co.zw*) is recommended for arranging activities and budget accommodation, as is the friendly and well-informed Kandahar Canoeing Safaris in the distinctive caboose opposite Soper's Arcade, Parkway (☎013/3589, 2279 or 4502, fax 2014, mobile ☎011/405930, *adrift@africaonline.co.zw*).

Taxis Tatenda (mobile ☎011/209141), Host (☎013/2238) and Alois (mobile ☎011/719359) are recommended. There are taxi ranks behind the Spar supermarket and on Parkway.

Telephones Card phones are to be found outside the post office and near the tourist information office on Parkway. You can buy cards at bureaux de change or the post office.

Livingstone and the Zambian Falls

Livingstone has seen a significant growth in tourism over the past five years, with visitors finding Victoria Falls town over commercialized and coming to appreciate the laid-back charm of the Zambian side. Unlike Victoria Falls, Livingstone is an authentic African town that was built by the British as an administrative centre and had little tourism till the late 1990s. Most visitors can get a special one-day pass without undue formality to cross to the Zambian side of the Falls.

Mosi-oa-Tunya National Park

The most compelling reason to venture over to Zambia is to see the Falls from the vantage of the **Mosi-oa-Tunya National Park** (6am–6pm; US$3). Once across, head for **Knife Edge Point** which is, without doubt, the most awesome view of the Falls. You reach it on a path that winds down to a slippery, spray-dashed footbridge and onto an island of high ground where the water roars deafeningly around you. You can also descend to the very bottom of the **Boiling Pot** gorge and watch from a safe distance as the powerful river surges into a terrific whirlpool.

These oblique views from Zambia are very different to the head-on aspect from the Zimbabwean side, and the gorges can be seen much more clearly. The "tourist show" on this side of the Falls, however, is more tatty: no well-kept national park to grace the scene here, just a half-broken, sad memorial plinth to the Northern Rhodesian war dead. The **Field Museum**, built around a small archeological dig, has prehistoric hand tools and elementary wall displays of information about local finds.

Next door, the **Craft Village** – its stallholders desperate to sell – offers much run-of-the-mill stuff, but also some items that are quite different from Zimbabwean craftwork. There's excellent **basketry** and colourfully decorated **wooden guinea fowls**. If you're into bartering, take along any spare clothes, particularly T-shirts, as they are much sought after.

The entrance to the **game reserve** section of the park is near the boat club, departure point for the Zambian sundowner cruises. While you will see game here and it's a rewarding enough place to go if you've time to kill in Livingstone, the park isn't in the same league as the really great reserves, such as Hwange and Chobe, both within rel-

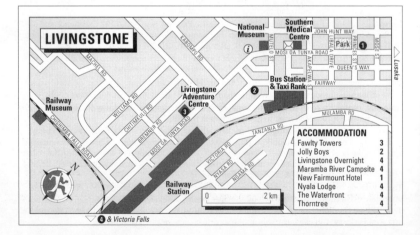

LIVINGSTONE

ACCOMMODATION

Fawlty Towers	3
Jolly Boys	2
Livingstone Overnight	4
Maramba River Campsite	4
New Fairmount Hotel	1
Nyala Lodge	4
The Waterfront	4
Thorntree	4

CROSSING INTO ZAMBIA: SOME TRAVEL TIPS

Apart from British and New Zealand passport holders, all Commonwealth citizens entering Zambia are exempt from visa requirements. A day **visa** costs US$10 or £5 (sterling is cheaper). For overnight stays it's US$25 for single entry and US$40 for multiple entry, unless you're British, in which case you'll pay a hefty £35 for single and £45 for a multiple-entry visa. But all isn't lost, as anyone travelling across and staying with a bona fide tour operator, such as *Jolly Boys* or *Fawlty Towers*, can be issued with a **Zambian manifest**, which gives exemption from visa payments. The operator applies on your behalf, so you must give them your passport details 24 hours before you travel so they have time to make arrangements. You can book this through any travel agent or activity company on the Zimbabwean or Zambian side. Note that this doesn't exempt you from **Zimbabwean visa requirements** (see Basics, p.14).

• **Border opening** times are 6am to 8pm; the distance across the bridge is easily walkable, but allow plenty of time to clear both sets of customs and immigration.

• **Currency** is the **kwacha** (K), but you can use Zimbabwe or US dollars for most things. Note that there's an export limit of Z$2000 when leaving Zimbabwe, so you'll need to take most of your money in US dollars. At the time of writing there were roughly 2350 kwachas to the US dollar and 3800 kwachas to the pound sterling.

• Be sure to check whether any **price** you have been quoted at accommodation, restaurants and elsewhere includes the ten percent government **tax**.

• If **driving** into Zambia, be sure to buy vehicle insurance at the agency at the border (8am–5pm; US$15). Border officials don't tell you you'll need this, but if you fail to do so you may get nabbed at a police road block a few kilometres down the road, where you could be fined and sent back to the border to buy the insurance. Make sure you are wearing your seat belt and that all your vehicle papers are in order.

• As in Victoria Falls, it's a poor idea to **change money** on the street – it's invariably a sting. You can change banknotes or travellers' cheques at any of the **banks** or bureaux de change in Livingstone. The *New Fairmount Hotel*, on the main road in the centre of Livingstone, also changes money.

• Government **hospitals** aren't recommended; rather opt for one of the inexpensive private **clinics** (see Livingstone Listings, p.212) which are quicker and better stocked.

• The international **phone code** for Zambia is ☎260 and the area code for Livingstone is ☎03.

atively easy reach of the Falls. Makora Quest Safaris in Livingstone (☎03/324253 or 321679), as well as *Gecko's Guest House*, 84 Limilunga Rd (☎03/322267), and *Fawlty Towers*, 216 Mosi-o-Tunya Rd (☎03/323432, mobile ☎011/708184), do day-trips to the park, museums and historical parts of the town.

Livingstone

For a peek at Zambia proper, make a sortie into **LIVINGSTONE**, 11km on from the Zambian side of the Falls. Now run-down, this former Falls capital remains a more convincing urban centre than its upstart successor in Zimbabwe, its main attraction being the **National Museum**, which displays a host of beautiful artefacts from all over Africa. Mosi-o-Tunya Road runs all the way from the border, slicing through Livingstone's centre; about halfway along, you pass the **Maramba Cultural Centre**. Once across the Maramba River, you meet Livingstone's industrial suburbs trailing into the countryside – you'll know you're close to the **centre** of town when you can hear shouts from the sidewalks offering packets of Zambian kwacha for dollars; people openly play the black market here, and you'll often be approached.

Getting there

The best way to get to Livingstone for a day or two is to arrange a transfer with one of the **backpackers' hostels** on the Zambian side, such as *Fawlty Towers, Gecko's Guest House* or *Jolly Boys*. *Fawlty Towers* picks up their guests daily at 9am and 5pm in Victoria Falls from Backpackers' Bazaar travel agency, and *Hitch Haven, Victoria Falls Backpackers* and *Shoestring* backpackers' lodges and will also arrange for a manifest that exempts you from paying for a visa (see box, p.209). Expect to pay about US$5 for a **taxi** from Vic Falls to Livingstone, depending on where in town you are, and about US$1 to the border. UTC charges US$4 and Riti Transfers US$1.50 to the Bridge; UTC will take you to Livingstone for US$8. Going **by bike** into Zambia is reasonably safe but there have been a few muggings, so to be on the safe side stick with other people, as it is less likely that you will encounter any trouble and be sure your bike has a lock. **Hitching** is safe during the day but not recommended at night. Cheap **minibuses** from the Zambian side ply the route between the Falls entrance to Livingstone. A number of **upmarket lodges** on the Zambian side will transfer their guests from Victoria Falls.

Accommodation

If Victoria Falls is booked out, you may have no option but to cross the border and stay in Livingstone, which fortunately has some cheap **accommodation** and a **campsite**, as well as good transport links with the Falls. See box on p.209 for the Zambia and Livingstone telephone codes. As in Victoria Falls, most places are all too happy to help you arrange safaris and activities for no charge and provide a wealth of information.

CENTRAL

Fawlty Towers, 216 Mosi-o-Tunya Rd, Livingstone (☎03/323432, mobile ☎011/708184, *ahorizon@ zamnet.zm*). Highly recommended clean and spacious backpackers' lodge, about 5min walk from town, in the Livingstone Adventure Centre. Run by friendly, well-informed staff, it has dorms (maximum six beds), doubles and camping under large mango trees. The popular *Funky Munkey* restaurant (see p.212) is at the bottom of the garden, and there's a congenial bar and pool. Email, phone and fax facilities available, as well as bicycle and tent rental. They also arrange regional safaris and local tours and provide free pick-ups from Victoria Falls town daily at 9am. Camping and dorms ①, doubles ②.

Gecko's Guest House, 84 Limilunga Rd, Livingstone (☎03/322267, fax 320586). Dorms and doubles and a grassy campsite at a run-of-the-mill backpackers' lodge that welcomes families, 2min from the train station in a quiet residential area. Option of self-catering or buying breakfast or supper, plus free border transfers and bike rental. Email, fax, phone and message service are also on offer. They run Livingstone Safaris, which offers local tours and game drives for about US$25. Camping and dorms ①, doubles ②.

Jolly Boys International Backpackers, 559 Mokambo Rd, Livingstone (☎03/324229, *quinn@outpost. co.zm* or *jboys@zamnet.zm*). Four- to six-bed dorms in a colourfully decorated hostel with plenty of cupboards in a quiet area a few hundred metres south of the town centre. A large and well-equipped kitchen makes self-catering easy or you can order breakfast or dinner. Fax facilities, bicycle rental and free transport to and from activities. An excellent US$10 package includes transfer from Victoria Falls town, a dorm bed for a night, an evening meal with a beer, and free entry to the Zambian Falls. ①.

New Fairmount Hotel, Mosi-o-Tunya Road (☎03/320723 or 320728, fax 321490, *nfhc@zamnet.zm*). One of Livingstone's most salubrious hotels, bang in the centre of town. ⑤.

The Jungle Junction, 21 Obote Ave, Livingstone; PO Box 61122 (☎ & fax 03/324127, *jungle @zamnet.zm*). With a good reputation on the backpacker grapevine, the *Junction* offers camping or huts on a lush island in the middle of the Zambezi, where you camp or stay in a hut. Palm trees, sandy beaches, hammocks and simple accommodation give a real castaway atmosphere, while still offering comfort. Shelters are rough, the flushing toilets are environmentally friendly and the bush showers are lit by African starlight. Basic supplies and booze are available for self-catering, or you can bring your own – or order a reasonably priced meal from the kitchen. A US$50 per-person cover charge includes transfers to and from border posts or Livingstone to the island, guided canoe activities, email holding and immigration formalities. Due to its popularity, booking is essential. Camping ①, double huts ②.

OUT OF TOWN

Livingstone Overnight, about 6km from the border, adjacent to the Mosi-oa-Tunya National Park (☎ & fax 03/320371, *overnight@outpost.co.zm*). Choice of self-catering twin cottages, A-frame thatched en-suite chalets or camping at a friendly place that has wildlife wandering through. The shady, lawned campsite has two spacious ablution blocks and a separate entrance, but all facilities are open to campers. Great home-cooked grills, chicken, steak, burgers, breakfasts and three-course dinners available. To get there, turn left off the main road into Livingstone, at the unmiss-ably large sign about 6km from the border post, and continue down the track for about 500m. Camping ①, cottages ⑤, A-frames with half-board ⑦.

Maramba River Campsite, 5km from the border post on the banks of the Maramba River, Livingstone (☎ & fax 03/324418-9, *maramba@zamnet.zm*. Promising option for self-catering families in the Mosi-oa-Tunya National Park, with self-contained en-suite chalets that sleep four in two twin beds and a double bunk. Tents for rent (US$5 per night), swimming pool and licensed bar. To get there, turn off at the Maramba Cultural Centre. Camping ①, chalets for two - four sharing ②.

Nyala Lodge, 5–6km from the border post, Livingstone (☎03/322446, fax 321248, *nyala@zamnet.zm*). Spacious luxury meru tents under thatch with their own private verandahs overlooking grassy, shaded grounds. You can drink or eat in the open thatched restaurant and bar area and there's a kids' playground. Transfers (including to Victoria Falls airport) can be arranged for an extra charge. To get there, turn west from the road to the border onto Sichango Road to Batoka Sky, continue for about 1km, then turn right at the "Nyala" sign and proceed for about 300m. Camping ①, luxury tents ⑥.

Thorntree, in the Mosi-oa-Tunya National Park. Book through Safari Par Excellence, Phumula Centre, Parkway Victoria Falls (☎013/2054, 4424 or 2190, fax 4510, *spevfa@africaonline.co.zw*); or Livingstone Adventure Centre, 216 Mosi-o-Tunya Rd, Livingstone (☎ & fax 03/321320, *atd@zamnet.zm*). Luxury tents under thatch, with river views. The price of about US$260, per per-son (mid-June to mid-Jan), or US$220, per person (rest of year), is inclusive of food, drinks, game drives and river cruises.

Waterfront, roughly 6km from the border post on the banks of the Zambezi River (booking as above for *Thorntree*). Camping or en-suite chalets, with a pool as well as a restaurant, bar and enter-tainment under a thatched dome. Cruises on a double-decker pontoon can be arranged. To get there, turn west onto Sichango Road to Batoka Sky. Camping ①, rooms ⑥.

The Town

The main attraction of Livingstone is the fusion of a sepia-toned colonial heritage, build-ings with tin roofs and wraparound verandahs, and its authentic African town life that owes just about nothing to tourism. If you've got time to kill and money to burn, you can pass a while at one of the two museums, of which the National Museum is the more interesting.

THE NATIONAL MUSEUM

The **National Museum**, Mosi-o-Tunya/Mutelo Street (daily 9am–4.30pm; US$5), is a peculiar place, containing some of the most interesting ethnological items in the region, yet with little explanation, making it stimulating and mystifying by turn. Helpful Zambian visitors, however, might offer illumination – this is the country's main muse-um and highly popular. Among its many and varied collections are displays of weapon-ry, hunting equipment, reconstructed villages and David Livingstone's cape, trunk, thermometer and surgical instruments.

The collection of **religious fetishes** is fascinating and ghoulish, one remarkable figurine bristling like a hedgehog with nails hammered into it. There's also a very fine range of **Tonga artefacts** from the Gwembe Valley, collected before it was flooded to create Kariba, including headrests, stools and a finely decorated waist-high drum used to send long-distance messages at night. On the ground floor, one of the most interest-ing exhibits is the **Broken Hill Man of Kabwe**, a copy of the 110,000-year-old Neanderthal skull found in 1921. The original was stolen by the British and the Zambians are still trying to get it back. In return, the British want David Livingstone's case and instruments – negotiations continue.

In the same part of the museum as the Livingstone memorabilia are some revealing old **photographs**. Don't miss the picture of four Arab traders examining an African slave. The hopeless look on the manacled man's face is painful, while the arrogance of those around has to be seen to be believed. Nearer the present, the story of Zambia's path to **Independence** is told through press cuttings and photos.

THE RAILWAY MUSEUM

The turning to the **Railway Museum**, Chishimba Falls Road (daily 8.30am–4.30pm; US$5), is clearly signposted on your left as you approach the centre of town. Opened in 1987, it aims to educate Zambians about the importance of the railways. A yard full of decrepit coaches and engines lets everyone indulge childhood fantasies, while inside, rooms full of antique rail souvenirs evoke the old days: wood and brass Morse code machines and gleaming brass signal lamps. Exhibits also give accounts of the development of railways in Europe and Africa, along with loads of photos.

Eating, drinking and nightlife

Livingstone has a number of decent **restaurants**; for takeaways, there are a number of typical joints in the centre of town.

Funky Munkey, 216 Mosi-o-Tunya Rd, behind the Livingstone Adventure Centre. It's difficult to ignore a reputation that extends into Zimbabwe and Botswana as *the* place to eat in Livingstone, and you'll find a wide and reasonably priced menu that includes soups and salads. Reminiscent of a Spanish villa, the restaurant has a courtyard and enormous trees but the thatched bar leaves you in no doubt that you're in Africa.

Kelvan's Kitchen, Mosi-o-Tunya Road near the central post office. Inexpensive breakfasts and dinners; serves up nice starters, such as smoked salmon and mussels, plus fish, steak and chicken mains.

New Fairmount Hotel, Mosi-o-Tunya Road. Moderately priced meals and night-time entertainment in the bars, with snooker and pool tables as well as a disco.

The Pig's Head, Kabompo Road, west of Mosi-o-Tunya Road. Pub and restaurant that stays open till midnight and has mid-priced daily specials, and pub food such as burgers, chicken and chips. Closed Sun.

Pilgrims Tea Room, outskirts of town west of Mosi-o-Tunya Road. A pleasant, airy tearoom which serves good, quality food at reasonable prices. Besides good coffee, they serve breakfast, light meals such as quiches, pies, vegetable bakes, as well as cakes and other tasty treats.

Listings

Groceries Shoprite Checkers supermarket, Kaponda Avenue, across from the taxi ranks (Mon–Fri 8am–7pm, Sat 8am–5pm, Sun 9am–1pm), is the best stocked, but there are also many small shops on the main road.

Hospitals and clinics The state hospital in Akapelwa Street is best avoided; rather go to one of the inexpensive clinics, which accept payment in any currency and where you'll get swifter and superior treatment: Southern Medical Centre, Mosi-o-Tunya Road between the post office and Akapelwa Street in the centre of town; or the clinic at 20 A.S. Sananga Rd (☎03/322038), about 100m from *Jolly Boys*, run by Dr Tigdi, who lives on site and can be roused at awkward hours in an emergency. You can get malaria tests here for about US$3 and the treatment, should you need it, will cost about US$20.

Internet Cyberian Outpost, the Livingstone Activity Centre, 216 Mosi-o-Tunya Rd, incorporates an Internet café, games and a business centre.

Photography Photo Express, Mosi-o-Tunya Road next to *Megabites Fast Foods* in the centre, has a same-day photo service.

Police The station is at Tanzania Road, near the train bridge crossing (☎03/320318).

Post office, Zambia State Insurance Building, next door to *Kelvan's Kitchen* and the Southern Medical Centre.

Taxis You can usually hail taxis in town, but the rank outside the Shoprite Checkers Supermarket in Kaponda Avenue is a dead cert.

HWANGE NATIONAL PARK

Once regarded as a vast wasteland, useless for farming, **HWANGE NATIONAL PARK** is now Zimbabwe's premier wildlife showcase. During August, September and October, the **game watching** can be truly spectacular: the park has an estimated shifting population of around 30,000 elephants, and a huge variety of animals and birds. And the great advantage of Hwange is that it is accessible, whether on a tour or doing it your own way – using National Park budget accommodation or staying in one of the many privately run safari camps. Hwange's thornbush, savannah, mopane and teak forests aren't as spectacular as the landscapes of the great East African parks – there are no huge mountains, craters or vast plains – but the bush savannah has its own modest beauty, the tracks are considerably less worn and you'll be able to see much the same game without being surrounded by other tourists.

It's only fair to point out, however, that you need to have luck on your side if you're dead set on seeing the big cats, or action as exciting as a lion kill. Frustratingly, you may repeatedly hear about the wonderful things seen by others the day before, or the bounding cheetah and the lion cubs you just missed. If you visit during the **rains**, you may not even clock an elephant. There's the story of a foreign tourist who complained that he had spent a whole day in the park and seen nothing except a pair of tortoises; the game ranger replied that he was actually very lucky, as they're not often seen in pairs. Don't be too big-game oriented – take your binoculars and a good field guide, and relax.

Although Hwange National Park spreads across a total of 14,620 square kilometres of dry bush country, only the eastern edge is accessible to the public. Here

---

TIPS FOR GAME VIEWING AT HWANGE

Hwange's highest concentrations of game occur during the **dry season** (May–Oct) when animals congregate around the pans. Once the rains come and there's surface water, they disperse all over the park, while long grass after the start of the rains tends to screen the animals from view. If you plan to do some serious game viewing, it is well worth getting hold of some field guides (see Books, p.391, for recommendations).

• **Early morning** is the best time of day for animal watching, when you'll see some of the nocturnals slinking off and others feeding before they hide away in the shade. **Dusk** is almost as good and certainly the best time to see elephants drinking. The usual pattern for safari operators is two game drives a day: dawn and dusk. An appetite-whetting chart at Main Camp reception shows exactly what you'll see when and each beast's cycle: lions, for example, usually drink early, rest in the heat and hunt in the late afternoon.

• Because it's on the edge of the Kalahari, **temperatures** in Hwange are extreme, particularly just before the rains and during the summer dry season, when it can soar to the high thirties (°C) during the day. Nights, however, are always cool, and in the dry season can drop below freezing. Whatever the season, always take a sweater on game drives, especially in the early morning. During winter (June–Aug), a sweater, anorak and scarf are essential, and gloves and a woolly hat won't come amiss.

• **Binoculars** are a must for scanning the horizon when you're out viewing. Don't try consciously to spot animals – many are well disguised. Instead, watch for any movement or something that strikes you as a bit out of place. Driving really slowly also pays off, particularly if you stop often. You can sometimes see more in a stationary hour alongside a pan than in a day's frantic driving.

• **Viewing platforms** at the major pans frequently provide the best chance to see something. High off the ground, they give good unobscured panoramas of the surroundings. All animals have to drink at some time.

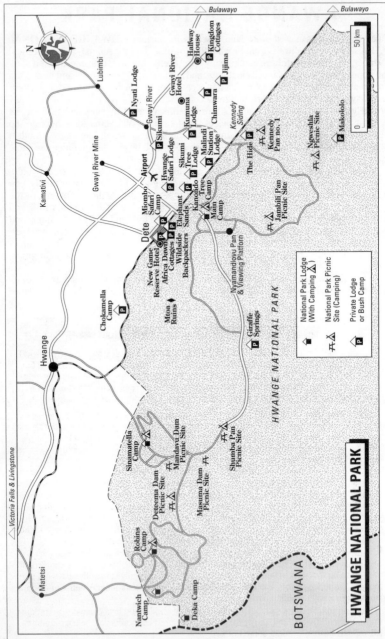

HWANGE NATIONAL PARK

many waterholes have been created to attract animals, and roads built for game viewing – all sand surfaces apart from 10km of tar at Main Camp. The dams, or **pans** as they're more usually known, are pumped with water throughout the year and remain the best places to spot animals. Surrounding the park boundaries are buffer zones, massive tracts of land used for forestry, game ranching and safaris, as well as hunting. The park itself is not fenced, and animals wander freely between it and the buffer zones, mostly attracted by the availability of water. The three major National Parks camps – Main, Sinamatella and Robins – act as the **main entry points** into the park.

Some history

On the easternmost edge of the Kalahari, Hwange was formerly peopled by **San** hunter-gatherers, able to survive with little water. The national park was created in 1929, largely because the land was hopeless for agriculture, and borehole water pumped into over sixty pans began attracting large numbers of animals. It's to these pans, several of which are around Main Camp, that visitors too are drawn.

Before adventurers and hunters arrived, parts of Hwange formed a royal **Ndebele hunting reserve**. Dete Vlei, where *Hwange Safari Lodge* is now sited, was later a favourite elephant-hunting ground for **Frederick Courteney Selous**, the most famous of Zimbabwe's Victorian adventurers. Three hunting areas still adjoin the park, where the rich pay thousands to bag trophies.

Main Camp and around

For most people, the gateway into Hwange is **MAIN CAMP**, where you can arrange walks, campsites and onward bookings for other Hwange camps. Touring the park by car you'll most likely start or finish here, and without your own transport this is one of the best places to get onto a game drive. But you don't need to venture much further to get an eyeful of game. The immediate surroundings of the camp have the park's highest concentrations: the **Ten-Mile Drive** between Main Camp and **Nyamandlovu Pan** regularly shows off all the animals one could hope for. Lions occasionally lie on the road in the evening – the fact that it's tarred doesn't seem to deter them – and elephants often water at Nyamandlovu Pan and nearby **Dom Pan**. Even if the lions evade you, you're bound to see giraffe, zebra, wildebeest, waterbuck, sable, impala, kudu and buffalo.

Main Camp is situated on Kalahari sand, shaded by aptly named *Acacia giraffae*, arching over the bar and restaurant. The camp is surrounded by teak **forests** that gradually

---

HWANGE NATIONAL PARK ESSENTIALS

Accommodation bookings National Parks **bookings** for Main Camp, Sinamatella or Robins camps are best arranged in **Harare** in advance through: Central Reservations Office, Borrowdale Road/Sandringham Drive, adjacent to the Botanic Gardens; PO Box CY 826, Causeway, Harare (Mon–Fri 8am–4pm; ☎04/706077–8, fax 726089 or 724914, *NationalParks@gta.gov.zw*). You can also book in **Bulawayo** (although they still have to refer to Central Reservations) through: National Parks, Herbert Chitepo Street/Tenth Avenue (☎09/65592).

Fees Day entry US$10, week entry US$20

Daily opening hours Park gates: Feb–April & Aug–Oct, 6am–6.30pm, May–July 6am–6pm, Nov–Jan 5.30am–7pm; Office: 7am–6pm

Speed limit 40kph

merge into Kalahari woodlands of thorn trees, mixed scrub and grassy clearings. Assuming you're up in the morning, go for a stroll around the clearings to look for antelope: there are certainly always hundreds of **impala** about. Come to Hwange in the rainy season and you're sure to see their young, just delivered and utterly appealing. Many animals give birth at the onset of the rains when the new grass springs up, but impala can prolong gestation by up to two months if the rains are late or inadequate. If you walk to the edge of the Main Camp offices you may also spot **giraffe**, heads above the trees, and you're bound to see **zebra** and **wildebeest** on the plains; these two species always graze in company.

Access and arrival

As its name suggests, **Main Camp** is the largest of the camps and the major focus for activity in Hwange, not simply because of its size, but also because it's the most easily accessed point in the park (tar all the way from Bulawayo or Victoria Falls) and also promises the best game viewing. Main Camp is the only public camp reachable by **public transport**, with luxury, Volvo and chicken buses, as well as trains and flights coming within easy striking distance.

The only town in the vicinity of Main Camp is **DETE**, 19km to its northwest along a tarred road that runs parallel to the train line, a dusty and functional place built around the station serving the park. Many of the park and safari industry workers live at Dete, which has a post office, shops selling basics, the offices of several companies offering low-cost game drives into the park, as well as a decent hotel and a number of backpackers' hostels, one of which is a Baz Bus stop, making the town a focus for budget travellers. **Hwange Safari Lodge**, 10km north of Main Camp and **Miombo Safari Camp**, 2km south of Dete, are both official Blue Arrow bus stops, making them alternative transport hubs to Dete (see p.220 & p.221).

Apart from the handful of highly desirable upmarket establishments that are inside the park itself, the majority of **private safari lodges** lie within a 25-kilometre-wide trapezoid of land squeezed between the park's eastern boundary and the main Bulawayo–Victoria Falls road. This lozenge stretches from Dete in the north to the *Halfway House Hotel* in the south, which is 66km from Main Camp. Be aware that, while all these private lodges claim to be at Hwange, few are less than fifteen minutes drive from the park gates, and even fewer are actually inside it. The cheaper lodges generally entail longish drives, often along poor roads, before you enter the game reserve. If money's no object, opt for one of the lodges inside the park.

By luxury bus

Blue Arrow **luxury buses** running between Bulawayo and Victoria Falls drop passengers at *Hwange Safari Lodge* and *Miombo Safari Camp*. They also stop at *Gwayi River Lodge*, which is useful if you're being collected by one of the safari operators in that area. To get to Main Camp from *Hwange Safari Lodge*, charter a UTC shuttle or hop on one of the game drives that meets the bus, neither of which is cheap (see below). There is also a Hertz office outside the lodge, where you can **rent a car**, mainly for use around Main Camp where the roads are good. From *Miombo*, backpackers can get free transfers to the lodges in Dete village, from which game drives into the park will be laid on.

By backpacker bus

Of the two **backpacker buses** that run between Bulawayo and Victoria Falls, only the Baz drops off passengers in the vicinity of Hwange National Park. Their official stop is at *Africa Dawn Safaris'* cottages in Dete (see Accommodation, p.219), a budget hostel that provides drives into the game reserve. The cottages are close enough to make getting to other accommodation in town fairly straightforward.

By Volvo bus

Volvo buses, of which there are one or two an hour, run along the Bulawayo–Victoria Falls road but don't deviate off the highway, so you'll need to get off at the turn-off known locally as Safari Crossroads if you're going to Main Camp, or Dete Crossroads if you're headed for Dete village. You can arrange beforehand for UTC to collect you from the main road at Safari Crossroads and take you to *Hwange Safari Lodge* (US$6) or Main Camp (US$12). Regular commuter omnibuses ply the route between Dete Crossroads and Dete village, a one-way trip that shouldn't cost much more than US$0.50.

By air

Air Zimbabwe **flights** go three times a week from Harare via Kariba to Hwange National Park airport. Most safari lodges will meet their guests at the airport by prior arrangement.

By car

Travelling in your own vehicle gives you by far the most flexibility when it comes to exploring Hwange and opens up the northern section as a viable possibility. **Main Camp** is two and a half hours from Victoria Falls, and three hours from Bulawayo, on an excellent and lightly used highway, which has virtually no settlements en route – petrol and facilities are only available at Gwayi River and Hwange Town.

By train

An increasing number of backpackers now take the **train** to the park's nearest station at Dete, despite the fact that from Victoria Falls it's timetabled to arrive at Dete at 00.13am; coming from Bulawayo, it pulls in at the even more inconvenient time of 1.26am. In any case, the precision suggested by these times is rather an illusion. There is no phone at the station, so you'll need to arrange to be collected before you arrive. Alternatively, a number of operators who have budget accommodation and provide drives into the park meet these trains. Whatever you do, don't try walking into town alone after dark, as wild animals (including lions that in the past have consumed their kills in suburban gardens) can be at large.

Accommodation, eating and shops

Main Camp has decent facilities, including a **shop** that sells basic foods, such as bread, milk, frozen goods, canned drinks, a selection of South African wines, and a limited choice of fruit and vegetables, although it's still best to bring your own supplies, especially fresh produce. Alternatively, you can eat all your meals at the inexpensive *Waterbuck's Head* **restaurant**, which does filling mains, toasted sandwiches and snacks, including vegetarian options, which you can have inside or outside. The adjacent **bar** is a regular hangout for local safari operators, who sit around with their drinks by the fire in the evenings. The camp **bookshop** sells a fair choice of mammal field guides and natural history books as well as postcards and photographic film and batteries. A public **telephone** and **petrol station** are also on hand. As all these facilities are outside the gate, you don't need to pay an entrance fee to use them.

Hwange provides **budget accommodation** in its **National Parks chalets** and **self-catering lodges**, built for the local market rather than for foreign tourists, which is not to say they're not frequently used by overseas visitors. They provide the only way to overnight in the park on the cheap. The other budget option is the **backpacker hostels** in banal railway workers' bungalows in Dete village, which are probably the least atmospheric option of all, but have the advantage of proximity to the park and easy access to organized game drives. **Mid-range accommodation** tends to be in hotels and safari lodges some distance from the park, but which are usually in private wilderness, where they attempt to foster a safari atmosphere. Of the expensive camps and lodges, a growing number operate in land concessions inside the park or in the bordering forest lands and safari areas which share Hwange's wildlife. If you can afford it, these work hard to feed safari fantasies and generally offer excellent wildlife experiences. **Hotels** in the service towns of Gwayi River, Hwange Town and Dete sell themselves, a little disingenuously, as springboards for Hwange as well as en-route stops and are detailed in the accommodation listings below. The most adventurous route into Hwange is on one of the **mobile safaris**, which drive through the park under the leadership of an armed guide, or on **"adventure walks"** led by a professional hunter-guide (see p.222).

National Parks accommodation

Booking for National Parks accommodation beforehand through the Central Office in Harare is virtually essential (see box p.46 for addresses), although if you turn up on the off chance you may be lucky – any vacant lodges are let from 4pm onwards, but they can be annoyingly bureaucratic whether you've made a reservation or not – be patient. Main Camp has a **campsite**, the only one you can get to without your own car; camping is also permitted at the fenced-in **picnic sites** inside the park, but needs to be prebooked, as the picnic sites are heavily in demand from mobile safari companies. Further details on each of the National Parks camps are given below and on p.224 and p.225.

CHALETS AND LODGES

Main Camp has twelve single **chalets** (①) with twin bedrooms and washbasin but shared washing and kitchen facilities; eight single **cottages** (①) with their own kitchen, but shared washing facilities; and eighteen en-suite, fully self-contained single **lodges** (①), which have lounge-diners and verandahs. There are also eight **family** chalets (①), cottages (①) and lodges, which have two bedrooms (②) and would be very cheap if there were four of you sharing. Accommodation is pretty basic, but comfortable, clean and good value if you can get a booking.

PICNIC SITES

Areas have been fenced off at **Jambili**, **Kennedy 1** and **Ngweshla**. They have outdoor braai facilities and toilets, hand basins and running water. You can **camp overnight**, provided you have a tent – wildlife can, and does on occasion, leap over the chicken-wire fencing in the enclosure.

Private accommodation

Budget accommodation is geared to backpackers and the local market. It comes with none of the posh trimmings of the upmarket camps and generally won't have the atmosphere of being in the wilderness. You also need to bear in mind that, while your accommodation may cost less than US$10, you still have to get into park. All the budget accommodation offers game drives, but you're unlikely to get away with paying much less than US$50 per day for your accommodation and a drive, and closer to US$100 per day if you take two game drives (recommended) and include the cost of food.

The **mid-priced** lodges cost US$135–180, covering accommodation, all meals and game activities, which isn't wildly more expensive than the budget options, when you take into account what's included. Of the places listed here, only *Elephant Sands* and *Miombo* are in the immediate vicinity of the national park.

Expensive safari camps (US$200–325) offer packages to a limited number of guests at a time, and are located either inside the park, or on private land adjoining it. Often in exclusive regions, they have the added attraction of expert guidance once you're there. Rates typically include all meals, drinks, snacks, laundry and game-viewing activities, though transfer fees to and from Hwange airport are extra. You can be assured of plenty of pampering, excellent service, and a degree of formality. Closed to casual visitors, the camps should be booked in advance.

BUDGET

Africa Dawn Safaris' Dete Cottages, 19 Duiker St, Dete (bookings ☎ & fax 09/74941, *afdawn@ telconet.co.zw*, direct ☎018/328, fax 588). Four three-bedroom bungalows, about 1km from town, with five-bed dorms, doubles and family rooms. Full bed linen provided, basic self-catering facilities and reasonably priced meals available. Half-day game drives US$35, full-day including lunch US$70, plus children's discounts on accommodation, meals and game drives. The cottages are the official Baz Bus stop in Dete; they provide free transfers from the Blue Arrow stop and will also collect free from the airport, if you've prebooked a game drive. ②.

Wildside Backpackers Hostel, 1 Duiker St, Dete (☎ & fax 018/446 or 395, *miombo@acacia. samara.co.zw*). One double room and two dorms, which sleep four each, in a coral-coloured former railway worker's bungalow. Owned by Paul de Montille, an experienced professional hunter-guide, it offers good budget game drives for US$35 per person, and free transfers from the more upmarket parent camp, *Miombo*, which is an official Blue Arrow bus stop. ①.

MID-PRICED

Elephant Sands, PO Box 52, Dete (☎018/326 or 247, fax 428, *elesands@acacia.samara.co.zw*). A small establishment, 12km from Main Camp, that accommodates twelve guests in square, stone-and-thatch chalets arranged around a garden with a small pool. A simple and welcoming place which admits children, it has no electricity, and lighting is by means of oil lamps. A resident labrador and cat add to the family friendly atmosphere, and game, which you can see from the camp's viewing platform, is free to wander through. Activities include game drives into the national park or night drives and walks on the camp's property. US$150 per person.

Kingdom Cottages, 1km east of Halfway House (☎089/321 or 226, *colmas@id.co.zw*). Rustic solar-powered bush camp 500m off the main road, in a beautiful setting under huge acacias on the banks of seasonal Gwayi River, but some distance from the national park. Twelve brick-and-timber chalets (two of them family units) with thatched roofs are raised on stilts and have flyscreens across a generous opening (no glass) that opens onto a balcony overlooking the river course. Midway between Bulawayo and Victoria Falls, this is a good refreshment stop (they do cheap snacks and teas) or place to overnight. It's a 30min drive along tar to the national park, making it an inconvenient, but nevertheless viable, base for game drives. Kingdom Safaris, whose owner is a professional hunter-guide, goes into Hwange twice a day and also offers walking safaris and cultural tours. B&B rate US$14, fully inclusive including full board and a half-day drive into Hwange US$77, full board and a full-day drive US$137.

Kumuna Lodge, PO Box BN 19, Gwayi (☎ & fax 018/541, mobile ☎011/409518, *lionsden@easynet.co.uk*). The most child-friendly of the Hwange camps, 54km from Main Camp and a rough 40min drive from Kennedy Gate. Comfortable, thatched rondavels and rooms in blocks are set in extensive lawns that tail off into bush and trees, with a dam that attracts wildlife. Meals are served under an enormous thatched marquee, which also houses a bar and TV lounge. *Kumuna* has its own mineral spring which feeds the swimming pool and Jacuzzis, and there's a decent-sized kids' playground. Transfers are available from the Blue Arrow bus stop or the airport. Despite the state of the road it can be negotiated in an ordinary car provided you go slowly along the 14km of dirt road, signposted from the main road. Rates for full board inclusive of two game-viewing activities for US$158 per person. A self-drive, full-board rate is approximately half that.

Miombo Safari Camp, 2km south of Dete on the main road, PO Box 90, Dete (☎ & fax 018/446, *miombo@acacia.samara.co.zw*). Nuzzling right up to the park boundary, with its own entrance on the cards, *Miombo* is one of the best-positioned camps in the area, has the added convenience of being an official Blue Arrow bus stop, and enjoys an excellent reputation for the quality of its game drives. Accommodation is in simple but comfortable pine "tree houses" raised on stilts and over-looking a waterhole among stands of *mukwa* and msasa trees. They're not for the faint-hearted: there are no windows, and leopards, hyenas and elephants pass through the camp occasionally. More down-to-earth are the salmon-pink breeze-block ground lodges, which have their own external showers and toilets. A large thatched central dining complex overlooks a fair-sized swimming pool surrounded by small area of lawns. Game drives go into the national park and walking safaris can be arranged. B&B US$72, fully inclusive rates in tree houses US$180 or ground lodges US$160.

New Game Reserve Hotel, in the centre of Dete; PO Box 2, Dete (☎018/543 or 546, fax 564). The least expensive hotel on the edge of Hwange gets most of its custom from packaged South African bus tours and makes little pretence of being a safari lodge. Staff are very friendly, the comfortable rooms are decorated with jolly African motifs, and, although it's not terribly stylish, it does have a swimming pool surrounded by lawns as well as a restaurant and convivial bar. Poor value unless you're from Southern Africa, in which case you can take advantage of their sizable regional discount. 3hr game drives can be arranged through the hotel with Dete-based Singing Bird Safaris for US$42 per person. ⑦.

Nyati Lodge, Gwayi Valley Safaris, PO Box 17, Gwayi (☎ & fax 018/515). Relaxed and welcoming family-run ranch 45km from Hwange Main Camp, set on an impressive ridge overlooking the Shangani River. A very different experience to the other Hwange lodges, its accommodation is simple but comfortable, some of it en suite, in brick-and-thatch chalets with verandahs, rooms in the garden or a self-contained family lodge. You can choose any combination of self-catering, partial or full board (worth considering, as the food is great). Game drives are available, but there's enough to do here to make it a good place to hang out for a few days, including swimming, tennis, horse-riding, visits to a local village or the farm's brick factory. To get there from the Bulawayo–Vic Falls road, take the turn-off 1km west of the *Gwayi River Hotel* and head north for 6km of dirt road to the farm. Free transfers available from Gwayi bus stop and the airport for US$15 per person, half-day game drives cost US$40 and full-day ones with lunch US$82. Self-catering and B&B ⑤, full board ⑦.

EXPENSIVE

Chimwara Camp, Run Wild, 3rd Floor, Southampton Life Centre, Jason Moyo Avenue (☎04/795841, *runwild@africaonline.co.zw*). Comfortable tented camp on the seasonal Gwayi River, 15km from the *Gwayi River Hotel*, 40min rough drive from the Kennedy Gate entrance. Often guides take picnics and spend the day out watching game. Armed walks are done on the large Chimwara property itself, where you'll see mostly plains game, with possible glimpses of big game. Closed during the rainy season. Return transfers to and from the airport US$44. US$225 per person per day.

Chokamella Camp, Landela Safaris, Travel Plaza, 29 Mazowe St, Harare, PO Box 66293, Kopje, Harare (☎04/734043–6, fax 708119, *res@landela.co.zw*). Located 35km from Hwange airport, due west of Main Camp entrance. Accommodation for up to twenty people in thatched bungalows set on sand cliffs above the (usually dry) Nkamella River. Their rooms are beautiful and the food excellent, but the camp's best feature is its low ratio of guests to professional guides, who lead walks and drives. One excursion is to the Chakabika area, near Sinamatella, where you may sight some of the few black rhinos left in Hwange, intensively protected by game scouts. Low season US$220, high season US$275.

Giraffe Springs, Wilderness Safaris, PO Box 288, Victoria Falls (☎013/3371 or 4527, fax 2020, *wildlodges@telconet.co.zw*). One of the most stylish yet most relaxed Hwange camps, overlooking an enormous plain and two waterholes right inside the park. Accommodation is in huge luxurious tents decorated using authentic Moroccan rugs and artefacts and Indian-print fabrics. They have two showers – one outside to allow you to watch game while scrubbing up; each tent also has its own raised deck offering further opportunities to laze about and watch animals, or you can cool off in the fair-sized pool. No children. Jan–June US$250 per person; July–Dec US$325.

The Hide, 27–29 James Martin Drive, PO Box ST 274, Southerton, Harare (☎04/660554 or 660555, fax 621216, *presgrou@mail.pci.co.zw*). One of Hwange's top private camps and one of the few actually inside the park, *The Hide* occupies an enviable location right next to the quieter Kennedy Gate park entrance overlooking plains full of game. Once you've travelled the 90min from the airport, you don't need to go anywhere else. Accommodation is in ten East African-style meru tents, furnished to evoke a colonial atmosphere, with nothing between their tiled patios and the game-rich waterhole less than 50m away. Four game activities daily, mostly drives conducted by professional guides, underline the emphasis on game viewing. No children. US$316 per person.

Hwange Safari Lodge, Zimbabwe Sun Hotels, Travel Centre, 93 Jason Moyo Ave, Harare (☎04/736644–5, fax 736646, *zimsuncro@zimsun.gaia.co.zw*). As close to Main Camp as you can get, and all the comfort you'd expect from a luxury three-star hotel with en-suite rooms and drinks by the swimming pool. Game drives are provided and you can watch elephants frolic in the lodge's own drinking hole. Both the lodge itself and UTC run game drives (US$44 for 3hr) that start here and pull in at Main Camp; the hotel can also arrange game trails on foot. Non-residents are charged an admission fee, but it could be worth having access to a poolside drink if you've arrived from a long hot trek. There's also a viewing platform, which overlooks a pan where you'll usually see some game, and a small playground. Very suitable for families. B&B rate US$93 per person.

Jijima, overlooking Jijima Vlei on a private estate bordering the national park. Book through Wild Horizons, PO Box 159, Victoria Falls (☎113/4219, fax 4349). *Jijima* is owned and operated by a family of two generations of professional guides, so if you want to hear ripping yarns about close shaves with lions, this is just the place. *Jijima* uses the Kennedy pan, which is less crowded than the Main Camp area, for game viewing, though it's a 40min drive. Swimming pool and walks on the extensive property. Accommodation is in safari tents under thatched canopies and the number of guests is limited to sixteen. High season (July 1–Jan 4) US$275, low season (Jan 5–June 30) US$240 per person per night.

Kanondo Tree Camp, Touch the Wild, 46 George Silundika St, PO Box 3447, Bulawayo (☎09/540922, 540944, 540967–8 or 540797 fax 229088 or 74589, *touchwld@harare.iafrica.com* or *ttw@acacia.samara.co.zw*). A bush camp with no pools, electricity, fences or lawns. Just 15min by vehicle from Hwange airport and an equal distance from Main Camp, it's one of the quickest private camps to reach, set among a stand of teak and camelthorn acacias on a private concession adjacent to the game reserve. Seven en-suite twin-bedded pine cabins on stilts that have no windows, just openings with blinds. A small log palisade encloses a rustic lounge and dining area, while above the bar a 40m walkway leads to a platform concealed in the spreading branches of a teak tree. The platform provides views of the waterhole, which is regularly visited by a special herd of elephants, protected in perpetuity by a presidential decree. The guides are good and the emphasis here is on walking and game viewing. No children. Jan–June & Nov–Dec US$197, July–Oct US$207 per person.

Makololo Camp, Wilderness Safaris, PO Box 288, Victoria Falls (☎013/3371 or 4527, fax 2020, *wildlodges@telconet.co.zw*). Remotest and most beautifully located of all the Hwange camps, *Makololo* is also one of the few actually deep within the park and makes a highly desirable destination. Set under ilala palm trees, the camp sleeps a maximum of eighteen guests in luxury en-suite tents, in a remote area of wide, grassy plains that is rarely visited, so you won't be sharing your game sightings with anyone else. A real feeling of African wilderness is guaranteed, justifying every cent of the price tag. Three professionals and two trainee hunter-guides are on hand to take guests on walks, game drives or to hides. Because of its location, guests either fly in from Hwange (US$40 per person) or Victoria Falls airport (US$125). No children. US$265.

Malindi Station Lodge, 186 Fife Ave, Harare, PO Box 2728 (☎04/705551–3, fax 732540, *malindi@utande.co.zw*). Train-themed lodge in four railway carriages under thatch, in a private concession that sees passing game, 20km from Main Camp. En-suite accommodation in carriage compartments, arranged along a mock platform that leads onto a viewing deck, will thrill train buffs but not claustrophobics. The standard of guiding is good and activities include game drives, morning breakfast picnics in the park, sundowners watching elephants at a waterhole, nature walks and visits to a local village. No children. US$266 per person.

Sikumi Tree Lodge, Touch the Wild (see *Kanondo Tree Camp* above). Signposted 19km south of the *Safari Lodge* turn-off followed by a 20min drive. Accommodation is in en-suite luxury huts done out in very pleasing decor (there's nothing rustic about the place), which rise on stilts from manicured lawns. One of the most beautifully set of the Hwange lodges, arranged around a pool, the chalets are shaded by a grove of huge camelthorn acacias overlooking the waterhole, which is just outside the perimeter fence and just metres from the dining area, where you can enjoy your meal watching wildlife. Guided walks and night drives in the forest are among the activities offered, as well as routine drives into the national park. One of the handful of lodges permitting children. Jan–June & Nov–Dec US$250, July–Oct US$318 per person; under 12s half-price. They also offer a self-drive rate for full-board without activities, which saves almost US$100 on the rates given.

The Park

Getting into the park itself is pretty easy, and not too expensive, with numerous operators vying to provide game drives. A far more exciting option is to go in on foot – there are some outstanding hunter-guides who take small groups doing just this. Several companies also operate camping and vehicle-based mobile safaris

Game drives and escorted walks

The hassle-free, but not always most satisfying, way to see game is to hop onto one of the vehicles that go into the national park via Main Camp. Several companies tout from the reception area for business, some meet the Blue Arrow bus at *Hwange Safari Lodge* and others operate out of Dete village. Finding an operator isn't the problem: the challenge is to make sure you don't end up in the clutches of a "**jeep jockey**" – a local term for someone who's not terribly knowledgeable about wildlife, but can steer a vehicle. Several otherwise reputable companies subcontract to freelancers, so even then you can't be sure who you're getting. Your best bet is to talk to other punters before committing yourself. Prices are between US$35 and US$45 for a half-day drive. Safer still is to go with Africa Dawn Safaris or Wildside, two recommended companies that run game drives from their backpackers' lodges in Dete (see Accommodation, p.219).

National Parks **escorted walks** are great value, going out for an hour or two in a group of no more than six, accompanied by an armed game ranger. Because of their popularity, they are frequently rationed to one outing per person. The guides often do the two-kilometre walk to the hide at Sedina pan, where you sit a while and watch; few cars ever come here, so it's wonderfully quiet.

For **longer safaris**, Zindele, 6 Caithness Ave, Eastleigh, Harare (☎04/746875, fax 776136, *zindele@pci.co.zw*), are recommended for their tailor-made, vehicle-based outings. Accommodation is in comfortable walk-in tents and trips cost about US$185 per person per day, which includes all transport, meals and accommodation.

Adventure walking

The most exciting way to experience any of Zimbabwe's game reserves is on foot and a handful of professional guides are licensed to take small groups walking in Hwange. Nights are generally spent at picnic sites or campsites where there's minimal development, making for a very elemental encounter with the wilderness. Guides are invariably armed and highly knowledgeable. Packages include meals and transfers.

Baobab Safaris, PO Box 196, Victoria Falls (☎ & fax 013/4283, mobile ☎011/404981 or 209576, *baobab@telconet.co.zw* or *safaris@telconet.co.zw*). Budget three-day/two-night camping and walking safaris in Hwange under the leadership of professional guide Steve Bolnick. Departures every Tuesday morning from Victoria Falls. The rate for the three days – inclusive of entry fees, transfers from the Falls, meals and camping gear – is US$230.

Khangela Safaris, PO Box FM 296, Famona, Bulawayo (☎09/49733, fax 78081, mobile ☎091/234676 or 023/406981, *scott@gatorzw.com*). Walking adventures with Mike Scott, one of the few professional guides licensed to walk the entire length and breadth of Hwange. Tailor-made trips with possible packages spending two nights each in the Main Camp, Sinamatella and Robins subregions. Can also be combined with other national parks. Good value at US$130 per person per day.

Leon Varley Walking Safaris, Backpackers' Bazaar, Shop 5, Victoria Falls Centre, Parkway (☎013/5828, fax 2208, mobile ☎011/404960, *backpack@africaonline.co.zw*). Four-day hiking adventures in Hwange, exploring the Main Camp area by vehicle, walking around Sinamatella tracking black rhinos, and travelling to the Zambezi National Park through the Matetsi wildlife area. May–Oct US$770, Nov–April US$640 per person for the whole trip.

MAIN CAMP TO SINAMATELLA

Driving through the national park from Main Camp seems like a great idea – game viewing all the way for 120km, and the 82km closest to Main Camp is marked on maps as
tarred. But don't be fooled: the cartographers clearly haven't been this way for some
time. The purportedly tarred section is so ravaged that you spend most of your time
dodging craters or leaving the road because the paths on the verge are more easily negotiated. The worst section is between Main Camp and Shumba picnic site, which has
become severely potholed due to a combination of spring-hare excavations and heavy
rains. It's quicker and more pleasant to leave the park and make your way from the one
camp to the other via the main Bulawayo–Vic Falls road. If you remain unconvinced and
are determined to torture your car's suspension, National Parks require you to leave by
2pm to make sure you have ample time to complete the journey before dusk, but you'd
be well advised to set out before noon. A tough vehicle is advisable, especially during the
rains, although people do successfully complete the journey in an ordinary car. And take
food and water – there are no shops en route.

Northern Hwange

Although the game viewing in northern Hwange can't routinely match Main Camp's
Ten Mile Drive, the region has a lot going for it. For one thing, it's less of a bun fight,
with few visitors and even fewer operators haring about, and some of the most striking
landscapes. The closest urban centre to the northern section of the national park is
HWANGE, a coalmining town that announces itself from some distance with its great
concrete chimneys pumping grey smoke in the middle of a vast panorama of blue sky
and rolling wilderness. In winter, the town itself is pleasanter than you might expect,
with surprisingly well-watered and colourful gardens, but in summer it can be stifling.
It's only on account of its status as the sole town of any size along the flank of the national park that you're likely to visit – a couple of well-stocked supermarkets make it the
best and cheapest place to buy supplies if you're going to Sinamatella or Main Camp. If
you need to stay in Hwange, head for the *Baobab Hotel* (☎081/2323 or 2493, fax 3481;
③), on top of a hill on the Bulawayo side of town; it's very pleasant and good value and
also does reasonably priced plain meals such as omelettes and Southern African-style
curry and rice.

Sinamatella

The hub of northern Hwange is **SINAMATELLA**, the largest camp in the region, but
still much smaller than Main Camp, 120km to its south, and by far the most attractive-
ly sited of all Hwange's camps, spectacularly teetering on the edge of a high ridge with
views over a distant river bed and grassy plains favoured by buffalo and elephants.
Nowhere else do you get as good a sense of just how extensive the national park is.
Several potentially rewarding **drives** are within very easy striking distance of
Sinamatella, with organized picnic sites along the way, where you can stretch your legs,
have a braai or use the kettle that's always on the boil to make some tea or coffee and
watch game from the hides or viewing areas. A note of caution, though: as elsewhere
in Hwange, drives are always unpredictable, although the drier it gets the better the
game viewing is likely to be as animals concentrate at the scarce water sources.

You can also camp here (see p.224), the best option being the beautifully sited
Mandavu Dam, 9km south of Sinamatella along a highly recommended short drive. A

INTENSIVE PROTECTION ZONES

An **Intensive Protection Zone** (IPZ) was created around Sinamatella in 1994 in an attempt to avert the extinction of Zimbabwe's remaining small population of black rhinos. Large numbers of game scouts were brought into the park to look after the animals and a dehorning campaign was carried out in 1994–95 in the hope that this would deter poachers. While there are black rhinos about, you're most unlikely to see them, unless you go on a walking safari that expressly looks for them, as they inhabit thickets, are solitary and exceedingly shy, although highly aggressive and dangerous when threatened. You may see one of the handful of white rhinos (six, at the time of writing) brought to Hwange from the Matopos in 1999.

thatched gazebo and viewing area overlooks a small lake that draws thirsty elephants in their hundreds in the dry season; it also has resident crocs and hippos. **Masuma**, roughly 10km further south, is smaller and less attractive than Mandavu but has the advantage of a hide extremely close to the waterhole, which gives very good sightings of animals. About another 15km will bring you to **Shumba** picnic site, which also has a hide at a waterhole and some basic facilities.

Practicalities

The closest public transport runs up and down the main Bulawayo–Victoria Falls road, which is 45km from Sinamatella, reached along a corrugated dirt road that can take up to an hour to negotiate; it's only realistic if you have your own transport, though a 4WD vehicle isn't necessary. The turn-off is just south of Hwange Town off the main Bulawayo–Hwange road. Self-catering **accommodation** consists of self-catering chalets (①) or lodges (②), and camping (①). You can also stay at any of the **picnic sites**, which can be a thrilling way to spend the night, particularly as game tends to come to the waterholes around sunrise and sunset, when most visitors are confined to the camps. All are fenced off with gates that are closed at night to keep wildlife at bay, and all have running water, toilets, showers and braai places. The most comfortable and best maintained is Mandavu, which has the luxury of hot water.

Other facilities include the *Elephant and Dassie* **restaurant** and **bar**, incredibly sited on the lip of a ridge overlooking an endless valley. You can get breakfast, lunch and dinner here (main courses are all under US$5) with standard chicken, steaks, burgers and sandwiches on the menu. More importantly, you can easily while away an afternoon with a couple of beers and a pair of binoculars watching **game** way below. Even without binoculars, the immediate environs have a lot to offer: the birdbath attracts a passing clientele, including a variety of seed-eaters; above the valley fish eagles and other raptors ride the thermals; dassies sun themselves on rocks in front of diners; and you'll spot some colourful lizards, one species being notable for its strategy of crawling under rocks, where it inflates itself to prevent predators dragging it out. If you're lucky, you may even see one of the aggressive honey badgers that wander through the camp to the kitchen, where they raid the garbage and terrorize the staff. A **curio shop** next to the restaurant sells postcards, stamps, souvenirs and a small selection of field guides, while a **kiosk** near reception sells absolute basics such as a few tins and drinks, but no fresh fruit or vegetables: it shouldn't be relied on for your supplies. Alongside are a public telephone and a filling station. There are no organized game drives from the camp but you can book at reception to go on **escorted walks** with Parks guides.

Robins and Nantwich

ROBINS and **NANTWICH** camps lie within 11km of each other in the northwest of the park – closer to Victoria Falls than Hwange. People sometimes drive the 70km

ELEPHANTS AT HWANGE

With the densest population in Africa, you'd be very unlucky not to see **elephants** in Hwange. During the rains, however, they can be elusive, disappearing to fresh vegetation in remote zones of the park.

Hwange's elephants are in fact a conservation over-success story. By the time the park was created, hunting had reduced the number of elephants to less than a thousand and their extermination was on the cards. But, by the 1970s, the elephant count had bounced back dramatically to twenty thousand – an **overpopulation** that led to habitat destruction. **Culling programmes**, a euphemism for controlling elephants by wiping out whole families, targeting the breeding females and youngsters, were started and continue today, along with a controlled level of trophy-hunting. The park can only properly support around 12,000 elephants, although there are still far more than that even today.

The question of elephant management is more than merely a moral dilemma (shootings are arguably as traumatic for the animals as they would be for defenceless human families) but also leads into arcane **ecological puzzles** in which new factors are continually emerging. While animal overpopulations are usually the result of old migration routes being cut off, forcing the creatures into new, unnatural reserves, the consequent foliage destruction caused by crowded herds also puts new life into the soil: experiments carried out at Hwange have shown that four times as many camel acacia seeds sprouted after being eaten and dunged by elephants than a control sample, which was left on the ground. Dung beetles, of which Zimbabwe is blessed with a multitude of varieties, gratefully tackle the football-sized elephant droppings, breaking them into pellets and pulling them into their burrows, where the seeds later germinate. Elephants also dig up driedout waterholes, providing moisture for other animals.

More mysteriously, there's evidence of a new natural adaptation to unnatural pressures – **tuskless cow elephants** – which present less attractive targets for poachers. This may change feeding habits, and even breeding cycles, as an elephant uses its tusks (and is either right- or left-tusked) to dig for essential minerals and strip tree bark.

along slow roads from Sinamatella during the dry season (you must set out by 3pm) or, less recommended, from Main Camp (leave in the morning). Preferably gain access along a gravel road 48km south of Victoria Falls on the Bulawayo road; from the turnoff it's 62km to Robins. En route you'll pass the track to Mpandamatenga, just over the border in Botswana. Robins is small and more remote than Sinamatella and the least attractive of the National Parks camps, though it's the only one to have its own waterhole in the camp itself. Game isn't especially good either, so there's no need to feel too disappointed if you can't make it here. Nantwich, administered by Robins, situated on a small bluff overlooking a natural pan, is smaller still and only has three lodges. **Accommodation** at Robins is in lodges and chalets or camping (all ①), while Nantwich has three two-bedroom lodges.

WESTERN KARIBA

The **western half** of **Lake Kariba** is much less developed than the east, and all that most people experience of it is a view from the cross-lake ferry. This side of the immense lake has as fine scenery as the area around Kariba town (see p.119), which is accessed from Harare, but the resorts here are low-key and, in the main, self-catering. More significant is the fact that this side is linked to Victoria Falls and Hwange by a tarred road, making it possible to visit the lake as part of a tour of western Zimbabwe, avoiding Harare altogether if you wish.

The main tourist development hinges on the small fishing resorts of **Binga**, which has several self-catering lodges and even some budget village accommodation, and

Mlibizi – the Kariba ferry terminus. Forty kilometres southeast of Binga, as the fish eagle flies, is **Chizarira National Park**, the least-visited but arguably most beautiful and isolated of all Zimbabwe's game reserves. Until very recently, this was a major sanctuary for black rhinoceros but, sadly, the few rhinos that survived the poaching were translocated to safer areas in 1995. The best way to see the park is to walk it with a safari company such as Khangela or Leon Varley Walking Safaris, who organize hiking adventures with excellent professional hunter-guides: it is not the most rewarding park to see game if you're in your own vehicle, as the thick bush hides the animals. If camping and walking doesn't appeal, a spell in a luxury lodge, perched on a hill just outside the national park, might.

Maps show scant settlement along the road that strikes out east from Binga, passing the northern boundary of Chizarira. In fact, the area is not uninhabited: between Binga and Karoi, a commercial farming area, lies a tract of semi-desert where the post-Kariba **Batonga** were dumped. Long stretches are just bush, with the odd tree thrown across the track by elephants; schools form the nuclei of dotted settlements announced by home-made bus stop signs tacked onto baobab trees.

You won't find tourists in the villages (there's nowhere to stay anyway), except for the odd person foraging for Batonga crafts or perhaps hoping to photograph the old women, bones through noses and minus front teeth, smoking long *mbanje* (marijuana) pipes. Kariba town and the western half of the lake is covered in Chapter Two.

Binga

The Kariba speed ferry calls by request at **BINGA** village, an isolated and interesting settlement with Chizarira Mountain views. If you're feeling intrepid you can also get there overland or on the DDF ferry. A scenic place, as yet undeveloped, it spreads over a couple of hills and along the lakeshore. Like Kariba, it has no real centre, so without a car you'll find yourself doing long sandy trudges to get around.

Getting there

The **DDF ferry** (☎015/229) runs across the lake from Kariba to Binga twice a month and takes two and a half days to complete the journey, stopping at fishing villages along the way, so take food and water. If you're planning on staying at *Chilangililo Co-operative* (see p.227), ask to be dropped off at the fishing cooperatives near Chilila, from where it's a short walk. The **passenger speed ferry** runs six days a week between Kariba and Mlibizi, but will pull into Binga provided you request this when booking (see box on p.120 for ferry details). The easiest way to get to Binga by **bus** is from Bulawayo or Harare, with several companies running direct services (see the box opposite). For *Chilangililo* and *Chilila Lodge*, get off the bus at the stop after Chilila Gate, 6km before Binga. Head straight through the gate and up the gravel road for *Chilila*; for *Chilangililo*, take instead the parallel road nearer the bus stop and follow the arrows on yellow signs.

The Town

Binga was created as an **administrative centre** for Batonga resettlement, though, ironically, despite the dam's creation for hydroelectric power, electricity has only recently arrived, and the water supplies, piped uphill, don't always work.

Missionaries, however, are well ensconced, and a **hospital** and foreign-aid worker village, secondary school and surprisingly well-stocked **supermarket** near the main bus stop form an ensemble of public buildings. The **school** is interesting, with an

THE WILDLIFE
OF EAST AND
SOUTHERN AFRICA

A ROUGH GUIDE

This field guide provides a quick reference to help you identify the larger mammals likely to be encountered in East and Southern Africa. It includes most species that are found throughout these regions, as well as a limited number whose range is more restricted. Straightforward photos show easily identified markings and features. The notes give you clear pointers about the kinds of **habitat** in which you are most likely to see each mammal; its daily rhythm (usually either **nocturnal or diurnal**); the kind of **social groups** it usually forms; and general **tips about sighting** it on safari, its rarity and its relations with humans.

◪ HABITAT ◪ DIURNAL/NOCTURNAL ◪ SOCIAL LIFE ☑ SIGHTING TIPS

Photographs © Bruce Coleman Picture Library. Text © Rough Guides, 1996.

Baboon *Papio cynocephalus*

🔲 open country with trees and cliffs; adaptable, but always near water

🔲 diurnal

🔲 troops led by a dominant male

✔ common; several subspecies, including Yellow and Olive in East Africa and Chacma in Southern Africa; easily becomes used to humans, frequently a nuisance and occasionally dangerous

Eastern Black and White Colobus
Colobus guereza

🔲 rainforest and well-watered savannah; almost entirely arboreal

🔲 diurnal

🔲 small troops

✔ troops maintain a limited home territory, so easily located, but can be hard to see at a great height; not found in Southern Africa

Patas Monkey *Erythrocebus patas*

🔲 savannah and forest margins; tolerates some aridity; terrestrial except for sleeping and lookouts

🔲 diurnal

🔲 small troops

✔ widespread but infrequently seen; can run at high speed and stand on hind feet supported by tail; not found in Southern Africa

Vervet Monkey *Cercopithecus aethiops*

🔲 most habitats except rainforest and arid lands; arboreal and terrestrial

🔲 diurnal

🔲 troops

✔ widespread and common; occasionally a nuisance where used to humans

PRIMATES

White-throated or Sykes' Monkey/Samango
Cercopithecus mitis/albogularis
- ⊠ forests; arboreal and occasionally terrestrial
- ⊠ diurnal
- ⊠ families or small troops
- ☑ widespread; shyer and less easily habituated to humans than the Vervet

Aardvark *Orycteropus afer*
- ⊠ open or wooded termite country; softer soil preferred
- ⊠ nocturnal
- ⊠ solitary
- ☑ rarely seen animal, the size of a small pig; old burrows are common and often used by warthogs

Spring Hare *Pedetes capensis*
- ⊠ savannah; softer soil areas preferred
- ⊠ nocturnal
- ⊠ burrows, usually with a pair and their young; often linked into a network, almost like a colony
- ☑ fairly widespread rabbit-sized rodent; impressive and unmistakable kangaroo-like leaper

Crested Porcupine
Hystrix africae-australis
- ⊠ adaptable to a wide range of habitats
- ⊠ nocturnal and sometimes active at dusk
- ⊠ family groups
- ☑ large rodent (up to 90cm in length), rarely seen, but common away from croplands, where it's hunted as a pest

PRIMATES – AARDVARK – RODENTS

Bat-eared Fox *Otocyon megalotis*

◪ open country

◪ mainly nocturnal; diurnal activity increases in cooler months

◪ monogamous pairs

☑ distribution coincides with termites, their favoured diet; they spend many hours foraging using sensitive hearing to pinpoint their underground prey

Black-backed Jackal *Canis mesomelas*

◪ broad range from moist mountain regions to desert, but drier areas preferred

◪ normally nocturnal, but diurnal in the safety of game reserves

◪ mostly monogamous pairs; sometimes family groups

☑ common; a bold scavenger, the size of a small dog, that steals even from lions; black saddle distinguishes it from the shyer Side-striped Jackal

Hunting Dog or Wild Dog
Lycaon pictus

◪ open savannah in the vicinity of grazing herds

◪ diurnal

◪ nomadic packs

☑ extremely rare and rarely seen, but widely noted when in the area; the size of a large dog, with distinctively rounded ears

Honey Badger or Ratel
Mellivora capensis

◪ very broad range of habitats

◪ mainly nocturnal

◪ usually solitary, but also found in pairs

☑ widespread, omnivorous, badger-sized animal; nowhere common; extremely aggressive

African Civet *Civettictis civetta*
- ⬚ prefers woodland and dense vegetation
- ⬚ mainly nocturnal
- ⬚ solitary
- ☑ omnivorous, medium-dog-sized, short-legged prowler; not to be confused with the smaller genet

Common Genet *Genetta genetta*
- ⬚ light bush country, even arid areas; partly arboreal
- ⬚ nocturnal, but becomes active at dusk
- ⬚ solitary
- ☑ quite common, slender, cat-sized omnivore, often seen at game lodges, where it easily becomes habituated to humans

Banded Mongoose *Mungos mungo*
- ⬚ thick bush and dry forest
- ⬚ diurnal
- ⬚ lives in burrow colonies of up to thirty animals
- ☑ widespread and quite common, the size of a small cat; often seen in a group, hurriedly foraging through the undergrowth

Spotted Hyena *Crocuta crocuta*
- ⬚ tolerates a wide variety of habitat, with the exception of dense forest
- ⬚ nocturnal but also active at dusk; also diurnal in many parks
- ⬚ highly social, usually living in extended family groups
- ☑ the size of a large dog with a distinctive loping gait, quite common in parks; carnivorous scavenger and cooperative hunter; dangerous

Caracal *Caracal caracal*

▨ open bush and plains; occasionally arboreal

▨ mostly nocturnal

▨ solitary

☑ lynx-like wild cat; rather uncommon and rarely seen

Cheetah *Acinonyx jubatus*

▨ savannah, in the vicinity of plains grazers

▨ diurnal

▨ solitary or temporary nuclear family groups

☑ widespread but low population; much slighter build than the leopard, and distinguished from it by a small head, square snout and dark "tear mark" running from eye to jowl

Leopard *Panthera pardus*

▨ highly adaptable; frequently arboreal

▨ nocturnal; also cooler daylight hours

▨ solitary

☑ the size of a very large dog; not uncommon, but shy and infrequently seen; rests in thick undergrowth or up trees; very dangerous

Lion *Panthera leo*

▨ all habitats except desert and thick forest

▨ nocturnal and diurnal

▨ prides of three to forty; more usually six to twelve

☑ commonly seen resting in shade; dangerous

Serval *Felis serval*

⬕ reed beds or tall grassland near water

◩ normally nocturnal but more diurnal than most cats

◪ usually solitary

☑ some resemblance to, but far smaller than, the cheetah; most likely to be seen on roadsides or water margins at dawn or dusk

Rock Hyrax or Dassie *Procavia capensis*

⬕ rocky areas, from mountains to isolated outcrops

◩ diurnal

◪ colonies consisting of a territorial male with as many as thirty related females

☑ rabbit-sized; very common; often seen sunning themselves in the early morning on rocks

African Elephant *Loxodonta africana*

⬕ wide range of habitats, wherever there are trees and water

◩ nocturnal and diurnal; sleeps as little as four hours a day

◪ almost human in its complexity; cows and offspring in herds headed by a matriarch; bulls solitary or in bachelor herds

☑ look out for fresh dung (football-sized) and recently damaged trees; frequently seen at waterholes from late afternoon

CATS – HYRAX – ELEPHANT

Black Rhinoceros *Diceros bicornis*

◪ usually thick bush, altitudes up to 3500m

◪ active day and night, resting between periods of activity

◪ solitary

☑ extremely rare and in critical danger of extinction; largely confined to parks where most individuals are known to rangers; distinctive hooked lip for browsing; small head usually held high; bad eyesight; very dangerous

White Rhinoceros *Ceratotherium simum*

◪ savannah

◪ active day and night, resting between periods of activity

◪ mother/s and calves, or small, same-sex herds of immature animals; old males solitary

☑ rare, restricted to parks; distinctive wide mouth (hence "white" from Afrikaans *wijd*) for grazing; large head usually lowered; docile

Burchell's Zebra *Equus burchelli*

◪ savannah, with or without trees, up to 4500m

◪ active day and night, resting intermittently

◪ harems of several mares and foals led by a dominant stallion are usually grouped together, in herds of up to several thousand

☑ widespread and common inside and out-side the parks; regional subspecies include *granti* (Grant's, East Africa) and *chapmani* (Chapman's, Southern Africa, right)

Grevy's Zebra *Equus grevyi*

◪ arid regions

◪ largely diurnal

◪ mares with foals and stallions generally keep to separate troops; stallions sometimes solitary and territorial

☑ easily distinguished from smaller Burchell's Zebra by narrow stripes and very large ears; rare and localized but easily seen; not found in Southern Africa

Warthog *Phacochoerus aethiopicus*
☒ savannah, up to an altitude of over 2000m
☒ diurnal
☒ family groups, usually of a female and her litter
☑ common; boars are distinguishable from sows by their prominent face "warts"

Hippopotamus *Hippopotamus amphibius*
☒ slow-flowing rivers, dams and lakes
☒ principally nocturnal, leaving the water to graze
☒ bulls are solitary, but other animals live in family groups headed by a matriarch
☑ usually seen by day in water, with top of head and ears breaking the surface; frequently aggressive and very dangerous when threatened or when retreat to water is blocked

Giraffe *Giraffa camelopardalis*
☒ wooded savannah and thorn country
☒ diurnal
☒ loose, non-territorial, leaderless herds
☑ common; many subspecies, of which Maasai (*G. c. tippelskirchi*, right), Reticulated (*G. c. reticulata*, bottom l.) and Rothschild's (*G. c. rothschildi*, bottom r.) are East African; markings of Southern African subspecies are intermediate between *tippelskirchi* and *rothschildi*

African or Cape Buffalo *Syncerus caffer*

⊠ wide range of habitats, always near water, up to altitudes of 4000m

⊠ nocturnal and diurnal, but inactive during the heat of the day

⊠ gregarious, with cows and calves in huge herds; young bulls often form small bachelor herds; old bulls are usually solitary

☑ very common; scent much more acute than other senses; very dangerous, old bulls especially so

Hartebeest *Alcelaphus buselaphus*

⊠ wide range of grassy habitats

⊠ diurnal

⊠ females and calves in small, wandering herds; territorial males solitary

☑ hard to confuse with any other antelope except the topi/tsessebe; many varieties, distinguishable by horn shape, including Coke's, Lichtenstein's, Jackson's (right), and Red or Cape; common, but much displaced by cattle grazing

Blue or White-bearded Wildebeest
Connochaetes taurinus

⊠ grasslands

⊠ diurnal, occasionally also nocturnal

⊠ intensely gregarious; wide variety of associations within mega-herds which may number over 100,000 animals

☑ unmistakable, nomadic grazer; long tail, mane and beard

Topi or Tsessebe *Damaliscus lunatus*

⊠ grasslands, showing a marked preference for moist savannah, near water

⊠ diurnal

⊠ females and young form herds with an old male

☑ widespread, very fast runners; male often stands sentry on an abandoned termite hill, actually marking the territory against rivals, rather than defending against predators

Gerenuk *Litocranius walleri*

◩ arid thorn country and semi-desert

◪ diurnal

◪ solitary or in small, territorial harems

☑ not uncommon; unmistakable giraffe-like neck; often browses standing upright on hind legs; the female is hornless; not found in Southern Africa

Grant's Gazelle *Gazella granti*

◩ wide grassy plains with good visibility, sometimes far from water

◪ diurnal

◪ small, territorial harems

☑ larger than the similar Thomson's Gazelle, distinguished from it by the white rump patch which extends onto the back; the female has smaller horns than the male; not found in Southern Africa

Springbok *Antidorcas marsupalis*

◩ arid plains

◪ seasonally variable, but usually cooler times of day

◪ highly gregarious, sometimes in thousands; various herding combinations of males, females and young

☑ medium-sized, delicately built gazelle; dark line through eye to mouth and lyre-shaped horns in both sexes; found only in Botswana, Namibia and South Africa

Thomson's Gazelle *Gazella thomsoni*

◩ flat, short-grass savannah, near water

◪ diurnal

◪ gregarious, in a wide variety of social structures, often massing in the hundreds with other grazing species

☑ smaller than the similar Grant's Gazelle, distinguished from it by the black band on flank; the female has tiny horns; not found in Southern Africa

Impala *Aepyceros melampus*

◼ open savannah near light woodland cover

◼ diurnal

◼ large herds of females overlap with several male territories; males highly territorial during the rut when they separate out breeding harems of up to twenty females

☑ common, medium-sized, no close relatives; distinctive high leaps when fleeing; the only antelope with a black tuft above the hooves; males have long, lyre-shaped horns

Red Lechwe *Kobus leche*

◼ floodplains and areas close to swampland

◼ nocturnal and diurnal

◼ herds of up to thirty females move through temporary ram territories; occasionally thousand-strong gatherings

☑ semi-aquatic antelope with distinctive angular rump; rams have large forward-pointing horns; not found in East Africa

Common Reedbuck *Redunca arundinum*

◼ reedbeds and tall grass near water

◼ nocturnal and diurnal

◼ monogamous pairs or family groups in territory defended by the male

☑ medium-sized antelope, with a plant diet unpalatable to other herbivores; only males have horns

Common or Defassa Waterbuck
Kobus ellipsiprymnus

◼ open woodland and savannah, near water

◼ nocturnal and diurnal

◼ territorial herds of females and young, led by dominant male, or territorial males visited by wandering female herds

☑ common, rather tame, large antelope; plant diet unpalatable to other herbivores; shaggy coat; only males have horns

Kirk's Dikdik *Rhincotragus kirki*

◩ scrub and thornbush, often far from water

◩ nocturnal and diurnal, with several sleeping periods

◩ pairs for life, often accompanied by current and previous young

✓ tiny, hare-sized antelope, named after its alarm cry; only males have horns; not found in Southern Africa except Namibia

Common Duiker *Sylvicapra grimmia*

◩ adaptable; prefers scrub and bush

◩ nocturnal and diurnal

◩ most commonly solitary; sometimes in pairs; occasionally monogamous

✓ widespread and common small antelope with a rounded back; seen close to cover; rams have short straight horns

Sitatunga *Tragelaphus spekei*

◩ swamps

◩ nocturnal and sometimes diurnal

◩ territorial and mostly solitary or in pairs

✓ very localized and not likely to be mistaken for anything else; usually seen half submerged; females have no horns

Nyala *Tragelaphus angasi*

◩ dense woodland near water

◩ primarily nocturnal with some diurnal activity

◩ flexible and non-territorial; the basic unit is a female and two offspring

✓ in size midway between the Kudu and Bushbuck, and easily mistaken for the latter; orange legs distinguish it; only males have horns; not found in East Africa

DWARF ANTELOPES · BUSHBUCK ANTELOPES

Bushbuck *Tragelaphus scriptus*

■ thick bush and woodland close to water

■ principally nocturnal, but also active during the day when cool

■ solitary, but casually sociable; sometimes grazes in small groups

☑ medium-sized antelope with white stripes and spots; often seen in thickets, or heard crashing through them; not to be confused with the far larger Nyala; the male has shortish straight horns

Eland *Taurotragus oryx*

■ highly adaptable; semi-desert to mountains, but prefers scrubby plains

■ nocturnal and diurnal

■ non-territorial herds of up to sixty with temporary gatherings of as many as a thousand

☑ common but shy; the largest and most powerful African antelope; both sexes have straight horns with a slight spiral

Greater Kudu *Tragelaphus strepsiceros*

■ semi-arid, hilly or undulating bush country; tolerant of drought

■ diurnal when secure; otherwise nocturnal

■ territorial; males usually solitary; females in small troops with young

☑ impressively big antelope (up to 1.5m at shoulder) with very long, spiral horns in the male; very localized; shy of humans and not often seen

Lesser Kudu *Tragelaphus imberbis*

■ semi-arid, hilly or undulating bush country; tolerant of drought

■ diurnal when secure; otherwise nocturnal

■ territorial; males usually solitary; females in small troops with young

☑ smaller than the Greater Kudu; only the male has horns; extremely shy and usually seen only as it disappears; not found in Southern Africa

Gemsbok *Oryx gazella gazella*
- ⊠ open grasslands; also waterless wastelands; tolerant of prolonged drought
- ⊠ nocturnal and diurnal
- ⊠ highly hierarchical mixed herds of up to fifteen, led by a dominant bull
- ☑ large antelope with unmistakable horns in both sexes; subspecies *gazella* is one of several similar forms, sometimes considered separate species; not found in East Africa

Fringe-eared Oryx *Oryx gazella callotis*
- ⊠ open grasslands; also waterless wastelands; tolerant of prolonged drought
- ⊠ nocturnal and diurnal
- ⊠ highly hierarchical mixed herds of up to fifteen, led by a dominant bull
- ☑ the *callotis* subspecies is one of two found in Kenya, the other, found in the northeast, being *Oryx g. beisa* (the Beisa Oryx); not found in Southern Africa

Roan Antelope *Hippotragus equinus*
- ⊠ tall grassland near water
- ⊠ nocturnal and diurnal; peak afternoon feeding
- ⊠ small herds led by a dominant bull; herds of immature males; sometimes pairs in season
- ☑ large antelope, distinguished from the Sable by lighter, greyish colour, shorter horns (both sexes) and narrow, tufted ears

Sable Antelope *Hippotragus niger*
- ⊠ open woodland with medium to tall grassland near water
- ⊠ nocturnal and diurnal
- ⊠ territorial; bulls divide into sub-territories, through which cows and young roam; herds of immature males; sometimes pairs in season
- ☑ large antelope; upper body dark brown to black; mask-like markings on the face; both sexes have huge curved horns

Grysbok *Raphicerus melanotis*

thicket adjacent to open grassland

nocturnal

rams territorial; loose pairings

✔ small, rarely seen antelope; two
subspecies, Cape (*R. m. melanotis*, South
Africa, right) and Sharpe's (*R. m. sharpei*,
East Africa); distinguished from more
slender Steenbok by light underparts;
rams have short horns

Oribi *Ourebia ourebi*

open grassland

diurnal

territorial harems consisting of male and
one to four females

✔ localized small antelope, but not hard to
see where common; only males have
horns; the Oribi is distinguished from the
smaller Grysbok and Steenbok by a black
tail and dark skin patch below the eye

Steenbok *Raphicerus campestris*

dry savannah

nocturnal and diurnal

solitary or (less often) in pairs

✔ widespread small antelope, particularly in
Southern Africa, but shy; only males have
horns

Klipspringer *Oreotragus oreotragus*

rocky country; cliffs and kopjes

diurnal

territorial ram with mate or small family
group; often restricted to small long-term
territories

✔ small antelope; horns normally only on
male; extremely agile on rocky terrain;
unusually high hooves, giving the
impression of walking on tiptoe

SMALL ANTELOPES – KLIPSPRINGER

WESTERN KARIBA TRANSPORT

ECONOMY BUSES

Public transport is minimal, with wildly erratic bus timetables, so keep asking around to get a reasonable idea of what's going on. However, Volvos and chicken buses can get you to Bulawayo, Hwange National Park and Victoria Falls with minimal hassle.

Binga–Hwange National Park/Victoria Falls
Country Boy buses run a daily service from Binga to Victoria Falls (1 daily at 5am; 7hr). The bus goes via Mlibizi, the speed ferry's western terminal, providing a link with the ferry and Vic Falls. For Hwange National Park (4hr), get off at Dete, where you'll find accommodation and guided drives into the game reserve.

Binga–Bulawayo
Four buses run by Country Boy and Kukuru-Kurerwa (known as "the cheetah bus") ply the route daily from Binga to Bulawayo. They leave Bulawayo between 5am and 6am, arriving around lunchtime in Binga, from where they turn around and head back to Bulawayo. In addition there are buses from Siabuwa to Bulawayo that pass through Binga (about 7am & noon) on their way south. The only drawback is that in Bulawayo they all leave from and arrive at B terminus, near the shops at the *renkini* in Entumbane, a high-density suburb about 10km west of the city centre; however, it's on the Luveve road, so most commuter omnibuses serving the western suburbs pass by.

Binga–Harare
Chawasarira runs buses from Binga to Harare via Siabuwa and Gokwe. Coming to Binga, they leave from the Gokwe stand at Mbare after 6am and sometimes as late as 8am, but it's better to be there early to get a comfortable seat behind the driver. The journey is longer and more tortuous than the one from Bulawayo, taking in 100km of dirt track.

BY CAR OR HITCHING

With your own car, Binga is easily accessible thanks to a tarred road all the way from Hwange town (188km), completed in the mid-1990s. Hitching is not easy, as traffic is sparse: start out early in the morning and take the bus if nothing else has materialized. For details on flights, ferries and other transport from Kariba town to the western lake see p.120.

impressive library open to the community, and innovative farming experiments are under way. The Batonga used to cultivate millet on the riverbanks, which doesn't thrive inland, so agriculturalists are trying poor soil crops like **manioc**, with the hard work done by schoolchildren in exchange for remission of their school fees. Pupils come from both Batonga and Ndebele communities. Teachers notice big differences in the children's responses to authority. The Ndebele, who come from a highly organized culture, accept what they are told without demur, whereas the Batonga, whose social system of virtually autonomous homesteads is much looser, question everything.

The Binga area is the source of the much-sought-after **Batonga handicrafts** sold at Victoria Falls; you'll find them being sold by several roadside traders dotted along the road from Hwange towards Chizarira. Prices are so low that bargaining is not on. The best items are the wide-mouthed **winnowing baskets** with plaited square bottoms, tricoloured V-patterned **beadwork** and the **carved stools** you see people sitting on under the trees. The Batonga are people who really know about travelling and roadside waits, and they make wonderful, portable stools with carrying handles. You won't be able to stash one of the free-standing Batonga **drums** in your baggage, but they're worth seeing (or even playing) all the same. Traditionally decorated with beautiful, archetypal zigzag motifs, they are now, sadly, a disappearing art.

Binga has a few lakeside villas – holiday homes for the affluent from Bulawayo – which the locals refer to as "The Palaces", and a couple of dozen houseboats for the

THE BATONGA

The **Batonga** are some of Zimbabwe's poorest rural people, still living mostly outside the influences of the modern nation. Cut off for centuries in the Gwembe section of the Zambezi Valley, upriver from Portuguese trading stations, they maintained a subsistence lifestyle until the building of the **Kariba dam**. In 1959, when the last lorry – piled high with evicted villagers and their belongings – was on the point of departure from the doomed valley, a small green bush was tied to the vehicle's tailboard to trail along behind. Villagers explained this was to allow their ancestral guardian spirit to ride until they reached their new home: it was essential that this spirit remained on the ground during the journey for it to settle comfortably into its new surroundings and maintain a relationship with the ancestors.

The **removal of the Batonga** created considerable anguish abroad (not to mention among the people themselves). Anthropologists rushed to amass details of Batonga society before everything changed. Some interesting theories about their **origins** still question whether they ever migrated to their present area in Southern Africa, as other Bantu people are supposed to have done. Uniquely among Bantu speakers, the Batonga have no migration myth, so the puzzle arises: have they forgotten their history, or have they been in the Gwembe Valley since much more ancient times? Anthropologists have suggested that they were indigenous hunter-gatherers who adopted the language stock and farming methods of Bantu immigrants, but not enough research has been done to be sure. Certainly, **Tonga** is a very old language, apparently a proto-form of Shona, though they may both derive from an earlier Bantu tongue, Shona having undergone more profound changes over the last millennium.

Little of this heritage seems to have found its way back to enrich the Batonga today. The people no longer engage in beadwork because they can't afford to buy the imported beads. Indeed, many have sold off their beaded family heirlooms, as well as some very beautiful stools and carved hut doors, in order to raise money for the next meal. There's no evidence of traditional dress, either, and the cosmetic practice of knocking out women's front teeth has (perhaps mercifully) died out. You may see the occasional old woman with a bone through her nose, but it's just as likely to be a stalk of grass.

fishing and drinking crowd are moored here and available for charter rental. **Boats** are fully equipped and come with a skipper who knows the lake; for details, contact Enzo Rossi (☎015/2405).

Accommodation

For **accommodation**, the former District Commissioner's residence down at the lakeside (5km downhill from the administrative centre and bus terminus) is now the *Binga Rest Camp* (☎015/244, fax 245; ③), a very uncommercialized outfit away from the lake but with a swimming pool filled from a nearby hot spring making it a distinctly reviving place; exotic gardens provide a wonderful respite from the dust. Extremely inexpensive en-suite chalets are available, and even cheaper ones if you're prepared to share washing facilities, plus there's a campsite and restaurant. More comfortable are the fully equipped, two-roomed self-catering cottages, *Kulizwe Lodge* (☎ & fax 015/286; sleeps four; ④), 5km from the police station on the lakefront. There are gardens, a swimming pool, a children's playground and a campsite (①).

Eight kilometres east of the village, a road leads off the Kamativi–Binga route along the lakeshore, where there are three more places to stay, all of them clearly signposted. For backpackers there's a great opportunity at *Chilangililo Co-operative* (☎015/563; ①), closest to the turn-off, to stay in a traditional Tonga hut built on stilts, where you can enjoy the lake as well as meet locals in the nearby family compound. Not much more is on offer, so you'll need to be self-sufficient and ready to adapt to African life,

After this checklist of loss, at least the layout of villages and **architectural techniques** remain much as they've always been. The thatching is an untidy affair, not groomed into flawless sections like Ndebele huts. The small huts on stilts are for chickens or children, with ladders removed at night to keep the precious charges safe from attack by wild animals. Huts on stilts in the fields are baboon watchtowers, occupied all day long before the harvest. These days, high-status building materials like cement and corrugated iron are used if someone has the money. **Baskets** are certainly still being made either for domestic use or for cooperatives, which distribute them through the mainstream curio centres.

The Batonga live over the border in Zambia, too, both in the Zambezi Valley and on the plateau (before the existence of political frontiers, valley people crossed the river in dugouts). But studies of the language and culture have concentrated on the plateau Batonga, who have always been broadly integrated with the rest of the country. In contrast, the isolation of the Gwembe Valley inhabitants has earned them the label "backward" among urban Zimbabweans. An obvious target for **aid money**, they attract attention from organizations like the Save the Children Fund, who have concentrated on improving **sanitation and water supplies** to communities with some of the worst child mortality rates in the country. Land-Rovers shuttle between villages transporting pipes and machinery for other projects like collective grain winnowing. And the government's desire to see universal primary **education** has seeded schools in many settlements. People no longer have to walk for days to get to a secondary school. One worker at Bumi Hills, remembering his schooling, recounted walking three days at the start and end of each term, accompanied by his older brother, armed with axe and spear to fend off wild animals.

However, nothing can compensate the Batonga for the forced substitution of a viable – even flourishing – farming and fishing economy on the Zambezi, for the poor soils and uncertain rainfall of the interior. Evicted overnight from familiar, well-watered ancient lands, the Batonga have floundered ever since in their new and alien home.

An ironic postscript to the story of the Batonga is the **trendiness** they've accumulated. Perhaps it's their *mbanje*-smoking (women, from long calabash pipes; men, from shorter clay ones) that's created a special niche for these people in colonial mythology: you will occasionally hear tales of young middle-class whites who became strange and went to live among the "Tonkies".

but it's a rare opportunity to get under the skin of a local community. Safe boiled water is available and two basic rural shops near *Chilangililo* can provide necessities.

A little further on, *Chilila Lodge*, Box FM 65, Famona, Bulawayo (☎09/67821, fax 60518, direct ☎ & fax 015/580, *chilila@acacia.samara.co.zw*; ③), attracts a boating and boozing crowd. Set in magnificent gardens, it has two-roomed brick-and-thatch chalets on the lakeshore with their own private outdoor area and braai stands, and boat rental can be arranged. In the same vicinity and most luxurious of the lot is the gorgeous *Masumu River Lodge*, Box 8247, Belmont, Bulawayo (☎015/585; full board ⑤), the only place around Binga that doesn't offer self-catering. Seven lovely bungalows and two-storey thatched lodges with lake views are constructed of wood or stone. A small lawned campsite has space for five tents (①).

Mlibizi

Most people see the western side of the lake because they're travelling on the ferry between Kariba town and Victoria Falls or Hwange. If you're catching the Kariba ferry (see box on p.120), you'll have to overnight at **MLIBIZI** for the 9am departure. The *Mlibizi Zambezi Resort*, booked through Galaxy Travel, PO Box 1511, Bulawayo (☎09/65061, fax 77842, direct ☎015/272), at the ferry terminal has self-contained and fully equipped Spanish-style **chalets** (①; minimum US$20) of various sizes that sleep two to eight. If these are too expensive there is a campsite (①) and some "camp rooms" (①), which consist of two mattresses on the floor, basic furniture, private verandahs and braai stands on request; you must provide your own linen. A small general store sells bread, milk, frozen meat and booze, but no fresh fruit or vegetables. You can rent catamaran rafts with drivers for about US$4 an hour.

Chizarira National Park

Very few travellers make it to **CHIZARIRA** (open year-round; day entry US$10, week entry US$20), Zimbabwe's most remote national park. Isolated and undeveloped, it is a spectacular region, a kingdom on top of the steep Zambezi Escarpment well watered by rivers cutting sheer gorges through the mountains and full of natural springs. The usual Zambezi Valley game is to be seen, including elephant, buffalo, zebra, kudu, waterbuck, bushbuck, grysbok and impala. It's not a great place for lions, though you will hear them and are more likely to see them in the south. There have been some exceptional daytime sightings of leopard, less shy here than in other parks because tourists are few and far between. But when people talk about the park, it's invariably the beautiful **scenery** that makes them wax lyrical.

This becomes understandable as soon as you approach the reserve. From a long way off, the jagged mountains of Chizarira are visible, dominated by **Tundazi** – home, local legend has it, to an immense and powerful serpent. Once you've arrived, the views across to Lake Kariba, 40km north, are equally magnificent. The **Chizarira Mountains** give you a clue to the nature of the place. Their name derives from a Tonga word meaning "to close off" or "create a barrier", defining the craggy edge of their baobab-wooded world, the **Gwembe Valley**. The escarpment's roof is another world altogether, of slender trees spaced out across grasslands and well-watered scrub savannah, and the **river gorges**, such as Mucheni and Lwizilukulu, are really exciting, with their thick

---

RHINO POACHING

Until recently, Chizarira offered your best chance of seeing the virtually extinct **black or hook-lipped rhinos**, which used to browse freely around thick bush and wooded gulleys in the northern part of the park. In 1995, however, following decades of ruthless **poaching**, the last few remaining animals were translocated to more intensively protected zones (IPZs) in other parts of the country, where they are guarded day and night.

Zimbabwe has the world's last viable breeding herd of black rhinos, yet nothing seems able to halt their steady extermination. Twenty years ago there were 40,000 in Africa, while in early 1992 it was estimated that fewer than 3000 individuals survived on the continent, of which 2000 were in Zimbabwe. However, in November 1992, a count throughout Zimbabwe found only 250 black rhinos living in the wild. Experts predict that Zimbabwe's last rhino will be finished off in the next few years. Despite the international ban on the trade in rhino horn, it is, even today, widely available in markets in Hong Kong and Taiwan at sky-high prices. The market for knife handles in the Yemen and apothecarial ingredients in the Far East continues to propel their unrelenting slaughter.

In 1985, the Zimbabwean government began shooting poachers on sight and capturing and translocating rhinos to safer parks, but this strategy hasn't worked. Poachers move quickly on foot, cutting out only the horn before ferrying back to their camps in Zambia. In an area of dense bush, they often escape undetected. The poachers themselves – many of them unemployed Zambians – are not the ones to cream off vast amounts of money, but are offered enough by middlemen to make it worth risking their lives. Zimbabwe's next step in the early 1990s was a massive **dehorning programme**. Since then, sadly, dehorned rhinos have been killed simply for their stumps.

vegetation cascading down places too steep for any vehicle. This doesn't stop the **elephants**, however: you'll notice their paths, less than a metre wide, cutting into slopes held together by the determined roots of stunted trees. On the escarpment in the north are plateaux of typical highveld Brachystegia woodland and mopane scrub as you move southwards. The southern boundary is marked by the Busi River, flanked by plains of characteristic *Acacia albida* trees.

Chizarira also offers superb prospects for ornithologists, with no less than 406 of Zimbabwe's 580 species of **birds** recorded here, among them the rare and beautiful Angola pitta, the Livingstone flycatcher, African broadbill, Taita falcon and elusive black stork. From mid-June to August, fish eagles make sorties from the shores Lake Kariba to the Busi Valley (a 1hr flight) to feed on catfish struggling in the mud of oxbow lakes that dry up in the winter.

Getting there

You won't have much company at Chizarira: it's just too far for most people, when other parks are far more accessible and better stocked. Most of those visitors who do come, drive from Victoria Falls or Hwange, an eight-hour journey mostly on dirt roads. While 4WD isn't essential for the north, except during the rains, it is necessary for the south, where you have to cross sandy rivers to reach Busi camp. The nearest **petrol and supplies** are 90km away at Binga, so bring all you need. From Harare, Chizarira is reached via 300km of dirt road, once you turn off at Karoi, with Siabuwa the only place en route for petrol.

Accommodation and walking safaris

Guests fly in to *Chizarira Wilderness Lodge*, the only tourist place. The lodge has eight thatched stone **chalets** shaded by a grove of mountain acacia dramatically overlooking the Zambezi Valley. It's just outside the park, half an hour's drive from the park headquarters, and is managed by Brian Johnson, a fully licensed professional guide who can take walks into the reserve and does game drives and birdwatching. The lodge itself now has a **tented camp**, slap in the centre of the park itself and an ideal base for hikes. Fully inclusive daily rates are US$230 in high season and US$190 in low, with an additional US$200 for transfers from anywhere in Zimbabwe. Book through Run Wild, 3rd Floor, Southampton Life Centre, Jason Moyo Avenue (☎04/795841, *runwild@africaonline.co.zw*).

If you want to do more hiking and tracking, contact Backpackers' Bazaar or Khangela Safaris (see below and p.232), who camp right in the park and, unlike most other operators, venture into the south. Their walking safaris in Chizarira offer guaranteed solitude and some of the most inspiring hiking in Zimbabwe. Most of the safaris are fully backed up – a 4WD carries camp attendants, who put up the tents, make the fires, prepare all the food and heat the water for your portable washbasins and bush showers. You don't have to carry anything besides your binoculars and camera. Nor is the walking uncomfortable – you're not pushed excessively and you rest up during the heat in the middle of the day. Bookings for Leon Varley Walking Safaris can be made through Backpackers' Bazaar, Shop 5, Victoria Falls Centre, Parkway (☎013/5828, fax 2208, mobile ☎011/404960, *backpack@africaonline.co.zw*). Expect to pay from US$130 per day all in, carrying your own kit, or US$190 for more comfortable safaris with vehicle backup (discounts available Nov–April). If this sounds too cushy, Khangela does safaris where you carry everything yourself and are free to walk into areas far from any roads or designated campsites; they also offer an easier option for those who'd rather have their gear carried. Their professional guide is excellent and the food's good. Prices are around US$130 per day all in, and trips normally last five nights/six days: discounts are available to groups. Bookings should be made direct through Khangela, PO Box FM 296, Famona, Bulawayo (☎09/49733, fax 78081, mobile ☎091/234676 or 023/406981, *scott@gatorzw.com*).

With either company, an African tracker walks with the armed guide and you spend a good deal of time identifying and following game tracks. It's a fascinating experience, estimating how far ahead the elephants are by feeling the warmth of their dung (it's mainly grass, after all), or how old the remains of a lion kill are, and noticing the insects and birds you miss when driving. While you can do a walking trip just to Chizarira, Backpackers' offers a twelve-day "Tundazi Trail" once a month, which takes in the Zambezi National Park, Hwange, and Kazuma pan, as well as Chizarira. Khangela offers a combined trip that usually starts at Bulawayo and ends at Victoria Falls and spends four nights in Chizarira and three in Hwange National Park.

If you're visiting the park under your own steam, you can ask an armed **National Parks game scout** to take you walking. They will take groups out for a small fee. Unlike Mana Pools, however, you can't wander off on your own.

National Parks camps

The National Park headquarters are in the northern part of the park, 22km up the escarpment from the Binga–Siabuwa road. There are no chalets or lodges here, but three **camping sites** are located nearby, the most developed of which is at **Kasiswi** on the Lusilukulu River, 6km from the park HQ, which has thatched shelters on stilts. Two spectacular sites overlooking the Mucheni Gorge have no facilities. Only one party at a time is allowed in each; booking is through National Parks' Central Reservations office in Harare (see p.33) and costs are, as usual, reasonable.

Mabolo Bush Camp on the Mucheni River, below the Manzituba spring, 6km from the camp HQ, has running water, a flush toilet and shower. If you prefer flood plains and lowveld vegetation, go 35km over very rough roads to **Busi Bush Camp**, which has thatched sleeping shelters, but no running water (you have to dig water from the river bed and boil it). It's a marvellous site under *Acacia albidas*, with herds of impala wandering around and a night chorus of hyenas and lions.

Siabuwa

The land **south of Lake Kariba** is among Zimbabwe's poorest and most remote. Travelling around the region, unless on an organized tour or with your own vehicle, you are dependent on a very few local buses – somewhat erratically scheduled and none too comfortable. **Hitching** is very chancy – traffic is very sparse and about your only hope would be to find an aid vehicle prepared to take you. Carry food and plenty of water, and expect long delays.

It's best not to get off except at villages, as wild animals abound in this region. A familiar sight along the roadsides are aid-built pumps where locals fill buckets, and Blair toilets, built behind huts in every settlement. These are an ingenious Zimbabwean design, solving the problem of flies and smell that plague the traditional long-drops; painted black inside and spiral-shaped with a chimney air vent, they trap flies escaping to the only source of light – the gauze-covered air vent, which also allows air to circulate.

SIABUWA, 100km east of Binga, is the halfway staging post on the 340-kilometre trip from Binga to Karoi – it's a sizable agglomeration of huts, schools and a basic store or two. A daily **bus** sets off in the early hours of the morning for Bulawayo via Binga on what must be the longest haul in the country: people sleep at the stop to ensure catching it, as the drivers leave when they get up. Another bus plies the route between Siabuwa and Harare.

PARKS VERSUS PEOPLE

As elsewhere in Zimbabwe, there's extreme tension between villagers and the National Parks over **wildlife** – a conflict which has deep roots.

Game parks were set up from the 1930s to maintain game populations that had been decimated by hunting and habitat removal for commercial farming. White rhinos had been completely exterminated and diaries of early settlers reveal obscene hunting excesses – 25 giraffe in an afternoon was nothing. To create the parks, however, people were moved out and banned from subsistence hunting. Long-established balances had enabled people to coexist with wild animals for thousands of years, yet, suddenly, wildlife had become a luxury for the rich. Colonial legislation stated that wildlife in communal (black) areas was State property, while on private (white) farms it was not.

Shortly after Independence, a host of new conservation measures were introduced, but the problem of human versus animal interests remains unresolved and **poaching** is still heavy in all the national parks. One major way forward is the **Campfire Project** (Communal Areas Management for Indigenous Resources), which has a philosophy of sustainable rural development to enable rural communities to manage, and benefit directly from, indigenous wildlife and other resources. Getting a community interested in the Campfire programme rests on changing the belief that the State owns the wildlife to the belief that the wildlife is owned by the community who lives with it.

The first Campfire Project to be set up was the **Nyaminyami Wildlife Trust** in the Omay Communal Lands, adjoining Matusadona National Park. Wild animals tend to be viewed either as food or as a crop menace by peasant farmers, who resent wildlife getting so much land, while they're forced to keep livestock numbers low to prevent encroachment on game areas. As hunting is forbidden, National Parks and the District Council are frequently called out to shoot "problem animals" that are endangering either lives or crops in the fields. From this arrangement, the people get the meat, while National Parks sells the tusks or hides on behalf of the council (elephants are frequently the culprits and victims). One difficulty is that the number of claims for crop compensation, paid in cash, tends to exceed the budget and may be open to abuse. Another is that people spend compensation money on other necessities and then lack the funds to buy the equivalent in grain.

The Campfire Project is also trying to make people aware that, although they want to acquire cattle, it's in their interests to limit numbers as wildlife is potentially more lucrative. In the Omay Communal Lands, the number of goats is roughly equal to the number of impala, even though the meat value alone of the latter far exceeds that of the former, and the hunting of impala brings in considerable revenue.

On the hunting front, to provide local people with the incentive not to poach, and to foster the perception of wild animals as having a high commercial value, Campfire channels revenue from game back to the communal lands. The council receives in the order of fifteen percent of the proceeds from hunting – money that can then be deployed to erect solar electric fences to protect crops, or to build clinics and schools. Privately run safari camps recently established on communal lands also pay a percentage of their income to the local council to fund projects, or for distribution to individual families. Sadly, towards the end of the 1990s, the whole Campfire Project began to run out of steam. The grapevine is full of stories of officials misappropriating Campfire-generated income intended for the community and there's a bizarre footnote from the southern Kariba area, where people have misunderstood the name Campfire, and believe that the scheme is responsible for blazes that have destroyed crops.

travel details

Trains

Note that the daily Bulawayo–Victoria Falls train arrives in Dete in the early hours of the morning in both directions, but travellers do still use it.

Dete to Bulawayo (1 daily; 8hr); Victoria Falls (1 daily; 6hr).

Victoria Falls to: Bulawayo (1 daily; 14hr).

Luxury coaches

Dete to: Bulawayo (Mon, Sat & Sun; 3hr 45min); Victoria Falls (Mon, Sat & Sun; 2hr 15min).

Hwange Safari Lodge to: Bulawayo (Mon, Sat & Sun; 3hr 30min); Victoria Falls (Mon, Sat & Sun; 2hr 30min).

Victoria Falls to: Bulawayo (Mon, Sat & Sun; 6hr); Dete (Mon, Sat & Sun; 2hr 15min); Gwaai River Lodge (Mon, Sat & Sun; 3hr); Halfway House (Mon, Sat & Sun; 3hr 30min); Hwange Safari Lodge (Mon, Sat & Sun; 2hr 30min); Hwange Town (Mon, Sat & Sun; 1hr 15min); Windhoek (Wed & Sun; 18hr).

Volvos and chicken buses

Frequencies and journey times given below are very approximate; always check information at the bus station before leaving.

Binga to: Bulawayo (4 daily; 7hr); Dete Crossroads (4 daily; 4hr); Harare (1 daily; 12hr);

Mlibizi (4 daily; 2hr); Victoria Falls (1 daily; 7hr).

Dete Crossroads to: Binga (about 8 daily; 4hr); Bulawayo (8 daily; 3hr); Victoria Falls (8 daily; 3hr).

Victoria Falls to: Binga (1 daily; 7hr); Bulawayo (8 daily; 10hr); Dete Crossroads (8 daily; 3hr); Mlibizi (1 daily; 6hr).

Mlibizi to: Dete (1 daily; 3hr); Victoria Falls (1 daily; 6hr).

Ferries

Speed ferries cover the journey between the western shore and Kariba in 24 hours, while the cheaper DDF ferry does it less frequently and takes three days to cover the same distance. See p.226 for details.

Mlibizi to: Kariba (daily except Thurs; 24hr); calling in by request only at Binga, Bumi and Tashinga.

Binga to: Kariba (fortnightly Mon; 3 days).

Flights

Hwange National Park to: Harare (3 weekly; 2hr).

Victoria Falls to: Harare (3–4 daily; 1hr); Johannesburg (daily; 1hr 50min); Kariba (daily; 1hr 50min); Maun (4 weekly; 1hr); Windhoek (5 weekly; 2hr 25min).

CHAPTER FIVE

GREAT ZIMBABWE AND GONAREZHOU

Pyramids apart, **Great Zimbabwe** is Africa's biggest stone monument and, for the century of colonialism, it was a potent political weapon. The monument's authorship was long claimed for "the white races" by die-hard settlers, and for Africans by most archeologists – and the site's Shona inheritors. The archeology has, therefore, been as much about excavating a detritus of disinformation as about digging under the walls. The ruins are beautifully set, thrilling and unfathomable, deserving of a day or two in anyone's trip.

The existence of Great Zimbabwe is **Masvingo**'s great fortune. If not for the **National Monument**, 28km away, the town would be little more than a crossroads, one at which few travellers would alight. But in fact Masvingo is an essential port of call for anyone wanting to see the ancient walls, given that it's the only urban centre of any size for 100km in any direction and it's from here that most visitors will be planning their trips to the monument or around the lake. Masvingo is an important route centre lying on the main north–south highway between Harare and Johannesburg, and is connected with Bulawayo to the west and Chimanimani and the Eastern Highlands to the east. In itself, the town has little to detain you, though if you are driving from Harare it's well worth a short detour north to the captivating **Serima Mission** – home to some of Zimbabwe's most inspiring modern carvings. Masvingo is also an excellent springboard for encountering rural Zimbabwean life, with short tours available to a nearby village where people use traditional methods to keep bees, or longer stays with a family in Zaka, a small village in the back country south of town.

THE LOWVELD

Destinations covered in this chapter fall within an area frequently referred to as "the **lowveld**", a term which can be as perplexing as it is vague, strictly speaking referring to ecozones rather than a place. "lowveld" describes topography not more than 600m above sea level, characterized by soaring daytime temperatures, summer rainfall and a savannah landscape. The presence of baobab trees is the most obvious indicator that you're in the lowveld, while along rivercourses you'll encounter lush subtropical vegetation. Because of their unsuitability for farming, the lowveld regions tend to be excellent game-viewing destinations and their dryness means that wildlife predictably congregates around scarce water sources. The Zambezi Valley, including Mana Pools National Park in northern Zimbabwe, is typical lowveld, but when used in this chapter the term refers to the southern lowveld, which sweeps across the Limpopo from south of Bulawayo and includes a vast tract south from Masvingo to South Africa's Kruger National Park.

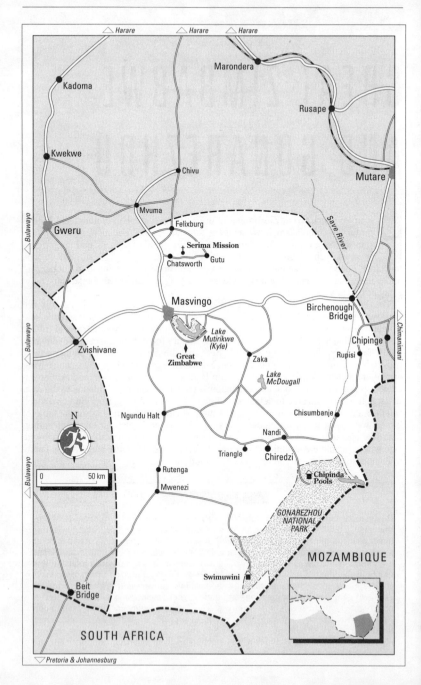

ACCOMMODATION PRICE CODES

Hotels and other accommodation options in Zimbabwe have been categorized according to the **price codes** given below, which indicate the cost, per person sharing, of a night's lodging. For a full explanation, see p.33.

① under US$7.50   ④ US$25–35   ⑦ US$55–75
② US$7.50–15   ⑤ US$35–45   ⑧ US$75–100
③ US$15–25   ⑥ US$45–55   ⑨ over US$100

Both Masvingo and Great Zimbabwe are sited near **Lake Mutirikwe**, an extensive artificial body of water surrounded by hills and large granite outcrops, with the small but well-stocked **Kyle Game Park** attached. Although not as compelling an attraction as Great Zimbabwe, Lake Mutirikwe is very pretty and its shores offer a handful of relaxing places to stay. The game park on its north shore is one of the most reliable places in Zimbabwe to see rhinos in the wild, and a 122-kilometre scenic drive around the lake takes you past Great Zimbabwe and through granite country and traditional villages.

Wildlife is the big incentive for anyone to head south of Masvingo and Great Zimbabwe, beyond the sugar boom town of **Chiredzi** to **Gonarezhou National Park** on the Mozambique border. Gonarezhou is renowned for its striking scenic wilderness, and although it's Zimbabwe's second largest game reserve, is little visited as it's very undeveloped and you'd need a 4WD vehicle and a good deal of confidence. Most visitors stay at one of the handful of luxury lodges in the private game reserves on the fringes of the park, or take a walking safari.

Masvingo

There's not much to keep you in **MASVINGO**, a humdrum town three hours by car from either Harare or Bulawayo, unless you happen to arrive as night approaches. But if you're travelling under your own steam you'll find it a solid enough base, and a useful place to stock up with supplies before camping or self-catering at the ruins or along Lake Mutirikwe – a more appealing prospect than the town itself.

Some history

Rhodesia's first white settlement, Masvingo was established in 1890 by pioneers trekking north, beyond the parched lowveld, to the cooler middleveld plateau. The settlers pitched and fortified their camp and named the spot **Fort Victoria** to link it with the global sisterhood of lakes, falls, towns, pubs and hotels named after the unamused queen. After some days of festivities – reportedly resembling an English village fair – the main force headed off, leaving the earthwork fort under heavily armed protection. When they realized there was little convenient water about, a new and stronger brick fort was built along the Mucheke River, a few kilometres away. One of its watchtowers, perforated with vertical gun-slits, still stands on Masvingo's main street, a reminder of frontier days.

Fort Victoria was the portal to southern Rhodesia for northward trekking fortune-hunters, and Mashonaland's gold centre: the town's early inhabitants had ambitious hopes of a big strike. In an ironic twist, however, the **Matabele War** of 1893 crushed these local aspirations. After an Ndebele raiding party entered Fort Victoria and, in a punitive raid, killed a number of local Shona who had avoided making tribute payments, a force was recruited to invade Bulawayo – a convenient excuse, as it turned out, to lay claim to the richer goldfields of Matabeleland. The destruction of Lobengula's kraal in Bulawayo subsequently served as a great pro-paganda coup in recruiting immigrants from the south. Enticed by the gold – not to mention the spoils of Ndebele farms and cattle – the whites had few reasons to return to Fort Victoria, condemning it to the small-time provincial status that has stuck ever since.

Arrival and information

The only public transport serving Masvingo are buses but, as the town lies at a cross-roads between Mutare and Bulawayo, and Harare and Johannesburg, it is extremely well connected for a provincial town. **Volvo** and **chicken buses** from Harare and Bulawayo stop in the town centre in Josiah Tongogara Avenue near the BP garage, and from Mutare on the corner of Tongogara and Robert Mugabe Way, before terminating in Mucheke township's *musika*, 2km west of the centre. Should you end up in Mucheke, it's no great disaster, as frequent commuter omnibuses buzz up and down between the bus station and the town centre. The only luxury **coaches** that pass this way are ones plying the route between Johannesburg and Harare (which by law aren't allowed to pick up passengers for journeys within Zimbabwe). From Johannesburg, Greyhound and Trans Zambezi coaches stop off at *Riley's Truck Inn* (aka "Shell City"), a filling station and mini-shopping complex 5km south of town, while Translux, also from Jo'burg, pulls in at the *Chevron Hotel* on the south side of the train line, all arriv-ing at horribly early hours of the morning.

MASVINGO

See map p. 245 for accommodation out of town centre

COMMERCIAL AREA

INDUSTRIAL AREA

Town Bus Terminal

Police

Edgars Clothes Store

Mutual Arcade

Meikles Department Store

Musika Bus Station

Police Station

MUCHEKE SUBURB

Publicity Bureau

Craft Centre

ACCOMMODATION	
Backpackers' Rest	5
Chevron Hotel	6
Clovelly	1
Flamboyant Hotel	8
Municipal Campsite & Caravan Park	4
Pa-Nyanda Lodge	9
Riverside Lodge	2
Sundowners	10
The Cottage	3
Titambire Lodge	7

EATING & DRINKING	
Ace Takeaway	A
Hidden Garden Cafe	C
Ritz Nite Spot	B

0   500 m

❶, ❷, *Gweru, Harare & Bulawayo*   *Hospital*   ❸

❹, *Lake Kyle Game Park & Birchenough Bridge*

❽, ❾, ❿, *Great Zimbabwe & Beit Bridge*

Across the road from the *Chevron*, the **Publicity Association office**, Robert Mugabe Way (Mon–Fri 8am–1pm & 2–4.30pm, Sat 9am–noon; ☎039/62643), has a helpful attendant and a small collection of leaflets, as well as information on local accommodation. For a more dynamic and backpacker-friendly information service, the **Masvingo Internet Café** in Old Mutual Arcade, Robert Mugabe Way (daily 8am–8pm; ☎039/63659, mobile ☎011/208043, *hippolodge@usa.net*), about 300m north of the Publicity Association, houses an agency that books activities in the area, including budget tours of Great Zimbabwe and Mutirikwe lake cruises. There's also a bureau de change, the Warthog curio shop and, of course, an Internet café.

Getting around and tours

Some of the budget accommodation provides **free transfers** to and from the centre; otherwise you'll have to rely on **taxis** for getting around town. They're not too expensive and line up on Simon Mazorodze Avenue behind the TM Supermarket and around Mucheke Bus Terminus – or you can phone for them (see p.243). Frequent and cheap commuter omnibuses connect Mucheke and the centre. For transport to Great Zimbabwe, see p.243.

A number of operators offer **Great Zimbabwe tours** that set out from Masvingo. *Sundowners* and *Hippo* backpackers' lodges offer free tours to their guests (although you still pay the entrance fee), while the *Masvingo Internet Café*, Old Mutual Centre, Robert Mugabe Way (same owners as *Hippo*), does budget Great Zimbabwe tours. Another operator taking visitors around the ruins is Heritage Tours (☎039/64256 or 62054–5), which has desks at the *Chevron* and *Great Zimbabwe* hotels. The Internet café also arranges **African Bee Village tours** in the dry season (May–Oct) in a settlement near Bondolfi Mission, where villagers keep the insects in traditional hives – baskets, crates or tree trunks. It includes a two-hour walk that involves a degree of serendipity as you never quite know what you'll see; it could be groundnuts drying or peasants ploughing, depending on the season. The tour is conducted by the village headman and half the fun is locating him, possibly working in a field or chatting around his hut; there's no phone in the settlement, so excursions can't be scheduled. For onsite tours of Great Zimbabwe and **lake cruises**, see p.243 and p.253.

Accommodation

Accommodation in Masvingo is a very mixed bag, but includes a number of backpackers' lodges, some hotels and self-catering places in the lower price ranges. In fact, it's far pleasanter to stay around Great Zimbabwe and Lake Mutirikwe (see p.245), which are, after all, the real reason for being here. Amongst these, *Hippo Lodge* (see p.252), owned by the *Masvingo Internet Café*'s Anthony Balliou, is a viable option for budget travellers, as daily transfers are offered to and from town – as are Great Zimbabwe tours.

Campsites and backpackers' lodges

Backpackers' Rest, First Floor, Dauth Building, Josiah Tongogara Street/Roberston Street (☎039/63960). The main point in favour of this crowded former block of flats is that the Harare and Bulawayo buses stop right outside before they go on to Mucheke, making it handy if you're arriving late without anywhere to stay. Dorms and doubles ①.

Clovelly, Glyntor Road, 6km from town on the Bulawayo road (☎039/64751 or 62346, *clovelly@mvo.samara.co.zw*). Excellent backpackers' lodge, with dorms and doubles on a shady out-of-town plot. The friendly owners collect and drop off guests at the post office in town, and keep a useful file of up-to-date information for travellers. A swimming pool and horse-riding in a nearby game park, where you can ride up to zebras, kudu and giraffe, are added attractions. Dorms and doubles ②.

ZAKA VALLEY RURAL HOMESTAYS

Some travellers reckon that the chance to spend two or more days with the **Madanhire family**, 65km southeast of Masvingo near **Zaka**, is a far better reason to get off the bus in Masvingo than the dry old stones of Great Zimbabwe. Aside from the beauty of the setting, off a ridge in a wide attractive valley, it gives you a chance to experience authentic rural Zimbabwean life. The family consists of Sekiwe Madanhire, his two brothers and six sisters, all of whom speak English, and their children (a total of thirteen people at last count).

The homestead consists of a collection of huts, one of which is a kitchen and the others sleeping quarters, granaries and barns, as well as a modern structure with some bedrooms and a lounge. Guest **accommodation** is either in a private room or one shared with family members; **food** is home-grown, cooked on an open fire and could include cabbage, spinach, beans, bread, fritters, pork, chicken, honey and peanut butter with *sadza*, plus lots of **tea**. There's a pit toilet, no electricity (apart a few solar-charged batteries), but there is a telephone.

Family members will take care of you and show you around the community and aspects of daily life such setting stone traps for bats, making mud bricks, livestock and farming methods and their irrigation scheme. If you want, you can meet the community, work in the fields or at other daily tasks.

GETTING THERE
By car from Masvingo, take the Mutare road for 42km to Roy's filling station, turn right to Zaka/Jerera/Buffalo Range; after 15km, turn right at Chimedza Primary School and follow the gravel road through Jichidza Township to Gunguvu Township; the Madanhire home is 200m from here. You can also get there on the daily Jichidza **bus** from Mucheke (ask to be let off at Gunguvu), or phone Sekiwe and see if he can meet you in Masvingo and accompany you on the bus.

COSTS AND CONTACTS
Apart from the bus fare you should expect to **pay** around US$5 per day including accommodation and all meals. You can **contact** Sekiwe Madanhire by writing to him at Gunguvu School, P/A Jichidza, Masvingo, Zimbabwe, or phone ☎034/22754, preferably in the evening.

Municipal Campsite and Caravan Park, 2km out of town on the Mutare road. A vast and incredibly clean site that is convenient for getting a lift to Mutirikwe's north bank and the game park. In some need of refurbishment, it is nevertheless conscientiously serviced and has good security behind its perimeter fence. ①.

Sundowners, Silver Oaks Farm, Old Great Zimbabwe road; signposted off the Beit Bridge road 6km south of town (☎039/65793, fax 62718, mobile ☎011/606563 or 707777), *sunbird@mvo.samara.co.zw*). Excellent backpackers' lodge on a farm beautifully set in the horseshoe of a river. It feels more like someone's house, which it is, than the average hostel, and you can stay in a choice of a double rondavels in the garden, three doubles in the house or two dorms that sleep five and eight, one of which can serve as an en-suite family room. Added perks are a plunge pool, satellite TV, free transfers from town and free guided tours of Great Zimbabwe as well as cheap Internet facilities. Self-catering ①, half-board ②.

Titambire Lodge, 14 Kirton St (☎039/62475). Suburban bungalow 5min walk from the town centre in a quiet area, with basic but clean dorms and doubles, whose lack of flair is justified by their very low price. A TV lounge and kitchen are available to guests. ①.

B&Bs and Hotels

Chevron Hotel, Robert Mugabe Street (☎039/62054, 64171 or 65978, fax 65961, *chevron@icon.co.zw*). The most central of Masvingo's hotels, opposite the publicity bureau, is a respectable place dating from the 1960s; its lack of modernization makes it look like the oldest swinger in town. ③.

The Cottage, 6 Citrus Rd (☎039/63340, fax 64277). Extremely comfortable cottage in the garden of a suburban house about 2km from the centre. Its three bedrooms (two twins and a single refurbished in 1999), and fully equipped kitchen, bath, shower, swimming pool and lounge with satellite TV, make it outstanding value for self-catering couples or families. Rate includes cereal, bread, eggs and cheese for breakfast. ②.

Flamboyant Hotel, 2km from the centre at the junction of the Beit Bridge road and the Great Zimbabwe turn-off (☎039/53085 or 52898). Clean and comfortable rooms at the best hotel in town. Owned by the large South African Protea chain, brimming with character it ain't, but it does bring the predictable reliability of the brand, including satellite TV, wall-to-wall carpets and slick service. ④.

Pa-Nyanda Lodge, PO Box 199, Masvingo, 11km south of town on the Beit Bridge road (☎039/63412 or after hours 63456, fax 62000, mobile ☎011/605512, *nrg-gr@icon.co.zw*). Five thatched chalets and a tree house, set amongst hills overlooking a waterhole on a beef farm that has some antelope and ostriches. The most luxurious accommodation around Masvingo, but you'll need your own car. Under-16s half-price and under-2s free. Half-board ⑨.

Riverside Lodge, Plot 12, Glynham (☎039/64725 or 64360, mobile ☎011/605576, *riversid@icon.co.zw*). Huge two-storey suburban house, 7km west of the centre off the Bulawayo road (turn left at Green Valley Store, 6.5km from town and continue for 500m). Comfortable accommodation in five double rooms sharing bathrooms, or two en-suite doubles. A full English breakfast is included in the rate and there are two kitchens for self-catering, a laundry service and free transport to town. ②.

The Town

In the typical style of colonial town planning, the train line (goods only) slices Masvingo in two: the more salubrious avenues and commercial centre lie to the north, with Mucheke township hidden on the wrong side of the tracks. In the **commercial centre** the focus is provided by **Mucheke market**. Though this doesn't stand out from its counterparts elsewhere in the country, it has lots of small stores, kiosks and the festive blare of local music. People lounge about waiting for long-distance buses on a grassy island between the shops and beer halls along Charumbira and Makuva streets.

Masvingo's only noteworthy sight is the **Chapel of St Francis**, known as the "Italian Chapel", 5km east of town off the main Mutare road. You can almost feel the homesickness of the Italian POWs who built it during the 1940s, in memory of 71 of their fellows who died in captivity in Rhodesia. The interior of the simple, corrugated-iron-roofed building breathes Italy, every surface covered with **paintings**. One elaborately worked shrine has nostalgic scenes depicting St Francis in Italian fields and the Virgin in an arcaded Tuscan courtyard. But the real stars of the show are the meticulously painted **mock mosaics**, which you'd swear are real until you get closer. The chapel is an easy stopoff on the way to Kyle Game Park, just a short walk from the main road, next to an army base. Hitch, or catch any **bus** going beyond the Copota Mission turn-off on the Birchenough Bridge road.

Eating, drinking and nightlife

The inexpensive *Hidden Garden Café*, 30 Hughes St, next to Roselli Gallery (Mon–Fri 8.30am–4.30pm, Sat 8.30am–1pm), is the best place in town for **lunch**, both for its shady outdoor seating and the straightforward menu of chicken wings and chips, toasted sandwiches, pastas and salads. Of the several places that do cheap **takeaways** and snacks, *Ace Takeaway* in Josiah Togogara Avenue is much visited by overland trucks for its good burgers and chips. The coffee shop in the CNA newsagent in Robert Mugabe Way isn't bad for a quick cup of tea and a toasted sandwich or pie, and you'll find similar offerings but slower service at the *Tea Cosy* in the Meikles department store in the same road. For traditional Zimbabwean **sadza and stew**, *Dees Restaurant and Takeaway*, Shop 2, CABS Building in Simon Mazorodze Avenue, is conveniently central. The only place worth considering for **evening meals** is the *Flamboyant*, which does good English-style standards such as steaks and chicken and some decent vegetarian options.

Apart from that, the only other **nightlife** in central Masvingo takes place at the *Ritz Nite Spot* in Hellet Street (between Josiah Tongogara Street and Leopold Takawira Avenue), which has live music at weekends and is the only place in the town centre to jive. You'll hear local bands here, and although the musicians aren't always the most polished and the equipment not the best, it's an easy-going place that stays open till the early hours. On Sunday afternoons you can catch jazz and have a pub lunch or play pool at the *Picadilly Bar and Garden* at the same place.

Shopping

For provisions, the grocers along Robert Mugabe Street have **fresh produce**, or check out Mucheke market, alongside the bus terminus, which offers greater choice. You could also stock up at one of the big supermarkets: Balmain Spar, on the corner of Robert Mugabe Way and Simon Mazorodze Avenue, next to the Shell garage, has a reasonable selection of groceries, while Tsungai Supermarket in Hofmeyr Street (daily 7am–8pm) is handy for its long opening hours and good choice of tinned goods, pulses, grains, fresh fruit, vegetables and meat. On the way to Great Zimbabwe, the D.B. Stopover, 6.5km southeast of the *Flamboyant* along the Great Zimbabwe road, has a 24-hour garage and good Quik Spar supermarket (daily 7am–8pm), with a bakery and a range of groceries and alcohol, while at the rear you'll find a tiny market where small-time traders sell vegetables.

Other shopping tends to be equally functional. Locally made **handicrafts** are available at the stalls just past the publicity bureau; mainly crochet work and anonymous soapstone carving. There are better baskets – and a huge variety of crafts – for sale from the huge conglomeration of marketeers who gather in a 200-metre swath outside the entrance to Great Zimbabwe. The only shop that makes any real concessions to the taste of passing tourists is the Roselli Gallery, 39 Hughes St (Mon–Fri 9.30am–4pm, Sat 9.30am–12.30pm), which stocks local paintings, sculpture and ceramics.

Listings

Banks Barclays, Standard Chartered and Zimbank, all down Robert Mugabe Street, are open Mon, Tues, Thurs & Fri 8am–3pm, Wed 8am–1pm, Sat 8–11.30am.

Books and stationery are sold at several shops, and CNA in Robert Mugabe Way and Belmont Press in Josiah Tongogara Avenue have a fair collection of maps and travel guides as well as a range of South African publications.

Bureaux de change Travellers, Edgars clothes store, Robert Mugabe Way/Josiah Tongogara Avenue is conveniently central and open during normal shop hours; Avos at the *Chevron Hotel*, opposite the Publicity Association in Robert Mugabe Way, is open daily (7am–9pm).

Car rental Travelworld, 43 Hughes St (☎039/62131, fax 64205), represent Rent-a-Car and Hertz.

Doctor Dr Makurira (surgery ☎039/63460, home ☎62783).

Hospital Hay Robertson Street (☎039/62112).

Internet café Old Mutual Centre, Robert Mugabe Way (☎039/63659, mobile ☎011/208043, *hippolodge@usa.net*).

Pharmacies Masvingo Pharmacy, Kubatana Centre, 14/15 Hughes St (☎039/63884, after hours ☎64136); Barry Nell Chemist, 264a Josiah Tongogara Ave, between Hughes and Hofmeyr streets (☎039/62869, after hours 65787).

Police Robertson Street/Josiah Tongogara Avenue (☎039/62222 or 62223, hotline ☎64911).

Post office Hughes Street, between Leopold Takawira and Josiah Tongogara Avenue (Mon–Fri 8.30am–1pm & 2–4pm, Sat 8–11.30am).

Taxis Taxis line up outside the TM Supermarket, Simon Mazorodze Avenue, or around Mucheke Bus Terminus. Otherwise, phone Rixi (☎039/63453), who have the newest cabs in Masvingo, or Masvingo Taxis (☎039/65866).

Telephones There are card phones outside the main post office in Hughes Street and cards are widely available – the post office or newsagents/bookshops are usually a reliable bet. The Message Centre, at the back of Old Mutual Arcade in Robert Mugabe Way (Mon–Fri 8am–5pm, Sat 8am–noon), has a public phone, where you pay after completing your call.

Travel agents Travelworld, 43 Hughes St (☎039/62131 or 62456, fax 64205, *travlwld@samara.co.zw*), does coach bookings, car rental and can also arrange accommodation. The Internet Café, Old Mutual Centre, Robert Mugabe Way (☎039/63659, mobile ☎011/208043, *hippolodge@usa.net*), is especially good for backpackers wanting to arrange tours or other activities in the area.

Great Zimbabwe National Monument

On a continent more used to impermanent buildings of mud, wood and grass, **GREAT ZIMBABWE**, 28km southeast of Masvingo (daily 6am–6pm; US$5) is almost miraculous. For nearly a thousand years, ever since it was built, this mysterious city has exercised the imaginations of those who held it, and right up until the nineteenth century it inspired hundreds of other Shona stone palaces, in a unitary sphere of influence from the desert lands of the west to the Indian Ocean in the east. The first Europeans who saw it took it both as evidence of the rumoured riches of the country and proof that tentacles of classical civilization – Phoenicians, Egyptians, Gulf Arabs, they weren't sure who – had been here before and built in stone. And for nearly a hundred years, from the time of Rhodes's incursion to the present day, the struggle for symbolic possession of this central monument has shadowed the struggle for political liberation.

The word *zimbabwe* is derived from Shona phrases used freely to mean either "stone houses" or "venerated houses", which may have amounted to the same thing – buildings in stone being statements about permanence and power. Great Zimbabwe is the best known of the country's several hundred *zimbabwes*, the stone heart of a city of as many as 10,000 people, and the home of its ruler, who lived surrounded by his family, court and tributary rulers.

Getting there and site tours

Buses and minibuses run roughly every half-hour during the day from Masvingo to Morgenster Mission, dropping passengers at the turn-off, a kilometre from the monument. The best place to catch them is from outside the Technical College at the junction of the Beit Bridge road, about 1km south of Masvingo and the Old Great Zimbabwe road. Handier still, less frequent buses to Zano go right past Great Zimbabwe and continue along the lakeshore to beyond the dam wall, making them useful for all the accommodation along Mutirikwe's southern shore. **By car** from Masvingo, take the well-signposted turn-off on your left, about 4km out of town, and just keep going; car rental – not too expensive if there's a group of you – can be arranged through Travelworld (see Travel agents, above). **Hitching** the 26km from Masvingo isn't difficult either, though you may end up waiting for a while; stand opposite the craft sellers, past the Publicity Association office, or better still at the turn-off outside the Technical College. **Taxis** from Masvingo – hail them behind the TM Supermarket on Simon Mazorodze Avenue or around Mucheke Bus Terminus – cost around US$10 and will take up to four people.

A glossy and brief but solidly reliable **site guide** is available at the National Park entrance, where you buy your ticket: it's inexpensive, and pretty essential if you're not going on a guided tour. The entrance is also the place to latch onto one of the inexpensive **guided tours** that leave from around here (for tours from Masvingo to Great Zimbabwe, see p.239). You can easily make a day of Great Zimbabwe, so it's fortunate that there's a good **teashop**, with outdoor seating under some shady trees at the foot of the Hill Enclosure, where you can get cheap teas and toasted sandwiches.

Accommodation

Despite being one of Africa's most impressive ancient monuments and the inspiration behind the country's name, Great Zimbabwe has remained surprisingly undeveloped. That's starting to change, with the once-lone *Great Zimbabwe Hotel* now joined by a choice of lodges and self-catering **accommodation**, as well as a campsite – some options being within the bounds of the National Monument. Much of the accommodation along the southern Mutirikwe lakeshore is also very convenient for the ruins, most of it less than 10km away and generally far cheaper than the immediate environs of the ruins. Less handy are a couple of places on the north shore (see p.252), which also sell themselves as bases for visiting Great Zimbabwe but are actually some distance away, nearer the game park.

Around Great Zimbabwe

Great Zimbabwe Chalets and Campsite, within the grounds of Great Zimbabwe; book through Private Bag 9158 Masvingo (☎039/7055 or 7059). Clean, no-nonsense rondavels set on a low rocky ridge that has views of the monument, with twin beds, a hot plate and private showers and toilets in outside units. The nearby campsite is very pleasant with clean washing facilities and braai places. Rondavels and camping ①.

Great Zimbabwe Hotel, adjacent to the National Monument (☎039/62274). Nostalgic old-fashioned hotel that retains some of the atmosphere of its 1960s heyday and a reputation for poor service. Forty-seven comfortable en-suite rooms. ⑧.

Great Zimbabwe Lodges, within the grounds of Great Zimbabwe, book through the *Great Zimbabwe Hotel*. Nine two-bedroomed, thatch-roofed National Parks-style lodges, but more stylishly furnished. A lounge with cable TV and a well-equipped kitchen makes this a very comfortable self-catering option, but you pay for the undoubted privilege of being inside the grounds of the monument itself. ⑤.

Lodge at the Ancient City, book through Touch the Wild, 46 George Silundika St, PO Box 3447, Bulawayo (☎09/540922 or 540944, fax 229088, *touchwld@harare.iafrica.com*). Adjacent to the ruins with distant views of the Great Enclosure, the lodge is themed around the fantasy that you are living in the style of Zimbabwe ancient royalty. Huge, luxurious mock-adobe chalets are built around granite formations with decoration in pastiche Shona stonework. Some of the private verandahs overlook an area of indigenous woodland and a vlei in which a herd of eight semi-domesticated eland wander around. Meals are served in a cavernous banqueting hall. To relax you can dip in the pool or go for walks around the property, but the ruins themselves are too far to reach on foot. Children welcome. Full board ⑨.

Southern Lake Mutirikwe

Inn on Great Zimbabwe, 8km east of Great Zimbabwe on the lake road (PO Box 196; ☎039/64879 or 65083, *nj@mvo.samara.co.zw*). The best-value accommodation along the southern lake, this collection of ten comfortable hotel rooms, five self-catering chalets and nine budget rooms was formerly the popular *Norma Jeane's*, but was taken over by the Inns of Zimbabwe group and given a complete makeover in 1999. Set in magnificent gardens on a hill, some of the hotel rooms have lake views from their verandahs. The budget accommodation is in simple twin rooms that share a kitchen, washing facilities and an outdoor eating area, where there's a fire to sit around at night. Budget rooms ②, self-catering chalets ③, rooms ④.

Mutirikwe Lake Shore Lodges, Right on the waterfront, 33km from Masvingo and 8km from Great Zimbabwe; PO Box 518, Masvingo (☎039/7151 or 64878). Two-storey, self-contained self-catering rondavels each with a twin and two single rooms that are pretty unstylish, but clean at least. A swimming pool and huge grounds with indigenous trees on the water's edge (Mutirikwe Lake Cruises leave from its jetty) makes the setting extremely pleasing. The important Southern African essentials of fresh fish, meat and liquor are on sale at the small shop, while a small, mid-priced

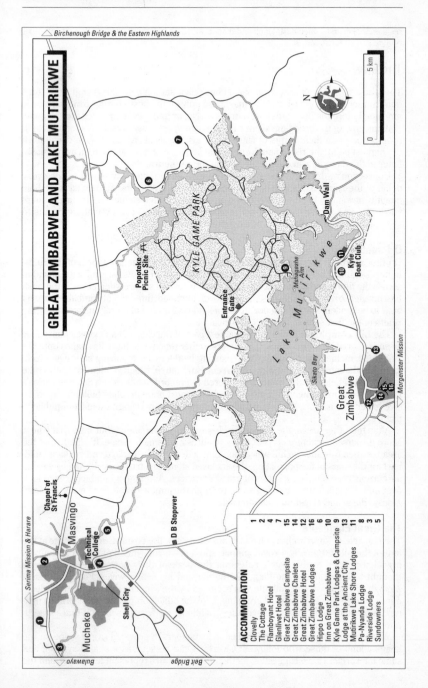

△ Birchenough Bridge & the Eastern Highlands

GREAT ZIMBABWE AND LAKE MUTIRIKWE

5 km

0

N

KYLE GAME PARK

Popoteke Picnic Site ⊼

Dam Wall

Kyle Boat Club

Entrance Gate

Lake Mutirikwe

Mshagashe Arm

Sikato Bay

Great Zimbabwe

▷ Morgenster Mission

Chapel of St Francis

◁ Serima Mission & Harare

Masvingo

Technical College

Muchecke

Shell City

D B Stopover

▽ Bulawayo

▽ Beit Bridge

ACCOMMODATION

Clovelly	1
The Cottage	2
Flamboyant Hotel	4
Glenlivet Hotel	7
Great Zimbabwe Campsite	15
Great Zimbabwe Chalets	14
Great Zimbabwe Hotel	12
Great Zimbabwe Lodges	16
Hippo Lodge	6
Inn on Great Zimbabwe	10
Kyle Game Park Lodges & Campsite	9
Lodge at the Ancient City	13
Mutirikwe Lake Shore Lodges	11
Pa-Nyanda Lodge	8
Riverside Lodge	3
Sundowners	5

restaurant is open for breakfast, lunch and dinner, with lake bream, chicken in a basket and other routine fare on the menu. ②.

The site

The whole Great Zimbabwe area has a nonchalant setting and, surprisingly, the ruins don't attract hordes of visitors. For maximum impact, the best **visiting times** are early morning before the heat and most tourists arrive, or in the evening, after they've gone. Walking among the brooding, silent rubble, you may even see how the Victorians could have been led on their flights of fancy about lost classical civilizations. At dawn, from the highest point, the rising sun drenches the expanse of bush and lake in a pink wash. Later in the day, you can escape the heat in the **museum**.

Unless you're driven by more than mere enthusiasm, you won't need to see every detail of the ruins; half a day is sufficient to see the highlights. There's an incredible quantity of walling, but it's mostly based on simple repeated elements. After a few hours you'll find you acquire a sort of architectural "vocabulary" and everything begins to seem, if no less alien, then part of a coherent vision.

Orientation

On first approach you can hardly discern more than the castellated form of the ruins' hilltop section. This is one of three main complexes of **walls**, spread with abandon across the lifting and dipping contours, covering several square kilometres. If the bush has invaded over the centuries, it was never intended thus: Great Zimbabwe wasn't built to be hidden, nor for defence. It was a loud declaration of power and wealth by the rulers of the first state in this part of Africa.

The **hill complex** is probably the earliest part of the city, and an extraordinary *tour de force* of organic architecture. Its builders, rather than try to force its shapes onto the landscape, melded their masonry with existing boulders, harmonizing nature and technology in the most beguiling way. The **Great Enclosure**, which you'll most likely come to first, down below to the south, has entered the record books as sub-Saharan Africa's greatest stone monument. It is also Zimbabwe's most photographed building, the massive tower and narrow, snaking parallel passage instantly recognizable from publicity pictures.

After the other areas, the **Valley Enclosure** offers variations, but little that's new. More dispersed structures repeat many features on a smaller scale. It's likely that the area between this and the hill was at one time a dense maze of *daga* and wooden buildings for the mass of the population, the enclosed stone constructions erected by wealthier citizens accessible via a series of grand entrances. Although a humbler area to look over now, it's still worth rambling about through the jumble of collapsed walls, set amid grassy thorn- and aloe-dotted countryside.

The Great Enclosure

The pinnacle of Rozvi architecture (see box on p.248), the **Great Enclosure** sits at the foot of the hill. Originally a **royal palace** and a powerful symbol of the community, it provided privacy to the state's rulers; at the peak of their power, the enclosure is thought to have housed the king, his mother and his senior wives. Following Great Zimbabwe's collapse, the building was occupied by the Mugabe dynasty, who headed a minor nineteenth-century tribal grouping. Like the other complexes, its walls are a mixture of fourteenth- to nineteenth-century traditional work, with some (at times inaccurate) modern reconstruction.

Whatever the **conical tower** signified to its builders, it provided ample scope for the imaginations of those who followed. Clearly, it can be seen as a phallic symbol, and some interpreters have suggested, further, that the **stairs** represent femininity, and the

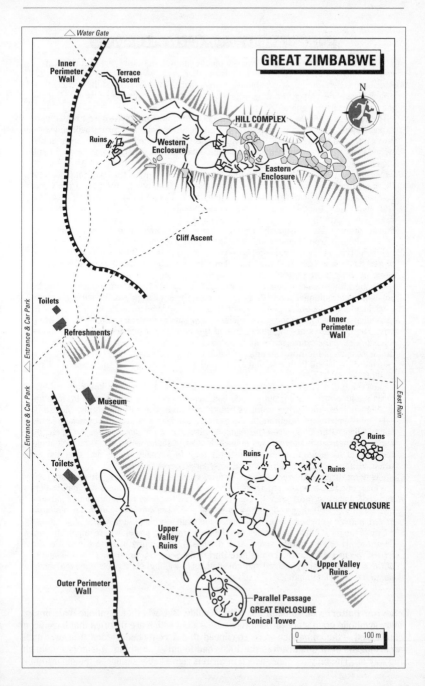

THE "LANGUAGE" OF ROZVI PLANNING

The architecture of Great Zimbabwe is a unique innovation of this part of Africa. Under its spreading cultural influence, hundreds of other *zimbabwes* were built across Central Africa, from Botswana to Mozambique. **Kame**, near Bulawayo, took up the architectural principles and developed the style, which became the means for any self-respecting ruling class to gain recognition and publicize itself.

The **walls** meander with a disturbing licence, confounding all Western architectural expectations. Their function was mainly symbolic; they twist and turn at will and were never intended to carry roofs. It was these walls that separated commoners from nobility, and you can still see the remains of monumental entrances that gave access to the ruling-class homesteads.

One of the reasons it's assumed that Great Zimbabwe wasn't a fortification is that there's no evidence of any doors in the **entrances**. The north entrance of the Great Enclosure, in particular, warrants a good long look. The problem of finishing off a wall without an abrupt and jarring halt is brilliantly resolved by curving the wall back in on itself. The **stairs** that take you up into the elevated world of the ruler are, meanwhile, fully incorporated as sensuously curving courses, incorporated into the wall's depth – all pure sculpture. Around and about – usually at entrances and particularly on the wall facing the cliff ascent of the hill complex – you'll notice **stone pillars**. It's likely they were topped by totems, which told you which family lived inside – a kind of street address. The *zimbabwe* birds were probably the totem of the royal family.

Although the walls are monumental in scale, the architectural **"language"** used is an adaptation of traditional Shona domestic themes; the circular pole and *daga* hut was the fundamental element of the Shona homestead, as it remains today in the rural areas. In the ruling-class sector, stone walls adjoined *daga* huts to form an enclosed family living unit. The complexes are organized around the principle of **privacy**: important homes were located at the centre, and walls radiated out to provide secluded courtyards. As they do today, each of the **homesteads** consisted of several huts arranged in a swept, open courtyard – a useful firebreak, and clear space in which intruders, snakes and rodents could be spotted.

Each room had a function. At the heart of the home lay the **kitchen** building, with the hearth at its centre. Each group of huts had stepped platforms, still present in traditional Shona homes, to display a woman's **household pots**. The pots are highly valued vessels and the platforms celebrate the household, marriage and woman's centrality in the family. Close to the kitchen was the main **sleeping** unit, where married couples spent the night together, but in polygamous households the husband would rotate himself about the huts of his several wives. Adolescents slept in sexually segregated dormitories, where visitors would stay if there were no separate guest quarters.

The homestead also included places for **food storage** and **livestock**. The granary took the form of a hut, but had a metre-high raised floor as protection against damp, insects and rodents; all surfaces were thoroughly plastered to preserve the precious food supply. There was a chicken coop (often on stilts), and a kraal for cattle or goats, although prized animals were sometimes kept inside the main sleeping hut in a special partition.

One of the most important spaces was the **dare** (meeting place), where important family questions or community issues were discussed. Frequently beneath the shade of a tree, it was located near the homestead. During the Second Chimurenga the official title of the supreme military council and government-in-waiting, *Dare re-Chimurenga*, incorporated this ancient notion.

chevron patterns on some of the walls, fertility. But, whether symbolic male organ, hefty symbolic grain store or prototype safe – all of which are theories that have been considered – the romantics were convinced that it contained hidden treasure, until archeologists delved beneath in the 1920s and found . . . nothing. It is in fact solid all the way up. The bulging cone, which in form is remarkably similar to the pillar tombs of the East African coast, marks the highest accomplishment of Rozvi masonry skills, and was one of their last constructions. The top of the pillar, now decapitated, was once decorated with three zigzagging lines. Look on the east side of the outer wall for the best remaining example of these.

Leading out of the tower enclosure, a **parallel passage** stretches 70m to the north entrance. It gives a good idea of the value of privacy to the Rozvi rulers, screening their domestic arrangements from even the privileged few invited inside. You can walk to the tower enclosure, for example, or even to the central area, and still not see where the main huts were. Look, too, at the improvements in Rozvi masonry skills as they gained experience – the inner wall was built at least a century earlier than the smoother, more accurately laid, outer leaf.

The Hill Enclosure

The oldest inhabited part of Great Zimbabwe, the **Hill Enclosure** was for some time known as the "acropolis", a kind of Hellenic compulsion having gripped some of the early observers. It's perhaps even more intriguing than the Great Enclosure, with its slender entrances and passages working their way around enormous balancing boulders. It's also harder work to get to, requiring a steep ascent of one of several stepped routes: this deters a fair proportion of the visitors who ramble about the tower below. But the rewards – at the least, a peaceful view over the kopjes, vleis and beyond to Lake Mutirikwe – are well worth the effort.

This hill was the site of the earliest settlement of simple **daga** and **pole huts**, built some time around the eleventh century. The increasing wealth of the growing state later made the building of stone walls possible. Like the Great Enclosure, the Hill Complex was originally a **royal palace**. It seems likely, however, that it later became the seat of a Rozvi **spirit medium** – the religious counterpart to the secular king's court, some 80m below in the Great Enclosure.

The older hill site would naturally have had closer contact with the Rozvi **ancestors** who once dwelt there than the newer and more temporal great enclosure. A flight of **curved steps** leads to a space sealed off with a huge rock, probably the domain of spirit mediums who communed with the ancestors here and participated in healing ceremonies. It feels a powerful place and it's wonderful to investigate the crevices, openings and warren of passages that sometimes bring you unnervingly close to sheer drops.

The museum

Like all great archeological sites, the ruins of Great Zimbabwe have been diligently pillaged over the years and bits and pieces from it have turned up all over the world, so you're not going to see the full array of finds here. Having said that, the site **museum** (daily 8am–4.30pm; free), near the entrance to the Great Enclosure, which was upgraded in 1999, has enough worthwhile exhibits to justify a visit. Most notable among these are the seven and a half **soapstone birds** – the inspiration behind the ubiquitous Zimbabwean symbol, and much copied these days by modern airport artists. Mystery surrounds the significance of these strange, composite creatures, which have been identified as badly executed fish eagles by ornithologists, though archeologists doubt they signify real birds at all, suggesting, rather, that they are mythological.

Iron tools such as hoes may seem pretty ordinary items nowadays, but the ones on display here were extremely valuable possessions, and very expensive to make in terms of labour and organization. A hoe was like a car – a tribute item of conspicuous royal wealth – and just one was valuable enough to seal a marriage. Other metal tools like gongs, strikers and spears were also royal regalia, and the

THE STRUGGLE FOR GREAT ZIMBABWE

For nearly four centuries, European knowledge of Great Zimbabwe was based entirely on hearsay. One of the earliest accounts came from the Portuguese, **Gaspar Veloso**, who wrote of "a fortress of the King of Monomotapa, which he is making of stone without mortar". Almost a hundred years later, a fellow countryman, **Brother Joas dos Boas**, had elaborated this modest account into a fantasy of biblical dimensions. He wrote that "these houses were in olden times the trading depots of the Queen of Sheba, and that from these depots they used to bring her much gold".

It was the gold that brought a glint to the eyes of European adventurers in the nineteenth-century scramble for Africa. **Adam Render**, a German hunter, was the first white to set eyes on the ruins of Great Zimbabwe, in 1871, later showing them to **Carl Mauch**, a compatriot geologist, who took the credit for "discovering" them. Clearly no stranger to embroidering the truth, Mauch went on to explain that "the fortress on the hill was a copy of King Solomon's Temple".

But it was in the 1890s that these overblown musings took on a serious significance that ran parallel to the ruthless **colonization** that was beginning in Rhodesia. Great Zimbabwe was a beacon that couldn't be ignored. Adventurers were eager to believe that it was the remains of a long-gone and wealthy civilization centred in Mashonaland, and that there were precious relics and gold for the taking. At the same time, none of the Victorian entrepreneurs or politicians who were poising themselves to exploit Mashonaland's wealth wanted to believe that the black people they planned to subjugate were capable of establishing a complex social system. To think otherwise would make nonsense of the supposed civilizing mission with which they wrapped the colonial ideology.

It was to resolve this glaring contradiction that the so-called "**Mystery of Zimbabwe**" evolved. The hard-headed Rhodes was the first to see the political importance of the issue, and in 1893 he employed an amateur antiquarian, **Theodore Bent**, to excavate the stones. After all his digging and delving, Bent was disgusted to find that "everything was native". This, however, didn't stop him concluding that an "ancient Mediterranean race" was responsible for the buildings. He nominated as candidates "the mythical Pelasgi who inhabited the shores of Greece", Britons, Phoenicians, Arabs, Romans, Persians, Egyptians or "Hebrews" – anyone, in fact, but Africans.

In 1905, **David Randall-McIver** became the first professional archeologist to investigate Great Zimbabwe. He concluded that the buildings were unmistakably African and of medieval date – and that there wasn't a shred of evidence for European or Oriental involvement. White outrage at this distasteful news was voiced by the journalist R.N. Hall, who lambasted McIver's lack of firsthand knowledge of local Africans, asserting that no "authority" believed in "McIver's hazarded hypothesis of 'the natural and unaided evolution of the negroid'". The battle lines were clearly drawn – the professionals standing their ground and building on the findings of McIver, while the white community and white politicians searched more and more frantically for some scrap of ammunition to shoot down the indigenous origin hypothesis.

As the **liberation struggle** escalated, the battle to reclaim the ruins as African heritage intensified. By the time of UDI in 1965 there was scarcely any doubt at the National Historical Monuments Commission that Great Zimbabwe was the work of a powerful indigenous culture that had once dominated the region. Responding to the discomforting onslaught of scientific findings, Colonel Hartley, MP for Victoria Province, rose in Parliament in 1969 to denounce the Commission, whose portrayal of the "ruins as only being of Bantu origin" he felt should be "corrected".

quantity discovered in the royal hoard shows the extent of the gulf between rich and poor at Great Zimbabwe. While the king had stacks of symbolic, but functionally useless, metal objects, an ordinary peasant would own just one or two utilitarian items.

The following year, **censorship** prevented official publications – guidebooks, museum displays, school textbooks, radio programmes, newspapers and films – from stating unequivocally that Great Zimbabwe was an African creation. Yet, while explanations like the Queen of Sheba fantasy implied BC origins, **radiocarbon dating** revealed that the state flourished after 1000 AD. The curator at the ruins commented that not since Nazi Germany had archeology been so brazenly censored, and for most Rhodesian archeologists it was the last straw. **Peter Garlake**, the leading expert on Great Zimbabwe, left Rhodesia. Throughout the 1970s the Rhodesian Front regime and its white supporters were left free to wallow in dreamland theories, without fear of informed contradiction.

CURRENT THINKING

Garlake returned home in 1981, following Independence, to continue his work, and, with censorship set aside, serious research into Great Zimbabwe resumed. Controversy certainly continues among researchers, but it's about detail rather than substance. It's generally agreed now that **Shona speakers** conceived and built Great Zimbabwe themselves, in response to local conditions.

One theory asserts that the **Zimbabwe state** was transformed from an undistinguished village to a regional power by its pivotal position near the head of the Save River, which placed it perfectly to control the thirteenth-century **gold trade** between Matabeleland and Sofala on the coast. Taxes increased the economic and political power of its ruling class, enabling it to employ craftsmen such as stonecarvers, goldsmiths and stonemasons. The rulers found themselves able to finance public works – the great walls – which enhanced their prestige and helped to cement the growing state that was evolving.

Peter Garlake, however, emphasizes the primacy of cattle in the growth of the Zimbabwe state, playing down trade as the kingpin of its economy. Garlake's scenario is less titillating than the idea of a trans-African gold trade focused on Great Zimbabwe, but it has a simple, compelling elegance. He points out that Great Zimbabwe, like a number of other similar centres, is positioned at the interface of the highveld and the lowveld, and he argues that the Great Zimbabwe state evolved to cope with a complex **herding system** that grazed huge areas of land. In the hot, wet season, cattle fed on the fresh grass of the highveld; in the winter they were herded to the better-watered lowveld when the risk of sleeping sickness was at its lowest. This method required a centralized state that was powerful enough to control a vast territory. The simplest way to coordinate cattle movement was as a single herd – the king's property, with animals granted to subjects for private use – moved en masse and protected by armies of men. Organized companies of men could also defend large territories and form a labour force to build walls.

The strength of Garlake's interpretation is that it corresponds to the way powerful cattle-owning states, like the Ndebele, were organized in recent times. Trade could simply have been a sideline, completely consistent with imported goods discovered at Great Zimbabwe. And in the end what made Zimbabwe great – **centralization** – was what destroyed it. Although Great Zimbabwe revolutionized the state, it failed to develop solutions to the problems of overpopulation that resulted. By the mid-fifteenth century, the lands around the capital had lost their fertility, game was hunted out, firewood was in short supply, and people began to drift away.

Although Great Zimbabwe collapsed, its culture continued. Some Rozvi migrants went west, and took their wall-building know-how with them, merging with the Leopard's Kopje platform-makers of the west at Kame, near Bulawayo (see p.178).

A small collection of **Oriental goods** provides evidence of Great Zimbabwe's trading links. From the twelfth century onwards, the Rozvis were indirectly in contact with the coast, the Islamic world and even China. Finds include Indian beads, crockery from China and Persia, and odds and ends brought via Swahili traders.

Lake Mutirikwe and the Kyle Game Park

LAKE MUTIRIKWE is an obvious destination to pair with Great Zimbabwe, just 6km away from its southern shore. Its north shore, a peaceful, undemanding place, has the draws of rhino and plains game in its game reserve. Southern Lake Mutirikwe is a collection of campsites and resorts, where people come to boat, fish and water-ski. Not as attractive as the north, the south bank's huge advantage is that it's near enough to walk or hitch to from Great Zimbabwe. Mutirikwe's much less developed north bank is most easily approached along the Masvingo–Birchenough Bridge road, rather than via the southern lake. While the route along the southern shore and the dam wall is highly scenic, you should ignore all the maps that show it as mainly tarred, as most of it is dirt track with some very poor sections. If you're taking this route, allow a couple of hours for the ninety-kilometre journey from Masvingo back to the main road.

Zimbabwe's second largest lake – artificial like almost all the rest – Mutirikwe has a varied shoreline of rocky beaches, wooded backdrops and sheer cliffs. Its small islands are secure refuge to a booming **bird** population, and the compact **Kyle Game Park** on the north bank hosts the country's biggest cross-section of **antelope** species, as well as a thriving herd of **white rhinos** – all free from predators.

The lake is not merely recreational – its *raison d'être* is to irrigate Hippo Valley and Triangle, the mammoth sugar estates to the south. When water levels dropped drastically after the failed rains of the early 1990s, rendering the lake a muddy pool by 1996, the plantations withered, causing shortages of sugar, food riots and leaving Zimbabwe with no other choice than to import sugar, at great expense. Happily, the good rains of 1997 and ensuing years brought it up to over seventy percent of its capacity in 1999 – its highest level since 1982.

Accommodation

North-shore **accommodation** is cheap and low-key and more about enjoying a lakeside retreat than seeing Great Zimbabwe, which is reached either along fifty-or-so kilometres of sometimes pretty rough dirt road, or a more circuitous but much faster 70km via Masvingo, mostly on tar. North-shore accommodation is more convenient for the game park, which is some 40km away, or you can stay in the park itself. If you're self-catering, bring all your supplies as there are no shops around here. For places to stay along the southern shores see the listings under Great Zimbabwe on p.245.

Glenlivet Hotel, 38km east of Masvingo and 54km from Great Zimbabwe (☎ & fax 039/66041). A 1960s hotel with a neglected atmosphere that some might find attractive – the setting at the foot of a large hill with lake views certainly is. Its ten en-suite rooms are plain, clean and furnished with old, but serviceable, furniture. A cheap self-catering cottage is also available. Too far to be a convenient base for Great Zimbabwe, it's a place for some undemanding leisure, aided by the swimming pool, tennis court and sauna. Self-catering cottage ①, rooms ②.

Hippo Lodge, 37km east of Masvingo and 6km south of the Masvingo–Birchenough Bridge road (☎039/63659, mobile ☎011/208043, *hippolodge@usa.net*). Simple but well-organized en-suite thatched accommodation 500m from the shore on the eastern side of Lake Mutirikwe share a braai place and outdoor eating enclosure. Open-plan twin chalets have a bedroom, kitchenette, sitting area, shower and verandah. Further up the hill are more spacious family chalets that sleep two or four people. Features a backpacker special package of free transport to Great Zimbabwe and a morning guided tour; also an afternoon transfer from town to lodge and from lodge to bus terminus. Also offers 15min free Internet access. Half-board backpacker rate, sharing chalets ① exclusive use of chalet ②.

Kyle Game Park Lodges and Campsite, 37km southeast of Masvingo in the game reserve; advance booking through National Parks Central Bookings in Harare or Bulawayo; standby booking at Kyle (☎039/62913). One- and three-bedroom fully equipped self-catering lodges along the water with enchanting views – better than the resorts on the south shore. Elephant Lodge at the

---

GAME CRUISES

Mutirikwe Lake Cruises launches onto the lake daily from *Mutirikwe Lake Shore Lodges* on game-viewing excursions and offers two-hour morning, afternoon (US$10 per person) and lunchtime **cruises** (US$15), meandering along the shoreline of Kyle Game Park. Booze can be bought from the *Lake Shore Lodges* and brought on board. If you want to see wildlife drinking, the afternoon is best, but don't expect to see the park's rhinos – you'll stand a better chance of this on a game drive. Cruises can be booked at the *Great Zimbabwe Hotel* (☎039/62274) or on 039/62449, 64173 or 64187, mobile ☎011/209517 or 011/209516.

---

summit of the hill has the most commanding lake vista. If you're on a budget, bear in mind that you'll have to pay park entrance fees on top. Lodges and camping ⑤.

Kyle Game Park

Kyle Game Park on the north shore, 33km east of Masvingo (daily 7am–6pm; US$10), has no big cats or elephants, but you'll see a whole range of herbivores – including buffalo, warthog, white rhino, giraffe, zebra and an astonishing variety of antelope – as well as numbers of hippos. The terrain ranges from grassland to wooded clumps and rocky outcrops. Some of the kopjes in the southeast are adorned with **rock paintings**, though none is especially notable. The easiest to reach are the ones signposted above Kyle Boat Club, a couple of kilometres past the Mutirikwe Lake Shore Lodges.

For a real treat, take a ninety-minute **guided horse-ride** through the park. No experience is required, but if you're proficient you can get permission from the warden for serious riding. At any pace, though, you can get to within a whisker of the wildlife. Rides can be arranged at park headquarters near the campsite and are an excellent way to see rhinos. With a **car** you can meander around the park's 64-kilometre network of dirt tracks. The most reliable source of information is the *Tourist Map of Lake Kyle and Great Zimbabwe*, but park headquarters often runs out of this; if possible, plan ahead and try to buy one from the Surveyor General's Office in Harare. The Masvingo Publicity Association also has an adequate map (see p.239).

There are two **picnic sites** with braai facilities and toilets (camping not permitted) – **Mtilikwe**, on the point, and the more remote **Popoteke** on the river. The approach to the latter is often sentinelled by zebra along the road, who relish its wooded surroundings.

Even without your own transport, it is still possible to get around. The official **walking area** is **Mshagashe Arm**, a small peninsula around the lodges and campsite. The walks aren't in the game park proper, but you can get to the lakeside and see **hippos**. Stroll down to the water, sit quietly on the rocks and you may be lucky enough to get a close view through binoculars. Be cautious, though: it's easy to regard these amusing snorters as some kind of oversized aquatic pigs, but they kill more people than any other mammal in Africa. Generally they mind their own business but, if threatened, can attack viciously. The real danger is getting between them and their element – water. Be vigilant during their landing period after sunset, and especially at dawn, when they're plodding sleepily back to the lake or river.

Serima Mission

Central Mashonaland is an unlikely place for a medieval church, but the **Serima Mission**, north of Masvingo, 20km from the road to Mvuma, does a more than competent impersonation. One of the most striking buildings in Zimbabwe, its construction began in the 1940s and was completed during the following decade. In the spirit of Europe's medieval churches, the construction and interior decoration was carried out by members of the local community over an extended period of time.

The mission was founded by Swiss priest-architect **Father John Groeber** in 1948. The carved doors, beams and altar were all produced by pupils at the mission school between 1956 and 1959, training that was intended to further Christian beliefs. West and Central African carved masks were used as models for the students, and among former pupils of the school is Zimbabwe's leading stone sculptor, Nicholas Mukomberanwa. You step inside the church into a pure space that feels sculpted from the solid shafts of light patterning the walls from clerestory windows. Gloriously carved totem-like timber columns, worked into the forms of African angels, rise 10m from floor to ceiling, and at the centre a crucifix is similarly sculpted. The materials are all pared back: simple concrete, furnished with benches, makes the superb carvings on every wall stand out.

Serima is tricky to get to and poorly signposted. Without your own transport, the best bet is to get the **bus** that passes through Serima four times weekly on its way from Harare to Gutu. If you are **driving**, make for Chatsworth and keep going, turning left at the first dirt road after the river; the church is more or less straight down this road, but keep asking directions as you go. Or, much easier, take the Felixburg turn-off from the main Harare–Masvingo road; the mission is signposted from this dirt track. This turn-off is the best place to try **hitching** from, but expect to wait.

Triangle and Chiredzi

Neither **Triangle** nor **Chiredzi**, the main towns south of Masvingo, provide any incentive to venture deeper in the lowveld, but they do make diverting stops on the way to Gonarezhou, the ultimate destination in the southeast. Callow children of a 1960s sugar boom, with little evidence of rooted urban culture, both are useful places for refreshments or to stretch your legs, but have little more to offer.

Triangle
TRIANGLE, 164km south of Masvingo, is without doubt the sugar capital of Zimbabwe, its surroundings full of memories of **Thomas Murray MacDougall**, an old-style pioneering Scotsman who wrestled with hostile conditions to green the lowveld with endless expanses of cane (see box). Now the archetypal company town, all Triangle's trimly arrayed facilities – schools, hospitals, housing and recreational facilities – are out of the same packet. The Triangle corporate logo (the company is now owned by Anglo-American Corporation) is everywhere, on vehicles, buildings and signs. Local workers from Triangle speak very proudly about corporate excellence, and of the beautiful greenness of the place in times of plenty.

You can hang about a bit, but there's nowhere to stay and not really very much to do, except visit the **MacDougall Museum** in the pioneer's former house (daily 8.30–9.30am & 3.30–4.30pm; small entrance fee). His whole heroic life story is told with excellent old photographs and school-project stuff on how sugar is grown and refined.

Chiredzi
CHIREDZI, 20km east of Triangle, is a creation of the 1960s, established as a centre for the fast-growing lowveld region and still expanding today. It's neatly laid out and pretty, with baobab-specked hills, but there's nothing to do and the town's only interest for travellers is as a stopoff for Gonarezhou. You'll find the basics in the centre – **banks**, **post office** and **shops** – but what life exists is around the bus station. Turn down Msasa Drive and left into Lion Drive, about 1km from the centre: here you'll find cheap **food**, and **taxis** and **buses** for Harare, Bulawayo, Masvingo and Mutare.

MACDOUGALL SUGAR

Thomas Murray MacDougall first encountered sugar cane in Demarara, British Guyana, where he had arrived, aged 14, after running away to sea from Britain on an Argentine cattle boat. After World War I he fetched up in Rhodesia, where he was granted a vast tract of dry lowveld. Here he began by grazing cattle, under a registered brand – a triangle – bought from a bankrupt rancher, but his fortunes collapsed in 1924 and he turned to agriculture. Despite official scorn, he was determined to prove that, properly irrigated, the country's parched southeast could be productive.

He spent the next seven obsessive years boring 420m through granite to bring the waters of the Mutirikwe River onto his land and, in 1931, at last managed to grow wheat, cotton, fruit and tobacco. However, large flocks of quelea birds and swarms of locusts feasted on his crops. On the verge of despair, MacDougall recalled his Demarara days and applied to import sugar plants. The unhelpful government gave him permission to bring three pieces of cane from the Natal sugar estates in South Africa: MacDougall brought his three sticks, and a whole lot more, in bundles hidden beneath his car. The experiment was an unqualified success and the **Triangle Sugar Estates** company was formed in 1939 – just in time to profit from World War II.

Only then did the government take notice and begin work on the lowveld's comprehensive **irrigation scheme**. Although the land is dry much of the year, around a third of Zimbabwe's rainfall run-off flows through the Save and Runde River catchment areas. There was enough water – it just needed storing on its way to the Indian Ocean – and Lake Mutirikwe was created from that need in 1961.

If you find yourself stranded and in need of a **hotel**, the business-oriented *Nesbitt Arms*, 238 Marula Drive (☎031/5071 or 5162–3; ③), a couple of minutes' walk from the main street, is the only option in town. They also do toasted snacks, drinks and teas on a very pleasant shaded terrace. A couple of alternatives to staying in Chiredzi are the *Hippo Valley Club*, about 10km southwest of town on a poorly maintained tar road (☎031/3360–1, fax 3363; ②), which has extremely reasonable chalets and a swimming pool surrounded by sugar-cane fields, or a further 8km along a dirt road the more luxurious *Mteri Lodges* (book through the club; half-board ④), on the shore of a small artificial lake; it's a good spot for families with a pool, fishing and birding.

Gonarezhou National Park

Designated a national park in 1967, remote and undeveloped **GONAREZHOU** is the second largest, yet least-known, game reserve in Zimbabwe. Adjoining Mozambique, this beautiful tract was closed for several years during the Mozambican civil war and subsequent droughts. During the 1990s, game populations made a gratifying recovery, especially around the Save–Runde river confluence. Despite the fact that the 5000-square-kilometre park encompasses an inspiring wilderness area, it attracts only the occasional tourist, a fact that reflects both its remoteness and its scant facilities, which amount to a few lodges in the southwest and some pretty basic campsites. During the 1980s and early 1990s, access was restricted to Zimbabweans and, these days, they and South Africans in their own 4WD vehicles are the only independent travellers you're likely to encounter here. Most other visitors come as part of an organized walking safari or stay in one of the handful of lodges in private game reserves just outside the park.

Some history

Gonarezhou (or Gona-Re-Zhou) derives from a Shona name meaning "place of the elephants", and has long been renowned as a source of highly marketable ivory, its tuskers being inordinately well endowed. In pre-colonial times, Arab ships are reputed to have navigated the Save River from the Indian Ocean to trade in ivory, gold and slaves. The region's current inhabitants, **Shangaan** people, migrated to southeast Zimbabwe and neighbouring areas of Mozambique in the early nineteenth century, fleeing from the storm of conquest unleashed by Shaka in what is now South Africa's Kwazulu-Natal province (see p.346). You'll still sometimes stumble across grain-grinding stones and remnants of huts left by the Shangaan, who were moved when the park was opened.

In the 1920s, the area was the stamping ground of the notorious poacher, **Cecil Barnard**, who felled the elephant Dhlulamithi ("Taller-than-the-Trees") here. As his name suggests, Dhlulamithi was huge; his tusks were reckoned to be the largest taken south of the Zambezi, with a combined weight of 110kg.

The 1980s and 1990s saw rifles replaced by automatic weapons and the park was ravaged by **poaching**, perpetrated by commercial poachers, soldiers from Zimbabwe, Mozambique and South Africa and, to a lesser extent, the Shangaan. Combined with drastic **culling** for tsetse fly control, and the ring-barking of beautiful trees, the illegal slaughter seriously depleted game stocks. Given the extent of the blood-letting, it's little surprise that Gonarezhou's **elephants** still either charge or run away and according to National Parks, they "bear a grudge against man due to persecution and harassment

over the years". Visitors are warned to be extremely cautious when encountering them, a warning you should not take lightly.

The good news is that animal numbers have been increasing over the past few years, due mainly to local **conservation initiatives** such as the Mahenye Campfire Project; combined with dynamic conservation work in the adjoining Malilangwe Game Reserve, this has given local people a stake in game preservation and helped to curb poaching.

Getting there and transport

Two distinct regions have been developed for visitors to Gonarezhou: **Chipinda Pools** in the Save–Runde subregion to the north, accessed via Chiredzi, roughly 50km to its north, and **Mabalauta** in the Mwenezi subregion to the southwest, reached from the Masvingo–Beit Bridge road. The best way to reach the south of Gonarezhou is to turn off at Mwenezi police station, 20km south of Rutenga on the main Masvingo–Beit Bridge road: 105km of dirt track brings you to the warden's office at Mabalauta, while Swimuwini Camp lies 8km further on. Sedan cars can make it, but a high-clearance vehicle is recommended as it will allow you to see more of the park. Note, too, that the road running through Gonarezhou from the north is awful and visitors are not advised to use it. As the park is so large and the road between these two regions virtually impossible to traverse, you basically have to choose between them.

Unless you are highly experienced, intrepid and equipped with a 4WD vehicle, Gonarezhou is not a place to attempt on your own. There are scant facilities and no shops, filling stations or even running water in most of the park. Unless you come as a guest at one of the private lodges or on an organized safari, there's no transport to get you there and no game drives once you arrive.

Accommodation

Most visitors to Gonarezhou stay in one of the **lodges** in the conservancies bordering the park, and take advantage of resident professional guides. An equally recommended alternative is to join a walking safari (see box, p.258) on which you'll camp, led by a licensed hunter-guide and tracker, whose knowledge will hugely enrich your experience.

Private lodges

There are no **private lodges** inside Gonarezhou itself; the best are on its borders in one of the neighbouring conservancies. They offer far greater luxury than Parks lodges as well as good, if not better, game-viewing prospects.

Chilo Gorge Safari Lodge Zimbabwe Sun Hotels, Travel Centre, 93 Jason Moyo Ave, Harare (☎04/736644–5, fax 736646, *zimsuncro@zimsun.gaia.co.zw*). Situated along the Save, adjacent to the northeast boundary of Gonarezhou, Chilo has fourteen twin-bedded en-suite lodges on the edge of a gorge with spectacular views down to the river. Electricity, faxes and phones suggest that it's geared to a business clientele, who don't quite want to get away from it all. Apart from the usual game walks and drives, you can also visit a nearby Shangaan village. Guests fly in by light aircraft to the landing strip 5km away, from which they are transferred by safari vehicle. US$215 per person per night.

Nduna Safari Lodge, PO Box HG940, Highlands, Harare (☎04/734293, fax 703633–4, *safari@icon.co.zw*). The pick of the private lodges, located in the Malilangwe Private Game Reserve on the northern edge of the park, the camp is set beneath shady trees on the edge of a rocky outcrop. Six luxury stone chalets enjoy spectacular views over a 7km lake. Activities include game viewing by vehicle, on foot or by canoe, as well as visits to San rock-art sites. The only private lodge you can drive to, it's 30min on tar from Chiredzi. US$200 per person per night.

Mahenye Safari Lodge, Zimbabwe Sun Hotels (see *Chilo Gorge* above). Situated close to the Save–Runde confluence, this luxurious lodge is set among riverine trees on the edge of a wide, though invariably dry, river. Arguably the most beautiful section of the park, the surrounding countryside is a birdwatcher's paradise, and ideal for the walks and game drives run for hotel guests. US$200 per person per night.

National Parks chalets and campsites

Gonarezhou's only **National Parks chalets**, each with its own baobab overlooking the Mwenezi River, are at Swimuwini in the southern Mwenezi subregion. The remaining accommodation throughout the park is at **campsites** where facilities are often pretty primitive and you may even have to dig in dry river beds for drinking water. Most people who camp do so in the northern Save–Runde subregion at **Chipinda Pools**, where the site is set under trees overlooking pools that are alive with crocs and hippos (but not that great for other animals). It's the best equipped of all the campsites, with the luxury of hot showers and flush loos, gazebos and braai places. Open throughout the year, it's accessible with an ordinary car, although anywhere beyond is 4WD territory that is only open from May 1 until October 31. The site lies equidistant from Harare and Bulawayo (550km), and 59km from Chiredzi: take the signposted dirt road 20km east of Chiredzi. As there are no stores or filling stations beyond Chiredzi, bring everything you need. Elsewhere in the Save–Runde subregion, there are campsites along the Runde River, with room for one party only at each spot. Facilities are basic, with long-drop toilets, water has to be drawn from river pools, and all rubbish taken away with you. Book through the National Parks offices in Harare and Bulawayo.

The Park

Gonarezhou's dominant features are the Save and Runde rivers (more often than not mere sandy swaths dotted with pools), embracing the northeastern third of the park between them and the towering Chilojo cliffs, just south of the Runde. Most visitors enter the park at **Chipinda Pools**, about 50km southeast of Chiredzi, and spend the night here at the campsite. From here you can drive to the rudimentary campsites near the Save–Runde river confluence, a difficult four-hour journey passing through kilometres of dull mopane and combretum woodland. En route, however, two hours from Chipinda Pools are the much-photographed **Chilojo Cliffs**, towering red-and-ochre sandstone precipices that are as impressive when seen from the road below as from the viewing platform erected by Operation Raleigh on top of the escarpment. Look out for nesting storks soaring about the castellated formations of the outcrops. Once at the **Save–Runde confluence**, you're greeted by a wild and beautiful landscape of rich riverine vegetation, huge nyala berry and fever trees, ancient baobabs and dense thickets of ilala palms. Here you stand a much better than average chance of sighting big game.

WALKING SAFARIS

Khangela Safaris offer a **walking adventure** to Gonarezhou led by outstanding professional guide, Mike Scott, who'll not only take you out to track dangerous game, but also cooks superb bush meals and will tell you everything you could want to know about local flora and fauna. Taking in the Chilojo Cliffs and beautiful riverine areas around the Runde and Save, prices are US$130 per person per day. Khangela also offers a Wild East adventure package, walking in some of the most unexplored regions of Zimbabwe's southeast, spending four nights each in **Gonarezhou** and the **Chimanimani Mountains**, and one night each at **Great Zimbabwe** and **Chirinda Forest**. The fully inclusive price for the ten nights is US$1000. For information and booking, contact Mike or Anna Scott, PO Box FM 296, Famona, Bulawayo (☎09/49733, fax 78081, mobile ☎091/234676 or 023/406981, *scott@gatorzw.com*).

The highlight of the southern **Mwenezi subregion** is Buffalo Bend on the Mwenezi River, close to Mabalauta National Park camp, which has a reputation for attracting large concentrations of game in the dry season.

In the vicinity of the park, a number of private conservancies complement Gonarezhou. One of the most ambitious and successful is the 400-square-kilometre **Malilangwe Private Game Reserve**, abutting Gonarezhou's northeast, owned by the Malilangwe Conservation Trust, a non-profit organization dedicated to creating a model for conservation in Africa. Underpinning the project is the belief that the best way of ensuring the survival of wildlife is by creating a contented local community that benefits from it.

As far as **wildlife** goes, Gonarezhou is best known for its tetchy elephants, of which there are estimated to be between 7000 and 8000, but there are also respectable numbers of buffalo, impala, kudu, giraffe, zebra and hippos. Amongst the antelope that inhabit the park, eland, sable, roan and reedbuck are fewer than one might expect for a wilderness of this size. On the other hand, the diverse habitat of the lower Runde harbours no less than six species of very pretty antelope not normally found together: duiker, steenbok, oribi, grysbok, klipspringer and suni, collectively known as "the small six". Rare nyala antelope are another prize of this park, often found in the woodland at the Save–Runde river confluence. Lions stalk the park but aren't seen that often, and the odds of seeing cheetah are low: there are thought to be fewer than thirty.

Birdlife flourishes in the park – an impressive four hundred species have been recorded. Notable sightings include green coucal, Pel's fishing owl, brown-throated golden weaver, narina trogon and mottled spinetail.

Towards the Eastern Highlands

Masvingo is well connected by road to the Eastern Highlands, with Mutare, its principal town (297km distant; see p.264), and Chimanimani, its ultimate mountain getaway (280km away; see p.294), accessible via Birchenough Bridge. The journey offers rewarding scenery, dominated by granite kopjes towering over traditional villages. Leaving Masvingo, you gradually slide off the escarpment into the **lowveld**. The only place to break your journey for refreshments or the night as you head east from Masvingo is *Mapari Ranch*, 12km west of Birchenough Bridge (PO Box 352, Mutare; ☎0248/2218), where you'll find the *Stop-In*, 200m from the main road, which has six spick-and-serviceable en-suite A-frame **chalets** (②) with five beds in each and a **campsite** (①).The *Stop-In Restaurant*, an ideal refreshment stop if you're driving, serves reasonably priced **food** including burgers, toasted sandwiches and stews under shady trees on tended lawns that are a real relief in the lowveld heat. The ranch also has the Sabi River Safari Camp, 16km from the main road, with chalets along the Save River which you can take on a fully inclusive basis including all meals and game drives (⑧) or self-catering (④).

Heading on east, progress is marked by increasing numbers of baobab trees, donkeys and goats, and long views ahead of the silvery **Birchenough Bridge** arching across the wide **Save River**. In the brown water, sand shows through and crocodiles lurk, though people wash their clothes undeterred. The ribbed steel structure of the bridge, incongruous in the flat, thorny landscape, provides a vital link between the lowveld and the Eastern Highlands.

The drab village of **BIRCHENOUGH BRIDGE**, hard by the southern tip of the Save Communal Lands, is another of those needy, out-of-the-way places designated by the government as Growth Points, but not one that has offers any obvious reason to delay your journey. There are, however, some excellent wayside craft stalls with reasonably priced woven baskets, hats and mats in a style associated with the district. Just beyond Birchenough Bridge, the road forks, with the main branch heading 124km north to Mutare. The *Hot Springs Resort*, 40km towards Mutare, is a relaxing place to pull over, where you can have lunch rounded off with a bath in their open-air hot mineral tubs (for details see Chapter Six, p.304).

travel details

Volvos and chicken buses
Masvingo's historical role as a gateway to the hinterland has placed it in a pivotal transport position, from which you can get buses, but no other forms of transport, to almost any part of the country and even to South Africa. Frequencies and journey times given below are very approximate; always check information at the bus station before departure. You can catch buses at the city centre stops, but you stand a far better chance of getting a seat if you get on at Mucheke Terminus, though you'll have to contend with pretty fierce touting.

Masvingo (Mucheke Bus Terminus) to: Beit Bridge (throughout the day; 3–4hr); Bulawayo (4 daily; 3–4hr); Chimanimani (1 daily at 11am;

4–5hr); Harare (throughout the day; 4–5hr); Morgenster Mission for Great Zimbabwe (every 30min; 30min); Mutare (3 daily 8–10am; 4–5hr).

Luxury coaches
South African Greyhound, Translux and Trans Zambezi coaches all pass through Masvingo on their way from Harare to Johannesburg (the only direction you'd be catching them in, as they aren't allowed to carry passengers from one Zimbabwean destination to another). There are a total of nine per week on this route, but they all arrive and leave from Masvingo in the wee hours, which makes it a less than convenient mode of transport.

CHAPTER SIX

THE EASTERN HIGHLANDS

Ranged along the Mozambique frontier, the Eastern Highlands of Manicaland rise from the plains to form a natural barrier. Peaking at almost 2600m in the Nyanga belt, these mountains reminded the original settlers of the Scottish Highlands, and they set about creating dams and lakes and planting pines in the mist – features that induce a sense of familiarity for Europeans. However, the climate is thoroughly Zimbabwean, there are some real expanses of jungle – and the earth is an unmistakably African red.

What the Highlands lack is big game (this was shot out early here), or indeed any very real tourist highlights. The appeal of the region lies more in exploring the superb hiking trails and indigenous forest, waterfall swimming pools and national parks, each quite different in character. The **Nyanga National Park**, closest to Harare, has long been a major holiday resort for Zimbabweans, with its forests and trout fishing, but hasn't yet been packaged much for foreign visitors. Adjoining its southern edge, the less easily accessible **Mtarazi National Park** is a much wilder zone, with undisturbed indigenous forest and Africa's highest waterfall. Down below, the luxuriant and beautiful **Honde Valley** is an untouristy area where you can see small-scale traditional peasant farming, as well as green-hilled tea estates. The region also offers a couple of recommended rural Africa tours and homestays, and for outdoor enthusiasts there's whitewater rafting, kayaking and abseiling. And for total relaxation and rejuvenation, the mineral baths at **Hot Springs**, an hour south of Mutare, shouldn't be missed.

The southern reaches of these Highlands are a little out on a limb – several hours' drive from the capital and not on the road to anywhere else. They are, however, connected to Mutare by daily local buses and should on no account be missed. The **Chimanimani National Park**, accessible only on foot, has the best **hiking** in Zimbabwe, with spectacular mountains, and waterfalls and rivers to bathe in. Still further south, **Chipinge**, a workaday town in the centre of tea and coffee estates, serves as a base for **Chirinda Forest**, a primeval woodland reserve with ancient red mahoganies.

ACCOMMODATION PRICE CODES

Hotels and other accommodation options in Zimbabwe have been categorized according to the **price codes** given below, which indicate the cost, per person sharing, of a night's lodging. For a full explanation, see p.33.

① under US$7.50   ④ US$25–35   ⑦ US$55–75
② US$7.50–15   ⑤ US$35–45   ⑧ US$75–100
③ US$15–25   ⑥ US$45–55   ⑨ over US$100

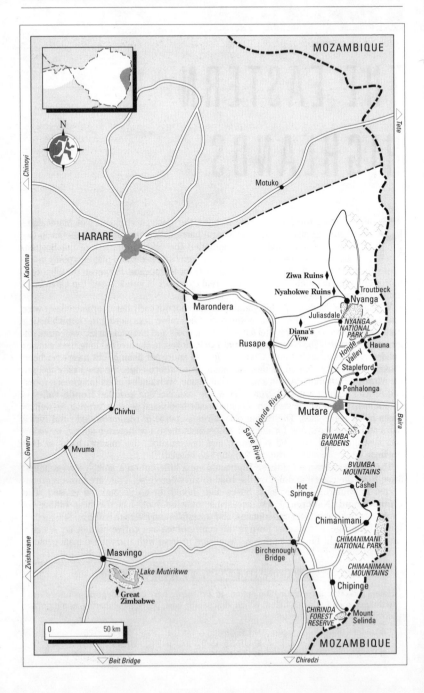

As for more urban attractions, **Mutare**, Zimbabwe's third city and the capital of Manicaland, is beautifully sited in a broad, mountain-rimmed valley on the Mozambique border, with the wonderful **Bvumba Botanical Gardens** and little-visited **Bunga Forest Reserve** within easy day-trip reach.

The road from Harare

Getting to the Eastern Highlands from Harare is easy enough, with regular trains and buses covering the 263km to Mutare. On the way you can linger at strategically placed tea gardens and craft shops, a couple of the nicest sited around **Marondera**, about an hour's drive from Harare, and there are a few hotels should you get stranded. **Rusape**, midway, offers the opportunity of heading straight to Nyanga National Park, as well as a highly recommended detour to the controversial rock paintings at **Diana's Vow**.

Marondera

MARONDERA, 74km east of Harare, was set up as a staging post between Mutare (or Umtali as it was then known) and the capital, and for travellers to the Eastern Highlands this remains its main, and perhaps only, interest. The town, the highest sited in the country, stands at the centre of a prosperous farming region, amidst a green and pleasant landscape of grazing sheep, pear and apple orchards, and vineyards.

Mukuyu Winery, 32km south of town off the Hwedza road (Mon–Fri 6am–4.30pm; ☎079/25001; tours by appointment), is the more notable of Zimbabwe's two wineries, producing quaffable plonk under the Symphony, Select, Meadows, Vat 10 and Mukuyu labels. Although you can buy at the winery, the modest saving over the supermarkets in towns all over Zimbabwe makes it only really worth the effort of trawling out if you intend taking a **tour** (by prior arrangement; Mon–Fri free, Sat & Sun US$1), which will let you taste before deciding. You'll also get a chance to see the vineyards and the processing plant, where crushing, pressing, centrifuging and blending take place. Although Zimbabwe is some way off being a great wine-producing nation, during the 1990s it managed to shake off its status as the viticultural joke of Southern Africa, with the introduction of modern equipment and internationally trained winemakers. There are some decent reds, but whites tend to be what Zimbabwe does best; the authoritative John Platter's South African Wines rates their delicious fermented-in-the-bottle Brut de Brut bubbly (US$3) as "pick of the bunch". There's a large lawned area at the winery with outdoor seating and braai facilities, where you can have a picnic (bring your own supplies) after the tour.

To get to Mukuyu, take the tarred Hwedza road out of town for about 17km till you reach the clear signpost to the winery, which is reached after 15km down a sandy dirt road. In the same vicinity is **Imire Safari Ranch** (see p.102), more usually taken as an excursion from Harare, where you can spend the night, go on game drives and feed baby rhinos or ride fully grown elephants.

If you're not pulling into Mukuyu or Imire, the pleasantest stop between the Eastern Highlands and Harare is the *Malwatte Farmhouse Restaurant* (☎079/23239, fax 20309), beyond Marondera at the 82-kilometre peg on the main Harare–Mutare road, where you can take tea in the garden or browse around their good craft shop. They also have double en-suite rondavels (③) and camping facilities.

Rusape and Diana's Vow

At the next stop, **RUSAPE**, 170km from Harare, the road splits, heading northeast to Nyanga or southeast to Mutare. If you're here for the night, you could stay at the *East*

Guest House (☎025/2945; ②), which offers respectable B&B accommodation in the heart of town, in a former hotel refurbished in 1999. However, the main reason for stopping off at this now nondescript town is to make a detour to the magnificent **Diana's Vow** – site of some of the finest, and certainly amongst the most unusual, rock paintings in the country.

You'll need a car to get to get there; from Rusape, take the road to Juliasdale. On the edge of town, just past the church on the left, a sign points left to **Diana's Vow Farm**, a 28-kilometre drive, mostly on a tarred road of variable quality. The paintings are indicated by a very discreet sign at a farm gate on your right; drive through the gate for half a kilometre until you reach a fenced enclosure around the painted overhang, set in a dramatic circle of granite boulders.

A large recumbent figure, evidently in ceremonial dress and a sable antelope mask, dominates the tableau. According to Peter Garlake (see Contexts, p.390), it depicts a **ceremonial dance** in which the life force *n/um* is being activated. The stretched figure is shown in an advanced state of trance – elongation being a sensation commonly reported by modern-day San dancers on achieving altered consciousness. While the oval attached to the bodies is believed to represent potency. A now discredited interpretation had the central figure as a dead king wrapped in bandages, and about to be buried.

Mutare and the Bvumba

MUTARE lies in a majestic location but has a distinctly provincial air, with scarcely a hint of high-rises on its main street, and the rest of the town centre a neatly organized grid of flower-bedecked avenues. It is at its best in September and October, when the hills around the town are a burnished red and yellow with spring msasa leaves. There is not much to see in the town itself, but some minor local attractions lie within easy reach, including **Murahwa's Hill Reserve**, **La Rochelle** and **Penhalonga**. Mutare is also the jumping-off point for the **Bvumba Mountains** and **Botanical Gardens**, which can be reached by car in less than half an hour, and, further afield, **Hot Springs**, on the road to Birchenough Bridge.

Some history

Mutare's nineteenth-century history is bound up with **gold** and **railways**. The traditional head of the area was one **Chief Mutasa**, a man much courted by both Portuguese and British settlers wanting to prospect for gold in the **Penhalonga Valley**, north of modern Mutare. Two days after the British occupied Mashonaland in 1890, however, they took over the granting of prospecting rights and rapidly constructed a fort to "protect" the chief from the Portuguese. A year later, as numbers began to swell, the fort was abandoned and a new township, **Old Umtali**, was established on the Mutare River. At the same time, the **rail** line begun in Beira was approaching the surrounding hills. These proved too big an obstacle, and everyone packed up and moved 14km south into the wide valley of Mutare's present position. The **American Methodist Church** took over Old Umtali, with a mission and school that are still going (on the left on the way to Penhalonga). In 1982 the name of the city was revised from "Umtali" to the more accurate "Mutare".

Chief Mutasa's descendants remain in the area today. In beautiful granite country on the Nyanga–Mutare road, a hand-painted sign with an arrow points "To Chief Mutasa". The present chief's sphere of influence is said to be extensive, although rural areas are now under the official control of rural and district councils. As ex officio members of the district councils, chiefs are still consulted and retain a certain amount of status and power, but the kingpins are government-appointed District Administrators, who have replaced the colonial District Commissioners. One of the main functions of chiefs is their right to settle out-of-court disputes.

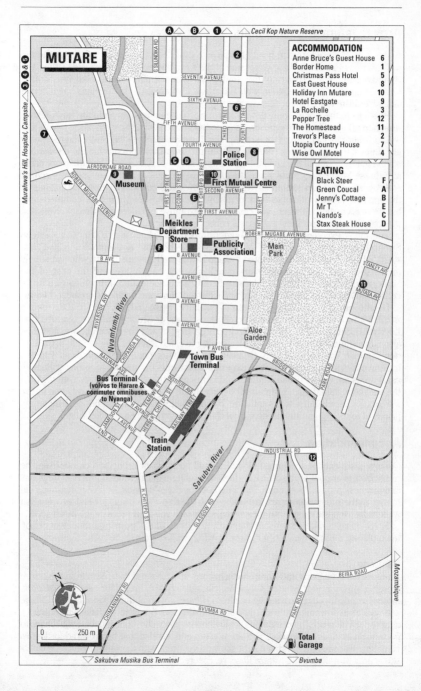

MUTARE

△ Cecil Kop Nature Reserve

ACCOMMODATION

Anne Bruce's Guest House	6
Border Home	1
Christmas Pass Hotel	5
East Guest House	8
Holiday Inn Mutare	10
Hotel Eastgate	9
La Rochelle	3
Pepper Tree	12
The Homestead	11
Trevor's Place	2
Utopia Country House	7
Wise Owl Motel	4

EATING

Black Steer	F
Green Coucal	A
Jenny's Cottage	B
Mr T	E
Nando's	C
Stax Steak House	D

Murahwa's Hill, Hospital, Campsite

SILUNDIKA RD

SEVENTH AVENUE

SIXTH AVENUE

FIFTH AVENUE

THIRD STREET

FOURTH AVENUE

AERODROME ROAD

Police Station

Museum

First Mutual Centre

ROBERT MUGABE AVENUE

FIRST STREET

SECOND STREET

HERBERT CHITEPO STREET

SECOND AVENUE

FIRST AVENUE

FIRST STREET

Meikles Department Store

B AVE

B AVENUE

ROBERT MUGABE AVENUE

Publicity Association

Main Park

C AVENUE

D AVENUE

E AVENUE

RIVERSIDE AVE

Nyamfumbi River

CHIPANDA S

STANLEY AVE

MUTASA AVE

Aloe Garden

F AVENUE

PARK ROAD

Town Bus Terminal

RAILWAY AVE

BRIDGE RD

Bus Terminal (volvos to Harare & commuter omnibuses to Nyanga)

H AVENUE

INSTITUTE AVE

HERBERT CHITEPO ST

RAILWAY STREET

JAMESON ST

END AVE

A AVENUE

Train Station

Sakubva River

INDUSTRIAL RD

GLASGOW RD

H CHITEPO ST

CHIMANIMANI RD

Mozambique

BEIRA ROAD

BVUMBA RD

PARK ROAD

Total Garage

N

0   250 m

▽ Sakubva Musika Bus Terminal   ▽ Bvumba

Arrival, information and tours

Arriving in Mutare **by road** from Harare or Nyanga is a real event: as you hit the top of Christmas Pass, the whole panorama of the town lies below you in a wide valley, the Bvumba Mountains rising to the southeast. Like all Zimbabwean towns, Mutare remains informally segregated, with **Sakubva** township, the factory and sawmill, set apart from the more salubrious city centre.

Buses from the **north** come down Christmas Pass before pulling into the **town terminus**; hop off here, before the bus roars off to Sakubva Musika (4km out of the town – and with nowhere to stay). From the **south**, most buses continue to the centre after stopping at Sakubva; if yours doesn't, take any **commuter omnibus** from outside the *musika* bus station gates, or one of the **taxis** that are always lined up. Blue Arrow and the more erratic Express Motorways **luxury coaches** from Harare pull in at the conveniently central *Holiday Inn*. The **train station**, arrival point for the overnight service from Harare, lies on the opposite (south) side of town, a longish walk from most of Mutare's accommodation, but there's a restaurant where you can have a restorative cup of tea and a snack. Note that the majority of backpackers' lodges will collect guests for free.

The city's excellent **Publicity Association** on Market Square, Herbert Chitepo Street/Robert Mugabe Avenue (Mon–Fri 8.30am–12.45pm & 2–4pm, Sat 8.30–11am; ☎020/64711, fax 67728), is operated by helpful and well-informed staff, who can supply information and photocopied maps (small charge) on Mutare and the rest of the Eastern Highlands. They will help with finding accommodation in town, have a list of cottages to rent in Bvumba, Nyanga and Chimanimani, and details of organized tours.

Of the **tour companies**, Green Travellers (☎020/61758, fax 62128, mobile ☎023/500048; ask for Dennis Borerwe) does tours of Mutare and the Bvumba, the Eastern Highlands, Hot Springs, Birchenough Bridge and Great Zimbabwe, and they also run a transport service for people needing to catch trains or buses or cross the border. Vimbiso Touring Company (☎020/60595 or 63692, fax 64238) is dedicated to giving travellers an authentic African experience, introducing people to Shona culture in rural areas as well as urban Mutare, and combining these cultural tours with visits to the well-established places of natural beauty in the Eastern Highlands; it is one of the few outfits which does tours into the Honde Valley. Both companies will negotiate prices of tours depending on the size of the group and where you want to go.

Accommodation

Mutare has plenty of accommodation to suit all pockets, including two **campsites**. The nicest **hotels** are out of the centre in the hills, and tend to cater for commercial travellers and business people. As a bunch, Mutare's **backpackers' lodges**, located in rambling old houses in the suburbs, compare favourably with the rest of the country. Most are a longish walk away from the centre, but their owners will pick you up if you arrange in advance.

For a more rural, inexpensive alternative, try one of the growing number of out-of-town places, most of which offer game viewing, walks and trips to rock paintings.

Camping

Mutare's **caravan park and campsite** is halfway up Christmas Pass, 6km from the centre (reservations through Mutare City Council; ☎020/64412, fax 61002, *donaldn@mutare. intersol.co.zw*). If you're arriving by bus from Harare, get off at the Christmas Pass Garage and walk 2km downhill to the site, just off the main road. Alternatively, take a taxi back up again once you reach the central bus station; unless you've brought supplies, you'll have to go to town to stock up anyway. The site is clean and wooded, but be prepared for lorries rumbling past all night offering a light show on your tent with their headlights. The campsite is near Murahwa's Hill Nature Reserve, covered on p.270.

There's a quieter site at Tiger's Kloof Dam, 3km north of the centre at Cecil Kop Nature Reserve (see p.269), where you'll be close to game and have a good chance of seeing samango monkeys.

Backpackers' lodges and rooming houses

Anne Bruce's Guest House, 99 Fourth St/Sixth Avenue (☎020/63569). Ever popular and fun spot, hosted by owner Ann Bruce, dogs Sasha and Bovril, and cats Custard Pie and Bonnie. Among the nicest of the budget options, this homely establishment has an en-suite double room in the garden, and doubles and shared rooms inside the house. Excellent food and the latest on developments in other places, including current information on the route to Mozambique and places to stay once you're there. All accommodation ①.

Border Home, 3a Jason Moyo Drive, off Third Street (☎020/63346, *borderhome@hotmail.com*). Clean, if slightly drab and cramped, hostel under the eye of friendly owner Nev Borradaile. Accommodation, amounting to a small settlement, consists of three dorms, six double rooms (one en suite) plus several single rooms inside the house and in timber sheds and cottages in the garden – they sleep up to four people and have their own bath and toilet. Laundry facilities and cheap meals are available, as well as free lifts to and from town, when there's a vehicle. ①.

East Guest House, Fourth/Fifth avenues (☎020/60794, fax 65769). Although not the homely "guest house" its name might suggest, this basic, cheap self-catering rooming house in a converted row of flats, a stone's throw from the Publicity Association, offers cheap, clean beds that are fine for a night. All rooms have a TV, and each apartment has a kitchen and bathroom which is shared with other guests in the unit. Best value are the en-suite family rooms with a double and two single beds. Rooms rented as dorms, doubles or family suites. ①.

The Homestead, 52 Park Rd (☎020/65870). Budget rooming house in the corrugated-iron buildings occupied by Mutare's first school, which was established in 1897, and some rambling annexes. Rooms are basic but serviceable for an overnight stay and there's a swimming pool, TV, large patio at the back and a kitchen for guests' use – or you can order meals. Rooms without bath or en suite. ①.

Pepper Tree, 25 Park Rd/Industrial Road (☎020/66509, fax 64708, mobile ☎091/331133, *jade@syscom.co.zw*). Three brightly decorated, double rooms and one single with en-suite showers, attached to Jade Health Studios. In the industrial part of town, but don't be put off, as the setting is a pleasant huge lawned garden, with the owners living in separate house on the premises. You can enjoy a wake-up sauna or use of the gym for less than US$1.50. Reasonably priced continental or English breakfast available, and, at the time of writing, a coffee bar was on the drawing board which will serve pastas, pizzas and salads, coffee and cake till 10pm. Best budget alternative to the backpackers' lodges. Doubles ①, singles ②.

Trevor's Place, 119 Fourth St (☎020/67762). A gently run-down house with double and triple rooms. Cheap and pleasant enough, and there's a kitchen for self-catering. ①.

Utopia Country House, 13 Robert Mugabe Way (☎ & fax 020/66056 or 67390). Ten unpretentious, pleasant and well-serviced double rooms, about half of which are en suite, as well as two family rooms in a clean airy suburban house close to the centre. A respectable family-friendly place, it targets Mozambicans crossing the border on shopping trips and makes a good alternative to the town's backpacker accommodation. Facilities include a kettle in each room and a well-equipped kitchen for self-catering, or you can buy cheap breakfasts and snacks such as toasted sandwiches. ①.

Hotels

Christmas Pass Hotel (☎020/63818, fax 63875). Decent mock-Spanish hotel with rather dated furnishings, on the brow of the hill at Christmas Pass, 5km from Mutare. Used mainly by travelling reps, it's virtually unoccupied over weekends, when they offer small discounts. Street-facing rooms are rather close to the main road into town with a constant background rumble of traffic, but the gardens are nice and there's a swimming pool. ③.

Hotel Eastgate, Simon Mazorodze/Aerodrome roads (☎020/65769, 60108 or 61812, fax 65769). Eighteen rooms and suites in a four-storey former block of flats less than 1km from the town centre. Bedrooms are comfortable but furnished with garish artificial velvet decor reminiscent of an Indian restaurant. Each apartment has a kitchenette, seven-channel TV and a phone. Very good value if you want the anonymity, facilities and privacy of a hotel. ②.

Holiday Inn Mutare, Aerodrome Road/Herbert Chitepo Street (☎020/64431, fax 64466). Very central accommodation straight out of the Holiday Inn mould. The only upmarket hotel in town, it's usually full of business travellers during the week. Ask about hefty weekend discounts (up to fifty percent). ⑦.

La Rochelle Hotel, Imbesa Valley Road, 14km north of Mutare (☎ & fax 020/22250, mobile ☎011/605474, *rochell@syscom.co.zw*). The accommodation bargain of Mutare in the former mansion of the fabulously wealthy Sir Stephen and Lady Virginia Courtauld, set in the middle of the beautiful and tranquil La Rochelle Gardens. Although the furnishings are nowhere near as opulent as when occupied by the Courtaulds, they remain faithful at least to the spirit of the 1950s. Four self-catering cottages in the garden aren't quite as lavish as the main house, but they are certainly amongst the best and most beautifully set in the area. B&B in the main house ③, self-catering cottages ②.

Wise Owl Motel, near the campsite on Christmas Pass (☎020/64643, fax 62995). A fairly sizable motel with 69 well-maintained but unmodernized 1960s-style rooms and a somewhat apathetic atmosphere. A restaurant, two bars, swimming pool and children's play area make it reasonable value if you're travelling as a family. ③.

Out of town accommodation

Drifters, PO Box 1646, Mutare (☎020/62930, fax 62964). Camping, dorms and pleasant double rondavels in a thatched game farm development in the hills, 21km west of Mutare off the Harare road. Meals are provided, or you can self-cater. Activities include day-trips to Bvumba and Nyanga, and walks up the adjacent mountain to look at rock paintings. Full bar and breakfast and dinner available; bed linen is provided, but not soap or towels. ①.

Mapor Estates, PO Box 98, Odzi (☎020/03013). Budget farmhouse accommodation, 15km from Odzi village (or 48km from Mutare), with two en-suite twin bedrooms and camping. Breakfasts available, but other meals must be self-catered (equipment is provided). The environs offer good mountain walking and plentiful birdlife, as well as rock art and archeological sites. If you can get through on the phone, the owners will collect you, and if you're driving yourself, the farm is a good, if remote, stopoff en route to the Highlands; the turn-off for Odzi is off the main Harare–Mutare road, 32km west of Mutare. ①.

Musangano Lodge, 26.5km west of Mutare (☎020/42267, fax 42263, *musangano@odziicon.co.zw*). Four self-catering lodges and five B&B chalets set in msasa woodland surrounded by hills, with views of the Eastern Highlands. Beautifully decorated units are set far apart for maximum privacy, with lots of pine furniture and great attention to detail. The soft furnishings are by Mutare artist Leanne Bray; each unit has a fireplace and verandah with deck chairs. There are wheelchair-friendly ramps and a children's playground, fenced-off swimming pool and cots available. To get there, take the Champion Mine turn-off about 25km west of Mutare and continue for 1.5km. Discounts for three nights or more, and lower regional rates. B&B ⑤, half-board or self-catering ⑥.

The town and around

Mutare has no grand sights, but, with its parks and surrounding natural landscape, plus a surprisingly good museum and art gallery, it's a pleasant place to pass a leisurely day before moving on into the Highlands proper, or across the border to Mozambique. As the capital of the province, a transport hub and a border town, its a good place to shop and attend to the practicalities you can't easily deal with out in the mountains.

The compact **park** and **aloe gardens**, on the corner of Fifth Street and Robert Mugabe Road two blocks east of the Publicity Association, are great places to picnic and while away hot afternoons. The park is shaded by numerous trees and has a palm-lined stream running down its centre, while at the heart of the botanic collections are some ten thousand **aloes** – large tropical succulents at their best when they flower in fiery tones in June and July. Besides aloes you'll find ancient and protected **cycads**, one of the slowest-growing and most primitive plants on earth.

Mutare Museum

About 1km north of the Publicity Association, the **Mutare Museum** (daily 9am–5pm; US$2), on Aerodrome Road, is worth a visit, if only to marvel at the goriness of its collection of stuffed animals. The taxidermist in Mutare was clearly fascinated by the hunt, and the more dramatic and fearful the better: in his tableaux, eagles sink talons into quivering hares, owls pounce on terrified rodents, and red-eyed serpents prey on petrified rats. The museum also has an enormous collection of **weaponry**, from inlaid silver pistols to crude trading rifles, and there's a hall packed with **vintage vehicles**, some of which look like the thirty-year-olds still going strong on Zimbabwean roads. The more serious historical exhibits are good, too, with explanations of the successive farming cultures in the region and examples of **trade goods** from the Arabs and Portuguese on the coast.

Lastly, don't leave without stepping into the **walk-in aviary**, a large enclosure bursting with birdsong, where you'll spot one of the most striking birds of the Highlands – the vermilion and jade **purple-crested lourie**, whose beautiful appearance is so at odds with its harsh, grating croak of a call.

National Gallery of Zimbabwe in Mutare

It's worth the two-kilometre trip northeast from the Publicity Association up Third Street (parallel to and a block east of Herbert Chitepo Street) to the **National Gallery of Zimbabwe in Mutare**, between Tenth and Eleventh avenues (daily 9am–5pm; US$1), just to see the restoration of the classic colonial-style **Kopje House**. Now the venue for the National Gallery, the building served as Mutare's first nursing home in the late nineteenth century, and reputedly hosts a couple of (benign) ghostly nurses, who are sometimes seen floating along the verandah.

The first phase of restoration was completed in 1999, saving the ailing historic building from imminent collapse, and forms part of an ambitious work-in-progress that will turn the gallery into more than just a venue for art. Under the curatorship of Traude Rogers, the gallery's mission is to foster "**Manicaland Art**", a reference to the Eastern Highlands of Zimbabwe and adjacent districts of Mozambique which share a common culture. It aims to encourage excellence in metalwork, woodcarving, painting, ceramics and textiles, which will be showcased at an annual Manicaland Exhibition.

In an effort to attract as wide an audience as possible, the gallery will also serve as a place of entertainment, with a children's **adventure playground** and **interactive sculpture area**, an outdoor **amphitheatre** that will provide a venue for drama, traditional dance and music, and **studios** on site to provide a space where artists and visitors can meet. Perhaps one of the highlights will be the gardens themselves, which will represent the **indigenous flora** of Southern Africa, promoting awareness of the relationship between art and the environment. This is a big issue in a country where hardwoods are disappearing fast due to their overuse in tourist-oriented carvings, and baobab trees are dying because their bark is harvested to create *gudza* baskets, rugs and other woven crafts. There will also be a **tearoom** and **shop**.

Cecil Kop Nature Reserve

Under 1km northwest of the art gallery up Herbert Chitepo Avenue, which becomes Arcadia Road, the **Cecil Kop Nature Reserve** (daily dawn–dusk; US$1) is a pleasant teatime venue, and popular with locals over the weekend. It's a contrived place, perhaps, but very pretty: in the late afternoon, you can sit overlooking a **dam** where elephant, buffalo, giraffe, wildebeest, zebra and antelope are drawn to food laid out for them at 4pm each day. Alternatively, go earlier and have the place to yourself: you won't see the same number of animals, but with luck you may spot shy blue duiker, or samango monkeys, darker and with longer tails than the common vervet. These are species endemic to the Eastern Highlands and you may well spot them in the wild.

Murahwa's Hill Nature Reserve

If you've a few more hours to kill and feel energetic, **Murahwa's Hill** – behind the most obvious kopje in the valley as you look from the town centre towards Christmas Pass – is a beautiful place to wander around. The drawback is the hour-long walk from town, though Murahwa is easy to get to from the campsite.

To walk around the kopje will take you quite some time: the path initially snakes through the thick draping forest at the base, but then it tracks fairly steeply up to the rocky summit, where you find the **remains of a village** protected on three sides by immense granite boulders. This abandoned settlement is thought to be of about the same vintage as Great Zimbabwe; its few remaining artefacts are now in the Mutare Museum. In a nearby cave there's a collection of unexceptional paintings – evidence of a much earlier settlement.

One way **to get there** is to take a commuter omnibus or walk to the *Wise Owl Motel*, where a road on the valley side climbs to one of the park entrances; there's also a gentler incline from the rear of the showgrounds in Jan Smuts Drive. A **map** of sorts at the reserve entrance shows the locations of the archeological titbits, but it's quite easy to get lost. Leave yourself plenty of time to get down while it's still light.

Eating

Though not the most lively of cities, Mutare has plenty of snack joints open during the day, several late-ish South African chicken and steak franchises, and a couple of good nightspots where, as well as drinking, you can pick up something to eat. The compact town centre makes most places easy to get to. **Breakfast** options range from basic eggs and toast at *Mr T* to the expensive and overwhelming morning menu at the *Holiday Inn* and the similar *Wise Owl Motel*, near the campsite. For a tea-and-bun breakfast while you're waiting for a bus, try one of the places at the *musika*, or hard-boiled eggs, mealies and fruit from vendors there and at the bus terminus.

Restaurants and snack bars

Apache Spur, *Holiday Inn*, Aerodrome Road/Victory Avenue. Reliable burgers, steaks and chips, from the family-friendly South African franchise. Daily 11am–11pm.

Black Steer, downstairs in Meikles department store, Herbert Chitepo Street. More mid-priced steaks, cheap burgers and chips from another popular South African franchise. Mon & Sun–Fri 11.30am–10.30pm, Sat 8.30am–11.30pm.

Jenny's Cottage, 130 Herbert Chitepo St/Eighth Avenue. Recommended for light lunches and tea on the verandah. Closed Sun.

Green Coucal, 111 Second St/Ninth Avenue. The nicest place in town for a quiet cup of coffee or tea and muffins in the shady gardens of a suburban house about 1km north of the centre; it doubles as the excellent Nyasa Seedcracker craft shop. They also do good light lunches and salads. Mon–Fri 9am–4.30pm, Sat 9am–2.30pm.

Holiday Inn, Aerodrome Road/Herbert Chitepo Street. The best place in town for gargantuan – though not cheap – buffet breakfasts, which will fill you up for the day. On Fridays, a traditional African buffet on the pool terrace is accompanied by a marimba band and dancing (12.30–2pm).

La Rochelle Restaurant, Imbesa Valley Road, 14km north of Mutare. Snacks and light English-style meals (daily 10am–4.30pm) on the terrace or lawns of the lovely La Rochelle Gardens, and à la carte fish and steak dinners inside the restaurant (daily 7–9.30pm).

Nandos, 16 Aerodrome Rd. Excellent but not cheap grilled peri-peri chicken, to take away or eat in, from South Africa's most successful fast-food franchise. Daily 9am–11pm.

Mr T, Manica Arcade, Second Avenue. Enjoy hamburgers and sandwiches indoors or out, served until 7.30pm during the week, later over weekends at a cheapo snack bar dead in the centre of the city.

Station Kiosk, Railway Street. Inexpensive *sadza* and *nyama*, handy if you're waiting for the 9pm Harare train.

Stax Steak House and Coffee Bar, First Mutual Centre, Herbert Chitepo Street. Apart from the hotels, one of the few restaurants open in the evenings, around the corner from the *Holiday Inn*. The steaks hang over the edge of the plate, and they do delicious veggieburgers, pizzas and have a kids' menu. There's also a cheaper takeaway section. Daily 7.30am–9.30pm.

Wimpy, shopping mall, Herbert Chitepo Street/Third Avenue. Familiar burgers and fast food from this worldwide franchise.

Wise Owl Motel, near the campsite on Christmas Pass. Known for its moderately priced flambé steaks and Sunday braais. Open daily.

Drinking, nightlife and entertainment

Both Mutare's **cinemas**, the Rainbow Vistarama and Rainbow Elite 200, as well as its theatre, are to be found in Robert Mugabe Avenue. The two cinemas show a fairly meagre selection of popular stuff (usually daily 2.15pm, 5.30pm & 8.30pm), but you might strike it lucky if there is a visiting (foreign) performance at the Courtauld Theatre, Queensway.

Bulldog's Pub, Meikles department store, Herbert Chitepo Street. Out-of-a-box English-style pub that's part of a franchise.

The Nite Place, Robert Mugabe Avenue, between Fourth and Fifth streets. Spot with a local flavour that's worth a visit if someone good is playing – otherwise, expect the usual mix of disco and drink.

Mutare's markets and shops

Mutare's **markets** are worth exploring, even though they're on nothing like the scale of those in Harare or Bulawayo. The **Sakubva Musika**, by the long-distance bus terminus, is entertaining when you're killing time waiting for transport. Handicrafts on sale are generally utilitarian, but you can rummage around for something interesting and try to guess a use for some of the unidentifiable objects.

Elsewhere, due to the abundant forests of the region, good **wooden crafts** are easy to find at Jairos Jiri, 41 First St, which has ebony snuffboxes and vials, and wooden platters, bowls and spoons in ebony and other hardwoods. Their stylish brown-and-white **woven hats** are also great – with narrow brims, white zigzags and pleated crowns. Arguably the best place for **high-quality crafts** is Nyasa Seedcracker Designs, 111 Second St, which sells literally unique pieces, made by local craftworkers to the specifications of owner Leanne Bray, who is a graphic designer and injects an exciting element of the unusual, surreal or modern into these traditionally produced items.

For more mundane requirements, the **Green Market** – just past the railway bridge on the right before the Bvumba turn-off – is a good place to stock up on fruit and vegetables; macadamia nuts are a particularly fine regional speciality. Regular shops include the TM Supermarket, on the station side of town at Herbert Chitepo Street/B Avenue, and Omar's Hyper, near the *Holiday Inn* on Herbert Chitepo Street/Aerodrome Road. Mutare is also home to Mitchells Bakery, producers of the best biscuits in Zimbabwe.

MUTARE SOUL

Mutare dies on Sunday unless you go to **church**, in which case you could be raising the rafters listening to the spirited and **spiritual singing** you'll catch at several churches around the centre, where worship owes scant resemblance to an English Home Counties village service and everything to African rhythm. The blue Elim Pentecostal Church, 30 Second St, probably offers the city's highlight, every second Sunday from about 10am till 1pm, with its evangelical services that consist of unadulterated African singing, accompanied by wild clapping in the aisles. St Columba's Presbyterian Church, Third Street/B Avenue, fills the air with spiritual singing and a great youth band, as does the Mutare Baptist Church, 19 Plantation Drive, in the suburb of Morningside, about 1km northeast of the centre. If you happen to be in town during the **August** school holidays, watch the press for details of an annual choral event in which ten to fifteen congregations get together for a massive **one-day jam session**.

Listings

American Express Handled by Manica Travel Services, Aerodrome Road/Second Avenue (☎020/64171–2).

Automobile Association Fanum House, Robert Mugabe Avenue/Fourth Street (☎020/64422, fax 64478).

Banks Barclays, First Banking Corporation, Grindlays and Zimbank are all in Herbert Chitepo Street, while CBZ (Commercial Bank of Zimbabwe) is at 31 Second St.

Books and stationery Best of the town's bookshops is Time Stationers, 85 Herbert Chitepo St, which sells a small but respectable selection of pulp and African novels, children's books, guidebooks, field guides, maps, newspapers, magazines, postcards, stationery. Book Centre, Norwich Union Centre, Herbert Chitepo Street/First Avenue, sells a small choice of African and British novels, and Kingstons, 93 Herbert Chitepo St, has the usual selection of books, magazines and stationery.

Bureaux de change Most banks have a foreign exchange counter and there are also around a dozen dedicated bureaux de change in town, all legal, licensed and safe. Among these are Barnford's, Meikles Building, 75 Herbert Chitepo St/B Avenue (daily 8am–5pm); FX Moneycorp, Shop 3, Herbert Chitepo/Second Avenue (Mon 8.15am–1pm & 2–5pm, Sat 8.15am–1pm); Otanya Foreign Exchange Bureau, 89a Herbert Chitepo Ave (Mon–Fri 8am–5pm, Sat 8am–noon) and at the *Holiday Inn* (daily 8am–8pm).

Car rental Cheapest is the locally based Club Car Hire, Herbert Chitepo/Fifth Avenue (☎020/62108, fax 60467), which has a fully inclusive unlimited mileage rate of US$27 per day on a three-day rental. Hertz, based at the *Holiday Inn* (☎020/64784), offer discounts at weekends, if cars are available, but only on a stand-by basis – you can't book ahead. Other firms include Europcar, at Grant's Service Station, 1 Josiah Tongogara Rd/Robert Mugabe Road (☎ & fax 020/62367).

Emergencies Police ☎995; ambulance ☎994; fire ☎993; general ☎999; MARS private ambulance ☎020/66466.

Hospital The best first port of call is the private Seventh Avenue Surgical Unit, 123 Herbert Chitepo St (☎020/64635, 66958 or 66397).

Immigration department Second Floor, Manica Chambers, Herbert Chitepo Street/Second Avenue (☎020/65653).

Internet and email The only dedicated Internet café in town is the *Internet Cyber Café*, Waller's House, 63–67 Fourth St (daily 7am–5pm; ☎020/67939, fax 62381, mobile ☎011/700465), which has seven terminals and a leased line that offers the fastest link you'll get in Zimbabwe. Another option is Web Solutions, Fifth Floor, Fidelity Life Centre, Herbert Chitepo/Aerodrome roads (☎020/68603, mobile ☎091/304095).

Petrol Grants Service Station, on Robert Mugabe Avenue, is open 24hr.

Pharmacies Lancasters Pharmacy, 95a Herbert Chitepo St (☎020/62579 after hours). Central Pharmacy, Cuthbert Building, Herbert Chitepo Street (☎020/61211 after hours).

Police Aerodrome Road, opposite *Holiday Inn* (☎020/64212).

Post office and phones Robert Mugabe Avenue (Mon–Fri 8.30am–4pm, Sat 8–11.30am).

Swimming pool Off roundabout on Robert Mugabe Avenue (Tues–Sun 6–7am & 10am–5pm; closed May 15–Sept 1; nominal admission).

Taxis Ranks outside the Publicity Association on Market Square, bus terminus and *musika*. Rixi ☎020/65451, 68227 or 65809.

Train station Ticket office (Mon–Fri 8am–12.30pm & 2–4pm; ☎020/62801). For first- and second-class tickets on the day of travel, if the office has closed, queue up at the economy-class ticket booth a couple of hours before departure.

Travel agents Manica Travel Services, Aerodrome Road/Second Avenue (☎020/64171–2), sells tickets for the Blue Arrow coach to Harare.

Visas Those for Mozambique are best arranged through the Mozambican embassy in Harare. They can be organized in Mutare, although your passport will have to go to Harare and you should expect it to take seven working days to be processed. Enquire at Mitchell Cotts Freight & Travel, 70 Herbert Chitepo St (☎020/63291).

MOVING ON TO MOZAMBIQUE: THE BEIRA CORRIDOR

The port of **Beira**, 300km east of Mutare on the coast of Mozambique, is the obvious outlet for landlocked Zimbabwe's trade, and was used extensively as such until 1974, as well as being the place where many Rhodesians took their seaside holidays. However, the overthrow of the Portuguese and the establishment of the Marxist **Frelimo** government obliged Rhodesia to export its goods via the long, expensive rail link with Durban in South Africa.

In response, Smith's intelligence agency set up a 500-strong destabilization force, the Mozambique National Resistance Movement (MNR), or **Renamo**. When majority rule emerged in Zimbabwe, Renamo was handed on to the South Africans, who built it into a monster of (according to some estimates) twenty thousand fighters. During the 1980s, South Africa used Renamo as an instrument of foreign policy, supplying it by means of parachute drops, its main function being to bring Mozambique to its knees. In this it was devastatingly successful: large parts of Mozambique were overrun by Renamo, whose grisly attacks helped to grind the country down into its status as one of the world's poorest nations, and one easily manipulated by its neighbour.

After Independence, Zimbabwe began once again exporting goods by rail to Beira. But Renamo attacks on the line brought traffic to a standstill in 1984. The crisis led to pragmatic cooperation between Zimbabwe's socialist leadership and predominantly white, capitalist interests, who formed the **Beira Corridor Group** to oversee the rehabilitation of the coastal link. Hundreds of millions of US dollars were pumped into the programme in a concerted effort to break apartheid South Africa's stranglehold on the economies of both countries.

Up to seven thousand Zimbabwean troops were sent in to guard the route, costing around US$70 million annually. Meanwhile, Renamo carried out its own atrocities against Zimbabwean border villages, as well as continuing the civil war in Mozambique. The peace accord brokered in 1992 stipulated that government soldiers and Renamo fighters be disarmed and formed into a unified army. Thankfully, a successful reconstruction is now under way and traffic along the Beira Corridor is once again on the increase.

Border practicalities

Forbes border post, ten minutes' drive east of Mutare, is the gateway to the Beira Corridor and the obvious crossing point for overland travel into Mozambique. As recently as the early 1990s, the civil war made this road hazardous, but tourists are now passing through safely.

Minibuses leave from **Machipanda border post**, on the Mozambique side, 10km from Mutare, taking passengers to Chimoio, from where you can get connections to points all over the country. Check out the current situation with the Mutare backpackers' lodges, or with the town's helpful Publicity Association. If you're driving, make sure all your vehicle documents are in order and stick to the speed limit.

Note that to enter Mozambique you must already have obtained a **visa**, either issued in Harare through one of many travel agents who can arrange things on your behalf (see below) or a Mozambican embassy abroad; allow seven days or more for it to be processed.

Penhalonga and La Rochelle

A good day's excursion north from Mutare easily combines **Penhalonga** – an attractive village with run-down period buildings, trading stores and its own working gold mines – and the pleasant **La Rochelle Gardens**, with the option of overnighting (or even spending a few days) at one of the charming cottages at La Rochelle, or just having tea or lunch at their restaurant.

Penhalonga

Hidden in a valley on the old scenic route to Nyanga, 17km from Mutare, **PENHALONGA** feels like a neglected outpost of the 1940s. It was the first of the settlers' **gold-prospecting** sites (gold is still mined here) and retains the appearance of a trading post. All the shops have dark interiors, with tailors on the pillared verandahs sewing with old treddle Singers, and, inside, lengths of cotton-print hanging from the ceiling. Two of the town buildings are particularly handsome – the corrugated-iron **church**, built on pillars, and the red-roofed **school**. Dating from the beginning of the century, the church is in Victorian-Gothic style, a tin version of an English country chapel.

Getting to Penhalonga is straightforward. **By car**, you take Robert Mugabe Avenue out of town and continue up Christmas Pass, following the clear signposts. Several **buses** a day also pass on the way to Stapleford and Honde Valley from Mutare's *musika*, while three buses (at 6am, 11am & 3pm) go to Penhalonga itself from the town terminus. Alternatively, catch any of the numerous buses up Christmas Pass from Robert Mugabe Avenue, get off at the Christmas Pass Service Station – where the road to Penhalonga begins – and **hitch**, or catch another bus, from there. The **campsite** and caravan park is sadly under threat of closure: despite its backwater charm, few visit Penhalonga these days.

La Rochelle

LA ROCHELLE, 4km south of Penhalonga in the Imbeza Valley, is a pleasant drive or walk from the main Mutare road (3km), past farms and smallholdings and some beautiful stands of *Acacia abyssinica* in the valley. Although not a patch on Bvumba, the cultivated gardens nevertheless make a pleasant and easy trip from Mutare if you have your own vehicle, and its a lovely place for **tea** on the lawn, surrounded by flowers and trees. A network of pathways, with scented plants and braille directions for the blind, is one of only two such garden trails in Africa (the other is at Cape Town's Kirstenbosch). There are rather elegant rooms in the main house and some inexpensive **cottages** for rent in the garden (see Mutare Accommodation, p.268), as well as a **caravan and camping site** nearby.

An infrequent **bus** goes to the Imbeza Valley from Mutare's **town terminus**; otherwise take any Penhalonga-bound bus and walk from the signposted turn-off.

Bvumba

When people in Mutare talk about "the mountains", they generally mean the **BVUMBA**, which lie south of Mutare. Bvumba – the name derives from a seventeenth-century Shona kingdom that spread well beyond the range into Mozambique – is often used simply to refer to the famous **botanical gardens** right at the top of the mountains, though it's actually a large area encompassing coffee, fruit and nut farms and commercial forestry stations.

The Bvumba is also a popular mountain resort, far less developed than Nyanga, with **cottages** to rent, a few **hotels** that wouldn't be out of place in the English countryside, and the **Mountain Meander**, a route that links together a number of craft workshops, tea gardens and activities such as walking or riding. Many of these are on the lower reaches of the Bvumba along either the **Laurenceville road** that goes past the *White Horse Inn* and terminates at a fence that defines the Mozambique border, or the circular **scenic route** that branches out east from the road to gardens at Cloudlands and passes into the Burma Valley before returning to Mutare.

Accommodation

Bvumba has **accommodation** to suit most pockets, ranging from the ultra-luxury *Leopard's Rock Hotel*, which boasts its own casino, down to an excellent backpackers'

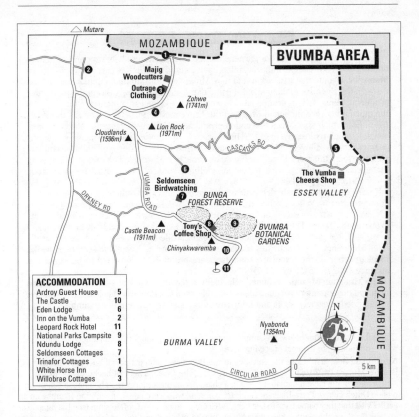

Map key:

BVUMBA AREA

- Mutare
- MOZAMBIQUE
- Majig Woodcutters
- Outrage Clothing
- Zohwe (1741m)
- Lion Rock (1971m)
- Cloudlands (1596m)
- CASCADES RD
- The Vumba Cheese Shop
- Seldomseen Birdwatching
- BUNGA FOREST RESERVE
- ESSEX VALLEY
- ORKNEY RD
- VUMBA ROAD
- Castle Beacon (1911m)
- Tony's Coffee Shop
- BVUMBA BOTANICAL GARDENS
- Chinyakwaremba
- MOZAMBIQUE
- Nyabonda (1354m)
- BURMA VALLEY
- CIRCULAR ROAD
- N
- 0   5 km

ACCOMMODATION

Ardroy Guest House	5
The Castle	10
Eden Lodge	6
Inn on the Vumba	2
Leopard Rock Hotel	11
National Parks Campsite	9
Ndundu Lodge	8
Seldomseen Cottages	7
Trinafor Cottages	1
White Horse Inn	4
Willobrae Cottages	3

lodge and campsites. Many of the places to stay are strung along the main road leading to the gardens. In addition, the Tourist Information Office in Mutare has a full list of reasonably priced self-catering **cottages** to let in the Bvumba and Essex Valley. They're usually fully booked during the school holiday season and are not places you can expect rent on spec, but ring ahead from town and you may strike lucky. Its best to go to the cottages for a minimum of two nights.

CAMPING AND BACKPACKERS' LODGES

Ardroy Guest House, Blue Mountain Road (☎020/217121). An atmospheric farmhouse on a coffee estate, 34km from Mutare, that has views over the plains of Mozambique. It once belonged to novelist Doris Lessing's late son, and has been left much as it was when he died: minimally maintained, and with an air of gentle decay. In one of her short stories, Lessing describes its trellised verandah with "creepers weighing down the roof". Small dorms and doubles are available. There are no cooking facilities, but tasty, inexpensive meals are served. Getting there by car from Mutare takes about 1hr, much of the route along winding dirt roads that can be tricky when wet: best phone for directions. Without a car you can still get there on the 6am Mapofu bus or the 11am one headed for Burma Valley. ①.

National Parks Camping and Caravan Site, Bvumba Botanical Gardens. This attractive National Parks campsite is set amid thick, shaded lawns that are scented in the summer by magnolia blossom. The bathrooms are spotless, and there's no shortage of hot water from the wood boiler outside. In the evening, you have the whole estate to yourself and the views over Mozambique's Lake

THE MOUNTAIN MEANDER

Several cottage industries, tea gardens, coffee shops, and craftworkers and operators offering activities such as walks or riding have ganged together as part of the **Mountain Meander**, a route that enables you to tour Mutare and the winding circular scenic road through the Bvumba, making stops at some of the studios tucked away in the mountains producing items such as printed fabrics, woodwork and cheese. Among the highlights is the thoroughly recommended Majig on the Laurenceville Road, 5km beyond the *White Horse Inn*, which specializes in wooden products and produces fantastic African animal puzzles, which make perfect gifts. There's a shop to browse around, you can watch carpenters at work, a lovely café serves tea and muffins in the garden, and children will find plenty to keep them occupied. On the next property is Outrage, a clothes and craft shop that specializes in bigger sizes of women's clothing, some of it hand-dyed; they also stock some pottery and jewellery.

If you're into a longish **drive** through scenic tropical farmland, take the seventy-kilometre Burma Valley circular drive from the Essex Road which goes past the Vumba Cheese Shop with its excellent home-made cheeses, yoghurt, local and macadamia nuts grown in the valley. They also do teas and coffees, making it a good halfway stop. It has to be said that part of the drive is on dirt roads, while the places on the Laurenceville Road are on tar. Of the activities available on the Meander, the Seldomseen **bird walks** through forest at the top of the mountains are a highlight, and need to be booked in advance (☎020/215115 or 62837).

The Mountain Meander is aimed principally at day-trippers, and a handy **leaflet** with a map and description of participants is available from the Publicity Association in Mutare, Nyasa Seedcracker Designs and numerous outlets in Mutare and the Bvumba.

Chicamba Reial, 1000m below, are simply stupendous. Bear in mind that you'll need to add US$20 week entrance fee to the cost of staying here. ①.

Ndundu Lodge, just before the entrance to the Botanical Gardens; postal bookings through PO Box 62, Mutare (☎020/63777, *ndundu@yahoo.com*). The *Leopard Rock* of backpackers' lodges – a stylish and comfortable mountain retreat in a characterful three-storey thatched house run by hospitable Dutch couple Petra Ballings and Bart Wursten, who were so taken with the Bvumba on an earlier visit that they came back to live here. Adjacent to an excellent coffee shop (see Eating, p.278) and the Gardens, the place is filled with African masks, ethnic decor, timber furniture and has a cosy lounge with a fireplace. All accommodation sleeps two, with the choice of compact budget rooms with a double bunk, and large or small twin rooms. There's a bar and reasonably priced meals are available, including their African buffet speciality, which can be arranged in advance for groups. Mountain bikes are available for rent and you can go on a two- to three-day hiking trail with accommodation available en route. Free transfers from the Publicity Association in Mutare (collection Mon, Wed & Fri between noon and 12.30pm). ①.

HOTELS

The Castle, Private Bag V7401, Mutare (☎020/66726, *castle@icon.co.zw*). Splendid Italian-POW-built accommodation, 32km from Mutare, on a choice site 4km beyond the Botanical Gardens. Its owners only take one party of up to eight people at a time (minimum charge US$300), cooking lavishly for them. A wonderfully private secluded place to stay, but you need to book well ahead. Half-board ⑨.

Eden Lodge, Freshwater Road, off the Essex Valley road on the way to the Botanical Gardens; postal bookings through PO Box 881, Mutare (☎020/62000, fax 62001). Smart hotel, 21km from Mutare and halfway up the Bvumba Mountains, set in a forest overlooking the Zohwi Valley, with comfortable en-suite timber chalets. It's recommended for wildlife enthusiasts; you can watch birds and monkeys from the rooms. Their restaurant has an à la carte menu. ③.

Inn on the Bvumba, signposted off Bvumba road 8km from Mutare (☎ & fax 020/60722). Four two-bedroom cottages and eighteen suites in two blocks in a lovely old-fashioned hotel, 10min drive from Mutare, with views across the valley into Mozambique and homely touches like fresh flowers on tables and biscuits served with tea. A dining room, two lounges and a cocktail bar top it all off. It's a fair way from the Botanical Gardens, but good value. Highly recommended and often fully booked, so reserve in advance. Half-board ④.

Leopard's Rock Hotel, top of the Bvumba road; postal bookings through PO Box 2601, Harare; or PO Box 1322, Mutare (☎020/60177, 60198 or 60171, fax 61165, *lrock@syscom.co.zw*). Whether or not the Queen Mum got it right when she declared in 1953 that there was "nowhere more beautiful in Africa" than this superbly located upmarket hotel, you can't ignore its pink mock-chateau facade and matchless mountain views. The double-height entrance lobby has floor-to-ceiling windows framing the vines, huge trees and giant ferns, and all rooms have balconies overlooking the woodlands or the vast tended gardens. The hotel is internationally renowned for its exceptionally beautiful golf course, which you can enjoy even if you're not staying here (about US$10 for eighteen holes). Indoor pursuits include saunas, a gym and a casino; the terrace restaurant (one of three) is wonderful for a classy tea, or you can idle in one of the several plush drawing rooms with fires crackling all day when it's cold. Standard rooms ⑧.

White Horse Inn, Laurenceville Road, signposted at 14km peg along Bvumba road (☎020/60138 or 81083, fax 60325, mobile ☎011/404475). Prettily sited in the lower Bvumba, this pleasantly rambling formal country inn does its English-style thing very well. Most of the twelve rooms and suites done out with cottage decor have views of the garden and forest. Intimate, comfortable and cosy with a swimming pool, lovely gardens, bar with fire and restaurant overlooking the forest, which has the best food in the area: smart-casual attire is insisted upon. ⑤.

SELF-CATERING COTTAGES

Seldomseen Holiday Cottages, PO Box 441, Mutare (☎020/215115 or 688402, fax 020/62837). Four self-catering cottages, each different, surrounded by their own private gardens and paths into indigenous forest, with fantastic birdlife and guided bird walks; you'll find them a few kilometres from Leopard Rock and the Botanical Gardens. The cottages, which sleep 4–8 people (cot available), are 1km on a gravel road, signposted just after the 24-kilometre peg on the Bvumba Road. ②.

Trinafor Cottages, PO Box 201, Mutare (☎ & fax 020/65422, *throb@syscom.co.zw*). Four well-equipped self-catering cottages, each in a different part of the Haden-Tebb's fruit, flower and pecan-nut farm in the lower Vumba, right on the border with Mozambique. Each serviced cottage has a little children's playground and braai stand: you have the use of swimming pool with unimpeded views onto a valley in Mozambique. Cots are available. Trinafor is 10km along the tarred Laurenceville Road, which you take at the 14km peg on the Bvumba road from Mutare. ②.

Willowbrae Farm Cottages, PO Box 3167, Paulington, Mutare (☎020/219122, mobile ☎011/211517, *holiday@syscom.co.zw*). Three beautifully decorated cottages in the lower Bvumba in a forested setting close to running water; they sleep two to four people, with cots or extra beds available. Breakfast baskets, pre-cooked meals and braai packs are provided on request, and you can picnic around the rocky swimming hole. ②.

Bvumba Botanical Gardens

An annual rainfall higher than that of London has created lush cloud forest in the **Bvumba Mountains**, known in Manyika as "the mountains of the mist". Such dreamlike connotations have inspired the **Bvumba Botanical Gardens** (daily 7am–5pm; day entry US$10, week entry US$20), which lie 32km south of Mutare, harmoniously landscaped in the best romantic tradition of the English garden. Surrounded by indigenous forest, they were the creation of a former Mutare mayor and his wife, who lived here from the 1920s to the late 1950s and called them – in true homesick fashion – the Manchester Gardens. Remarkably, throughout the mayhem of the bush war, the gardens were kept in immaculate condition; they are now run by National Parks.

Paths meander through flowering shrubs and trees gathered from all over the world, waterlilies float on the central ornamental lake, scattered gazebos invite contemplative rests, and pristine lawns and flowerbeds give way on the fringes to a more African feel where giant tree ferns adorn streams – as they do all over the Eastern Highlands. The full range of Zimbabwe's upland flora is represented at Bvumba, including many varieties of orchid.

Summer downpours can flood everything in sight and it's a lot chillier up here than in Mutare. Weather permitting, a **teashop** is open every day from 10am until 4.30pm, but a far more exciting option is the fabulous and highly eccentric *Tony's Coffee Shop* close to the entrance outside the gardens (see below).

THE RAINFOREST
You can explore the **rainforest** that adjoins the gardens along a number of waymarked paths; maps are available at the main entrance. A **path** from the edge of the campsite takes you through the forest and back to the gardens – a two-hour circuit. It begins by leading down into jungly forest, where the indigenous trees rise about you – all darkness and silence until the monkeys catch sight of you and the birds screech in alarm. Further on you begin to hear the sound of chattering streams cascading over slippery rocks. For a shorter walk, several paths branch off the main trail.

GETTING TO THE GARDENS
Bvumba is not well served by public transport and the only reliable means of getting there apart from driving is by **taxi**, which shouldn't cost more than US$10 for a whole vehicle. The only **bus** to the gardens is a purportedly weekend service that departs from Mutare's E Street terminus, opposite the Customs House, on Fridays, Saturdays and Sundays, but in practice follows a rather arbitrary and changeable schedule. Prospects for **hitching** are reasonable, especially over the weekends, when the gardens are a popular teatime trip; on weekdays, a number of people living on smallholdings and farms in the mountains also go into Mutare to work, so late afternoon would again be a good time. Wait at the Bvumba Service Station on the corner of Park and Bvumba roads, where you'll get cars from the centre bypassing the bottom end of town. Many of these lifts, however, don't go all the way to the gardens, so be prepared for a longish walk.

At Cloudlands, the road forks, uphill to the gardens and down to the Essex and Burma valleys, where there are commercial farms and communal lands. The **walk** from here to the gardens is a rewarding though steep hike through smooth green hills, flower-specked pastures and thick stands of forest and pine trees. Modern-day Bvumba comprises indigenous woodland as well as commercial wattle forest, interspersed with farmhouses, cottages and workers' huts that have inviting English-style country gardens. On the Bvumba road, before you reach the gardens, you'll pass through **Bunga Forest Reserve**, an extension of the rainforest preserved in the gardens and also waymarked.

Eating and drinking
The unquestionable tea- or coffee-highlight of the Bvumba, and indeed of Zimbabwe, is **Tony's Coffee Shop** (daily 9am–5pm), near the entrance to the Botanical Gardens and adjacent to *Ndundu Lodge*. A compulsory port of call on any visit to the Bvumba, it provides a Baroque extravaganza of lethally decadent confections masquerading as cakes,

---

CHINYAKWAREMBA (LEOPARD'S ROCK)

Outside the gardens, it's possible to climb **Chinyakwaremba**, or **Leopard's Rock** hill. A path from a lay-by on the right of the main road leads up 1.5km from the turn-off to the Botanical Gardens. It's an easy twenty-minute walk up to the top, where there are lovely views into Burma Valley, across to Mozambique, and down to the chateau-like *Leopard's Rock Hotel* below (see Accommodation, p.277).

accompanied by a choice of over 25 types of coffee (mostly involving large dashes of alcohol), an equal variety of hot chocolates and over fifty choices of tea (including uncharacteristically healthy herbal ones). Housed in a fantastically quaint timber, stone and thatch-roofed woodland cottage that could be made of gingerbread, its crystal chandeliers, starched tablecloths, silver cutlery, fine china, brocaded upholstery and fresh roses give it a slightly unreal Brothers Grimm atmosphere. Expect to pay US$4–5 for a coffee and cake. At a more mundane level, all the Bvumba hotels have à la carte **restaurants** and cosy **pubs**, where you'll get a good meal in invariably beautiful surroundings. The *White Horse Inn* is a favourite Sunday lunch outing for Mutare residents and is reliable for a mid-priced meal any day of the week. For teas, possibilities include the tea room at the Botanical Gardens, or the pleasant tea garden at Majig Woodcutters, 5km beyond the *White Horse Inn*.

Nyanga region

Ninety minutes' drive north of Mutare on good tarred roads (and just 3hr from Harare), the **Nyanga region** attracts Zimbabwean outdoor enthusiasts, who come for the mountains and forests, and for trout fishing. The inevitable focus of the district is the **Nyanga National Park**, with several recreational dams overlooked by National Parks chalets and lodges and, less developed, the **Mtarazi National Park** on its southern edge, which most people experience from viewpoints on the Scenic Road. On the edges of the park itself are the tiny functional centres of **Juliasdale**, **Troutbeck** and **Nyanga**, serving the surrounding resorts, which feature a few hotels and numerous self-catering cottages and chalets. The region is scattered with intriguing **ruins and forts**, mostly unrestored and hidden beneath shrouds of ferns and undergrowth. On the grandest scale, Van Niekerk's ruins, now known as **Ziwa ruins**, straggle across at least fifty square kilometres of open country northwest of the park borders, in a jumble of rubble-strewn stone terraces and levels.

Below the Nyanga mountains, and visible from them, lies the tropical **Honde Valley**, a beautiful area of communal farms and tea estates with some superb walks. The area began to open up tentatively to visitors at the end of the 1990s, with some good and reasonably priced accommodation, but it remains pretty untouched by tourism. While an overnight stay in the valley is recommended, you can also take a drive through it as a day-trip from Nyanga.

The disparate character of the Nyanga region makes it ideally suited to **driving**, with the possibility of exploring its scenic routes on day excursions. Without a car you'll almost certainly have to make for tiny Nyanga village which, despite its diminutive size, is the transport hub of the region (Volvos, chicken buses and commuter omnibuses stop here).

The best **seasons** to visit the uplands are either side of the April to May and August to September school holidays. The scenery then is especially lovely and the weather as warm and dry as it ever gets. Be prepared, however, for cold nights all year round, and – if you come during the rainy season – for wet weather that can sometimes last for days on end, though it never snows. The valley is far warmer throughout the year.

Accommodation

Accommodation in the district is restricted to holiday-resort **hotels**, National Parks **lodges**, of which *Udu* and *Pungwe Drift* are especially nice, some **self-catering cottages** (see box on p.281), **camping** at the National Parks camps and cheap doubles and

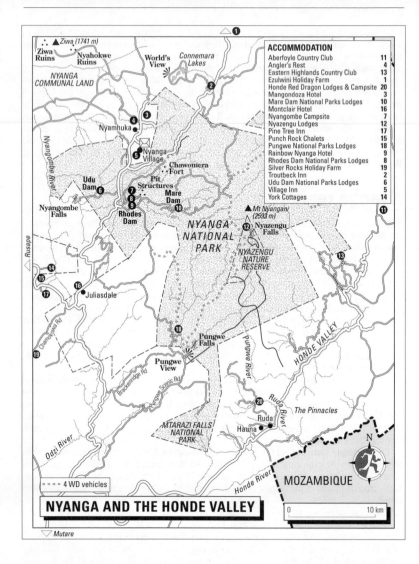

ACCOMMODATION

Aberfoyle Country Club	11
Angler's Rest	4
Eastern Highlands Country Club	13
Ezulwini Holiday Farm	1
Honde Red Dragon Lodges & Campsite	20
Mangondoza Hotel	3
Mare Dam National Parks Lodges	10
Montclair Hotel	16
Nyangombe Campsite	7
Nyazengu Lodges	12
Pine Tree Inn	17
Punch Rock Chalets	15
Pungwe National Parks Lodges	18
Rainbow Nyanga Hotel	9
Rhodes Dam National Parks Lodges	8
Silver Rocks Holiday Farm	19
Troutbeck Inn	2
Udu Dam National Parks Lodges	6
Village Inn	5
York Cottages	14

NYANGA AND THE HONDE VALLEY

0   10 km

dorms in Nyanga village if you're backpacking. The Honde Valley, one of the region's best-kept secrets, offers accommodation on tea estates or at the pleasant *Red Dragon* at Hauna.

National Parks lodges and campsites

The most convenient concentrations of overnight options are at **Rhodes Dam** and **Udu Dam** – at the western edge of the park, within a few kilometres of the main entrance and headquarters – and at **Mare Dam**, further afield to the east. Apart from

SELF-CATERING COTTAGES AND CHALETS

Unless otherwise specified, the cottages below are fully equipped and serviced, and lie outside the national park. Prices per cottage are between US$20 and US$40 per night (a minimum stay of two nights is the rule), depending on how many the cottages sleep, what facilities are offered and the time of year; public holidays are usually more expensive and you must book ahead. There are also the National Parks cottages, listed under the park (see p.285), which offer a reliable and pleasant stay, and one of the remotest and best options in the Nyazengu Private Nature Reserve (see p.288).

Brackenridge Cottage, PO Box 27, Juliasdale (☎029/26321). On a fruit farm 3km from Pungwe Falls, making it a good place to explore the Mtarazi area or hike into the Honde Valley. The cottage sleeps ten. Bring towels, cutlery and toilet rolls.

Ezulwini Holiday Farm, PO Box 12, Troutbeck (☎029–8/61121). Fully equipped and serviced cottages that sleep five, six or eight people on a working potato, apple and blueberry farm on the slopes of Rukotso Mountain; there are views of the Nyamaropa Valley and Mozambique. Turn left at the 26.5-kilometre peg 11.5km beyond the *Troutbeck Hotel* and follow the signs for about 4km down a dirt track. Pretty far from the National Park, so suitable for a few nights' stay.

The Follies, PO Box HG 760, Harare (☎04/746875 or 776136, fax 776137). High in the mountains overlooking the Connemara lakes near World's View, this cottage can sleep up to ten people.

Ivivi, Tintagel Road, close to the *Montclair Hotel* (☎04/308229, *rcunliffe@mango.zw*; keys must be collected in Harare). Artistically decorated and comfortable large one-roomed timber cottage owned by Harare painter Vivienne Jedeikin, with

a deck overlooking a beautiful valley. Depending on your outlook, its basic facilities – wood-fired hot water provided by an attendant, and oil lamps – will prove either too rustic or thrillingly romantic.

Punch Rock Chalets, 8km from Juliasdale on the Rusape road (☎029/224424). One thatched and two asbestos-roofed cottages set under a stand of shady flat-topped *Acacia abyssinica* trees overlooking a pretty dam. Fri & Sat minimum stay of two nights.

Silver Rocks Holiday Farm, PO Box 27, Juliasdale (☎029/21719). Located 10km south from the Juliasdale–Rusape road with two-, four- and six-bed cottages on a picturesque farm with the added enticements of a swimming pool, hikes and fresh farm produce.

York Cottages, adjacent to *Punch Rock*, 9.5km from Juliasdale on the Rusape road (☎029/2360). Two-storey newish timber chalets that sleep up to four people, with fireplaces and balconies set in sixteen square kilometres of Forestry Commission land with kudu, hares and bushpigs present. There are good views of granite formations and the Nyanga Mountains, and you're free to hike on the property.

the single luxury hotel in the national park (situated in its north), the only roofed **accommodation** consists of one- and two-bedroomed **lodges** (note that *Udu* has large lodges only). These can sleep up to eight people, and each is fully serviced, right down to there being loads of chopped wood and laid fires. During school holidays or long weekends, it's virtually impossible to get lodge accommodation without having **booked** six months or more ahead (you can do this through the National Parks Booking office in Harare; see p.96). In the off season, though, or during the week, you stand a fairly good chance of a place just turning up at the Parks' office at Rhodes Camp. **Camping** is cheap and space never a problem.

Budget hotels and rooms

Angler's Rest, 3km north of Nyanga village (☎0298/436). A 1950s hotel converted into eight en-suite lodges with kitchenettes, six en-suite double rooms and pretty rudimentary backpackers' dorms. No meals are served. If you phone, receptionist Charles Mutowa can arrange transfers from the bus station and he will also organize budget outings to World's View (US$3 per group) and day-tours to the national park (about US$22 per group, excluding entrance fee). Rooms and dorms ①, lodges ②.

Mangondoza Hotel, along the main road, about 4.5km north of Nyanga village (☎0298/588). Rural hotel in the middle of communal lands offering an alternative perspective to resorts. Concrete floors and iron bedsteads give the basic rooms a slightly school-dorm feeling, but it's a decent place managed by the affable David Nyamangodo, with a beautiful backdrop of huge granite formations. To the front it opens out to sparsely peopled communal lands that you can safely stroll in. Traditional meals such as *sadza* and *nyama* or chicken and rice are served in the dining room, making it more a cultural experience than just an overnight stay. ①.

Mid-range and expensive hotels

Montclair Hotel & Casino, in the middle of Juliasdale (☎029/2441–6, fax 2447). Seriously upmarket 84-room, four-star hotel with an evening dress code for the casino, attracting the glitz and Mercedes from Harare. However, you don't have to be a guest, or smartly dressed, to enjoy its valley-sided gardens for tea or drinks, or go one-armed-banditing in its darkened gambling hall. ⑥.

Pine Tree Inn, 5km west of the *Montclair* along the Rusape road (☎ & fax 029/2388 or 2259, fax 2388, *pinetree@pci.co.zw*). Stone cottages arranged around gardens overlooked by Susurumba kopje, and decorated in English country style. Cosy bar and lounge with fires and a restaurant with a top reputation for its à la carte menu. Half-board ④.

Rainbow Nyanga Hotel, on the south side of Rhodes Dam in the northwest corner of Nyanga National Park (book through central reservations in Harare: ☎04/733781, fax 708125, mobile ☎011/205 588, *reservations@rainbowgrp.co.zw*; hotel: ☎0298/376–7, fax 477). The only private hotel inside the national park itself is an atmospheric old-fashioned institution. Its 1950s and 1960s heyday is reflected in the Rhodesian high-colonial style of polished cement floors, tin roofs and verandahs, and Morris chairs overlooking terraced lawns. En-suite rooms. ④.

Troutbeck Inn, Nyanga village (☎0298/305–6, fax 474). Very much a mountain resort amid the pines, with all sorts of leisure activities, from croquet to riding. The conspicuously rich take their holidays here, bringing the nanny along to look after the kids, though it still manages to be relaxed and informal. ⑧.

The Village Inn, Nyanga village (☎0298/336, 339 or 506). Comfortable, unpretentious family hotel with nicely furnished en-suite rooms amid grassy gardens that have a small watercourse running through them, and a fenced-in swimming pool. It's the only place to stay in the village. Full board ④.

Juliasdale, Nyanga village and around

Straggling along the main road to Nyanga, **JULIASDALE** lies on the west of the park, 10.5km south of Rhodes Camp. A regional centre, it consists of little more than Hogan's Supermarket, a branch of Zimbank (Mon, Tues, Thurs & Fri 8am–3pm, Wed 8am–1pm; Sat 8–11am), a petrol station and post office. The area around is a popular retirement location for white Zimbabweans; Robert Mugabe, too, has a country retreat somewhere among the forests and fruit farms. Lower down, there are splendid granite valleys, msasa trees and tempting *gomos* to climb. **Nyanga village**, 23km from Juliasdale on a good tarred road, is a bigger centre, tucked into a salient that eats into the north of the park and services the nearby communal lands with shops and buses, and the region's cheapest hotels. Some 17km to its north on a tarred road that passes through the park, **Troutbeck** is little more than the *Troutbeck Inn* and a few self-catering cottages, known for their proximity to **World's View** and its heady vistas.

Nyanga village

NYANGA village nestles in a valley surrounded by mountains and extensive grasslands. A charming if unexciting place, it makes a good base, with fine walks nearby and easy hitching to the national park. It's also the jumping off point for the Matema Village Visits which give you an experience of rural Zimbabwean life in the communal lands beyond *Troutbeck Inn*. The **Three Sisters** mountain, its slopes dotted with smart houses, dominates the village, with the huge rampart of the Troutbeck Massif beyond. The village itself straggles between two distinct characters: at the more upmarket end is *The Village Inn*, at the other the **Nyamhuka** township and the *Mangondoza Hotel*.

The only public transport to Nyanga are **Volvo and chicken buses** from Mutare and Harare which arrive at the bus terminal in **Nyamhuka township**, just off the main road. Near Nyamhuka, your eyes will be drawn to a series of brightly painted huts proclaiming a **craft village**, which is surrounded by a lake of stone sculptures and some carvers busily chipping away.

Less than a kilometre away is Nyanga's tiny formerly white village centre, where you'll find the **tourist information bureau** (Mon–Fri 9am–1pm & 2–4.30pm, Sat 9–11.30am) in the library building on the east side of the green. **Shops and banks** are clustered in a huddle that consists of a filling station; a branch of the Standard Chartered Bank (Mon–Fri 8am–12.30pm, Sat 8–11am); the Nyanga Pharmacy, which dispenses medicines and sells newspapers and magazines; the Rochdale Stores, where you can buy a limited range of basic groceries such as fresh bread, milk, eggs, frozen meat and canned goods; and the **Zuwa Weaving Co-op** which has lovely handmade stuff in wool, cotton and gudza (a fibre made from chewed baobab bark), subtly coloured with local plant dyes.

Ziwa and Nyahokwe

The remote (and tricky to reach without a car) **ruins** at ZIWA spread for kilometres across the hillsides north of Nyanga. Their central reserve is forty square kilometres in extent but this vast complex rambles very much further than that. They are also, confusingly, known by their old colonial name, **Van Niekerk's ruins** – after the Boer major of nearby Bideford Farm, who led the archeologist Randall McIver around the site in 1905.

Visiting the ruins without your own car is pretty well impossible, as there is no public transport, and few vehicles, if any, pass this way. The ruins and museum are 29km from Rhodes Camp and signposted. The best route is to travel north out of Nyanga village for 14km, turning left to reach the Nyahokwe Village 5km on site (see p.284); from here it's a further 8km to Ziwa.

THE RUINS

Exploring **the ruins** you meander on and on, drawn by yet another pathway or area of terracing to the next hill. Little restoration has taken place: stepping about the stone-littered bush you can feel what it must have been like for early archeologists. At first it all seems somewhat puzzling, but after a time patterns do begin to emerge, with Ziwa Mountain a point of orientation back to the road. To help out, there's a small **museum** on site, and guides to show you around.

The settlement's seventeenth- and eighteenth-century builders may have been influenced by Great Zimbabwe masonry techniques. But these are no monuments to a wealthy ruling class, rather the **homesteads and farms** of ordinary people. When the uplands over to the east lost fertility and crops began to fail, people shifted westwards into the valleys. They built **terraces** for crops and **enclosures** for huts and livestock; platforms for huts are less common than in the uplands as the abundance of stone meant that surrounding walls could be used for protection. Typically, entrances are lintelled and you may notice slots in the inner doorway for a wooden drawbar. **Grooves** are worn into some flat stones within enclosures where women ground grain. You can walk down the networks of walled **lanes**, probably for driving livestock and still in good condition, but with candelabra trees and aloes growing out of the heavy stonework. And, if you've visited the Rhodes Dam reconstruction, you'll quickly be able to spot the tree-spouting **pit structures**.

Standing back and trying to grasp the extent the ruins, it's tempting to imagine an enormous community inhabiting the hills and valleys. However, it's more likely that these structures were the work of a relatively few agriculturalists, spread over two centuries, who had to move on every few years when the soil lost its fertility. Although scant excavations have been carried out, it is clear that the stonework was done by **Bantu-speaking people** and not by Portuguese or Arabs.

NYAHOKWE

The granite-built **Nyahokwe Village Site** lies crouched under the cliff face of the top of Nyahokwe Mountain and has similar characteristics to the other Nyanga ruins. One really interesting feature is a **dare**, or meeting place for elders – a large circular area with upright stones around it. Also, about 100m below the ruins (on a bare granite plateau just off the path), there are some eighty or so **grinding hollows** in groups. Probably several people would have sat around each group grinding down iron-bearing rock for smelting. The remains of **furnaces** have been found in the area and trade was certainly pursued with border-crossing Portuguese.

Some of the nearby granite outcrops – as at Ziwa – are **sacred mountains**, probably centres of the old **Mwari Cult** and not a good idea to climb. Two North Korean officers who were training Zimbabwean brigades in the 1980s took a disdainful attitude to local prohibitions about Ziwa, climbed it, and were never seen again.

Troutbeck, World's View and Matema village

Up in the mists beyond the northeast boundary of the national park, **TROUTBECK**, 17km from Nyanga village, was the fantasy creation of one Major McIlwaine, an Irishman who established the very swish **Troutbeck Inn** (see p.282), planted acres of forest on the bare hills – in the early days of the inn he made each visitor plant a tree – and created several lakes. Almost in conspiracy with the artifice, the weather up here can be cool and drizzly when the rest of the country is sweltering; they claim at *Troutbeck* that the log fire in the foyer has been kept burning since the place was built in 1950. Non-residents are able to rent **horses** to ride up through the bracken and ferns to **World's View** – a thrilling scarp-edge panorama.

Opposite the gates of *Troutbeck Inn*, you'll find a general store selling basics, a garage, bus stop and a very quaint post office. Beyond *Troutbeck Inn*, off the Nyamaropa road, is a predominantly white dairy and fruit-farming area with a couple of cottages for rent. If you continue along the Nyamaropa Road you reach the communal lands and **MATEMA village**, with shops, a school, church and grinding mill, which you can visit on a rural village tour.

Getting to Troutbeck without your own car is not too difficult. Occasional **buses** run from Nyanga village to Troutbeck and Nyamaropa Communal Lands, or it's a rather more reliable **hitch** from the Troutbeck turn-off, a couple of kilometres south of Nyanga on the main road. Buses back to Nyanga leave from outside the trading store opposite the hotel. If you're just up for the day and get to World's View early enough, you can **walk** 10km directly back to Nyanga village. Just below the World's View car park, a steep, narrow path leads down the mountain for 4km until it reaches a prominent dirt road, from where it's another 6km to Nyanga village.

WORLD'S VIEW

World's View – not to be confused with the World's View where Cecil Rhodes is buried – is a seven-kilometre hike, or ride, from Troutbeck. At the summit of the steep neighbouring high ground, the remains of a **fort** are connected to the mountain by a narrow ridge. With precipices on three sides, this is definitely the wettest and windiest stonework site of all. In the wide-open treeless moorland of this lakes district, you can get an idea of what the country was like before the *Troutbeck* transformation. The lakes, disappointingly, aren't for public use.

VSO-supported **Matema Village Visits** run every day, and start either from Nyanga village, where a guide can meet you at the bus terminus and accompany you on the bus for the 30–45 minute ride to Matema, or closer by at Troutbeck. Reasonably priced, with fifty percent of the proceeds going into a community fund, a half-day outing includes a walking tour of the village, visiting traditional homes, meeting people and finding out about activities such as brick-making, thatching and market gardening. A full-day tour includes a traditional meal of *sadza* and relish cooked on an open fire, while the overnight option allows you to stay with a family, and have more time to absorb village life. To book, contact Spiwe Matema at the Nyanga Tourist Office (☎029–8/435).

Nyanga National Park

Devoid of big game but with plenty of unthreatening smaller animals and antelope, **NYANGA NATIONAL PARK** lends itself perfectly to hiking along the hundreds of well-defined footpaths or the fishing roads that crisscross its surface. There are less energetic pursuits on offer, too, such as lazing around the pools and waterfalls at one of the National Parks' three camps (see p.280). The most developed section of the park lies in the **northwest**, where the majority of accommodation is located near the shores of **Rhodes**, **Udu** and **Mare dams**. Within hiking distance of the dams you'll find some archeological sites, the most interesting of which are the **Rhodes Dam Pit Structure**, a reconstructed indigenous homestead, and the **Chawomera** and **Nyangwe fort**, two of a series of puzzling structures that despite their appearance don't seem to have been used for defence.

In the **eastern sector** of the park, the looming, myth-bound mass of **Mount Nyangani** (2592m) is a simple enough summit to scale. At its base, in the middle of the national park, an exceptionally beautiful lozenge of land constitutes the **Nyazengu Private Nature Reserve**, which has accommodation, but can only be reached on foot or by 4WD vehicle. The southern sector of the park takes in remote **wilderness territory**, where you could easily spend several days hiking, although most people tour the park by car, and during rounds of teas and lunches, inevitably driving along the approximately thirty-kilometre Scenic Road from the *Rainbow Nyanga Hotel* to **Mtarazi Falls**, which takes in the fabulous views of **Pungwe Gorge**, the **Honde Valley** and the Mtarazi Falls themselves. The road is unsealed and can be rough, or slippery during the summer months of high rainfall.

Entry fees to the park are US$10 for one day and US$20 for week entry. You will need to bring most provisions with you. There is just one park **shop** (daily 9am–2pm), on the south side of Rhodes Dam, which sells essential food supplies, but nothing fresh, though you can get all you need at either Juliasdale or Nyanga village. The national park has no **moneychanging** facilities, but there is a bank in Nyanga village, as well as Juliasdale, and petrol at both centres. The river water throughout Nyanga is bilharzia-free and drinkable.

Rhodes Dam and around

RHODES DAM is the most convenient, though the least exciting, of the camps, close to the main road and near the shop and hotel, and site of the local Parks office (office open daily 7am–6pm; ☎0298/274 or 384). The **lodges** here, tucked between the pines, face onto a small lake, one of several recreational lakes in the park. The area is tame, but pleasing, and it provides easy access to some historical sites as well as walks around the rest of the park.

NYANGOMBE CAMPSITE AND BRIGHTON BEACH

A couple of kilometres from the office, on the main Nyanga road, is **Nyangombe campsite**, reached via a short cut over the Nyangombe River. Along the river you'll see a natural pool known – by the local expat community at least – as **Brighton Beach**, complete with changing rooms and gazebo. A small waterfall and rock slide culminate in a large pool of icy water surrounded by a river-sand beach – good for sunbathing, and not as crowded as the name might suggest.

RAINBOW NYANGA HOTEL AND MUSEUM

After visiting the Nyanga area in 1896, Cecil Rhodes wrote to his agent:

> *Dear McDonald*
> *Inyanga is much finer than you described. I find a good many farms are being occupied. Before it is all gone, buy me quickly up to 100,000 acres and be sure to take in the Pungwe Falls. I would like to try sheep and apple growing. Do not say you are buying for me.*
> *Yrs. C.J. Rhodes*

The old colonialist was successful in acquiring a substantial slice of territory and, indeed, the park was known up until Independence as "Rhodes Inyanga".

Rhodes's former residence, a simple Georgian-style stone house set among English oaks and chestnuts, stands just across the lake from Rhodes Dam. It is now incorporated into the **Rainbow Nyanga Hotel** (see p.282): non-residents are allowed to drift into the rose garden and look round the **Nyanga Historical Exhibition** in the old stables (daily except Wed 9am–1pm & 2.30–5.50pm; US$0.10), where, alongside a fair amount of Rhodes memorabilia, an interesting photo exhibition gives the history of colonization in the area from the Portuguese and British up to recent resistance. There's a comprehensive display in homage to **Chief Rekayi Tangwena**, one of Zimbabwe's nationalist stalwarts, buried at Heroes' Acre in Harare. Tangwena fought against the eviction of his people from their land in the Nyafara area beyond Troutbeck during the Smith era, gave considerable assistance to guerrillas throughout the **bush war**, and provided a link with the spirit mediums who encouraged resistance. In 1975 he helped **Robert Mugabe** and **Edgar Tekere** escape into Mozambique and, after Independence and his appointment as a senator, he participated in a programme here to resettle orphaned and homeless children.

THE RHODES DAM PIT STRUCTURE

A common sight throughout the Nyanga area are sixteenth-century **pit structures**, or "slave pits" – roofless, two- to three-metre-deep enclosures that are something of a mystery. No archeological evidence has been found to support the notion that they were used to detain slaves – certainly no one seems to know who kept the slaves, who the slaves were and why they didn't escape. Other interpretations suggest they were fortified refuges for women and children, grain stores, gold-washing tanks or symbolic representations of the Phoenician fertility goddess Astarte's womb. The most widely accepted theory is that the pits were livestock pens, some say for miniature cattle that Portuguese travellers were supposed to have seen. But in view of the reputation of the Portuguese explorers for tall stories, and in the absence of any supporting material, most people keep an open mind about this. It's more likely that ordinary goats, sheep and pigs were corralled in the enclosures.

At the **Rhodes Dam Pit Structure**, a dry-stone wall pit on an earth platform is partially cut into the side of a hill and held back by a retaining wall on the lower slopes. This was the centre of the homestead, and from here you can creep into a pit, through a narrow, curved tunnel, roofed with flat stone slabs. You can't see the exit from the entrance, but halfway along the sky penetrates through a gap that used to open into the largest hut on the platform above: a nifty floor slot enabled the occupants to block and unblock the passage at will with a timber pole. According to one theory, the master of the house had his headrest at the top of the pole and no one could tamper with the security system without waking him. Evidence of a drainage system in the pits reinforces the idea that animals rather than grain were kept in them.

There are thousands of pit structures in Nyanga which you'll stumble across, sometimes literally, on walks. They occur singly or in groups of as many as twelve or more – look out for an isolated clump of trees or thick bush when you're walking in the region. If you're interested, it's as well to visit the developed Rhodes Dam Pit site first so you know what you're looking for.

CHAWOMERA FORT

The other ruins at Nyanga, equally mysterious, are of fort-like hilltop structures, always commanding superb views across the valleys and plains. From the pit structure exhibit, there's an agreeable ninety-minute walk to **Chawomera Fort** and pits, one of the easiest hilltop fort ruins to reach.

The function of these so-called forts, which are invariably sited next to a few pits, is uncertain, as all sorts of things indicate that they weren't actually built for defence. While all the walls have small, square **loopholes**, reminiscent of gun-slits, when you look through them the views are restricted and no weapon could effectively have been fired from them. Assailants, moreover, would have quite easily been able to fire through the wide inside openings. And, although the forts are in easily defensible positions, none has a nearby water supply, so inhabitants couldn't have withstood a siege for long. One theory suggests they were a series of beacons or signal points, from where a kudu horn sounded messages carried across the valleys. It is in fact possible to see several forts from one site, once you can recognize the hills on which they're constructed.

As you head for Chawomera from the Rhodes Dam Pit Structure, you'll see a dirt road leading to workers' houses attached to the **Government Experimental Orchard**. Follow it for a few metres and, just before a fence, take a well-defined path next to a pine plantation on your left. This path continues down to the **Nyangombe River**, hugging the riverbank and passing several bathing spots along the way. Cross the river at the second bridge and continue uphill along the path until it hits the gravel road from Rhodes Dam.

Mare Dam, Mount Nyangani and Nyazengu

MARE (pronounced "mah-ree") is the camp closest to Mount Nyangani and the isolated areas between the "back" of Nyangani and the Pungwe Falls in the south. Despite its proximity to these remote parts, though, pine-forested Mare Dam itself has no hint of the back of beyond. In a rare flight of fantasy, National Parks have built the well-sheltered **lodges** like Swiss chalets, complete with pitched roofs, wooden finishings and laid log fires (bring your own matches). If you're into riding, Mare is a convenient camp, just 3km from the national park's stables.

NYANGWE FORT

Nyangwe Fort, thirty minutes' uphill trudge (or a rather easier ride) above Mare Dam, is worth visiting for the view alone. It is also, however, the most complex of the forts here, five enclosures surrounding the original one on the summit. Within the structure – possibly dating back to the sixteenth century – are the remains of nineteen circular stone bases for huts or granaries.

From Nyangwe you look straight across to **Chawomera Fort** (see above), a good two hours' walk away. To reach it, head down the hill just before the pony trails office and stables on the main road, from where a well-defined path on your right skirts pine plantations and heads straight across the grassy valley, over the Nyangombe River to the fort's twin hills.

FISHING, HORSE-RIDING AND TENNIS

Boat rental is possible at any of the dams – more for an afternoon drifting in the sun rather than any serious rowing (the lakes are pretty small). You need to claim a boat quickly, though, as many are taken by trout fishermen. The **fishing** is good, too: rainbow, brook and brown trout can be hooked all year – you need a licence from Rhodes Dam office, and your own rod. **Horse-riding** can be arranged at Rhodes, Udu or Mare camps; the stables are an hour's walk from Rhodes, on the Mare road. The horses come with a guide, who'll take you on paths through the park for ninety minutes to the pit structures, Nyangwe Fort or the experimental orchard. Proficient riders can also book a horse for a full day's escorted ride. The terrain is ideal for brisk gallops and the Nyangombe River provides delightful picnic sites. **Tennis** rackets can be rented at the rather under-used courts at Rhodes Camp.

MOUNT NYANGANI

Unlike Mount Ziwa in the north, which rises abruptly from the plain, **MOUNT NYANGANI**, long and flat-topped, seems scarcely higher than the mountains around it. Nevertheless, at 2592m it's a substantial mountain, Zimbabwe's highest, and often mist-wrapped and shadowy. According to local legend it has frightening people-eating tendencies, and one or two walkers have disappeared without trace over the years. The mountain holds considerable religious significance for Shona people. Locals from the Honde Valley say the mountain should be approached very respectfully – one should never shout or make a noise on it – and that they wouldn't dream of climbing it themselves.

Despite the taboos, Nyangani is frequently climbed as a morning's hike. The two-hour **ascent** is clearly marked from the car park, and there are white cairns along the way to guide you where the path becomes indistinct. The climb reveals spectacular panoramas into Mozambique, and around the summit you'll find lots of water; several rivers rise here. There are areas of quicksand up here, too – it's certainly marshy towards the summit – and it's not difficult to see how the people-swallowing reputation might have arisen. Go up only in fine weather and take something warm in case the mist comes down. The very active **Mountain Club of Zimbabwe** does this climb regularly and has its own hut on Nyanga.

To get to the **trailhead** without a car, you have to hitch the 10km from Mare. If you decide to walk, it means making camp at the base, which is in any case ideal if you intend to hike for a few days beyond Nyangani to Mtarazi National Park and into the Honde Valley. An ambitious and very beautiful three-day hike of 48km will take you from Nyangani to the Pungwe Falls, Mtarazi Falls and into the Honde Valley (see p.290), from where you can catch a bus back to Mutare.

Nyazengu Private Nature Reserve

Perhaps the most rewarding way to explore the Nyangani area and beyond is to camp and hike through the privately owned, and very remote, **Nyazengu Private Nature Reserve** in the national park. The reserve, at the base of Nyangani, has exceptionally beautiful views of the mountain and across the grasslands towards the Pungwe Gorge. There's a choice of several well-marked trails, some of which take you to waterfalls and clear pools of amber rocks. The **Nyazengu Falls**, deep in forest, are easily as dramatic as the better-known Mtarazi Falls. One trail takes you right to their valley base, or you can climb upwards to the top of Nyangani.

While it's possible to go for a day's hike in the reserve, for a modest fee per vehicle and per person, it makes an ideal base for a couple of days' walking. The main **campsite**, near the office, is spectacularly situated and completely undeveloped, apart from a long drop. Staff provide water for cooking, though – all the river water is safe to drink. It's also possible to camp at the Nyazengu Falls, in a sheltered forest site, though there are no facilities at all. If camping doesn't appeal, there are two lovely **cottages** for rent, sleeping six (US$35) or four people (US$20), perched on the side of the mountain: book through Dr Trace, Nyazengu (☎04/339679, *vet@samara.co.zw*).

Unless you hike in on foot, which takes a full day from Mare Dam, you'll need a high-clearance 4WD vehicle to get to Nyazengu – you have to ford a river, but the rough road is passable all year round. Take the road marked "no entry", on the right just before the road climbs to the Nyangani car park. From here it's 8km to the office where you obtain a permit to walk. There are no shops or supplies available in the reserve, but you can buy fresh trout at the office.

Udu Dam

Unlike Rhodes and Mare, **Udu Camp**, in the far west corner of the park, provides the opportunity to get out of the pines and into granite and indigenous vegetation. The **lodges**, with long sloping roofs, based on traditional Nyika thatching, overlook the dam and ruin-capped hills, and *Acacia abyssinicas* grow in a smooth V-shaped stand, up the facing slopes. The **Udu River** flows through here, too, forming an exquisite, wide valley where waterbuck feed, before leading into the dam and out into a bathing pool, and eventually joining with the Nyangombe.

The **Udu Valley** preserves the gentle steps of ancient terracing, and remains dotted with pit structures, including one outside the back door of the Parks office. The chunky **Nyangombe Falls** with square-cut rocks are near Udu and make a nice walk. And it's easy to find your way around Udu: wandering in the encircling hills you can always spot the valley.

The two-kilometre **walk to the camp** from the main Nyanga road, opposite the Nyangombe **campsite**, is pretty, heading first uphill, then opening out into a view of the camp in the valley; you'll invariably get a lift from a passing car, if you want it. Well-worn short cuts between the loops in the road take you straight to the nearest **shop** – at Rhodes Hall.

NYANGOMBE FALLS

The **Nyangombe Falls** are an impressive cubist plunge, thirty minutes' walk if you take the dirt road, or ninety minutes if you go over the saddle of the hills facing the

---

NYANGA'S FLORA AND WILDLIFE

The vast grassy areas of Nyanga hold a fantastic range of **wild flowers**. Look out for Zimbabwe's national bloom, the delicate **flame lily** (here more often yellow than red), **gladioli**, **ground orchids** and different kinds of **heather**. **Aloes** of all sizes grow in the various ruins, forming beacons in June and July when they flower red and orange. After grass fires, the red **fire lily** springs up with extraordinary vigour in the blackened stubble. South Africa's floral emblem, the furry **protea**, grows well here too; eight species are native to Zimbabwe and three endemic to the Eastern Highlands. They are easily recognizable – small trees with white or pinkish-white flowers surrounded by rose, or deeper pink bracts covered with silvery hairs.

There's an amazing diversity of local **wildlife**. It's not as spectacular as in the big game parks, but kudu, reedbuck, klipspringer, leopard, hyena and herds of wildebeest all inhabit the park, and Nyanga is well-known for its populations of samango monkeys and blue duikers, which are found nowhere else in Zimbabwe. One of the former wardens compiled a check list of mammals and birds – including rare sightings of buffalo, which occasionally penetrate into the Pungwe Gorge, and even lion passing secretively through. However, you're highly unlikely to meet any of these travellers.

lodges. The Nyangombe tumbles dramatically over steep blocks before smoothing out into a densely wooded gorge below. Inviting as it looks, several people have been killed trying to climb down the walls of the gorge or edging too close to the waterfall, where the rocks are treacherously wet. You can see the waterfall quite clearly from dry rocks, a short downhill walk from the car park.

To reach the falls over the hills, take the path that starts at the back door of Udu Camp reception and keep bearing right to cross the river, then cut up to the saddle between two hills through woodland with dwarf bonsai-like msasas, wild fruit trees and the odd antelope. Follow your nose down until you turn right onto the dirt road to the falls. Instead of descending, you could carry on to the top of the highest hill to inspect a collapsed **fort** marked by a single big tree, clearly visible from the Udu Camp office. A path from the ruins leads back down through trees, across the dam wall (next to the pool) and to the lodges.

Mtarazi National Park

Adjoining Nyanga Park's southern edge, the **MTARAZI NATIONAL PARK** is essentially considered part of the Nyanga region. It is, however, a much wilder zone, with undisturbed indigenous forest, and is somewhat difficult to reach without a car. But, if you've time you can hike there: two recently rebuilt National Parks cottages in the dramatic **Pungwe Gorge**, plus the unparalleled views into the luxuriant **Honde Valley** and Mozambique, provide strong incentive. It's magnificent country.

Most people tend to get only as far as the viewpoints along the **Scenic Road** which loops eastwards from the main Mutare–Nyanga Village road. These take in the much-photographed vistas of the **Pungwe Falls** and Gorge, the 762-metre drop of the **Mtarazi Falls** and the deep seat of the **Honde Valley**. If you're **hiking**, it's possible to penetrate these panoramas, either from the ridge of the Scenic Road itself or, more adventurously, walking the park from Rhodes Camp to Nyangani in the west, south to Pungwe and Mtarazi falls, then dropping into the Honde Valley – approximately 60km in all.

Traffic is light along the Scenic Road and you'll end up walking much of it if you're car-less. Hikers have got stranded along this route – not an experience to be recommended, as it's very wild, entirely without facilities, and patrolled by leopards and even the odd lion.

Accommodation

Places to stay in the area are thin on the ground and it's advisable to make arrangements before you arrive. Above Mtarazi Falls, most accommodation, apart from the National Parks lodges, lies along the Scenic or Brackenridge roads. For the latest details on private cottages, contact the Publicity Association in Mutare. **National Parks accommodation** is available at the **campsite** (①), above Mtarazi Falls, just past the national park entrance, where you'll find basic facilities, but it's a definite option if you're intrepid, or in a car. **National Parks Lodges** (②) are located at Pungwe Drift, above the Pungwe Falls (book through National Parks Central Booking in Harare or Bulawayo). If you're after solitude and natural beauty, these are the choicest places to stay anywhere in the Nyanga–Mtarazi area. Limited to a pair of two-bedroom, fully equipped self-catering lodges set idyllically on either side of the river (for up to five people), they're in great demand at peak season.

Pungwe Gorge and Falls

The first obvious stop on the Scenic Road is for the bird's-eye view of **Pungwe Gorge** and the top of the Falls before the Pungwe River, which rises at the foot of Mount Nyangani and flows southwards through the park before plummeting 240m into a dramatic tree-gridded gorge and eventually descending into the Honde Valley and Mozambique. Although you can't see the falls themselves, you'll certainly hear their roar. Getting down to the Pungwe River at Pungwe Drift isn't as daunting as it looks from the top. From the Scenic Road, a couple of kilometres north of the viewpoint, follow the signposts to the Pungwe Drift, where you'll find the National Parks cottages (40min on foot – the rough road needs a high-clearance vehicle), then walk another twenty minutes along a riverside path to the top of the Falls. There's a great swimming spot in the river above the Falls; the current here won't tow you over the edge and you can float downstream and safely duck out before the flow gathers speed. The bush comes right to the water's edge amid smooth rocks and clean river sand.

Basing yourself here, or hiking around the park, you can continue northeast along the **Drift Road** as it follows the valley and climbs onto the escarpment: high mountains rear up on your right and fantastic views open into the gorge all the way to the car park at the base of Mount Nyangani (24km). From this track you can drop into some very wild montane forest down in the gorge.

If you've less time, a couple of disused fishing roads leading off the Scenic Road make good shorter walks. Some 4km north of the turn-off to Pungwe Drift, a no-through road leads 1km down to **Thomborutedza Falls**. Here, the fast-flowing river rushes over sink holes, which create an effervescent, natural Jacuzzi. Two kilometres beyond, a similar dead-end track passes various pit structures, and trails the Pungwe nearer to its source on Nyangani.

Mtarazi Falls and Honde View

Mtarazi Falls – the highest in Zimbabwe – are at the end of the line for Scenic Road view-spotters and a fair walk from their signposted car park. They spout from the cleaved edge of the vertical green cliff to disappear in virgin forest 1km below. The best time to be here is late afternoon, when the sun behind the water makes the slender falls gauzy and golden. To **swim** nearby, make your way to the river above the falls, marked by beautiful tree ferns, where brown rocks, sloping into the river pools, warm the water a little. On the road to Mtarazi, don't miss the turn to the **Honde View**; the aerial view of the Honde Valley, where its contours relax to enter Mozambique, is stunning.

MTARAZI ADVENTURE

If you thought Victoria Falls was the only place in Zimbabwe for **whitewater rafting and adventure**, then the Eastern Highlands will surprise you. Far and Wide runs a range of outdoor adventure activities which are more challenging than those at the Falls, whitewater rafting and kayaking being the most popular options. One-day trips start at the Pungwe Gorge in the Honde Valley and traverse a series of rapids – many of them with steep drops – including seven grade fours. On the **rafts**, you're not rowed by a guide, as at the Falls, but navigate yourself in a two- or four-person inflatable instead – more difficult, and consequently more rewarding. **Kayaks** along the same route are single-person crafts. Safety kayakers accompany the trips, which cost US$60–70 for a full day; a less difficult one-day "family" rafting trip through grade-two and -three rapids starts at US$35. Finally, if – and only if – you're an expert, you may want to try a specialist kayaking option along the Gairezi River, taking in grade-six rapids.

Other activities include half-day guided **mountain-biking** trips through the Nyanga Wilderness, **abseiling** off the Honde Valley escarpment, **rock climbing** and **guided walks**. Guides on all activities are knowledgeable about the flora and fauna of the area, and fully inclusive prices start at US$35 per day. Book through Far and Wide, Box 14, Juliasdale (☎029/3011–2, fax 3011, mobile ☎011/717 583, *farnwide@pci.co.zw*).

FOREST TRAILS

Several well-trodden **trails** lead down from the escarpment into the **Honde Valley**: two used by workers from the valley connect the Pungwe and Honde viewpoints, but you'd really need a local person to show you. One of the overgrown paths is about 500m from Mtarazi, heading east into the valley; without a guide, it's hard to know which fork to take when the path splits. The other equally teasing trail drops right into the Pungwe Gorge and hugs the river bank into the Honde Valley below. If you find someone to show you the way, though, either walk makes a good, day-long hike to the valley floor and back, through awesome **montane forest** which opens into clearings with views of the valley. From Honde you can catch a bus to Mutare if you're moving on.

The mountainous regions of Nyanga have over one hundred species of **fern**, including four different types of the giant tree fern. Overhead, epiphytes – orchids of many varieties – dangle from the branches. This kind of forest, increasingly whittled away by tree clearance, once covered the whole of Nyanga. **Hardwood species** include mlanje cedar and yellowwood, while **flowering trees** to look out for are cape chestnut, the forest fever tree with its giant leaves and sweet-scented flowers, the glossy-leaved wild holly and the tube-flowered notsung.

While you admire the canopy above, spare the odd glance for the forest floor, which has its own absorbing interest and occasional dangerous encounter. The **gaboon viper**, brightly patterned with white, buff, purple, pink and deep-brown diamonds and triangles, spends its days half-buried in the leaves and litter of the forest floors of the Eastern Highlands. Although less aggressive than other vipers, it's the largest of the family and heavily built: up to 1.5m long, gorgeous and deadly.

The Honde Valley

Stretching across the foot of the Nyanga range and adjoining Mozambique, the tropically verdant **HONDE VALLEY** stands in striking contrast to the tamer resorts that look down on it. While the Nyanga area is best known for its uplands, with their mountain air and winter log fires, the Honde is a fertile hothouse of tropical vegetation flourishing under humid summer temperatures that often exceed 30°C. Apart from taking a scenic drive along the valley floor past **traditional villages**, there are a number of possible hikes, including ones to the **Pungwe River** and to the foot of the **Mtarazi Falls**, as well as visits to **tea and coffee estates**. Just opening up after decades of political woes, the Honde Valley is exceptionally interesting and beautiful, accessible on a tarred road, with a handful of places to stay.

Some history

During the Zimbabwean **liberation struggle** of the 1960s and 1970s, some of the bloodiest fighting and atrocities took place in the Honde, due to its proximity to Mozambique, which provided refuge to anti-Smith guerrillas, a fact which remains the sum of what most people know of it. For nearly two decades, villagers found themselves drawn into the war between pro- and anti-government forces. By the conclusion of the conflict at the end of the 1970s, large numbers of valley dwellers had been confined by the white government to **"Protected Villages"** (aka "PVs", known more simply by Africans as "the cages"), fenced settlements under armed guard resembling concentration camps. Agriculture ceased and villagers were forced to live on rations provided by Smith – a potent tool of political control. You can still see relics of the PVs all over the valley in the form of dilapidated fence posts and water tanks.

The peace brought by Zimbabwean Independence was slow in coming to the Honde, as **Renamo** guerrillas (see Contexts, p.359) fighting against the Mozambique government replaced the previous dogs of war, periodically slipping across the border to scavenge and steal, frequently murderously. The Zimbabwean **army** was sent in to clear out the bandits in the 1990s, but in their turn overstayed their welcome. Having achieved their task, boredom set in, and incidence of undisciplined soldiers harassing villagers became common. Under pressure from the local community and management at the tea estates, the army eventually withdrew in the late 1990s, leaving the Honde to the first real peace it has enjoyed in three decades.

Getting there
Despite being literally a stone's throw from the Nyanga National Park on the higher reaches of the escarpment, the Honde Valley has remained pretty isolated from the rest of Zimbabwe. This isn't to say it's inaccessible: a good tarred road winds down into the valley and continues for 62 picturesque kilometres before petering out near the Mozambique border. The possible hiking **trails** from Mtarazi National Park into the valley are detailed above (see box opposite). By **bus**, the easiest approach is to take any Mutare-bound bus from Nyanga to the Honde turn-off, then pick up one of the buses from Mutare into the valley; there are no direct buses from Nyanga. If you're **driving**, take the turn-off for the valley, 25km south of Juliasdale on the Mutare road.

Accommodation
There are a few places in the Honde offering cheap or reasonably priced **accommodation**, all in extremely beautiful settings. The two country clubs were established in colonial days to provide accommodation to visiting staff, while *Red Dragon Lodges* is the only place in the valley built to accommodate tourists.

Aberfoyle Country Club, 90km from Juliasdale in the Honde Valley (☎028/385, or contact their Harare HQ and ask for Mrs Donette Kruger ☎04/728255 or 728256, fax 729457). Situated on the Aberfoyle tea estate, right at the end of the valley, this once elegant club, now a bit neglected, retains its 1950s colonial outpost feel. Its situation, high on a green hill with thick, verdant forest, is peaceful and beautiful. You can visit the tea factory, go birding or walking in the area, as well as use the golf course and other sporting facilities. The road is tarred all the way, apart from the last 6km stretch to the club, which is very rough indeed, and extremely slippery in the rainy season. You can also turn up for tea, lunch or a drink, even if you're not staying. ②.

Eastern Highlands Country Club (ask for Wellington the barman, or Mr Driscoll at the clubhouse ☎028/251–3). Two quaintly old-fashioned log cabins on a mountain overlooking tea estates and the Nyawamba Dam. Pillows and basic furniture are provided and braai packs, eggs, milk, bread and butter are for sale, but you'll need to bring your own bedding and any other food, especially fruit and vegetables. The shower and toilet facilities inside the clubhouse are available to guests, and you can also use the fully equipped kitchen. A pleasant, lawned campsite enjoys some shade under trees near the swimming pool and braai area. ①.

Honde Red Dragon Lodges & Campsite, 4km from Hauna (daytime ☎028/288 or 264, after hours ☎251–2, fax 04/307407). Run by the animated Iris Driscoll (aka the "Welsh Dragon" as she jokingly likes to tell guests), who was health and safety training officer at Eastern Highlands Tea Estates for twenty years. Accommodation is peacefully sited along the Ruda River in the middle of very traditional communal lands. Three comfortable new two-storey stone lodges, a family bungalow and the "Chieftain's Lodge" honeymoon suite, which luxuriates in its sunken bath draped with plants, are all surrounded by guava trees and lit by oil lamps; the fact that there's no electricity is part of the atmosphere. Facilities include a bar and restaurant (open to passers-by), but the key attraction of the place is Mrs Driscoll's knowledge of the area and her good relations with the local community. She can arrange tours of the tea and coffee plantations and processing plants; hikes into the Pungwe Gorge, where you can swim in rock pools, eat a picnic lunch and look at butterflies and fish; or village visits. Camping ①, B&B ②, fully inclusive rate (three meals and activities) ④.

Hauna to the tea estates
Dramatic landscape and temperature changes occur as you wind down the single tarred road from the main Mutare road into the valley. The main settlement, **HAUNA**, 34km east of the Mutare road, is little more than a few modest general dealers, a police

station, clinic and some houses. One of the most rural pockets of Zimbabwe, the tarred road through the valley leads through a succession of photogenic **traditional villages** surrounded by small-scale rice, maize, banana, cotton, sugar, papaya, avocado, mango and groundnut plantations. A common sight is peasants patiently waiting along the roadside with baskets fulls of produce to be collected by the daily trucks that come to transport the fruit and vegetables to processing plants or supermarkets in the towns. While the land is very productive, villagers have a hard time deterring wild pigs and baboons, which ravage their crops, while the absence of roads to some of the settlements, and thinly spread facilities, force people to trek up to 10km to the nearest shop or clinic. No strangers to foot-slogging, those who live closest to the mountains climb two to three hours to the top every day to work on commercial farms or private homesteads.

From Hauna, the centre of the valley is visually dominated by the **Masimike** – sacred sentinel granite pinnacles up to 100m high, which make good orientation points. Climbing them is taboo, and shouldn't be undertaken without permission from the local headman. The **Pungwe River** flows through the valley, with rope footbridges crossing the clear water in a couple of places: the final section of the forested river gorge is well worth exploring if you're based in the valley.

At the northeast end of the valley, kilometres of smooth green hills under the looming massif of the Nyanga Mountains signal Zimbabwe's large commercial **tea and coffee estates**, providing a major source of employment; the largest of the three, Eastern Highlands Tea Estates, employs 3000 people and supports an estimated 10,000. The estates were established in the 1950s when planters crossed Mount Nyangani on foot into the roadless vale. It's possible to tour the estates, visit the processing plants and even stay on them: go to personnel at Eastern Highlands or head straight for the signposted factories.

Chimanimani to Chirinda Forest

At the southern end of the Eastern Highlands, the **Chimanimani Mountains** are completely different from the rest of the range, and geologically unique in Zimbabwe. The apparently modest size of the peaks – Binga, the highest, is 2240m – gives no idea of their scale, the mountains rising in rugged ridges. Sheltering in this fortress, the **Chimanimani National Park** is an enthralling wilderness of rocks, caves, waterfalls and gentle valleys.

Chimanimani village

The village of **CHIMANIMANI**, 148km south of Mutare, comprises a small collection of shops, a hotel, a post office and a group of houses gathered around a red-earthed "village green". The 1899 administration building is a handsome example of an early colonial type that seems all roof – dominated by ruddy corrugated iron. Basically a centre serving the farms and forestry estates in the vicinity, the village is surrounded by mountains, with the **Chimanimani Rampart** in the blue distance; on some evenings the mountains appear to catch fire with a pink glow as the rays hit the rose quartz embedded in the rock face. It is a wonderful place to idle away a few hours, or even several days: so pleasant, indeed, that visiting government officials reportedly ask to be put up here rather than in Chipinge, the region's real administrative centre.

White settlement in the region began after the pioneer **Dunbar Moodie** visited in 1890, and told his friend Marthinus Martin about the beauty and potential of the countryside south of Umtali (Mutare). It sounded too good to pass up and, true to colonial form, Martin led a party from South Africa to take over the area in 1894. Sinking roots, they named the district **Melsetter**, after Moodie's family home in the Orkney Islands.

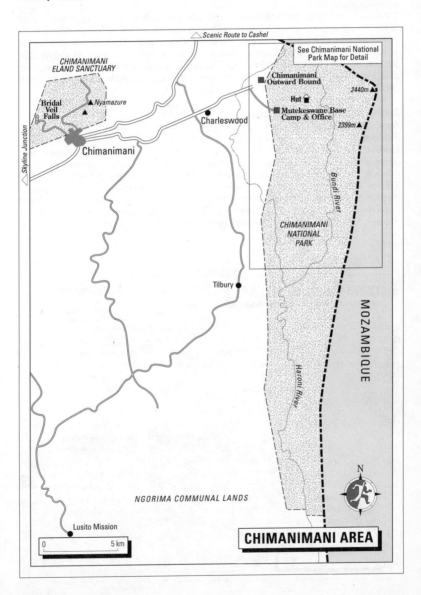

After Independence, "Melsetter" became "Chimanimani", a name previously reserved for the nearby mountains. One version of the name's meaning has it that the main footpath between Zimbabwe and Mozambique runs closely in parallel to the Msapa River and is so tight in places that you have to walk single file or even sideways: a *chimanimani*.

Chimanimani holds few full-blown tourist attractions, but the local **craft shop** next to the trendy Msasa coffee shop on the village green is excellent, with a number of well-priced gifts to take away, including *gudza* dolls, bags and mats and fun, articulated wooden snakes. *Gudza* products are woven from bark that's been chewed and dyed in browns, ochres and oatmeal. No trip to Chimanimani is complete, either, without sampling the village's delicious, home-made **cheese and jam**, available from *Frog and Fern B&B*, signposted off the Bridal Veil Falls road.

Arrival, information and transport

Buses arrive outside Nyamatanda Supermarket at the local **market**, where you can buy ridiculously cheap fruit and vegetables. It's conveniently located next to the **Publicity Bureau** (daily except Wed & Thurs 9am–1pm & 2–5pm), which can provide information about places to stay and transport to the national park; there's also a **phone** outside or you can use the phone and fax facilities at the Chimanimani Bushwalking Co (Mon–Fri 7.30am–4.30pm, Sat 7.30am–1pm), adjacent to the Publicity Bureau, which runs daily shuttles to the Chimanimani Mountain base camp (see Getting to the park, p.301) and also operates the village's only **Internet café**. You can buy **petrol** in town, but if you're planning to self-cater or are shopping for an expedition, buy **provisions** in one of the

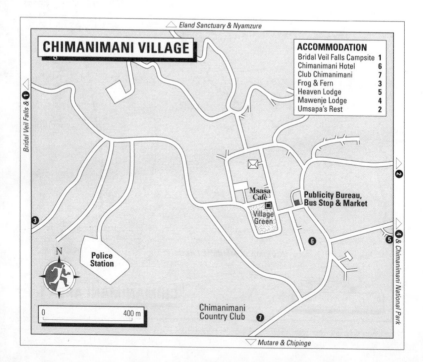

CHIMANIMANI VILLAGE

Eland Sanctuary & Nyamzure

Bridal Veil Falls & ▲❶

ACCOMMODATION

Bridal Veil Falls Campsite	1
Chimanimani Hotel	6
Club Chimanimani	7
Frog & Fern	3
Heaven Lodge	5
Mawenje Lodge	4
Umsapa's Rest	2

Msasa Café

Village Green

Publicity Bureau, Bus Stop & Market

❸

❻

❺ & Chimanimani National Park

N

Police Station

0   400 m

Chimanimani Country Club ❼

Mutare & Chipinge

SECURITY IN CHIMANIMANI

Although daytime incidents in Chimanimani have been nonexistent up to now, travellers are warned to take care at night, as there have been a number of muggings in the village, some involving knives. Be conscious of cultural differences, particularly the fact that locally it isn't usual for unmarried black men and women to casually mix; what may seem like plain friendliness may well be read here as a come-on. Locals recommend the following precautions after dark:

- Walk in groups of not less than five.
- Don't carry your possessions where they are obviously visible.
- Beware of approaches by strangers.
- Don't accept offers to escort you, even if refusal seems rude or racist.

larger centres before you arrive – the local stores are poorly stocked, especially when it comes to fresh meat. If you're stuck, the best choice of groceries available is at the small Chimanimani Bottle Store which, apart from being the only place in the village to sell alcohol, also has bread and milk, some frozen goods, snacks such as crisps and a small selection of fruit and vegetables, but is most notable for being the sole outlet in the village centre for the excellent locally produced cheeses, yoghurts and honey. For changing money, the only **bank** is CBZ (Mon, Tues, Thurs & Fri 8am–2.30pm, Wed 8am–1pm, Sat 8–11am), on the southwest corner of the green, which can change foreign banknotes and travellers' cheques (but won't handle Visa or Mastercard) and will inexplicably insist on seeing your passport even if you're changing cash.

Finally, regarding the **weather**, although it never snows you should bring warm clothes; especially in July and August, when the mountains can be very chilly indeed. During the rainy season, a waterproof is recommended for hiking and evenings are cool enough for jumpers.

Accommodation

As well as the **accommodation** options listed below, there are a couple of self-catering cottages to rent in Chimanimani – enquire at the Publicity Bureau.

Bridal Veil Falls Campsite. The nicest place to camp in Chimanimani, at a very beautiful sheltered green site near the waterfall. The road to the site is rough but you'll find the luxuries of hot and cold running water once you get there. It doesn't work out cheap when you add the US$10 park entrance fee you'll have to pay. ①.

Chimanimani Rainbow Hotel, PO Box 5, Chimanimani (☎026/2511 or 2513, fax 2515). The only hotel in town has 26 en-suite rooms, a casino and a 1950s lounge, polished floors and wicker chairs. It's worth spending a little extra for one of the twelve rooms that have glorious views of the mountains – and baths rather than showers. They also serve inexpensive meals, and have a pricey bar. ③.

Club Chimanimani, 1km west of town along the main road (☎ & fax 026/2266). A quieter and more intimate budget alternative to *Heaven Lodge*, under the accommodating management of Buck Rogers, in timber sheds in the garden and a family room inside the village club, which has a bar, television, squash and tennis courts and a golf course as well as a children's playground. Men's and women's ablutions are inside the clubhouse. Self-catering isn't available but good cheap breakfasts and bar food are, and it can be a good spot in the evenings. ①.

Frog and Fern, 2.5km from town off the Bridal Veil Falls road (PO Box 75, Chimanimani ☎026/2840, fax 2294, *frogfern@uz.zw*). Deservedly popular accommodation in three very comfortable self-contained stone cottages with kitchenettes in a garden that has views of the mountains. Hosts Jane and Dee are extremely knowledgeable about the area, and can take you golfing or horse-riding. Their attention to detail is reflected in the breakfast basket of local cheeses and yoghurt, and the packet of freshly ground mountain coffee. Children welcome. B&B or cheaper self-catering rate ④.

Heaven Lodge, just out of town on the national park road (☎026/2701). Gloriously located dorms, double or single rooms and A-frame double chalets in the garden of a hostel that is known for being one of the highest in Zimbabwe (and not just because of the altitude). But if you're self-driving you can park next to your chalet and avoid becoming involved in the main-lodge action. Meals are available at the lodge bar, but they aren't as good as the ones at the café in town. ①.

Mawenje Lodge, 13km from the village on the road to the national park (PO Box 160, Chimanimani ☎ & fax 026/2710 or 2709). Beautifully done stone lodge and chalets at the foot of the mountains, along the banks of the Haroni River, which provides a natural swimming pool. The riverine forest is excellent for birds and butterflies, some of which are rare; the lodge, which sleeps a maximum of twelve people, is well run; and the food – included in the rate – is excellent. Transfers to the base camp, 3km away, are provided for guests who are hiking. No children. Full board ⑨.

Musapa's Rest, north of the village on the Cashel scenic road (☎026/22314). Self-catering or B&B accommodation in a stone A-frame cottage, in the homestead garden of a coffee plantation run by a very hospitable Afrikaner family who make the brilliant cheeses and yoghurts that are sold in Chimanimani. An ideal base for exploring the Corner section of the mountains, but the road to the farm is awful and you'll need a high-clearance sturdy vehicle to get there with your suspension intact. ①.

Eating and entertainment

Most people eat where they stay, but there's also *The Msasa Café*, a surprisingly good **restaurant** on the north side of the green (daily 9.30am–3.30pm & 5.30–9.30pm) that seems to have benefited hugely from a visit to the hamlet in 1998 by a French chef on an overland jaunt. Their pastas are excellent and Mexican food such as nachos, tacos and enchiladas are sometimes on the inexpensive menu – with the added attraction of a pool table and occasional live bands. Food at the *Chimanimani Rainbow Hotel* isn't bad either, and their highlight is the Thursday-night "indigenous evening" when waitresses dress up in traditional costume with dolls standing in for babies strapped to their backs; the menu consists of oxtail, *sadza*, mopane worms and fried locusts (when available). Another option is *Club Chimanimani*, where the fare tends to be cheap and tasty pub grub.

Apart from the annual **Chimanimani Arts Festival**, when the hamlet absolutely hums for a few days in April, with visitors descending from all over Zimbabwe for free performances and markets around the village green, for the rest of the year the only consistent way to kill time at night is gambling in the **casino** at the *Rainbow Hotel*. The more salubrious section is inside, where there are roulette and pontoon tables. It's most fun at the beginning of the week when they have the informal and backpacker-friendly **"Monday Madness"** in the evening, with chips going for Z$1 (compared with a normal Z$10). In the section outside the hotel, ragged locals queue up to feed the one-armed bandits, in the hope of making their fortune.

The Eland Sanctuary and Bridal Veil Falls

There are a couple of good **walks** out of Chimanimani Village that are worth considering if you're not in a rush to move on to the national park. For these and other possibilities, it's a good idea to invest at the craft shop in the excellent local **map** produced by Milkmaps in aid of the rural hospital; alternatively, *Heaven Lodge* provides its own local maps. A single ticket costing US$5 per person provides day entry to the Eland Sanctuary, Nyamzure and Bridal Veil Falls, and is available at the entrance gate to any one of the three. If you're feeling energetic, the best way to take full advantage of the ticket is to take in Bridal Veil in the morning and Nyamzure in the afternoon (3–4pm is perfect). This gives you views of the whole range.

THE ELAND SANCTUARY

The **Eland Sanctuary** (daily 6am–6pm), a large area north of the village on the slopes of **Nyamzure** (or "Pork Pie" as it's also known), is a rugged terrain of cliffs, waterfalls and dense bush. It was created to provide a refuge for **elands**, Africa's largest antelopes, which are indigenous to the area and were coming into conflict with the timber-growing industry. The elands are now successfully kept away from the bark and

HORSE-RIDING AND BIRDWATCHING AT CHIMANIMANI

Horse-riding at Chimanimani is terrific: you can enjoy huge views with the wind in your hair, on well-trained, responsive horses. Rides are primarily geared for experienced riders who can enjoy a gallop or canter up a mountainside, and go for two hours or full days – or overnight to Corner. They cost US$7 per hour. For the trip to Corner, you need to be riding-fit – it's more than five hours in the saddle to get there. In the afternoon, while the horses relax, you go to the waterfall and prepare for the night's braai and camping. Book for rides in advance through Jane at *Frog and Fern* (8am–1pm; ☎026/2840, fax 2294).

If you're interested in **birdwatching** at Chimanimani, you can take advantage of the excellent services of the affable and knowledgeable Kevin Donaldson, formerly of National Parks, at *Club Chimanimani* (see p.297). Prices are negotiable, depending on group size and the type of birding activity.

buds of pine saplings behind a fence in an eighteen-square-kilometre tract. You'll also see zebra, waterbuck, bushbuck, klipspringer and noisy troops of baboons. Antelope can be spotted, too, roaming wild in the surrounding farmlands, though in considerably smaller numbers than the vast herds locals remember.

There are two **roads to the Sanctuary**, but you can explore it further on foot along the ridge. Alternatively, scale Nyamzure, either from the village or from the car park halfway up if you're driving (you'll need a tough vehicle). To get onto the Nyamzure road, drive past the garage (on your right) and post office (on the left); take the first turn left, then right. To park, continue for 300m past the entrance gate – you can't drive to the summit. Allow two hours to walk up and ninety minutes for the descent.

BRIDAL VEIL FALLS

The showpiece of the sanctuary, the **Bridal Veil Falls** (daily 6am–6pm) cascade down a sheer rock face into an inviting pool of beautifully clear water that looks as if it ought to be inhabited by water sprites draping themselves across the mossy rocks. The Falls are at the bottom of a green, wooded valley where there is a beautiful picnic site and campsite (see Accommodation on p.297) under the trees.

It's a two-hour **walk** to the falls on a seldom used dirt road which meanders through msasa-clad valleys full of birds. You need to take the road leading out of town with the Beverley Building Society on your left, and then just keep going. If you want a challenging and longer walk back, take the ridge route, which runs to the south of the Eland Sanctuary.

Chimanimani National Park

The only way to penetrate the **CHIMANIMANI NATIONAL PARK** (day entry US$10, week entry U$S20) is by scaling the blue rampart you see from Chimanimani village. It's possible to do this route as a day's hike, if you have your own transport to get to the foothills and back to the village, but you'll enjoy the trip more if you spend some days exploring the mountains.

Between the Parks mountain hut (at the centre of the park) and the soaring peaks shared with Mozambique, spreads the ample **Bundi Valley**. Spliced by the Bundi River, this is covered in grass, which changes from wet-season green to maizy yellow and dried brown after the rains subside. Its downhill course is broken by a series of waterfalls splashing into icy cola-coloured pools, with smooth rocks to bask on. Giant **tree strelizias** (wild bananas), **tree ferns** and **cycads** fringe the banks, while the grass slopes are dotted with bright-yellow helichrysum, grass aloes and small mauve gladioli.

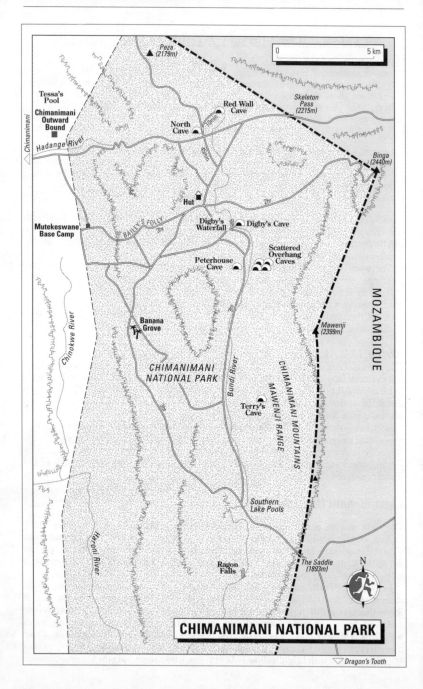

CHIMANIMANI NATIONAL PARK

But it's the **rocks** on the way up the valley that are most astonishing. Completely different from the granite formations peppering much of Zimbabwe, the folded and faulted silvery schist and quartz has been sculpted into fantastic stone forms. In the fine white soil, wild hibiscus, heather, aromatic tree shrubs and fiery pincushions grow.

Getting to the park

Although the first 9km of the road from Chimanimani village to **MUTEKESWANE** base camp is tarred, parts of the remaining 10km are shocking, and unless you have a high-clearance vehicle you'll be best off taking advantage of the twice-daily **shuttles** (about 8am & 3.30pm; US$5.50 one way) offered by the Chimanimani Bushwalking Co (aka Bushwalkers), which collect passengers outside the entrances to the *Chimanimani Rainbow Hotel* and *Heaven Lodge*. Bushwalkers also offer two- to four-day **guided hikes**, which include meals and transfers, but not park entrance fees, for US$25–60. If you're going up of your own you'll need to report to the base camp, give details of your length of stay and agree to foot the bill if you get hopelessly lost and a search party comes looking for you. The **Ordnance Survey map** (1:50,000 Melsetter 1932 D4 and 1933 C1, C3, available from the Surveyor-General's office in Harare) is invaluable, although the Publicity Bureau also supplies hiking maps (see p.298).

Accommodation

Camping is permitted anywhere in the **national park**. If you arrive too late in the day to go into the mountains you can **camp** at Mutekeswane, which has the usual facilities but no roofed accommodation. However, you don't have to lug a tent around.

The **mountain hut** (②), in a beautiful spot overlooking the Bundi Valley, two hours up from the base camp, has wooden beds and thin mattresses, plus two gas cookers and washing facilities. You can choose one of the two dorms to sleep in (they are not segregated) or use the verandah. This is the place to meet other walkers and line up a lift back to Chimanimani village. An **attendant** lives nearby, down a discreetly camouflaged path (to give the feeling that he's not really there). Don't break in if you find the hut shut up – there's always someone around to unlock the door. If you plan to do daytrips from the hut, it's safe to leave all your gear, but if you want to be extra-cautious bring a padlock: the benches in the central area double as lockers. Bring all your **food** with you – and a torch – as there's no shop in the park.

There are also several well-used **caves** (see map), which you don't have to pay for, but are consequently very popular and may well already be occupied by the time you get there. Each has its own informal name, and one or two are floored with dried grass and are beginning to become a little tatty through inconsiderate camping practices (see box on p.302).

Routes to the peaks – and Tessa's Pool

Three routes head up to the mountain hut and peaks. **Bailey's Folly** is the most direct, leading straight up behind the Parks Office. It takes about three hours to the hut, with several false tops on the way – whenever you think you're nearly there, another ridge appears. The route is waymarked with cairns, which should be diligently followed; when the path braids, keep going left. **Banana Grove** – the "bananas" are actually tree strelizias – is a much gentler approach, good if you're heading for the **caves** along the Bundi River on the way to the Southern Lakes. From Mutekeswane, follow the fire break until you meet the path going up from Dead Cow, the former base camp. **Hadange River**, the third route, leads to Tessa's Pool (see p.302), but isn't recommended as it has become seriously degraded, causing several hikers to break their ankles. You should enquire locally about its state before embarking on it, and when it's **wet** the Hadange route is definitely not advised, given the way it cuts through a very slippery forested ravine and crisscrosses the river, which is impassable after a storm.

HIKING IN CHIMANIMANI: THE PRACTICAL LIMITS

Two-thirds of the Chimanimani range is actually in Mozambique. On the Zimbabwean side, **hiking** is confined to a long thin stretch from the peaks in the north, scaleable on day-trips from the hut, down the Bundi Valley to **Dragon's Tooth** and beyond in the south. In the north, local mountaineers often ignore the border, which is drawn through Skeleton Pass, and head off to Martin's Falls, Valley of the Wizards and endless deserted peaks. There's no way up from Mozambique to this northern side of the park but Mozambicans do cross over at the **Saddle** in the far south, on a well-worn track to the store at Tilbury. It's not been unknown for women to be seen carrying a bed on their heads, making their way back over the mountains to Mozambique – an incredible feat given the distance and steepness. It's not a good idea to go beyond the **Saddle and Ragon Falls** as the path fizzles out on the Zimbabwean side and you have to cross into Mozambique to get further south.

SAFETY

The Chimanimani Mountains are small compared with European and North American peaks, which tends to give hikers a false sense of confidence. Several hikers have died up here (one tourist stepped to his death in the dark off a 70m cliff) and there have been numerous casualties. Mountain rescue teams don't go out till 24 hours after a person or party has failed to return, so avoid problems rather than rely on them to extricate you. Following a few easy tips should help minimize your risk.

MAKE SURE YOU . . .
• Don't climb alone.
• Inform someone where you're going if you plan to deviate from the route you filed at base camp.
• Leave early enough to give yourself time to complete your route during daylight.
• Don't try to descend via an unknown route. If you get lost in poor weather, seek shelter, keep warm and wait for help.
• Stick to the main paths.
• Don't venture into Mozambique; if you run into trouble it may not be possible to rescue you there.

Tessa's Pool is to be found down a clearly marked path off the main driveway. Surrounded by luxuriant palm trees, lianas and ferns at the bottom of a waterfall, it is the perfect spot to cool your heels after the descent. Picnicking isn't allowed and you should get permission at Chimanimani Outward Bound before you swim.

Peaks, caves and pools

Like all mountain climbs, once you've made it to the top there are still more tops. **Peza** and **Binga** (Kweza on some maps) are each a couple of strenuous hours' climb from the hut on good paths, with fantastic views. Peza is easier and you go along beautiful open stretches of the Bundi Valley to the waterfall at North and Red Wall caves before you start climbing. Both caves are big enough to sleep a troop of boy scouts. **North Cave** is located right above the waterfall, while **Red Cave** is a bit higher up on the other side of the river and not quite as easy to find. A path leading straight down from the hut goes right across the valley and up formidable Binga. **Skeleton Pass** is an easy walk from here, but the views are not as exceptional as you might have expected.

If you want to **swim** and laze about, there's a waterfall, pool and a small overhang – **Digby's Cave**, a good night shelter – a steep half-hour down from the hut on the main path to Southern Lakes. A little further on is yet another waterfall and **Peterhouse Cave**.

For a **full-day trip**, you could continue on the path all the way to the **Southern Lakes**, where the swimming is exceptional. On your left, slate-blue **Mount Mawenje**

WEAR
- Suitable clothes
- Good footwear; boots are recommended
- A broad-brimmed hat

TAKE
- Enough food; there's no shop up there
- High-energy snacks such as glucose sweets, nuts, dried fruit, juice
- A water bottle
- A warm jersey
- A windbreaker
- A raincoat
- Sunglasses
- High-factor sunscreen
- Plasters for blisters
- A map
- A trowel
- A sturdy plastic bag

WASTE AND WASHING

The growing use of the mountain by hikers is taking its toll in the form of lingering toilet paper, candles melted into cave walls and garbage decorating the mountainside. If you're camping wild you can do your bit to preserve Chimanimani by following some simple pointers. Remember that there's only one river in the valley and often there will be several people camping along it and drawing their drinking water from it.

- Don't leave turds or leftover food lying around; both should be buried.
- Take everything back with you; even the smallest scrap of rubbish, including bottle tops, cigarette ends, tampons and toilet paper. You can dump these at the National Park office at base camp, where they will be incinerated.
- Pick up any other litter, even if it's not yours, and take it down.
- Don't wash in the river; fill a receptacle and wash away from the banks.
- Don't clean pots in the river; wash and rinse away from it.
- Don't throw food into the river.

(also called Turret Towers) dominates the horizon, while the river widens into a big oxbow creating reed-fringed, wine-dark pools – the "lakes".

Midway is **Terry's Cave**, set under a massive boulder, and with two compartments in the unlikely event of two parties arriving. No one seems to know who was responsible for building them. One theory is that a priest spent some time here before leaving the country, and this was his goodbye present. Terraces have been built to keep out the draughts, a fireplace made and the floor covered with masses of dried grass.

The snag is that the cave is difficult to find. If you want to spend the night here, locate it before going down to the lakes. It's in a very rocky area, quite a long way from the main north–south path; there's no direct route to get from it to the lakes, so you have to come back to rock-jump the river. To get to the cave you must rock-jump the river. One path to it veers off opposite a small tributary; the other, where a minor path back to Banana Grove joins the north–south one. Another (and possibly easier) route is to take a path on the east side of Peterhouse Cave. From Southern Lakes it's a three-hour-plus hike back to base camp; there are no caves at the lakes themselves.

Corner and the Cashel Road

The only part of the national park accessible by car is the northeast corner – known as **CORNER** – approached along an extremely rough, unsignposted road through communal lands, entailing the use of a high-clearance vehicle. Despite, or perhaps because of, the poor access, it's a beautiful, unspoiled area, with several waterfalls

---

HOT SPRINGS

Excellent food is one good reason to visit **Hot Springs Resort** (☎026/2367 or 2361, *loanda@hotspring.icon.co.zw*), 85km south of Mutare in baobab country on the Birchenough Bridge Road; another is the open-air mineral pools where you can melt off the indulgence. One pool, shaded by duikerberry and mopane trees, is 40–45°C, while there's a cooler, large pool at about 30°C, surrounded by lawns and loungers, to do lengths in. Run by the Nel family who're all trained in a variety of natural therapies, you can also get treatments ranging from massage, acupuncture, facials and nutritional counselling, to **Watsu** – a wonderful stretching massage treatment done in the warm pool. **Accommodation** is in nine modest thatched chalets at an extremely reasonable full-board rate of US$35 per person including all meals, but not treatments or drinks. Day-trippers (US$1) are welcome to pull in for a soak and swim, though no picnicking is allowed. As a day-tripper, you can get a full lunch, but need to book in advance. Failing that, there is a snack menu. **Camping**, aimed at backpackers rather than families, is allowed, out of sight of the main complex, and a more upmarket resort on the banks of the nearby Odzi River is being planned. Transfers to the springs from Mutare can be arranged at US$10 per person one way.

---

and pools to swim in. While there are no cottages, there is a campsite a short hike from a waterfall, close enough to walk to. There are no facilities, so you'll need to be self-sufficient.

To get there, take the Cashel Road out of Chimanimani village, turn right at the Chikukwa village sign and follow meandering roads, and locals' directions, to Corner. The Chimanimani Bushwalking Co takes one- and two-day excursions to Corner that cost US$25 or US$45 including meals (see p.301). If you have a rugged vehicle, and time in hand, the scenic route from Chimanimani to Cashel, which hugs the Mozambique border, is the most spectacularly scenic mountain drive in Zimbabwe, but the road is very rough.

South to Chipinge and Chirinda

CHIPINGE, 64km southeast of Chimanimani, is a working town that sees little tourism. Its small centre hides bottling plants, a brewery and storage depots down the backstreets, and two banks in the centre – hinting at the wealth produced from this industry and from the surrounding commercial tea and coffee plantations. Chipinge is also the nearest town for the sugar plantations of the extreme eastern lowveld. However, its main attraction for visitors is its proximity to the **Chirinda Forest**.

If you're driving, the nicest **accommodation** for exploring the forests is the *Kiledo Lodge*, 18km east of Chipinge on the Eastern Border Road, which has eight thatched lodges set in rainforest with views of the Chimanimani Mountains; book through Inns of Zimbabwe in Mutare (☎020/67449, fax 60722; *kiledo@pci.co.zw*; full board ④). Excellent guided walks are taken from the lodge through the indigenous forest, and the food and service are uniformly of a very high standard.

Chirinda Forest Reserve

All that remains of a large primeval woodland is preserved in the tiny enclave of **CHIRINDA FOREST RESERVE**, 30km south of Chipinge. It is almost a fantasy African jungle, with thick, dark undergrowth, lofty trees reaching skywards, science fiction plants with outsized leaves, and loud bird calls.

Getting to Chirinda – and camping

The forest surrounds a hilltop mission, known as **Mount Selinda**. On the road to Mozambique, the mission, which provides education and basic health care to the local community, is passed by a fair amount of traffic, including a number of **buses** from Mutare, Bulawayo and Masvingo, all of which pass through Chipinge en route. Chipinge's bus stop is just outside Ron's Motors on the corner of Main Street and Seventh Avenue. By far the best idea, though, is to travel up in one of the many fare-charging **pick-ups** that can be taken from the corner of Chipinge's main drag and the Mount Selinda road. Many of these rides terminate at Chako Township, but try to make your way 2km further on to the mission hospital, close to the (signposted) "**Big Tree Path**" that heads into the forest. If your lift ends at Chako, get off at the T-junction and walk uphill to the signposted forest entrance.

Chirinda has a **campsite** with forest cabins (①), and trees felled to give a view. At the campsite you can buy a map and booklet about the forest. There's also a small rural **store** at the Chako T-junction, but it makes more sense to pick up supplies from the better-stocked shops in Chipinge.

Mount Selinda

There's no mountain as such at **Mount Selinda**; just a big forested hill visible from some distance. It's a steep climb from Chipinge's farmlands; you'll see maize fields, grazing cattle and neat rows of coffee bushes on the way. The mission was founded by Americans in 1889, but its main claim to fame is as the point of arrival in 1919 of Africa's first agricultural missionary. One of his big successes was the Nyanadzi irrigation scheme on the Birchenough Bridge to Mutare road – long before Triangle and Hippo Valley estates undertook their complex water diversions. Peasant agriculture thrives at Nyanadzi today: good grain and fruit yields are achieved in an otherwise dry and unpromising environment.

Across the tarred road from Mount Selinda, and a little further toward the mission hospital, is the overgrown plinth of **Swynnerton's Memorial**, another evocation of good colonial works. Apparently forgotten, Swynnerton was an English entomologist who settled in Chimanimani in 1898. He researched tsetse flies and butterflies, and was appointed Tanzania's first game warden in 1919. His researches there led to an acclaimed paper on the reclamation of tsetse-afflicted districts, but he's best known in Zimbabwe for his work as a naturalist, and gave his name to a number of plants and birds.

Into the forest

A web of paths weaves through the forest. From the picnic site, marked trails lead to the **Big Tree** and the **Valley of the Giants** – both routes worth taking.

The Big Tree, 70m high and 16m round, is probably the oldest living thing in the forest. The wildest estimates claim it as a contemporary of Christ, a nice myth for a tree near a mission. More realistic stabs reckon it's a thousand years old – and in decline, judging by the large sections of dead wood. Like many Valley of the Giants goliaths, it's a red mahogany, *Khaya nyasica*, used by Africans to produce massage oil from the seeds and an anti-colds infusion from the quinine-bitter bark.

Another remarkable lumber-type at Chirinda is the orange-, yellow- and black-timbered **zebra wood**, found nowhere else. And, on the wildlife front, you may encounter the **forest elephant shrew**, which is unique to a small part of the southeast. This rat-like creature has kangarooish back legs and a mini-trunk, and beneath each lower eyelid a fluorescent spot acts as a recognition signal for other shrews in the forest's evening gloom. The more common **samango monkeys** emerge from the treetops at dawn and, after catching some sun, head off to breakfast on Chirinda's leaves, fruits and berries.

travel details

Trains
Mutare to: Harare (daily at 9pm; 9hr).

Volvos and chicken buses
There are several **buses** daily to all the destinations listed below. As a general rule of thumb, there will be more buses along the main arteries than to smaller destinations, and more in the morning than the afternoon. From Mutare to Harare, for example, you can expect at least one bus an hour. Journey times given below are approximate; and it's advisable to confirm all bus information before setting out.

Chimanimani to: Mutare (4hr).

Mutare to: Beit Bridge (8hr); Bulawayo (8hr); Chimanimani (4hr); Chipinge (4hr); Harare (4hr); Masvingo (4hr); Nyanga (3hr 30min).

Nyanga to: Harare (7hr); Mutare (3hr 30min).

Luxury coaches
The only reliable service is run by Blue Arrow, departing from the *Holiday Inn*, **Mutare**, to **Harare** (daily except Tues & Thurs at 1pm; 4hr 30min), via **Rusape** (1hr) and **Marondera** (3hr). Book at Manica Travel Services (see Mutare Listings, p.273).

CHAPTER SEVEN

CHOBE AND
THE OKAVANGO DELTA

Botswana's main appeal lies in its wild outdoors, and most visitors concentrate on the accessible northern and eastern sections of the country. The top attractions in the north are the seamlessly joined Okavango Delta, Moremi Wildlife Reserve and Chobe National Park, all of which are most easily accessed from Zimbabwe's Victoria Falls.

About an hour's drive from the Falls, **Chobe National Park** is renowned for its massive number of elephants, often seen watering along the picturesque Chobe River running past **Kasane**, on the northern side of the park. To explore the park, you'll need your own 4WD and a tent, or a booking in one of the luxury safari camps along the river, or to the south in the remote **Savuti** region. If you don't have your own transport, it's worth considering one of the **overland expeditions** that travel through the park from Victoria Falls through Kasane to Maun.

Touching the southwest corner of Chobe, the **Moremi Wildlife Reserve** can plausibly claim to be the most desirable wildlife destination in Africa, poised between dryland

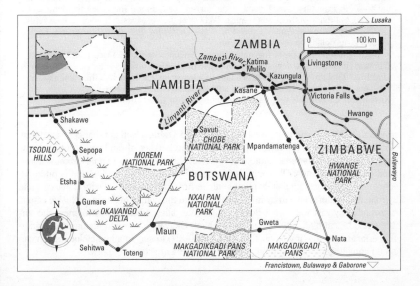

TIPS ON TRAVEL IN BOTSWANA

• **Accommodation** Apart from camping (US$7), there's no cheap accommodation in northern Botswana, although you will find a few moderately priced hotel-style places (US$25–30) in the springboard towns of Kasane and Maun. In the national parks, which is after all the reason for being here, the distinction is starker still, with a choice between basic National Parks campsites (US$7), usually in fantastic locations, and luxury lodges that will set you back up to US$800 per night.

• **Banks** You can change travellers' cheques at banks or the larger hotels in big centres. However, there are no banks in the vast tracts of the rural countryside: change money when you're in towns and make sure you're carrying enough cash with you. The following towns offer full banking facilities: Francistown, Gaborone, Ghanzi, Jwaneng, Kanye, Kasane, Lobatse, Mahalapye, Maun, Mochudi, Molepolole, Palapye, Selebi-Phikwe and Serowe.

• **Costs** Unless you want simply to trek along the deserted backways of Botswana, it's going to be difficult to get around on a shoestring. The government's policy of low-density high-cost tourism, instituted in mid-1989 in an attempt to maximize revenue while minimizing the harmful impact of too many visitors, has made things more difficult than they were before. In Chobe, Okavango and all the major game reserves, it costs over US$15 a day just to be there and to use an ill-equipped campsite – at the time of writing an increase of over 100 percent was mooted.

• **Currency** is the **pula (P)**, the Setswana word for "rain", demonstrating the enormous value of water in a dry land. Each pula is divided into a hundred thebe (t). At the time of writing, the exchange rate was US$1 to P4.5; £1 to P7.5; AUS$1 to P3; R1 to P0.75. As the pula is effectively a hard currency, and residents are permitted to export considerable sums, there's no black market in Botswana.

• **Driving** Foreign drivers' licences are valid for six months, You must be able to cope with difficult road conditions and know how to mend punctures (of which you'll have many) and to effect minor repairs. Above all, **four-wheel driving** requires a fair amount of expertise, and you should familiarize yourself with what's involved before undertaking any major expedition into the wilderness. Many places are trackless and if you get stranded you may not see another human being for some time. Botswana's main north–south artery is a very good, wide, tarred road, as are the roads to Maun and Shakawe, but many of the roads require 4WD or at the very least a high-clearance vehicle. Some roads are seasonally passable – ask locally for up-to-date information. Each section gives details on the road situation.

• **Getting there** Britain is the only country outside Southern Africa that has direct flights to Botswana, and very few travellers use those. Most visitors enter Botswana overland from Zimbabwe or South Africa and to a lesser extent from its other neighbours, Namibia and Zambia. There are easy surface connections between Victoria Falls and Kasane and it's possible to get from Johannesburg or Cape Town to Maun on the regu-

savannah to its east and to its west the **Okavango Delta**, a wetland that appears miraculously in the heart of the Kalahari Desert, the parched sea of sand and scrub that covers two-thirds of Botswana. Some 15,000 square kilometres of channels, oxbow lakes, flood plains and islands, Okavango is traversed by wildlife in a setting that is undoubtedly one of the most exquisitely photogenic in Africa. Much of the Delta is inaccessible by road and visitors have to fly in by small plane to the couple of dozen exclusive camps surrounded by vast waterways floating with water lilies, where at any moment the surface could be cut by a crocodile or an elephant. Okavango is worth making a considerable effort to get to – if you can't afford US$300–400 to stay in a luxury lodge, you can get an equally good taste of it on a mobile safari at a quarter of the price.

lar Route 49 backpackers' bus. For quicker connections, Air Botswana has flights from Victoria Falls and Johannesburg to Maun.

• **Phones** Botswana's telephone system works well. To phone Botswana from outside its borders, dial the international gateway code (UK 00; US 011; Australia 00; South Africa 09), then its country code **267**, followed simply by the destination number (there are no area codes). Phoning out from Botswana, the international access code is **00**. This is followed by the country and area codes and finally the destination number. Country codes are the same as those dialled from Zimbabwe (see p.45).

• **Passports and visas** No visas are required for citizens of the US, the EU or Commonwealth countries (including South Africa) to enter Botswana for up to ninety days. Botswana issues a one-month entry visa initially and visitors aren't allowed to stay longer than three months in any year. Entering Botswana from South Africa is particularly hassle-free, as the two countries are part of the Southern African Common Customs Union, which means there is no internal customs control between them.

• **Public transport** isn't extensive in Botswana, but economy buses and flights connect Kasane and Maun, the main springboards for Chobe and Okavango, to the rest of the country.

LANGUAGE
SETSWANA GREETINGS AND RESPONSES

People customarily **greet** each other, whether strangers or not, with the older person greeting the younger one first. Greet people courteously in all situations – at roadblocks, when asking directions, or meeting people at the roadside, or when talking to the person servicing your room. The magic word is *dumêla* (pronounced "doo-meh-la" with the stress in the middle) which means "hello" and can be said at any time. Onto *dumêla* you tag *Mma* for women and *Rra* for men; thus *dumêla Mma* and *dumêla Rra*. Use *Mma* and *Rra* after questions (even when speaking English) like "Where is the station, Mma?", "How much is it, Rra?" The pronunciation of the "a" is short, close to the "u" in *fun*. The "Rr" is slightly rolled if you are up to that. To round off a conversation or to indicate everything's OK, say *Go siame*.

Hello (to one/many)	*Dumêla/dumêlang*	Goodbye	*Sala sentlê*
Hello (in response)	*Dumêla/dumêlang*	(person leaving)	
How are you?	*A o sa tsogile sentlê?*	Goodbye	*Tsamaya sentlê*
Fine thanks	*Ee, ke sa tsogile*	(person remaining)	

BASICS

Yes	*Ee*	Thank you	*Kea itumêla*
No	*Nnyaa*	Please	*Tsweetswee*

CHOBE NATIONAL PARK

The small town of **Kasane** is the obvious base if you don't have your own transport and want to get into **Chobe National Park**, Botswana's premier game reserve. It has ample accommodation and camping, and is the only place you'll catch Chobe **game drives** and **river cruises**. With your own transport, Kasane is a pleasant enough town to relax in, as well as being the place to stock up with fuel and supplies before going into big game country.

Chobe National Park itself is a far cry from the paradise of the Okavango Delta or the watery Moremi Wildlife Reserve (see p.338): it's a raw and compelling wilderness packed with game. The park was created in 1968, and named after the river that defines its northern boundary. Confusingly, however, this river itself has a number of different names. Where it rises in Angola it's called the Kuando; where it first enters Botswana it's the Linyanti. It then becomes the Itenge and only when it reaches Ngoma, back on the Caprivi Strip in Namibia, does it become the **Chobe**. Even its life as the Chobe is short-lived; it soon joins up with the **Zambezi**, which eventually hits the chasm at Victoria Falls.

Chobe National Park consists of three very distinct main areas – the **riverfront**, the **Ngwezumba region** and the **Mababe Depression**, usually known simply as **Savuti**. The best time to visit the river is during the dry season from June to October, when animals come from the interior to the northern part of the park for water. Savuti and Ngwezumba are good from November to May.

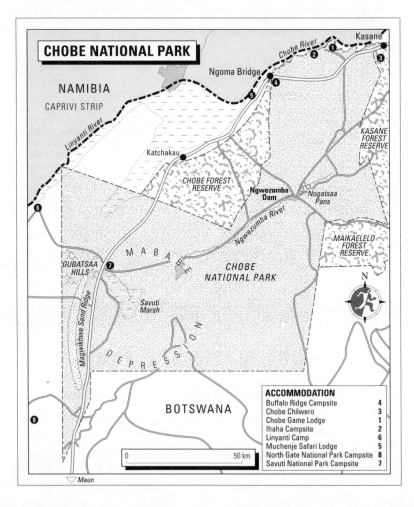

CHOBE NATIONAL PARK

NAMIBIA
CAPRIVI STRIP

Kasane

Chobe River

Ngoma Bridge

KASANE FOREST RESERVE

Linyanti River

Katchakau

CHOBE FOREST RESERVE

Ngwezumba Dam

Nogatsaa Pans

Ngwezumba River

MAIKAELELO FOREST RESERVE

GUBATSAA HILLS

M A B A B E

CHOBE NATIONAL PARK

Savuti Marsh

Magwikhwe Sand Ridge

D E P R E S S I O N

N

BOTSWANA

0   50 km

ACCOMMODATION

Buffalo Ridge Campsite	4
Chobe Chilwero	3
Chobe Game Lodge	1
Ihaha Campsite	2
Linyanti Camp	6
Muchenje Safari Lodge	5
North Gate National Park Campsite	8
Savuti National Park Campsite	7

▽ Maun

CHOBE PRACTICALITIES

Chobe National Park is **open** throughout the year. **Fees** at the time of writing were US$11 for **entry** per person per day (with a reduction if you're doing a drive or cruise with a registered safari company); US$2.50 for foreign-registered **vehicle** per day; and use of National Parks **campsites** was US$4.50 per person. A substantial increase of over 100 percent was mooted in 1999, so make enquiries before you travel.

The park's northern **gate**, 8km west of Kasane, is where you enter and pay your fees if you're camping at Ihaha, or driving via Nogatsaa to Savuti and Maun.

BOOKING CAMPSITES

If you're camping, **booking** your site is essential as several campsites were closed down in the late 1990s and their replacements offer limited space. They fill up fast, especially during holiday periods and the peak months of September and October. Unfortunately, getting any sense out of most of the PARRO (Parks and Reservations Offices) can be difficult. A common complaint is that staff say sites are full when in fact they turn out to be anything but that.

The **Gaborone office** appears to be the most efficient, so as a last resort you can try working through them. Contact Catherine Motsatsi or Jan Boroekhuis at PARRO, PO Box 131, Gaborone (☎580774, fax 580775, *dwnpbots@global.bw*). Officially, for Chobe you're supposed to book through the **Maun office**, PARRO, PO Box 20634, Boseja (☎661265, fax 661264), but getting any sense out of them may tax your patience. If you're already in **Kasane**, you can also try going through the Department of Wildlife and National Parks, Kasane (☎650235, 650486 or 650799, fax 661332), but this is a slightly long shot. If you need help, Heather at Kasane Enterprises can help with bookings. If there are places available at campsites, you can sometimes make a booking on arrival – another, rather risky, option.

Of the various **National Parks camps** (basic facilities only) scattered across the varying terrain of the park, the closest to Kasane, and the most popular, is **Ihaha**, ribboning along the Chobe River about 33km from Kasane. Although the whole park is called Chobe, you'll frequently hear it used to refer just to this river area. Just outside the national park, 55km from Kasane at Ngoma Bridge, is the privately run *Buffalo Ridge* campsite; at the other end of the scale in terms of style and cost, the park is served by a handful of **luxury safari lodges**.

From about 10km west of the park entry gate, two routes splay out southwards, before converging again on Savuti. The first runs west, parallel to the Chobe River, before bearing south into the heart of the national park. The second takes you through Ngwezumba with its mopane forests to **Nogatsaa Pans** and several newly created waterholes. But the ultimate destination in Chobe is the **Mababe Depression**, a dead-lake area comprising the **Savuti Channel and Marsh**. It's renowned for the unusually gentle bull elephants roaming around the campsite, plus the prides of lions that prowl the marsh – a grassy plain formed during the years when this part of Botswana was under the big lake.

Kasane and Chobe riverfront

Graced by big trees and the beautiful Chobe River, **KASANE** provides a pleasant respite from the dust and dryness of the rest of the country. It was once the imperial centre of the Makololo – eighteenth-century invaders from what is now South Africa, who conquered the local Lozi people – although no evidence of that period remains. A bunch of dusty administrative buildings, a small mall, a bank, public phone, hospital, a couple of takeaways and some traditional huts are strung out desultorily along the main road. There's a centre of sorts at the western end of the village, the one closest to the park entrance. Here you'll find a small supermarket, a garage, car rental and the *Chobe Safari Lodge*.

Getting there

Because Kasane is a border town, you're most likely to hit it as you arrive from one of the neighbouring countries, although there are a few buses that head up here from Francistown, which is in the southeast of Botswana.

By bus

Most visitors arrive in Kasane by road from Victoria Falls, and numerous operators, among them African Sport & Leisure (Victoria Falls ☎013/2145 or 5976, fax 2145), Safari Excellence (Kasane ☎650992, *safexcel@info.bw*) and Chobe Safari Lodge (Kasane ☎650336, *chobelodge@info.bw*), offer return transfers between the two centres for around US$35, usually for a minimum of two people, with advance booking generally required. One of the few companies that will do transfers at short notice if they have a free vehicle is Janala Tours (Kasane ☎650234 or 650576), which, at US$60 return, is more expensive than the others. For day-trips from Vic Falls to Chobe, see Getting around Chobe on p.315. **From Zambia** you cross the Zambezi from Livingstone on the Kazungula ferry to the Botswana border post. If you're not in your own vehicle, try to line up a lift into town while you're on the ferry – it's too far to walk. **From Namibia**, there's a border post at Ngoma Bridge, 55km west of Kasane itself, with *Buffalo Ridge*

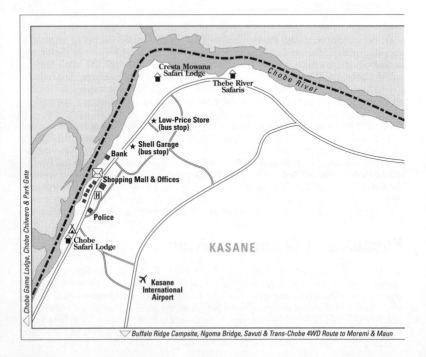

◁ Chobe Game Lodge, Chobe Chilwero & Park Gate

Cresta Mowana
Safari Lodge

Thebe River
Safaris

Chobe River

★ Low-Price Store
(bus stop)

★ Shell Garage
(bus stop)

Bank

Shopping Mall & Offices

H

Police

△ Chobe
Safari Lodge

KASANE

✈ Kasane
International
Airport

▽ Buffalo Ridge Campsite, Ngoma Bridge, Savuti & Trans-Chobe 4WD Route to Moremi & Maun

Campsite (☎ & fax 650430) – conveniently adjacent on the western boundary of Chobe – run by a Botswana game veteran. The road from Kasane to Ngoma is tarred, with plans to take the tar further. A few daily economy buses ply the route **from Francistown and Nata** to Kasane, arriving at the Shell petrol station near the Hot Bread Shop and at the corner of Mabele Road and President's Road (the main road through town), near the Low Price shop in the shopping area. **From Johannesburg**, the most convenient, reliable and comfortable bus service is operated Route 49, which goes to and from Victoria Falls twice a week in each direction and passes through Kasane, where you can alight or get on at *Chobe Safari Lodge* (Kasane ☎650336, fax 650437) or *Thebe River Safaris* (Kasane ☎650314, *thebe@info.bw*), both of which arrange bookings.

By air

Kasane **airport** makes the northeast of Botswana easily accessible without long road journeys, especially for travellers coming from South Africa, with direct passenger flights from Maun, Gaborone and Johannesburg. If you're booked into one of the lodges you'll be met; otherwise, transfers for US$10 can be prearranged through African Odyssey (☎ & fax 650601).

Accommodation

At present, the *Chobe Safari Lodge* is the only central place to stay in Kasane. Most of the other places nearby are luxury lodges with hefty price tags, in the national park

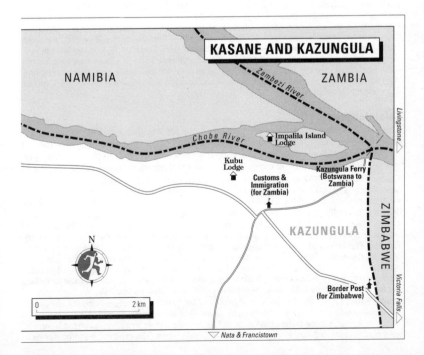

itself. At the other end of the scale there are several reasonably priced campsites, often with permanent tents to rent, on or close to the banks of the Zambezi but (with the exception of Ihaha) outside the hallowed boundaries of Chobe.

Campsites

Apart from the places listed here, camping is also available at *Chobe Safari Lodge* and *Kubu Lodge* (see below and opposite).

Buffalo Ridge Campsite, about 55km from Kasane; turn right towards Ngoma Bridge then left as you descend down the hill (☎650223, fax 650430, mobile ☎082/659 1232). Peaceful and isolated backpackers' and overlanders' campsite on a ridge overlooking the Chobe River flood plain. There is hot and cold water, but ablutions are otherwise rudimentary. A thatched bar with views of the water sells snacks and drinks, and you can get essentials from the camp shop. A professional guide is on hand to take walks and day or night game drives for about US$20. ①.

Ihaha National Park Campsite, roughly 30km west of Kasane (see box on p.311 for booking details). Friendly campsite with two ablution blocks and space for ten tents. Facilities include flush toilets, hot water and braai stands. ①.

Livingstone Camp, Northern Quarries, Private Bag K15, Kasane, Botswana (☎ & fax 650821). Backpackers' and overlanders' campsite on eight islands in the Zambezi River with a capacity of forty people. Facilities include ablutions with hot and cold running water, a fully stocked cash bar, a kitchen serving meals or available for self-catering, a shop with essential supplies selling braai packs, natural pools to swim in, hammocks and mobile phone and radio communication with their Kasane head office. Activities include nature walks, mokoro and inflatable-canoe trips and micro-light flights from the islands. The islands are only accessible by boat, with pick-up points at Mambova village in Zambia and Kasane; transfers can be arranged from Livingstone, Kasane and Vic Falls. Camping with own tent ①, thatched reed shelters with mosquito net, two-person tents with mattresses and bedding ②, dome tents with mattresses and bedding ③.

Thebe River Safaris, PO Box 5, Kasane (☎650314, *thebe@info.bw*). Campsite used mainly by over-landers, but open to individuals with permanent tents for rent. Located around 12km from the Kazangula border and 5km from the Chobe park gate on the main road into Kasane. The site is large, with lots of shade, bush-style washing areas made of hessian, mesh and cement, and some *letaka* (reed) walls with showers heated by wood-fired boilers. There are flush toilets and the facilities are clean and more than adequate for a comfortable stay. There is a braai area, four fire pits and a lovely pool near the river's edge, as well as an open bar and dining area under a reed roof. With advanced booking, catered meals can be arranged. They also run safaris (see p.316). Camping ①, permanent tents ②.

Safari lodges

The only en-suite rooms anywhere around Chobe for less than US$150 per person are at *Chobe Safari Lodge*, where you can stay for around US$35 – a bargain, despite the fact that you're outside the national park. Unless otherwise specified, all prices are per person per night inclusive of all meals, game drives and transfers from Kasane Airport.

Chobe Chilwero, PO Box 22, Kasane (☎651632, *chobe@icon.co.za*). A small, intimate camp with eight thatched bungalows and fantastic views over the river from the hill near the park gate. The camp offers excellent river trips, on which you can see birds and monitor lizards at close quarters, as well as game drives as part of the all-inclusive price of US$390.

Chobe Game Lodge, PO Box 32, Kasane (☎650340, fax 650280 or 650223, *chobe@fast.co.za*). On the riverbank inside the park itself, Botswana's most famous and elegant hotel still trades off the fact that Elizabeth Taylor and Richard Burton had their honeymoon here (after marrying each other for the second time). Of course, the elephants that drink from the river, within sight of the rooms, are a more satisfying reason to spend time in these luxurious surroundings. Even if you can't afford to stay, you're welcome for a drink or meal: their lavish Sunday brunches are worth shelling out for if you're already in the park. High season US$330, low season US$280.

Chobe Safari Lodge, PO Box 10, Kasane (☎650336, fax 650437). The original Chobe hotel – not to be confused with the glamorous *Chobe Game Lodge* – but considerably upgraded in the late 1990s, although it retains some budget rondavels and its campsite. More upmarket accommodation consists of air-conditioned double or family rooms with river views. The campsite is sandy, shaded by numerous trees and is right on the riverbank, with clean, well-maintained washing blocks. You can rent permanent two-person or family tents. Facilities include a dining area with an outdoor deck overlooking the river, a rather tatty bar (due to be renovated), and a travel agency. You can organize just about any activity possible here, including game drives (US$15), cruises (US$12), hot-air ballooning (from $140–250) and Chobe day-trips (US$60–80). Prices exclude park fees where applicable. Camping US$7 per person, permanent tents US$9 per person, budget rondavels with shared ablutions US$50 per unit, en-suite rondavels or rooms US$70 per unit, and upmarket rooms/family suites with river views US$90/100.

Cresta Mowana Safari Lodge, PO Box 335, Kasane (☎650300, fax 650301, *mowana@info.bw*). A safari hotel with the usual game activities. Service is nothing to write home about and it's the dullest of the Chobe accommodation places. US$235.

Impalila Island Lodge, Box 70378, Bryanston 2021, South Africa (☎ & fax 011/706 7207, ☎650794–5). Eight chalets in riverine forest, right at the meeting of all four neighbouring countries – you'll hear the river flowing by from your bed. Access is by boat from *Crest Mowana Safari Lodge*, though the lodge is technically in Namibia. Recommended. US$240.

Kubu Lodge, PO Box 43, Kasane (☎650312, fax 651092, *kubu@info.bw*). Some kilometres east of town on the river, near the Zimbabwean and Zambian borders, with en-suite rooms, rondavels and camping. Some of the campsites are separated by low *letaka* (reed) walls and the ablutions are tiled and spotless. There's a bar and a very good restaurant on site, with a terrace overlooking a lawn that slopes down to the river. *Kubu* can arrange game drives and river cruises into Chobe through African Odyssey. Chalets US$155 per person, camping US$10.

Muchenje Safari Lodge, Private Bag K31, Kasane (☎ & fax 636000). Superb, luxury lodge set high above the river on the edge of the escarpment with a commanding view, 65–70km from Kasane through Chobe along the tar road, about 10km beyond *Buffalo Ridge Campsite*. Chalets are decorated with tiled flooring and ceramic bowls in the bathroom sinks, and the dining room/bar area has a well-stocked library and a viewing deck overlooking a small floodlit waterhole. You can watch the sun set from the deck or down on the shores of the river. Activities include game drives and walks, night drives, river cruises and village visits. US$225.

Getting around Chobe

The nicest way to see Chobe is in your own vehicle and at your own pace. Without your own 4WD, and if you don't mind being in a group, the best option is to join one of the **mobile safari companies** who traverse the route as part of a Botswana–Victoria Falls trip.

Self-driving

Vehicles without 4WD can normally get to the riverfront around Ihaha camp, but no further, and you should check out the condition of the road to Ihaha before heading out. You can arrange **4WD rental** in Maun (see p.326) or Kasane, but you definitely need 4WD experience to cope with the heavy sand further south, and strong nerves for being in the wild. There are no mechanics, breakdown services, petrol stations or shops, and only very primitive campsites. **Car rental** can be arranged through Avis at the *Cresta Mowana Lodge* (☎650144) or Holiday Car Hire (☎650336, fax 650437, *holidayhire@info.bw*), next to *Chobe Safari Lodge*. Prices for a 4WD start at around US$50 per day, plus additional charges for mileage, and about half that for a sedan.

Mobile safaris, day drives and river cruises

Without your own vehicle, you can still easily get into Chobe and the other wilderness areas around Kasane. If you're short of time or cash, the obvious option is to go on one of the half- or-full-day outings that will include a game drive, river cruise or both. Many operators will transfer clients from Victoria Falls, although it may be more expensive than leaving from Kasane.

The least expensive **multi-day safaris** through Chobe – and even they are certainly not cheap – are overland adventure trips of seven to sixteen days. Departures are usually offered from Victoria Falls or Maun. Without your own 4WD, these trips are the best way to get into remote game parks and have the experience of camping in the bush and sitting around campfires. **Prices** for half-day trips start at US$15 but are more typically around US$25, whereas full safaris will set you back around US$110–320 per day and are mostly all-inclusive. On the cheapest "participation" safaris, clients usually pitch their own tents and help with some of the chores like cooking, while at the top of the range you just sit pretty, with some of the accommodation in luxury camps or luxury hotels. This price ensures hot showers, sheets on your camp bed and iced drinks. Children under the age of 12 are normally not permitted on safaris.

African Odyssey, *Kubu Lodge* (☎ & fax 650601). Recommended operator offering three-hour game-viewing boat cruises and game drives, including refreshments, but not park fees, for US$25; half- or full-day drive or cruise with lunch, and return transfers to the Botswana border, park fees and drinks for US$50/US$70; overnight trips into the park and participation overland camping from Chobe to Okavango Delta for a minimum of seven days, or five-day camping safari in Chobe for US$150 per day, including transfers to and from Vic Falls.

Go Wild Safaris, *Chobe Safari Lodge*, PO Box 56 (☎650468). One-day safaris for a minimum of two people, including a boat cruise, game drive and lunch cost US$75; adventure safaris, including wine and beer, are US$230 per day; luxury safaris go for US$320 per day.

Into Africa Mowana Safaris, run from *Cresta Mowana Safari Lodge*, PO Box 266 (☎650478, fax 650469). Day and night game drives and mokoro trips to African villages for around US$20, and boat cruises for about US$25.

Janala Tours, PO Box 55, Kasane (☎650234 or 650576, fax 650223). A small local operator offering budget safaris. Overnight in Chobe for US$120–150 per person (depending on numbers) including park fees, game drives, camping, meals and drinks; inclusive day-trips for US$50.

Mantis Safaris and Nkwazi Fishing Safaris, Private Bag K48, Kasane (☎650051, mobile ☎71/304150). The only Kasane-based fishing company registered in Namibia can take you to the prime spots to fly fish from 5m fibreglass boats. 5hr trips can be scheduled to fit in with other safaris/activities and cost US$90 per boat, while a full day costs US$135, including tackle, rods, fuel and a guide. Boats take up to four people. They also offer a full-day walking trail to a Namibian village for US$20 and Chobe river trails for US$6 per hour.

Nsundano Travel Tours, PO Box 16 (☎650901, mobile ☎71/612559). Small, local operator offering day-trips for US$45 and full-day trips into Zambia to traditional villages for around US$40, including food and soft drinks.

Safari Excellence, Private Bag K33, Kasane (☎ & fax 650992). Full-/half-day luxury Chobe overland safaris with lunch for US$80/60, including transfers from Vic Falls; 3hr walking safaris with lunch $55; 3hr game drive or cruise from *Chobe Safari Lodge* at US$15, including soft drinks but not park fees.

Safari Thanda Manzi, Private Bag K24, Kasane (☎ & fax 650881). Tailor-made luxury safaris in Chobe, Moremi, Okavango and Kalahari, with prices dependant on itinerary and group numbers, but roughly US$250 per day fully inclusive, plus one- to three-night camping trips out of Vic Falls.

Thebe River Safaris, PO Box 5, Kasane (☎650314, *thebe@info.bw*). Day-trips including a game drive and cruise from Kasane for US$100, or from Vic Falls for US$125; budget, luxury or tailor-made safaris in Botswana cost from US$110 to US$190 per day, excluding drinks; a nine-day Botswana–Zambia safari starting from Victoria Falls, including nights spent in Chobe and on an island in the Zambezi, will set you back US$1500.

Chobe riverfront

Afternoons are usually the favoured time for **elephant herds** to make their way to the river, and consequently a wonderful time to see them, en masse, in lovely surroundings. Chobe's 50,000-strong population is legendary: at water they provide excellent slapstick entertainment, as their playfulness comes to the fore in the elephantine equivalent of a booze-up. Bear in mind that the rainy season can be disappointing, especially for seeing elephants, so if the pachyderms are your target go in the **dry season**. The best way to see something of the Chobe River is to take a **cruise** that goes slowly along

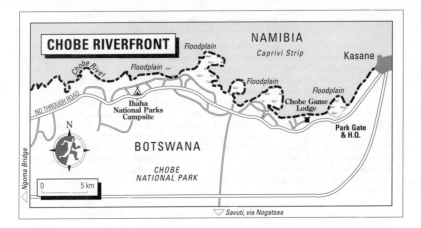

the river. As you skirt the flood plains you'll see a wealth of animals and birds from the deck of the launch, and you can have a drink at the same time. The flood plains, with their different vegetation types – thickets of bush, open grassland and riverine forest – are ideal for **game viewing**. Besides herds of elephant and buffalo, look out for tsessebe, waterbuck, roan and sable antelopes, eland, sable, rhinoceros, giraffe, hyena, kudu and bushbuck.

Common **water birds** you'll spy on the margins include herons, storks, geese, ducks, jacanas and skimmers. One of the greatest delights is a huge colony of **carmine bee-eaters** that nests in holes in the bank, although not always in the same place each year.

Close to the water, you may spot one of the rarest Botswanan antelope, the **puku**, which bears a passing resemblance to the impala but lacks the latter's distinctive black and white markings. **Red lechwe** are far more commonly sighted antelope in northern Botswana's wetlands – their southernmost range. Although still one of Chobe's common sights, the species faces extinction due to competition with humans for its specialized waterside habitat. Hippos loll in the water and you may spot water monitor lizards or crocodiles basking on the sandy edges of the flood plains.

Ihaha campsite and around

At *Ihaha* (see p.314 for details) you'll be surrounded by animals, especially elephants, in the dry season; never fall asleep outside your tent or leave it open, however warm the night. Ihaha is on the old road from Kasane to Ngoma, the crossing point into Namibia. From this road there are several loops, through varied landscapes – down to the **flood plains**, into areas of **thicket**, or inland into **mopane forest**.

Near the camp, you can sit on the riverbank and watch **elephants** drinking and frolicking 100m away, but be on your guard and never get too close. If you're very lucky and patient, you could see some of the river's beautiful **otters**. For some curious reason, the airstrip near *Chobe Game Lodge* is a preferred spot for **lions** (perhaps because it provides them with a cleared area from which to watch game) and you can usually hear their chilling roars at night. **Baboons** are the louts of the animal world. They sometimes destroy tents left up during the day – the best tactic is to collapse your tent every morning and take everything with you in the car, if you don't want to return to find it ripped to shreds by their sharp nails.

THE CHOBE ELEPHANTS

The big issue at Chobe is **elephants**. The Botswanan government prohibited elephant hunting and rejected a culling policy for some years, though it now allows the hunting of a certain number. The original hunting ban was motivated by the notion that if the elephants have nothing to fear outside reserves they'll migrate freely beyond the national park boundaries, and thus ease the pressure on parkland itself.

The reason for the policy change is that the available land cannot support the official count of 75,000–80,000 elephants, although this number includes migrating elephants from neighbouring Zimbabwe, Zambia and Namibia: the Chobe Wildlife Trust estimates 50,000. The elephants threaten other species and cause serious environmental damage, especially along Chobe's riverfront, where you'll see wrecked mopane trees, ravaged by elephants, which are turning woodland savannah into degraded bushveld. In Botswana there's a passionate anti-culling lobby, which argues that elephants cause change, not simple destruction, of habitat, and that the park will establish its own balance without the stress of slaughtering whole family groups of elephants. In Zimbabwe, most people involved in wildlife management argue for culling. Both countries are in favour of the ivory trade, arguing that their well-managed herds have become so big that regulated trade is in the best interests of the species and the countries' economies. The Southern Africa Centre for Ivory Marketing has agreed a system for marking legally culled tusks: a self-adhesive strip with a hologram, plus a bar code and number. The hope is that illegal traders and poachers will be unable to copy the official hologram on poached ivory.

Kasane to Savuti

From Kasane, there are two routes to choose from for the half-day, 4WD-only **drive to Savuti**. Leave early in the day, be entirely self-sufficient in fuel, water, food and spares, and remember you're in one of the wildest places in the world.

The shorter and more usual, though not especially scenic, route heads west on tar towards **Ngoma Bridge**, the border post with Namibia, with the *Buffalo Ridge Campsite* close by (see p.314). There's then good gravel to the village of **Katchakau**, where the route turns south into the Chobe Forest Reserve. Here the road deteriorates into thick sand ruts for the two-hour journey on to Savuti, and 4WD is essential. Expect the whole journey to take four hours, but don't make it in the hope of good game sightings – you'd be far better off driving around the northern section of the park close to the river, where the game viewing is far better.

The alternative route via Nogatsaa, though it takes around six hours, has several advantages: the road is less sandy, and you'll see more game on the way. Crossing the depression during the rains, however, when the Mababe Depression's "black-cotton" soil is wet, is heavy going, if not impossible, and definitely not recommended for novices. It's another four or five hours to Maun from Savuti.

Nogatsaa, about 70km south of the Chobe River, is part of an extensive complex of pans set in forest that attracts herds of buffalo and elephant, particularly during the rainy season. There is no campsite but you could do it as a day-trip from Kasane; it's game all the way on the two-hour stretch to Nogatsaa, and there's a hide overlooking a dam where you can spend a couple of hours. The Nogatsaa region isn't as spectacular as the riverfront area, but you'll see antelope on the wide-open plains and, in clearings in the mopane woodlands near the pans, you may glimpse **oribi**. This is the only place these compact, dun-coloured antelope occur in Botswana. They live in small parties of two to five, in distinct territories, which the male marks out by rubbing glandular secretions on twigs and grass stems. You're most likely to see them in the early morning, when they're feeding. During the day, and when danger threatens, they lie quietly in tall grass or by a bush or rock.

After Nogatsaa Pans, the route runs parallel to the Ngwezumba River, which flows when rains are good; the Ngwezumba Dam near Tjinga is a fine place to watch elephant and buffalo.

Savuti and the Mababe Depression

SAVUTI is on the route of every four-wheel-drive expedition to Botswana, though it can be frighteningly dry and harsh, and there's been no water in the Savuti Channel for many years. During the rainy season, there's enough other water around to lure the game, but in drought years animals move off to more permanent water sources. Besides **camping and driving** around the **Mababe area**, you can fly in by light aircraft and stay at a **luxury bush camp**, usually as part of a package to Moremi and the Okavango Delta. And overland trips from Maun to the Chobe River and Victoria Falls invariably spend a night or two at Savuti.

Savuti lies within the **Mababe Depression**, a plain covered with grass and scattered bush that was once the bed of the primeval lake that covered large parts of the Kalahari. If you've driven south to Savuti via Ngoma Bridge, you'll have crossed the **Magwikhwe Sand Ridge**, which curves across the track and then runs southwards, parallel to it. You'll also see the low sandy bank on your right as you head toward Maun; the ridge is believed to have formed the western shoreline of the former lake. Progress through the deep, soft sand around here is slow and bumpy.

The **Savuti Channel**, part of which runs through the campsite, periodically carries water over 100km from the Linyanti (Chobe) River through a gap in the Magwikhwe Sand Ridge, and spills it onto the floor of the depression, creating the small **Savuti Marsh**. Sometimes it's deep in water, and other times it's cracked dry. The ebb and flow of the Savuti Channel is something of a mystery. It doesn't flow as a matter of course and has been dry since before 1980. Connected as it is to the Linyanti River, it would seem to stand to reason that when the river's in flood its waters would push through and fill the channel. But, as with other waterways in Botswana, nature conspires to confound logic. In some years of exceptional flood the channel has remained dry, and it seems that the flow has more to do with shifts beneath the earth's surface than the state of the waterways themselves. The caprice of the channel leaves its own scarring mark on the landscape. Trees that eagerly took root in the dry bed now stand gnarled and dead – drowned when the waters unexpectedly came flooding down.

The **Gubatsaa Hills** are Savuti's other notable geographical feature, just as intriguing as the channel. These dispersed, rocky outcrops have almost sheer northeastern faces formed by powerful waves crashing into them during the lake days. Seasmoothed pebbles, rounded by the long-gone tides, can still be found on the lee side. On some of the hills there are rock paintings: not easy to find unless someone who knows directs you – ask one of the game scouts at Savuti camp.

The area has a dazzling display of **wildlife**. Once the first rains have greened the yellow grass, and allayed the dust, magnificent stretches of grassland fringed with mopane woodland attract elephant, buffalo, wildebeest, impala, giraffe, tsessebe, hartebeest, kudu, warthog, jackal and zebra. When the water disappears on the marsh there is adequate grazing for some time, and when that has gone many animals move off to the riverfront. You can spot **prides of lions** on the plain until the grass grows long during the rains, hiding them. A lion research team, and an intrepid Englishwoman who crept around at night studying **hyenas**, are among the scientific groups to have spent time here.

Savuti campsite

The name *Savuti* casts an almost mythical spell in the minds of seasoned Botswana veterans. Every one of them has a tale of a close shave with one animal or another and you're assured of some sort of wildlife action at the campsite. It really has the flavour of big-game country, not a place where you'd contemplate stumbling to the loo after dark.

Elephants stroll about the **campsite**, which is no more than a large unfenced area of bush along the Savuti Channel. There are rudimentary toilets and taps, which are regularly destroyed by thirsty elephants, who in the past have torn off the roof of the washing facilities to get at the water. Fresh fruit, particularly oranges, also bring out the mischievous element in elephant populations, so don't carry them with you and don't feed the elephants, no matter how appealing they seem. A number have had to be shot because their appetite for citrus had them tusking open car boots.

Hyenas also do the rounds at the campsite every night. It's unnerving to hear them sniffing around the tent, centimetres from where you lie, but they won't bite through tents and they go away if you shout at them. **Baboons** are a more serious menace and, as at all campsites, will lay into tents in search of booty. You'll almost certainly be treated to the roars of lions in the distance, too.

MAUN AND THE OKAVANGO DELTA

The country was one intricate labyrinth of swamp, with many small streams moving outward from the river into the sandy wastes of the southwest. Where all this water goes to is a mystery.

Aurel Schultz, explorer, 1897

The **Okavango River**, which rises in Angola, flows inland across 1300km of sand and never makes it to the sea. Instead it forms one of the largest inland deltas in the world, trapped between deep fault lines and imperceptibly dammed by rising land in the east. Most of the river's water evaporates on its way downstream, and on the fringes it seeps into the desert. The mighty river dies in a sandy trickle in the Kalahari. The **Okavango Delta** is a luxuriant oasis in the desert – a place of lagoons, palm islands and secret waterways weaving through papyrus and water lilies. At the bottom of the clear waters are the white sands of the Kalahari Desert. On the edges of the Delta, once riverine trees give over to desert thorn and grass, it's hard to imagine that you're so close to so much natural bounty.

The Delta alters its character seasonally – most people visit in the **dry season** (April–Oct) when the flood waters from the Okavango River have pushed through to the southernmost fingers. Up at the Panhandle (between the Caprivi Strip and the main delta) the water arrives two or three months earlier. The channels are at their lowest during the rainy season before the flood waters have come down from Angola.

The papyrus-matted **eastern delta** is what most people mean when they talk about "Okavango". This is where most of the lodges are found, in the depths of the exciting island and waterway landscapes that positively teem with wildlife. The way in is through **Maun** – a dusty frontier town of hunters, safari operators and tourists, superimposed on a sprawling traditional village which was the seat of the king of the Batawana (an offshoot of the main Tswana tribal grouping) for most of this century. It's simply not possible to go it alone in the swamps, but you'll find all the contacts you need for Delta travel in Maun.

The real heart of the Delta is **Moremi Wildlife Reserve**, an exclusive zone (which charges a daily fee of P50 per head) with one foot in the water and the other in savannah. It includes the two high-ground land masses of **Chief's Island** to its west and the **Moremi Tongue** jutting out of the mainland to the east. Between the two is a changing landscape of both permanent and seasonal wetland that ebbs and flows with the Delta's waters. The contact of extreme drylands with the quenching Okavango gives Moremi the richest variety of habitats in Southern Africa, and access to it is both tightly controlled and bitterly fought over.

Maun

MAUN (pronounce to rhyme with *town*), raw and remote, is the sort of place you reach with a sense of achievement. However, although you're finally at the edge of the Okavango Delta, don't be fooled by the maps: you're not in the swamps yet, and access can be expensive. Nevertheless, you'll find everything you need here for the final push into the Okavango.

A sprawling town straddling the Thamalakane River, Maun has grown around the traditional capital of the Batawana that was first established here in 1915 (see box on p.323). The traditional village is still there and you're bound to see Herero women – relative newcomers from Namibia, who sought refuge among the Batawana – sweep the dust with their colourful bustled Victorian dresses. Superimposed on the original village, unfortunately without any apparent plan, and ever growing, is the main town.

You can't really speak of Maun having a "centre", and it has no street names. There are three dispersed shopping malls, with untethered goats and donkeys wandering about, and everything is stretched out along a three-kilometre strip between the malls. Everything to do with tourism, bar a few exceptions, clusters around the airport: car rental, travel agents, air charter outfits and curio shops. You'll find a bank and supermarket nearby at the **Ngami Centre**, opposite which is the **BGI Mall**, where there's a petrol station, photographic shop and supermarket. A couple of kilometres south of the airport, the **Old Mall** is the focus for a sprinkling of other shops and offices, one of which is the pretty useless **tourist information office** (☎660492, fax 661676) on the main road across from the Riley's Garage Complex. A better reason to head here is the **post office**, bus stop and the Shoprite shopping complex. Despite its isolation, Maun's **supermarkets** are well stocked, albeit with South African fruit, vegetables and dry goods. You'll find everything you need for a camping trip (see Listings, p.326). Beyond the airport, continuing east for 14km, you reach **Matlapaneng** on the **Thamalakane River**, effectively a suburb of Maun with some of the area's few affordable places offering **accommodation** for travellers; on the opposite side of town, on the road to Toteng, you'll find a couple of other options.

Maun's white residents value the town's **frontier image** – rough, tough, remote and hard-drinking: there was a time when you needed 4WD to drive through the town centre. These days there's a tarred road, which allows people to roar in smoothly from places like Johannesburg, but 4WDs continue to predominate because, once you're off the tar, you're on desert roads.

Arrival

Air Botswana has **flights** to Maun from Gaborone, Johannesburg (US$420 return), Kasane (US$113) and Victoria Falls (US$113) and, although the **airport**, at the north end of town, is the busiest in Botswana (mainly charters flying in and out of the Delta), it's small enough to bring you instantly into the heart of things.

Driving from Nata

Short of taking the cross-Chobe route, most trips to Maun by road from Kasane in the north or from Francistown in the south, pass through **Nata**. From here, the once notoriously rough Nata–Maun road, now tarred, hauls through 300km of desert plains and scrubland. The main **landscape** interest on this road is the gentle transition from dense bush and stunted trees to vast, open **grasslands** with stately palms. Gweta is an access point for the **Makgadikgadi Pans** and the grasslands. Keep your eyes

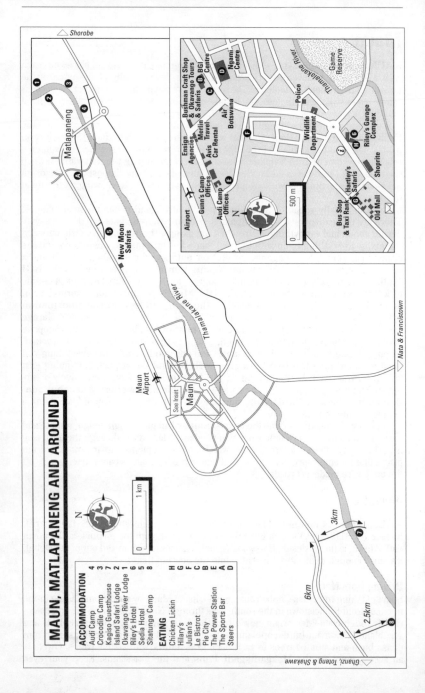

MAUN, MATLAPANENG AND AROUND

ACCOMMODATION
Audi Camp	4
Crocodile Camp	3
Kagiso Guesthouse	7
Island Safari Lodge	2
Okavango River Lodge	1
Riley's Hotel	6
Sedia Hotel	5
Sitatunga Camp	8

EATING
Chicken Lickin	H
Hilary's	G
Julian's	F
Le Bistrot	C
Pie City	B
The Power Station	E
The Sports Bar	A
Steers	D

peeled for game as you make your way from Gweta to Maun; the road goes right through the gap between the boundaries of the Makgadikgadi Pans Game Reserve and Nxai Pan National Park, and you can regularly spot **giraffes**, **zebras**, **ostriches** and various **antelope** species. You also cross part of the **Pans complex** – a hostile white and grey skin of salty clay stretching to the horizon, where nothing grows.

By bus

Mahube **buses** run three times daily between Francistown and Maun (allegedly leaving Francistown at 8.30am, 10.30am & 3.30pm; 5hr) arriving at the bus/taxi rank at the Old Mall. In addition to this, Mercedes Sprinters commute between Kasane, Maun and Francistown; they shuffle around each town collecting passengers, can be caught at petrol stations or the bus rank, and leave when full. An excellent service aimed at backpackers, but handy for other travellers too, is the four-times-weekly **Route 49 shuttle bus** between Nata and Maun. The shuttle is scheduled to link up with the twice-weekly services (in each direction) between Johannesburg and Victoria Falls. Departures are from hostels in Johannesburg and Pretoria on Tuesdays and Saturday evenings (arriving Maun at 5.30pm the same day), and from Vic Falls on Monday and Friday mornings (arriving Maun at 2.30pm the same day).

MAUN – TRADITIONAL CAPITAL OF THE BATAWANA

Since 1915, **Maun** has been the capital of the **Batawana** people. The Batawana are now one of the main Batswana groupings, having emerged through strife at the end of the eighteenth century, when they broke away from the Bangwato over a succession dispute.

The disagreement among the Bangwato arose when their king married out of the clan. The bride, who was merely a minor wife, had a son called Tawana. Trouble came when the king declared that Tawana was to be his successor, rather than Khama, the son of his principal wife. The clan split and, following an attack on Tawana by Khama, the king took Tawana away on a migration. After wandering for some years, the king took his leave to return home, leaving the breakaway band under his son's leadership, and the tribe became known as the Batawana.

During their migrations, the Batawana intermarried with other tribes and so managed to swell their numbers. Around 1824 they settled on the banks of Lake Ngami, gathering strength and building a powerful state and military force, which dominated the other people of the region: the Bangologa, Bayei and San. In 1830, now under Moremi I, they moved on to escape the marauding Bakololo, who were sweeping north from South Africa. The Bakololo pursued and eventually caught up with the fleeing Batawana on the Linyanti River, surrounding them and taking them as captives to the Chobe River. After a few years the dispossessed Batawana escaped, and eventually managed to re-establish themselves and to rebuild their cattle herds.

Their recovery was impressive. By the mid-nineteenth century the Batawana had forged an effective state that stretched across northern Botswana and extended as far south as Ghanzi. They established their capital at Maun in 1915, with the settlement developing along traditional Tswana lines – it became enormous by absorbing foreigners, who were incorporated in geographically distinct wards. The adobe huts were arranged around courtyards, at the centre of which was the ruling family. Further out were the wards of the Batswana who had split off from other groups, and people from other tribes like the Herero and Mbukushu were on the very outskirts: the San were outcasts, not allowed to live in the village unless as servants. Those who chose the settled life had their own separate villages within the orbit of the main settlement.

Accommodation

The only **place to stay** in central Maun is *Riley's Hotel*; most of the other **accommodation** is at lodges – usually with campsites – 10–14km from town on the Thamalakane River, most of which have bars and serve food. Roughly 12km east of town at **Matlapaneng** on a tarred road, the lodges and camping sites cluster along the waterway, paradoxically dry in the rainy season before the flood waters come down. **West of Maun**, you'll find another two lodges. All the lodges have bars and serve food, and, although thoroughly pleasant, are only points of passage, the real destination being the Delta. Most, however, run packages into the Delta that are in fact the cheapest way of penetrating into the exclusive waters (see Mobile safaris and day excursions, p.332).

Audi Camp, Shorobe Road, 12km from Maun at Matlapaneng; Private Bag 28, Maun (☎660599, fax 660581, *audicamp@info.bw*). The best Matlapaneng campsite, with friendly management and a clean, beautiful swimming pool. The two reed-walled ablution blocks have plenty of toilets and showers open to the sky creating a nice bush-type atmosphere. If you don't have your own tent, there are permanent two-person tents with or without mattresses, fans, bedside tables, and tables and chairs on a deck leading off. A thatched dining room/bar area on a terrace is the most charming place to dine or have a drink, and you can get pretty good food (including vegetarian options) at reasonable prices. They run budget safaris into the Delta (see p.332). Camping ①, permanent tent ②, bedded tent ③.

Crocodile Camp, Matlapaneng; PO Box 46, Maun (☎660265, fax 660793, *info@botswana.com, sales@botswana.com*). The grounds at this Matlapaneng camp, 15km from Maun on the Shorobe Road, are lush, beautifully landscaped and well-maintained. Most of the eight en-suite double chalets have verandahs overlooking the gardens and there's a family chalet that sleeps five. The campsite has reed enclosures with lots of shade trees, but the washing area is rather dreary, although clean. A range of safaris is on offer, one of the most interesting being a four-night semi-participation trip, combining horseback riding, mokoro trails and game walks. Tailor-made safaris of minimum seven days start at US$145 per day. Camping ①, chalets ③.

Island Safari Lodge, Matlapaneng; PO Box 116, Maun (☎ & fax 660300, *island@info.bw*). Maun's most family-friendly lodge is also the most wonderfully set: it's on a riverbank. Helpful staff, under the management of owners Kay and Phil Potter; the comfortable chalets and campsite were refurbished and upgraded at the beginning of 2000. There's a swimming pool and boat for rent, which you can take onto the river, water levels permitting, and they also run budget and luxury trips into the Delta (see p.332). Camping ①, chalets ④.

Kagiso Guesthouse, about 7km west of Maun; PO Box 158, Maun (☎663466, *kagiso@info.bw*). A range of accommodation at a modern house overlooking the Thamalakane River, along the Toteng/Shakawe/Ghanzi road (turn left at sign and continue for 3km along a dirt road), and rondavels in the garden. A double en-suite room leads off of the dining room of the main house, with a lovely stone verandah overlooking the river. In the garden there are two en-suite rondavels, one of them self-catering and a third four-bed rondavel geared mainly to backpackers, with thin mattresses, breeze block and wood shelves, and separate ablutions. Breakfasts and dinners are available by prior arrangement and transfers to or from Maun cost US$5. Note that you must cross the river to get to Kagiso, which poses no problem when the river bed is dry, but when it's flowing you must approach from the other bank or arrange to park at a neighbouring house and be transported across the river. En suite ③, backpacker rondavel ①.

Okavango River Lodge, Matlapaneng, adjacent to Crocodile Camp; Private Bag B010, Maun (☎660298, mobile ☎71/603753, or book through Bathusi Travel & Safaris or Travel Wild; see Listings, p.326). Friendly down-to-earth place with en-suite chalets, a backpackers' dorm and camping with clean but indifferent washing facilities. A snack menu is available, as are continental breakfasts, and you can get reasonably priced suppers by prior arrangement, but the party piece they're known for is their "beer in a bucket" (six beers packed in ice in a tin bucket) to drink while watching rugby and cricket on TV. A great spot for the sports fans, whether resident or not. They organize Delta trips for about US$90 per day all-inclusive. Camping and backpacker dorm ①, en-suite chalets ③.

Riley's Hotel, opposite the Old Mall; PO Box 1, Maun (☎660320, fax 660580, *rileys@info.bw*). Maun's most luxurious hotel has gone through innumerable changes since its original makeshift construction on the banks of the Thamalakane by the hunter Harry Riley. There's a great outdoor bar in the garden alongside the swimming pool – an escape from Maun's omnipresent tar and sand. ⑥.

Sedia Hotel, about 5km out of Maun on the Matlapaneng Road; Private Bag 058, Maun (☎ & fax 660177, *sedia@info.bw*). Modern, boring hotel, which may nevertheless do the trick if you're after something near the centre that's cheaper than *Riley's*. A large campsite has clusters of small trees giving some degree of privacy, but it's essentially pretty dismal – although improved by its extension in 1999 by some 100m to the river's edge. The ablutions are new, modern and clean and there's a volleyball court and pool. Campers have use of the hotel's bar, restaurant, terrace menu, pool and Internet facilities. Camping ③, en-suite rooms ④.

Sitatunga Camp, 6km west of the Kagiso turn-off, then turn left for 2.5km (*jillandgazza @hotmail.com*). Large campsite, under renovation at the time of writing, on a terrific site with lots of shade and a separate (more secluded) area adjoining it. Aimed principally at overlanders, individual campers are welcome and some walk-in *meru* tents are available for rent. Basic supplies are available from a little shop. A two-night mokoro trail can be organized for around US$130 per person, including park fees, one meal, some drinks and transport. Camping ①.

Eating, drinking and entertainment

In the centre of town, the *Power Station* (Mon–Sat 9am–11pm), on the road running along the airport behind the *Audi Camp* offices, is a hugely popular one-stop **eating** and entertainment emporium where you'll catch broadcasts of international sports events on their large screen as well as recent-release videos (Mon, Wed, Fri & Sat nights), or you can play chess and sometimes hear live music. Apart from serving the best burgers in town, they also have a bar, snack foods and an eclectic lunch and dinner menu that includes salads, Indian dishes and baklava. *Le Bistrot*, in the shopping area near the airport, is another reliable joint with a nice atmosphere and is good for lunch or dinner, but can be a bit pricey. Less expensive but also recommended is *Julian's*, a daytime venue up the road from the *Power Station*, west off the main road through town, which does good East Asian food. More mundane grub in the centre is available at *Steers*, in the Ngami Mall (daily 8.30am–9pm), which does the usual franchised burgers and steaks – there's also *Pie City* in the BGI Mall, which serves exactly what its name suggests, as does *Chicken Lickin*, near Riley's Garage and Service Station (daily 9.30am–9pm).

As recently as the late 1990s, **entertainment** in Maun came down to drinking, which was pursued as an acrobatic fine art: one Matlapaneng lodge used to have guests climbing a pole in the middle of the bar and drinking beers whilst doing handstands. Things have calmed down a bit since then, particularly with the arrival of TV. The hottest **drinking** spot on Fridays and Saturdays is *The Sports Bar*, 6km from Maun on the road to Matlapaneng, which is a major hangout for guides and pilots, and is also recommended for its pizzas – the best in town. Out of the centre, all the lodges and camps have bars that are open to non-residents and serve food.

Transport

Remote as it is, Maun is nevertheless the focus for most travel in Botswana. One consequence of its isolation is that modes of transport are strictly limited: four-wheel drive, boat or air.

Self-drive vehicles, notably **4WDs**, can be rented at Avis for adventurous travel into the northern game parks and pans, up to Shakawe or westwards to Ghanzi. **Air charter** isn't as expensive as you'd expect, but can be difficult to arrange in the high season without prior booking. In low season the charter companies are more flexible about taking you to places like Tsodilo Hills and waiting while you look round, as long as they haven't got queues of clients gathering back in Maun. Five-seater planes can be chartered, which is a real option if there's a group of you, for a trip to the Tsodilo Hills (see Air charter on p.326 for recommended companies). These companies also run charter flights to Gaborone, Kasane, Victoria Falls and Johannesburg and can arrange **game flights**, offering the chance to see the Delta from above – a memorable vision, but one you'll be rewarded with anyway if you're flying into one of the Delta's camps. From the air, you see the rich patchwork of green and brown ink-blot islands, spiked with upright palms, their dense green centres bleaching out to sandy rings that seep into the water. You may also see large herds of game scattering away. **Motorboats** provide an alternative way of penetrating the Delta, but aren't significantly less expensive, and consequently aren't recommended.

Listings

Airlines Air Botswana is situated on the airport turn-off, in a stand-alone thatched building on your left (☎660391).

Air charter The most highly recommended company is Mack Air, PO Box 329 (☎661508, ☎ & fax 660675, *mack.air@info.bw*), which does flights to most of the camps in the Delta and has the reputation of having the best-trained and most professional pilots. Another reliable outfit is Delta Air (☎660044), owned by Okavango Tours and Safaris. For lifts or sharers for a plane charter, leave messages on the notice board at Shoprite, on the main road next to Okavango Tours and Safaris, or on the noticeboard at *Le Bistrot*.

Banks Standard Chartered (Mon–Fri 8.30am–2.15pm, Sat 8.15–10.30am) and Barclays (Mon–Fri 8.30am–3.30pm, Sat 8.15–10.45am) are both just southwest of the Mall, while First National (Mon–Fri 9am–12.45pm & 2.15–3.30pm, Sat 8.30–11am) is at the Ngami Centre.

Bookshop Botswana Book Centre, in the Old Mall, has a small selection of books about the country and a few novels.

Bureau de change Sunny's at the Ngami Mall (daily 7am–6pm); La Cuvette at the Old Mall (daily 7.30am–6.30pm).

Camping equipment Try Kalahari Canvas, parallel to the runway just outside the airport perimeter fence for rental; one or two campsites around Maun and in the Delta will also rent equipment to their clients.

Car rental Avis are at the end of the left branch just before the airport, next to Kalahari Canvas camping shop, Box 130, Maun (☎660039, fax 661596). You'll find Holiday Safaris Car Rental at the airport (☎ & fax 662429, *holidayhire@info.bw*).

Dentist Dr Ajayi, Top Floor, Roots Tower, the Mall (☎661226).

Doctor Dr Jourdan (☎660482); Dr Akhiwu, Delta Medical Centre, near Shoprite (☎661411).

Garage Riley's Garage and Service Station near *Riley's Hotel*.

Groceries Shoprite near the Old Mall; Score at the BGI Centre; and the Spar at Ngami Mall – all good bets for buying supplies.

Hospital 2km along the main Ghanzi road.

Immigration In one of the lone buildings on your right as you head toward Matlapaneng, 1km before the airport turn-off.

Internet services The Computer Shop, the Old Mall, next to *Hilary's*, provides email and Web-surfing facilities; the *Internet Café* (daily till 7pm or later by request; *icafe.maun@info.bw*) at the *Sedia Hotel* has four state-of-the-art machines and plans for satellite reception.

Pharmacy Okavango Pharmacy, the Old Mall and on main road near Ngami Mall, can dispense prescriptions and sells the usual chemist's stuff (☎660043 or 662049).

Police Located in one of the buildings near Immigration, heading for Matlapaneng on the right, just before the airport turn-off.

Post office Along the main road in front of the Mall slightly towards Francistown (Mon–Fri 8.15am–1pm & 2.15–4pm, Sat 8.30–11.30am).

Telephones Outside the Wildlife Department; the post office; the BGI Centre; Ngami Mall; and at the airport.

Travel agents For bookings into the Delta, Travel Wild at the airport, PO Box 236, Maun (☎660493), are probably the most helpful; Okavango Tours and Safaris, directly opposite the airport (☎660339) and at the *Power Station* (☎660220, fax 660589, mobile ☎71/303674, *okavango@icon.co.za*), are another efficient and helpful outfit; Merlin Travel, PO Box 13, Maun (☎660635), opposite the airport, can book most things; and Bathusi Travel & Safaris, Riley's Garage Complex (☎ & fax 660647, *bathusi@info.bw*) is a well-regarded company that can organize pretty much anything in Botswana or the Victoria Falls area.

The Okavango Delta

Although the **OKAVANGO DELTA** looks like a large lake on the map, it is in fact the most complex of mazes – channels twisting and turning in on themselves through the thick wetland vegetation, some rejoining main river channels, others coming to a dead end of matted papyrus as far as the eye can see.

The archetypal Okavango, of islands, lagoons and secret waterways, is the eastern Delta, incorporating the eastern sanctuary of Moremi Wildlife Reserve, which straddles both wet and dry terrain (see below and p.338). Due to the sizable **park entrance fees**, however, budget travellers are often forced to satisfy themselves with the region outside Moremi's boundaries. The cheapest deals can get you as far as the borders of Moremi, north of Maun, which have a very similar geography and vegetation to the reserve itself.

Up in the far north, where the Okavango River enters Botswana as a wide, strong river, is the area known as the Panhandle. Here, close to the border with Namibia, are a number of **fishing camps**. Along the remote west bank of the Okavango River, you'll still find traditional villages, in an exotic region of palm trees and thick riverine vegetation, reachable from the tarred road to **Shakawe** and Namibia's **Caprivi Strip**.

Some geology

The stillness of the slow-flowing Okavango Delta (a one-in-several-thousand gradient) masks a turbulent character beneath the deep sands over which it drifts. Not only does the Delta change with the seasons, its level varying as the flood waters come down from Angola, but it's also **geologically unstable**, its base shifting, twisting and turning, constantly but imperceptibly.

The region also suffers **earthquakes** – 38 minor ones in one ten-year period – which have brought frequent dramatic changes to the Delta's shape. Channels open and close, one suddenly becoming dry as another bursts forth: one large tremor in Maun in 1952 restored the flow of the bone-dry Boro River. Over the last century these movements have caused the Delta's boundaries to shift over 100km, a fact revealed by the distribution of **papyrus** and **palms**. Papyrus is fast-growing and quickly establishes itself where conditions are suitable, whereas the phoenix palm grows much more slowly. Whenever the swamp extends, papyrus marks the new map until the palm catches up. The limits of the two plants are 150km further south than the current perennial swamp on the Thaoge River, while on the Ng-gokha River the papyrus growth far outstrips that of the palm, indicating that the eastern extent of the swamp is recent.

Behind these mysterious shifts and changes lies a deep and ancient past. Long ago, some experts believe, when the Kalahari was wetter and the rocky plate at its base was tilted differently, the Okavango River drained into the Limpopo, which flowed into the Indian Ocean. At this time, much of northern Botswana was flooded by a **super-lake**. As the lake silted up, sedimentation led to the current drainage patterns, and the Delta was left behind as a remnant.

Access, safaris and accommodation

It's easy to get lost in the Okavango Delta, and not just in the mazes of islands and papyrus – negotiating the tour operators, and trying to get what you want without facing bankruptcy can be equally confusing. There's virtually no way of getting onto the waters on your own, so, to set out into the Delta, you'll have to go on some kind of **package**. Although booking well ahead ensures a place, you can usually organize something from Maun, which, together with Matlapaneng, is the hopping-off point for most of

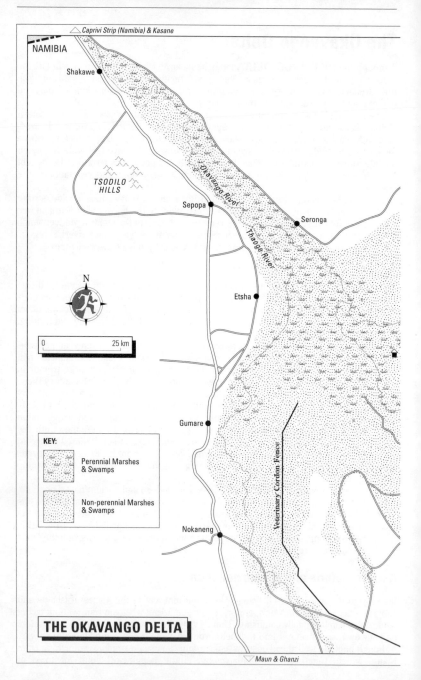

THE OKAVANGO DELTA

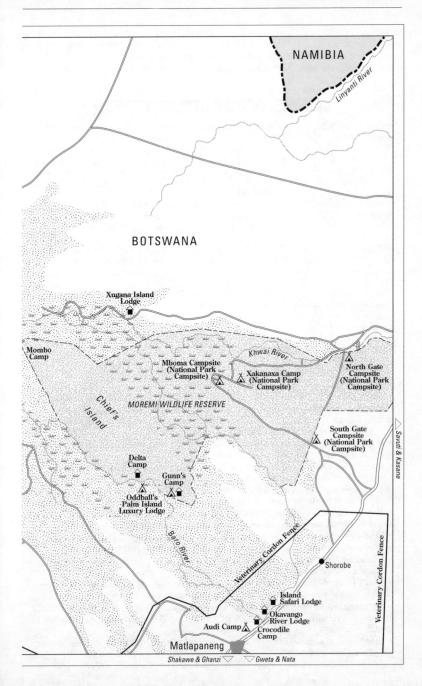

Okavango's camps and mokoro packages. Beware, however, of local operators making a quick buck out of this. There are reports of unsuspecting or ill-informed travellers being taken into areas outside of Moremi by ill-equipped guides, where not only are there no controls over littering and general environmental degradation but where

---

GETTING THE MOST FROM THE DELTA

Although the luxury lodges are highly recommended if you can afford them, the best way fully to experience **Okavango** remains the traditional one; that is, to get into the depths of the wilderness by going out on a mokoro for several days. You should take the Okavango as slowly as you possibly can. People who fly in for a night and out the next day are usually disappointed – and are wasting their money. We suggest an absolute minimum of two nights' **camping** in the Delta. It is a unique and special place and it takes a while to synchronize with its rhythms.

What you get out of your mokoro expedition depends firstly on yourself, and secondly on your poler. If you know what you want, are enthusiastic and are prepared to make an effort, you stand a good chance of having a wonderful time – and one that begins to touch the essence of the Delta. Do not regard your poler as simply a taxi driver. His familiarity with the waterways, his abilities at manoeuvring the craft and his knowledge of fauna and flora make you completely dependent on him. The greater the rapport you develop, the more you'll see and learn. As far as tasks go, polers are expected to take you on game-viewing walks and to find an island to camp on at night. They may well do more, such as cooking, fishing or making coffee in the morning. These are extras, and you should reciprocate by sharing your food, or in some such way as tipping.

Some aficionados suggest throwing yourself headlong into the experience by taking the minimum of food – a little maize meal – and relying on the fruits of the Delta. You eat the fish you catch, and gather wild foods with your poler – delicacies like palm nuts, water lilies and honey. But this is strictly for the hardy, must be arranged beforehand and you should offer your poler a decent tip.

SOME PRACTICAL TIPS

• **Don't rush off into the Delta.** Spending a couple of days in Maun, just relaxing and talking to people who have come back from the Delta, is an investment that will pay dividends. Get an idea of what is available, what people did there and what's going to suit you. This will give you an idea of which operator to go for.

• **Find out which polers gave people a good service**, and which camp they work from. Seek them out and ask to go out with them.

• **Fly to your Delta camp.** It's not much more expensive than boating in, and you get a superb overview of Okavango; and you'll have plenty of time on the water once you go out in a mokoro. There's a ten-kilogramme baggage allowance, however; leave tents and heavy items in Maun (booking agents will look after it) to make space for food supplies.

• **Buy supplies in Maun.** Prices are inflated inside the Delta. Maize meal, packet soups, rice and tinned foods are convenient. Don't forget matches and a torch.

• **Find out whether your poler is provided with rations** before you leave Maun. If in doubt, assume that you'll be feeding him and take enough food for the trip.

• **Spend at least a night at the camp** before launching out into the waters, to give yourself a chance to adjust to the environment.

• **Don't swim without asking:** most places are too risky for swimming. If you want a dip, say so, and you can be taken to safe shallow waters.

• **Be prepared to walk to see game.** Most animals are likely to be on the islands and dry areas. It requires some effort to see them, but you'll probably welcome a chance to stretch your legs.

• **Sleep under a mosquito net.** Leave your tent behind – it's bulky and unnecessary out of the rainy season.

there's little or no game. The **fees** to enter Moremi have been raised sharply a couple times over the past decade in an attempt to cut down the number of visitors and minimize destruction of the environment. In practice, however, the effect seems to have been that the ecological danger has been shifted out of the parks and into areas where there is no jurisdiction at all.

There are no bargain deals into Okavango. You won't get away spending much under US$100 for two or three days in a mokoro, and even this won't get you deep into the really desirable regions. For this kind of money, you'll be transferred from Maun and around to the Delta's edge in a 4WD vehicle or a powerboat, and from there be poled around the Delta north of Maun. This gives a good feel of Okavango, although it's not the ideal way to get the most out of your visit; the game viewing is a far cry from the sights inside Moremi Wildlife Reserve, though it can be very good in September and October. You will, however, be spared the stiff fees to enter and camp in the Moremi.

Moremi – the ultimate destination – is geared mainly towards the well-off. It incorporates the large **Chief's Island** and **Moremi Tongue**, which has the advantage of both wetland and dryland habitats, and hence attracts a large variety of game. There is only one **lowish-budget option**: the self-catering camp at the popular *Gunn's Bush Camp*. The usual scheme of things is to base yourself at the camp (in a tent), where you rent a mokoro to spend several days on the water, camping on islands. All the other places in Moremi are **luxury camps**, with tariffs that include all meals, all mokoro trips and, at the dryland camps, all game drives. They average US$400 per day in high season.

WASTED WATERS

Okavango is now regarded as one of the world's great wildernesses, but it wasn't always so. As recently as 1955 it was described as a useless swamp by one J.H. Wellington, who proposed its wasted waters be turned "into one of the richest gardens in Africa". He planned to throw up a mud dyke, the considerable distance from Sepopa to Chief's Island, in order to drain about 12,000 square kilometres to the southeast, which would be farmed.

Before that, **Cecil Rhodes**, too, had his eye on the swamps as a block in his great empire-building schemes. Convinced that Ngamiland was rich in diamonds and minerals – a belief that proved correct after Independence, when diamonds were found at Orapa – Rhodes planned to settle the swamp area with Boer families who would farm it using the plentiful supply of water. But the British government was reluctant to get involved with Okavango, which they saw as a watery wasteland that would be an administrative liability. Placing people in Ghanzi, on the border of Namibia, to nip any German expansion in the bud, seemed a far better investment.

The Delta has remained a contentious issue ever since, with some outlandish proposals to utilize its seemingly **wasted waters**. In a country that suffers badly from low rainfall, the water promises to be a wonderful resource for farming and mining. There are demands for water from nearby Maun, which has no permanent supply – the water runs out in the taps occasionally – and the Orapa diamond mine, a big currency-earner, is looking for more water. Irrigable land in the west could be utilized to provide great self-sufficiency in crops; the Eastern Corridor, too, needs far more water.

But tapping off the waters is liable to create major **ecological changes** in the region and international conservation agencies are lobbying for protection of the wetland habitat. If it goes, they argue, so will some endangered species and thousands of wild animals and birds. Already cattle are encroaching – the veterinary **cordon fence**, passing across the southern edge of the Delta, just north of Maun, marks the present boundary between domestic and wild animals – and tsetse-fly-spraying has had undesirable effects on the ecology.

HORSEBACK SAFARIS

One of the most thrilling ways to explore Okavango is on horseback, and a couple of reputable operators run riding trips from camps based in the Delta.

Okavango Horse Safaris, Private Bag 23, Maun (☎661671, fax 661672, *ohsnx@global.bw*). The longest-established riding operator is owned by Barnie and P.J. Bestelink, who have twenty years' experience and an intimate knowledge of the Okavango. Rated one of Africa's top riding safaris, trips are generally booked out well in advance, so plan ahead. A maximum of eight guests are taken at a time for five- or ten-day safaris; four to six hours daily are spent in the saddle, with afternoons being given over to leisure activities such as swimming, game drives or bird walks. On a ten-day ride, three different camps are used, depending on water levels and game movements. There are fixed departure dates and safaris cost US$330 per night in high season (Jan, Feb & June–Oct) and US$300 in low season (March–May, Nov & Dec). A flexible alternative with no set departure dates or duration is to stay at a fixed camp and take daily game rides for US$300 per person in high season and US$250 in low. Only proficient riders are accepted. Children are welcome as long as they have passed a pony-club riding test. Additional costs are concession fees of US$12 per day and return air transfers for $145.

African Horseback Safaris, PO Box 20538, Maun (☎663154, fax 660912, *sjhorses@info.bw*). Run and owned by Sarah-Jane Gullick; safaris run out of *Macatoo Camp* in the Delta, which is open all year except February. Activities at the camp include horseback safaris, game drives, bird walks, night drives and mokoro trips. Seven-, ten- or eleven-night safaris (to accommodate transfer schedules), which include riding to a second Okavango camp. You need to be an experienced rider and have the choice of English or Western trail saddles. Arrivals and departures are on Tuesdays and Fridays, making the minimum stay three or four nights: in high season (June–Sept) US$425; in low (Jan, March–May & Oct–Dec), $330. A one-way transfer or game flight is US$125.

Mobile safaris and day excursions

Apart from offering one of the cheapest ways of getting into the Delta, although you're still looking at US$60 and up per day for rock-bottom budget trips, **mobile safaris** can also be a thrilling experience. If you're short of time as well as money, there's always the less-than-ideal option of a **one-day excursion** from Maun.

Audi Camp, Private Bag 28, Maun, opposite the airport (☎660599, fax 660581). A comprehensive range of no-frills camping trips, including ones into the Okavango fringes and Moremi. One- to three-day mokoro trips, for which you bring your own gear and food, will set you back US$60–120; two-day fly-in safaris into the Delta are US$200; and three-day mobile safaris to Moremi cost from US$170.

Crocodile Camp Expeditions. One of the Matlapaneng lodges (see Accommodation, p.324). This place rents out mokoro, and runs more upmarket overland or motorboat mobile safaris in Moremi. Rates are on a sliding scale depending on group numbers – the more clients, the cheaper the rate per head.

Island Safari Lodge, PO Box 116, Maun (☎ & fax 660300, *island@info.bw*). Budget participation tours from Maun in which you're are taken by powerboat or land cruiser to the edge of Moremi and set off on a mokoro with a poler for two nights' camping for US$148. You supply your own food and camping gear. A luxury version, in which everything is provided, is also available.

New Moon Safaris, about 4km out of Maun along the Shorobe/Matalapeng Road; Private Bag 210, Maun (☎ & fax 661665, *newmoon@info.bw*). Small company offering Delta trips and a few unusual activities at reasonable prices. Most trips cost about US$100 per person per day, including food, transport and guide (but not drinks or camping and park fees). For example, a one- to three-day mokoro trip in the Delta costs US$60–120 including transfers, poler fees and entrance fees, but you provide your own food and equipment. Among their more unusual safaris are day-trips to see elephants ($105–160), and visits to a local Bushman community, where you go out with a band gathering food and learn about their culture, at night listening to stories and watching trance dancing (minimum four days; US$120 per day).

Phakawe Safaris, Private Bag 210, Maun (☎ & fax 661665, mobile ☎71/606984, *steve@phakawe. demon.co.uk*). Tailor-made budget safaris covering the whole of Botswana, taking maximum groups of six people, and mini-tours usually lasting at least ten days (from US$100 per day). Activities include mokoro trips, day-walks with elephants, four-day bush walking safaris, a Bushman survival course and canoe trips down the Okavango River.

Quadrum Safaris, *Sedia Hotel* (☎ & fax 662574, *icafe.maun@info.bw*). Mokoro trips and mobile safaris; from a one-day mokoro trip for US$95 including cold drinks, picnic lunch, pick-up and park fees, to a three-day trip costing US$125, for which you bring all your own food and camping equipment. They also run mobile safaris throughout Botswana at very competitive prices.

Camping

Apart from *Gunn's Bush Camp*, one of the few other places offering the moderately priced option of camping in the Delta is *Oddballs* (see p.334), which is more expensive.

Gunn's Bush Camp, on Ntswi Island; Private Bag 33, Maun (☎660023, fax 660040, *gunnscamp@info.bw*). The only budget accommodation in the Delta proper is at the bush camp attached to *Gunn's* luxury lodge, but it will still set you back US$200–300 to get onto the water. Bringing your own camping equipment reduces your costs, but you're fairly limited by the 10kg baggage allowance that is usual for the small planes that do the transfers. Fortunately, you can rent anything you need on site, right down to bedding and towels. The ablutions have flush bush loos and plenty of hot water, and a small, well-stocked shop can supply basic non-perishable goods for self-catering, or you can arrange for meals at the simple restaurant. Special overland safari packages are available for groups of ten or more. Camping costs US$15 and you can rent mekoro by the day at US$60 or take a sunset powerboat cruise for US$35 (minimum three people). Camping safaris going out in a mokoro cost from US$255 for three nights, including return flights, accommodation and park fees; you bring your own food as well as camping and cooking gear, or rent it from the bush camp. Return transfers from Maun cost US$120.

Luxury camps and lodges

If you're after something more luxurious in Moremi, you have to be prepared to pay for it, with minimum inclusive prices upwards of US$275 per person per day in the low season (Jan–June) and up to US$1000 in high season (July–Dec). The **lodges** are comfortable, bush-camp style, with a limited number of guests. For the price, you can expect food, drink and activities (game drives, mokoro outings or walks) to be included, and you'll be hosted and taken good care of. Flights from Maun are usually extra. All camps and lodges have single supplements.

You're unlikely to be disappointed if you do choose this option. Some camps are plusher than others, but all are beautifully set in the Delta. Depending on whether they're land or wetland camps, the emphasis is on game drives or getting onto the water. They offer similar basics: game viewing, birdwatching, boating of some kind and usually fishing. There are several safari operators, usually running a combination of land or wetland camps, some offering packages that take in several camps with a variety of terrain. A typical minimum stay in the Delta would cost US$1350 per person in high season, for three nights, including flights from Maun into the Delta, flights between camps, game park fees, food and accommodation. All are bookable through travel agents in Europe or North America, but you could save yourself a lot by booking directly. None of the camps caters for casual drop-ins and all must be booked in advance.

With over two dozen camps in the Delta, making a **choice** can be a serious headache – the short list below is our pick of the bunch based on location, and on their excellent reputation.

Delta Camp, Chief's Island; Okavango Tours and Safaris, directly opposite Maun Airport (☎660339) and at the Power Station (☎660220, fax 660589, mobile ☎71/303674, *okavango@icon. co.za*). One of the oldest of the luxury camps, relaxed and beautiful in the permanent swamp waters, is small and compact. A maximum of seventeen guests are accommodated in spacious thigh-high reed-walled chalets with blinds that can be lowered for privacy. Comfortable wicker chairs furnish the lounge, which has a well-stocked bar, extensive library, a spotlight for night viewing and a hammock, while a raised viewing deck overlooks the flood plain and offers quite stunning sunsets. Days centre around guided walks and mokoro outings or there's the more adventurous option of going out with a poler on a mokoro and camping for a few days in the bush, where the service matches that back at camp. The wine and food are superb and stylishly served. Low season (March, May, June, Nov & Dec) US$360; high season (April & July–Oct) US$420; return flights US$120.

Gunn's Bush Camp, Ntswi Island, Private Bag 33, Maun (☎660023, fax 660040, *gunnscamp@ info.bw*). Luxury tents under thatch in a central, grassy area connected by stepping stones, with twin beds and en-suite bathrooms. The dining room, lounge and bar are in a separate area in a two-storey thatch-and-wood building overlooking the flood plain, offering good game viewing. Activities include mokoro trips, walking and motorboat outings. There is a pool and braai area set amongst vegetation, dotted with wooden head sculptures. Dinner is either a braai or a three-course meal. US$275.

Mombo Camp, northern tip of Chief's Island; Wilderness Safaris, PO Box 5219, Rivonia, South Africa (☎011/807 1800, fax 807 2110, *enquiry@wilderness.co.za*). Southern Africa's ultimate, and one of its most expensive, game lodges, right in the Moremi Wildlife Reserve, amid wide expansive plains vegetated with umbrella thorns and ilala palms. Situated alongside marshes and flood plains, fabulous game sightings are virtually guaranteed, which probably explains why BBC and National Geographic film crews have in the past based themselves here. Primarily a land camp, offering 4WD game drives rather than mokoro trips, it takes a maximum of sixteen guests in its ten luxury en-suite walk-in tents. A dining area, lounge and pub are raised on a teak deck and overlook the flood plains. Foot trails are available, with the possibility of sighting elephant, buffalo, lion, leopard and cheetah, which are fairly common in the region; one of the other highlights is a pack of resident wild dogs. Low season US$660, high season US$795.

Oddballs Palm Island Luxury Lodge, Chief's Island; Okavango Tours and Safaris, directly opposite Maun Airport (☎660339) and at the Power Station (☎660220, fax 660589, mobile ☎71/303674, *okavango@icon.co.za*). Comprises a two-storey en-suite tree house, chalets built around tree trunks and walk-in tents on the edge of the flood plain – which have beds raised to allow you to recline and enjoy the view. The tents on concrete platforms have small verandahs, beds with thin mattresses and pillows, while the ablutions are constructed from reed and timber and there's the option of taking your shower with a view of the flood plain. The atmosphere is languid and you can kick back in a hammock in your chalet or at the dining room, which overlooks the water with a deck for game viewing. Food is good with plenty of fresh vegetables and fruit and the bar is well-stocked but pricey. Chalets (including meals, guide and mokoro excursions) cost US$280. Camping (minimum of two nights and must be taken in conjunction with a mokoro excursion, including meals, tent, bedding; on trail includes a guide, mokoro, camping equipment, food) US$150. Additional nights camping at *Oddballs* US$70. Park fees are included for all these rates. Return air transfers $120.

Xakanaxa Camp, Moremi Safaris and Tours, Central Reservations, Johannesburg (☎011/465 3842–3, fax 465 3779, *moremi@yebo.co.za*) or Private Bag 26, Maun, (☎660351, fax 660571, *ensign@info.bw*). Spacious luxury tents raised on wooden platforms with large en-suite bathrooms and a deck with chaises longues overlooking the river. The camp enjoys the best of both worlds in a stunning part of Moremi which can offer land and water-based game viewing throughout the year. Lion and elephant sightings are common, while wild dogs, cheetahs and leopards are less frequently seen prizes. Because of its siting at the cusp of wetland and dryland habitats, the birding is equally excellent. Enquire about standby discounts. High season $395, low US$295.

Xugana Island Lodge, northern Okavango overlooking Xugana Lagoon; Hartley's Safaris, the Old Mall, Maun; Private Bag 48, Maun (☎661806, fax 660528, *hartleys@info.bw*). Eight twin-bedded reed-and-thatch *msasa* (huts on stilts) on one of the largest lagoons and loveliest settings in Okavango, where Prince Charles stayed in 1984. Although you're in the wild you still get the luxuries of an en-suite shower, toilet and handbasin as well as hot and cold running water. From here you can set out on luxury mokoro trails for a maximum of six people, following the river during the day from one temporary camp to the next. Stops are made en route to explore islands and look for birds and wildlife. Accommodation is in luxury walk-in, twin-bedded tents and camp is struck each morning and tents pitched again at your next overnighting spot. One of the highlights is the bush showers, offering the thrill of standing exposed to the stars, with lions roaring and leopards calling. The food is delicious – a real feat given the rudimentary facilities. Permanent camp in low season US$300, high season US$400, mokoro trails US$350.

Seeing the Delta

When you're in the middle of it, **Okavango** seems an impenetrable jungle of papyrus, rising dense from the waters and reaching fine brush-like ends into the air. In the major channels the flow is fast enough to inhibit the establishment of aquatic plants, and it's through these that experienced navigators steer their craft. Getting lost is easy but people have been living in these waters for centuries. Their esoteric knowledge of routes is something you'll come to appreciate: channels come and go and a few hours floating merges it all into a seamless vision of waterways, weeds and islands. Some channels are so narrow you feel you're heading straight into the weeds as plants spring back to brush past your face, but you finally break through into another channel or a lagoon.

The **lagoons** or *madiba* (singular *lediba*) are relatively fixed features of Okavango. These large and beautiful expanses of open water, often isolated from the main river routes, are frequently the sites for lodges. It's hard to avoid feeling as though you're in an illustration in a coffee-table book in this stillness and isolation, where the surrounding forests are perfectly reflected on glassy water. In contrast, many of the **islands** are there only during low water, often raised above the surrounding waters by a fraction of a metre. Sometimes you'll find yourself poled across a lake that a few months previously was savannah grazed by antelope. On the higher islands (those that still hold back the enclosing flood waters), you can hop off for a picnic or camp for the night. Many islands are no more than termite mounds, often only large enough for a single tree.

It's on the **permanent drylands** and islands that you get huge **trees** and an incredible variety of animal species. From your low angle of vision in the mokoro, the only indications of the islands dotted about are the towering boughs: **hyphaene palm savannah** is one of the common land features in the Delta's depths. Often you'll find antelope grazing in open grasslands surrounded by thick forest – the palms dominating with, in the damp woods, strangler figs webbing themselves round host trees. Ninety percent of all trees in Moremi are mopane, but you'll also see rain trees, which are a mass of pink blossoms in the spring; combretum bush willows (lead wood); African ebony or jackal berry; wild fig; and, near North Gate, camel thorn.

Mekoro are hewn from ancient trees in these forests: large trunked wild ebony is a favourite, specimens between one and five centuries old being used. These craft have been used by the Bayei on the Delta since the middle of the eighteenth century, and with their rounded hulls require quite some skill to balance and manoeuvre. Sitting low in the water the dugouts sway wildly every time you move and it's not a little hair-raising at first. But with experience, you get the hang of being a passenger and take cheer from the rhythmic confidence of the skilled **polers** who have not only to pole, but to balance standing up as well. Be warned, though, that all mekoro leak – you will end up sitting in a puddle unless a seat has been provided (standard practice at the luxury lodges).

Although the mirror-still surface is deceptively tranquil, this is still wild Africa. Beneath the delicate waxy **lilies**, in all their pale pinks, mauves, blues and whites, are **crocs and hippos**. At one time the swamps were a crocodile hunters' free-for-all, and it's reckoned that as many as 20,000 may have been shot in a fifteen-year period. The big two crocodile killers are said to have divided the Delta between them in the late 1950s and 1960s and to have taken every one of the reptiles they came across. One of them, Bobby Wilmot, died from a black mamba bite in the swamps.

Crocodiles notwithstanding, local children wade through the water collecting the rhizome, stems and flowers of **water lilies**. The rhizome and lower stem are roasted (six make a good meal for an adult), while the flower is eaten raw and is used to flavour porridge. During drought, people crack open dry stems of papyrus reeds to chew the sweet pith; it tastes rather like sugar cane.

PEOPLE OF THE WATERS

The first people of the waters were the **Banoka** – sometimes called the River Bushmen – of whose origins little is known. The **Mbukushu** and **Bayei**, who arrived in the area in the eighteenth century, appear to be fairly closely related, both being adept wetland farmers and fishermen with the unusual matrilineal system of a chief's succession passing onto his eldest sister's son. From oral traditions it's reckoned they were living in close proximity around the seventeenth century. Both made similar **migrations** from Central Africa and in recent times fled southwards to escape the tyranny of Lozi conquest on the Zambian side of the Zambezi Valley. By 1800, the Bayei appear to have moved into Okavango and to have surrounded the Delta. The Mbukushu, too, fled from the expanding borders of the Lozi first to the Kuando River, dividing Botswana from Caprivi, then westwards to Andara on the Okavango River, just south of Angola.

Things in Andara were no better and possibly worse. **Mambari traders** (sons of Portuguese men and African women) arrived on the quest for ivory, and Mbukushu leaders began selling their own people as slaves. The subjects got fed up and left their leaders, paddling down the Okavango River until they arrived around the Panhandle area of the Delta, where most still live today. **Mekoro** remain the means of getting around on water, poling (like punting) in the shallows, and paddling where the water is deep, in the Panhandle area.

The Mbukushu were more reliant on **farming** than the predominantly fishing Bayei, their methods better suited to the deep waters, where they could plant on riverbanks without the floods rising to spread over the plains. They continue to till the alluvial soils deposited in flood zones, planting, as the waters recede, sorghum, millet, maize and cane in the wet earth. Mbukushu **architecture** is unusual in the use of rectangular rather than round buildings surrounded by high reed fences, and the women are justly renowned for their fine **basketry**. In the past Mbukushu chiefs were great **rainmakers**. So widespread was their reputation that distant rulers paid handsome tributes for the benefit of their services. Their use of child sacrifice in rain ceremonies and the involvement of the Mbukushu kings in slaving are said – understandably – to have been major factors in precipitating the departure of their subjects. When the migrating Mbukushu arrived in Botswana they brought their fame for opening the skies with them; the custom of sending tribute for rainmaking was taken up by the Bayei and continued by the Batawana in the early nineteenth century, once they had penetrated the northern Delta.

The Bayei are flood-plain farmers who excel at **fishing and hunting** – far more important to their subsistence than for the Mbukushu. Bayei hunters developed elaborate methods for catching fish and game, particularly hippo, the meat of which was a great delicacy. Two methods were used for **hippo hunting**. The more inventive used a spear weighted with rocks and triggered by a tripwire. The more dangerous involved floating down the river into a herd and harpooning the animals, a rope attached to the weapon then being tied to a tree. Once the struggling animal had exhausted itself, the hunters would move in for the kill.

When the **Batawana** arrived in the Delta, toward the middle of the last century, they conquered the Bayei and forced them into servitude. The vanquished Bayei, who'd previously lived only in small groups, began to adopt the lifestyle of their masters and are now found in large villages, where many raise cattle. The Mbukushu were less affected by contact with the Batawana, but colonialism brought changes to the whole region, probably the most significant being migration to the great economic magnet of Southern Africa: the Johannesburg gold **mines**. The mines had recruitment agencies deep in the bush, flying out new workers. Many men still work in the mines, while a number of people are employed in tourism – as polers, bush guides, cooks, cleaners and hunting-safari attendants.

Keep your eyes open along the water's edge and you may see the leguans or **water monitors** – large dragon-like lizards whose terrifying looks are all show. They skirt between wet and dry, scavenging for birds' eggs, chicks and anything they can catch.

Delta species

The variety of habitats thrown together produces a wide spectrum of game – 114 species of large mammal. The actual numbers that can be supported by the delicate ecosystem, however, are relatively few. In fact, if you're simply after game your visit to Okavango could prove a disappointment – especially if you don't move far from Maun.

As elsewhere, the **dry season** is best for game viewing and the variations in game from season to season are enormous. Some species, like sable antelope, increase their numbers nearly thirtyfold from their nucleus of only a hundred in the wet season. Nomadic elephants, too, converge here in increased numbers in the dry season. Elephants are mainly seen in the Moremi Tongue between Third Bridge, Xakanaxa and Hippo Pool on the Khwai River. Other species are here more or less permanently – not only water-dwellers like hippos, but also warthog and antelope such as lechwe and sitatunga.

Red lechwe are an endangered water antelope occurring in pockets of Zaire, Zambia and Botswana, with Okavango now being the furthest south they're found. Like sitatunga, they have become highly adapted to wetland living, following the ebb and flow of the flood waters, sometimes going belly-deep to graze on submerged grasses. Dusk and dawn feeders, they retreat to reed-hidden termite mounds to rest up during the day. Their hooves are long and spread sideways, an adaptation that facilitates rapid passage through mud and enables them to venture onto mats of floating papyrus. **Lions**, **leopards** and **hunting dogs** will pursue lechwe into the wetlands for food. But their real danger has been of slaughter by humans, not for their unappetizing meat, but for their lovely skins, which are greatly prized as sleeping mats, aprons and cloaks. In Botswana, the Bayei and Basubiya developed their own technique for hunting lechwe using mekoro. A team on land would herd the animals into a lake where an awaiting party in dugouts would pole at speed into the animals, stabbing in all directions. Nowadays, only licensed hunters are allowed to kill lechwe, and a much greater threat is the one to the wetland habitat itself.

The rarest and most fascinating of all the animals you might see is the **sitatunga**, a medium-sized antelope completely adapted to the world of water and papyrus. Shy and rarely seen, this denizen of the reeds has unusually widely splayed hooves that perform well on mud, and when frightened it completely submerges itself, leaving only its nostrils protruding for air. One cruel technique used to hunt them is to set fire to their reedland habitat to flush them out.

If the variety of mammals is broad, the range of **birds** is overwhelming – something around 400 species. With wetland, forest, savannah and desert in such close proximity, the assortment of ecological niches makes this possibly the most concentrated cross-section of birds in the world. Every season in Moremi is unique and, depending on the water level, different waves of animals and birds move through to feed and to breed. Most spectacular of all are the **breeding colonies** in the Xakanaxa and Godikwe lagoons, where marabou, open-bill, yellow-bill and saddle-bill **storks**, purple, goliath, grey, black-headed and squacco **herons**, as well as egrets and pelicans, breed in August and September. Intra-African migrants like **carmine bee-eaters** and various **kingfishers** arrive in the summer, filling the skies. At mokoro-level, African jacanas with stretched-out toes trot over the lily pads as if they're on ballroom floors. The usual waterside **birds of prey** occupy the trees – the fish eagles and the Pel's fishing owl, large and specially adapted, with featherless legs for dips in the water and extra-long claws for gripping fish of up to two kilogrammes.

The best chance you'll get of seeing a **fish eagle** doing its famous downward swoop and liftoff is at the camps, where they toss fish on the water and whistle for obliging birds. The **lilac-breasted roller** is here too, one of the subcontinent's most beautiful birds and familiar from drier areas like Hwange National Park in Zimbabwe. It was held in high regard by the Ndebele, whose king, Mzilikazi, reserved the use of its vivid lilac, blue and green feathers for himself.

After dark, once the people have retired, the wilderness matches urban energy. Night sounds pierce the darkness, with distant hyenas whooping and lions roaring far off – sounding far more like wind blowing over an open bottle than the MGM snarl you might expect. But one of the most surprising sounds of all is the loud chorus of tiny reed **frogs** piping their message into the night – not froggy croaking, but like melodic, amplified wind chimes.

Moremi Wildlife Reserve

The **MOREMI WILDLIFE RESERVE** is the centrepiece of the Okavango Delta, the most desirable destination for travellers in Botswana – if not all of Southern Africa. In 1963, after extensive depletion of game populations in Botswana due to hunting and habitat destruction, the **Batawana** declared a reserve on 1800 square kilometres of their tribal land. It was named in honour of their leader, Moremi, as was Chief's Island.

In Moremi, you'll find all the major Okavango **ecotypes**: savannah woodland, mopane forest, riverine woodland, flood plain, reed beds and permanent swamp. The reserve breaks down into three main areas, roughly corresponding to broad terrain types: the **dryland peninsula** bounded by the Khwai River to the north, the **seasonal swamp** dominated by Chief's Island, and the **permanent flood lands**, which comprise everything else. This impressive range of habitats means a prodigious variety of **animals**. Large herds of elephant, buffalo, giraffe, zebra, kudu and impala are regularly seen, as well as lions, hyenas and hippos; less frequent, but by no means scarce, are magnificent sable antelope, leopard, wild dogs and large crocodiles. As far as **birds** go, Moremi has no equal. Bee-eaters, darters and kingfishers flock among the reeds and dead wood in the channels. Fish eagles are commonly positioned on their "sentry posts" around lagoons and oxbows, and you'll see some very fine heronries at Xakanaxa. The Moremi pans are a sure bet for birdwatchers, always jostling with ducks, waders, storks and as wide a range of waterfowl as you could hope for.

The **prime visiting time** is April to November, out of the rainy season. Many camps close after Christmas until March, though some of them do stay open all year. November and February can sometimes produce soaring temperatures, up to 40°C, and, from December to March during the rains, flooding can occur. The roads traced over thick sand may be submerged, and the only practical route by car is to go straight from South to North Gate. Midwinter (June & July) can be very chilly in the mornings, although the days are generally bright and sunny. **Mosquitoes** are always a problem in the rainy season. And don't let the beauty of the place lull you into a false sense of security. Tourists have been killed here: for example, one swam in the river and met a large crocodile, and another slept in the open, without the protection of a tent, and was taken by lions.

The Moremi camps

The only independent way into Moremi is to travel across the dry landmasses by **4WD** and **camp**, although the substantial entrance and camping fees make even this far from cheap. For companies that bring **mobile safaris** into the park and for **luxury safari camps** in Moremi, see p.333. Moremi is one of the few places in the region where you can camp on your own (but not without a tent), and follow small tracks into thick bush – in an open vehicle if you wish. Although driving is an effective way to see animals, it doesn't help you get onto the Delta proper and, while many parts of Moremi are accessible by 4WD, you do need to be fully self-sufficient.

A popular route is **northwards from Maun** through Moremi to Savuti, and then on to the Chobe riverfront, camping all the way. There is no petrol or food en route, so take everything you need. While you're in Moremi, it's worth spending at least four days and doing a circuit around the four **public campsites** – from South Gate (aka

Magwee) to Mboma, Third Bridge, Xakanaxa and round to North Gate (aka Khwai). If you're not going to fly into the Delta, visiting Third Bridge and Xakanaxa at its edge will give you magnificent views of flood plains, open lagoons and reed banks, and the birdlife is stupendous. There are no facilities in Moremi; the private camps will help in emergencies, such as minor repairs to broken vehicles, but they're otherwise out of bounds.

At the **campsites** drinking water is available but should be boiled, and facilities are rudimentary to say the least. All the camps have water heated by a wood-fired boiler, but you may well find that you have to feed it and stoke it up yourself. Many ablutions are poorly maintained and you may want to bring cleaning material so you can give them a clean before use. Watch out for the monkeys that help themselves to anything left unattended, and the troops of baboons that breeze through. Driving after dark is prohibited and camping restricted to official sites, which you must book in advance. Unless you've prebooked a site, you may be turned back to Maun (see box on p.321). This is part of Botswana's policy to restrict the numbers of people using the parks.

Third Bridge can get fairly full, especially in July. But it has earned its reputation as the best of the campsites, with some wonderfully secluded shady spots to dream away a couple of days. Swimming isn't permitted anywhere around the camps, and be on the lookout for crocs: a visitor was attacked there in 1989. **Baboons** at the campsite are a real menace – they'll do anything to get at food, including ripping tents apart, opening trunks, turning over trailers, and even confronting humans. You'd best collapse your tent if you're out for a few hours, and remove your food to your vehicle. The **bridge** at Third Bridge consists of rough-hewn poles sitting on heavy logs, which shudder as you trundle over them. **Lions** cross here as well as vehicles – in fact Third Bridge is a regular lion hangout, especially at the end of their hunting season after September. At this time there is no more food in the hunting grounds, and more lions return to Moremi, especially males that are too lazy to hunt most of the time. Moremi lions are buffalo-killers, which makes for exciting game viewing, but the buffalo themselves – not surprisingly – tend to be skittish.

There are two **routes** from South Gate to North Gate: the longer one going via the other two public camps is recommended as being in far better condition than the more direct track, which has been steadily deteriorating over the years. A new ablution facility and hide was being built between Xakanaxa and North Bridge at the time of writing.

The routes between the campsites are all game drives in themselves. Coming from Maun, it's three hours to Third Bridge from the South Gate entrance, and an hour or so from Third Bridge to **Xakanaxa**, making a total of 130km from Maun. At the crescent-shaped lagoon there's a public campsite as well as an exclusive one: look out for elephants and hippos at night and baboons during the day. At the western extremity of the Moremi peninsula is **Mboma**, about 30km from South Gate and 7km from Third Bridge. Mboma Road from Third Bridge is quite different from the Third Bridge/Xakanaxa area, the former being surrounded by open grass and trees, and the latter by dense trees and mopane forest.

North Gate, the nicer of the park entrance camps, is 50km from Xakanaxa, taking three or four hours along the Khwai flood plain past large hippo pools. The North Gate

---

DELTA NAMES

Many of the **names** in the Delta date back to earlier San-speaking inhabitants and are characterized by the large number of "x"s and "c"s, which represent the click sounds released by air escaping when the tongue pulls away from the palate or teeth. Most Europeans find the sounds impossible, and you'll hear place names like *Xakanaxa* pronounced as "Ka-cun-icka" or *Xugana* as "coo-gunner".

camp is well wooded and, on the edge, looks onto a large plain where impala often graze. Leopards slink through the camp at night and there have been extraordinary sightings, like a wild-dog kill, right in camp. Another clattery log bridge crosses the River Khwai with clear, Delta-brown water and water lilies. One of North Gate's disadvantages is noise in the evenings from the local village – radios and domestic racket – but it never goes on too long.

travel details

Buses and minibuses

There are several **buses** a day between Francistown, Maun and Kasane. Schedules tend to be flexible, so it's best to enquire locally when you want to travel. Generally speaking, it's best to turn up at the bus station early in the morning to ensure getting a place.

Route 49

The most reliable surface transport to Maun is on the **Route 49 bus**, which connects Victoria Falls with Jo'burg and Cape Town. A shuttle bus seamlessly transfers passengers from the Jo'burg–Vic Falls bus (twice a week in each direction) at Nata, and takes them to Maun. You can also get from Jo'burg to Kasane on the Victoria Falls bus.

Flights

Apart from scheduled flights, you can also often get a seat on one of the many **chartered flights** that leave Maun. For these ask around the travel agents, and the air charter companies.

Kasane to: Johannesburg (Mon, Wed & Fri; 2hr); Maun (Mon, Wed & Fri; 1hr 15min).

Maun to: Johannesburg (daily; 2hr); Kasane (Mon, Thurs & Sat; 50min); Victoria Falls (Tues, Wed, Fri & Sun; 1hr); Windhoek (Wed & Sun; 2hr).

PART THREE

THE
CONTEXTS

THE HISTORICAL FRAMEWORK

Pre-colonial Zimbabwe enjoyed a political continuity unique in sub-Saharan Africa, being dominated, from the tenth century on, by a succession of Shona states. In successive centuries, the influence of these states stretched east to the coast of Mozambique and west into Botswana's desert lands. It was only in the 1890s, with the arrival of white colonists and the creation of "Rhodesia", that the country's modern boundaries were drawn.

ROCK ARCHIVES

Zimbabwe's **Stone Age** leaps the millennia through the vivid records of its **rock art**. These paintings, often finely realized, most commonly express religion and ritual – suggesting a long-gone spiritual world that respected all living things as equal in creation. But they also give firm clues about their **hunter-gatherer** artists, depicting the bows and stone-tipped arrows of the male hunter and the digging sticks and bags of the female gatherer. Who exactly were the successors of these, the plateau's first people, remains in some dispute: some theories suggest they were San, like the remaining handful of the region's hunter-gatherers in Botswana; others favour a people more akin to today's Bantu speakers.

Farming was the plateau-dwellers' first social revolution – a quantum leap into a vastly different existence that was firmly established by around 200 BC. Although hunter-gatherers had mastered subsistence existence – needing no more than twenty hours a week to forage – farming provided more security and a stable lifestyle, which enabled people to accumulate produce against barren years. It was, though, the slowest of transitions. Hunter-gatherers already possessed the elements of farming, burning grass to bring new shoots to attract animals, and protecting useful plants.

Following the establishment of farming, occasional pictures of sheep appear on cave walls. People still moved about with their herds, but agriculture meant a slower, more static way of life – tilling, seeding and reaping is a lengthy process. Some discovered that ore from certain rocks could be used to make labour-saving tools, and weapons; the first **miners and iron-workers** were farmers. And then came trade, with people who had access to iron (and later gold) bartering their minerals for other goods.

LINEAGES

Hunter-gathering supported only small nomadic bands, but farming culture gradually created more complex societies as people began to map relationships within communities, and to trace back family trees to their first ancestors – the spiritual guardians of each piece of land.

Late **Iron Age** people lived in collections of homesteads, which belonged to **lineages**. Each lineage had its own ancestor, but there was a single major figure – the big daddy of them all. The more direct the relationship to him, the more senior the lineage, so daughters from senior lineages began to command a high bride price, as they brought a large number of cattle into the lineage.

In questions of marriage, therefore, the balance of trade favoured the senior lineage every time, and these groups, in consequence, could become quite rich. Around the **tenth century**, the first **towns** emerged in the cattlelands of Zimbabwe's southwest and in eastern Botswana. The lands here were too dry for horticulture, but great for cattle, with plenty of grass and mopane trees – juicy leaves perfect for the dry season when grass dies back.

THE SHONA STATES

It was from the senior lineages that the large herd-owning **ruling classes** came. Their wealth and power catapulted traditional society from subsistence to a patronage system that could muster large armies to build the great public works of the plateau – the **stone-walled towns**. Few other sub-Saharan countries have such imposing evidence left by powerful states over the last thousand years.

THE ZIMBABWE STATE

Toward the end of the eleventh century, Iron Age Shona speakers settled at the hilltop site of **Great Zimbabwe**, building a village of pole and *daga* huts. Despite large cattle herds, they weren't inordinately wealthy, but by the fourteenth century this had changed. The lineage **herds** had grown to unprecedented numbers and so the power of the rulers had increased. They began to organize their subjects into armies of builders, herders and soldiers.

Although the wealth of Zimbabwe's rulers rested on cattle, the state also developed a **gold trade**, trading on the Mozambique coast. Zimbabwean armies policed the trade and the rulers charged a toll, supplementing their growing riches, which they used to build the famous walls – today's national symbol.

Great Zimbabwe itself became the largest regional centre, with over ten thousand inhabitants. The reason for its eventual **decline** is another disputed issue, but current evidence favours the theory that the area suffered from overpopulation – too many people and cattle and too much farming. The land lost its fertility and by the sixteenth century the site of Great Zimbabwe was deserted.

THE MUTAPA STATE AND THE FIRST PORTUGUESE ENCOUNTERS

The **Mutapa State**, a looser confederation of ruling families, rose as the Zimbabwe State was sliding, to span the fifteenth to twentieth centuries. Better placed for the gold trade, near

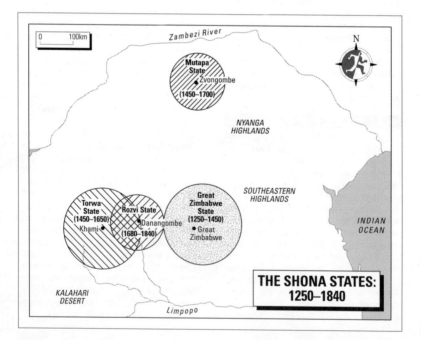

the northern gold fields and the coast, they surrounded their homesteads with stone walls.

Written accounts of the state come from **Portuguese** sailors, who first heard of central African empires, gold and untold riches, from Arab traders. The Portuguese had a tendency to exaggerate, perhaps to encourage backers to give financial support to expeditions – one very apocryphal story had the adventurer Vasco da Gama dubbing the Zambezi "the river of good omens" in 1497, after encountering gold-dust-laden Arab dhows in its Indian Ocean delta.

By 1505 the Portuguese were in control of Sofala on the Mozambique coast, and soon their attention turned to the hinterland, heralding a history of **colonial interference** that was to last over the next four centuries.

In Zimbabwe the Mutapas were the first to taste contact with Europeans; sweet at first, it was soon to sour. The whites were enthralled by tales of Mutapa wealth, the elite garbed in gold and silver embroidered cloths and so overladen with precious bangles that they could hardly move their arms. Their wealth was in fact quite great, stemming from their ability to impose taxes on gold-seekers, ivory-hunters and traders.

Mutually beneficial **barter** between the two powers took place until the Portuguese decided they could no longer brook Swahili competition. In 1569 an army of one thousand led by **Francisco Barreto** set out from Portugal to invade the Mutapa State. Defeated by disease and starvation, the expedition flopped before it arrived, but toward the end of the sixteenth century the Portuguese seized a new opportunity to gain a foothold, when they took advantage of successive ruling-class splits in Mutapa. In exchange for military help, they eventually gained a free hand in the territory.

In 1629 the Mutapa (or king) became a **vassal of the Portuguese** monarchy, and the Portuguese occupied several towns along the Zambezi, notably Tete and Sena. At its height, their influence extended along the river beyond Kariba and south of Harare to the Kadoma goldfields. Territory was divided into *prazos* – minifiefdoms controlled by ruling families. Each of these formed private armies and raided the countryside, taking slaves and land, and building markets all over the north.

This first colonial nightmare ended, however, in 1663, when the Mutapa was assassinated

and the new ruler rejected Portuguese domination. Forming an alliance with the Rozvi Changamire in the southwest, he drove the Portuguese from Zimbabwe, and they never returned as a credible political force. When they did, it was to Manyika on sufferance of the Manyika rulers, and they had to content themselves with trading through African go-betweens.

For the next 250 years Portuguese influence in the region was very tenuous, with small stretches of coast and a handful of islands coming under their control. It was only after the Berlin Congress of 1884 that they succeeded in getting recognition for the colony of Mozambique and set up an administration to control the entire territory.

TORWA AND THE ROZVI

In its declining years, Great Zimbabwe was eclipsed by a new state – the **Torwa** – in the southwest around present Bulawayo.

As an offshoot of Great Zimbabwe, the Torwa State carried the tradition of **stone construction** to new heights. The ruling dynasty kept apart from the peasantry, intermarrying only within the ruling classes and setting up centres throughout the country. Its *mambos* or rulers wore spun cotton garments and gold, copper and ivory jewellery. They taxed peasants, traders and farmers, and controlled most of the state's cattle. By the seventeenth century, though, the economy was crumbling – mainly through a slow-down in gold exports – and the rulers began to lose their grip. The building of stone walls stagnated, coming to a complete standstill by the end of the century.

There is uncertainty about the origins of the next dynasty, the **Rozvi**. They may have been invaders from the north who conquered the Torwa, or perhaps just a new Torwa dynasty under a different name. Their capital was at **Danangombe** – the walls are still standing – and although the size of the state was relatively small, the extent of their influence was considerable. The state's wealth was based on its powerful army and its capacity to exact tribute even beyond its own borders. This differed from the Mutapa State, which was far more dependent on trade.

Rozvi **military power** took it into Mutapa territory, where it attacked the ruling dynasty in the 1680s. In the nineteenth century, Rozvi might began to weaken from within, and the exaction of tribute became progressively more difficult. The situation was compounded by waves of invading Nguni, and culminated in **Zwangendaba**'s hordes sweeping through on their way north.

THE MFECANE

Through the preceding millennium, Zimbabwe's affairs had been determined largely by the Shona speakers, who dominated the plateau. At the onset of the nineteenth century, however, an explosion of external events reverberated into the region, bringing the first serious threat from **non-Shona elements**. Over the Drakensberg Mountains, in what is now South Africa's Natal Province, a storm was brewing among the small **Nguni** groups who, as a result of land hunger – aggravated by the encroachment of white settlers – had entered into a virtually constant state of feud with each other.

In 1818, **Shaka**, the illegitimate son of a minor Nguni chief, turned his father's small **Zulu** clan into the most powerful fighting machine in Southern Africa. A shrewd commander and ruthless absolute ruler, he tolerated no opposition and during the 1820s his army swept through the subcontinent, conquering and expanding his power base. Many clans fled, hence the term *mfecane*, meaning "forced migration".

Some of these were the marauding hordes that passed through Shona territory, pillaging but enforcing few lasting changes on the communities they encountered. But two of these raiding armies stayed, exerting very much longer-term effects. In the east, Shoshangane set up the iron-handed **Gaza State**, but it was the **Ndebele State** that made the most lasting impression.

THE NDEBELE STATE

In 1822, an army of the **Khumalo** clan, under their ruler, Mzilikazi, left Natal to escape Shaka's conquests. Wherever they went, however, they were pursued by the unrelenting Zulu *impi*, which moved throughout the region, raiding well into Zimbabwe. Unable to settle and farm, these refugees, who became the Ndebele, were forced to rely on seizing cattle and food as they marched. After years of wandering, which took them to Botswana and brought them into conflict with the

advancing Boers in the Transvaal, they eventually established a capital at **Bulawayo** in the 1840s.

Mzilikazi, who was succeeded by his son, Lobengula, in 1870, had forged a united state from disparate elements. Although at core Zulu, his **Ndebele State** comprised Nguni, Sotho, Tswana and Shona people, who'd been picked up on the Khumalo's northward migration. Far from resenting cultural eclipse, Shona youth was eager to be identified with this go-ahead society, to the extent that in 1888 a missionary, Reverend Knothe, commented that:

> They have completely taken over the language, costume and customs of the Ndebele and do not want to know that they are descendants of the Karanga [Shona speakers].

Although Ndebele status was affected by ethnic origins, Mzilikazi wisely ensured that all captives were fully incorporated into the state. Women and children went to live with Ndebele families to learn their language and customs and had the same rights and duties as everyone else. When the boys were ready to marry, the king provided them with the necessary bridewealth cattle.

Most Ndebele were cattle farmers living in homesteads; others were in the powerful army, which ensured Ndebele control well beyond the farms of its own people. A **tribute system** operated, whereby small states on the periphery signified their dependence on the Ndebele by offering food and cattle. The intention was not to cripple the subject states, which retained most of their wealth, but rather to symbolize their client status. The relationship was symbiotic. The Ndebele wanted peaceful states on their doorstep in which they could graze their cattle, but at the same time their army offered protection against hostile raiders to the smaller states.

THE GAZA INVASIONS

Also in the 1820s, **Shoshangane** fled north with one of the sections of the Zulu-shattered Ndwandwe (Nguni) State, eventually settling amid the **Ndau** (Shona dialect speakers), and completely disrupting their culture. Gaza words passed into the Ndau language, while Ndau men were conscripted into the army and women became Gaza wives.

Unlike the Ndebele, who successfully incorporated their conquered subjects into their state, the **Gaza** were themselves eventually absorbed. They treated the people they conquered as second- and third-class citizens. Subjects such as the Ndau from the southern Eastern Highlands, who accepted Gaza domination, were simply exploited, while others such as Mozambique's Tsonga and Chopi were often sold as slaves to the Portuguese.

A huge area of eastern Zimbabwe and parts of Mozambique were harassed and controlled by the small, permanent **Gaza army**. As in society, the forces were separated according to class. The elite were all born Nguni, while conquered people formed cannon-fodder regiments. In the

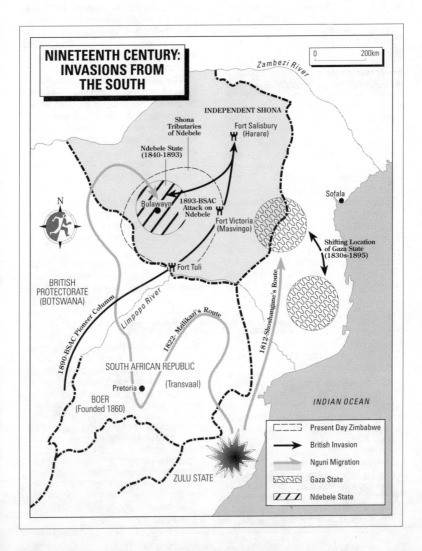

NINETEENTH CENTURY: INVASIONS FROM THE SOUTH

Zambezi River

0   200km

INDEPENDENT SHONA

Shona Tributaries of Ndebele

Fort Salisbury (Harare)

Ndebele State (1840-1893)

1893-BSAC Attack on Ndebele

Bulawayo

Sofala

Fort Victoria (Masvingo)

Shifting Location of Gaza State (1830s-1895)

N

Fort Tuli

BRITISH PROTECTORATE (BOTSWANA)

1890-BSAC Pioneer Column

Limpopo River

1822-Mzilikazi's Route

1812-Shoshangane's Route

SOUTH AFRICAN REPUBLIC

Pretoria

(Transvaal)

INDIAN OCEAN

BOER (Founded 1860)

ZULU STATE

	Present Day Zimbabwe
→	British Invasion
	Nguni Migration
	Gaza State
	Ndebele State

end the Gaza State was brought down by internal divisions and finally succumbed to **Portuguese** forces in 1895, becoming part of their Mozambique colony.

The Gazas' main mark on the area was the title *Shangaan*, a corruption of Shoshangane's name, which became prized by people of the east. Gaza identity was very attractive to many subjects, especially the youth, some of whom adopted Nguni clan names – which continue today. In military matters Gaza influence was total: the Ndau completely changed their uniform, and adopted the methods of their conquerors.

BRITAIN'S PRIVATIZED INVASIONS

A pair of British hunter-adventurers, Henry Hartley and Frederick Courteney Selous, arrived in Zimbabwe in the 1870s, possibly on the trail of Portuguese stories of gold wealth. They were to find the remains `of hundreds of **gold mines**, and wrote home that the country was rich in gold. But, as they were to learn, gold mines didn't necessarily signify the existence of gold – rather, its removal; most of the local shallow-cast mines had been exhausted.

Nevertheless, with the discovery of vast gold reefs on South Africa's Witwatersrand, speculators began to believe that something similar was waiting to be discovered in Zimbabwe, and interested parties gathered like flies to get in on the action. In the 1880s, **Boer** and **German** agents approached the Ndebele king, Lobengula. Meanwhile, along the Eastern Highlands, the **Portuguese**, too, were surreptitiously muscling in.

THE BRITISH SOUTH AFRICA COMPANY

In the end it was **Cecil John Rhodes** – with the backing of Britain – who gained control of the area north of the Limpopo. Britain was eager to block any expansion by rival powers, while Rhodes, for his part, having made a fortune in the Kimberley diamond mines in South Africa, but losing out on the Witwatersrand, saw rich pickings.

With powerful friends, Rhodes formed the **British South Africa Company (BSAC)**, with the express brief to exploit the lands north of the Limpopo. From the British government's point of view this was a convenient bit of privatized foreign policy, which they naturally endorsed. The BSAC was granted a Royal Charter for the territory north of South Africa and west of Mozambique, to:

> . . . make treaties, promulgate laws, maintain a police force, acquire new concessions, make land grants and carry on any lawful trade, commerce or business.

Rhodes's long-term plan was to occupy Zimbabwe, Zambia and Malawi – but his approach was gradual and intent on avoiding

---

"LET THEM EAT DOGS"

Speech by Chief Somabulana, rebel leader and spokesman at the 1896 Matopos *indaba* with Rhodes:

We, the Amandabili, the sons of Kumalo, the Izulu, Children of the Stars; we are no dogs! You came, you conquered. The strongest takes the land. We accepted your rule. We lived under you. But not as dogs! If we are to be dogs it is better to be dead.

I myself once visited Bulawayo. I came to pay my respects to the Chief Magistrate. I brought my indunas with me, and my servants. I am a chief. I am expected to travel with attendants and advisers. I came to Bulawayo early in the morning, before the sun had dried the dew, and I sat down before the Court House, sending messages to the Chief

Magistrate that I waited to pay my respects to him. And so I sat until the evening shadows were long.

I sent again to the Chief Magistrate and told him that I did not wish to hurry him in an unmannerly way; I would wait his pleasure; but my people were hungry; and when the white men visited me it was my custom to kill that they might eat. The answer from the Chief Magistrate was that the town was full of dogs; dog to dog; we might kill those and eat them if we could catch them. So I left Bulawayo that night; and when next I tried to visit the Chief Magistrate it was with my impis behind me; no soft words in their mouths; but the assegai in their hands. Who blames me?

(*The Nineteenth Century in Southern Rhodesia*, Terence Ranger)

immediate confrontation with Lobengula's powerful Ndebele State. In 1890, his private army, the "**Pioneer Column**", marched north to the site of Harare, skirting lands under Lobengula's control. Immediately the settlers set about looking for gold, which never materialized; many turned to farming instead, taking over traditional Shona lands.

LOBENGULA – AND WAR

Ndebele influence over large parts of Zimbabwe was, at this time, immense. So strong, in fact, that businessmen and politicians in South Africa concluded that it would have to be removed, and by means of war.

A shrewd statesman, **Lobengula** tried to concede as little as possible while keeping his regiments firmly in check. War, he knew, would bring to an end Ndebele pre-eminence in the region. But the forces he faced were insurmountable and Rhodes succeeded in outmanoeuvring him.

Several times Lobengula was deceived. **Moffat**, an agent of Rhodes, presented the king with a treaty that prohibited him from making further agreements with anyone but the British. He refused to sign, but Moffat claimed otherwise and the phoney document was used to keep out the Germans and Portuguese. To tighten the noose further, Lobengula was then lured into agreeing to the **Rudd Concession**, which allowed miners into Matebeleland and provided the means for white entrenchment in Mashonaland. The British made empty verbal promises that the concession would protect the Ndebele from further colonial pressure: only ten miners would prospect and notices would be put in all English and South African papers warning Europeans off. But the BSAC was simply waiting for the right time to invade Matabeleland – an action that began, with a fairly routine event, in 1893.

The first act in the drama was Lobengula's sending of a **Ndebele raiding party** to the Masvingo area, to punish Shona tributaries who had cut a telegraph wire and made mischief between the BSAC and the Ndebele. Similar raids in the past had always been ignored – as was this at first by the local BSAC commander, one Leander Starr Jameson.

But some weeks after, judging the time right for an invasion of Matabeleland, **Jameson** seized on the incident, told the British authorities that the Ndebele were planning to attack white settlers, and mustered an army of pioneers and black mercenaries. Reports were fabricated that this force had been ambushed by Ndebele troops, and the British sent in a powerful battalion from neighbouring Botswana. Jameson, eager to see the destruction of Lobengula's kingdom and concerned that his hands would be tied by less partial forces, hastened to pre-empt their arrival.

Aware of the impending disaster, Lobengula desperately tried to avoid war. Delegates were sent to Cape Town, stressing his **desire for peace** – but they were intercepted and shot. Furious at this, Lobengula, according to one account, appeared before his war-ready troops repeatedly shouting the salute, *Bayete*, before thrusting his assegai to the ground. Its shaft broke – a bad omen.

The **battle**, when it came, was swift. As Ndebele troops approached to meet the advancing enemy, they were mercilessly mowed down by machine guns. Their capital, **Bulawayo**, was subsequently razed, and Lobengula fled into the wilderness, where he died the following year.

THE FIRST CHIMURENGA

The Shona had not been conquered by the British in the way that the Ndebele were, and at first welcomed the settlers. **Trade** took place and successful Shona farmers generated sufficient surplus to feed the whites and earn themselves a tidy profit. Only after the gold dream turned to dust did the newcomers start farming seriously, nabbing any fertile land they fancied. For the Shona, too, the daydream was short-lived – the happy days of trade and neighbourliness turned into a reality of domination and eviction.

COMPANY LAW

Within years, both Ndebele and Shona found themselves trespassers in their own land, evicted by whites, and subject to British South Africa Company decrees.

Both peoples saw their rights whittled away as they were relegated to dry, infertile and tsetse-infested reserves. The Company, meanwhile, seized the majority of **Ndebele cattle** as spoils of war, claiming it had belonged to Lobengula. In fact the herd had been held in trust by the king on behalf of the whole community. Cattle were more than a treasury, resting at the very core of social relations, and this seizure was an attack on Ndebele culture and society itself. What cattle remained to them were wiped out in the 1895 Rinderpest epidemic, many of them shot by white ranchers eager to stem the spreading disease. The sight of whites randomly potting the dwindling Ndebele herds rankled.

And, if that wasn't enough, the colonials sought ways to bring the blacks into the cash economy. Only the payment of pittance wages made it possible for the whites to make the worn-out mines profitable, so a **hut tax** was devised to flush out the "idle natives" from their subsistence existence and into the job market. Blacks saw their traditions under fire and their way of life crumbling.

UPRISING

In 1896, when Rhodes's hatchet man Jameson staged an **abortive coup** against the Boer-controlled South African Republic, a large number of the British South Africa Police (the Company's army) were captured. Spotting their chance, the Ndebele initiated the **First Chimurenga** (liberation war), attacking and killing white farmers and traders.

Much to the surprise of whites, many **Shona** joined forces with the Ndebele, having developed a greater resentment towards the settlers than to their former overlords. The Shona **spirit mediums** of Kaguvi and Nehanda moved around the country inspiring the battle to regain ancestral lands. Whites fled to the forts in the main settlements.

For a while chiefs again controlled their traditional domains, but British reinforcements were sent to crush the Ndebele – a war that proved costly for both sides. Villages and crops were destroyed, while at the same time the conflict was a drain on BSAC coffers. Eventually, both parties came together in the infamous **Matopos indabas** – an agreement made between Rhodes and Ndebele *indunas* (captains). Rhodes made all sorts of promises, including the return of all occupied land; none were kept.

With the Ndebele subdued, the BSAC set about putting down the **Shona rebels**. Unlike the Ndebele, the Shona lacked political unity, and individual chiefs sometimes took sides with the British, happy to see rivals cut down to size

by the settlers. Clinically, systematically and with total ruthlessness, the colonial forces moved through Mashonaland, picking off the disunited groups one by one. By 1897 it was all over, though on the scaffold the defiant **medium of Nehanda** prophesied that "my bones will rise". For her, final victory was certain.

RHODESIA – LIMITED COMPANY

Until 1923 the **British South Africa Company** ran **Rhodesia** – as the colonists had dubbed the territories of Mashonaland and Matabeleland – and virtually everything in it.

The Company, and its associated white settlers and immigrants, had hopes that these territories would become a "white country" along the lines of Australia or New Zealand, or even South Africa. Blacks were regarded as somewhat incidental. But, in the eighty years following the British takeover, Rhodesia's white population reached only 270,000, alongside a black majority that grew from 700,000 in the 1920s to nearly 8,000,000 at Independence.

SELL-OFF: THE 1923 CONSTITUTION

The BSAC had anticipated huge profits from their African fiefdom, but by the 1920s these had signally failed to materialize, and they began looking for a way to rid themselves of the albatross. The solution was a referendum offering whites a new constitution. The recommendation of the British High Commission and the Company was to incorporate the territory into the more profitable Union of South Africa, which in 1910 had brought together the two British colonies of the Cape and Natal with the defeated pair of Boer republics.

The idea of being dominated by Afrikaners, however, horrified the Rhodesians, who voted instead for an option of so-called responsible government in a new state that became known as **Southern Rhodesia**. In effect, "responsible government" meant that they were responsible to no one but themselves. Although the British authorities technically reserved the right to veto any legislation that affected African rights, this was never invoked – despite decades of hut taxes, segregation and land-filching legislation.

The new constitution maintained power in the hands of whites while paying lip service to the idea of a non-racial democracy – a

qualified franchise based on British citizenship and a minimum annual income that worked to keep most Africans out of the polling booths. With insufficient numbers to maintain control simply through white administrators, the government set about creating a network of sympathetic chiefs by installing puppets and unseating those who didn't go along with official policies.

WEALTH AND INEQUALITY: THE LAND ISSUE

Rhodesia's mineral wealth proved a disappointment to early settlers, and soon after the turn of the century white immigrants looked instead to rewards from **large-scale farming**. The country, in their wake, became one of the most unequal in the world.

A BLACK WORKING CLASS: THE MINES

The Rhodesians' great white myth – developed at the turn of the century and maintained to the present – was that blacks were better off under them because of their modernizing influence. Yet, while it's true that colonialism brought benefits like modern medicine and technology, at the same time it robbed Africans of a way of life that had worked successfully. Poverty was not the natural condition of Africa that the colonials fondly imagined they were improving, and was in fact created by the destruction of the traditional economy.

At the root of these problems lay the land question and the deliberate, forcible creation of a black working class. Cheap black labour was the backbone of white commercial activity, and, through taxes and the restriction of African access to farmlands, blacks were forced out of communal farming into selling their labour as workers. When even that policy failed in the first decade of the twentieth century, blacks were simply rounded up and press-ganged into the mines – a system known as *chibaro*.

The **Rhodesian mines** were more notorious than even those in South Africa. Because they were extensively mined out, only very low wages could make them profitable – and working in them was to be avoided at all costs. Workers gave the mines their own coded names, warning of what could be expected. Celtic Mine was known as *Sigebengu* ("Thugs

are in charge"), Old Chum Mine was called *Makombera* ("You're closed in"); other names included *Maplanki* ("Planks for punishment") and *Mtshalwana* ("You will fight one another").

THE LAND APPORTIONMENT ACT

The **1930 Land Apportionment Act** set aside half of the country for whites – territory that invariably included the good fertile lands. Enclaves of poor land, meanwhile, became the so-called "**Native Reserves**" (later called the Tribal Trust Lands – many still refer to them as TTLs). Land pressure combined with infertile soils gradually forced many more people off the land and into the white economy.

It was from observing the destruction of the reserves through over-cultivation that many whites later drew the conclusion that Africans were bad farmers, forgetting that blacks had farmed these lands effectively for millennia, some accumulating tidy profits by selling off their surplus to white settlers at the turn of the century. For settler farmers, things were pretty rosy, with huge farms and help from the Land Bank to assist commercial agriculture – plus revenue from taxes extracted from Africans.

FEDERATION

Following the 1923 Constitution, the influence of the BSAC gradually waned. The mines were bought by the government in 1933 and the railways taken over by South Africa shortly after World War II. Also, despite black opposition, the **Central African Federation** of Southern Rhodesia, Northern Rhodesia (Zambia) and Nyasaland (Malawi) was forged, providing the means for Southern Rhodesia to cream off the mineral riches to the north. The copper wealth of Northern Rhodesia did a lot for Southern Rhodesia, accounting for much of modern Zimbabwe's infrastructure – roads, hospitals and public works such as Lake Kariba.

Through its brief life, the Federation was dogged by black opposition, especially from nationalist movements in Northern Rhodesia and Nyasaland, which brought its collapse in 1963, followed by the Independence of the two northernmost members the following year.

NO LEFT TURN

In 1951, in an attempt to counter the overcrowding caused by the Land Apportionment

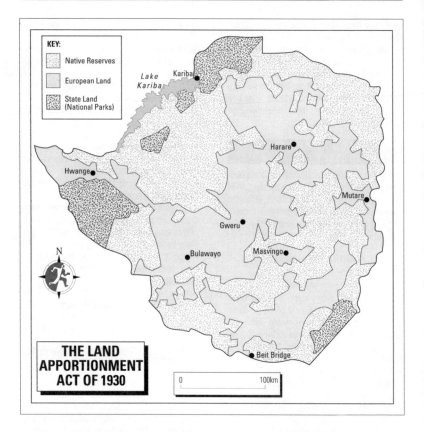

KEY:
Native Reserves
European Land
State Land
(National Parks)

Lake Kariba Kariba

Harare

Hwange

Mutare

Gweru

Bulawayo Masvingo

N

Beit Bridge

**THE LAND
APPORTIONMENT
ACT OF 1930**

0   100km

Act, the **Land Husbandry Act** was passed, causing further resentment. To make space for thousands evicted from white-designated lands, the common grazing areas in the "Native Reserves" were divided into smallholdings of private land. Households were forced to reduce their herds to six head of cattle – most small-scale African farmers ended up worse off than before.

During the 1950s, however, there seemed the possibility of liberalization, as **Garfield Todd**'s ruling United Rhodesia Party discussed the idea of black suffrage. Although Todd saw liberalization essentially as a way to secure a peaceful place for whites, the electorate perceived him as a traitor and booted him out in the 1958 election. While the rest of the country drifted to the

right, his sympathies for the nationalists grew and he ended up house-arrested by Ian Smith in the 1960s.

Each government after 1958 was more reactionary than its predecessor, not only putting the brakes on African advancement, but shifting into reverse gear. The crown prince of white domination was **Ian Smith**, whose Rhodesia Front Party led the country down the dead-end road to UDI in 1965. His "thousand-year republic" barely hobbled its way to mid-adolescence.

NATIONALISM: THE GATHERING STORM

In the early years of colonization, black campaigners hoped to use **persuasion** to get the British authorities to give them rights. Before

1923 there was little activity apart from unsuccessful demands by Lobengula's son, Nyamanda, for the return of his father's cattle. In the 1920s, though, a proliferation of pressure groups were set up to represent middle-class black professionals. The government simply ignored what they had to say. But during the 1940s, Benjamin Burombo's **African Voice Association** heralded a more militant phase, spreading resistance among workers and peasants, demanding improved working conditions, higher wages, parliamentary representation and better education.

CONSTITUTIONALISM: THE 1950s

It was under the Central African Federation that a **mass nationalist movement** was born, bent on action. The first major challenge was presented by the City Youth League, formed in Harare in 1955 and later expanded into the **African National Youth League**. Its newspaper *Chapupu* was used to galvanize support – which focused on the land question. In 1956 the League organized a bus boycott in Harare against fare increases. The following year it merged with another organization to form the **African National Congress (ANC)** under **Joshua Nkomo**.

Nkomo's ANC attempted a **broad-based approach** covering worker and peasant issues. In the rural areas it organized resistance to unpopular measures like the Land Husbandry Act, while in the urban areas meetings and demonstrations were held. 1959 was a year of expansion and protest against the Federation, prompting Sir Edgar Whitehead's governing United Rhodesia Party to ban the organization, declare a state of emergency, slap nearly 500 members behind bars and introduce a range of legislation to put an end to African demands. Nkomo narrowly escaped arrest because he was in Britain at the time canvassing support.

1960: ZHII, THE NDP AND ZAPU

Far from ending black political activities, this course of repression caused black frustrations to erupt in the resounding explosion of **Zhii**. The term has no direct English translation: it is basically a drastic act against an arch-enemy and signifies total annihilation, complete destruction or reduction to rubble.

A result of the largest uprising since the First Chimurenga, *Zhii* swept the cities when three

leaders of the newly formed **National Democratic Party (NDP)** were arrested, and the party responded with the **Salisbury March**. The government banned all meetings, and popular outrage, involving almost 50,000 protesters, spread to Bulawayo, where workers went on strike and symbols of government were attacked. After a week, government bullets put a temporary end to *Zhii*, taking eighteen lives and leaving hundreds injured.

The Federation consequently swung into the 1960s, cracking visibly at the edges. Northern Rhodesia and Nyasaland were on target for Independence, but the settler government of Southern Rhodesia was intransigent on majority rule. At a conference in Britain a **constitution** was proposed giving blacks fifteen seats in a 65-seat parliament. The four NDP representatives accepted the proposal, but on their return were fiercely rebuked by the domestic leadership and party rank and file. The NDP continued to organize against the government until it was banned and its assets seized in 1961.

A week later it re-emerged as the **Zimbabwe African People's Union (ZAPU)**, led by Joshua Nkomo. Sabotage replaced demonstrations, though Nkomo was still convinced that diplomatic pressure could be put on Britain to grant Independence to Southern Rhodesia under a majority government. Inside the country, rural dwellers were organized in campaigns of burning the fields of unpopular farmers and destroying equipment, and others squatted white-designated unoccupied lands. In 1962 ZAPU was banned and the leadership exiled to remote rural areas for three months.

SPLITS IN THE RANKS: ZAPU AND ZANU

There was some doubt about where to go from the banning of ZAPU. Nkomo favoured the idea of setting up a government in exile to lobby international support, while others urged remaining inside the country and organizing local action.

Under Nkomo's instructions the government in exile headed for Dar es Salaam, only to receive a lukewarm reception from President Nyerere; they returned home. There were rumblings about Nkomo's leadership on questions of both judgment and the principle of operating from exile. After some arguments, Nkomo suspended four members of the ZAPU executive:

Robert Mugabe, Ndabaningi Sithole, Moton Malianga and Leopold Takawira. In 1963 this "dissident" group formed the **Zimbabwe African National Union (ZANU)**, with Sithole as president and Mugabe as secretary-general.

An outbreak of fighting between the two organizations provided a convenient excuse for the government to ban them both in 1964 and to declare a state of emergency once again in some urban centres. Various top leaders were arrested, while the organizations set up headquarters in exile in Zambia and Tanzania, and began looking at broadening the struggle to all classes — and to the use of guns.

TALKING TOUGH: UDI

To pacify an increasingly alarmed white electorate, Prime Minister Ian Smith moved swiftly to demonstrate that he was made of stern stuff. Raising two fingers to the nationalists and an increasingly hostile world, he issued the **Unilateral Declaration of Independence (UDI)** in 1965, promising white Rhodesians:

> We have struck a blow for the preservation of justice, civilization and Christianity and in the spirit of this belief we have this day assumed our sovereign independence. God bless you all.

Alongside this defiance of Britain, Smith refused to speak to the nationalist leaders. Instead, he installed a council of chiefs, paid by his government but which he insisted represented the people.

CHIMURENGA PHASE ONE

UDI was the signal to the nationalist organizations to begin armed action. The **Second Chimurenga** began on April 28, 1966, when seven ZANU guerrillas engaged Rhodesian forces at Chinoyi — and were killed. This episode set the pattern for the next four years of commando hit-and-run actions. The guerrillas were no match for the Rhodesian army and enjoyed virtually no support organization within the country.

The following year, fighters from South Africa's ANC joined forces with ZAPU and operated for some months in Hwange National Park. A number of **ZAPU-ANC camps** were also established inside the country, but once discov-

ered they were fairly easily destroyed by Rhodesian forces – themselves now assisted by South African units. Overall, this first phase of the war remained low-key, and continual setbacks for the nationalists served to encourage the white belief in their own invincibility.

Britain, meanwhile, despite Rhodesian intransigence, was still eager for some kind of negotiated settlement and Ian Smith and British Prime Minister Harold Wilson met on two occasions on the British warships HMS *Fearless* and *Tiger*. Wilson wanted a few more rights for blacks and moves to majority rule in some far-flung future, but Smith always maintained there would never be a black government in Rhodesia in his lifetime – or those of his children. Both meetings achieved little, except to add Wilson to the Rhodesian demonology of degenerate socialist sellouts.

THE 1969 CONSTITUTION

As the 1960s came to a close, Smith still had everything to play for. The guerrillas were looking pretty impotent and British-imposed **sanctions** were a distinctly half-hearted affair – white Rhodesians could boast the boycott was actually stimulating Rhodesia's internal economy, while the flow of trade remained more or less unchanged in the five years after UDI. South Africa was openly defying sanctions and several multinational companies continued trading: with the knowledge of the British government, Shell and BP were both supplying Rhodesia with oil.

Smith tried to pre-empt any further negotiations by taking matters into his own hands. Yet another constitution was put forward, giving blacks a derisory 8 elected seats in a 66-seat parliament. This was Smith's starting point for further discussions with the mother country. But Britain insisted on testing black opinion on the new dispensation prior to any further talks. **Lord Pearce** was despatched to the rebel colony to probe opinion in the cities and the remote rural areas.

Organizing a response was a problem for the nationalist movement, most of whose leaders were either in jail or in exile – but it was also a golden opportunity. ZANU and ZAPU united to form an internal campaigning body under the leadership of **Bishop Muzorewa**. While Rhodesia's government pumped massive resources into cajoling a positive response from blacks, they banned ANC views from the national media. However, this small chance to campaign openly was exploited by the nationalists to set up internal networks – the lifeline in the final stage of the liberation struggle.

This was, in fact, the first time in Rhodesia's history that whites heard an authentic voice of black opinion. Having always assumed that they "knew their Africans", they refused to believe the resounding "NO!" that echoed across the country. The Rhodesian Broadcasting Corporation reflected the white prejudice that they alone were in touch with reality:

The British Government's report revealed very clearly the extreme naivety of the British approach to the test of acceptability, and of the basic assumption that uneducated tribesmen could comprehend a complicated constitutional arrangement.

THE EARLY 1970S: LEARNING THE LESSONS

The early 1970s were a time of rethinking and consolidation. The Pearce Commission findings had shown that, contrary to the regime's beliefs, blacks fully comprehended the constitutional arrangement. The bush war of the 1960s had vividly demonstrated the futility of a struggle fought without popular support.

FIGHTING FISH

Early in the 1970s, **Josiah Tongogara**, the commander of ZANU's military wing, **ZANLA**, went to China for training. He came back with Maoist doctrines and strategies, remarkably well suited to Rhodesia. As in China, the Rhodesian revolution was primarily rural, playing on decades-old resentments – the eviction from ancestral lands – and it was in these areas that the liberation movement needed support.

ZANLA adopted the Maoist principle of "guerrillas swimming like fish in the water of the people" – without water they would flounder. Mutual trust and cooperation between farmers and fighters was vital to military success, while at the same time helping to spread political ideas. Young boys were recruited as *mujibas* to spy for the guerrillas and carry messages; girls became *zvimbwidos*, who carried weapons and cooked for them. In the end, so effective were the networks that guerrilla intelligence far outstripped the information the Rhodesian forces were gathering.

ZIPRA – ZAPU's military wing – followed a different strategy that relied less on villagers and more on infiltrated reception committees. Internal divisions hampered their implementation and their battle plan wasn't fully operational until the war was well advanced in 1977. Some observers put down ZANU's subsequent electoral success to their better wartime organization and integration with the people.

PLAYING FOR TIME

The 1974 **Portuguese coup** and consequent liberation of Mozambique and Angola were catalysts that changed the geopolitics of Southern Africa almost overnight. Suddenly the minority regimes in South Africa and Rhodesia found themselves flanked by independent black governments. The South Africans became concerned about the prospects of radical nationalists coming to power in Rhodesia and began tightening the screws on Smith to force him to the negotiating table.

In a most unlikely bout of cooperation, Kenneth Kaunda of Zambia united with South African Prime Minister Vorster in persuading Smith to release nationalist leaders like Nkomo and Sithole. **Talks** were held in 1975 on the Victoria Falls railway bridge in the no-man's land between Rhodesia and Zambia. Smith refused to include majority rule on the agenda, and observing that there was a temporary let-up in fighting he saw little reason to pursue the talks, which collapsed like all the previous ones.

THE FINAL PHASE OF WAR

The collapse of the Victoria Falls talks heralded an intensified, no-holds-barred, armed struggle. The Smith regime's complacency about controlling the situation was soon translated into increasingly bitter repression and resistance. In 1975, the ZANU chairman, **Herbert Chitepo**, was blown up in Lusaka by the Rhodesian Central Intelligence Organization. Amid this and other assassinations and disappearances, continued government claims to be fighting for civilization rang extremely hollow.

PEOPLE'S WAR

In white farming areas, **guerrilla attacks on farmers** increased, and a siege existence became the norm, with a whole industry developing around the supply of security equipment, fences, communications networks and an array of "counter-insurgency" devices – tripwire-triggered grenades, mine-proofed vehicles and cars bristling with elaborate "anti-terrorist" weaponry for use on the road. Throughout many areas of the country, whites could travel along main roads only in armed convoys, and even these were frequently ambushed. Guerrillas also hit hotels and tourist centres, while missions and schools could be arbitrarily closed or opened by armed nationalists, who would often demand tithes from teachers in the rural areas.

In the shadowy world of attack and retribution, countless sickening **massacres** occurred – frequently at schools or mission stations – with each side blaming the other. The people who invariably suffered most were ordinary villagers, trapped in a nightmare of guerrilla appearances under cover of darkness and armed visits by day from the Rhodesian forces, who would brutally beat and torture suspected nationalist sympathizers. The law laid down heavy sentences for people who failed to report the presence of guerrillas – by the end of the war, death was routine punishment for helping armed nationalists. On the other hand the guerrillas were frequently ruthless with informers and government collaborators.

TOTAL WAR

The **Rhodesian army** solution was to hold whole villages responsible for the presence of guerrillas, and army units would storm settlements when nationalists were suspected of being present. In the first half of 1977, Combined Operations HQ reported the killing of 58 "curfew breakers", 53 "running with or assisting terrorists", 13 "failing to halt" and 54 "caught in crossfire".

Official policy, as espoused by the suave right-wing Minister for Information P.K. van der Byl, was:

If villagers harbour terrorists, and terrorists are found running about in villages, naturally they will be bombed and destroyed in any manner which the commander on the spot considers desirable in the suitable prosecution of a successful campaign.

A different approach was the introduction of the dubiously named **protected villages** –

intended to isolate the guerrillas from their lifeblood, the peasantry. These "PVs," supposedly to protect villagers from the nationalists, were known by their inhabitants as "the cage" – little more than concentration camps, with guards, curfews, poor sanitation and walks of up to 10km to their livestock and land. Such measures only served to increase their hatred of the government.

By 1976 things were already looking dire for the Smith regime. The war was by now costing over US$1 million a day and the close of 1978 saw over half the country under **Patriotic Front** control. White males were being called up for increasingly lengthy stints, a "Dad's Army" of everyone up to 60 years old found themselves involved in the war, while conscription for blacks drove many over the border to join the nationalists. Only by employing a force of 10,000 **mercenaries** – mainly British and South Africans – was Smith able to keep things afloat.

CONTEMPLATING THE IMPOSSIBLE – ELECTIONS

Smith by now admitted that majority rule was inevitable and hoped for a negotiated settlement on his own terms, which would simultaneously bring international recognition. His favoured "moderate" candidate, **Bishop Muzorewa**, seemed a sharp choice at the time – malleable in a way which Nkomo and Mugabe were not, but also with some apparent street credibility through his part in trouncing Smith over the 1969 Constitution.

Smith negotiated an internal settlement with Muzorewa and other tame black "leaders". In a 1979 ballot, which excluded ZANU and ZAPU, Muzorewa's **UANC** swept the board. In fact the bishop's campaign was financed by Smith's government, and most of the cleric's speeches and statements were written by an advertising company. Muzorewa, however, became prime minister, while Smith continued to control all the instruments of power: the army, police, judiciary and civil service. The now supposedly liberated country was called **Zimbabwe-Rhodesia** – jokingly called Rhobabwe by some.

No one was fooled. The accolades of international recognition failed to materialize, and nor did the expected hordes of demoralized ZANLA and ZIPRA personnel. Instead the **war** rose to an unprecedented ferocity. In May 1979 a relieved and grateful white Rhodesian public joyfully welcomed the election of Margaret Thatcher in Britain, but their elation was short-lived when she proved as unsympathetic as her "socialist" predecessors – the Iron Lady had no intention of recognizing the "Internal Settlement".

LANCASTER HOUSE AGREEMENT

Under siege, the Smith-Muzorewa team found themselves in Britain, and by the end of the year were discussing a new constitution with the Nkomo-Mugabe Patriotic Front at the **Lancaster House conference**. Eager for a rapid settlement in the wake of some Conservative opposition at home, Britain's foreign secretary, Lord Carrington, succeeded in bulldozing through an agreement in just fourteen weeks.

Patriotic Front demands were toned down in the agreement. One man, one vote was diluted by allowing the whites, a mere three percent of the population, to hang on to twenty of the one hundred parliamentary seats. The Rhodesian army would form the core of the new defence force and pensions would continue to be paid to civil servants, even if they left the country. Perhaps the biggest concession the PF made was to agree that unoccupied **white farmlands** could not be expropriated without compensation. As the central issue of the liberation struggle, this was – and indeed remains today – a potential post-Independence time bomb.

THE ELECTION

Following the Lancaster House Agreement, the **Patriotic Front split**, and **ZANU** and **ZAPU** launched separate campaigns. The election that followed was crammed with drama, edgy nationalist troops corralled at assembly points, while Rhodesian troops were freely deployed by the interim governor-general. Neatly collected in one place, the guerrillas were sitting ducks, but a post-election **coup plan** to massacre them was jettisoned once the extent of the ZANU victory emerged. Several attempts were made on Mugabe's life, while the government and South Africa pumped enormous quantities of cash into Muzorewa's campaign – the slickest razzmatazz ever in Central Africa.

Despite a four-day pro-Muzorewa rally, with bands, free food, films, prizes and all, attracting over a million people, the cool cleric failed to win more than three of the eighty seats. ZAPU took twenty, and whites, for decades accustomed to believing their own propaganda, woke on **March 4, 1980** to the nightmare of a 57-seat **ZANU landslide**.

INDEPENDENCE: THE FIRST DECADE

Independence and majority rule failed to mark the immediate decline of civilization that whites had predicted, as it soon became apparent that **Robert Mugabe** wasn't going to turn the protected villages into re-education camps. In stark contradiction to Ian Smith's shock-horror predictions, churches were not turned into barracks and concentration camps. In fact, for those whites who remained, standards of living remained at their previous high level.

A CAUTIOUS ADVANCE

Robert Mugabe managed to transform his image from that of a hardline Marxist guerrilla leader into that of a statesman after he appeared on national television on March 4, 1980, following his party's victory in the national elections. "There is a place for everyone in this country," he told viewers. "We want to ensure a sense of security for both the winners and the losers." A year later, once things had settled and it was apparent that no hasty radical reforms were under way, Mugabe, on a visit to Britain, was asked whether he was heading towards a "new Kenya" or a "new Mozambique", to which he replied, "a new Zimbabwe", indicating that Zimbabwe would tread a "middle way" between capitalism and socialism.

The government was restrained from carrying out a radical transformation of the country by several factors, including the Lancaster House Agreement, the fact that seventy percent of investment came from outside the country and by South Africa's hostile apartheid regime breathing over its shoulder. Perhaps the strongest influence came from Mozambique's President Samora Machel, who advised Mugabe to avoid alienating whites, as had happened in his country, where most of the colonists followed a vindictive scorched-earth tactic of sabotaging infrastructure before leaving for Rhodesia, South Africa or Portugal.

Mugabe included minority representatives from ZAPU and the white community in his cabinet and he raised the minimum wage for farm workers by fifty percent, but industrial workers made fewer gains. While moves were made to reassure white farmers and foreign investors, other efforts were made to Africanize Zimbabwe. Segregation was ended, education was enormously extended and free health care was provided to low earners – most of the population.

Zimbabwe raved into the 1980s, with Bob Marley offering his final performance at the **Independence celebrations** on April 17, 1980. The first years were euphoric and the London *Times* reported that the economy had taken off "like a rocket", with GDP advancing at an impressive eight percent for two successive years following the nil growth of the final Smith years. But by 1982 a drought brought growth down to zero and the precarious national unity began to fracture.

DISSIDENTS

In the ZAPU stronghold of **Matabeleland** there were rumblings of discontent and fighting broke out between ZANU and ZAPU supporters. Joshua Nkomo spoke out against Mugabe's efforts to establish a one-party state. Shortly afterwards, the government claimed to have uncovered arms caches on farms owned by Nkomo's party and all members of ZAPU, including Nkomo, were dropped from the cabinet. ZIPRA guerrillas loyal to ZAPU drifted back to the bush and carried out violent anti-government protests. Among the more widely publicized incidents were the kidnapping and murder of six foreign tourists and the killing of several white farmers.

It looked as if the country would again be torn apart by civil war and, in sinister moves that looked like a carbon copy of Smith tactics, the government insisted that the dissidents were simply armed terrorists and refused any negotiations. The ruthless Korean-trained **Fifth Brigade** of the national army was sent in to put down the rebels: it killed thousands of civilians in brutal attempts to flush out the dissidents. Credible estimates put the Matabeleland deaths higher than 20,000 – a grievous human-rights atrocity that left scars on the country that still fester.

This repression only served to strengthen ZAPU support in Matabeleland, and the government realized the dangers of a tactic that played into the hands of an apartheid South Africa eager to destabilize its neighbours. Mugabe admitted the error and began talks with Nkomo.

In 1987 the two **parties merged**, although some felt that it was more a case of ZANU swallowing the opposition. Nkomo was given a senior position and Mugabe was upgraded to executive president. By May 1988, the dissidents had given themselves up under an **amnesty**, and all attacks ceased. Emerging from years in the bush, Mhkwananzi, a dissident spokesman, optimistically declared:

Disunity does not pay. We have gone on operations twice, first against the white colonizers and then against the party. We have liberated everybody and now we must forge ahead with our lives.

THE LATE 1980S: UNITY AND DISAPPOINTMENT

The merger of the two parties meant that Mugabe came very close to achieving his goal of a **one-party state**, but his troubles were not over. There was an uproar in Parliament over accusations of **corruption** at Air Zimbabwe, with some MPs maintaining that money ought to be spent on buses for the people rather than planes for the privileged. The usually tame press published articles attacking the government for professing socialism while pursuing capitalism for the elite. There were frustrations, too, over the pace of reform, with the pre-colonial inequities still remaining firmly in place.

In 1988, the Bulawayo-based *Chronicle* newspaper itself became the centre of the news by breaking a corruption scandal. Senior cabinet ministers were exposed for having made large profits on cars they had procured by pulling rank from the State-owned Willowvale car assembly plant. The so-called **Willowgate scandal** outraged the public, while Minister of Defence Enos Nkala made threats against the *Chronicle* but, in the end, it was Nkala who eventually bit the dust, along with four other ministers.

On the University of Zimbabwe campus, students joined in the protests over government corruption, but were quelled, first by police and then by the removal of grants from student leaders. Believing that the president was on their side, with his "leadership code" aimed at keeping the government clean, the students were surprised when Mugabe returned from a foreign trip and rebuked them for "childish behaviour". Only after apologizing for embarrassing him were the grants restored. Meanwhile, support gathered for the rabble-rousing freelance parliamentary opposition led by **Edgar Tekere** – who was expelled from ZANU in 1988.

But the biggest problem of all remained **apartheid-ruled South Africa**, which was constantly making veiled threats against Zimbabwe, and occasionally sending in agents to bomb alleged African National Congress (ANC) personnel. Most of Zimbabwe's trade went through its southern neighbour's ports, and South Africa was able to use this fact to apply pressure. The Zimbabwe government tried to shift trade to the Mozambican port of Beira and deployed 10,000 troops in Mozambique to defend the **Beira corridor** railway. As a result, South African-backed **Renamo (MNR)** rebels declared war on Zimbabwe. At the end of the 1980s, Renamo guerrillas made several raids on Zimbabwean villages in the Eastern Highlands bordering Mozambique.

THE 1990S: DECADE OF DISCONTENT

If Zimbabwe kicked off the 1980s in a mood of euphoria and heady optimism, the 1990s began as the decade of disillusion and discontent. In the first ten years of Independence the government made remarkable headway in improving conditions for ordinary people. Health care was made more accessible, average life expectancy rose and infant mortality fell, free primary-school education was provided and for many people wages increased.

By the end of the 1980s, however, the country faced a series of economic problems. Dissatisfaction with the government found expression in **strikes** and demonstrations by nurses, students and trade unionists. When a student anti-corruption meeting was banned in October 1989, **Morgan Tsvangirai**, leader of the Zimbabwe Congress of Trade Unions (ZCTU), spoke out against the "naked use of force to suppress the growing disenchantment of the masses over the rising cost of living, transport problems, unemployment, destitution and other negative socio-economic developments". Tsvangirai was arrested on unspecified charges, though later released.

The hottest issue, however, was the **land question**, which remains unresolved two decades after liberation. The Lancaster House Agreement failed to make funds available to buy out white farms for redistribution to small-scale farmers, and there were rumblings of dissatisfaction among some landless ex-combatants, who felt betrayed by the revolution. In its first decade in power, Mugabe's government only managed to **resettle** 52,000 families, less than a third of the 162,000 targeted for the first three years following Independence. In March 1990, Mugabe announced that the government was drafting a plan to provide for the landless, but at the same time he assured nervous white property-owners that the process would be fair. Under the Lancaster House Agreement, Zimbabwe's constitution ensured that for a decade after Independence the government could buy only land that was offered for sale.

Mugabe announced, as a prelude to the March 1990 elections, that the government was planning to amend this restriction to coincide with the tenth anniversary of Independence on April 18, 1990. But for Mugabe the heart of the election campaign was to gain a mandate for his cherished ideal of establishing a **one-party state**, and, aware of the importance of the land issue, he hoped to capture vital rural support.

THE 1990 ELECTION

In the event, the **1990 election** campaign was an ugly affair. As Edgar Tekere had promised, his fledgling **ZUM (Zimbabwe Unity Movement)** fought the election, standing on a capitalist and multi-party ticket. Small and poorly funded, it was never a serious threat to ZANU, though, surprisingly, Mugabe seemed to take the opposition threat very seriously. One of the grimmest series of events centred on the Gweru North constituency, where vice-president Simon Muzenda was locked in a tight campaign against ZUM's Patrick Kombayi. On the Saturday before the ballot, Kombayi suffered a sharp setback when Mugabe issued a presidential proclamation altering the electoral boundaries to exclude his stronghold. Later that week Kombayi was shot and seriously wounded. Several other ZUM candidates withdrew from contests in other constituencies.

The ballot failed to live up to the excitement promised by the campaigning. As was widely expected, ZANU won a massive victory, taking

116 of the 119 contested seats to ZUM's mere two. In the presidential race against Tekere, Mugabe took 78 percent of the votes cast. But the most powerful statement of the poll was apathy, with around half the electorate failing to vote. Mugabe described his victory as a mandate for the establishment of a **one-party state**. When he put the idea to the ZANU Central Committee, however, it was roundly defeated.

ESAP: LET THEM EAT KODACOLOR

The real issue for Zimbabwe was the problem of **economic growth** and **job creation**. The economy had stagnated in the late 1980s and by 1990 nearly 300,000 young people each year finished their O Levels with little hope of finding jobs. The government recognized it had to do something. After years of holding out against those bastions of capitalism, the IMF and the World Bank, the Mugabe government finally agreed to their principles of economic restructuring and accepted a five-year **Economic Structural Adjustment Programme** in October 1991. The plan, known in Zimbabwe by its acronym **ESAP**, sought to liberalize the economy, encourage market forces and make imports easier, to help rebuild the country's ageing infrastructure. It marked a significant retreat from socialism for the Mugabe government.

The most visible effect of the plan was the appearance of previously unavailable **imported goods** and it was apparent that the structural adjustment plan worked for business and particularly the tourist industry, which was now able to modernize and make international consumer goods available. Less visible was the really serious hardship caused to ordinary people, for whom maize meal and bread, not Kodacolor Gold, were the big issues.

The IMF and the World Bank pressed Mugabe to slash government spending, but instead of cutting the defence budget, now that the threat from apartheid South Africa had gone, the Zimbabwean government chose to cut health and education expenditure. This caused a major reversal of the gains in living conditions that had been achieved in the 1980s. Free education ended and the public health-care system ceased to deliver affordable care. The lifting of price controls saw the cost of staple foods rocket. According to some analysts, living standards fell below those of the mid-1970s under the

Smith regime. For instance, the maternal death rate – a key health indicator showing the number of women dying in childbirth – rose above pre-Independence levels. A major reason was because women could no longer afford to go to the hospitals for childbirth and instead had their babies at home, without proper care.

The government argued that structural adjustment was short-term pain in the interests of long-term gain, but its timing could not have been worse. The launching of the plan coincided with the most severe **drought** for a century. Dams became puddles and the "great, grey, green, greasy Limpopo" was reduced to a dirty, desperate, dry dustbowl. Zimbabwe, once the grain basket of the region, struggled in the grip of a **famine** in which two million lives were at risk.

The seriousness of the situation was as much due to failures of government policy as natural disaster. Encouraged by the IMF, Zimbabwe had sold off its contingency maize supplies to pay off the interest on its debt. Maize had to be reimported to feed the starving – at a considerably higher price.

In 1992, after a visit to her homeland, Doris Lessing wrote that "this year may make or break Zimbabwe". In the dry lowveld, wildlife began to die off and farmers were forced to shoot starving cattle. The country's tobacco crop (a major forex earner) was devastated, maize (the staple food) withered, and the entire national sugar crop was wiped out. At the end of the year relief did come: 1993 brought normal rains – and respite.

THE MID-1990S: HARD TIMES

Life in the **mid-1990s** became tougher for most Zimbabweans. Some, including Mugabe, blamed this on the drought, but many economists argued that government economic mismanagement was the cause. The economic liberalizations of the structural adjustment plan made virtually any imported good available – for those who could afford it. But, for peasants and many workers at the bottom of the pile, bread itself became an unaffordable luxury. When prices rose in 1993, there were **bread riots** followed by consumer boycotts in some high-density suburbs (townships), while joblessness continued to grow, with no concrete steps from the government to create employment.

Discontent grew, with the normally loyal *Herald* declaring that "what the government calls cost recovery is seen by the people as total neglect and betrayal of the liberation struggle". Even government minister Didymus Mutasa hit out against ESAP, saying that the structural adjustment had given the country "ten indigenous millionaires against ten million poor workers".

Yet the government went on to enjoy its biggest victory ever in the **1995 general election** – a far more peaceful one than five years earlier, but with widespread evidence of vote rigging by the government. Certainly the election victory did not produce a sense of euphoria in ZANU – rather there was disquiet at the high level of abstentions and the feeling that the government had lost its legitimacy.

INTO THE MILLENNIUM: WHISPERS OF CHANGE

Although the country began the decade filled with disillusion and despair, as Zimbabwe entered the new millennium several civic groups were working to change the status quo and give people hope of better times. At the end of the century Zimbabwe faced its most serious economic crisis since Independence, which in turn caused political problems. Cracks in the ruling party widened and **Robert Mugabe's** status as a national leader became tarnished.

In response, Mugabe attempted to talk up his popularity with a series of outspoken **attacks on gays**. As a result, the international community's perception of Mugabe changed; his image as a statesman has become one of an anachronistic despot, unable to hold a candle to South Africa's enlightened former ruler, Nelson Mandela. Mugabe's double standards did nothing to repair his tattered image when the country's first state president, Canaan Banana, stood trial for the homosexual rape of bodyguards and police officers. It seemed clear that Mugabe knew what had been going on, but had covered up for his colleague.

Mugabe also returned to the **land issue** and in 1998 promised that his government would seize white-owned properties and would not "pay a penny for the soil". Desperate peasants began squatting on lush white-owned farms, but were soon evicted by the government: it was revealed that land supposedly designated for resettlement had not gone to poor peasant farmers but to well connected cabinet ministers, army generals and top civil servants.

In August 1998, Mugabe surprised the world by sending 10,000 troops to the distant **Democratic Republic of Congo** (formerly Zaire) to prop up the tottering regime of Laurent Kabila, who was under attack from rebels backed by neighbouring Uganda and Rwanda. The Congo war was unpopular with Zimbabweans from the start and drew the government deeper into debt, leading to a currency crash: the Zimbabwe dollar lost more than fifty percent of its value almost overnight. In a significant sideshow, in January 1999 an independent Sunday newspaper, the *Standard*, reported that 23 army officers had been arrested for allegedly plotting a coup to end the Congo war. Infuriated army officials illegally arrested the paper's editor Mark Chavunduka and reporter Ray Choto, allegedly torturing them. Yet Mugabe stood up for the army, saying they had been provoked by the journalists. The government pressed specious charges against the two journalists but did nothing to investigate the charges of torture.

By the end of 1999, Zimbabwe's **economic problems** had become severe – inflation at seventy percent, interest rates at sixty percent and unemployment at fifty percent – and most urban Zimbabweans blamed the Congo adventure and the Mugabe government.

The economic decline, corruption and abuse of power that had become associated with the Mugabe regime by the end of the 1990s led a coalition of civic organizations to focus on Zimbabwe's core problem: its weak constitution. Through the **National Constitutional Assembly** they pressed for a new constitution and brought together an impressive collection of church groups, women's groups, human rights activists, trade unions and many others. Placed on the defensive, Mugabe hijacked the process by forming his own constitutional commission. Meanwhile the Zimbabwe Congress of Trade Unions (ZCTU) became an increasingly vocal opponent of the government, and ZCTU leaders Morgan Tsvangirai and Gibson Sibanda formed a new political party, the **Movement for Democratic Change**.

The opening months of 2000 were dominated by the growing **economic crisis** and the campaign for the **new constitution**, which aimed not to extend human rights but rather curtail them while giving Mugabe more power. And while the president continued to pour resources into the Congo war, at home corruption and mismanagement in the state oil procurement agency literally brought the country to a standstill as diesel and paraffin – used to run buses and many other vehicles – ran out. The **fuel crisis** continued right up to the constitutional referendum in February. The campaign that led up to the ballot became a test of popularity for the government which was confident of its ability to manipulate the poll through its monopoly over the broadcasting media – and by repeating the tired promise that peasants would be resettled on white owned farms if they voted "yes". Against all odds the Movement for Democratic Change campaigned against the highly flawed constitution and delivered a major setback for Mugabe, with 55 percent of those who voted rejecting the constitution – a fact taken by many comentators to be a vote of no-confidence in Mugabe and ZANU-PF. Mugabe's first electoral defeat in his twenty-year presidential career provided an electrifying curtain-raiser to the general election, due for April 2000, and suggested that the whispers of change might be substantiated

WILDLIFE

Zimbabwe and northern Botswana are perhaps the most exciting places in Africa to see wildlife. While neither is as efficiently geared up or well funded as neighbouring South Africa and you won't find the prodigious quantities of animals you get in East Africa, the compensations are immeasurable: lower densities of visitors mean the game reserves still feel wild; you won't have to share your experiences with busloads of package tourists; and the standards of game guiding are by far the best in Africa. That's not all – Zimbabwe and Botswana host huge herds of animals that are heading for extinction elsewhere on the continent, with parks that are literally trampled by elephants, while the full range of African predators are here plus herbivores such as giraffe, zebra, buffalo, hippo and many species of antelope.

This account supplements the colour field guide to "The Wildlife of East and Southern Africa" in the centre of the book (to which bracketed page numbers refer) and will help you get the most from watching big game and smaller species. It aims to inspire you to go beyond check lists, to appreciate the interactions of the bush and get more out of your

Page numbers below refer to the **colour guide** to "The Wildlife of East and Southern Africa" in the centre of this book.

safari. Beyond the scope of this account are the hundreds of colourful bird species that are an inseparable part of the African landscape and whose calls are a constant element of its soundtrack. Taking an interest in these will immeasurably add to your experience of the country's wildlife. Some outstanding **field guides** are listed on p.391.

PRIMATES

Southern Africa has the lowest diversity of **primates** on the continent, a mere five species (compared with Kenya's twelve) excluding our own, *Homo sapiens*. They include two varieties of bushbaby, two monkeys and one species of baboon – the largest and most formidable of Southern Africa's primates. Great apes such as gorillas and chimpanzees are only found much further north in countries such as the Democratic Republic of the Congo and Uganda.

CHACMA BABOONS

Apart from humans, **chacma baboons**, *Papio ursinus* (p.2), the local subspecies of these common savanna monkeys, are the primates most widely found in Zimbabwe and Botswana; indeed their range extends from Cape Point in South Africa into southern Zambia. On safari you'll have plenty of opportunity to watch baboon troops up close.

Large males can be somewhat intimidating in size and manner and are frequently bold enough to raid vehicles or accommodation in game reserves in search of food – undeterred even by the close presence of people. Baboons are highly gregarious and are invariably found in troops, which can number as few as fifteen or as many as a hundred members, but an average of around forty is more common. Baboon social relations are complex and fascinating, and revolve around their jockeying either to climb the social ladder or to avoid being toppled from its upper rungs. Rank, gender, precedence, physical strength and kin ties determine an individual's position in this mini society, which is led by a dominant male. Baboon males are unreconstructed chauvinists and every adult male enjoys dominance over every adult female. Days are dominated by the need to forage and hunt for food: baboons are highly opportunistic omnivores, who will as happily tuck into a scorpion or a newborn antelope in

Hwange National Park as they will ravage the maize crop on a peasant smallholding in Zimbabwe's communal lands.

Grooming is a fundamental part of the social glue during times of relaxation. When baboons and other monkeys perform this massage-like activity on each other, the specks which they pop into their mouths are sometimes parasites – notably ticks – and sometimes flecks of skin.

VERVET MONKEYS

Another widespread primate you'll encounter in wilderness throughout the region covered by the Guide is the **vervet monkey**, *Cercopithecus aethiops* (p.2). Although happy foraging in grasslands, they rarely venture far from the refuge of woodland, particularly along river-courses. You can frequently see them outside reserves, where they often live around farms and even come into the suburban fringes, where the opportunities for scavenging are promising. Vervets are principally vegetarians, but they are not averse to eating invertebrates, small lizards, nestlings and eggs as well as being partial to processed foods, such as biscuits and sweets – when they're able to snatch them from unsuspecting visitors. Vervet society is made up of family groups of females and young defended by associate males, and is highly caste-ridden. A mother's rank determines that of her daughter from infancy, and lower-ranking adult females risk being castigated if they fail to show due respect to these "upper-crust" youngsters.

SAMANGO MONKEYS

Far rarer and considerably shyer, **samango monkeys**, *Cercothpithecus mitis* (p.3), are found only in the narrow strip of Zimbabwe's Eastern Highlands. Although they bear a passing resemblance to vervets, samangos are larger and have long cheek hair that gives them the passing appearance of Darth Vader masks. Samangos tend to hang out in the higher reaches of gallery forest, although they will on occasion venture into the open to forage. Like vervets, they are highly social animals that live in troops of females under the proprietorship of a dominant male, but unlike their relatives they are more inclined to fan out when looking for food. In striking contrast with the cheekier, upfront disposition of vervets, they are shy animals that may only give themselves away through their loud explosive call or the breaking of branches as they go about their business through the canopy.

BUSHBABIES

With their soft fluffy pelts, huge saucer-like eyes, large rounded ears and superficially cat-like appearance, bushbabies are the ultimate in cute, cuddly looking primates. Of the half-dozen-plus species endemic to Africa, only the **thick-tailed bushbaby**, *Otolemur crassicaudatus*, and, at about half the size, the **lesser bushbaby**, *Galago moholi*, are found south of the Zambezi. The former is restricted to the eastern third of Zimbabwe, while the latter is found throughout Southern Africa.

If you're staying in, amongst others, the Okavango Delta, Hwange or Mana Pools, you stand a fair chance of seeing a bushbaby after dark as they emerge from the dense tangles of the forest canopy where they rest in small groups, for spells of lone foraging for tree gum and fruit. Even if you don't see one you're bound to hear their piercing scream cut through the sounds of the night. Although thick-tails will eat insects – unlike other bushbabies, including the lesser, which leap with ease and speed – *crassicaudatus* is a slow mover that hops or walks along branches, often with considerable stealth. They habituate easily to humans and will sometimes come into lodge dining rooms scavenging for titbits.

CARNIVORES

Almost three dozen species of **carnivore** are found in Southern Africa, ranging from mongooses and weasels to hyenas, dog-relatives and seven species of cat.

DOG-RELATIVES

Southern Africa's five dog-relatives, *Canidae*, consist of two foxes, two jackals and the wild dog. The **black-backed jackal**, *Canis mesomelas* (p.4), is distributed throughout most of Botswana and western Zimbabwe, where Hwange National Park is the most likely place you'll see one. It bears a strong resemblance to a small, skinny German Shepherd, but with a more fox-like muzzle, and is distinguished from the grey, **side-striped jackal**, *Canis adjustus*, by the white-flecked black saddle on its back, to which it owes its name. As both occur in Hwange there's a possibility of confusing the two, but the fact that the black-backed seeks a drier habitat, in contrast to the side-striped's preference for well-watered woodland, is an additional identification pointer. Both species are omnivorous, with diets that take in carrion, small animals, reptiles, birds and insects as well as wild fruit and berries, and both are most commonly spotted solitary or in pairs, but you'll occasionally spot family groups.

The **bat-eared fox**, *Otocyon megalotis* (p.4), found in most of Botswana and a tiny section of western Zimbabwe, including Hwange, can be easily distinguished from the jackals by its out-sized ears, shorter, pointier muzzle, its considerably smaller size and black Zorro mask. Like other dogs, the bat-eared fox is an omnivore, but it favours termites and larvae, which is where its large radar-like ears come in handy. Using them it is able by triangulation to pinpoint the precise position of dung beetle larvae up to 30cm underground and to dig them out. Bat-eareds tend to live in pairs or family groups, an arrangement which affords mutual protection.

Once widely distributed hunters of the African plains, **wild dogs**, *Lycaon pictus* (p.4), have been brought to the precipice of extinction through persecution by humans. They are rarely sighted in Chobe, Hwange and Mana Pools national parks. For many years dogs were shot on sight, having gained an unjustified reputation as cruel and wanton killers of cattle and sheep. More recent scientific evidence reveals them to be economical and efficient hunters – and more successful at it than any other African species. You would be extremely lucky, though, to see a pack trotting along in the evening for a hunt. Capable of sustained high speeds (up to 50kph) over long distances, wild dogs lunge at their prey en masse, tearing it to pieces – a gruesome finish, but perhaps no slower or more grisly than the suffocating muzzle-bite of a lion. The entire pack of ten to fifteen animals participates in looking after the pups, bringing back food and regurgitating it for them.

CATS

Apart from **lions**, which very notably live in social groups, all the cats are solitary carnivores and, with the exception of the cheetah, which is anatomically distinct from the other cats, the remaining members of the family are so similar that Richard Estes comments in *The Safari Companion* (see Books, p.391) that big cats are just jumbo versions of the domestic cat, "distinguished mainly by a modification of the larynx that enables them to roar".

Perhaps it's just a question of size, but the most compelling of the *Felidae* for most people on safari are **lions**, *Panthera leo* (p.6), the largest cats and, indeed, the most massive predators in Africa. It's fortunate then that, despite having the most limited distribution of any cat, lions are the ones you're most likely to see. Of the public reserves, Moremi, Chobe, Hwange and Mana Pools national parks have healthy populations. Lazy, gregarious and sizable, lions rarely make any attempt to hide or move away from vehicles, making them relatively easy to find, especially if someone else has already spotted them – a gathering of stationary vehicles frequently signals lions. Seeing lions hunting is another matter: their fabled reputation as cold, efficient hunters is ill-founded, as lions are only successful around thirty percent of the time and even in this instance only when operating as a group. Males don't hunt at all if they can help it, and will happily enjoy a free lunch courtesy of the females of the pride.

The lion may be king, but the most successful and arguably most beautiful of the large cats is the **leopard**, *Panthera pardus* (p.6), which survives from the southern coastal strip of Africa all the way to China. Highly adaptable, they are able to subsist in extremes of aridity or cold as well as near human habitation, where they will happily prey on domestic animals. They are present in the surreal whaleback Matobo Hills near Bulawayo, but you are most unlikely to encounter these secretive, solitary animals here. Your best chance of sighting one is with a keen-eyed guide at one of the private lodges. Powerfully built, leopards can bring down prey twice their mass and can drag an impala their own weight up a tree. The chase is not part of the leopard's tactical repertoire; they hunt by stealth, getting to within 2m of their target before pouncing.

In the flesh, the **cheetah**, *Acinonyx jubatus* (p.6), is so different from the leopard that it's hard to see how there could ever be any confusion. Cheetahs are the lightly built greyhounds of the big-cat world, with small heads, very long legs and an exterior decor of fine spots. Unlike leopards, which are highly arboreal, cheetahs never climb trees, being designed rather for activity on the open plains. Cheetahs live alone, or sometimes briefly form a pair during mating. Hunting is normally a solitary activity, down to eyesight and an incredible burst of speed that can take the animal up to 100kph for a few seconds. Because they're lighter than lions and less powerful than leopards, cheetahs can't rely on strength to bring down their prey, instead having to resort to tripping or knocking the victim off balance by striking its hindquarters and then pouncing. Cheetahs were once common in Southern Africa but now are only widespread across Botswana, and you stand a chance of seeing them at Hwange.

The other *Felidae* are usually classified as small cats, although the **caracal**, *Caracal caracal* (p.6), is a substantial animal, which occurs, but isn't often seen, across Zimbabwe and Botswana. An unmistakable and awesome hunter, it's able to take prey such as adult impala and sheep, which far exceed its own mass of 8–18kg. More commonly, it will feed on birds, which it pounces on, sometimes while still in flight, as well as smaller mammals including dassies, which its climbing and jumping agility make it uniquely well adapted to catching.

Long-legged and spotted, **servals**, *Felis serval* (p.7), are higher at the shoulder but lighter than caracals and are equally rarely seen, although they are present throughout most of Zimbabwe and in northern Botswana. Efficient hunters, servals use their large rounded ears to pinpoint prey (usually small rodents, birds or reptiles), which they pounce on with both front paws after performing impressive athletic leaps. Of the genuinely small cats, the **African wild cat**, *Felis lybica*, is distributed throughout Southern Africa and is easily mistaken for a domestic tabby, although its legs are longer and it has reddish ears. First domesticated six thousand years ago by the Egyptians, wild cats are still so closely related to the domestic version that the two are able to interbreed freely.

HYENAS

The largest carnivores after lions are **hyenas**, and, apart from the lion, the **spotted hyena**, *Crocuta crocuta* (p.5), is the meat-eater you will most often see. Although considered a scavenger *par excellence,* the spotted hyena is a formidable hunter, most often found where antelopes and zebras are present. Exceptionally

efficient consumers with immensely strong teeth and jaws, spotted hyenas eat virtually every part of their prey, including bones and hide and, where habituated to humans, often steal shoes, unwashed pans and refuse from tents. Although they can be seen by day, they are most often active at night, when they issue their unnerving whooping cries. Clans of twenty or so animals are dominated by females, which are larger than the males and compete with each other for rank. Curiously, female hyenas' genitalia are hard to distinguish from males', leading to a popular misconception that they are hermaphroditic. They occur in Moremi, Chobe, Hwange and Mana Pools national parks, south into South Africa and north into East and West Africa.

The **brown hyena**, *Hyaena brunnea*, is restricted to parts of Namibia, Botswana, Zimbabwe and South Africa, where it's not commonly seen. That it's usually seen singly also distinguishes this shaggier, slightly larger hyena from its spotted cousin. The hyena-like **aardwolf**, *Proteles cristatus*, is smaller than the spotted hyena and far lighter (about two-thirds the height at the shoulder and roughly a tenth of its weight), as well as being less shaggy, with vertical dark stripes along its tawny body. It is further distinguished from the hyena by its insectivorous diet and its particular preference for harvester termites, which it laps up en masse (up to 200,000 in one night) using its broad sticky tongue. Far more widely distributed in South Africa than the hyena, this nocturnal animal is sometimes active in the cooler hours just before dusk or after dawn. Although they aren't often seen, you could keep an eye open at Chobe and Hwange.

SMALLER CARNIVORES

Among the smaller predators, the unusual **honey badger**, *Mellivora capensis* (p.4), is related to the European badger and has a reputation for defending itself extremely fiercely. Primarily an omnivorous forager, it will tear open bees' nests (to which it is led by a small bird, the honey guide), its thick loose hide rendering it impervious to their stings. **Small-spotted** (or **common**) **genets**, *Genetta genetta* (p.5), are reminiscent of slender elongated cats and were once domesticated around the Mediterranean (but cats turned out to be better mouse hunters). In fact they are viverrids, related to mongooses, and are frequently seen after dark around national park lodges, where they live a semi-domesticated existence. Distributed widely in Botswana and western Zimbabwe, they are difficult to distinguish from the **large-spotted genet**, *Genetta tigrina*, which has bigger spots and a black (instead of white) tip to its tail and is found throughout Zimbabwe and northern Botswana.

Most species of **mongoose** (p.5), of which there are nearly a dozen in the region covered by the Guide, are also tolerant of humans and, even when disturbed out in the bush, can usually be observed for some time before disappearing. Their snake-fighting reputation is greatly overplayed: in practice they are mostly social foragers, fanning out through the bush like beaters on a shoot, rooting for anything edible – mostly invertebrates, eggs, lizards and frogs.

One of the best places to see the **Cape clawless otter**, *Aonyx capensis*, a large heavily built species, is in the Okavango Delta, where it feeds on crabs, fish and frogs. It is also found in Chobe and near water in the southern half of Zimbabwe.

The **civet** (or **African civet**), *Civetticus civetta* (p.5), is a stocky animal, resembling a large terrestrial genet. It was formerly kept in captivity for its musk (once an ingredient in perfume), which is secreted from glands near the tail. Distributed throughout Zimbabwe and northern Botswana, civets aren't often seen, but they are predictable creatures that wend their way along the same path at the same time night after night.

ANTELOPES

Antelopes represent the most regularly seen family of animals in the game reserves, and you'll even spot some on farmland. Because antelopes are so common, it's easy to become blasé and to stop looking at them in the search for more exciting species such as the large carnivores. But, given that such sightings can be relatively infrequent, you'll be doing yourself a favour if you take an interest in these herbivores, which provide a ready means of entertainment in every game reserve. Zimbabwe and Botswana have roughly a third of all the antelope species that occur in Africa. These can be subdivided into a number of tribes and, like buffaloes, giraffes and domestic cattle, they are ruminants.

THE BUSHBUCK TRIBE

Among the **bushbuck**, tribe horns, in curving spirals, are restricted to males, the exception being the eland, in which both sexes have straight horns but are still marked by distinctive spiralling. The tribe is the only one among the African antelope that is non-territorial. Look for them in the shadows of thickets and bush cover, which they use as a means of defence against predators. Largest of the tribe, and, indeed, the largest living antelope, is the **eland**, *Taurotragus oryx* (p.14), which is solidly built like an ox and moves with slow deliberation of one, but, in striking contrast, is a great jumper. Once widely distributed throughout Southern Africa, herds survive in most of the game reserves described in the Guide. The magnificent **kudu** (or **greater kudu**), *Tragelaphus strepsiceros* (p.14), is more elegantly built, and the male of the species is adorned with sensational spiralled horns that can easily reach 1.5m in length; it's these you'll often see mounted in old-fashioned country hotels. Female groups usually include three or more members and will sometimes combine temporarily to form larger herds, while males form similarly sized but more transient groupings, although it's not uncommon to encounter lone bulls. Despite a distinct family resemblance, you could never confuse a kudu with a **bushbuck**, *Tragelaphus scriptus* (p.14), which is considerably shorter and has a single twist to its horns, in contrast to the kudu's two or three turns. They also differ in being the only solitary members of the tribe, which is one reason why you're less likely to spot them in the undergrowth. They're found in Moremi, Chobe and Mana Pools national parks. **Nyala**, *Tragelaphus angasi* (p.13), are midway in size between the kudu and bushbuck, with which they could be confused on first glance. Telling pointers are their size, the sharp vertical white stripes on the side of the nyala (up to fourteen on the male or eighteen on the female) and in the males a short stiff mane from neck to shoulder. Females tend to group with their two last offspring and gather with other females in small herds of rarely more than ten, while males become more solitary the older they get. You tend to see males and females separately, as they only deliberately congregate for mating. They occur only in northern and southern fringes of Zimbabwe.

HORSE ANTELOPES

Widely distributed throughout Zimbabwe and northern Botswana, the **sable**, *Hippotragus niger* (p.15), is easily as magnificent as the kudu. A sleek black upper body set in sharp counterpoint to its white underparts and facial markings, as well as its massive backward-curving horns, makes this the thoroughbred of the ruminants, particularly when galloping majestically across the savannah. Highly hierarchical female herds number between one and three dozen, while territorial bulls frequently keep their distance, remaining under cover, where you could easily miss them. The **roan**, *Hippotragus equinus* (p.15), is a very similar-looking animal, but larger than a sable (it's Africa's second largest antelope), with less impressive horns and lighter colouring. You're more likely to see them in open savannah than sables, which prefer woodland. Geographically more restricted, **gemsbok** (also known as the **oryx**), *Oryx gazella* (p.15), are only to be seen in Zimbabwe in the desert regions of Hwange and Botswana. If you encounter a herd of these highly gregarious grazers, you should be left in no doubt as to what they are. Like the roan and sable, they have thick-set bodies and superficially similar facial markings, but their greyish-fawn colouring, black and white underbody markings and long, slender, almost-straight backward-pointing horns make them unmistakable. Gemsbok are highly adapted for survival in the arid country they inhabit, being able to go for long periods without water, relying instead on melons and vegetation for moisture. They can tolerate temperatures above 40°C by raising their normal body temperature of 35°C above that of the surrounding air, thus allowing them to lose heat by conduction and radiation; at the same time they keep their brains cool by drawing warm blood into their bodies and using cool blood from their noses as a coolant for this most vital organ.

HARTEBEESTS

With their bracket-shaped, relatively short horns (certainly when compared with the two previous antelope tribes) and ungainly appearance, the **hartebeests** look vaguely like elongated cows – particularly their faces. All hartebeests are gregarious, particularly the **blue wildebeests**, *Connochaetes taurinus* (p.10), which in East Africa gather in hundreds of thousands for their annual migration. You won't see these kinds of numbers in Southern Africa, but you'll regularly see smaller herds in most game reserves.

Rather inelegant, like the wildebeests, the **red hartebeest**, *Alcelaphus buselaphus* (p.10), the extremely rare **Lichtenstein's hartebeest**, *Sigmocerus lichtensteinii*, and the far more common **tsessebe**, *Damaliscus lunatus* (p.10), are highly similar in appearance, but confusion is only likely to arise at Hwange, which is the one place red hartebeest are found in the same range as tsessebes. The key distinction is in the horns, which in the hartebeest curve round to almost touch each other, while the tsessebe's are more splayed.

DUIKERS AND DWARF ANTELOPES

Duikers and the dwarf tribe are non-herding antelopes that live either in solitary or as pairs. Despite their diminutive size (or perhaps because of it), males tend to be highly aggressive and are able to use their straight, stiletto-sharp horns to deadly effect. The smallest Southern African antelope, the **blue duiker**, *Philantomba monticola*, weighs in at around 4kg, has an arched back and stands 35cm at the shoulder (roughly the height of a cat). Extremely shy, it is seldom seen in the Eastern Highlands forests where it lives. The member of this tribe you're more likely to see, though, is the **common duiker** (sometimes called the grey duiker, reflecting its colouring), *Sylvicapra grimmia* (p.13), which occurs all over Southern Africa, often outside reserves, and is one of the antelope most tolerant of human habitation. When under threat it freezes in the undergrowth, but if chased will dart off in an erratic zigzagging run designed to throw pursuers off balance.

This type of fast darting movement is also characteristic of the dwarf antelopes, particularly **Sharpe's grysbok**, *Raphicerus sharpii*, which occurs in Hwange and Mana Pools national parks, but is nocturnal and so is not often sighted. A relative of the grysbok, the **steenbok**, *Raphicerus campestris* (p.16), can be spotted day or night all over their range, which includes South Africa, all of Botswana and large parts of Zimbabwe. Its large, dark eyes, massive ears and delicate frame give this elegant half-metre-high antelope an engaging Bambi-like appearance. Another dwarf antelope you could well see in Zimbabwe is the **klipspringer**,

Oreotragus oreotragus (p.16), whose Afrikaans name ("rock jumper") accurately reflects its goat-like adaptation to living on kopjes and cliffs – the only antelope to do so, making it quite unmistakable. It is also the only antelope to walk on the tips of its hooves. Keep your eyes peeled at the Matobo National Park (or any wilderness areas where there are rocky outcrops) for their large bounding movements to scale steep inclines or their hopping from rock to rock. The largest of the dwarfs is the **oribi**, *Ourebia ourebi* (p.16), which could be taken for an outsized steenbok, to which its faster smoother movements, when compared to other dwarfs, are more akin. Not commonly seen, they live in small parties of a ram and several ewes. You may hear their short sharp warning whistle as you approach, before you see them, although they will frequently stop, after fleeing a little way to look back at you.

IMPALA

Impala, *Aepyceros melampus* (p.12), are a one-off antelope in a tribe of their own. Elegant and athletic, they are prodigious jumpers that have been recorded leaping distances of 11m in length and 3m in the air. Only the males carry the distinctive lyre-shaped horns. They are so common in most reserves that jaded rangers refer to them as "Hwange goats", a perception that carries more than a germ of truth as these flexible feeders are both browsers and grazers. Ewes and lambs form tight herds that can number over a hundred animals, which move about in a home range that may overlap the territory of several rams. During the rut, which takes place during the first five months of each year, these males will cut out harem herds of around twenty ewes and will expend considerable amounts of effort herding them and driving off any potential rivals.

NEAR-AQUATIC ANTELOPE

Only the males of the near-aquatic Kob tribe have horns; all species inhabit countryside close to water. The largest of the tribe, **waterbuck**, *Kobus ellipsiprymnus* (p.12), are sturdy antelope (1.3m at the shoulder) with shaggy reddish-brown coats and a white horseshoe-shaped marking on their rumps. They are found in most reserves, always in proximity to permanent water that is close to woodland. Sociable animals, they usually gather in small herds of up to

ten, but on occasions as many as thirty. The **reedbuck**, *Redunca arundinum* (p.12), roughly two-thirds the height of waterbuck, is a tan-coloured antelope that favours a habitat of tall grass or reedbeds to offer it refuge.

OTHER HOOFED RUMINANTS

Along with cattle, sheep and goats, antelope, buffalo and giraffes are hoofed **ruminants** – animals that have four stomachs and chew the cud. Bacteria in their digestive systems process plant matter into carbohydrates, while the dead bacteria are absorbed as protein – a highly efficient arrangement that makes them economical consumers, far more so than non-ruminants such as elephants, which pass vast quantities of what they eat as unutilized fibre. Species that tend to concentrate on eating grasses are known as **grazers**, while those that eat leaves are called **browsers**.

BUFFALO

You won't have to be in Hwange or most of the other reserves in Zimbabwe or Botswana for long to see **buffalo**, *Syncerus caffer* (p.10), a common and much-photographed safari animal that, as one of the "Big Five", also appears on every hunter's shopping list. Don't let their resemblance to domestic cattle or water buffalo (to which they are not at all closely related) or their apparent docility lull you into complacency: lone bulls in particular are noted and feared even by hardened hunters as dangerous and relentless killers. In other words, don't assume that, just because there are no carnivores about, it's safe to go walking without a guide.

Buffalo are non-territorial and highly gregarious, gathering in their hundreds or even sometimes thousands. Herds under one or more dominant bulls consist of clans of a dozen or so related females under a leading cow, and you'll be able to spot such distinct units within the group: at rest clan members will often cuddle up close to each other. There are separate pecking orders among both females and males, the latter being forced to leave the herd during adolescence (at about three years) or once they're over the hill to form bachelor herds, which you can recognize by their small numbers. Evicted old bulls (sometimes called "*daga* boys" on account of their penchant for mud baths), who have been stripped of their social position and active sex lives, understandably become resentful and embittered loners and are to be avoided at all costs. To distinguish males (as shown in the colour guide) from females, look for their heavier horns bisected by a distinct boss, or furrow.

GIRAFFE

Giraffes, *Giraffa camelopardalis* (p.9), are among the easiest animals to spot because their long necks make their heads visible above the low scrub. The tallest mammals on earth, giraffes spend their daylight hours browsing on the leaves of trees too high for other species: combretum and acacias are favourites. Their highly flexible lips and prehensile tongues give them almost handlike agility and enable them to select the most nutritious leaves while avoiding deadly sharp acacia thorns. At night they lie down and spend the evening ruminating. Non-territorial, they gather in loose leaderless herds; if you encounter a bachelor herd, look out for young males testing their strength with neck wrestling. When the female comes into oestrus, which can happen at any time of year, the dominant male will mate with her. She will give birth after a gestation of approximately fourteen months. Over half of all young, however, fall prey to lions or hyenas in their early years. Moremi, Chobe and Hwange reserves are all good places to see them; they are notably absent from Mana Pools and the Zambezi Valley.

NON-RUMINANTS

Non-ruminating mammals have more primitive digestive systems than animals that chew the cud. Although both have bacteria in their gut that convert vegetable matter into carbohydrates, the less efficient system of the non-ruminants means they have to consume more raw material and process it faster. The upside is they can handle food that is far more fibrous.

ELEPHANTS

Zimbabwe and Botswana have the largest populations of **elephants**, *Loxodonta africana* (p.7), in Africa, numbering tens of thousands. You'll see them in all the major reserves and potentially in large numbers at Hwange and Chobe game reserves. Elephants are the most engaging of animals to watch, perhaps because their interactions, behaviour patterns and personality have so many human parallels. Like people they lead complex, interdependent social lives, growing from helpless infancy, through self-conscious adolescence, to adulthood. Babies are born with other cows in close attendance, after a 22-month gestation. The calves suckle for two to three years from the mother's two breasts between her front legs.

Elephants' basic family units are composed of a group of related females, tightly protecting their babies and young, led by a venerable matriarch. It's the matriarch that's most likely to bluff a charge – though occasionally she may get carried away and tusk a vehicle or person. Bush mythology has it that elephants become embarrassed and ashamed after killing a human, covering the body with sticks and grass. They certainly pay much attention to the disposal of their own dead relatives, often dispersing the bones and spending time near the remains. Old animals die in their seventies or eighties, when their last set of teeth wears out and they can no longer feed.

Seen in the flesh, elephants are even bigger than you would imagine – you'll need little persuasion from those flapping warning ears to back off if you're too close – but they are at the same time amazingly graceful silent animals on their padded, carefully placed feet. In a matter of moments a large herd can merge into the trees and disappear, their presence betrayed only by the noisy cracking of branches as they strip trees and uproot saplings.

DASSIES (HYRAXES)

Dassies look like they ought to be rodents, but amazingly, despite being fluffy and rabbit-sized, their closest relatives (some way back) are elephants rather than rats. Their name (pronounced like "dusty" without the "t") is the Afrikaans version of *dasje*, meaning "little badger", given to them by South Africa's early Dutch settlers. **Rock dassies**, *Procavia capensis* (p.7), are commonly sighted in their areas of distribution in the southern half of Zimbabwe, having thrived with the elimination of predators. They hang out in suitably rocky habitat and you're bound to spot some in the Matobo National Park. One of the most striking places you'll see them is sunning themselves among the rocks of the Hill Enclosure at Great Zimbabwe. Like reptiles, hyraxes have poor body control systems and rely on shelter against both the cold and hot sunlight. They wake up sluggish, and first thing in the morning seek out rocks, where they can catch the early-morning sun – this is one of the best times to look out for them. One adult stands sentry against predators and issues a low-pitched warning cry in response to a threat. Dassies live in colonies of a dominant male and eight or more related females and their off-spring.

RHINOS

Two species of rhinoceros are found in Africa: the **hook-lipped** or **black rhino**, *Diceros bicornis* (p.8), and the much heavier **square-lipped** or **white rhino**, *Ceratotherium simum* (p.8). Both have come close to extinction in the African wild and have all but disappeared. "Hook-lipped" and "square-lipped" are technically more accurate terms for the two rhinos than "black" and "white", which are based on a linguistic misunderstanding. Somewhere along the line, the German term *weid,* that actually refers to the square-lipped's wide mouth, was misheard as "white", a term which has stuck despite the fact that both rhinos are a greyish muddy colour.

The shape of their lips is highly significant, as it indicates their respective diets and consequently their favoured habitat. The cantankerous and smaller black rhino has the narrow prehensile lips of a browser, suited to picking leaves off trees and bushes, while the wide, flatter mouth of the heftier (twice the weight) white rhino, is more like a lawnmower and well suited to chomping away at grasses. Diet and habitat also account for the greater sociability of the white rhino, which relies on safety in numbers under the exposure of open grassland, while the solitary black rhino relies on the camouflage of dense thickets, which is why you'll find them so much more difficult to see.

Rhinos give birth to a single calf after a gestation period of fifteen to eighteen months, and the baby is not weaned until it is at a least a year old, sometimes even two. Their population growth rate is slow compared with most animals – another factor contributing to their predicament.

HIPPOS

Hippopotamuses, *Hippopotamus amphibius* (p.9), are highly adaptable animals that once inhabited Zimbabwe's waterways from the Limpopo in the south to the Zambezi in the north. Today they're more restricted and tend to be found (in fair numbers) around the fringes of the country and in the waterways of northern Botswana. You will find them elsewhere, where they've been introduced, in places such as Lake Mutirikwe near Great Zimbabwe. Hippos need fresh water deep enough to submerge themselves in where there's a surrounding of suitable grass to graze. By day they need to spend most of their time in water to protect their thin, hairless skin. After dark, hippos leave the water to spend the whole night grazing, often walking up to 10km in one session.

Their grunting and jostling in the water may give the impression of lovable buffoons, but throughout Africa they are feared – rightly so, as they are reckoned to be responsible for more human deaths on the continent than any other animal. When disturbed in the water or on land, lone bulls and cows with calves can become extremely aggressive. Their fearsomely long incisors can slash with ease through a canoe and on land they can charge at speeds up to 30kph and have a tight turning circle.

ZEBRAS

Zebras are closely related to horses and, together with wild asses, form the *Equid* family. Of the three species of zebra, one, **Burchell's** or **plains zebra**, *Equus burchelli* (p.8), lives in Zimbabwe and Botswana. It has small ears and thick black stripes, with lighter "shadows", and survives in Zimbabwe in a crescent that sweeps from the Zambezi in the north down the west, taking in Hwange and through to the southern third of the country. They are also found in northern Botswana. Zebras congregate in family herds of a breeding stallion and two mares (or more) and their foals, while unattached males will often form bachelor herds. Offspring leave the family group at between one and two years.

PIGS

Two species of wild pig are found in Zimbabwe and Botswana. If you're visiting the Chobe, Hwange, Mana Pools or Matobo parks, families of **warthogs**, *Phacochoerus aethiopicus* (p.9), will become a familiar sight, trotting across the savannah with their tails erect like communications antennae. Family groups usually consist of a mother and her litter of two to four piglets, or occasionally two or three females and their young. Boars join the group only to mate. They are distinguished from sows by their prominent face warts, which are thought to be defensive pads protecting their heads during often violent fights. Warthogs shelter in holes in the ground, usually porcupine or aardvark burrows, although they are quite capable of digging their own. **Bushpigs**, *Potamochoerus porcus*, are more widely distributed in Zimbabwe than warthogs, but because they're nocturnal aren't seen as often. Much like hairier versions of domestic pigs, they live in harems called "sounders", consisting of a boar with several females and their piglets. Fathers drive out male offspring when they approach adolescence.

OTHER MAMMALS

Despite their common taste for ants and termites, their nocturnal foraging and their outlandish appearance, aardvarks and pangolins are quite unrelated. The **aardvark**, *Orycteropus afer* (p.3), is one of Africa's – indeed the world's – strangest animals, a solitary mammal weighing up to 70kg. Its name, Afrikaans for "earth pig" is an apt description, as it holes up during the day in large burrows – excavated with remarkable speed and energy – and emerges at night to visit termite mounds within a radius of up to 5km to dig for its main diet. It's most likely to be common in bush country well scattered with termite mounds: holes dug into the base of these are a telltale sign of the presence of aardvarks.

Pangolins, *Manis temminckii*, are equally unusual – scale-covered mammals resembling armadillos that feed on ants and termites. Under attack they roll themselves into a ball. Pangolins occur widely (but aren't often seen) in Zimbabwe and Botswana.

A number of species of rabbits and hares bounce about the Southern African landscape, but the **scrub hare**, *Lepus saxatilis*, distinguished by its exceptionally long ears, is the commonest and one you'll undoubtedly see in scrubby, wooded country throughout the region.

If you go on a night drive you'd be most unlucky not to see the bright glint of eyes bouncing through the dark like some frenetic computer game. The glare of a halogen beam will reveal the form of **spring hares**, *Pedetes capensis* (p.3), which, despite their resemblance to rabbit-sized kangaroos, are in fact true rodents. Throughout the region you'll spot **tree squirrels**, *Paraxerus cepapi*, scurrying about during the day looking for roots, seeds and bulbs. The most singular and largest of the African rodents is the **porcupine**, *Hystrix africae-australis* (p.3), which is quite unmistakable with its coat of many quills. Porcupines are widespread and present in most reserves in both countries, but because they're nocturnal you may only see evidence of them in shed quills lying along the path or in front of their burrows.

Scores of different **bats**, either fruit or insect eaters, leave their roosts each night and take off into the Southern African night, but all you're likely to see of them is some erratic flying against a moonlit sky. Despite their image in the popular imagination as gruesome bloodsuckers, no such bats live in this part of the world and some are rather useful members of the community. The foxy-faced **Egyptian fruit bat**, *Rousettus aegyptiacus*, for instance, is virtually single-handedly responsible for pollinating baobab trees, thus keeping them from extinction.

While **rats** and **mice** are probably not what brought you on safari, it's worth noting that over thirty different species are found in Zimbabwe and Botswana.

MUSIC

Zimbabwe resounds to music – traditional, reggae, soul, funk, rock, rap and rave. Loudspeakers bounce songs off the pavements outside the downtown record bars; night-time city streets echo with the discos of the central hotels; and transistor radios crackle with ZBC's Radio Two – even out at Nyaminyami on the remote banks of Lake Kariba.

The music is varied but dominated by one style today: **local jive**. After years of flirtation with Europe and the Americas, popular music has returned to its roots. Zimbabweans have discovered that their traditional rhythms are as danceable as any in the world – and as marketable. Zimbabwean musicians often add a touch of South African, Congolese or East African influence that makes the mix lively and truly African. The music scene is exciting for musicians and music lovers alike: many hotels in Harare, Bulawayo and other major centres have a band of sorts performing live six nights a week, while numerous restaurants, bars, beer halls, community halls and stadiums provide venues for nights and days of good live music. There is no shortage of talent; equipment, however, is not so plentiful.

And that's where the fairy tale of music falls apart in Zimbabwe. Not many bands can afford to maintain the sparse musical equipment that's available, so people with money buy the gear, then overwork musicians and underpay them. The record companies play it pretty much the same way, paying some of the lowest royalties

in the world. Inevitably, some enterprising groups and individuals do manage to escape this web of exploitation, but for the majority it's a hard way to earn a living. But it's also an age-old way of having a good time, telling a story, and quite romantic into the bargain, so the bands plug away, the joints are jumping, records are selling and music videos are being made.

TRADITIONAL MUSIC

Zimbabwe's most popular form of **traditional music** is based on the rhythms and melodies of the **mbira** or thumb piano – basically a small sound box, held between the hands, with a row of metal strips of different lengths plucked by the thumbs. Mbiras are used in traditional rituals and players are often spirit mediums, communicating with ancestral spirits through music. The music therefore tends to be hypnotic and repetitive, encouraging simple responses from the audience and inviting participation. Its melody lines run through trilling treble patterns while the bass bounces about in spongy steps reminiscent of a reggae bass line. Because mbiras are played with the thumbs only, single notes rather than chords carry the songs. Traditional accompaniment consists of voices (lead and response), *hosho* (shakers and gourds filled with dried seeds and so on) plus drums and other forms of percussion – such as wooden blocks clapped together, or stamping feet.

MBIRA GROUPS

There are hundreds if not thousands of **mbira groups** in the country, and if you're lucky you may wander into some village and find one jamming at the local meeting place. Traditional music and dance groups take part in all the festivals and celebrations, from Independence Day to the annual agricultural shows.

Few of these musicians make the transition into the world of mass electronic media unadulterated, but some, such as **Ephat Mjuru**, still play and record within a strictly traditional cultural format. There are now many women mbira players in Zimbabwe. One of them, **Amai Muchena**, who performs with Mhuri yekwa Muchena (the Muchena family), has been playing since she was five years old. She views the instrument as a sacred thing: "I don't play in beer halls, because the spirit is like a God to go

MUSIC VENUES

The wealth of Zimbabwean music is not matched by first-rate venues. Most are pretty basic, but can be fun for drinking beer, dancing and soaking in the music. The club scene is very fluid, but there are a handful of other **clubs** that have been around for a while and a number of new players, many of which operate for a while, close down and then reopen under a new name. The best you can do is check out the entertainment pages in the local daily newspapers. Most just give the name of the club and who is going to play – no time, no address, no information about the cover charge, no phone number. Where the time is given it's mostly "till late", which in Zimbabwe means just that. Zimbabweans are legendary for consuming copious amounts of beer and staying upright; the more they drink, the longer the band must play. Many music buffs like going to performances on Sunday afternoons. The crowds, although they do drink, don't get as rowdy as on Saturday night and a good time is had by all. In addition to nightclubs, there are often concerts at the Harare International Conference Centre and other halls.

Like clubs in other countries, Zimbabwean nightclubs also attract those whose agenda is not music: pickpockets abound. There are also plenty of would-be Romeos who will be very forward and persistent with women. Remember Zimbabwe has one of the world's highest AIDS infection rates: with one in four adults HIV positive, there is no margin for error.

FESTIVALS

As Zimbabwe's music scene becomes better known, a number of **festivals** have sprung up that offer music and other cultural events. The best of these is the **Harare International Festival of the Arts (Hifa)**, which takes place at the end of April and beginning of May. Hifa offers a fabulous array of local and international acts and is well worth a visit. Then there's the Zimbabwe Musicians Day in August/September when there are special concerts; the Chimanimani Arts Festival offers music in a beautiful mountain setting in April; the Zimbabwe National Jazz Festival features a great selection of jazz for a week in October; and in May there's the Inxusa Festival at Bulawayo's Amakhosi Theatre complex.

---

to if there are problems, but I can play in the *Sheraton* – there are no drunks there."

In contrast, **Beulah Djoko**, a quiet but serene woman who believes strongly in the message of her music, plays in beer halls in Chitungwiza: "Some people don't know mbira, like youths in bars, so I take mbira to them."

Stella Chiweshe is perhaps the best-known mbira player outside Zimbabwe – she's based half the time in Germany, and performs more often overseas than at home. She bends the boundaries by occasionally combining pure mbira or marimba (a wooden xylophone) with electric bass and a Western drum kit, underpinning her truly regal voice and presence with dreader-than-dread rhythms. She has provoked some criticism for her avant-garde mixture of sacred and commercial music – controversial in a country where music is so close to the spiritual centre of life. She certainly uses the mystique of the instrument in her shows to good effect, sometimes going into a trance on stage. The newest of Zimbabwe's "mbira queens" is **Chiwoniso Maraire**, the daughter of renowned traditional musician Dumi Maraire. In 1998 she burst onto the local scene with a haunting CD, *Ancient Voices*, that combined her traditional mbira playing with contemporary music. She won a prestigious award in France and a following in Zimbabwe.

Electric guitars slot easily into mbira music: turn up the treble, cuff the strings lightly, pluck sequences with a plectrum and a reasonable facsimile of the mbira sound is created. A lot of local jive revolves around this technique, the best-respected exponent of which is **Thomas Mapfumo**.

Probably the finest mbira-style guitarist was the late **Jonah Sithole** – a veteran of Mapfumo's band, who sometimes played with his own band. His over-tracked lead sequences on Mapfumo's *Shumba* album bear repeated listening.

MARIMBA GROUPS

The **marimba** (or African xylophone) is another widely used traditional instrument, usually made of wooden blocks, which can sometimes be arranged over resonators made from dried gourds. Visitors to the Victoria Falls are served up endless renditions of *Auld Lang Syne* and *When the Saints Go Marching in* played on marimbas, while trying to enjoy a quiet hotel lunch. Marimbas are not meant for such martial music – and it shows (painfully). For the real thing, check out Stella Chiweshe's *Ambuya* album, which uses marimba extensively and to brilliant effect.

Authentic **marimba groups** are also found throughout the country, often in schools and community centres. The best-known of these is the **St Peter's Kubatana** school band in Harare.

DANCE, DRUM AND CHORAL GROUPS

Dance, **drum** and **choral groups** exist all over Zimbabwe, too. The **National Dance Troupe**, based in Harare, performs at festivals and special venues. Many songs and dances were created by guerrillas in the 1970s in order to politicize the masses, and can be heard on the **Chimurenga Songs** series of LPs.

Interestingly, one of the former ZANLA choirmasters became the contemporary pop singer **Comrade Chinx**, who combines political lyrics with mbira and drum machines (see p.376). The **Tumbuka Dance Company** leaped into the dance scene in 1992 and immediately became the country's most vibrant contemporary dance group. Springing from a township outreach programme by the conservative (and virtually all-white) National Ballet, Tumbuka developed a distinctive dance style that mixes traditional African movements with contemporary styles in a fusion that is at once African, abstract and universal. Tumbuka's black male dancers have won raves in South Africa and Europe. Any Tumbuka performance in Zimbabwe is highly recommended.

BEST JIVE ALIVE

Most foreigners think **Jit Jive** is a generic name for contemporary Zimbabwean music – it's not. *Jit Jive* was coined by the internationally successful **Bhundu Boys** to identify their brand of upbeat jive. Local bands play music influenced by mbira, rhumba, zouk, reggae, salsa, kwela, rock, jazz and soul. What emerges is a complex but coherent mix, shot through with occasional pure strains of Hendrix or Charlie Parker. The combination of influences from South Africa, the Congo and East Africa means that Zimbabwean music is hard to pigeonhole. And there's something new every day.

THE BHUNDU BOYS

Jive kings who in the 1980s seemed on the verge of conquering half the Western world (starting with London), and catapulted Zimbabwean jive into the big league, the **Bhundu Boys** were for some years great heroes at home (when they *were* home), playing the very biggest venues. The music which brought them their fame was hard, fast and always melodic, rippling guitars on solid bass and drums beneath multiple vocal harmonies. Their full five-piece sound, regrettably overproduced and overdubbed on their British-recorded *Jit Jive*, was heard at its best on their first two LPs, *Bhundu Boys* and *Hupenyu Hwepasi*, as well as on singles such as "Simbimbimbo", "Chemedzevana", "Chimaninmani" – and stacks more. They have, however, in the last few years suffered a series of staggering blows, including the deaths of three successive bass guitarists, and an acrimonious break-up with charismatic front man Biggie Tembo, who later committed suicide.

ANDY BROWN AND THE STORM

Andy Brown started off as a member of Ilanga (see Comrade Chinx below) and, after a stint in South Africa in the 1990s, he came back to Zimbabwe and formed his own band. **The Storm** quickly became one of Zimbabwe's most exciting live acts. While the South African influence is sometimes obvious, Brown happens to be one of the most adventurous Zimbabwean musicians, taking traditional songs and transforming them into a heady brew of ragga, hip hop and searing rock guitar solos à la Carlos Santana. The Storm also features rising mbira star **Chiwoniso Maraire** on background vocals. In addition, **Potato**, a gruff-voiced rapper/deejay, performs a rap sequence that is very popular with local audiences.

SIMON "CHOPPER" CHIMBETU

"Chopper" Chimbetu is hugely popular in Zimbabwe. Doing time for car theft (Chimbetu claims he is innocent of the charges) in the mid-1990s did not diminish his popularity and everything he has released since coming out of prison in 1995 has turned to gold. In October 1999, *African Panorama Chapter 1* was certified platinum on the day it was released, after his record company shipped 38,000 cassettes (sales of 30,000 earn a platinum disc in Zimbabwe). It was also the month Chimbetu celebrated nineteen years in the music business. Chimbetu and his band, the **Orchestra Dendera Kings**, play music that is heavily influenced by East African guitar patterns and their appeal lies in their repetitive but infectious lead guitar underpinned by rapid-fire drumming and a solid bass.

COMRADE CHINX

An ex-ZANLA choirmaster with a foghorn voice, **Comrade Chinx** is a great entertainer, strutting the stage in combat fatigues, beret and sunshades, as well as an incisive social commentator. His early singles – "Zvikomborera", "Nerudo", "Magamba Ose" and others – experimented with sequencers and drum machines mixed into traditional mbira/chant.

Chinx also broke into synthesizer pop; his biggest-selling record *Roger Confirm*, about love through a short-wave radio, was made with the help of the group Ilanga. Even with six singles and an excellent LP behind him, however, he can't make music pay and works five days a week for the Zimbabwe Broadcasting Corporation. **Ilanga** themselves were a talented bunch of session musicians, responsible in their own right for a number of LPs, of which the first, entitled simply *Ilanga*, is the best. Shortly after a rather sour split from Chinx, they went their separate ways.

THE FOUR BROTHERS

The Four Brothers are a straightforward fast Shona band, lyrics above rippling guitar riffs, and strongly influenced by Mapfumo (one of them, Marshall Munhumuwe, who recently suffered a stroke, is Mapfumo's uncle, and learned the drums and singing from him). Their first hit, "Makorokoto" (Congratulations), was dedicated to the freedom fighters at Independence, and they became one of the top Zimbabwean bands during the 1980s. ·

They call themselves The Four Brothers so that they remain equal and no one brother becomes "big" – a fate that has split too many Zimbabwean bands apart in the past. And, despite their prolonged exposure in the West, they stick firmly to their traditional roots, claiming to have "learned from the lesson of the Bhundu Boys". They deliberately choose to record in Harare rather than the technically superior studios of the UK.

THE JAIROS JIRI SUNSHINE BAND

The **Jairos Jiri Sunshine Band** (or **JJB**) have been around for many years but have been relatively inactive in the past couple of years. The band originated in a welfare organization founded by Jairos Jiri to assist disabled Zimbabweans in their full integration into the local culture and economy. They too are no longer the force they used to be, following the imprisonment for rape of their former leader, the blind singer-songwriter Paul Matavaire. However, their back catalogue is extensive, and their songs are renowned for acute social observations: "Our music differs from overseas music. It has moral lessons telling you how to behave. Songs from overseas are only for entertainment." Look out for their 1980 single "Take Cover" (the story of a guerrilla group's journey through the war zone), "JJB Style" from the 1987 LP *Amatshakada*, their 12" versions of "Taurai Zvenyu" (remix), "Handirambi", and 7" singles such as "Muphurisa".

MUSIC AND FILM

Although Zimbabwe is well used as a location by foreign film-makers, the indigenous film industry is still small. However, when local films do appear they're invariably backed by lively soundtracks featuring Zimbabwean musicians.

Jit (Michael Raeburn, 1990) is set in the beer garden at the *Queens Hotel*, which at the time was the epicentre of Harare music, but now, sadly, is closed. A light-hearted look at Shona tradition and how some people abuse it in their greed, it includes a long string of performances by the top Zimbabwean bands, unfortunately all playback music rather than real performance, with Oliver Mtukudzi in a leading role. Mtukudzi also wrote the soundtrack of **The Winds of Change**, 1992.

The Spirit of the People (Simon Bright, 1990), named after Ephat Mjuru and his band, examines the links between traditional mbira music and modern electric jit. It demonstrates the transition from Ephat Mjuru playing traditional mbira music, with singing and dancing at the fireside in the rural areas, to the electrified stage sound of Thomas Mapfumo, in an urban commercial show with lights, electronic instruments and microphones, but still featuring unmistakable mbira strains. The sound quality is poor but the film gives a good overview of different music styles in Zimbabwe. Other Zimbabwean films, notably **Neria** and **Everyone's Child**, feature Zimbabwean music to good advantage.

ZEXIE MANATSA AND THE GREEN ARROWS

The **Green Arrows** played roots jive for about twenty years, but their upbeat mix of groaning lead vocals (**Zexie**), shrill vocal chorus and solid rhythm unit remained entertaining and danceable. In 1988 a car accident killed two band members and injured others, including Zexie. Fortunately Zexie and the band are back, but they have found religion and are known as the **Gospel Arrows**. Instead of playing nightclubs they play at church halls, but their music has retained its energy and drive.

THOMAS MAPFUMO AND THE BLACKS UNLIMITED

Thomas Mapfumo is a musical and political veteran, having been jailed some time before Independence for his protest songs and populist stance. A hypnotic-eyed, dreadlocked vocalist, he is backed by some of the finest musicians around – and was one of the first Zimbabwean musicians to achieve star status overseas. Some of his **chimurenga** songs were directly political, while others used the Shona tradition

For love with love only I walked in my father's land, in my mother's land, in my grandmother's land
You can see for yourself love is enough
Mugabe said this and so did the comrades
Only love love is enough

Comrade Chinx and Mazana Movement

of "deep proverbs" to conceal messages of resistance. Mapfumo's earlier LPs are classics: *Hokoyo, Gwindingwi Rine Shumba* and *Ndangariro* stand out, as do 12" singles like "Kariba" and "Corruption" (which as a consequence of its subject received little airplay). Mapfumo's reggae outings can, by comparison, be a little tedious, but, if you enjoy dread beat, listen to "Mugara Ndega" (12") and the *Chimurenga for Justice* LP. Don't miss a chance to see him live, at the one of the venues in central Harare.

OLIVER MTUKUDZI

Performing with his band the Black Spirits, **Oliver Mtukudzi** (Tuku) is the other major contender for the title of giant of Zimbabwean music, with a deep soul voice and a high-energy, well-choreographed stage act. He has produced nearly forty LPs, and in 1999 his tape and CD *Tuku Music* became an all-time listening favourite. Influences include mbaqanga and rhumba beats, but Mtukudzi is a strong traditionalist who remains committed to his roots.

As with all Zimbabwean musicians, Mtukudzi is very conscious of the importance of his lyrics. A deeply moral man, he sang the first AIDS song in a (subsequently banned) Zimbabwean film. His lyrics deal with tradition, and place an emphasis on discipline.

SOLOMON SKUZA AND THE KWENJANI BAND

In the same vein as Oliver Mtukudzi, both physically and musically, the late **Solomon**

WOMEN MUSICIANS

I have been going around looking for girls but when I find one she can't come to the stage and perform because she's scared of what people will say about her.

Oliver Mtukudzi

The conservatism and chauvinism of Zimbabwean society has meant that women musicians have had a difficult time, and some brilliant musicians are unable to make their way. In a society that looked down upon musicians, male or female, attitudes towards women musicians are changing slowly. Dimunitive but dynamic **Busi Ncube**, formerly with Ilanga, has been in the music business for sixteen years, the last nine as leader of the Rain Band. "I do get quite a lot of respect from fellow musicians and record companies are also starting to treat me with respect." The public, according to Ncube, remains ambivalent: "There are still a lot of people who think a woman has no business being a musician, they think you must be in the kitchen at home or in an office making tea for a male boss." Emerging from the shadows of providing background vocals, where the majority of women are condemned, has meant all the decision-making is on her shoulders. That includes dealing with the four male members of her seven-member band. "I just use my charm when we have a problem." Her

charm and diplomacy seem to have served her well, because during the nine years she has led the Rain Band, only two members have left. "The bass player went to Botswana and another guy died," she said.

Her comments are frequently echoed by other women musicians, many of whom feel frustrated by their lack of freedom. Few women make decisions within their band, often finding that the band will not release them to perform alone, and they tend to get a poor deal with money and recording rights. Sexual harassment by band managers and even the audience is also a problem.

In 1990, however, a Women Musicians' Advisory Group was set up. Amongst its members are the top female Zimbabwean musicians: Stella Chiweshe, Busi Ncube, Doreen Ncube, Virginia Jangano (Harare Mambos), Amai Muchena and Beulah Djoko. The group aims to educate women about their rights and advise on discrimination. As Stella Chiweshe puts it, "we are slow but we are coming up – you will see us.

Skuza had a classic blues/soul crooner's quality. He and his band came from Bulawayo. Their LP *Zihlangene* is varied and accomplished, and they issued wonderful singles such as "Iquino Aliso", "Jennifer" and "Sobukhu".

LEONARD ZHAKATA

Leonard Zhakata is one of the fastest-rising Zimbabwean artists. His allure is his focus on topical issues and fine use of lyrics, delivered in a distinctive plaintive wail. But, like the Congolese soukous from whom he draws inspiration, he will transform a song midway through by letting loose those long, hard-to-resist guitar solos that the Congolese genre is famous for. On stage he cuts a colourful figure in tailormade, shimmering iridescent outfits, which recall the 1970s disco era.

PROPONENTS OF ELECTRIC MBIRA

Ephat Mjuru and The Spirit of the People are one of the best electric mbira groups around. Their music borders on the chimurenga beat, as

well as a variety of other influences: Afro-jazz, soca and reggae. **Pengaudozoke**, a very dancey new band with a fast rhythm borrowing from rhumba as well as chanting traditions, is Oliver Mtukudzi's favourite group – "people thought they wouldn't go far but I could sense they had a unique touch in their music. They are different from the others."

Vadzimba adopt a similar approach to Thomas Mapfumo – drawing from traditional songs and treating them with a mbira-guitar translated beat – though with less success. At one time Thomas threatened to sue them for infringement of copyright, but, as Vadzimba member Farai put it, "Our music is not Thomas's music – just as reggae is not only Bob Marley. The traditional tunes belong to everyone."

The powerfully voiced **Robson Banda**, who plays instantly infectious music with **The New Black Eagles**, has also been influenced by Mapfumo's electric mbira music, as well as strains of South African mbaqanga and rhumba beats.

She's the girl I was telling you about
Vimbai is a beautiful girl
A heart snatcher – God's masterpiece
It's not only my idea; many praise her
Her eyes reflect real tenderness
Vimbai has a warm heart, warm as a
    winter blanket
Her neck is as smooth as the King's
    horse
She is a nice girl

The Four Brothers

RHUMBA

The Zairean-born **Lumbumbashi Stars** claim to be "the rhumba kings of Zimbabwe" and they certainly have the brass to prove it, bopping till they drop in fine rhumba style, Ray-Bans and all. Now resident in Zimbabwe (at the whim of the Ministry of Home Affairs), they blast away with heart-warming good vibes.

JOHN CHIBADURA

John Chibadura, backed by the Tembo Brothers, has been one of the biggest-selling artists in recent years. Shy, private, introverted, and posing as an "anti-star", he has had amazing success, winning the following of young Zimbabweans with the result that all records routinely turn gold. His music combines fast-moving Zimbabwean dance music and rhumba. His lyrics are a grim reflection of social conditions, but, with typical Zimbabwean stoicism, are sung over a defiantly happy beat.

DEVERA NGWENA JAZZ BAND

Long-standing local top-sellers, **Devera Ngwena** play under contract to one of Zimbabwe's big mines. Their music is mainly rhumba with occasional infusions. Since they're based outside the cities it's difficult to catch them live. They tend to play larger venues. Their numerous records are all just called *Devera Ngwena Jazz Band*, and are numbered sequentially.

JAZZ AND THE SOUTH AFRICAN INFLUENCE

Jazz groups are coming up fast in Zimbabwe, particularly in Bulawayo, where the close proximity of South Africa can be clearly heard in the music. **Dorothy Masuka** ("Auntie"), the "mama" of jazz from Bulawayo with a musical career that spans over forty years, sang with Miriam Makeba and Hugh Masekela in South Africa in her early days, later fleeing to London to escape Ian Smith's Rhodesia, and then campaigning for Zimbabwe all over Southern Africa.

Like many Bulawayan musicians, she draws a lot on South African influences, playing a mixture of jazz swing and local melodies in a style known as **marabi**. She is now living and performing in South Africa, a far more lucrative market, but occasionally returns to Zimbabwe.

Two notable Zimbabwean jazz groups are **Mhepo** and **Savannah Cruise.** Both bands play music that is a mix of South African township jazz, American old-style jazz with some Zimbabwean elements thrown in. Both bands play good lively gigs.

BLACK UMFOLOSI

Black Umfolosi, an a cappella group of singers and dancers from Bulawayo, are an amazing sight live, with their precise and acrobatic singing and dancing to a strong Zulu beat. They even perform the rarely seen South African miners' gumboot dance, and are Zimbabwe's answer to South Africa's Ladysmith Black Mambazo.

• *Written by Michael Philips and Judy Kendall; updated by ish Mafundikwa, a freelance Zimbabwean journalist and Radio One DJ. His shows include* Africa International, *broadcast on Saturday afternoons.*

ESSENTIAL LISTENING: A DISCOGRAPHY

BANDS

Bhundu Boys
Shabini AFRILP02 – at their best
Hupenyu Hwepasi Gramma
True Jit WX 129 (1987) (without Biggie)
Absolute Jit AFRILP09 (1990)
Live at King Tut's Wah Wah Hut 09
Black Umfolosi
Unity WCB020
(featured on *Boiling Point – Musicians from Hot Countries* WCB022)
John Chibadura and the Tembo Brothers
The Essential CSLP5002
More of the Essential CSLP5004
Simon "Chopper" Chimbetu
Survival L4KSALP 173
Zuwa Raenda DMCLP001
Pachipamwe DALP900
Lullabye KSALP177
African Panorama Chapter 1
James Chimombe and the Ocean City Band
Munakandafa ZIL218
Stella Chiweshe
Ambuya ZMC ORB029
Comrade Chinx
Ngorimba (with Ilanga) ZMC
The Four Brothers
Bros COOK023
Makorokoto COOKC014
Rudo Chete KSLP124
Rugare KSLP111
Ilanga
Ilanga ILGLP2
Lovemore Majaivana
Istimela
Amandla! ZIM003
Thomas Mapfumo
Hokoyo (Thomas Mapfumo and the Acid Band), Gramma
Gwindingwi Rine Shumba Gramma

Shumba EWV22 (compilation of early work)
Chimurenga Singles (1976–1980) ELP 2004
Greatest Hits ASLP5001
Zimbabwe-Mozambique TML100
Corruption MLP51059
Chamunorwa M1075
Chimurenga 1998
Lion of Zimbabwe L44TML110
Dorothy Masuka
Pata Pata Mango Island Records
Paul Matavaire and the Jairos Jiri Sunshine Band
Amatshakada
Take Cover! Various Artists AFRILP01
Ephat Mjuru
Ndiani Waunoda Baba Namai
(*The Spirit of the People*) ZML1003
Oliver Mtukudzi
1980 Afrika ZMC
Sugar Pie CSLP5001
Psss Psss Hallo CSLP5005
Africa TEL2015
Live at Sakubva RTP TKLP4
Neria RTP TKLP7
Svovi Yangu RTP TKLP19
Tuku Music OMCD001
Devera Ngwena
(In Zimbabwe they have produced a series of numbered LPs, all titled *Devera Ngwena Jazz Band*)
Taxi Driver KK01
The Nyami Nyami Sounds
Kwira Mudenga ZML 1030
The Pied Pipers
People of the World Unite WIZ 5000
Southern Freeway
Southern Freeway RTP (second album includes compositions from other members)
Leonard Zhakata
Maruva Enyika CKLZ1/KLZ1
Greatest Hits CDKLZ5

COMPILATIONS

Virgin Records Zimbabwe Frontline 88 EWV9. Includes Thomas Mapfumo, Four Brothers, Jonah Moyo and Devera Ngwena, Zexie Manatsa, Oliver Mtukudzi, Susan Mapfumo and Robson Banda.
Spirit of the Eagle Zimbabwe Frontline Vol. 2 EWV 18. Includes Robson Banda, Thomas Mapfumo, The Four Brothers, Nyami Nyami Sounds.
Under African Skies REQ 745. Includes the Bhundu Boys, Comrade Chinx, Ilanga and

Lovemore Majaivana.
Zimbabwe Frontline Vol. 3 – Roots Rock Guitar Party STEW40CD. Includes John Chibadura, the Tembo Brothers, Muddy Face, The Four Brothers, Max Mapfumo and Dopiro Band and Zimbabwe Chachacha Kings. *Mahube* – a great compendium of jazz stars from throughout Southern Africa, including Oliver Mtukudzi, Stevie Dyer ex of Southern Freeway and many other prominent South African musicians.

WRITING FROM ZIMBABWE

Zimbabwe has long possessed a rich oral literature, but until the 1890s Shona and Ndebele were not written, and although before Independence there may have been blacks ready to bare their souls about the experience of being colonized, the printing presses were in white hands. Black writers, therefore, had limited possibilities for publication. All manuscripts were vetted by the Rhodesia Literature Bureau, which allowed for more than direct government censorship: through its workshops, pamphlets and advice to authors, it forced the creative production of several decades through particular, restricted channels. Anything political was, naturally, quite out of the question.

During the **liberation struggle**, some fiction and its authors found their way to Britain and acclaim. Writers such as **Dambudzo Marechera** appeared in print outside the country. But at home, throughout the war, non-fiction and music proved more effective voices than literature, for the story that had, with increasing urgency, to be told.

With **Independence** in 1980, however, poets came home from foreign universities and from the guerrilla camps. From the offices, factories and classrooms people came together in workshops and a writers' union was formed.

I scratched around in the rubbish dump with other kids, looking for comics, magazines, books, broken toys, anything that could help us kids pass the time in the ghetto . . . You could say my very first books were the books which the rabidly racist Rusape whites were reading at the time.

I took to the English language like a duck takes to water. I was therefore a keen accomplice and student in my own mental colonization . . . For a black writer, the language is very racist: you have to have harrowing fights and hair-raising panga duels with it before you can make it do all you want it to do.

Dambudzo Marechera, **Dambudzo Marechera 1952–1987** (Baobab Books, Harare 1988).

The liberation struggle was naturally enough a major concern for most writers, combined with an optimism for the new order. Creative opportunities seemed unlimited.

Two decades on, despite the occasional reappearance of government censorship, the result is a stimulating mixture: fine, crafted works from masters such as **Charles Mungoshi** are published alongside fast, trashy township **gangster stories**; **war novels** alongside **love poems**; plus the first stabs at **satire** in a new black state. Perhaps most fascinating are the **autobiographies** out of the silenced past – prison life, existence on farms, on the front line, behind guns, or simply picking veld flowers – from a society that was divided and remains so. These are still early days in Zimbabwe's search for its voice. Expect everything, especially surprises.

CHARLES MUNGOSHI

Charles Mungoshi is arguably the finest voice of pre-Independence black despair. His characters face each other across a desolate silence that language cannot bridge – a historical or human condition, depending on your reading. "Words are handles made to the smith's fancy and are liable to break under stress," he wrote. "They are too much fat on the hard unbreaking sinews of life."

The story below is from the Coming of the Dry Season – not overtly a political work, but nevertheless banned by the Smith regime.

THE LIFT

When they were tired of going round the factories and shops in search of jobs, the boys went to the tall buildings at the heart of the city for their daily ride in the lifts. It was the only fun they had and it made them forget a little their burning bellies and tired feet.

There were lots of clouds flung about the sky like cotton balls in a field. It was rather chilly and the boys felt sharply the pleasant warmth of the sun when it came out of the clouds, and both of them unconsciously looked up irritably when it darted behind another cloud.

At present, their minds, usually the colour of the changing streets and just as desolate, were fixed on the ride in the lifts.

Pearl Assurance Building, one of the tallest buildings in the city, had a guard at the wide entrance.

'Can I help you?' the guard asked.

'We would like to go up.'

'Floor?'

'Tenth.'

'What for?'

The boys looked at each other and hazarded an answer.

'We are doing correspondence courses.'

The guard looked at them suspiciously and then dismissed them with a flick of the hand.

'You are not allowed up there.'

The boys looked at the guard as if they had not heard him. Then their eyes turned to gaze at the wall above the lift where numbers went on and off in amber to show the lift coming down.

'There has been much stealing up there lately,' the guard said.

'We are not thieves.'

The guard's eyes swept over their heads and he dismissed them from his attention.

'Go away, boys.'

The boys turned to go. They passed two European boys of their own age. Looking back, the boys saw the guard take off his cap to the Europeans who did not answer him and quickly entered the lift and disappeared.

'Why did you allow those two to go up?'

'*You* are not allowed up there.'

The boys went out onto the street. It was not yet noon and they had nowhere to go and nothing to do to kill the time until night when they would go home to sleep.

'Wish I had kept that shilling after all,' one of them, thinner than the other, said.

'We had to have something to eat.'

'All the same, we could have used it now. It's so much nicer to have something to eat when you don't have anything to do.'

They were moving toward Salisbury Park. They had not talked of the park yet both of them knew that that was the only place left to go and rest.

'I was a fool to use that shilling,' the thin one said again.

His friend didn't answer because he always felt irritated by his companion's mourning for things that could have been. He felt like shouting at him to stop it but he controlled himself. He didn't care for words when he was tired. They made him even more tired than he really was.

'This is unbearable,' the thin one said once more.

But his friend kept quiet. He was hungry and there was nowhere to get money from. The thin one looked at him, knew that he would be asked why he was looking at him, and kept quiet, knowing that this would only lead to a quarrel. But all the same, it could have been so much better if his friend would talk, then he wouldn't have to think and feel that he was not wanted, so lonely and so hopeless. The park was almost deserted except for two or three people lying on the forbidden grass, asleep or pretending to be asleep.

The thin one said, 'They are going to start trouble with the authorities.'

His friend answered him this time. 'It's silly to forbid people from lying on the grass. What is it there for?'

'It's the rules.'

'To hell with the rules.'

They found a bench under some bamboos and sat down. Immediately they had sat down, the talkative one said, 'They are not allowed to lie on the grass.'

'You have said that already.'

The thin boy looked at his friend and said nothing more. His friend leaned back on the bench and closed his eyes, pretending to go to sleep but the other one knew that this was the cue for him to keep quiet. Both of them were under a strain. They wanted to be somewhere else; the swimming pool, the beer hall – anywhere where there were people and fun and a chance to forget themselves. But there was only the wide empty park and themselves.

The sleepless one looked around the park. He tried to steady his thoughts on the flowers and the trees and the light in the leaves of the trees on the grass and the tall buildings of the city beyond the trees and the immense space of sky above the city, but there was nowhere his thoughts could rest and he was forced to come back to himself.

But he was tired of looking into himself, of asking himself why he was like this and not like that, tired of examining himself, of finding faults with himself, tired of judging and condemning himself. He was tired of the whole circling process of his thoughts, so tired that he wanted movement – any movement, to feel that he was going somewhere and not just stationary. The feeling of doing nothing, of being nothing, oppressed and frightened him. He must talk at least: that gave him a sense of direction, a feeling of really moving towards something. But his friend would not talk.

'That guard was just a nuisance. We wanted nothing except a ride. Only one ride in the lift.'

His friend stirred impatiently and said, 'Perhaps he was right. Lift rides are so short anyway.'

'But sometimes you get off a lift and find the sun has set.'

'Why don't you try to get some sleep? The sun would set faster.'

'I can't sleep during the day.'

'Then shut up please and let me sleep.'

The thin boy watched his friend as he moved towards the further end of the bench after these words. He moved towards the other end and closed his eyes. But he opened them again, worried about the space between them and the empty space that had opened up in him on closing his eyes.

'Can't we do something?' he asked.

Without a word, his friend rose and walked away to another bench and sat down, staring through the trees across the park toward the city. The thin one stayed in his place and struggled to keep himself seated, afraid to stand up and follow his friend, afraid to make even the smallest movement with his body that he knew before he had made it would fall into the pattern of yesterday, today and tomorrow.

So he tried to hurry the night when the darkness would hold his thoughts together and he wouldn't be worried by the distance between their two benches, the space that isolated them; so that looking at the two of them from afar, he saw that they were not friends. Not quite friends.

Reproduced, with permission, from **Coming of the Dry Season** (Zimbabwe Publishing House, Harare 1981).

FREEDOM T.V. NYAMUBAYA

Writers published after Independence are invariably involved in the debate as to whether a writer should be primarily concerned with burning political issues, or with "art". The poet Freedom T.V. Nyamubaya fought with ZANLA in the Second Chimurenga. Military comparisons in her work are irresistible: the poems are forceful, direct and bullet-like. Despite her political objectives, her poems remain funny, perceptive and tender.

The poem below is the opening piece of her first collection, On the Road Again, which establishes Comrade Freedom's position in the argument for a literature of commitment:

> Now that I have put my gun down
> For almost obvious reasons
> The enemy still is here invisible
> My barrel has no definite target
>   now
> Let my hands work –
> My mouth sing –
> My pencil write –
> About the same things my bullet
>   aimed at.

Reproduced, with permission, from **On the Road Again** (Zimbabwe Publishing House, Harare 1986).

CHENGERAI HOVE

Chengerai Hove, too, calls for engaged, progressive writing: authors who identify with the lives and struggles of the people. The following extract from his Noma Award-winning novel Bones (interestingly, narrated by a woman) addresses, as do his poems, the issues and experiences of the Independence War.

FROM BONES

Do you know Chisaga? He is a good man, but his greed for women is a bit too much. He came to me and pleaded that he will do anything if he can sleep with me. I said that was also my idea for a long time. But since he was the first to mention it, I want him to do something before he can sleep with me. I said he should steal some money for me from Manyepo's safe in the house where he cooks for him every day. Since Manyepo trusts him so much, he will not think it is him. Manyepo will think of other people who have been caught stealing mangoes, but not Chisaga. So Chisaga has stolen the money for me. He expects to sleep with me when he is not working, one of these days. But he will have nobody to sleep with because I knew what I was doing. Do not open your mouth so much, child. The things men will do to satisfy the desire of their things are very surprising. Men will kill their own mothers if they stop them from satisfying the desire of their things. They can dig a hole through a mountain if you tell them you will be waiting the other side of the hill to give them your thing. Men are like children, my mother used to say. They rule everything, like children. Do they not say children are like kings? You let them play with fire, but you always keep looking. You always keep looking at them so that they do not burn their fingers. This is what we do all the time. Look and watch over them. If it were not for men, do you think your grandfather would have died in places where they could not return his body for burial? Did your mother not say that your grandfather died fighting a war started by a man called Hikila who wanted to rule the whole earth? Think of that, a man who does not even know how to cook for himself wants to rule the whole earth. That is what men are like. They look after their things erect in front of them and think they are kings. They do not know that it is just desire shooting out of them, nothing else. So child, you do what you can with the weaknesses of men, but do not let them play with your body. It is your last property, you will die with it. So do not let people waste it like any rubbish they pick up in the village rubbish heap. I know this because my mouth has eaten medicines which even a dog would vomit. My ear has heard things even a witch would faint to hear . . .

*****

The fighters leave him to go home without making any promises. Then after a few days of walking and seeing with their own eyes the poverty of the people, they decide they cannot wait much longer. The people did not have much to give them. If the fighters do not feed, Marita says, they will stop fighting and go working in the fields. But they had seen so much poverty that it became harsh to their eyes. Let us leave, they said to each other. Let us look for better areas where there are fields that can give something to the farmers. Our hopes will die if we continue to see children dying every day and the cattle licking the soil as if it contains salt. We have learnt that we must free our people from poverty. Poverty is worse than war, they say. You can stop war through talking. You can't stop poverty through talking.

So we must fight with all we have so that our people cannot continue to be buried in this ant-hill of poverty.

Reproduced with permission, from **Bones** (Baobab Books, Harare 1988).

DAMBUDZO MARECHERA

Not all Zimbabwe's literary figures share Hove's and Nyamubaya's view of the artist's role. Most flamboyant and controversial among the dissenting was Dambudzo Marechera, well-known outside Zimbabwe since his novella and short stories, House of Hunger, won the Guardian Fiction Prize.

Before his death in 1987 at the age of 35, Marechera was the enfant terrible of Zimbabwean letters. Genius or madman – public opinion remains undecided, although he had become a minor cult figure by the time of his death. Some refuse to label him an "African writer" – and they include Marechera himself: "I would question anyone calling me an African writer. Either you are a writer or you are not. If you are a writer for a specific nation or a specific race, then fuck you."

IDENTIFY THE IDENTITY PARADE

I am the luggage no one will claim;
The out-of-place turd all deny
Responsibility;
The incredulous sneer all tuck away
  beneath bland smiles;
The loud fart all silently agree never
  happened;
The sheer bad breath you politely confront
  with mouthwashed platitudes: 'After all,
  it's POETRY.'
I am the rat every cat secretly admires;
The cat every dog secretly fears;
The pervert every honest citizen surprises
  in his own mirror: POET.

THE FEAR AND LOATHING OUT OF HARARE

What is it about Harare . . .?
Is it the nightlife, the hotels,
the nightclubs? Or the melancholy
solitary walk back to the flat
when a tawny, almost rubescent dawn

is signalling from within the dark
confines of another pent-up night? For four
years I had not ventured out of the City –
the rest of the country only existed in news
reports about dissidents,
co-operatives, and Blair toilets,
not to mention Binga
where it was reported that the main meal
of each drought-stricken day was a tray of
fried grass.

THE TREES OF THE DAY

Trees too tired to carry the burden
Of leaf and bud, of bird and bough
Too harassed by the rigours of
    unemployment
The drought-glare of high rents
And the spiralling cost of water and
    mealie-meal
Trees shrivelled into abortion by the forest
    fires
Of dumped political policies
Trees whose Kachasu-veined twig-fingers
Can no longer clench into the people's fist
But wearily wipe dripping noses, wearily
    wave away
The fly-ridden promises issuing out of the
    public Lavatory
Trees under which, hungry and homeless
I emerge from seed to drill a single
    root into the
Salt stone soils
The effort a scream of despair.

Reproduced, with permission, from **Dambudzo
Marechera 1952–1987** (Baobab Books, Harare
1988).

TSITSI DANGAREMBGA

**Tsitsi Dangarembga is a formidable talent
from the same generation as Marechera:
her first novel, Nervous Conditions,
excerpted below, won the 1989
Commonwealth Literature Prize. The book
is a triumph for women's writing as well as
for Zimbabwean literature. Its opening
sentence, "I was not sorry when my brother died", signals its defiance of what is
acceptable in a dutiful daughter in its tale
of a young black woman growing up in
Rhodesia. This extract is about the return
of the young narrator's uncle, Babamukuru,
from university in Britain.**

FROM NERVOUS CONDITIONS

Babamukuru came home in cavalcade of motor
vehicles, sighted four miles away on the main
road by three jubilant pairs of eyes. Netsai
I and little Shupikai, whose mother was one of
the relatives gathered to celebrate the occasion of Babamukuru's return, watched as the
cavalcade progressed, distressingly slowly,
now disappearing behind clumps of trees, now
reappearing hours later, or so it seemed, no
more than a few hundred yards nearer. The vigil
lasted twenty minutes. We watched from a
rock on the hill behind the homestead until the
carts disappeared for the last time into the
home-stretch. Then we went wild. We slid off
our rock, skinning elbows and knees on the
way, scrambled oblivious through bushes that
scratched our legs, dashed out on to the road
and ran on. 'Ba-ba-mu-ku-ru! Ba-ba-mu-ku-ru!'
we chanted, running and jumping and waving
our skinny arms about all at the same time,
skirts swirling, bottoms jutting as we capered.
Shupikai, several yards behind, started to cry,
still tottering along and chanting through her
sobs, because we had left her behind and
because she was excited. Her crisis was so
inconvenient. I considered ignoring her, which
could not be done. Dashing back, I snatched her
up to continue the mad welcome with her
perched on my hip.

My aunt Gladys, the one who is my father's
womb-sister, older than him but younger than
Babamukuru, came first, her husband behind the
wheel of a gallant if rickety old Austin. They
hooted long and loud. We waved and shouted
and danced. Then came Babamukuru, his car
large and impressive, all sparkling metal and
polished dark green. It was too much for me. I
could have clambered on to the bonnet but, with
Shupi in my arms, had to be content with a song:
'Mauya, mauya. Mauya, Babamukuru!' Netsai
picked up the melody. Our vocal cords vibrating
through wide arcs, we made an unbelievable
racket. Singing and advancing we ushered
Babamukuru on to the homestead, hardly noticing Babamunini Thomas, who brought up the
rear, not noticing Maini Patience, who was with
him, at all.

Slowly the cavalcade progressed towards
the yard, which by now was full of rejoicing relatives. My father jumped out of Babamukuru's
car and, brandishing a staff like a victory spear,
bounded over the bumpy road, leaping into the

air and landing on one knee, to get up and leap again and pose like a warrior inflicting a death wound. '*Hezvo!*' he cried 'Do you see him? Our returning prince. Do you see him? Observe him well. He has returned. Our father and benefactor has returned appeased, having devoured English letters with a ferocious appetite! Did you think degrees were indigestible? If so, look at my brother. He has digested them! If you want to see an educated man, look at my brother, big brother to us all!' The spear aimed high and low, thrust to the right, to the left. All was conquered.

The cars rolled to a stop beneath the mango trees. Tete Gladys disembarked with difficulty, with false starts and strenuous breathing; because she was so large, it was not altogether clear how she had managed to insert herself into the car in the first place. But her mass was not frivolous. It had a ponderous presence which rendered any situation, even her attempts to remove herself from her car, weighty and serious. We did not giggle, did not think of it.

On her feet at last, Tete straightened herself, planted herself firmly, feet astride, in the dust. Clenched fists settling on hips, elbows jutting aggressively, she defied any contradiction of my father's eulogy. 'Do you hear?' she demanded, 'what Jeremiah is saying? If you have not heard, listen well. It is the truth he is speaking! Truly our prince has returned today! Full of knowledge. Knowledge that will benefit us all! Pururu.u!' she ululated, shuffling with small gracious jumps to embrace my mother. 'Pururuu!' They ululated. 'He has returned. Our prince has returned!'

Babamukuru stepped out of his car, paused behind its open door, removed his hat to smile graciously, joyfully, at us all. Indeed, my Babamukuru had returned. I saw him only for a moment. The next minute we were drowned in a sea of bodies belonging to uncles, aunts and nephews; grandmothers, grandfathers and nieces; brothers and sisters of the womb and not of the womb. The clan had gathered to welcome its returning hero. His hand was shaken, his head was rubbed, his legs were embraced. I was there too, wanting to touch Babamukuru, to talk, to tell him I was glad that he had returned. Babamukuru made his fair-sized form as expansive as possible, holding his arms out and bending low so that we all could be embraced, could embrace him. He was happy. He was smiling.

'Yes, yes,' he kept saying. 'It is good, it is good.' We moved, dancing and ululating and kicking up a fine dust-storm from our stamping feet, to the house.

Babamukuru stepped inside, followed by a retinue of grandfathers, uncles and brothers. Various paternal aunts, who could join them by virtue of their patriarchal status and were not too shy to do so, mingled with men. Behind them danced female relatives of the lower strata. Maiguru entered last and alone, except for her two children, smiling quietly and inconspicuously. Dressed in flat brown shoes and a pleated polyester dress very much like the one Babamukuru bought for my mother the Christmas before he left, she did not look as though she had been to England. My cousin Nyasha, pretty bright Nyasha, on the other hand, obviously had. There was no other explanation for the tiny little dress she wore, hardly enough of it to cover her thighs. She was self-conscious though, constantly clasping her hands behind her buttocks to prevent her dress from riding up, and observing everybody through veiled vigilant eyes to see what we were thinking. Catching me examining her, she smiled slightly and shrugged, 'I shouldn't have worn it,' her eyes seemed to say. Unfortunately, she had worn it. I could not condone her lack of decorum. I would not give my approval. I turned away.

Reproduced, with permission, from **Nervous Conditions** (The Women's Press, London/Zimbabwe Publishing House, Harare 1988).

BRUCE MOORE-KING

The work of a new white writer, Bruce Moore-King, White Man Black War has had a considerable impact within Zimbabwe and abroad. A former soldier in one of Rhodesia's crack regiments, Moore-King questions the society and the interests he fought for and for which so many died, interspersing military experiences of terrible brutality, recounted in unflinching deadpan style, with philosophical deliberations.

FROM WHITE MAN BLACK WAR

A man hangs spreadeagled, handcuffed to a steel bed-frame. Outside the small, pre-fabricated rondavel, the land is wet and soaked, a quagmire of mud, farm roads turned into river beds. Half a mile from the rondavel an army truck stands buried to the axles in clay. Twenty yards from the rondavel stands the main ranch house. Over the gate leading into the garden a sign reads "Makorski River Ranch — Manager". In the garden around the rondavel, bedraggled rose bushes, thick clumps of bougainvillea, a group of tattered banana trees.

The bed-frame is standing propped against the interior of the rondavel, almost vertical. The man is naked, handcuffs tight at each hand and each ankle, stretching him. His head is lolling, face gazing blindly down at his feet, but shortly the frame will be rotated and he will hang upside-down.

Around the ranch house a maze of trenches and barbed wire meanders, dotted with green canvas tents and heavily covered ammunition pits. There are numerous mortar craters, the freshest having arrived the night before. The ranch manager and his wife have elected to stay, a show of deliberate defiance, and the man on the bed-frame is their boss boy, they've known him for nine years.

There are three elements of the security forces present on the ranch, a company of territorials on call up, a platoon of special police constabulary — black men in blue overalls — under the command of an eighteen-year-old white policeman, and the troop of Grey's Scouts that have been helicoptered in because of the deteriorating situation on the ranch.

There are two men in the rondavel with the prisoner, an SB officer, and the commander of the Grey's troop. The latter is a short, very powerfully built man in his early forties, a professional soldier, ex-British SAS, ex-Foreign Legion, former Warrant Officer in the Rhodesian SAS. The two are sitting on camp stools, drinking Cokes.

The special police constables are equipped with old .303s, but their commander has taken their magazines away from them, as they have developed a tendency to fire somewhat erratically when the base comes under mortar attack. The night before the Grey's commander had found himself under fire from two directions, as the enemy fired into the base, and the constables fired out from the centre, with the troops in the middle.

The man on the bed-frame groans, and the troop commander speaks: "Give us a hand." Together they rotate the bed-frame until the man is hanging upside-down. The troop commander, Kelly, picks up a length of thick, high-pressure compressor hose and hits the prisoner across the thighs and testicles with it. The prisoner screams.

"I thought that would wake you up, you sonofabitch!".

A corporal enters, muddy and wet. He glances at the two men, nods to the SB officer, then sits down, propping his rifle beside him. He opens a Coke, picks up a *Playboy*, and begins reading it.

*****

I do not think my memories of the reality of the society we held before the war are incorrect.

I can understand, now, why our countrymen took up arms against us. And if these actions and attitudes and forms of selective ignorance displayed by my tribe once caused blood and fire to spread across the land called Rhodesia, what will these same actions and attitudes and forms of selective ignorance produce in this land called Zimbabwe?

Must my tribe reinforce their Creed of racial superiority by denying these, the victors of the war, the basic humanness of the ability to Anger?

Reproduced, with permission, from **White Man Black War** (Baobab Books, Harare 1988).

BOOKS

Reading up on Zimbabwe before you go poses few problems, and there's no need to take everything with you, either – the country has a flourishing high-quality domestic publishing industry producing both fiction and non-fiction. The best-covered topics, not unexpectedly, are colonization, the two chimurengas (liberation struggles), and post-Independence disillusion, but you'll find material on most subjects. Zimbabwe-produced books aren't always easy to get hold of outside the country, but specialist African/Third World bookshops sometimes stock them, and will certainly be able to order them. The biggest publishing concerns are Zimbabwe Publishing House (ZPH), Baobab Books and Mambo Press.

Botswana is another story, with no real indigenous book publishing apart from branches of big British companies involved in educational books. Several glossy tomes are, however, published outside the country, covering natural history and landscape.

ZIMBABWE'S HISTORY

A number of good school texts give a quick and easy **overview** of Zimbabwe's history. They include:

David Beach *Zimbabwe: A New History for Primary Schools* (College Press, Harare 1982). Account by one of the country's leading historians, giving reliable, readable and condensed coverage of 15,000 years of history.

Peter Garlake and Andre Procter *People Making History* (2 vols; ZPH, Harare 1985). The first volume covers pre-colonial history, the second the twentieth century. Aimed at secondary schools, they go into more depth than Beach's *Zimbabwe*, with considerable emphasis on class analysis.

PRE-CHIMURENGA

David Beach *The Shona and Zimbabwe 900–1850: An Outline of Shona History* (Mambo Press, Gweru 1980). The history of the Shona groupings in their heyday and of events on the Zimbabwean plateau before the arrival of the Ndebele and their conquests in the southwest.

David Beach *War and Politics in Zimbabwe 1840–1900* (Mambo Press, 1986). A kind of sequel to the above, covering the crumbling at the edges of Shona domination of the region with the arrival of Nguni raiders and finally the *coup de grâce* of British colonial conquest.

Stanlake Samkange *On Trial for My Country* (Heinemann African Writers Series, Oxford 1967). Set up as two trials, this classic dramatized account has Rhodes and Lobengula called in the afterlife to account for their conduct in the events leading up to the BSAC's colonization of Matabeleland.

Elizabeth Schmidt *Peasants, Traders and Wives: Shona Women in the History of Zimbabwe, 1870–1939* (James Currey, London 1992). Fascinating documentation of the lives of women in Southern Rhodesia.

Charles van Onselen *Chibaro: African Mine Labour in Southern Rhodesia 1900–1933* (Pluto, London 1976). Don't be put off by the dry, academic-sounding title. *Chibaro* means "forced or slave labour", and in van Onselen's inimitable way this lively book reveals exactly how the colonial system's tentacles reached into workers' everyday lives, and details their response to it.

THE SECOND CHIMURENGA

The **Second Chimurenga** was a significant formative phase in the birth of independent Zimbabwe, so it's no surprise that there's a lot of material on the war, the nationalist movement and the decade leading up to liberation.

During this period, white Rhodesians published a lot from their point of view, with no shortage of bizarre coffee-table books with dramatic pictures of Fireforce units swooping down on "terrs". Only since Independence has the other side of the story been told, and although sometimes the picture is again sometimes simplified, the reader now at least has the freedom to choose which view to take.

Julie Frederikse *None But Ourselves: Masses vs Media in the Making of Zimbabwe* (James Currey, London; Ravan Press, Joburg; ZPH, Harare; Viking Penguin, New York 1982). An amazing quantity of material, collected and collaged into a complex tapestry of interviews, photographs, quotes from contemporary media and commentary. Very highly recommended.

David Lan *Guns & Rain: Guerrillas & Spirit Mediums in Zimbabwe* (James Currey, London; University of California Press, Berkeley & LA Press: 1985). A fascinating excursion into the world-view of the people of Zimbabwe's remote Dande region along the eastern Zambezi River, and the role of spirit mediums in fostering the liberation struggle among the peasantry.

Terence Ranger *Peasant Consciousness and Guerrilla War in Zimbabwe* (James Currey, London; University of California Press, Berkeley & LA Press: 1985). Anything by Ranger (and he's prolific) is worth reading for the entertaining, rolling narrative argument and gripping insights. *Peasant Consciousness* draws comparisons between the anti-colonial struggle in Zimbabwe and those in Kenya and Mozambique.

Terence Ranger *Voices from the Rocks: Nature, Culture and History in the Matopos,* Baobab Books, Harare; James Currey, London: 1999. Highly readable and fascinating account of the history of the Matopos Hills, known largely for their wild beauty and as the burial site of Cecil John Rhodes. Ranger re-inserts culture and people into the hills, covering topics such as the ideological conflicts between early Christians and the followers of the Mwali rain shrine cult, the flow of white pilgrims to Rhodes's grave and black to Mzilikazi's, and the years of the guerrilla war, followed by dissension against the new government. What's for sure is that the research is ground-breaking, the insights fresh, and you'll never see the Matopos in the same way again.

Irene Staunton (ed) *Mother of the Revolution* (James Currey, London 1990). A vivid portrait of the war experiences of thirty Zimbabwean women, telling their stories in their own words.

POST-INDEPENDENCE ZIMBABWE

John Hatchard *Individual Freedoms and State Security* (James Currey, London 1993). An interesting look at the strength of the Zimbabwean state, and its hold over society.

Dr Peter Iliff *Health for Whom?* (Mambo Press). Easy to read and authoritative account of the effect of AIDS, poverty and the Structural Adjustment Programme on health and health care in Zimbabwe, with some chilling projections for the future. The author, a doctor in the health-care service, writes from his own close experience, incorporating thorough research.

Robin Palmer and Isobel Birch *Zimbabwe, A Land Divided* (Oxfam, 1992). A brief, lively and well-illustrated introduction to the country, which looks at culture as well as providing social information.

Colin Stoneman and Lionel Cliffe *Zimbabwe* (Pinter Publishers, 1989). Part of the Marxist Regime Series and aimed mainly at students, this somewhat dry account still provides a solid and up-to-date summary of available material on the country's politics, economics and society.

BOTSWANA'S HISTORY

There are few up-to-date histories of Botswana. The only easily available general history is the school text: **T. Tlou and A. Campbell** *History of Botswana* (Macmillan Botswana, Gaborone 1984). It gives solid coverage from prehistoric times through to developments in the early 1980s.

Bessie Head *Serowe: Village of the Rain Wind* (Heinemann African Writers Series, Oxford 1981). The story of Serowe over the last 100 years, largely collections of testaments by residents. There are also sound pieces on the Swaneng Project and the Brigades Movement.

Fred Morton and Jeff Ramsay (eds) *The Birth of Botswana* (Longman Botswana, 1987). A useful collection of essays on parties, rulers and regions up to 1966.

LIVES

D.N. Beach *Mapondera 1840–1904* (Mambo Press, Gweru 1989). More than simply biography, this account of one of Zimbabwe's last independent rulers, who resisted European conquest, also looks at life in the region just south of the eastern Zambezi River on the eve of colonization. Equally absorbing is the way the book is put together – a fascinating example of the art and craft of writing history. The author eschews "established facts", a notion which he says "involves no original thinking", and instead lays bare the contradictory accounts, which are his raw material.

Peter Godwin *Mukiwa: A White Boy in Africa* (HarperCollins, 1997). This evocative memoir of boyhood in Rhodesia charts the beginning of the guerrilla war and Godwin's reluctant participation in it, to Independence and beyond, ending with Mugabe's atrocities against the Matabele people, and Godwin's near capture as an investigative journalist. It's a compelling read, and there's nothing written to touch the personalized picture it gives of this period of recent history.

William Plomer *Cecil Rhodes* (David Philip, Cape Town 1984). There are countless books on Rhodes. Most feed the legend, although the distance of time has made some historians readier to regard him as a flawed colossus – but a giant nonetheless. This is a republication of one of the most interesting critical accounts, written several decades ago, against the prevailing grain, by a South African poet-novelist, when colonialism was still regarded as a good thing. It pulls no punches in presenting Rhodes as an immature person driven by his weaknesses.

Sir Charles Rey *Monarch of All I Survey: Bechuanaland Diaries 1929–1937* (Botswana Society, Gaborone; Lilian Barber, New York; James Currey, London 1988). These dashingly colloquial diaries by the energetic parvenu who was governor of Bechuanaland for eight years, reveal as much about his attitudes to his colleagues and associates as about colonial neglect of the territory. And all is brought alive by his humour and personal detail.

Frederick Courtenay Selous *Travel and Adventure in South East Africa* (Century, 1984). Reprint of an account by one of Africa's notorious Victorian hunters and adventurers, who spent time in Zimbabwe just prior to colonization and in the early colonial years.

ARCHEOLOGY, CRAFTS, ARTS AND ARCHITECURE

M. Arnold *Zimbabwean Stone Sculpture* (Books of Zimbabwe, Bulawayo). Altogether the most solid account of the subject, if less lavishly illustrated than Mor's (see below).

H. Ellert *The Material Culture of Zimbabwe* (Longman Zimbabwe; Sam Gozo, Harare 1984). Authoritative coverage of all aspects of Zimbabwe's traditional arts and crafts, including jewellery, vernacular architecture, carving, ceramics, tools and games.

Peter Garlake *Great Zimbabwe Described and Explained* (ZPH, Harare 1982). A useful little booklet by the leading authority on the topic, condensing his research into a guide for visitors and seemingly discussing every bit of stonework. It includes a useful bibliography for enthusiasts.

Peter Garlake *The Hunter's Vision* (British Museum, London 1995). A turning point in the interpretation of Southern African rock art: the author breaks with regional generalizations and begins to develop a unique understanding of Zimbabwean examples, which he believes are richer and more complex than those found in South Africa. Fascinating.

Peter Garlake *The Painted Caves* (Modus Publications, Harare 1987). A well-illustrated account of San rock art in Zimbabwe – essential reading for anyone with even the slightest interest in the topic, and the first attempt at a coherent analysis, with both interpretation and detailed instructions on where to find 38 of the finest painting sites.

Garlake has also produced another brief booklet called *Life at Great Zimbabwe*, which is in many ways the most accessible publication about the place, with pen and ink illustrations providing an impression of how it might have been, and discussion that succeeds in bringing the ruins alive.

And if you're very interested in the whole topic of unravelling the meanings of rock art, look at the large body of work by **J.D.Lewis-Williams**, a pioneer in the field and the starting point for Garlake. Although Lewis-Williams' research is based on rock art in South Africa, it's sufficiently related to be enlightening. Two of his books worth reading are *Believing and Seeing* (Academic Press, London 1981) and *The Rock Art of Southern Africa* (Cambridge University Press, 1983).

Peter Jackson *Historic Buildings of Harare* (Quest, Harare 1986). The only coherent assessment of colonial architecture in Zimbabwe, by one of the country's top architects. Apart from a catalogue of some of the finest examples of historic buildings, there's also a run-through of the development of Zimbabwe's distinct architectural styles.

F. Mor *Shona Sculpture* (Jongwe, Harare 1987). Written in idiosyncratic and at times impenetrable English by an Italian sculptor, this book is nevertheless good value for the copious outstanding colour photographs of sculptures.

B. Plangger *Serima* (Mambo Press, Gweru). Subtitled *Towards an African Expression of Christian Belief*, a well-illustrated account of the sculpture movement nurtured at Serima Mission.

Nick Walker *The Painted Caves: Rock Art of the Matopos* (Mambo Press, Gweru 1996). Indispensable field guide to the rock art of the Matopos, with excellent historical and scientific background on the paintings and the people who executed them, by a leading archeologist who has specialized in the field.

Celia Winter-Irving *Stone Sculpture in Zimbabwe: Context, Content & Form* (Roblaw, Harare 1991). An excellent account not only of Zimbabwe's stone sculpture, but also an overview of the visual arts in the country including ancient rock art, colonial and twentieth-century developments.

MUSIC

Chris Stapleton and Chris May *Africa All-Stars – the Pop Music of a Continent* (Paladin, London 1989). The best book on popular African music with country-by-country coverage . . . even though the section on Zimbabwean music is disappointingly brief.

Fred Zindi *Roots Rocking in Zimbabwe* (Mambo Press, Gweru 1985). A quick run-through of Zimbabwe's musicians by one of the country's major promoters.

NATURAL HISTORY AND FIELD GUIDES

Material on **flora and fauna** is a hugely vibrant publishing sector in the region, mostly emanating from South Africa. Amongst the wealth of material you'll find well-produced and accessible publications on anything from grasses, trees and butterflies to birds of prey and mammals. And, because numerous South Africans travel to their neighbouring countries, you'll find Zimbabwe and Botswana well covered. In addition to full-size field guides, **Struik** (known as New Holland outside the country) and **Southern** issue convenient and affordable pocket guides on seemingly every topic.

BIRDS

Gordon Lindsay Maclean *Robert's Birds of Southern Africa* (New Holland, London 1988).

The standard reference work on the subcontinent's entire avifauna population: if it's not in *Robert's* it doesn't exist. Alas, the weight of this tome makes it more a book to consult in a library than to carry with you.

Ian Sinclair *Field Guide to the Birds of Southern Africa* (HarperCollins, London 1985). A reliable and, thankfully, portable guide with good illustrations. Probably the most convenient to take along.

Ian Sinclair *Sasol: Birds of Southern Africa* (Struik, Baobab Books). Many professionals choose this book for the clarity of its illustrations. Compact and easy to carry on the move.

Michael P. Stuart Irwin *The Birds of Zimbabwe* (Quest, Harare 1981). Targeted on Zimbabwe, this is smaller than *Robert's* (although still quite heavy), but it nevertheless provides outstanding coverage.

MAMMALS

Richard D. Estes *Safari Companion* (Tutorial Press, Zimbabwe; Russel Friedman Books, South Africa: 1993). A long-needed guide on how to understand African wildlife, with interesting and readable information on the behaviour and social structures of the major species.

Theodor Haltenorth and Helmut Diller *Field Guide to the Mammals of Africa* (HarperCollins, London 1989); **Jean Dorst and Pierre Dandelot** *Larger Mammals of Africa* (HarperCollins, London). Less handy, but solidly researched, detailed and well-illustrated volumes.

Chris and Tilde Stuart *Field Guide to the Mammals of Southern Africa* (Struik, Cape Town; New Holland, London 1989). Unless you're visiting countries further north, this is the best book – with its local focus – to take along. It gives excellent background and has clear illustrations to help you recognize a species.

Chris and Tilde Stuart *Southern, Central and East African Mammals* (Struik, Cape Town; New Holland, London 1992). Inexpensive and slim pocket field guide with clear photographs and the usual reliable commentary you can expect from these authors. Perfect for casually interested amateurs who don't want to lug a large book around.

TREES AND PLANTS

Keith Coates Palgrave *Trees of Southern Africa* (Struik, Cape Town 1977). The authoritative book on the subject, but a hefty tome.

Eve Palmer *A Field Guide to the Trees of Southern Africa* (HarperCollins, London 1977). Covers South Africa, Botswana and Namibia, but not specifically the trees of Zimbabwe. On the other hand, it's smaller and easier to carry than Coates Palgrave (see above).

OKAVANGO AND THE KALAHARI

Duncan Butchart *Wild About Okavango* (Southern, Johannesburg 1997). Excellent easy-to-carry, all-in-one field guide to the Delta's geology, mammals, birds, reptiles, snakes, fish, insects and flora, with crisp photographs to accompany each species listed.

Michael Main *Kalahari: Life's Variety in Dune and Delta* (Southern, Johannesburg 1987). Fascinating and lively melange of personalized history, natural history, geology, sociology and anthropology, with great anecdotes, well-chosen photographs and a lightness of touch that belies its intelligence.

Mark and Delia Owens *Cry of the Kalahari* (Fontana, 1986). A thoroughly readable Botswana version of *Born Free* by two young US naturalists who spent seven years in the Kalahari studying lions and brown hyenas. Much more of a good yarn than straight natural history, the book has become something of a cult, with tours organized to Deception Valley where the authors worked. They tackle the thorny issue of fences in Botswana which protect cattle, but which they believe cause the deaths of countless wild animals.

Karen Ross *Jewel of the Kalahari: Okavango* (BBC Books, London 1987). Similar in scope to Main's text, this book of the BBC television series isn't quite as well written. On the other hand, coverage is very sound and it provides excellent and interesting background.

FICTION: ZIMBABWE

Only a fraction of the writing produced in Zimbabwe finds its way abroad, but if you've a taste for fiction prepare to splurge when you get there. For extracts from some of the best writers, see pp.381–387. Other names to look out for, besides the authors of the titles listed below, are: Samuel Chimsoro, Kristina Rungano, Musa Zimunya and Eddison Zvogbo (poetry); Barbara Makhalisa, Tim McLoughlin, Cont Mhlanga, Habbakuk Musengezi and Stanley Nyamfukudza (fiction).

Tsitsi Dangarembga *Nervous Conditions* (The Women's Press, London; ZPH, Harare 1988). A riveting story of race, class, gender and growing up in colonial Rhodesia, told with wit and great psychological depth. The best novel yet to emerge from Zimbabwe.

Chenjerai Hove *Bones* (Heinemann African Writers Series, Oxford 1991). Award-winning experiences of the war, from a politically engaged writer. His *Shadows* (Heinemann African Writers Series, Oxford 1991) is a tragic story of lovers who opt for death.

Wilson Katiyo *A Son of the Soil* (Longman African Classics). A compelling story of a young Zimbabwean's struggle against oppression and hardship, remarkable for its lack of bitterness.

Doris Lessing *The Grass is Singing* (Heinemann African Writers Series, Oxford 1973). A portrayal of white Rhodesia unmatched by any writer – as are her physical descriptions of the country. Equally powerful, and emotionally intense, are the novels in the later Children of Violence Masterwork Series: *Landlocked*, *Martha Quest*, *Proper Marriage* and *Ripple from the Storm* (Plume 1970). In the same vein, her *Collected African Stories*, published in two volumes, *This was the Old Chief's Country* and *Sun Between Their Feet* (Panther, 1979), are not to be missed. *Going Home* (Panther, 1968), which chronicles her return to witness the supposed transformation of the colony during the Federation in the 1950s, still rings unnervingly true to the hard-core sections of the white community today. Her latest book about Zimbabwe, *African Laughter* (HarperCollins, London 1992) tells of the changes she observed on four visits between 1982 and 1992.

Nevanji Madanhire *Goatsmell* (Anvil, 1992). A lively love story focusing on the conflicts dividing modern Zimbabwe – between the sexes, between the Shona and the Ndebele, and between the powerful and the powerless.

Dambudzo Marechera *House of Hunger* (Heinemann African Writers Series, Oxford 1978); *Black Sunlight* (Heinemann African Writers Series, Oxford 1980). Zimbabwe's internationally best-known writer shocks and amazes with his vigorous and often abrasive prose. His exploits and lifestyle attracted as much notoriety as his writing won acclaim. *Dambudzo Marechera 1952–1987* (Baobab Books, Harare 1988) is a posthumous collection of writing, quotations and tributes.

HEINEMANN AFRICAN WRITERS

Other books worth looking out for in **Heinemann's African Writers Series** include: *Stories from Central and Southern Africa* by Paul Scanlon; *Smouldering Charcoal* by Tiyambe Zeleza; and *Harvest of Thorns* by Shimmer Chinodya.

Bruce Moore-King *White Man Black War* (Baobab Books, Harare 1988). A courageous, semi-autobiographical work by an ex-soldier who, out of hindsight or guilt, switches sides and exposes the brutality of the liberation struggle and the underpinning ideology of white supremacy.

Charles Mungoshi *Waiting for the Rain* (Heinemann African Writers Series, Oxford 1977); *Setting Sun and The Rolling World* (Heinemann African Writers Series, Oxford); *Coming of the Dry Season* (Oxford University Press, 1972; ZPH, Harare 1981). In spare, aching prose, informed by traditional oral forms, Mungoshi explores the dusty, overworked "native reserves", the urban townships and the terrible bond of abandonment and empty hope between them. Masterly.

POETRY

It's worth looking out for the following editions:

Chenjerai Hove *Up in Arms* (ZPH, Harare 1982).

Kadhani and Zimunya (eds) *And Now the Poets Speak*.

Freedom T.V. Nyamubaya *On the Road Again* (ZPH, Harare 1986).

Colin and O'Lan Style (eds) *The Mambo Book of Zimbabwean Verses in English* (Mambo Press, Gweru).

CHILDREN'S LITERATURE

Hugh Lewin's Jafta series (Baobab Books, Lerner Publications) – *Jafta* (1988), *Jafta: The Journey* (1988), *Jafta and the Wedding* (1989) and *Jafta: The Town* (1994) – are all beautifully

illustrated books aimed at four- to six-year olds, and written with the poetic simplicity of a child that feels universal.

Tim Matthews *Tales of the Secret Valley* (Baobab, Harare 1988). A collection of Batonga tales, colourfully illustrated by Colleen Cousins, and interesting for coming out in Ndebele, Shona, Tonga and English, covering the mother tongues of most Zimbabweans.

Jacqui Taylor *An African ABC* (Jacqui Taylor, 1996). Elaborately illustrated full-colour alphabet, using Zimbabwean imagery, such as "L for lion, Limpopo and leguaan".

FICTION: BOTSWANA

There's little indigenous fiction in English from Botswana. The paradox is that a number of outsiders have been inspired by Botswana to write novels, while Setswana-speakers in South Africa have made their contribution in English to South African literature.

Bessie Head *When Rain Clouds Gather* (Heinemann, London 1989). Set in the heart of rural Botswana, this outstanding writer's first novel deals with a South African exile who becomes involved in an agricultural project. The book deals with love, friendship, drought and the fierce forces of tradition. Among her other books, *Maru* (Heinemann African Writers Series, Oxford 1987) is on one level about racial prejudice and loneliness, but a beautifully told love story that is also firmly in the mystical realm. *A Question of Power* (Heinemann African Writers Series, Oxford 1986) goes much further into subjective states and suffering, sliding in and out of sanity. By comparison, the short stories in *The Collector of Treasures* (Heinemann African Writers Series, Oxford 1977) are mostly light and amusing, and alongside her first novel are the best introduction to her work and village life.

Norman Rush *Whites* (Paladin, London 1987). Entertaining and well worth reading, these short stories by a US Peace Corps worker give vivid glimpses into the white sections of Botswana society.

LANGUAGES

Nearly seventy percent of Zimbabweans are mother-tongue Shona-speakers, spread across most of the country and beyond its borders, while Ndebele is the first language of fifteen percent, living around Bulawayo and the Matabeleland area of the southwest. Both are official languages, as is English – the most widely used language in Zimbabwe.

English is the language of the media, shop and street signs. You will need nothing else to book a room, eat out, make travel arrangements or ask directions – there's hardly anywhere in the country where you won't find someone who speaks it and, particularly in the cities, people speak it fluently.

Even between Africans, you'll hear English spoken – sometimes simply as a lingua franca, but also as a status symbol, especially among the middle class. In the city streets you may also hear a style of banter that lurches back and forth between English and Shona or Ndebele.

Although attempts to speak **Ndebele** or **Shona** as a means of communication may be more or less redundant, don't be put off trying – a symbolic attempt to greet people in their mother tongue is much appreciated, although also an invitation for you to be jokingly tested to the limits of your ability. Just mastering the greetings will open up channels of communication and assure friendly responses.

NDEBELE

As a young language derived from Zulu within the last 170 years, **Ndebele** is fairly homogenous and closely related to its ancestral roots. When Mzilikazi (founder of the Ndebele) fled north from Zululand in the 1820s, he forged a new state from his core of followers and Sotho, Pedi, Tswana and other elements that he collected on his way. Ndebele and Zulu, one of South Africa's most widely spoken languages, are mutually understandable – they're about 95 percent identical.

SHONA

Shona is a relatively ancient language that has had many centuries on the plateau to diversify into six main dialects, which are divided into over thirty minor ones. Of the major dialects, **Zezuru**, spoken in central Zimbabwe, has assumed the status of a prestige form because it's spoken in Harare and on the radio.

As a magnet for people from all over the country, Harare has become a linguistic melting pot, where a new Shona form, known as "Town Shona" or "ChiHarare", has begun to develop. Characteristics include borrowings from English and an informality, particularly in the disappearance of pronoun forms to denote respect.

CHILAPALAPA

Finally, it's worth mentioning **Chilapalapa**, a pidgin English/Ndebele that evolved so whites could give orders to their black workers. It has no proper grammar – all verbs exist only in the imperative form – and has now become unfashionable. It is nevertheless still used by some white households, and on farms.

SHONA AND NDEBELE WORDS AND PHRASES

Harald Vieth's Shona **phrasebook**, *Have a Nice Trip in Zimbabwe: A Colloquial Guide to Shona*, published by Mambo Press in Gweru, is a useful start. No similar book exists for Ndebele, but Zulu phrasebooks and grammars published in South Africa are very common and will easily give you enough basics to communicate with an Ndebele-speaker.

GREETINGS AND RESPONSES

Greetings are very important in both Shona and Ndebele society. They can also get quite complicated. The following greetings will be appropriate for most situations you'll encounter, and are the ones to use when you first meet someone or pass them on the road. Other greetings exist for use between people who know each other. When you approach someone's homestead or yard, it's polite to wait outside until you're invited in.

	SHONA	NDEBELE
A: Hello (sing.)	Mhoro	Sawubona
Hello (pl.)	Mhoroi	Salibonani
B: Hello (reply)	Ehoi	Yebo
A: How are you?	Makadii (sing.)/Makadini (pl.)?	Unjani (sing.)/Linjani (pl.)?
B: Fine, and you?	Tiripo makadiiwo?	Sikhona, unjani wena?
A: Fine	Tiripo	Sikhona
Good morning	Mangwanani	Livuke njani
Good afternoon	Masikati	Litshonile
Good evening	Manheru	Litshone njani
Thank you	Ndatenda/Masvita	Siyabonga kakulu
Come in/forward	Tiswikevo	Ekuhle!

AFTER GREETING

What's your name?	Munonzi ani?	Ubani ibizo lakho?
I am Tony	Ndini Tony	Elami igama ngingu (pronounced "nyingu") Tony
Pleased to meet you	Ndinofara ku-ku-ziva-i	Ngiya thaba ukukwazi
Where are you from?	Munobva kupi?	Uvelaphi?
I'm from Britain/ US/Germany	Ndinobva kuBritain/ kuAmerica/kuGermany	Ngivela e Bilithani/ Melika/Jelimana

SAYING GOODBYE

Stay well (person leaving)	Chisarai	U/Lisale kuhle
Go well (person staying)	Fambai zvakanaka	Uhambe kuhle (sing.)/ Nihambe kuhle (pl.)
See you	Tichaonana	Sizalibona njalo

TRAVEL

Where is the bus stop?	Chiteshi chiri kupi?	Singaphi isiteshi samabhasi?
When does the bus leave?	Bhazi richaenda rihni?	Izawuhamba nini ibhasi?
Is there a bus to Bulawayo today?	Nhasi pane bhazi ririkuenda kuBulawayo here?	Kunebhasi leya KaBulawayo lamuhla?
Does this bus go to Harare?	Bhazi iri rinoenda kuHarare here?	Lebhasi iyaya yini e-Harare?
Where's the road to Binga?	Mugwagwa unoenda kuBinga uri kupi?	Uphi umgwaco loya e-Binga?
Road	Mugwagwa	Mugwaco
Car	Motokari	Imoto
Train	Chitima	Isitimela
Station/bus stop	Chiteshi	Isiteshi
Go on foot	Ku-enda netsoka	Hamba ngonya wo

Continues overleaf

SHONA AND NDEBELE WORDS AND PHRASES continued

SHOPPING

	SHONA	NDEBELE
Where's the market?	*Musika uri kupi?*	*Ikuphi imakethe?*
Have you got . . .?	*Mune . . . here?*	*Une . . . yini?*
I'd like . . . please	*Ndipei/Wo*	*Ngicela*
How much is it?	*Imarii?*	*Yimalini?*

BASICS AND SIGNS

	SHONA	NDEBELE
Yes	*Ehe*	*Yebo*
No	*Aiwa*	*Hayi*
Thank you	*Tatenda/Masviita*	*Siyabonga*
Thank you (after a meal)	*Taguta*	
Please	*Ndapota*	*Uxolo*
Good/nice!	*Zvakanaka!*	*Kuhle*
Sorry	*Ndine urombo*	*Ncesi*
When?	*. . . rihni?*	*. . . nini?*
Where?	*. . . kupi?*	*. . . ngaphi?*
Now	*Zvino*	*Khathesi*
Today	*Nhasi*	*Lamuhla*
Tomorrow	*Mangwana*	*Kusasa*
Yesterday	*Nezuro*	*Izolo*
DANGER	*NGOZI*	*INGOZI*
MEN	*VARUME*	*AMADODA*
WOMEN	*VAKADZI*	*ABAFAZI*

FOOD

	SHONA	NDEBELE
Fruit	*Michero*	*Izithelo*
Orange	*Ranjisi*	*Ama-orintshi*
Peanuts	*Nzungu*	*Ama-zambane*
Guava	*Gwavha*	*Ama-gwava*

	SHONA	**NDEBELE**
	Grains	
Stiff porridge	*Sadza*	*Sadza*
Maize	*Chibage*	*Umbila*
	Drinks	
Tea	*Tii*	*Itiye*
Coffee	*Kofi*	*Ikofi*
Water	*Mvura*	*Amanzi*
Milk	*Mukaka*	*Uchago*
Beer	*Doro/Hwahwa*	*Utshwala*
Fruit squash	*Mazoe*	*Mazoe*
	Vegetables	
Potatoes	*Mbatatisi*	*Amagwili*
Tomatoes	*Matomasi*	*Utamatisi*
Leaves/greens	*Muriwo*	*Umbhido*
	Meat	
Meat	*Nyama*	*Inyama*
Meat of . . .	*Nyama ye . . .*	*Inyama ye . . .*
chicken	*huku*	*nkukhu*
beef	*mombe*	*nkomo*
goat	*mbudzi*	*mbuzi*
pork	*nguruve*	*ngulube*
	MISCELLANEOUS	
Bread	*Chingwa*	*Sinkhwa*
Salt	*Munyu*	*Uswayi*
Sugar	*Shuga*	*Ushukela*
Honey	*Uchi*	*Uju*
Butter	*Bhata*	*Ibatha*
Fish	*Hove*	*Inhlanzi*
Eggs	*Mazai*	*Amaqanda*

GLOSSARY

Ablutions Communal washing facilities found at campsites and National Parks rest camps.

African Indigenous Zimbabwean, distinct from the broader term "black"

Assegai Spears used by Zulu and Ndebele armies

Bakkie Light pick-up truck or van

Biltong Sun-dried salted strips of meat, chewed as a snack

Boerewors Spicy lengths of sausage that are *de rigueur* at braais

Boma Enclosure used for holding animals or for outdoor eating, usually with a fire at the centre

Boy Patronizing term used commonly and unthinkingly to refer to an adult African man who is a worker

Braai Barbecue

BSAC British South Africa Company; Cecil Rhodes's private company that colonized Zimbabwe in the 1890s

Bhundu See *bundu*

Bundu Wilderness or back country

Bush See *bundu*

Bushveld Country composed largely of thorny bush

Campfire Acronym for Zimbabwe's Communal Areas Management Programme For Indigenous Resources, a scheme that seeks to foster conservation by bringing benefits to local communities

Chibuku Bitter-tasting Zimbabwean beer brewed from malted grain

Communal Lands Collectively owned peasant farmlands in Zimbabwe's rural areas, previously known as Tribal Trust Lands under white minority rule

Dagga Marijuana

Dagha Adobe – mud used in traditional hut construction

Dassie Hyrax

Donga Dry, eroded ditch

Dwala Bald, whaleback granite rock formation

ESAP Economic Structural Adjustment Programme, the monetarist economic regime imposed on Zimbabwe by the International Monetary Fund

Gem squash Tasty, cricket-ball-shaped and -sized marrow

Girl Female equivalent of *boy* (see above)

Gomo See *dwala*

Gudza Textile made from chewed baobab bark and used to manufacture rugs, hats and other goods

Guti Light misty drizzle

High Density Suburbs Politically correct term introduced in Zimbabwe after Independence for African townships, which has only partially caught on

Highveld High-lying areas over 1200m above sea level, which tend to be cooler and more fertile than the rest of the country

Impi Zulu or Ndebele regiment

Jesse Dense, impenetrable bush

Just now In a while

Kapenta Small sardine-like fish introduced into Lake Kariba and frequently found in a dried form in supermarkets

Kgotla Meeting place for village discussions in Botswana

Kopje Hillock

Kraal (pronounced "crawl") Enclosure for farm animals or collection of traditional huts occupied by a family

Lapa Courtyard of group of Ndebele houses; also used to describe an enclosed area where braais are held at safari camps

Lediba (plural *madiba*) Lagoon

Lekker Nice

Letaka Reed

Lowveld Low-lying areas below 600m above sea level, which tend to be extremely hot

Madiba See *lediba*

Marimba African xylophone

Mbanje Marijuana

Mbira Thumb piano

Mealie Maize

Meru Large East African-style walk-in tent

Mesasa Huts on stilts

Middleveld Topographical region between 600m and 1200m above sea level

Mielie See *mealie*

Mokoro (plural *mekoro*) Dugout canoe

Mopane Type of tree; also used to describe terrain

Munt Highly objectionable term of abuse for Africans

Musika Market and bus station

Naartjie (pronounced "narchie") Tangerine or mandarin

Nyanga Traditional healer

Pawpaw Papaya

Pronk Characteristic jump of impala

Pula Botswana's unit of currency, literally "rain"

Robot Traffic light

Rondavel Thatched cottage, circular in plan

Sadza Maize porridge

Setswana Language of the Batswana

Shona Mother tongue of the majority of Zimbabweans

Tackies Sneakers or plimsolls

Thebe Unit of coinage in Botswana (a hundred thebe equals one pula)

Township Exclusively African areas of towns, created under colonial segregationist policies and characterized by high-density low-cost housing and scant facilities

Tribal Trust Lands African reserves in rural areas created under colonial segregationist policies

Tsotsi Villain

TTLs See *Tribal Trust Lands*

Vlei Marsh

ZANU Zimbabwe African National Union, the party that has ruled Zimbabwe since Independence

ZBC Zimbabwe Broadcasting Corporation

INDEX

ROUGH GUIDES: Travel

Amsterdam
Andalucia
Australia

Austria
Bali & Lombok
Barcelona
Belgium &
  Luxembourg
Belize
Berlin
Brazil
Britain
Brittany &
  Normandy
Bulgaria
California
Canada
Central America
Chile
China
Corfu & the
  Ionian Islands
Corsica
Costa Rica
Crete
Croatia
Cyprus
Czech & Slovak
  Republics
Dodecanese &
  the East Aegean

Dominican
  Republic
Ecuador
Egypt
England
Europe
Florida
France
French Hotels &
  Restaurants
  1999
Germany
Goa
Greece
Greek Islands
Guatemala
Hawaii
Holland
Hong Kong &
  Macau
Hungary
India
Indonesia
Ireland
Israel & the
  Palestinian
  Territories
Italy
Jamaica
Japan
Jordan

Kenya
Lake District
Laos
London
Los Angeles
Malaysia,
  Singapore &
  Brunei
Mallorca &
  Menorca
Maya World
Mexico
Morocco
Moscow
Nepal
New England
New York
New Zealand
Norway
Pacific
  Northwest
Paris
Peru
Poland
Portugal
Prague
Provence & the
  Côte d'Azur
The Pyrenees
Rhodes & the
  Dodecanese

Romania
St Petersburg
San Francisco
Sardinia
Scandinavia
Scotland
Scottish
  highlands and
  Islands
Sicily
Singapore
South Africa
South India
Southwest USA
Spain
Sweden
Syria

Thailand
Trinidad &
  Tobago
Tunisia
Turkey
Tuscany &
  Umbria
USA
Venice
Vienna
Vietnam
Wales
Washington DC
West Africa
Zimbabwe &
  Botswana

AVAILABLE AT ALL GOOD BOOKSHOPS

ROUGH GUIDES: Mini Guides, Travel Specials and Phrasebooks

MINI GUIDES

Antigua
Bangkok
Barbados
Big Island of
  Hawaii
Boston
Brussels
Budapest

Dublin
Edinburgh
Florence
Honolulu
Jerusalem
Lisbon
London
  Restaurants
Madrid
Maui
Melbourne
New Orleans
Rome
Seattle
St Lucia

Sydney
Tokyo
Toronto

TRAVEL SPECIALS

First-Time Asia
First-Time
  Europe
Women Travel

PHRASEBOOKS

Czech
Dutch

Egyptian Arabic
European
French
German
Greek
Hindi & Urdu
Hungarian
Indonesian
Italian
Japanese

Mandarin
  Chinese
Mexican
  Spanish
Polish
Portuguese
Russian
Spanish
Swahili
Thai
Turkish
Vietnamese

AVAILABLE AT ALL GOOD BOOKSHOPS

ROUGH GUIDES:
Reference and Music CDs

REFERENCE
Classical Music
Classical:
  100 Essential CDs
Drum'n'bass
House Music
Jazz
Music USA

Opera
Opera:
  100 Essential CDs
Reggae
Reggae:
  100 Essential CDs
Rock
Rock:
  100 Essential CDs
Techno
World Music
World Music:
  100 Essential CDs
English Football
European Football

Internet
Millennium

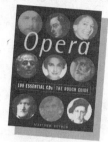

ROUGH GUIDE MUSIC CDs
Music of the
  Andes
Australian
  Aboriginal
Brazilian Music
Cajun & Zydeco

Classic Jazz
Music of
  Colombia
Cuban Music
Eastern Europe

Music of Egypt
English Roots
  Music
Flamenco
India & Pakistan
Irish Music
Music of Japan
Kenya & Tanzania
Native American
North African
Music of Portugal

Reggae
Salsa
Scottish Music
South African
  Music
Music of Spain
Tango
Tex-Mex
West African
  Music
World Music
World Music Vol 2
Music of
  Zimbabwe

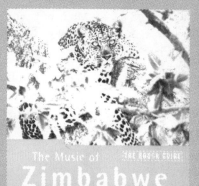

You've rafted the Falls, jumped from the bridge, canoed the Zambezi, now...

take a walk.

Guided hiking and camping safaris to Hwange, Chizarira, Matusadona and Gonarezhou National Parks, led by pro hunter-guide Mike Scott.

Just US$130 per person per day fully inclusive.

Dare yourself.

Real adventure in the wilds of Zimbabwe.

For information and booking, contact Mike or Anna Scott, Khangela Safaris, PO Box FM 296, Famona, Bulawayo. ☎+263 (09) 49733, fax 78081. Mobile ☎ (091) 234 676 or (023) 406 981.

scott@gatorzw.com

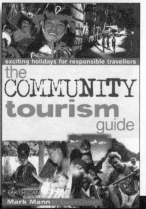

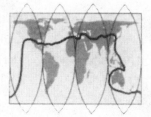

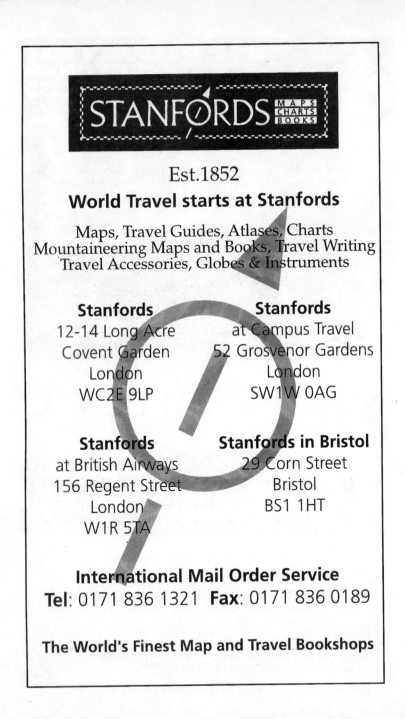